ABRAHAM LINCOLN

THE PRAIRIE YEARS

BY CARL SANDBURG

ABRAHAM LINCOLN: THE PRAIRIE YEARS

ABRAHAM LINCOLN: THE WAR YEARS

MARY LINCOLN: WIFE AND WIDOW

STORM OVER THE LAND

LINCOLN COLLECTOR

THE PHOTOGRAPHS OF ABRAHAM LINCOLN
(with Frederick H. Meserve)

THE AMERICAN SONGBAG

THE CHICAGO RACE RIOTS

STEICHEN THE PHOTOGRAPHER

POTATO FACE

HOME FRONT MEMO

Novel

REMEMBRANCE ROCK

Poems

SMOKE AND STEEL

SLABS OF THE SUNBURNT WEST

CHICAGO POEMS   CORNHUSKERS

GOOD MORNING, AMERICA

SELECTED POEMS
(edited by Rebecca West)

THE PEOPLE, YES

COMPLETE POEMS

For Young Folks

ROOTABAGA STORIES   ROOTABAGA PIGEONS

ABE LINCOLN GROWS UP

EARLY MOON

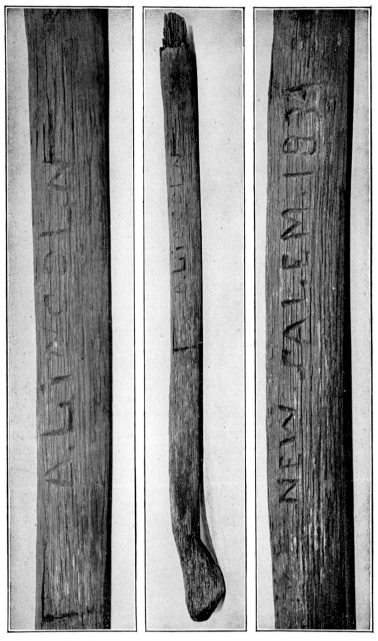

Jackknife signature of Abe Lincoln on his ax handle, New
Salem, Illinois, 1834.

ABRAHAM LINCOLN

THE PRAIRIE YEARS

BY CARL SANDBURG

WITH ILLUSTRATIONS FROM PHOTOGRAPHS
AND MANY CARTOONS, SKETCHES,
MAPS, AND LETTERS

ABRIDGED EDITION IN ONE VOLUME

HARCOURT, BRACE & WORLD, INC.

NEW YORK

PREFACE

For thirty years and more I have planned to make a certain portrait of Abraham Lincoln. It would sketch the country lawyer and prairie politician who was intimate with the settlers of the Knox County neighborhood where I grew up as a boy, and where I heard the talk of men and women who had eaten with Lincoln, given him a bed overnight, heard his jokes and lingo, remembered his silences and his mobile face.

The Mayor of Galesburg in 1858, Henry Sanderson, is the only individual of casual record who carried warm cistern water to a bathtub for Lincoln and saw Lincoln taking a bath. There in Galesburg Clark E. Carr, author of "The Illini," repeated Bill Green's remark about Lincoln, "He can make a cat laugh." And there Lincoln when bantered about his backwardness with women, answered, "A woman is the only thing I am afraid of that I know will not hurt me."

The folk-lore Lincoln, the maker of stories, the stalking and elusive Lincoln is a challenge for any artist. He has enough outline and lights and shadows and changing tints to call out portraits of him in his Illinois backgrounds and settings—even had he never been elected President.

Perhaps poetry, art, human behavior in this country, which has need to build on its own traditions, would be served by a life of Lincoln stressing the fifty-two years previous to his Presidency. Such a book would imply that if he was what he was during those first fifty-two years of his life it was nearly inevitable that he would be what he proved to be in the last four.

Then, too, the vortex in which he stood during the last four years of his life was forming in the years he was growing. The embryo of modern industrial society was taking shape. The history of transportation, of world colonization and world markets based on power-driven machinery, of international trade, finance, and standardization, weave through the destiny of Lincoln. He wore home-made moccasins as a boy, rawhide boots from a factory as a young man, and dressed calfskin shoes in still later years. A vast play of economic action, in whatever impressionistic manner, must move in the record of Lincoln.

And then Lincoln from a child on was intensely companionable, keenly sensitive to the words and ways of people around him. Therefore those people, their homes, occupations, songs, proverbs, schools, churches, politics, should be set forth with the incessant suggestion of change that went always with western pioneer life. They are the backgrounds on which the Lincoln life moved, had its rise and flow, and was moulder and moulded.

Of all the sources from which men are to gather impressions of the personality of Lincoln, the foremost singly important one is the collection of his letters and papers, the speeches and writings of the man himself. This is the high document, always, to be lived with and brooded over, to be scrutinized and forgotten and gone back to and searched again with all gifts of imagination, intuition, experience, prayer, silence, sacrifice, and the laughter next door to tears.

The first widely read biography of Lincoln, excluding campaign sketches, was by Josiah Gilbert Holland of New York, who characterized Lincoln as "a Christian gentleman." Ward Hill Lamon's book, in 1872, attacked the claims of Holland. Sixteen years later came the notable biography wherein William H. Herndon, the law partner of Lincoln, set forth a mass of documents, recollections, impressions. With the same period goes the ten-volume "History of Abraham Lincoln" by John G. Nicolay and John Hay, and Henry C. Whitney's "Life on the Circuit with Lincoln." The evidence seemed about complete when Ida Tarbell made her investigations that put fresh color into the early life of Lincoln, theretofore pictured as drab and miserable beyond the fact.

Death and time have obliterated people and houses that Miss Tarbell visited nearly thirty years ago with note book, camera, and portfolio; her services as a recorder and writer, her sketches, interviews, photographs, surveys, of that period of so many now vanished vestiges, are an achievement and a leading contribution.

Since then has come a friendly and human book on Lincoln from Jesse W. Weik, who had so loyally and ably collaborated with Herndon. The contributions of Dr. William E. Barton in many fields, notably that of the ancestry of Lincoln, mount into several books that form an important corner in all collections of Lincolniana.

Meantime the University of Illinois directed the production of a solid, crowded statement of the Lincoln-Douglas debates, followed by a monumental five-volume centennial history of the State of Illinois. Meantime also, the collection and classification of materials by the Illinois State Historical Society and the Chicago Historical Society has proceeded, while the Huntington, McLellan and Morgan collections and others such as those of Oliver R. Barrett, Joseph B. Oakleaf, Frederick H. Meserve, Clark Bissett, Emanuel Hertz, besides many more, have increased beyond all proportions at first considered probable.

Several thousand books, pamphlets, brochures, have been written and printed about Lincoln. The bibliography of Daniel Fish, published in 1906, listed 1,080 books. J. B. Oakleaf of Moline, Illinois, bringing the Fish enumeration to the year 1925, adds 1,600 items. A projected bibliography now under way by Emmanel Hertz will list several hundred additional items.

In a single private collection are biographies of Lincoln in French (five in number), German (four), Italian, Portuguese, Russian, Yiddish, Greek, Turkish, Japanese (three), Chinese (two), and Hawaiian.

At intervals and often with curious surprise, come new glints of illumination on Lincoln. Thus reminiscences gathered by Allen Thorndike Rice, Dorothy Lamon, A. K. McClure, Horace White; Eleanor Atkinson's haunting sketch of Dennis Hanks; the Old Salem league publications; the transcript by Henry C. Whitney of the "Lost Speech" of 1856; the reprint in 1921 by the Woman's Club of Elizabethtown, Kentucky, of the history of that community as written by Samuel Haycraft and published in a local newspaper in 1869.

Besides these materials I have used the reminiscences of Thomas G. Lowry, whose published volume was limited to 200 copies, and notes taken in extended conversations with Joseph W. Fifer, former Governor of Illinois and during many years an intimate of Leonard Sweet and Richard Oglesby.

In the McLellan manuscripts of the John Hay Library of Brown University, in the collections of the Chicago and Illinois Historical societies and in private collections, I have met sixty-five unpublished letters and papers in Lincoln's handwriting. I visited the Shenandoah Valley farm site of Lincoln's grandfather, the Lincoln birthplace and the Kentucky and Indiana regions, traveled down the Mississippi River, walked the docks of New Orleans, spent weeks in Springfield, Petersburg, New Salem, Bloomington, and towns in Illinois where Lincoln lived.

Lincoln's last speech in Illinois, at Tolono, I first met in a file of the *New York Herald*. Old newspaper files in the Chicago Public Library, and various source materials in the Newberry Library, were of service. The forty large volumes of newspaper clippings about Lincoln, gathered by the Chicago Historical Society during the centennial year of 1909, yielded letters, sketches, interviews, and memoirs of worthy authenticity. Local newspaper files such as *The Galesburg Republican-Register, The Galesburg Evening Mail, The Bloomington Pantagraph, The Alton Telegraph,* supplied quaint original material. Oliver R. Barrett loaned me an almost complete file of the *New York Herald* covering a critical period when that newspaper had at Springfield a correspondent with fine understanding of Lincoln; also Mr. Barrett supplied many rare copies of newspapers published in Illinois during the forty years previous to 1860.

Such items as letters and papers of Alexander Stephens characterizing Lincoln; the Lincoln & Herndon office as seen through the letters of Herndon to Theodore Parker in Joseph Fort Newton's book; the monographs of William H. Townsend on Lincoln as defendant and litigant; the diary of Orville H. Browning; the researches of Cole and Pease in Illinois history; the Tracy Uncollected Letters"; the studies of William E. Dodd in wheat, railroads, finance, from 1840 to 1860 and his remarkable paper, "The Fight for the Northwest"—these are but a few instances of documents and material, brought forth in the past eight years, that go to form the Lincoln impression.

We might list also the *Atlantic Monthly* publication of "The Bear Hunt" doggerel from the manuscript owned by J. Pierpont Morgan; the Black Hawk War history and the biography of Stephen A. Douglas written by Frank Stevens of Sycamore, Illinois; the Louis A. Warren brochure "From White House to Log Cabin"; biographies of James A. Buchanan and Lyman Trumbull; the Herndon broadsides and a letter of Mrs. Lincoln reprinted by H. E. Barker of Springfield, Illinois, besides that copy of the *Cleveland* (Ohio) *Plaindealer* which publishes for the first time the text of a letter written by Mrs. Lincoln to her husband; the Addison G. Procter recollections of the 1860 Chicago Republican convention; and the writings of Lincoln edited by Arthur Lapsley, with an introduction by Theodore Roosevelt. In so out of the way a volume as the autobiography of John James Ingalls of Kansas one comes across the first statement of an exact figure as to how much money Lincoln's campaign managers in Illinois spent to nominate him for president in 1860.

No letter—of length, or of importance as indicative of situations and characters—written by Lincoln to his wife has ever come to light publicly during all the years in which the streams of biography have run on endlessly. Such a letter, constituting a rarely fine document on the relationship between Lincoln and his wife, is loaned for use in this book through the courtesy of Alexander W. Hannah of Chicago. In the same year of 1925 we have seen the publication by Oliver R. Barrett of the 1858 address showing Lincoln with head bent in defeat just before the fall elections, hinting, with no cheap regrets, at the treachery of supposed friends and mentioning how he and his associates had been "bespattered with every imaginable odious epithet."

The Barrett collection began more than thirty-five years ago when Oliver R. Barrett as a boy of fifteen started to gather letters, manuscripts, photographs, of Lincoln and reminiscences from men and women who had met Lincoln in life. There in Pittsfield, county seat of Pike County, Illinois, the old settlers had heard Lincoln deliver speeches, had sat at turkey dinners with him, and had passed the Gilmer house, where Lincoln, going to a conference in the house, had lifted Lizzie Gilmer off the front gate, kissed her and put her back on the gate; they remembered the little red-headed boy, John G. Nicolay, who was a printer's devil at the office of the Pike County *Free Press*, and the boy John Hay who went to school and wrote "contributions" for the *Free Press*. There Barrett grew up; later he was a Peoria lawyer, familiar with the "orgmathorial" humor and savor of the old Eighth Circuit Bar and the stump politics of central Illinois; then he moved to Chicago. Keen in the scrutiny of evidence and shrewd in his analysis of documents; a man droll, inventive, quizzical and lovable in the company of children; a long distance walker, a fisherman, story-teller, bookman; a man who takes a ten or fifteen mile hike at midnight or dawn when the impulse moves him; a man who enjoys being ungrammatical when with ungrammatical people; with the restless urge of the pony express rider modulated by the peaceful preoccupations of the antiquarian—Oliver R. Barrett requires further portraiture. As a collaborator and commentator he has given honest values to some of these pages.

Frederick H. Meserve gave full access to his collection of 200,000 photographs and was ready with seasoned counsel on Lincoln photographs; he loaned the bronze life mask for the two photographs by Edward Steichen; they deliver the enigmatic Lincoln whose range of laughter and tears was far and deep.

Going farther month by month in stacks and bundles of fact and legend, I found invisible companionships that surprised me. Perhaps a few of those presences lurk and murmur in this book.

NOTE

WHEN I TRIED TO MAKE A COMPLETE LIST OF THE
PERSONS WHO GAVE VALUABLE TIME AND HELP TO-
WARD THE MAKING OF THIS BOOK, THE SERIES OF
NAMES GREW SO LONG THAT IT WOULD OVERBAL-
ANCE THE PLAN OF THE BOOK TO INCLUDE THEM IN
PROPER STYLE WITH JUST AND MEASURED ACKNOWL-
EDGMENTS. I CAN ONLY SAY THAT I AM GRATEFUL
BEYOND WORDS TO THE MANY WHO ASSOCIATED
THEIR EFFORTS, OFFERED FREE COMMENT, WORTHY
COUNSEL, AND PERFORMED ERRANDS.

*I first planned this book for one large volume.
When completed, however, it was necessary for initial
publication to issue it in two volumes. In its present
condensed edition it is made available to a large part
of the public I had in mind all the time.*

LIST OF PHOTOGRAPHS, CARTOONS, SKETCHES, MAPS, AND LETTERS

ABRAHAM LINCOLN

THE PRAIRIE YEARS

CHAPTER 1

In the year 1776, when the thirteen American colonies of England gave to the world that famous piece of paper known as the Declaration of Independence, there was a captain of Virginia militia living in Rockingham County, named Abraham Lincoln.

He was a farmer with a 210-acre farm deeded to him by his father, John Lincoln, one of the many English, Scotch, Irish, German, Dutch settlers who were taking the green hills and slopes of the Shenandoah Valley and putting their plows to ground never touched with farming tools by the red men, the Indians, who had held it for thousands of years.

The work of driving out the red men so that the white men could farm in peace was not yet finished. In the summer of that same year of 1776, Captain Abraham Lincoln's company took a hand in marches and fights against the Cherokee tribes.

It was a time of much fighting. To the south and west were the red men. To the north and east were white men, the regiments of British soldiers, and Virginia was sending young men and corn and pork to the colonial soldiers under General George Washington. Amos Lincoln, a kinsman of Abraham, up in Massachusetts, was one of the white men who, the story ran, rigged out as Indians, went on board a British ship and dumped a cargo of tea overboard to show their disobedience, contempt, and defiance of British laws and government; later Amos was a captain of artillery in the colonial army.

There was a Hananiah Lincoln who fought at Brandywine under Washington and became a captain in the Twelfth Pennsylvania regiment; and Hananiah was a first cousin of Abraham. Jacob Lincoln, a brother of Abraham, was at Yorktown, a captain under Washington at the finish of the Revolutionary War. These Lincolns in Virginia came from Berks County in Pennsylvania.

Now Abraham Lincoln had taken for a wife a woman named Bathsheba Herring. And she bore him three sons there amid the green hills and slopes of the Shenandoah Valley, and they were named Mordecai, Josiah, and Thomas. And she bore two daughters, named Mary and Nancy.

This family of a wife and five children Abraham Lincoln took on horses in the year 1782 and moved to Kentucky. For years his friend, Daniel Boone, had been coming back from trips to Kentucky.

While Bathsheba was still carrying in her arms the baby, Thomas, it happened that Abraham Lincoln sold his farm, and in accordance with the laws of Virginia she signed papers giving up her rights to her husband's land, declaring in writing on the 24th day of September, 1781, that "she freely and voluntarily relinquished the same without the Force threats or compulsion of her husband." Then they packed their belongings, especially the rifle, the ax, and the plow, and joined a party which headed down the Wilderness Road through Cumberland Gap and up north and west into Kentucky.

Abraham and Bathsheba (or Batsab) Lincoln sign their names to a deed in the courthouse of Rockingham County, Virginia.

Tall mountains loomed about them with long blue shadows at sunup and sundown as they traveled, camped, broke camp, and traveled again. And as they watched the mountains they slanted their keenest eyes on any moving patch of shrub or tree—the red men who ambushed enemies might be there.

There had been papers signed, and the land by law belonged to the white men, but the red men couldn't understand or didn't wish to understand how the land was gone from them to the white men. Besides, the red men had been fighting among themselves for favorite hunting grounds and fishing waters; there had been hundreds of years of fighting; now they were fighting white men by the same weapons, ways, and ambushes as they fought red men.

Some towns and villages then were paying a dollar to two dollars apiece for Indian scalps.

Coming through safe to Kentucky, Abraham Lincoln located on the Green River, where he filed claims for more than 2,000 acres. He had been there three or four years when, one day as he was working in a field, the rifle shot of an Indian killed him. His children and his children's children scattered across Kentucky, Tennessee, Indiana, and Illinois.

Tom Lincoln, the child of Abraham and Bathsheba, while growing up, lived in different places in Kentucky, sometimes with his kith and kin, sometimes hiring out to farmers, mostly in Washington County, and somehow betweenwhiles managing to learn the carpenter's trade and cabinet-making. He bought a horse—and paid taxes on it. He put in a year on the farm of his uncle, Isaac Lincoln, on the Wautauga River in East Tennessee. He moved to Hardin County in Kentucky while still a young bachelor, and bought a farm on Mill Creek, paid taxes on the farm, kept out of debt, and once bought a pair of silk suspenders for a dollar and a half at a time when most men were using homemade hickory-bark galluses.

As Tom Lincoln came to his full growth he was about five feet, nine inches tall, weighing about 185 pounds, his muscles and ribs close-knit, so that one time a boy joking with him tried to find the places between his ribs but couldn't put a finger in between any place where a rib ended and the muscle began. His dark hazel eyes looked out from a round face, from under coarse black hair. He was a slow, careless man with quiet manners, would rather have people come and ask him to work on a job than to hunt the job himself. He liked to sit around and have his own thoughts.

He wasn't exactly lazy; he was sort of independent, and liked to be where he wasn't interfered with. A little slab of bacon with hoecake or a little corn-bread and milk every day, and he was satisfied. He drank whisky but not often. The sober Baptists saw more of him than those who were steady at licking up liquor. He was a wild buck at fighting, when men didn't let him alone. A man talked about a woman once in a way Tom Lincoln didn't like. And in the fight that came, Tom bit a piece of the man's nose off. His neighbors knew him as a good man to let alone. And his neighbors knew him for a good workman, a handy man with the ax, the saw, the drawknife, and the hammer. Though he was short-spoken, he knew yarns, could crack jokes, and had a reputation as a story-teller when he got started. He never had much time for the alphabet, could read some, and could sign his name.

Church meetings interested him. He had been to cabins on Sunday mornings; the worshipers sat where it was half dark. Windows hadn't been cut in the walls; light came in through the door; words of the sermon came from a preacher in half-shadows. And he had gone to service in the evening when the cabin was lighted by the burning logs of the fireplace. Sometimes he felt stirred inside when a young woman kneeling on the floor would turn a passionate, longing face to the roof of the cabin and call, "Jesus, I give everything to thee. I give thee all. I give thee all. I am wholly thine!"

He had heard different preachers; some he liked better than others; some he was suspicious of; others he could listen to by the hour.

CHAPTER 2

DURING those years when Tom Lincoln was getting into his twenties, the country in Hardin County and around Elizabethtown was still wilderness, with only a few farms and settlements. Kentucky had been admitted to the Union of states; there were places in the state where civilization had dented the wilderness; but it was still a country of uncut timber, land unknown to the plow, a region where wolves and bear, wild animals and the Indians still claimed their rights and titles, with tooth and fang, claw and club and knife.

They talked in Elizabethtown about Miles Hart, who lived near by, and how he was killed by the Indians after he had used up his powder, how his wife Elizabeth and her two children were taken by the Indians, and how, on an outdoor march with the Indians, she was sent away, as Indian squaws were, by herself, to build a fire in the snow and give birth to her child. The child lived six months, but its mother was several years in the hands of the Indians before a Frenchman bought her near Detroit and sent her back to her relatives in Kentucky, where she again married and was raising a family. It was nearly twenty years since Elder John Gerrard, the Baptist preacher, had come to Hardin County. He preached nine months, and then one day, when a hunting party was surprised by Indians, all got away except Elder Gerrard, who was lame, and whether the Indians killed him, burned him at the stake, or took him along as a slave, nobody ever heard. There were many things to talk about around Elizabethtown. There was a negro living there called General Braddock, a free man; he had been given his freedom because, when his master's cabin was attacked by Indians, he had killed nine of the red men and saved the lives of his owner's family.

There was the time when Henry Helm and Dan Vertrees were killed by the Indians; a red man wrestled a gun away from a white man and had his war-ax raised to bring down and split the head of the white man; it was then Nicholas Miller, quick as a cat, made a jump, snatched the white man away and killed the Indian. One man who saw it, John Glenn, said, "Miller snatched the white man from the Indian as he would a chicken from a hawk." There was talk about how, even though the wilderness life was full of danger, men kept coming on, the Wilderness Road and the Ohio River bringing more and more settlers year by year, some speaking in one form or another the language of Daniel Boone, calling himself "an instrument ordained by God to settle the wilderness."

As the crossroads grew into settlements in Hardin County, there was hard feeling between the crowd around Elizabethtown and the settlers in the valley over near Hodgen's mill, about where the county seat should be located and the courthouse built. On election days, when the members of the county board were chosen, the voters clashed. The hard feeling lasted nearly ten years. At least fifty combats of fist and skull took place, though it was generally understood that the only time the fighting was not strictly fair and square rough-and-tumble combat was when a young man named Bruce tried to gash his enemies by kicking them with shoes pointed with sharp iron pieces shaped like the "gaffs" which are fastened to the feet of fighting cocks, Bruce himself being a rooster-fight sport.

The first jail in Elizabethtown cost the county $42.60. The sheriff was discouraged with it, and in 1797 a new jail was built, costing $700.00, with stocks and whipping-post. Many of the prisoners were in for debt and both white and black men were lashed on their naked backs at the public whipping-post. The stocks were built so that each prisoner had to kneel with his hands and head clamped between two grooved planks. If the prisoner was dead drunk he was laid on his back with his feet in the stocks and kept there till he was sober.

The same year the jail was built, it happened that a man in for debt set fire to it when the jailer was away; the prisoner was nearly roasted to death but was saved, though the jail burned down; after which he was indicted for arson, and acquitted because he was a first-rate bricklayer and the town needed his work.

The time of the grand "raisin'" of the courthouse in 1795 in the middle of August was remembered; on that day forty strong men raised the frames and big logs into place while many women and children looked on, and at noon the men all crowded into the Haycraft double log-house to eat hearty from loaves of bread baked in a clay oven, roast shotes, chickens, ducks, potatoes, roast beef with cabbage and beans, old-fashioned baked custard and pudding, pies, pickles, and "fixin's."

Grand juries held their sessions in the woods alongside the courthouse. In 1798 their entire report was, "We present Samuel Forrester for profane swearing"; on several occasions they mention Isaac Hynes, the sheriff, for "profane swearing." The sheriff was a distiller and his still-house was in one year recommended for use as the county jail.

When people spoke of "the time Jacob was hung," they meant the year 1796 and the negro slave Jacob, who was "reproved for sloth" and killed his owner with an ax; a jury fixed the value of the slave at 80 pounds, or $400; he broke jail, was taken again, and on hanging day the sheriff hired another black man "to tie the noose and drive the cart from under," leaving the murderer hanging in mid-air from the scaffold. A large crowd came in Sunday clothes, with lunch baskets, to see the law take its course.

If in that country they wished to speak of lighter things, they could talk about pancakes; it was a saying that a smart woman, a cook who was clever, could toss a pancake off the skillet up through the top of the chimney and run outdoors and catch it coming down. Eggs were five cents a dozen. And one year a defendant in a case at law got a new trial on showing that in his case the jury, after retiring and before agreeing on a verdict, "did eat, drink, fiddle, and dance." Such were some of the community human cross-weaves in the neighborhood where Tom Lincoln spent the years just before he married.

CHAPTER 3

Tom Lincoln was looking for a woman to travel through life with, for better or worse. He visited at the place of Christopher Bush, a hardworking farmer who came from German parents and had raised a family of sons with muscle. "There was no back-out in them; they never shunned a fight when they considered it necessary; and nobody ever heard one of them cry 'Enough.' "

Also there were two daughters with muscle and with shining faces and steady eyes. Tom Lincoln passed by Hannah and gave his best jokes to Sarah Bush. But it happened that Sarah Bush wanted Daniel Johnson for a husband and he wanted her.

Another young woman Tom's eyes fell on was a brunette sometimes called Nancy Hanks because she was a daughter of Lucy Hanks, and sometimes called Nancy Sparrow because she was an adopted daughter of Thomas and Elizabeth Sparrow and lived with the Sparrow family.

Lucy Hanks had welcomed her child Nancy into life in Virginia in 1784 and had traveled the Wilderness Road carrying what was to her a precious bundle through Cumberland Gap and on into Kentucky.

The mother of Nancy was nineteen years old when she made this trip, leaving Nancy's father, who had not married her, back in Virginia. She could croon in the moist evening twilight to the shining face in the sweet bundle, "Hush thee, hush thee, thy father's a gentleman." She could toss the bundle into the air against a far, hazy line of blue mountains, catch it in her two hands as it came down, let it snuggle to her breast and feed, while she asked, "Here we come—where from?"

And after they had both sunken in the depths of forgetful sleep, in the early dark and past midnight, the tug of a mouth at her nipples in the gray dawn matched in its freshness the first warblings of birds and the morning stars leaving the earth to the sun and the dew.

And while Nancy was still learning to walk and talk, her mother Lucy was talked about in and around Harrodsburg, Kentucky, as too free and easy in her behavior, too wild in her ways. A grand jury had taken up the case of Lucy Hanks at one session in Harrodsburg and named her to be investigated for immoral tendencies.

And whether some man on the jury or some officer of the law had a spiteful heart against Lucy or whether it was a roistering, jesting grand jury like the one that before agreeing on a verdict "did eat, drink, fiddle and dance," was not clear.

What was clear in the years that had passed was that Lucy Hanks was strong and strange, loved love and loved babies, had married a man she wanted, Henry Sparrow, and nine children had come and they were all learning to read and write under her teaching. Since she had married the talk about her running wild had let down.

After she married Henry Sparrow her daughter Nancy went under the roof of Thomas Sparrow, a brother of Henry, and Elizabeth Hanks Sparrow, a sister of Lucy. Under the same roof was an adopted boy named Dennis Hanks, a son of a Nancy Hanks who was one of three sisters of Lucy. There were still other Nancy Hankses in Hardin County and those who spoke of any Nancy Hanks often had to mention which one they meant.

Tom Lincoln had seen this particular Nancy Hanks living with the Sparrows and noticed she was shrewd and dark and lonesome. He had heard her tremulous voice and seen her shaken with sacred desires in church camp-meetings; he had seen her at preachings in cabins when her face stood out as a sort of picture in black against the firelights of the burning logs. He knew she could read the Bible, and had read in other books. She had seen a few newspapers and picked out pieces of news and read her way through.

Her dark skin, dark brown hair, keen little gray eyes, outstanding forehead, somewhat accented chin and cheek-bones, body of slender build, weighing about 130 pounds—these formed the outward shape of a woman carrying something strange and cherished along her ways of life. She was sad with sorrows like dark stars in blue mist. The hope was burned deep in her that beyond the harsh clay paths, the everyday scrubbing, washing, patching, fixing, the babble and the gabble of today, there are pastures and purple valleys of song.

She had seen tall hills there in Kentucky. She had seen the stark backbone of Muldraugh's Hill become folded in thin evening blankets with a lavender mist sprayed by sunset lights, and for her there were the tongues of promises over it all.

She believed in God, in the Bible, in mankind, in the past and future, in babies, people, animals, flowers, fishes, in foundations and roofs, in time and the eternities outside of time; she was a believer, keeping in silence behind her gray eyes more beliefs than she spoke. She knew . . . so much of what she believed was yonder—always yonder. Every day came scrubbing, washing, patching, fixing. There was so little time to think or sing about the glory she believed in. It was always yonder. . . .

The day came when Thomas Lincoln signed a bond with his friend, Richard Berry, in the courthouse at Springfield in Washington County, over near where his brother, Mordecai, was farming, and the bond gave notice: "There is a marriage shortly intended between Thomas Lincoln and Nancy Hanks." It was June 10, 1806. Two days later, at Richard Berry's place, Beechland, a man twenty-eight years old and a woman twenty-three years old came before the Reverend Jesse Head, who later gave the county clerk the names of Thomas Lincoln and Nancy Hanks as having been "joined together in the Holy Estate of Matrimony agreeable to the rules of the Methodist Episcopal Church."

After the wedding came "the infare," the Kentucky style wedding celebration. One who was there said, "We had bear-meat, venison, wild turkey and ducks, eggs wild and tame, maple sugar lumps tied on a string to bite off for coffee or whisky, syrup in big gourds, peach-and-honey; a sheep that two families barbecued whole over coals of wood burned in a pit, and covered with green boughs to keep the juices in; and a race for the whisky bottle."

The new husband put his June bride on his horse and they rode away on the red clay road along the timber trails to Elizabethtown. Their new home was in a cabin close to the courthouse. Tom worked at the carpenter's trade, made cabinets, door-frames, window sash, and coffins. A daughter was born and they named her Sarah. Tom's reputation as a solid, reliable man, whose word could be depended on, was improved after his quarrels with Denton Geoheagan.

He took a contract to cut timbers and help put up a new sawmill for Geoheagan; and when Geoheagan wouldn't pay he went to law and won the suit for his pay. Geoheagan then started two suits against Lincoln, claiming the sawmill timbers were not cut square and true. Lincoln beat him in both suits, and noticed that afterward people looked to him as a reliable man whose word could be depended on.

It was about this time the building of the third Hardin County jail was finished in Elizabethtown, with an old-time dungeon underground. The first jailer was Reverend Benjamin Ogden, who was a Methodist preacher, also a chair-maker and worker in wood.

In May and the blossom-time of the year 1808, Tom and Nancy with little Sarah moved out from Elizabethtown to the farm of George Brownfield, where Tom did carpenter work and helped farm.

The Lincolns had a cabin of their own to live in. It stood among wild crab-apple trees.

And the smell of wild crab-apple blossoms, and the low crying of all wild things, came keen that summer to the nostrils of Nancy Hanks.

The summer stars that year shook out pain and warning, strange laughters, for Nancy Hanks.

CHAPTER 4

THE same year saw the Lincolns moved to a place on the Big South Fork of Nolin's Creek, about two and a half miles from Hodgenville. They were trying to farm a little piece of ground and make a home. The house they lived in was a cabin of logs cut from the timber near by.

The floor was packed-down dirt. One door, swung on leather hinges, let them in and out. One small window gave a lookout on the weather, the rain or snow, sun and trees, and the play of the rolling prairie and low hills. A stick-clay chimney carried the fire smoke up and away.

One morning in February of this year, 1809, Tom Lincoln came out of his cabin to the road, stopped a neighbor and asked him to tell "the granny woman," Aunt Peggy Walters, that Nancy would need help soon.

On the morning of February 12, a Sunday, the granny woman was there at the cabin. And she and Tom Lincoln and the moaning Nancy Hanks welcomed into a world of battle and blood, of whispering dreams and wistful dust, a new child, a boy.

A little later that morning Tom Lincoln threw some extra wood on the fire, and an extra bearskin over the mother, went out of the cabin, and walked two miles up the road to where the Sparrows, Tom and Betsy, lived. Dennis Hanks, the nine-year-old boy adopted by the Sparrows, met Tom at the door.

In his slow way of talking—he was a slow and a quiet man—Tom Lincoln told them, "Nancy's got a boy baby." ** A half-sheepish look was in his eyes, as though maybe more babies were not wanted in Kentucky just then.

The boy, Dennis Hanks, took to his feet, down the road to the Lincoln cabin. There he saw Nancy Hanks on a bed of poles cleated to a corner of the cabin, under warm bearskins.

She turned her dark head from looking at the baby to look at Dennis and threw him a tired, white smile from her mouth and gray eyes. He stood by the bed, his eyes wide open, watching the even, quiet breaths, of this fresh, soft red baby.

"What you goin' to name him, Nancy?" the boy asked.

"Abraham," was the answer, "after his grandfather."

Soon came Betsy Sparrow. She washed the baby, put a yellow petticoat and a linsey shirt on him, cooked dried berries with wild honey for Nancy,

** These words are from the Eleanor Atkinson interview with Dennis Hanks. Throughout this work conversational utterances are based word for word on sources deemed authentic.—The Author.

put the one-room cabin in better order, kissed Nancy and comforted her, and went home.

Little Dennis rolled up in a bearskin and slept by the fireplace that night. He listened for the crying of the newborn child once in the night and the feet of the father moving on the dirt floor to help the mother and the little one. In the morning he took a long look at the baby and said to himself, "Its skin looks just like red cherry pulp squeezed dry, in wrinkles."

He asked if he could hold the baby. Nancy, as she passed the little one into Dennis's arms, said, "Be keerful, Dennis, fur you air the fust boy he's ever seen."

And Dennis swung the baby back and forth, keeping up a chatter about how tickled he was to have a new cousin to play with. The baby screwed up the muscles of its face and began crying with no let-up.

Dennis turned to Betsy Sparrow, handed her the baby and said to her, "Aunt, take him! He'll never come to much."

So came the birth of Abraham Lincoln that 12th of February in the year 1809—in silence and pain from a wilderness mother on a bed of corn-husks and bearskins—with an early laughing child prophecy he would never come to much.

And though he was born in a house with only one door and one window, it was written he would come to know many doors, many windows; he would read many riddles and doors and windows.

The Lincoln family lived three crop years on the farm where baby Abraham was born. It was a discouraging piece of land with yellow and red clay, stony soils, thick underbrush, land known as "barrens." It was called the Rock Spring farm because at the foot of one of its sloping hills the rocks curved in like the beginning of a cave; coats of moss spotted the rocks and rambled with quiet streaks of green over the gray; a ledge of rock formed a beckoning roof with room for people to stand under; and at the heart of it, for its centre, was a never-ending flow of clear, cool water.

With the baby she called Abe in her arms, Nancy Hanks came to this Rock Spring more than once, sitting with her child and her thoughts, looking at running water and green moss. The secrets of the mingled drone and hush of the place gave her reminders of Bible language, "Be ye comforted," or "Peace, be still."

Cooking, washing, sewing, spinning, weaving, helping keep a home for a man and two babies, besides herself, in a one-room cabin, took a good deal of her time. If there were flies creeping over the face of the baby Abe, she had to drop her work and shoo the flies away. There were few hours in the year she was free to sit with her child and her thoughts, listening to the changing drone and hush of Rock Spring saying, "Be ye comforted," or "Peace, be still."

The baby grew, learning to sit up, to crawl over the dirt floor of the cabin; the gristle became bone; the father joked about the long legs getting longer; the mother joked about how quick he grew out of one shirt into another.

Sparrows and Hankses who came visiting said, "He's solemn as a papoose." An easy and a light bundle he was to carry when the family moved to a farm on Knob Creek, eight miles from Hodgenville, on the main highway from Louisville to Nashville.

CHAPTER 5

On the Knob Creek farm the child Abraham Lincoln learned to talk, to form words with the tongue and the roof of the mouth and the force of the breath from lungs and throat. "Pappy" and "Mammy," the words of his people meaning father and mother, were among the first syllables. He learned what the word "name" meant; his name was Abraham, the same as Abraham in the Bible, the same as his grandfather Abraham. It was "Abe" for short; if his mother called in the dark, "Is that you, Abe?" he answered, "Yes, Mammy, it's me." The name of the family he belonged to was "Lincoln" or "Linkun," though most people called it "Linkern" and it was sometimes spelled "Linkhorn."

The family lived there on Knob Creek farm, from the time Abe was three or so till he was past seven years of age. Here he was told "Kaintucky" meant the state he was living in; Knob Creek farm, the Rock Spring farm where he was born, Hodgenville, Elizabethtown, Muldraugh's Hill, these places he knew, the land he walked on, was all part of Kentucky.

Yet it was also part of something bigger. Men had been fighting, bleeding, and dying in war, for a country, "our country"; a man couldn't have more than one country any more than he could have more than one mother; the name of the mother country was the "United States"; and there was a piece of cloth with red and white stripes having a blue square in its corner filled with white stars; and this piece of cloth they called "a flag." The flag meant the "United States." One summer morning his father started the day by stepping out of the front door and shooting a long rifle into the sky; and his father explained it was the day to make a big noise because it was the "Fourth of July," the day the United States first called itself a "free and independent" nation.

His folks talked like other folks in the neighborhood. They called themselves "pore" people. A man learned in books was "eddicated." What was certain was "sartin." The syllables came through the nose; joints were "j'ints"; fruit "spiled" instead of spoiling; in corn-planting time they "drapped" the seeds. They went on errands and "brung" things back.

Their dogs "follered" the coons. Flannel was "flannen," a bandanna a "bandanner," a chimney a "chimbly," a shadow a "shadder," and mosquitoes plain "skeeters." They "gethered" crops. A creek was a "crick," a cover a "kiver."

A man silent was a "say-nothin'." They asked, "Have ye et?" There were dialogues, "Kin ye?" "No, I cain't." And if a woman had an idea of doing something she said, "I had a idy to." They made their own words. Those who spoke otherwise didn't belong, were "puttin' on." This was their wilderness lingo; it had gnarled bones and gaunt hours of their lives in it.

Words like "independent" bothered the boy. He was hungry to understand the meanings of words. He would ask what "independent" meant and when he was told the meaning he lay awake nights thinking about the meaning of the meaning of "independent." Other words bothered him, such as "predestination." He asked the meaning of that and lay awake hours at night thinking about the meaning of the meaning.

CHAPTER 6

SEVEN-YEAR-OLD Abe walked four miles a day going to the Knob Creek school to learn to read and write. Zachariah Riney and Caleb Hazel were the teachers who brought him along from A B C to where he could write the name "A-b-r-a-h-a-m L-i-n-c-o-l-n" and count numbers beginning with one, two, three, and so on. He heard twice two is four.

The schoolhouse was built of logs, with a dirt floor, no window, one door. The scholars learned their lessons by saying them to themselves out loud till it was time to recite; alphabets, multiplication tables, and the letters of spelled words were all in the air at once. It was a "blab school"; so they called it.

The Louisville and Nashville pike running past the Lincoln cabin had many different travelers. Covered wagons came with settlers moving south and west, or north to Ohio and Indiana; there were peddlers with knick-knacks to spread out and tell the prices of; congressmen, members of the legislature meeting at Lexington, men who had visited Henry Clay at Ashland.

Coming back from a fishing trip, with one fish, Abe met a soldier who came from fighting in the Battle of New Orleans with General Jackson, and Abe, remembering his father and mother had told him to be good to soldiers, handed the soldier the one fish.

The Lincolns got well acquainted with Christopher Columbus Graham, a doctor, a scientist, who was beginning to study and write books about the rocks, flowers, plants, trees, and wild animals of Kentucky; Graham slept in the bed while the Lincolns slept on the floor of the cabin, more than once; he told in the evening talk about days camping with Daniel Boone, and running backward with Boone so as to make foot-tracks pointing forward to mislead the Indians; he talked about stones, leaves, bones, snake-skins he was carrying in a sack back to Louisville; he mentioned a young storekeeper at Elizabethtown, named John James Audubon, who had marvelous ways with birds and might some day write a great book about birds. The boy Abe heard traveling preachers and his father talk about the times when they held church meetings in cabins, and every man had his rifle by his side, and there were other men with rifles outside the cabin door, ready for Indians who might try to interrupt their Sabbath worship. And the boy never liked it when the talkers slung around words like "independent" and "predestination," because he lay awake thinking about those long words.

Abe was the chore-boy of the Knob Creek farm as soon as he grew big enough to run errands, to hold a pine-knot at night lighting his father at a job, or to carry water, fill the woodbox, clean ashes from the fireplace, hoe weeds, pick berries, grapes, persimmons for beer-making. He hunted the timbers and came back with walnuts, hickory and hazel nuts. His hands knew the stinging blisters from using a hoe-handle back and forth a summer afternoon, and in autumn the mash of walnut-stain that wouldn't wash off, with all the rinsing and scrubbing of Nancy Hanks's homemade soap. He went swimming with Austin Gollaher; they got their backs sunburnt so the skin peeled off.

Wearing only a shirt—no hat nor pants—Abe rode a horse hitched to a "bull-tongue" plow of wood shod with iron. He helped his father with seed corn, beans, onions, potatoes. He ducked out of the way of the heels of the stallion and brood mares his father kept and paid taxes on.

The father would ride away to auctions, once coming home with dishes, plates, spoons, and a wash basin, another time with a heifer, and again with a wagon that had been knocked down to the highest bidder for 8½ cents.

Life dripped with fat and ease. Or it took hold with hunger and cold. All the older settlers remembered winter in the year 1795, when "cold Friday" came; Kentucky was "cold as Canada," and cows froze to death in the open fields. The wilderness is careless.

In this Knob Creek neighborhood Abe Lincoln grew up from three to seven years of age, heard travelers talk, learned to write and sign his name, in fact, first learned the meanings of names and how to answer, "Yes, it's me," if his mother called in the dark, "Is that you, Abe?"

CHAPTER 7

In the year 1816 Tom Lincoln was appointed road surveyor. The paper naming him for that office said he was named in place of George Redman to repair the road "leading from Nolen to Pendleton, which lies between the Bigg Hill and the Rolling Fork." It further commanded "that all hands that assisted said Redman do assist Lincoln in keeping said road in repair." It was a pasty red clay road. That the county was beginning to think about good roads showed that civilization was breaking through on the wilderness. And that Tom Lincoln was named as road surveyor showed they were holding some respect for him as a citizen and taxpayer of that community. At the county courthouse the recorder of deeds noticed that Thomas Lincoln signed his name, while his wife, Nancy, made her mark.

Thomas Lincoln
Nancy X Lincoln
her mark

Knob Creek settlers taking their corn to Hodgen's mill or riding to Elizabethtown to pay their taxes at the court or collect bounties on wolf-skins at the county courthouse, talked a good deal about land-titles, landowners, landlords, land-laws, land-lawyers, land-sharks. Tom Lincoln about that time was chopping down trees and cutting brush on the Knob Creek land so as to clear more ground, raise corn on it and make a farm out of it. And he wasn't satisfied; he was suspicious that even if he did get his thirty acres cleared and paid for, the land might be taken away from him. This was happening to other settlers; they had the wrong kind of papers. Pioneers and settlers who for years had been fighting Indians, wolves, foxes, mosquitoes, and malaria had seen their land taken away; they had the wrong kind of papers. Daniel Boone, the first man to break a path from civilization through and into the Kentucky wilderness, found himself one day with all his rich, bluegrass Kentucky lands gone, not an acre of his big farms left; he had the wrong kind of papers; that was why he moved from Kentucky to Missouri.

Though Tom Lincoln was paying taxes on his thirty-acre farm, he was sued as a "tresspasser." He had to prove he wasn't a squatter—which he did. He went to court and won his suit. His little thirty-acre piece was only one of many pieces of a 10,000-acre tract surveyed in 1784 and patented to one man, Thomas Middleton, in 1786.

Poor white men were having a harder time to get along. Hardin County had been filling up with negroes, slave black men, bought and sold among the rich and well-to-do. The Hodgens, La Rues, and other first families usually had one or two, or six or a dozen, negroes. More than half the population of Hardin County were colored. And it seemed that as more slave black men were brought in, a poor white man didn't count for so much; he had a harder time to get along.

While these changes were coming in Kentucky, the territory of Indiana came into the Union as a state whose law declared "all men are born equally free and independent" and "the holding any part of the human creation in slavery, or involuntary servitude, can only originate in usurpation and tyranny." In crossing the Ohio River's two shores, a traveler touched two soils, one where the buying and selling of black slaves went on, the other where the negro was held to be "part of human creation" and was not property for buying and selling. But both soils were part of the Union of states.

Letters and reports reaching Hardin County about this time told of rich, black lands in Indiana, with more bushels of corn to the acre than down in Kentucky, Government land with clear title, the right kind of papers, for two dollars an acre. This helped Tom Lincoln to decide in the year 1816 to move to Indiana. He told the family he would build a flat-boat, load the household goods on it, float by creeks to the Ohio River, leave the household goods somewhere along the river while he went afoot up into Indiana, located his land, and registered it. Then he would come back, and the family, afoot and on horseback, would move to the new farm and home.

CHAPTER 8

THE boy, Abe, had his thoughts, some running ahead wondering how Indiana would look, some going back to his seven little years in Kentucky. Here he had curled around his mother's apron, watched her face and listened to her reading the Bible at the cabin log-fire, her fingers rambling through his hair, the hands patting him on the cheek and under the chin. God was real to his mother; he tried to make pictures in his head of the face of God far off and away in the sky, watching Kentucky, Hodgenville, Knob Creek, and all the rest of the world He had made. His thoughts could go back to the first time on a winter night around the fire when he lay flat on his stomach listening to his father as he told about his brothers, Mordecai and Josiah, and their father, Abraham Lincoln, who had staked out claims for more than 2,000 acres of land on the Green River. One day Abraham Lincoln and his three boys were working in a field; all of a sudden the father doubled up with a groan of pain and crumpled to the ground, just after the boys had heard a rifle-shot and the whining of a bullet. "Indians," the boys yelled to each other.

And Mordecai ran to a cabin, Josiah started across the fields and woods to a fort to bring help, while Tom Lincoln—little knee-high Tom—stooped over his father's bleeding body and wondered what he could do. He looked up to see an Indian standing over him, and a shining bangle hanging down over the Indian's shoulder close to the heart.

The Indian clutched upward with his hands, doubled with a groan and crumpled to the ground; Mordecai with a rifle at a peephole in the cabin had aimed his rifle at the shining bangle hanging down close to the Indian's heart, and Tom was so near he heard the bullet plug its hole into the red man.

And for years after that Mordecai Lincoln hated Indians with a deadly hate; if he heard that Indians were loose anywhere in a half-day's riding, he took his best rifles, pistols, and knives, and went Indian-killing.

There was Dr. Christopher Columbus Graham from Louisville, telling how the Indians were chasing Daniel Boone, and Boone saw a grapevine climbing high up a big oak; and he cut the grapevine near the root, took a run and a swing and made a jump of forty feet, so the Indians had to lose time finding sight and smell of his foot-tracks again.

And there were caves, worth remembering about in that part of Kentucky, and especially the biggest one of all, Mammoth Cave, fifty miles south; they said a thousand wagons could drive in and there would be room for another thousand.

And there was the foxy Austin Gollaher, his playmate. Up a tree he climbed one time, Abe dropped a pawpaw down into a coonskin cap; he guessed it was Austin's cap he was putting a smear of pawpaw mash in, but Austin had seen the trick coming and changed caps. So he had to wipe the smear out of his own cap.

Once he was walking on a log across Knob Creek when the rains had raised the creek. Just under the log, and under his feet, was the rush of the yellow muddy water. The log was slippery, his feet slippery. His feet went up in the air, he tumbled to the bottom of the creek; he came up, slipped again, came up with his nose and eyes full of water, and then saw Austin Gollaher on the bank holding out a long pole. He took hold of the pole and Austin pulled him to the bank.

Maybe he would grow up; his feet would be farther away from his head and his chin if he grew up; he could pick apples without climbing a tree or throwing clubs—if he grew up. Maybe then, after growing up, he would know more about those words he heard men saying, "in-de-pend-ent," "pre-des-ti-na-tion." Daniel Boone—yes, he could understand about Daniel Boone—wearing moccasins and a buckskin shirt. But George Washington and Thomas Jefferson, and the President in Washington, James Madison—they were far off; they were sort of like God; it was hard to make pictures of their faces.

How many times he had gone to the family Bible, opened the big front cover, and peeped in at the page which tells what the book is! There were the words: "The Holy Bible, containing the Old and New Testaments, with Arguments prefixed to the Different Books and Moral and Theological Observations illustrating each Chapter, composed by the Reverend Mr. Osterwald, Professor of Divinity." And then pages and pages filled with words spelled out like the words in the spelling book he had in school. So many words: heavy words—mysterious words!

About wolf heads, he could understand. He saw a man in Elizabethtown one time carrying two big wolf heads. The man had shot the wolves and was going to the courthouse, where they paid money for wolf heads. Yes, this he could understand. Wolves kill sheep and cattle in the fields; they come to the barns for pigs and chickens; he had heard them howling and sniffing on winter nights around the Knob Creek cabin and up the hills and gorges.

And there was his mother, his "mammy," the woman other people called Nancy or Nancy Hanks. . . . It was so dark and strange about her. There was such sweetness. Yet there used to be more sweetness and a fresher sweetness. There had been one baby they buried. Then there was Sally—and him, little Abe. Did the children cost her something? Did they pull her down? . . . The baby that came and was laid away so soon, only three days after it came, in so little a grave: that hurt his mother; she was sick and tired more often after that. . . . There were such lights and shadows back in her eyes. She wanted—what did she want? There were more and more days he had to take care of her, when he loved to bring cool drinking water to her—or anything she asked for.

Well—a boy seven years old isn't supposed to know much; he goes along and tries to do what the big people tell him to do. . . . They have been young and seen trouble: maybe they know. . . . He would get up in the morning when they called him; he would run to the spring for water. . . . He was only seven years old—and there were lots of frisky tricks he wanted to know more about.

He was a "shirt-tail boy." . . . Three boys teased him one day when he took corn to Hodgen's Mill; they wouldn't be satisfied till he had punched their noses. . . . A clerk in the store at Elizabethtown gave him maple sugar to sit on a syrup keg and suck while his mother bought salt and flour. And the clerk was the only man he knew who was wearing store clothes, Sunday clothes, every day in the week. . . . The two pear trees his father planted on the Rock Spring farm . . . the faces of two goats a man kept down in Hodgenville . . . Dennis Hanks saying, "Abe, your face is solemn as a papoose."

It wouldn't be easy to forget that Saturday afternoon in corn-planting time when other boys dropped the seed-corn into all the rows in the big seven-acre field—and Abe dropped the pumpkin seed. He dropped two seeds at every other hill and every other row. The next Sunday morning there came a big rain in the hills; it didn't rain a drop in the valley, but the water came down the gorges and slides, and washed ground, corn, pumpkin seeds and all clear off the field.

CHAPTER 9

In the fall of the year 1816, Abe watched his father cut down trees, cut out logs, and fasten those logs into a flatboat on Knob Creek. Abe ran after tools his father called for, sometimes held a hammer, a saw and a knife in his hands ready to give his father the next one called for. If his father said, "Fetch me a drink of water," the boy fetched; his legs belonged to his father. He helped carry chairs, tables, household goods, and carpenter's tools, loading them onto the flatboat. These, with four hundred gallons of whisky, "ten bar'ls," Tom had loaded onto the boat, made quite a cargo. Tom Lincoln, who was not much of a drinking man, had traded his farm for whisky, which was a kind of money in that day, and $20.00 cash.

Nancy Hanks and Sarah and Abe stayed on the farm while the husband and father floated down Knob Creek to Salt River and into the Ohio River. Tom was out of luck when the flatboat turned over so that the tool chest, household goods and four barrels of whisky slid out of the boat. Most of the whisky and some of the other goods he managed to fish up from the river bottom. Then he crossed the Ohio River, landed on the Indiana side at Thompson's Ferry and left his whisky and household goods at the house of a man called Posey.

He started off on foot into the big timbers of what was then Perry County, later divided into Spencer County. He decided to live and to farm on a quarter-section of land on Little Pigeon Creek; he notched the trees with his ax, cleared away brush and piled it, as the Government land-laws required. This was his "claim," later filed at the Land Office in Vincennes, Indiana, as the Southwest Quarter of Section Thirty-two, Town Four South, Range Five West, to be paid for at $2.00 an acre. His Indiana homestead was now ready for a cabin and a family; he walked back to the Knob Creek home in Kentucky and told the family he reckoned they'd all put in the winter up in "Indianny."

They had fifty miles to go, in a straight line "as the crow flies," but about one hundred miles with all the zigzags and curves around hills, timbers, creeks, and rivers.

Pots, pans, kettles, blankets, the family Bible, and other things were put into bags and loaded on two horses. Nancy and Sarah climbed on one horse, Tom and Abe on the other. When it was hard going for the horses, the father and mother walked. Part of the way on that hundred-mile ride made little Abe's eyes open. They were going deeper into the wilderness.

In Kentucky there were ten people to the square mile and in Indiana only three. As Abe sat on the horse plodding along, he saw miles and miles of beeches, oaks, elms, hard and soft maples, hung and run over with the scarlet streamers and the shifting gray hazes of autumn.

Then they came to the Ohio River. The Frenchmen years before named it "La Belle Rivière," meaning it was a sheen of water as good to look at as a beautiful woman. There she lay—the biggest stretch of shining water his eyes had ever seen. And Abe thought how different it was from Knob Creek, which he could walk across on a log—if he didn't let his feet slip from under. They crossed the river, and at the house of the man called Posey they got a wagon, loaded the barrels of whisky and the household goods, and drove sixteen miles to their "claim." The trail was so narrow that a few times Tom Lincoln got off the wagon with an ax and cut brush and trees so the wagon could pass through. It was a hired wagon and horses they came with, and the wagon and horse-team were taken back to Posey.

Tom Lincoln, his wife, boy, and girl, had arrived on a claim at Little Pigeon Creek, without a horse or a cow, without a house, with a little piece of land under their feet and the wintry sky high over. Naked they had come into the world; almost naked they came to Little Pigeon Creek, Indiana.

The whole family pitched in and built a pole-shed or "half-faced camp." On a slope of ground stood two trees about fourteen feet apart, east and west. These formed the two strong corner-posts of a sort of cabin with three sides, the fourth side open, facing south. The sides and the roof were covered with poles, branches, brush, dried grass, mud; chinks were stuffed where the wind or the rain was trying to come through. At the open side a log-fire was kept burning night and day. In the two far corners inside the camp were beds of dry leaves on the ground. To these beds the sleepers brought their blankets and bearskins.

Here they lived a year. In the summer time and fair weather, the pole-shed was snug enough. When the rain storms or wind and snow broke through and drenched the place, or when the south or southwest wind blew the fire-smoke into the camp so those inside had to clear out, it was a rough life.

The mother sang. Nancy Hanks knew songs her mother, Lucy, had heard in Virginia. The ballad of Fair Ellender told of the hero coming home with the Brown Girl who had lands and gold. Fair Ellender taunted: "Is this your bride? She seemeth me plagued brown." And for that, the Brown Girl leaped over a table corner and put a slim little knife through Fair Ellender's heart. Then out came the hero's sword and he cut off the Brown Girl's head and "slung it agin the wall." Then he put the sword through his own heart.

And there was the ballad of Wicked Polly, who danced and ran wild and told the old folks, "I'll turn to God when I get old, and He will then receive my soul." But when death struck her down while she was young and running wild, she called for her mother, and with rolling eyeballs, cried, "When I am dead, remember well, your wicked Polly screams in hell."

Tom chopped logs for a cabin forty yards away while Abe did the best he could helping Nancy and Sarah trim the branches off the logs, cut brush, clear ground for planting, hoe weeds, tend the log-fire. The heaviest regular chore of the children was walking a mile away to a spring and carrying a bucket of water back home. Their food was mostly game shot in the woods near by; they went barefoot most of the year; in the winter their shoes were homemade moccasins; they were up with the sun and the early birds in the morning; their lighting at night was fire-logs and pine-knots. In summer and early fall the flies and mosquitoes swarmed.

In the new cabin Tom Lincoln was building, and on this little Pigeon Creek farm, the Lincoln family was going to live fourteen years.

CHAPTER 10

As Abe Lincoln, seven years old, going on eight, went to sleep on his bed of dry leaves in a corner of the pole-shed there on Little Pigeon Creek, in Indiana, in the winter of 1816, he had his thoughts, his feelings, his impressions. He shut his eyes, and looking-glasses began to work inside his head; he could see Kentucky and the Knob Creek farm again; he could see the Ohio River shining so far across that he couldn't begin to throw a stone from one side to the other.

And while his eyes were shut he could see the inside of the pole-shed, the floor of earth and grass, the frying-pan, the cooking-pot, the water-pail he and his sister carried full of water from the spring a mile away, and the log-fire always kept burning. And sometimes his imagination, his shut eyes and their quick-changing looking-glasses would bring the whole outdoor sky and land indoors, into the pole-shed, into the big shifting looking-glasses inside of his head. The mystery of imagination, of the faculty of reconstruction and piecing together today the things his eyes had seen yesterday, this took hold of him and he brooded over it.

One night he tried to sleep while his head was working on the meaning of the heavy and mysterious words standing dark on the pages of the family Bible; the stories his mother told him from those pages; all the people in the world drowned, the world covered with water, even Indiana and Kentucky, all people drowned except Noah and his family; the man Jonah swallowed by a whale and after days coming out of the belly of the whale; the Last Day to come, the stars dropping out of the sky, the world swallowed up in fire.

And one night this boy felt the southwest wind blowing the log-fire smoke into his nostrils. And there was a hoot-owl crying, and a shaking of branches in the beeches and walnuts outside, so that he went to the south opening of the shed and looked out on a winter sky with a high quarter-moon and a white shine of thin frost on the long open spaces of the sky.

And an old wonder took a deeper hold on him, a wonder about the loneliness of life down there in the Indiana wilderness, and a wonder about what was happening in other places over the world, places he had heard people mention, cities, rivers, flags, wars, Jerusalem, Washington, Baltimore.

He might have asked the moon, "What do you see?" And the moon might have told him many things.

That year of 1816 the moon had seen sixteen thousand wagons come along one turnpike in Pennsylvania, heading west, with people hungry for new land, a new home, just like Tom Lincoln. Up the Mississippi River that year had come the first steamboat to curve into the Ohio River and land passengers at Louisville. The moon had seen the first steamboat leave Pittsburgh and tie up at New Orleans. New wheels, wagons, were coming, an iron horse snorting fire and smoke. Rolling-mills, ingots, iron, steel, were the talk of Pennsylvania; a sheet copper mill was starting in Massachusetts.

The moon could see eight million people in the United States, white men who had pushed the Indians over the eastern mountains, fighting to clear the Great Plains and the southern valleys of the red men. At Fallen Timbers and at Tippecanoe in Indiana, and down at the Great Bend of the Tallapoosa, the pale faces and copper faces had yelled and grappled.

And how had these eight million people come to America, for the moon to look down on and watch their westward swarming? Many were children of men who had quarreled in the old countries of Europe, and fought wars about the words and ways of worshiping God and obeying His commandments. They were Puritans from England, French Huguenots, German Pietists, Hanoverians, Moravians, Saxons, Austrians, Swiss, Quakers, all carrying their Bibles. Also there were Ulster Presbyterians from North Ireland, and Scotch Presbyterians. They came by their own wish. Others who came not by their own wish were fifty thousand thieves and murderers sent from British prisons and courts. Dr. Samuel Johnson, the same man who said, "Patriotism is the last refuge of a scoundrel," had called Americans "a race of convicts." Convicted men in England, offered the choice of hanging or being shipped to America, had given the answer, "Hang me."

The moon had seen boys and girls by thousands kidnaped off the streets of English cities and smuggled across to America. And each year for fifty years there had come a thousand to fifteen hundred "indentured servants," men and women who had signed papers to work for a certain master, the law holding them to work till their time was up.

The moon had seen sailing-ships start from ports in Europe and take from six weeks to six months crossing the Atlantic. Aboard those ships often were "stench, fumes, vomiting, many kinds of sicknesses, fever, dysentery, scurvy, the mouth-rot, and the like, all of which come from old and sharply salted food and meat, also from bad and foul water."

Such were a few of the things known to the fathers and grandfathers of part of the eight million people in America that the moon was looking down on in the winter nights of 1816. And in the years to come the moon would see more and more people coming from Europe.

Seldom had the moon in its thousands of years of looking down on the earth and the human family seen such a man as the Napoleon Bonaparte whose bayonets had been going in Europe for fifteen years, shoving kings off thrones, changing laws, maps, books, raising armies, using them up, and raising new armies, until people in some regions were saying, "The red roses of this year grow from the blood-wet ground of the wars we fought last year."

When Napoleon sold to Jefferson the Great Plains between the Mississippi River and the Rocky Mountains, the moon saw only a few Indians, buffalo hunters and drifters, living there. The price for the land was fifteen million dollars; Jefferson had to argue with people who said the price was too high. Such things the moon had seen. Also, out of war-taxed and war-crippled Europe the moon could see steady lines of ships taking people from that part of the Round World across the water to America. Also, lines of ships sailing to Africa with whisky, calico, and silk, and coming back loaded with negroes.

And as the wagons, by thousands a year, were slipping through the passes of the Allegheny Mountains, heading west for the two-dollar-an-acre Government land, many steered clear of the South; they couldn't buy slaves; and they were suspicious of slavery; it was safer to go farming where white men did all the work. At first the stream of wagons and settlers moving west had kept close to the Ohio River. Then it began spreading in a fan-shape up north and west.

The moon could see along the pikes, roads, and trails heading west, broken wagon-wheels with prairie grass growing up over the spokes and hubs. And near by, sometimes, a rusty skillet, empty moccasins, and the bones of horses and men.

In the hot dog-days, in the long rains, in the casual blizzards, they had stuck it out—and lost. There came a saying, a pithy, perhaps brutal folk proverb, "The cowards never started and the weak ones died by the way."

Such were a few of the many, many things the moon might have told little Abe Lincoln, nearly eight years old, on a winter night in 1816 on Little Pigeon Creek, in the Buckhorn Valley, in southern Indiana—a high quarter-moon with a white shine of thin frost on the long open spaces of the sky.

He was of the blood and breath of many of these things, and would know them better in the years to come.

CHAPTER 11

DURING the year 1817, little Abe Lincoln, eight years old, going on nine, had an ax put in his hands and helped his father cut down trees and notch logs for the corners of their new cabin, forty yards from the pole-shed where the family was cooking, eating, and sleeping.

Once Abe took a gun as a flock of wild turkeys came toward the new log cabin, and, standing inside, shot through a crack and killed one of the big birds; and after that, somehow, he never felt like pulling the trigger on game-birds. A mile from the cabin was a salt lick where deer came; there the boy could have easily shot the animals, as they stood rubbing their tongues along the salty slabs or tasting of a saltish ooze. His father did the shooting; the deer killed gave them meat for Nancy's skillet; and the skins were tanned, cut, and stitched into shirts, trousers, mitts, moccasins. They wore buckskin; their valley was called the Buckhorn Valley.

After months the cabin stood up, four walls fitted together with a roof, a one-room house eighteen feet square, for a family to live in. A stick chimney plastered with clay ran up outside. The floor was packed and smoothed dirt. A log-fire lighted the inside; no windows were cut in the walls. For a door there was a hole cut to stoop through. Bedsteads were cleated to the corners of the cabin; pegs stuck in the side of a wall made a ladder for young Abe to climb up in a loft to sleep on a hump of dry leaves; rain and snow came through chinks of the roof onto his bearskin cover. A table and three-legged stools had the top sides smoothed with an ax, and the bark-side under, in the style called "puncheon."

A few days of this year in which the cabin was building, Nancy told Abe to wash his face and hands extra clean; she combed his hair, held his face between her two hands, smacked him a kiss on the mouth, and sent him to school—nine miles and back—Abe and Sally hand in hand hiking eighteen miles a day. Tom Lincoln used to say Abe was going to have "a real eddication," explaining, "You air a-goin' to larn readin', writin', and cipherin'."

He learned to spell words he didn't know the meaning of, spelling the words before he used them in sentences. In a list of "words of eight syllables accented upon the sixth," was the word "incomprehensibility." He learned that first, and then such sentences as "Is he to go in?" and "Ann can spin flax."

Fall time came with its early frost and they were moved into the new cabin, when horses and a wagon came breaking into the clearing one day. It was Tom and Betsy Sparrow and their seventeen-year-old boy, Dennis Hanks, who had come from Hodgenville, Kentucky, to cook and sleep in the pole-shed of the Lincoln family till they could locate land and settle. Hardly a year had passed, however, when both Tom and Betsy Sparrow were taken down with the "milk sick," beginning with a whitish coat on the tongue. Both died and were buried in October on a little hill in a clearing in the timbers near by.

Soon after, there came to Nancy Hanks Lincoln that white coating of the tongue; her vitals burned; the tongue turned brownish; her feet and hands grew cold and colder, her pulse slow and slower. She knew she was dying, called for her children, and spoke to them her last choking words. Sarah and Abe leaned over the bed. A bony hand of the struggling mother went out, putting its fingers into the boy's sandy black hair; her fluttering guttural words seemed to say he must grow up and be good to his sister and father.

So, on a bed of poles cleated to the corner of the cabin, the body of Nancy Hanks Lincoln lay, looking tired . . . tired . . . with a peace settling in the pinched corners of the sweet, weary mouth, silence slowly etching away the lines of pain and hunger drawn around the gray eyes where now the eyelids closed down in the fine pathos of unbroken rest, a sleep without interruption settling about the form of the stooped and wasted shoulder-bones, looking to the children who tiptoed in, stood still, cried their tears of want and longing, whispered "Mammy, Mammy," and heard only their own whispers answering, looking to these little ones of her brood as though new secrets had come to her in place of the old secrets given up with the breath of life.

And Tom Lincoln took a log left over from the building of the cabin, and he and Dennis Hanks whipsawed the log into planks, planed the planks smooth, and made them of a measure for a box to bury the dead wife and mother in. Little Abe, with a jackknife, whittled pine-wood pegs. And then, while Dennis and Abe held the planks, Tom bored holes and stuck the whittled pegs through the bored holes. This was the coffin, and they carried it the next day to the same little timber clearing near by, where a few weeks before they had buried Tom and Betsy Sparrow. It was in the way of the deer-run leading to the saltish water; light feet and shy hoofs ran over those early winter graves.

So the woman, Nancy Hanks, died, thirty-six years old, a pioneer sacrifice, with memories of monotonous, endless everyday chores, of mystic Bible verses read over and over for their promises, and with memories of blue wistful hills and a summer when the crab-apple blossoms flamed white and she carried a boy-child into the world.

She had looked out on fields of blue-blossoming flax and hummed "Hey, Betty Martin, tiptoe, tiptoe"; she had sung of bright kingdoms by and by and seen the early frost leaf its crystals on the stalks of button weed and redbud; she had sung:

> You may bury me in the east,
> You may bury me in the west,
> And we'll all rise together in that morning.

CHAPTER 12

Some weeks later, when David Elkin, elder of the Methodist church, was in that neighborhood, he was called on to speak over the grave of Nancy Hanks. He had been acquainted with her in Kentucky, and to the Lincoln family and a few neighbors he spoke of good things she had done, sweet ways she had of living her life in this Vale of Tears, and her faith in another life yonder past the River Jordan.

The "milk sick" took more people in that neighborhood the same year, and Tom Lincoln whipsawed planks for more coffins. One settler lost four milch cows and eleven calves. The nearest doctor for people or cattle was thirty-five miles away. The wilderness is careless.

Lonesome and dark months came for Abe and Sarah. Worst of all were the weeks after their father went away, promising to come back.

Elizabethtown, Kentucky, was the place Tom Lincoln headed for. As he footed it through the woods and across the Ohio River, he was saying over to himself a speech—the words he would say to Sarah Bush Johnston, down in Elizabethtown. Her husband had died a few years before, and she was now in Tom's thoughts.

He went straight to the house where she was living in Elizabethtown, and, speaking to her as "Miss Johnston," he argued: "I have no wife and you no husband. I came a-purpose to marry you. I knowed you from a gal and you knowed me from a boy. I've no time to lose; and if you're willin' let it be done straight off."

Her answer was, "I got debts." She gave him a list of the debts; he paid them; a license was issued; and they were married on December 2, 1819.

He could write his name; she couldn't write hers. Trying to explain why the two of them took up with each other so quickly, Dennis Hanks at a later time said, "Tom had a kind o' way with women, an' maybe it was somethin' she took comfort in to have a man that didn't drink an' cuss none."

Little Abe and Sarah, living in the lonesome cabin on Little Pigeon

Creek, Indiana, got a nice surprise one morning when four horses and a wagon came into their clearing, and their father jumped off, then Sarah Bush Lincoln, the new wife and mother, then John, Sarah, and Matilda Johnston, Sarah Bush's three children by her first husband. Next off the wagon came a feather mattress, feather pillows, a black walnut bureau, a large clothes-chest, a table, chairs, pots and skillets, knives, forks, spoons.

Abe ran his fingers over the slick wood of the bureau, pushed his fist into the feather pillows, sat in the new chairs, and wondered to himself, because this was the first time he had touched such fine things, such soft slick things.

"Here's your new mammy," his father told Abe as the boy looked up at a strong, large-boned, rosy woman, with a kindly face and eyes, with a steady voice, steady ways. The cheek-bones of her face stood out and she had a strong jaw-bone; she was warm and friendly for Abe's little hands to touch, right from the beginning. As one of her big hands held his head against her skirt he felt like a cold chick warming under the soft feathers of a big wing. She took the corn-husks Abe had been sleeping on, piled them in the yard and said they would be good for a pig-pen later on; and Abe sunk his head and bones that night in a feather pillow and a feather mattress.

Ten years pass with that cabin on Little Pigeon Creek for a home, and that farm and neighborhood the soil for growth. There the boy Abe grows to be the young man, Abraham Lincoln.

Abe Lincoln grows up. His father talks about the waste of time in "eddication"; it is enough "to larn readin', writin', cipherin' "; but the stanch, yearning stepmother, Sarah Bush Lincoln, comes between the boy and the father. And the father listens to the stepmother and lets her have her way.

CHAPTER 13

WHEN he was eleven years old, Abe Lincoln's young body began to change. The juices and glands began to make a long, tall boy out of him. As the months and years went by, he noticed his lean wrists getting longer, his legs too, and he was now looking over the heads of other boys. Men said, "Land o' Goshen, that boy air a-growin' !"

As he took on more length, they said he was shooting up into the air like green corn in the summer of a good corn-year. So he grew. When he reached seventeen years of age, and they measured him, he was six feet, nearly four inches, high, from the bottoms of his moccasins to the top of his skull.

These were years he was handling the ax. Except in spring plowing-time and the fall fodder-pulling, he was handling the ax nearly all the time. The insides of his hands took on callus thick as leather. He cleared openings in the timber, cut logs and puncheons, split firewood, built pig-pens.

He learned how to measure with his eye the half-circle swing of the ax so as to nick out the deepest possible chip from off a tree-trunk. The trick of swaying his body easily on the hips so as to throw the heaviest possible weight into the blow of the ax—he learned that.

On winter mornings he wiped the frost from the ax-handle, sniffed sparkles of air into his lungs, and beat a steady cleaving of blows into a big tree—till it fell—and he sat on the main log and ate his noon dinner of corn bread and fried salt pork—and joked with the squirrels that frisked and peeped at him from high forks of near-by walnut trees.

He learned how to make his ax flash and bite into a sugar-maple or a sycamore. The outside and the inside look of black walnut and black oak, hickory and jack oak, elm and white oak, sassafras, dogwood, grape-vines, sumac—he came on their secrets. He could guess close to the time of the year, to the week of the month, by the way the leaves and branches of trees looked. He sniffed the seasons.

Often he worked alone in the timbers, all day long with only the sound of his own ax, or his own voice speaking to himself, or the crackling and swaying of branches in the wind, and the cries and whirs of animals, of brown and silver-gray squirrels, of partridges, hawks, crows, turkeys, sparrows, and the occasional wildcats.

The tricks and whimsies of the sky, how to read clear skies and cloudy weather, the creeping vines of ivy and wild grape, the recurrence of dog-wood blossoms in spring, the ways of snow, rain, drizzle, sleet, the visitors of sky and weather coming and going hour by hour—he tried to read their secrets, he tried to be friendly with their mystery.

So he grew, to become hard, tough, wiry. The muscle on his bones and the cords, tendons, cross-weaves of fiber, and nerve centres, these became instruments to obey his wishes. He found with other men he could lift his own end of a log—and more too. One of the neighbors said he was strong as three men. Another said, "He can sink an ax deeper into wood than any man I ever saw." And another, "If you heard him fellin' trees in a clearin', you would say there was three men at work by the way the trees fell."

He was more than a tough, long, rawboned boy. He amazed men with his man's lifting power. He put his shoulders under a new-built corncrib one day and walked away with it to where the farmer wanted it. Four men, ready with poles to put under it and carry it, didn't need their poles. He played the same trick with a chicken house; at the new, growing town of Gentryville near by, they said the chicken house weighed six hundred pounds, and only a big boy with a hard backbone could get under it and walk away with it.

A blacksmith shop, a grocery, and a store had started up on the cross-roads of the Gentry farm. And one night after Abe had been helping thresh wheat on Dave Turnham's place, he went with Dennis Hanks, John Johnston, and some other boys to Gentryville where the farm-hands sat around with John Baldwin, the blacksmith, and Jones, the storekeeper, passed the whisky jug, told stories, and talked politics and religion and gossip. Going home late that night, they saw something in a mud puddle alongside the road. They stepped over to see whether it was a man or a hog. It was a man—drunk—snoring—sleeping off his drunk—on a frosty night outdoors in a cold wind.

They shook him by the shoulders, doubled his knees to his stomach, but he went on sleeping, snoring. The cold wind was getting colder. The other boys said they were going home, and they went away leaving Abe alone with the snoring sleeper in the mud puddle. Abe stepped into the mud, reached arms around the man, slung him over his shoulders, carried him to Dennis Hanks's cabin, built a fire, rubbed him warm and left him sleeping off the whisky.

And the man afterward said Abe saved his life. He told John Hanks, "It was mighty clever of Abe to tote me to a warm fire that night."

So he grew, living in that Pigeon Creek cabin for a home, sleeping in the loft, climbing up at night to a bed just under the roof, where sometimes the snow and the rain drove through the cracks, eating sometimes at a table where the family had only one thing to eat—potatoes. Once at the table, when there were only potatoes, his father spoke a blessing to the Lord for potatoes; the boy murmured, "Those are mighty poor blessings." And Abe made jokes once when company came and Sally Bush Lincoln brought out raw potatoes, gave the visitors a knife apiece, and they all peeled raw potatoes, and talked about the crops, politics, religion, gossip.

Days when they had only potatoes to eat didn't come often. Other days in the year they had "yaller-legged chicken" with gravy, and corn dodgers with shortening, and berries and honey. They tasted of bear meat, deer, coon, quail, grouse, prairie turkey, catfish, bass, perch.

Abe knew the sleep that comes after long hours of work outdoors, the feeling of simple food changing into blood and muscle as he worked in those young years clearing timberland for pasture and corn crops, cutting loose the brush, piling it and burning it, splitting rails, pulling the crosscut saw and the whipsaw, driving the shovel-plow, harrowing, planting, hoeing, pulling fodder, milking cows, churning butter, helping neighbors at house-raisings, log-rollings, corn-huskings.

He found he was fast, strong, and keen when he went against other boys in sports. On farms where he worked, he held his own at scuffling, knocking off hats, wrestling. The time came when around Gentryville and Spencer County he was known as the best "rassler" of all, the champion.

In jumping, foot-racing, throwing the maul, pitching the crowbar, he carried away the decisions against the lads of his own age always, and usually won against those older than himself.

He earned his board, clothes, and lodgings, sometimes working for a neighbor farmer. He watched his father, while helping make cabinets, coffins, cupboards, window frames, doors. Hammers, saws, pegs, cleats, he understood first-hand, also the scythe and the cradle for cutting hay and grain, the corn-cutter's knife, the leather piece to protect the hand while shucking corn, and the horse, the dog, the cow, the ox, the hog. He could skin and cure the hides of coon and deer. He lifted the slippery two-hundred-pound hog carcass, head down, holding the hind hocks up for others of the gang to hook, and swung the animal clear of the ground. He learned where to stick a hog in the under side of the neck so as to bleed it to death, how to split it in two, and carve out the chops, the parts for sausage grinding, for hams, for "cracklings."

Farmers called him to butcher for them at thirty-one cents a day, this when he was sixteen and seventeen years old. He could "knock a beef in the head," swing a maul and hit a cow between the eyes, skin the hide, halve and quarter it, carve out the tallow, the steaks, kidneys, liver.

And the hiding-places of fresh spring water under the earth crust had to be in his thoughts; he helped at well-digging; the wells Tom Lincoln dug went dry one year after another; neighbors said Tom was always digging a well and had his land "honey-combed"; and the boy, Abe, ran the errands and held the tools for the well-digging.

When he was eighteen years old, he could take an ax at the end of the handle and hold it out in a straight horizontal line, easy and steady— he had strong shoulder muscles and steady wrists early in life. He walked thirty-four miles in one day, just on an errand, to please himself, to hear a lawyer make a speech. He could tell his body to do almost impossible things, and the body obeyed.

Growing from boy to man, he was alone a good deal of the time. Days came often when he was by himself all the time except at breakfast and supper hours in the cabin home. In some years more of his time was spent in loneliness than in the company of other people. It happened, too, that this loneliness he knew was not like that of people in cities who can look from a window on streets where faces pass and repass. It was the wilderness loneliness he became acquainted with, solved, filtered through body, eye, and brain, held communion with in his ears, in the temples of his forehead, in the works of his beating heart.

He lived with trees, with the bush wet with shining raindrops, with the burning bush of autumn, with the lone wild duck riding a north wind and crying down on a line north to south, the faces of open sky and weather, the ax which is an individual one-man instrument, these he had for companions, books, friends, talkers, chums of his endless changing soliloquies.

His moccasin feet in the winter-time knew the white spaces of snow-drifts piled in whimsical shapes against timber slopes or blown in levels across the fields of last year's cut corn stalks; in the summer-time his bare feet toughened in the gravel of green streams while he laughed back to the chatter of bluejays in the red-haw trees or while he kept his eyes ready in the slough quack-grass for the cow-snake, the rattler, the cop-perhead.

He rested between spells of work in the springtime when the upward push of the coming out of the new grass can be heard, and in autumn weeks when the rustle of a single falling leaf lets go a whisper that a listening ear can catch.

He found his life thrown in ways where there was a certain chance for a certain growth. And so he grew. Silence found him; he met silence. In the making of him as he was, the element of silence was immense.

CHAPTER 14

IT was a little country of families living in one-room cabins. Dennis Hanks said at a later time, "We lived the same as the Indians, 'ceptin' we took an interest in politics and religion."

Cash was scarce; venison hams, bacon slabs, and barrels of whisky served as money; there were seasons when storekeepers asked customers, "What kind of money have you today?" because so many sorts of wildcat dollar bills were passing around. In sections of timberland, wild hogs were nosing out a fat living on hickory nuts, walnuts, acorns; it was said the country would be full of wild hogs if the wolves didn't find the litters of young pigs a few weeks old and kill them.

Farmers lost thirty and forty sheep in a single wolf raid. Toward the end of June came "fly time," when cows lost weight and gave less milk because they had to fight flies. For two or three months at the end of summer, horses weakened, unless covered with blankets, under the attacks of horse-flies; where one lighted on a horse, a drop of blood oozed; horses were hitched to branches of trees that gave loose rein to the animals, room to move and fight flies.

Men and women went barefoot except in the colder weather; women carried their shoes in their hands and put them on just before arrival at church meetings or at social parties.

Rains came, loosening the top soil of the land where it was not held by grass roots; it was a yellow clay that softened to slush; in this yellow slush many a time Abe Lincoln walked ankle-deep; his bare feet were intimate with the clay dust of the hot dog-days, with the clay mud of spring and fall rains; he was at home in clay. In the timbers with his ax, on the way to chop, his toes, heels, soles, the balls of his feet, climbed and slid in banks and sluices of clay. In the corn-fields, plowing, hoeing, cutting, and shucking, again his bare feet spoke with the clay of the earth; it was in his toenails and stuck on the skin of his toe-knuckles. The color of clay was one of his own colors.

In the short and simple annals of the poor, it seems there are people who breathe with the earth and take into their lungs and blood some of the hard and dark strength of its mystery. During six and seven months each year in the twelve fiercest formative years of his life, Abraham Lincoln had the pads of his foot-soles bare against clay of the earth. It may be the earth told him in her own tough gypsy slang one or two knacks of living worth keeping. To be organic with running wildfire and quiet rain, both of the same moment, is to be the carrier of wave-lines the earth gives up only on hard usage.

CHAPTER 15

HE took shape in a tall, long-armed cornhusker. When rain came in at the chinks of the cabin loft where he slept, soaking through the book Josiah Crawford loaned him, he pulled fodder two days to pay for the book, made a clean sweep, till there wasn't a blade left on a cornstalk in the field of Josiah Crawford.

His father was saying the big boy looked as if he had been roughhewn with an ax and needed smoothing with a jack-plane. "He was the ganglin'est, awkwardest feller that ever stepped over a ten-rail snake fence; he had t' duck to git through a door; he 'peared to be all j'ints."

His stepmother told him she didn't mind his bringing dirt into the house on his feet; she could scour the floor; but she asked him to keep his head washed or he'd be rubbing the dirt on her nice whitewashed rafters. He put barefoot boys to wading in a mud-puddle near the horse-trough, picked them up one by one, carried them to the house upside down, and walked their muddy feet across the ceiling. The mother came in, laughed an hour at the foot-tracks, told Abe he ought to be spanked— and he cleaned the ceiling so it looked new.

The mother said, "Abe never spoke a cross word to me in his life since we lived together." And she said Abe was truthful; when Tilda Johnston leaped onto Abe's back to give him a scare on a lonely timber path, she brought the big axman to the ground by pulling her hands against his shoulders and pressing her knee into his backbone. The ax-blade cut her ankle, and strips from Abe's shirt and Tilda's dress had to be used to stop the blood. By then she was sobbing over what to tell her mother. On Abe's advice she told her mother the whole truth.

As time went by, the stepmother of Abe became one of the rich, silent forces in his life. Besides keeping the floors, pots, pans, kettles, and milk-crocks spick and span, weaving, sewing, mending, and managing with sagacity and gumption, she had a massive, bony, human strength backed with an elemental faith that the foundations of the world were mortised by God with unspeakable goodness of heart toward the human family. Hard as life was, she was thankful to be alive.

Once she told Abe how her brother Isaac, back in Hardin County, had hot words with a cowardly young man who shot Isaac without warning. The doctors asked Isaac if they could tie him down while they cut his flesh and took out the bullet. He told them he didn't need to be tied down; he put two lead musket-balls in between his teeth and ground his teeth on them while the doctors cut a slash nine inches long and one inch deep till they found the bullet and brought it out. Isaac never let out a moan or a whimper; he set his teeth into the musket-balls, ground them into flat sheets, and spat them from his mouth when he thanked the doctors.

Sally Bush, the stepmother, was all of a good mother to Abe. If he broke out laughing when others saw nothing to laugh at, she let it pass as a sign of his thoughts working their own way. So far as she was concerned he had a right to do unaccountable things; since he never lied to her, why not? So she justified him. When Abe's sister, Sarah, married Aaron Grigsby and a year after died with her newborn child, it was Sally Bush who spoke comfort to the eighteen-year-old boy of Nancy Hanks burying his sister and the wraith of a child.

A neighbor woman sized him up by saying, "He could work when he wanted to, but he was no hand to pitch in like killing snakes." John Romine made the remarks: "Abe Lincoln worked for me, but was always reading and thinking. I used to get mad at him for it. I say he was awful lazy. He would laugh and talk—crack his jokes and tell stories all the time; didn't love work half as much as his pay. He said to me one day that his father taught him to work, but he never taught him to love it."

A misunderstanding came up one time between Abe Lincoln and William Grigsby. It ended with Grigsby so mad he challenged Abe to a fight. Abe looked down at Grigsby, smiled, and said the fight ought to be with John Johnston, Abe's stepbrother. The day was set for the fight; each man was there with his seconds; the mauling began, with the two fighters stripped to the waist, beating and bruising each other with bare knuckles.

A crowd stood around, forming a ring, cheering, yelling, hissing, till after a while they saw Johnston getting the worst of it. Then the ring of people forming the crowd was broken as Abe Lincoln shouldered his way through, stepped out, took hold of Grigsby and threw that fighter out of the center of the fight-ring.

Then Abe Lincoln called out, "I'm the big buck of this lick." And looking around so his eyes swept the circle of the crowd he let loose the challenge, "If any of you want to try it, come on and whet your horns." A riot of wild fist-fighting came then between the two gangs and for months around the Jones grocery store there was talk about which gang whipped the other.

After a fox-chase with horses, Uncle Jimmy Larkin was telling how his horse won the race, was the best horse in the world, and never drew a long breath; Abe didn't listen; Uncle Jimmy told it again, and Abe said, "Why don't you tell us how many short breaths he drew?" It raised a laugh on Jimmy, who jumped around threatening to fight, till Abe said quietly, "Now, Larkin, if you don't shut up I'll throw you in that water."

Asked by Farmer James Taylor if he could kill a hog, he answered, "If you will risk the hog I'll risk myself."

He had the pride of youth that resents the slur, the snub, besides the riotous blood that has always led youth in reckless exploits. When he was cutting up didoes one day at the Crawford farm-house, Mrs. Crawford asked, "What's going to become of you, Abe?" And with mockery of swagger, he answered, "Me? I'm going to be president of the United States." His father's yellow cur, which always yelped and gave warning when Abe and John Johnston tried to get off for a coon-hunt or a trip to Jones's store, was picked up and taken along one night on a coon-hunt. The skin of the coon they killed that night was sewed onto the "yaller cur," which ran for home, was caught by bigger dogs and torn to pieces. Sore at some action of Josiah Crawford, who had purple veins on a large nose, Abe nicknamed him "Blue Nose" so that the nickname stuck.

He drew a red ear at a husking bee, kissed Green Taylor's girl, and in a fight the next day hit Green Taylor with an ear of corn, making a gash and a scar for life. For the day of the marriage of his sister Sarah to Aaron Grigsby, he wrote "Adam and Eve's Wedding Song," telling in doggerel how the Lord made woman from a rib taken from Adam's side. The three final verses read:

> The woman was not taken
>   From Adam's feet, we see,
> So he must not abuse her,
>   The meaning seems to be.

> The woman was not taken
>   From Adam's head, we know,
> To show she must not rule him—
>   'Tis evidently so.

> The woman she was taken
>   From under Adam's arm,
> So she must be protected
>   From injuries and harm.

A farcical poem from Abe's pen was recited, with the climactic verse:

But Betsy she said, "You cursed baldhead,
    My suitor you never can be.
Beside, your ill shape proclaims you an ape,
    And that never can answer for me."

A favorite that Abe asked Dennis Hanks to sing began with the lines,
"The turbaned Turk that scorns the world, and struts about with his
whiskers curled," while Dennis had still another beginning, "Hail Columbia, happy land! If you ain't drunk then I'll be damned." But when Abe
tried singing, "Poor Old Ned," Dennis would say he had the tune wrong
and couldn't sing anyhow. Visitors to the Lincoln house were shown in
a copy-book the scribbling:

> Abraham Lincoln
> his hand and pen.
> he will be good but
> god knows When.

Driving a horse at the mill, he was sending the whiplash over the nag
and calling, "Git up, you old hussy; git up, you old hussy." The horse
let fly a hind foot that knocked down the big boy just as he yelled, "Git
up." He lay bleeding, was taken home, washed, put to bed, and lay all
night unconscious. As his eye winkers opened the next day and he came
to, his tongue struggled and blurted, "You old hussy," thus finishing what
he started to say before the knockdown.

He grew as hickory grows, the torso lengthening and toughening. The
sap mounted, the branches spread, leaves came with wind clamor in them.

CHAPTER 16

WHILE young Abe was growing up, he heard his father and John and
Dennis Hanks tell neighbors this and that about their families, what kind
of men and women they had for relatives, kinsfolk, blood connections. And
young Abe learned there were things the Lincolns and Hankses didn't care
to tell the neighbors concerning Abe's mother Nancy and his grandmother
Lucy.

About 1825 Lucy Hanks, the grandmother of Abe, had died, near to
sixty years of age, the mother of eight children, James, Thomas, Henry,
George, Elizabeth, Lucy, Peggy, and Polly. James and Henry had
become ministers of the gospel. The children were all well brought up,
and spoken of as honest, industrious, law-abiding and God-fearing citizens. Their father, Henry Sparrow, had married Lucy Hanks in 1791.
She could read and write though her father and brothers couldn't.

Such things the Lincolns and Hankses were free to talk about with
any of their neighbors, either in corn-shucking time or in the winter

around the stove in Jones's store. They were proud of Lucy Hanks and her husband and the eight children respectably brought up.

They were less free to say that Nancy Hanks, the mother of Abe, was born in Virginia in 1784 when Lucy Hanks was nineteen years old, and seven years before Lucy married. And Joseph Hanks, the father of Lucy, had taken his family to Kentucky that same year.

In November, 1789, a grand jury of Mercer County had named Lucy Hanks as a loose woman; the clerk of the court was ordered to issue a summons for her arrest by the sheriff. Then five months had gone by, and Lucy Hanks came to the courthouse in Harrodsburg, Kentucky, and signed a certificate that she would marry Henry Sparrow on that day or as she wrote it, "enny other day." And she had waited a year, to show him perhaps what kind of life she could lead for the sake of a man she wanted to marry. And at the end of that year came the wedding of Lucy Hanks and Henry Sparrow. "And it turned out to be a love match."

Then two years passed and Joseph Hanks, the father of Lucy, died and left a will. To his son William (father of the same John Hanks who worked in the cornfields with young Abe Lincoln) was bequeathed "one gray horse called Gilbert." And he left his son Thomas "one sorrel horse called Major," while the son Joseph fell heir to "one sorrel horse called Bald" besides 150 acres of land. To his daughter Elizabeth he gave "one heifer yearling called Gentle," to his daughter Polly "one heifer yearling called Lady," and to his daughter Nancy "one heifer yearling called Peidy." The residue then went to his wife Nanny.

Thus the dead man had remembered in his will and given a piece of his property to four sons, three daughters and his wife. He had named and mentioned all of his family—except Lucy. She was the disobedient child, the daughter who had erringly darkened his door sills, and he died with a heart hardened against her, unforgiving to the last.

Yet it seemed that his punishment of Lucy made little difference with his daughter, Nancy, who lived to make a mistake like that of Lucy. For in 1799 Nancy's son, Dennis Hanks (who later helped Abe Lincoln build corncribs around Gentryville) was born several years before his mother married Levi Hall and moved to Indiana to die in the same plague that took away her husband and her niece Nancy Hanks, the mother of Abe Lincoln.

Thus life came and went and there were men and women who seemed to have been candles lighted and to be seen till a sudden gust of wind had come and their lights no longer met the eyes; they had been; they no longer were.

One of the sisters of Lucy Hanks worth talking about was Betsy, the one given the heifer called Gentle. She had married Thomas Sparrow; they wanted children of their own but the wanted children didn't come; so they took into their house the children of others. When Lucy Hanks married Henry Sparrows, then Betsy and Tom Sparrow took in Nancy Hanks and raised Nancy Hanks till she married Tom Lincoln; to out·· siders Nancy Hanks was sometimes known as Nancy Sparrow. They took in Dennis Hanks when Levi Hall married Nancy Hanks, the mother of Dennis. Yes, one of the sisters worth talking about was the big-hearted, ready-handed Betsy Sparrow with her door open and welcome to the children not so welcome in the homes of her sisters. She it was who had gone two miles down the road the morning little Abe Lincoln was born, to help wash the new baby and put a yellow petticoat on him.

Such were tissues of fact twisted through and around the births and the deaths of the men and the women of the Lincoln and Hanks clan, talked about sometimes in hushed and sober moments, sometimes perhaps late at night when monotonous, multitudinous rain came on the roof in late winter and early spring, when a chill was still on the air and the frost not yet out of the ground, and the logs of the home fire threw shadows that lengthened, lessened, and lengthened again along the puncheon floor and among the rafters where seed corn hung.

Back in the shadows of the years had lived the dark, strange woman, Lucy Hanks, with flame streaks in her. And the years had beaten on her head, and circumstance had squeezed at her heart and tried to smother her hopes. And she had lived to pick a man she wanted to marry and borne him eight children and brought them up to read and write in a time when few could read and still fewer could write so much as their own names.

Young Abe Lincoln was free to have his thoughts about this mother of his mother. He could ask himself about what is called "good" and what is called "bad" and how they are criss-crossed in the human mesh. He could ask whether sinners are always as crooked as painted; whether people who call themselves good are half the time as straight as the way they tell it.

Maybe he ought to go slow in any deep or fixed judgments about people. Did the ghost of his lovable mother or the phantom of his lovely grandmother seem to whisper something like that?

CHAPTER 17

A MILE across the fields from the Lincoln home was the Pigeon church, a log-built meeting-house put up in 1822 after many discussions among members about where to locate. On June 7, 1823, William Barker, who kept the minutes and records, wrote that the church "received Brother Thomas Lincoln by letter." He was elected the next year with two neighbors to serve as a committee of visitors to the Gilead church, and served three years as church trustee. Strict watch was kept on the conduct of members and Tom served on committees to look into reported misconduct between husbands and wives, brothers and sisters, of neighbor against neighbor.

William Barker once entered the subscriptions for the support of the church as follows: "We the undersined do asign our names to pay the sevrial somes annexed to our names in produce this fall to be delivered betwixt the first and 20th of December the produce is as follows corn wheat whiskey pork Linnen wool or any other article or material to do the work with. the produce will be Dilevered at the meting hoas in good merchanable produce." Among the subscribers was recorded, "undersined" —"Thomas Lincoln in corn manufactured pounds 24."

Along with the earliest settlers in Indiana had come Catholic priests, and Baptist and Presbyterian preachers, and Methodist circuit riders. Churches had been organized, and the members, with prayer and songs, hewed the logs and raised the frames of their meeting-houses for worship.

Most of the church people could read only the shortest words in the Bible, or none at all. They sat in the log meeting-house on the split-log benches their own axes had shaped, listening to the preacher reading from the Bible by the light of fire-logs. The pronunciation of the words Egypt, Mesopotamia, Babylon, Damascus, set minds to work imagining places less real to them than Rockport, Boonville, Vincennes, Cincinnati.

Their own morning-glories, honeysuckle, and blooming perennials came to leafage out of the rhythmic text, "Consider the lilies of the field, how they grow; they toil not, neither do they spin; and yet I say unto you, that even Solomon in all his glory was not arrayed like one of these." They felt enough portents in the two words, "Jesus wept," for the arrangement of that as a verse by itself.

At the Pigeon church one of the favorite hymns was "How Tedious and Tasteless the Hours," and another, "Oh, to Grace How Great a Debtor!" and another began with the lines:

> When I can read my title clear
> To mansions in the skies.

To confess, to work hard, to be saving, to be decent, were the actions most praised and pleaded for in the sermons of the preachers. Next to denying Christ, the worst sins were drinking, gambling, fighting, loafing, among the men, and gossiping, backbiting, sloth, and slack habits, among the women. A place named Hell where men, women, and children burned everlastingly in fires was the place where sinners would go.

In a timber grove one summer Sunday afternoon, a preacher yelled, shrieked, wrung his hands in sobs of hysterics, until a row of women were laid out to rest and recover in the shade of an oak-tree, after they had moaned, shaken, danced up and down, worn themselves out with the "jerks" and fainted. And young Abe Lincoln, looking on, with sober face and quiet heart, was thoughtful about what he saw before his eyes.

The Sabbath was not only a day for religious meetings. After the sermon, the members, who rode horses many miles to the meeting-house, talked about crops, weather, births and deaths, the growing settlements, letters just come, politics, Indiana, and land titles.

Families had prayers in the morning on arising, grace at breakfast, noon prayers and grace at dinner, grace at supper, and evening prayers at bedtime. In those households, the manger at Bethlehem was a white miracle, the Black Friday at Golgotha and the rocks rolled away for the Resurrection were near-by realities of terror and comfort, dark power and sustenance. The Sabbath day, Christmas, Easter, were days for sober thoughts and sober faces, resignation, contemplation, rest, silence. Verses in the Gospel of St. John had rhythm and portent. "I am the way, the truth, and the life. . . . He that believeth in me shall not perish but shall have everlasting life."

Besides a wisdom of short syllables covering all the wants of life in the Lord's Prayer, they found a melodious movement of musical intention in the arrangement of its simple words. It was like a walk from a green valley to a great mountain to pronounce with thoughtful cadence: "Give us this day our daily bread. And forgive us our trespasses as we forgive those who trespass against us. And lead us not into temptation but deliver us from evil."

The glisten of dewdrops on wheat straws, in the gray chill of daybreak on harvest fields, shone in the solemn assurance of "Yea, though I walk through the valley of the shadow of death, I will fear no evil: . . . thy rod and thy staff they comfort me."

After a day of plowing corn, watching crop pests, whittling bean-poles, capturing strayed cattle and fixing up a hole in a snake-rail fence, while the housewife made a kettle of soap, hoed the radishes and cabbages, milked the cows, and washed the baby, there was a consolation leading to easy slumber in the beatitudes: "Blessed are the meek: for they shall inherit the earth. . . . Blessed are the pure in heart, for they shall see God. Blessed are the peacemakers: for they shall be called the children of God." It was not their business to be sure of the arguments and the invincible logic that might underlie the Bible promises of heaven and threats of hell; it was for this the preacher was hired and paid by the corn, wheat, whisky, pork, linen, wool, and other produce brought by the members of the church.

The exquisite foretokening, "In my Father's house are many mansions: if it were not so I would have told you," was but a carrying farther of the implications of that cry from the ramparts of the unconquerable, "O death, where is thy sting? O grave, where is thy victory?"

Beyond Indiana was something else; beyond the timber and underbrush, the malaria, milk-sick, blood, sweat, tears, hands hard and crooked as the roots of walnut trees, there must be something else.

Young Abraham Lincoln saw certain of these Christians with a clean burning fire, with inner reckonings that prompted them to silence or action or speech, and they could justify themselves with a simple and final explanation that all things should be done decently and in order. Their door-strings were out to sinners deep in mire, to scorners seemingly past all redemption; the Jesus who lived with lawbreakers, thieves, lepers crying "Unclean!" was an instrument and a light vivifying into everyday use the abstractions behind the words "malice," "mercy," "charity."

They met understanding from the solemn young Lincoln who had refused to join his schoolmates in torturing a live mud-turtle, and had written a paper arguing against cruelty to animals; who when eleven years old took his father's rifle and shot a prairie turkey and had never since shot any game at all; who could butcher a beef or hog for food but didn't like to see rabbit blood; who wanted to be a river steamboat pilot but gave up in simple obedience when his father told him he was needed at home; who as a nine-year-old boy helped get a traveling preacher to speak some sort of final ceremonial words over the winter grave of Nancy Hanks Lincoln; who would bother to lug on his shoulders and save from freezing the body of a man overloaded with whisky; who had seen one of his companions go insane and who used to get up before daylight and cross the fields to listen to the crooning, falsetto cackling and disconnected babbling of one whose brain had suddenly lost control of things done decently and in order.

The footsteps of death, silent as the moving sundial of a tall sycamore, were a presence. Time and death, the partners who operate leaving no more track than mist, had to be reckoned in the scheme of life. A day is a shooting-star. The young Lincoln tried to rhyme this sentiment:

> Time! what an empty vapor 'tis!
>   And days how swift they are:
> Swift as an Indian arrow—
>   Fly on like a shooting star,
> The present moment just is here,
>   Then slides away in haste,
> That we can never say they're ours,
>   But only say they're past.

His mother Nancy Hanks and her baby that didn't live, his sister Sarah and her baby that didn't live—time and the empty vapor had taken them; the rain and the snow beat on their graves. The young man who was in his right mind and then began babbling week in and week out the droolings of a disordered brain—time had done it without warning. On both man and the animals, time and death had their way. In a single week, the milk-sick had taken four milch-cows and eleven calves of Dennis

Hanks, while Dennis too had nearly gone under with a hard week of it.

At the Pigeon Creek settlement, while the structure of his bones, the build and hang of his torso and limbs, took shape, other elements, invisible, yet permanent, traced their lines in the tissues of his head and heart.

CHAPTER 18

PIONEERS are half gypsy. The lookout is on horizons from which at any time another and stranger wandersong may come calling and take the heart, to love or to kill, with gold or with ashes, with bluebirds burbling in ripe cornfields or with rheumatism or hog cholera or mortgages, rust and bugs eating crops and farms into ruin.

Down in Indiana, as Abe Lincoln grew up, he cherished his sweet dreams, and let the bitter ones haunt him, and tried to search out from the muddled hugger-mugger of still other dreams whether the meaning was to be sweet or bitter. His father had had portentous dreams; his father told how in a night's sleep once he saw a wayside path to a strange house; he saw the inside walls, the chairs, the table, the fireplace in that house; at the fireside a woman was sitting, and her face, eyes, and lips came clear; she was paring an apple; she was the woman to be his wife. This was the dream, and in his night's sleep it came again and again; he could not shake it off. It haunted him till he went to the path, followed the path to the house, went inside and there saw the woman, sitting at the fireside paring an apple; her face, eyes, and lips were those he had seen so often in his night sleep; and the rest of his dream came to pass. Tom Lincoln had told this to his son, Abe, and the boy searched his dreams for meanings. He learned to say of certain coincidences, "I'm superstitious," feeling that what had happened before under certain combinations of events would probably happen again.

Even the water underground, the streams and springs, were whimsical, unreliable, ran by luck, it seemed, in southern Indiana. Not far from the Lincolns was a region where rivers dipped down into limestone and faded out of sight. "Lost rivers," they were called. In Wyandotte Cave a walker could go fifteen miles around the inside. In some counties there was no telling when a good well would give out and say, "No more water here." Abe's father hired a man to come with a witch-hazel and tell by the way the magic stick pointed where to dig a well that wouldn't go dry. The well was dug where the witch-hazel said it should be dug. And that well went dry just as others before had on the Lincoln farm.

Besides superstitions there were sayings, to be spoken and guessed about, old pieces of whim and wisdom out of bygone generations of Kentuckians, of English, Scotch, and Irish souls. Potatoes, growing underground, must be planted in the dark of the moon, while beans, growing above-ground, must be planted in the light of the moon. The posts of a rail fence would sink in the ground if not set in the dark of the moon. If in planting corn you skipped a row there would be a death in the family. If you killed the first snake you saw in the spring, you would win against all your enemies that year.

When a man is putting up a crop of hay or shucking a field of corn or driving a load of wood, the weather has a particular interest for him. Out of the lives of farmers, timber-workers, ox-drivers, in Kentucky and Indiana, have come sayings:

If the sun shines while it is raining, it will rain again the next day; birds and hens singing during the rain indicate fair weather; if roosters crow when they go to roost it is a sign of rain; the first thunder in the spring wakes up the snakes from their winter sleep; when chickens get on a fence during a rain and pick themselves, it is a sign of clear weather.

"If a man can't skin he must hold a leg while some one else does," was a saying among the butcher gangs Abe Lincoln worked with. Men in those gangs would indicate a short distance by saying it was "far as you can throw a bull by the tail." A strong whisky "would make a rabbit spit in a dog's face." There were admonitions: "Spit against the wind and you spit in your own face," or "Don't see all you see, and don't hear all you hear."

Then, too, there were sayings spoken among the men only, out of barn-life and handling cattle and hogs; the daily chores required understanding of the necessary habits of men and animals.

And naturally in field and kitchen, among young and old, there were the phrases and epithets, "as plain as the nose on your face; as easy as licking a dish; as welcome as the flowers in May; as bare as the back of my hand; before the cat can lick her ear; as red as a spanked baby."

And there were eloquent Irish with blessings, maledictions, and proverbs. "Better be red-headed than be without a head." "No man can live longer at peace than his neighbors like." "I think his face is made of a fiddle; every one that looks on him loves him." "She's as dirty as a slut that's too lazy to lick herself." "A liar must have a good memory." "It's an ill fight where he that wins has the worst of it." "Hills look green that are far away." "It will be all the same after you're dead a hundred years."

Among the young people were whimsies often spoken and seldom believed. Fancy was on a loose leash in some of these. "If you can make your first and little finger meet over the back of your hand, you will marry." "If you spit on a chunk of firewood and speak your sweetheart's name, he will come before it burns out." "The new moon must never be seen through the trees when making a wish." "If a butterfly comes into the house a lady will call wearing a dress the color of the butterfly." "If you sing before breakfast you will cry before night." "If the fire roars there will be a quarrel in the family."

CHAPTER 19

THE farm boys in their evenings at Jones's store in Gentryville talked about how Abe Lincoln was always reading, digging into books, stretching out flat on his stomach in front of the fireplace, studying till midnight and past midnight, picking a piece of charcoal to write on the fire shovel, shaving off what he wrote, and then writing more—till midnight and past midnight. The next thing Abe would be reading books between the plow handles, it seemed to them. And once trying to speak a last word, Dennis Hanks said, "There's suthin' peculiarsome about Abe."

Maybe in books he would find the answers to dark questions pushing around in the pools of his thoughts and the drifts of his mind. He told Dennis and other people, "The things I want to know are in books; my best friend is the man who'll git me a book I ain't read." And sometimes friends answered, "Well, books ain't as plenty as wildcats in these parts o' Indianny."

This was one thing meant by Dennis when he said there was "suthin' peculiarsome" about Abe. It seemed that Abe made the books tell him more than they told other people. All the other farm boys had gone to school and read "The Kentucky Preceptor," but Abe picked out questions from it, such as "Who has the most right to complain, the Indian or the negro?" and Abe would talk about it, up one way and down the other, while they were in the cornfield pulling fodder for the winter. When Abe got hold of a storybook and read about a boat that came near a magnetic rock, and how the magnets in the rock pulled all the nails out of the boat so it went to pieces and the people in the boat found themselves floundering in water, Abe thought it was funny and told it to other people. After Abe read poetry, especially Bobby Burns's poems, Abe began writing rhymes himself. When Abe sat with a girl, with their bare feet in the creek water, and she spoke of the moon rising, he explained to her it was the earth moving and not the moon—the moon only seemed to rise.

John Hanks, who worked in the fields barefooted with Abe, grubbing stumps, plowing, mowing, said: "When Abe and I came back to the house from work, he used to go to the cupboard, snatch a piece of corn bread, sit down, take a book, cock his legs up high as his head, and read. Whenever Abe had a chance in the field while at work, or at the house, he would stop and read." He liked to explain to other people what he was getting from books; explaining an idea to some one else made it clearer to him. The habit was growing on him of reading out loud; words came more real if picked from the silent page of the book and pronounced on the tongue; new balances and values of words stood out if spoken aloud. When writing letters for his father or the neighbors, he read the words out loud as they got written. Before writing a letter he asked questions such as: "What do you want to say in the letter? How do you want to say it? Are you sure that's the best way to say it? Or do you think we can fix up a better way to say it?"

As he studied his books his lower lip stuck out; Josiah Crawford noticed it was a habit and joked Abe about the "stuck-out lip." This habit too stayed with him.

He wrote in his Sum Book or arithmetic that Compound Division was "When several numbers of Divers Denominations are given to be divided by 1 common divisor," and worked on the exercise in multiplication; "If 1 foot contain 12 inches I demand how many there are in 126 feet." Thus the schoolboy.

What he got in the schools didn't satisfy him. He went to three different schools in Indiana, besides two in Kentucky—altogether about four months of school. He learned his A B C, how to spell, read, write. And he had been with the other barefoot boys in butternut jeans learning "manners" under the school teacher, Andrew Crawford, who had them open a door, walk in, and say, "Howdy do?" Yet what he tasted of books in school was only a beginning, only made him hungry and thirsty, shook him with a wanting and a wanting of more and more of what was hidden between the covers of books.

He kept on saying, "The things I want to know are in books; my best friend is the man who'll git me a book I ain't read." He said that to Pitcher, the lawyer over at Rockport, nearly twenty miles away, one fall afternoon, when he walked from Pigeon Creek to Rockport and borrowed a book from Pitcher. Then when fodder-pulling time came a few days later, he shucked corn from early daylight till sundown along with his father and Dennis Hanks and John Hanks, but after supper he read the book till midnight, and at noon he hardly knew the taste of his cornbread because he had the book in front of him. It was a hundred little things like these which made Dennis Hanks say there was "suthin' peculiarsome" about Abe.

Besides reading the family Bible and figuring his way all through the old arithmetic they had at home, he got hold of "Æsop's Fables," "Pilgrim's Progress," "Robinson Crusoe," and Weems's "The Life of Francis Marion." The book of fables, written or collected thousands of years ago by the Greek slave, known as Æsop, sank deep in his mind. As he read through the book a second and third time, he had a feeling there were fables all around him, that everything he touched and handled, everything he saw and learned had a fable wrapped in it somewhere.

One book came, titled, "The Life of George Washington, with Curious Anecdotes, Equally Honorable to Himself and Exemplary to His Young Countrymen. Embellished with Six Steel Engravings, by M. L. Weems, formerly Rector of Mt. Vernon Parish." It pictured men of passion and proud ignorance in the government of England driving their country into war on the American colonies. It quoted the far-visioned warning of Chatham to the British parliament, "For God's sake, then, my lords, let the way be instantly opened for reconciliation. I say instantly; or it will be too late forever."

Such book talk was a comfort against the same thing over again, day after day, so many mornings the same kind of water from the same spring, the same fried pork and corn-meal to eat, the same drizzles of rain, spring plowing, summer weeds, fall fodder-pulling, each coming every year, with the same tired feeling at the end of the day, so many days alone in the woods or the fields or else the same people to talk with, people from whom he had learned all they could teach him. Yet there ran through his head the stories and sayings of other people, the stories and sayings of books, the learning his eyes had caught from books; they were a comfort; they were good to have because they were good by themselves; and they were still better to have because they broke the chill of the lonesome feeling.

He was thankful to the writer of Æsop's fables because that writer stood by him and walked with him, an invisible companion, when he pulled fodder or chopped wood. Books lighted lamps in the dark rooms of his gloomy hours. . . . Well—he would live on; maybe the time would come when he would be free from work for a few weeks, or a few months, with books, and then he would read. . . . God, then he would read. . . . Then he would go and get at the proud secrets of his books.

His father—would he be like his father when he grew up? He hoped not. Why should his father knock him off a fence rail when he was asking a neighbor, passing by, a question? Even if it was a smart question, too pert and too quick, it was no way to handle a boy in front of a neighbor.

In growing up from boyhood to young manhood, he had survived against lonesome, gnawing monotony and against floods, forest and prairie fires, snake-bites, horse-kicks, ague, chills, fever, malaria, "milk-sick."

A comic outline against the sky he was, hiking along the roads of Spencer and other counties in southern Indiana in those years when he read all the books within a fifty-mile circuit of his home. Stretching up on the long legs that ran from his moccasins to the body frame with its long, gangling arms, covered with linsey-woolsey, then the lean neck that carried the head with its surmounting coonskin cap or straw hat—it was, again, a comic outline—yet with a portent in its shadow. His laughing "Howdy," his yarns and drollery, opened the doors of men's hearts.

Starting along in his eleventh year came spells of abstraction. When he was spoken to, no answer came from him. "He might be a thousand miles away." The roaming, fathoming, searching, questioning operations of the minds and hearts of poets, inventors, beginners who take facts stark; these were at work in him.

Days came when he sank deep in the stream of human life and felt himself kin of all that swam in it, whether the waters were crystal or mud.

He learned how suddenly life can spring a surprise. One day in the woods, as he was sharpening a wedge on a log, the ax glanced, nearly took his thumb off, and left a white scar after healing.

"You never cuss a good ax," was a saying in those timbers.

CHAPTER 20

Sixteen-year-old Abe had worked on the farm of James Taylor, at the mouth of Anderson Creek, on that great highway of traffic, the Ohio River. Besides plowing and doing barn and field work, he ran the ferryboat across the Ohio. Two travelers wanted to get on a steamboat one day, and after Abe sculled them to it and lifted their trunks on board they threw him a half-dollar apiece; it gave him a new feeling; the most he had ever earned before that was at butchering for thirty-one cents a day. And when one of the half-dollars slipped from him and sank in the river, that too gave him a new feeling.

At Anderson Creek ferry, he saw and talked with settlers, land buyers and sellers, traders, hunters, peddlers, preachers, gamblers, politicians, teachers, and men shut-mouthed about their business.

Along the water-front of Louisville, Mike Fink had backed up his claim, "I can outrun, outhop, outjump, throw down, drag out, and lick any man in the country; I'm a Salt River roarer; I love the wimming and I'm chockfull of fight." They tried him for crimes in Louisville and acquitted him for lack of sufficient evidence; he waved a red bandanna for a good-by and told them he would come back to face their other indictments.

The Hope Distillery Company, capitalized at $100,000, was operating with grain from the near-by Kentucky and Scioto River valleys, while one Dr. McMurtrie called the Hope concern "a gigantic reservoir of damning drink; they manufacture poison for the human race; of what avail are the reasonings of philanthropists?"

So risky was travel that the Indiana legislature specifically permitted travelers to carry concealed weapons of any kind. There were traders from Cincinnati to New Orleans who were familiar with a regular dialogue, which they rehearsed to each other when they had the same room or bed in a tavern. "Stranger," one would say, "it's been a mighty long time since you and me slep' together." "Yep," came the regulation answer. "Got the same old smell you used to have?" "You *bet*." "Air you as lousy as ever?" "That's me." "Put 'er thar!" Then with a handshake and a swig from the jug they went to their sleep. There were tales of mosquitoes of a certain breed along the Ohio River; two could kill a dog, ten a man.

Men who had made trips up and down the river more than once had a song with a chorus:

> Hard upon the beach oar!
> She moves too slow.
> All the way to Shawneetown,
> Long time ago.

Lawyers with books in their saddlebags took the ferryboat across the Ohio; law and order was coming to that wild young country, they believed; they could remember only ten years back how the law of the Territory of Indiana provided that a horse-thief should have two hundred lashes with a whip on his bare back and stay in jail till the horse was paid for, and the second time he was caught horse-stealing he was shot or hanged; for stealing cattle or hogs the thief had his shirt taken off and was given thirty-nine lashes.

Hunters crossed Anderson Creek ferry who could tell how George Doty in 1821 up in Johnson County killed 300 deer. They said Noah Major, one of the first settlers in Morgan County, estimated there were 20,000 deer in that county when he came in 1820, six years before. Circuit riders could tell about Peter Cartwright, who twenty years before was riding the Salt River district in Kentucky, occasionally getting over into Indiana; once Cartwright labored with a community of Shakers till eighty-seven of that sect were "rescued from the delusion." Those circuit riders could tell about Samuel Thornton Scott, the Presbyterian wilderness preacher, who swam the White River, losing his hat and one boot, arriving at Vincennes, as one friend said, "neither naked nor clad, barefoot nor shod."

Old-timers came along who could tell how the Indians in 1809 were stealing horses, burning barns and fences, killing settlers, running off with cattle and chickens, and how General Hopkins with 1,200 soldiers burned the Indian villages along the Wabash, their log cabins, gardens, orchards, stationed rangers to hunt down every Indian they found, till the time came when there was not a red man on the Wabash or south of that river in the state of Indiana.

The ferry boy at Anderson Creek watched and listened to this human drift across the Ohio River, the bushwhackers and bad men who called themselves bad, and the others who called themselves good. Civilization went by, boats and tools breaking ways. Steamboats came past in a slow and proud pageantry making their fourteen- to twenty-day passage from New Orleans to Pittsburgh; geography became fact to the boy looking on; the flags on the steamboats were a sign of that long stretch of country the steamboats were crossing. Strings of flatboats passed, loaded with produce, pork, turkeys, chicken, cornmeal, flour, whisky, venison hams, hazel-nuts, skins, furs, ginseng; this was farm produce for trading at river ports to merchants or to plantation owners for feeding slaves. Other trading boats carried furniture, groceries, clothes, kitchenware, plows, wagons, harness; this was from manufacturing centres, consignments to storekeepers and traders. Houseboats, arks, sleds, flatboats with small cabins in which families lived and kept house, floated toward their new homesteads; on these the women were washing, the children playing. The life-flow of a main artery of American civilization, at a vivid line of growth, was a piece of pageantry there at Anderson Creek.

CHAPTER 21

YOUNG Abe was out with ax, saw, and draw-knife building himself a light flatboat at Bates's Landing, a mile and a half down the river from Anderson's Creek. He was eighteen years old, a designer, builder, navigator; he cut down trees, hewed out planks, pegged and cleated together the bottoms and sides of his own boat, wood from end to end.

Pieces of money jingled in his pockets. Passengers paid him for sculling them from Bates's Landing out to steamboats in the middle of the Ohio River.

He studied words and figurations on pieces of money. Thirteen stars stood for the first Thirteen States of the Union. The silver print of an eagle spreading its wings and lifting a fighting head was on the half-dollar. As though the eagle were crying high, important words, above its beak was inscribed "E Pluribus Unum"; this meant the many states should be One, young Abe learned.

Circled with the thirteen stars were the head and bust of a motherly-looking woman. On her forehead was the word "Liberty." Just what did *She* mean?

Waiting for passengers and looking out on the wide Ohio to the drooping trees that dipped their leaves in the water on the farther shore, he could think about money and women and eagles.

A signal came from the opposite shore one day and Lincoln rowed across the river. As he stepped out of his boat two men jumped out of the brush. They took hold of him and said they were going to "duck" him in the river. They were John and Lin Dill, brothers who operated a ferry and claimed Abe had been transporting passengers for hire contrary to the law of Kentucky.

As they sized up Abe's lean husky arms they decided not to throw him in the river. He might be too tough a customer. Then all three went to Squire Samuel Pate, justice of the peace, near Lewisport.

A warrant for the arrest of Abraham Lincoln was sworn out by John T. Dill. And the trial began of the case of "The Commonwealth of Kentucky versus Abraham Lincoln," charged with violation of "An Act Respecting the Establishment of Ferries."

Lincoln testified he had carried passengers from the Indiana shore out to the middle of the river, never taking them to the Kentucky shore. And the Dill brothers, though sore and claiming the defendant Lincoln had wronged them, did not go so far as to testify he had "for reward set any person over a river," in the words of the Kentucky statute.

Squire Pate dismissed the warrant against Lincoln. The disappointed Dills put on their hats and left. Lincoln sat with Squire Pate for a long talk. If a man knows the law about a business he is in, it is a help to him, the Squire told young Abe.

They shook hands and parted friends. Afterwards on days when no passengers were in sight and it was "law day" at Squire Pate's down the river, Abe would scull over and watch the witnesses, the constables, the Squire, the machinery of law, government, justice.

The State of Indiana, he learned, was one thing, and the State of Kentucky, something else. A water line in the middle of a big river ran between them. He could ask: "Who makes state lines? What *are* state lines?"

CHAPTER 22

In the year 1825, ox teams and pack horses came through Gentryville carrying people on their way to a place on the Wabash River they called New Harmony. A rich English business man named Robert Owen had paid $132,000.00 for land and $50,000.00 for live stock, tools, and merchandise, and had made a speech before the Congress at Washington telling how he and his companions were going to try to find a new way for people to live their lives together, without fighting, cheating, or exploiting each other, where work would be honorable yet there would be time for play and learning; they would share and share alike, each for all and all for each. In January, 1826, Owen himself with a party of 30 people came down the Ohio River in what was called the "boatload of knowledge."

More ox wagons and pack horses kept coming past the Gentryville crossroads; about a thousand people were joined in Owen's scheme at New Harmony on the Wabash. The scheme lighted up Abe Lincoln's heart. But Tom Lincoln had other plans for his son Abe.

Across the next three years the boy grew longer of leg and arm, tougher of bone and sinew, with harder knuckles and joints. James Gentry, with the largest farms in the Pigeon Creek clearings, and a landing on the Ohio River, was looking the big boy over. He believed Abe could take his pork, flour, meal, bacon, potatoes, and produce to trade down the Mississippi River, for cotton, tobacco, and sugar. Young Abe was set to work on a flatboat; he cut the oaks for a double bottom of stout planks, and a deck shelter, two pairs of long oars at bow and stern, a check-post, and a setting pole for steering.

As the snow and ice began to melt, a little before the first frogs started shrilling, in that year of 1828, they loaded the boat and pushed off.

In charge of the boat Mr. Gentry had placed his son Allen, and in charge of Allen he had placed Abe Lincoln, to hold his own against any half horse, half alligator bush-whackers who might try to take the boat or loot it, and leave the bones of those they took it from, at Cave-in-Rock on the Illinois shore, or other spots where the skeletons of flat-boatmen had been found years after the looters sold the cargo down the river. The honesty of Abe, of course, had been the first point Mr. Gentry considered; and the next point had been whether he could handle the boat in the snags and sand-bars. The two young men pushed off on their trip of a thousand miles to New Orleans, on a wide, winding waterway, where the flatboats were tied up at night to the river-bank, and floated and poled by day amid changing currents, strings of other flatboats, and in the paths of the proud white steamboats.

Whitecaps rose and broke with their foam feathers, a mile, two miles, beyond the limit of eyesight, as fresh winds blew along the Ohio River. Cave-in-Rock was passed on the Illinois shore, with its sign, "Wilson's Liquor Vault and House of Entertainment," with a doorway 25 feet high, 80 feet wide, and back of that entrance a cavern 200 feet deep, a 14-foot chimney leading to an upper room, where one time later were found 60 human skeletons, most of them rivermen lured and trapped by the Wilson gang that camped at Hurricane Island near by.

Timber-covered river bluffs stood up overlooking the river like plow-men resting big shoulders between the plow-handles; twisted dumps and runs of clay banks were like squatters who had lost hope and found rheumatism and malaria; lone pine trees had silhouetted their dry arms of branches on reefs where they dissolved and reappeared in river-mist lights as if they struggled to tell some secret of water and sky before going under.

The nineteen-year-old husky from Indiana found the Mississippi River tricky with sand-bars, shoals, and islands scattered along with the look of arithmetic numbers. Sudden rains, shifting winds, meant new handling of oars. A rising roar and rumble of noise might be rough water ahead or some whimsical current tearing through fallen tree-branches at the river side. A black form seems to be floating up-river through a gray drizzle; the coming out of the sun shows it is an island point, standing still; the light and air play tricks with it.

The bends of the river ahead must be watched with ready oars and sweeps or the flatboat naturally heads in to shore. Strong winds crook the course of the boat, sometimes blowing it ashore; one of the crew must hustle off in a rowboat, tie a hawser to a tree or stump, while another man on the big boat has a rope at the check-post; and they slow her down. Warning signals must be given at night, by waving lantern or firewood, to other craft.

So the flatboat, "the broadhorn," went down the Father of Waters, four to six miles an hour, the crew frying their own pork and corn-meal cakes, washing their own shirts, sewing on their own buttons.

Below Baton Rouge, among the sugar plantations known as the "Sugar Coast," they tied up at the plantation of Madame Duquesne one evening, put their boat in order, spoke their good nights to any sweet stars in the sky, and dropped off to sleep. They woke to find seven negroes on board trying to steal the cargo and kill the crew; the long-armed Indiana husky swung a crab-tree club, knocked them galley-west, chased them into the woods, and came back to the boat and laid a bandanna on a gash over the right eye that left a scar for life as it healed. Then they cut loose the boat and moved down the river.

At New Orleans they traded, sold the rest of their cargo of potatoes, bacon, hams, flour, apples, jeans, in exchange for cotton, tobacco, and sugar, and sold the flatboat for what it would bring as lumber. And they lingered and loitered a few days, seeing New Orleans, before taking steamer north.

On the streets and by-streets of that town, which had floated the flags of French, British, and American dominion, young Abraham Lincoln felt the pulses of a living humanity with far heartbeats in wide, alien circles over the earth: English sailors who sang "Ranzo" and "Boney," "Hangin' Johnny," and "O Fare-you-well, My Bonny Young Girls"; Dutchmen and French in jabber and exclamative; Swedes, Norwegians, and Russians with blond and reddish mustaches and whiskers; Spaniards and Italians with knives and red silk handkerchiefs; New York, Philadelphia, Boston, Rome, Amsterdam, become human facts; it was London those men came from, ejaculating, " 'Ow can ye blime me?"

Women in summer weather wearing slippers and boots; creoles with dusks of eyes; quadroons and octoroons with elusive soft voices; streets lined with saloons where men drank with men or chose from the women sipping their French wine or Jamaica rum at tables, sending quiet signals with their eyes or openly slanging the sailors, teamsters, roustabouts, rivermen, timber cruisers, crap-shooters, poker sharps, squatters, horse thieves, poor whites; bets were laid on steamboat races; talk ran fast about the construction, then going on, of the New Orleans & Pontchartrain Railroad, to be one of the first steam railroads in America and the world; slaves passed handcuffed into gangs headed for cotton fields of one, two, six thousand acres in size; and everywhere was talk about niggers, good and bad niggers, how to rawhide the bad ones with mule whips or bring 'em to N' Orleans and sell 'em; and how you could trust your own children with a good nigger.

As young Abe Lincoln and Allen Gentry made their way back home to the clearings of Pigeon Creek, Indiana, the tall boy had his thoughts. He had crossed half the United States, it seemed, and was back home after three months' vacation with eight dollars a month pay in his pocket and a scar over the right eye.

That year Indiana University was to print its first catalogue, but Abe Lincoln didn't show up among the students who registered. He was between the plow handles or pulling fodder or sinking the ax in trees and brush, and reading between times "Pilgrim's Progress," a history of the United States, the life of Francis Marion, the life of Ben Franklin, and "The Revised Laws of Indiana."

CHAPTER 23

READING the *Louisville Gazette* which came weekly to Gentryville, working out as a chore-boy, field-hand and ferryman, walking a fifty-mile circuit around the home cabin, flatboating down the Ohio and Mississippi, the young man Abraham Lincoln took in many things with his eyes that saw and his ears that heard and remembered. A Virginia planter named Edward Coles had quit Virginia and come down the Ohio River with his slaves, ending his journey in Illinois, where he had deeded a farm to each of his slaves with papers of freedom. The Erie Canal in New York, a big ditch for big boats to run on, was finished; it cost seven and a half million dollars but it connected the Great Lakes and the Atlantic Ocean and it meant that the north ends of Indiana and Illinois, besides other prairie stretches, were going to fill up faster with settlers. The first railroad in the United States, a stub line three miles long, was running iron-wheeled wagons on iron rails at Quincy, Massachusetts. A settlement, called Indianapolis had been cleared away. Glass and nails were arriving in southern Indiana now; there used to be none at all ten years back.

There had been the four years John Quincy Adams was President. He had been elected in a three-cornered fight that ended on election day with Andrew Jackson having the most votes cast for him but not a majority. This had put the contest into Congress, where Henry Clay had thrown his forces to Adams; and Adams's first move was to appoint Clay Secretary of State. The Jackson men said it was a crooked deal. Jackson had handed in his resignation as Senator from Tennessee and started work on his political fences for 1828, while his New York Tammany friend, Martin Van Buren, was booming him up North. All the four years Adams was President, the moves in Congress were aimed at bagging the Presidency in 1828. Investigating committees worked overtime; each side dug for the other's scandals: Adams's past personal record; Jackson's handling of six deserters at Mobile in 1815, when 1,500 soldiers were drawn up at parade rest to watch thirty-six riflemen fire at six blind-folded men, each man kneeling on his own coffin; Adams's bills for wall paper and paint in renovating the White House; Jackson's alleged marriage to his wife before she was properly divorced.

In the background of all the bitter personal feelings, the slander and the slack talk of politics, a deep, significant drift and shift was going on. Part of it was the feeling of the West and Southwest, the raw and new country, against the East and New England, the settled and established country. Added to this was a feeling that Jackson stood for the rough, plain people who work, as against the people who don't. That was the issue, as the Jackson crowd presented it, so that even Abe Lincoln in Spencer County, Indiana, was caught in the drive of its enthusiasm, and wrote:

> Let auld acquaintance be forgot
> And never brought to mind;
> May Jackson be our President,
> And Adams left behind.

Jackson rode to election on a tumultuous landslide of ballots. His wife, Rachel, said, "Well, for Mr. Jackson's sake, I am glad, but for my own part I never wished it." And the home women of Nashville secretly got ready dresses of satin and silk for her to wear in Washington as the first lady of the land; then death took her suddenly; her husband for hours refused to believe she had breathed her last; he had killed one man and silenced others who had spoken against her. One woman wrote, "General Jackson was never quite the same man afterward; her death subdued his spirit and corrected his speech."

Then the new President-elect sailed down the Cumberland River to the Ohio, stopped at Cincinnati and Pittsburgh, and went on to Washington for an inauguration before a crowd of ten thousand people, whose wild cheering of their hero showed they believed something new and different had arrived in the government of the American republic. Daniel Webster, writing a letter to a friend, hit off the event by saying: "I never saw such a crowd. People have come five hundred miles to see General Jackson, and they really seem to think the country is rescued from some dreadful danger." The buckskin shirts of Kentucky settlers and the moccasins of Indian fighters from Tennessee were seen in the crowd, and along with politicians, preachers, merchants, gamblers, and lookers-on, swarmed in to the White House reception, took their turns at barrels of whisky, broke punch-bowls of glass and chinaware, emptied pails of punch, stood on the satin-covered chairs and had their look at "Andy Jackson, Our President," who was shoved into a corner where a line of friends formed a barrier to protect the sixty-two-year-old man from his young buck hench-men.

Thus began an eight-year period in which Andrew Jackson was President of the United States. He came to the White House with the mud of all America's great rivers and swamps on his boots, with records of victories in battles against savage Indian tribes and trained Continental European generals who had fought Napoleon, with shattered ribs and the bullets of Tennessee duelists and gun-fighters of the Southwest in his body; he knew little grammar and many scars, few classics and many fast horses.

Jackson came taking the place of John Quincy Adams, who was asking large funds for a national university and a colossal astronomical observatory, "a lighthouse of the skies," a lovable, decent man who knew all the capes, peninsulas, and inlets of New England, who had been across the Atlantic and stood by the Thames and the Seine rivers, and had never laid eyes on the Mississippi nor the Wabash River. Harvard went under as against the Smoky Mountains and Horseshoe Bend. Jackson came in with 178 electoral votes as against 83 for Adams, after national circulation by his enemies of a thick pamphlet entitled, "Reminiscences; or an Extract from the Catalogue of General Jackson's Youthful Indiscretions, between the Age of Twenty-Three and Sixty," reciting fourteen fights, duels, brawls, shooting and cutting affairs, in which it was alleged he had killed, slashed, and clawed various American citizens. It was told of him that he asked a friend the day after the inaugural what the people were saying of his first message. "They say it is first-rate, but nobody believes you wrote it," was the answer. To which Jackson rejoined, "Well, don't I deserve just as much credit for picking out the man who could write it?"

One nickname for him was "Old Hickory"; he had lived on acorns and slept in the rain; now he sat in a second-story room of the White House smoking a cob pipe, running the United States Government as he had run his armies, his political campaigns, his Tennessee plantation, his stable of racing horses, with a warm heart, a cool head, a sharp tongue, recklessly, cunningly; he was simple as an ax-handle, shrewd as an Indian ambush, mingling in his breast the paradoxes of the good and evil proverbs of the people.

CHAPTER 24

ALL the way down the Mississippi to the Gulf and back, Abe Lincoln had heard about Andrew Jackson in that year of 1828 when Jackson swept that country with a big landslide. In the newspapers that came to the post office at Gentryville, in the talk around Jones's store, in the fields harvesting, and at meetings, Andrew Jackson was the man talked about. With Andrew Jackson for President, the plainest kind of people could go into the White House and feel at home; with that kind of man, who smoked a cob pipe, talked horse sense, and rode reckless horses, and who had whipped the British at New Orleans, the Government would be more like what was meant in the Declaration of Independence and the Fourth of July speeches. Thus the talk ran.

Young Abe Lincoln heard it. The personality and the ways of Andrew Jackson filled his thoughts. He asked himself many questions and puzzled his head about the magic of this one strong, stormy man filling the history of that year, commanding a wild love from many people, and calling out curses and disgust from others, but those others were very few in Indiana. The riddles that attach to a towering and magnetic personality staged before a great public, with no very definite issues or policies in question, but with some important theory of government and art of life apparently involved behind the personality—these met young Abe's eyes and ears.

It was the year he wrote in the front cover of "The Columbian Class Book" the inscription, "Abe Lincoln 1828." The preface of the book said it contained "pieces calculated to interest the attention of the scholar and impress the mind with a knowledge of useful facts." And he borrowed from Josiah Crawford "The Kentucky Preceptor," the preface of that book saying, "Tales of love, or romantic fiction, or anything which might tend to instil false notions into the minds of children have not gained admission." There were essays on Magnanimity, Remorse of Conscience. Columbus, Demosthenes, On the Scriptures as a Rule of Life, the speech of Robert Emmet on why the English government should not hang an Irish patriot, stories of Indians, and the inaugural address of President Jefferson twenty-four years previous to that year. Jefferson spoke of "the agonizing spasms of infuriated man, seeking through blood and slaughter his long-lost liberty" in the French Revolution. Let America remember that free speech, and respect for the opinions of others, are measures of safety, was the advice of Jefferson.

Then Abe Lincoln read the passage from the pen of Jefferson: "If there be any among us who would wish to dissolve this Union, or to change its republican form, let them stand as monuments of the safety with which error of opinion may be tolerated where reason is left free to combat it. I know, indeed, that some honest men fear a republican government cannot be strong, that this government is not strong enough. . . . I believe this, on the contrary, the strongest government on earth."

Young nineteen-year-old Abe Lincoln had plenty to think about in that year of 1828, what with his long trip to New Orleans and back, what with the strong, stormy Andrew Jackson sweeping into control of the Government at Washington, and the gentle, teasing, thoughtful words of Thomas Jefferson: "Sometimes it is said that man cannot be trusted with the government of himself. Can he then be trusted with the government of others?"

CHAPTER 25

IN the fall of 1829, Abraham Lincoln was putting his ax to big trees and whipsawing logs into planks for lumber to build a house on his father's farm. But his father made new plans; the lumber was sold to Josiah Crawford; and the obedient young axman was put to work cutting and sawing trees big enough around to make wagon-wheels, and hickories tough enough for axles and poles on an ox-wagon.

The new plans were that the Lincoln family and the families of Dennis Hanks and Levi Hall, married to Abe's step-sisters, thirteen people in all, were going to move to Macon County over in Illinois, into a country with a river the Indians named Sangamo, meaning "the land of plenty to eat." The Lincoln farm wasn't paying well; after buying eighty acres for $2.00 an acre and improving it for fourteen years, Tom Lincoln sold it to Charles Grigsby for $125.00 cash before signing the papers.

The milk-sick was taking farm animals; since Dennis Hanks lost four milk-cows and eleven calves in one week, besides having a spell of the sickness himself, Dennis was saying, "I'm goin' t' git out o' here and hunt a country where the milk-sick is not; it's like to ruined me."

In September Tom Lincoln and his wife had made a trip down to Elizabethtown, Kentucky, where they sold for $123.00 the lot which Mrs. Lincoln had fallen heir to when her first husband died; the clerk, Samuel Haycraft, filled out the deed of sale, declaring that she "was examined by me privately and apart from her said husband" and did "freely and willingly subscribe to the sale." And Tom, with the cash from this sale and the money from the sale of his own farm, was buying oxen, or young steers and trading and selling off household goods.

Moving was natural to his blood; he came from a long line of movers; he could tell about the family that had moved so often that their chickens knew the signs of another moving; and the chickens would walk up to the mover, stretch flat on the ground, and put up their feet to be tied for the next wagon trip.

The men-folks that winter, using their broadaxes and draw-knives on solid blocks of wood, shaping wagon wheels, had a church scandal to talk about. Tom Lincoln and his wife had been granted by the Pigeon church a "letter of Dismission," to show they had kept up their obligations and were regular members. Sister Nancy Grigsby had then come in with a "protest" that she was "not satisfied with Brother and Sister Lincoln." The trustees took back the letter, investigated, gave the letter again to Brother and Sister Lincoln, and to show how they felt about it, they appointed Brother Lincoln on a committee to straighten out a squabble between Sister Nancy Grigsby and Sister Betsy Crawford. And it was jotted down in the Pigeon church records and approved by the trustees.

The ox wagon they made that winter was wood all through, pegs, cleats, hickory withes, and knots of bark, holding it together, except the wheel rims, which were iron. Bundles of bedclothes, skillets, ovens, and a few pieces of furniture were loaded, stuck, filled and tied onto the wagon; early one morning the last of the packing was done. It was February 15, 1830; Abraham Lincoln had been four days a full-grown man, a citizen who "had reached his majority"; he could vote at elections from now on; he was lawfully free from his father's commands; he could come and go now; he was footloose.

At Jones's store he had laid in a little stock of pins, needles, buttons, tinware, suspenders, and knickknacks, to peddle on the way to Illinois.

And he had gone for a final look at the winter dry grass, the ruins of last year's wild vine and dogwood over the grave of Nancy Hanks. He and his father were leaving their Indiana home that day; almost naked they had come, stayed fourteen years, toiled, buried their dead, built a church, toiled on; and now they were leaving, almost naked. Now, with the women and children lifted on top of the wagon-load, the men walked alongside, curling and cracking their whip-lashes over the horns or into the hides of the half-broken young steers.

And so the seven-yoke team of young steers, each with his head in a massive collar of hardwood, lashed and bawled at with "Gee," "Haw," "G' lang" and "Hi thar, you! Git up!" hauled the lumbering pioneer load from the yellow and red clay of Spencer County, in Southern Indiana, to the black loam of the prairie lands in Macon County, Illinois.

They had crossed the Wabash River, the state line of Illinois, and the Sangamo River, on a two-week trip with the ground freezing at night and thawing during the day, the steers slipping and tugging, the wagon axles groaning, the pegs and cleats squeaking. A dog was left behind one morning as the wagon crossed a stream; it whined, ran back and forth, but wouldn't jump in and swim across; young Lincoln took off boots and socks, waded into the icy water, gathered the hound in his arms and carried it over.

Near the Indiana-Illinois state line, Lincoln took his pack of needles and notions and walked up to a small farmhouse that seemed to him to be "full of nothing but children." They were of assorted sizes, seventeen months to seventeen years in age, and all in tears. The mother, red-headed and red-faced, clutched a whip in her fingers. The father, meek, mild, tow-headed, stood in the front doorway as if waiting for his turn to feel the thongs. Lincoln thought there wouldn't be much use in asking the woman if she wanted any needles and notions; she was busy, with a keen eye on the children and an occasional glance at her man in the doorway.

She saw Lincoln come up the path, stepped toward the door, pushed her husband out of the way, and asked Lincoln what was his business.

"Nothing, madam," he answered gently, "I merely dropped in as I came along to see how things were going." He waited a moment.

"Well, you needn't wait," the woman snapped out. "There's trouble here, and lots of it, too, but I kin manage my own affairs without the help of outsiders. This is jest a family row, but I'll teach these brats their places ef I have to lick the hide off every one of 'em. I don't do much talkin' but I run this house, so I don't want no one sneakin' round tryin' to find out how I do it, either."

Around them as they crossed the first stretch of the Grand Prairie was a land and soil different from Indiana or Kentucky. There were long levels, running without slopes up or hollows down, straight to the horizon; arches and domes of sky covered it; the sky counted for more, seemed to have another language and way of talk, farther silences, too, than east and south where the new settlers had come from. Grass stood up six and eight feet; men and horses and cattle were lost to sight in it; so tough were the grass-roots that timber could not get rootholds in it; the grass seemed to be saying to the trees, "You shall not cross"; turf and sky had a new way of saying, "We are here—who are you?" to the ox-wagon gang hunting a new home.

Buffalo paths, deer tracks, were seen; coon, possum, and wolf signs were seen or heard. And they met settlers telling how the sod was so tough it had broken many a plow; but after the first year of sod-corn, the yield would run 50 bushels to the acre; wheat would average 25 to 30 bushels, rye the same, oats 40 to 60 bushels; Irish potatoes, timothy hay, and all the garden vegetables tried so far would grow. Horses and cattle, lean from short fodder through the winter, would fatten and shine with a gloss on their hair when turned loose in the wild grass in spring. Beds of wild strawberries came ripe in June and stained horses and cattle crimson to the knees. Wild horses and wild hogs were still to be found.

The outfit from Indiana raised a laugh as they drove their steers and wagon into the main street of Decatur, a county-seat settlement where court would hold its first session the coming May. To the question, "Kin ye tell us where John Hanks' place is?" the Decatur citizens told them how to drive four miles, where they found John, talked over old Indiana and Kentucky times, but more about Illinois. After the night stay, John took the Lincoln family six miles down the Sangamo River, where he had cut the logs for their cabin. There young Lincoln helped raise the cabin, put in the crops, split rails for fences. He hired out to Major Warnick near by, read the few books in the house, and passed such pleasant talk and smiles with the major's daughter, Mary, and with another girl, Jemima Hill, that at a later time neighbors said he carried on courtships, even though both girls married inside of a year after young Lincoln kept company in those parts. He was asking himself when he would get married, if ever.

He wrote back to Jones at Gentryville that he doubled his money on the peddler's stock he sold; he earned a pair of brown jean trousers by splitting four hundred rails for each yard of the cloth. With new out-looks came new thoughts; at Vincennes, on the way to Illinois, he had seen a printing-press for the first time, and a juggler who did sleight-of-hand tricks. John Hanks put him on a box to answer the speech of a man who was against improvements of the Sangamo River; and John told neighbors, "Abe beat him to death." More and more he was deliver-ing speeches, to trees, stumps, potato rows, just practicing, by himself.

Fall came, with miasma rising from the prairie, and chills, fever, ague, for Tom Lincoln and Sally Bush, and many doses of "Barks," a Peruvian bark and whisky tonic mixture, bought at Renshaw's general store in Decatur. Then came Indian summer, and soft weather, till Christmas week. And then a snowstorm.

For forty-eight hours, with no let-up, the battalions of a blizzard filled the sky, and piled a cover two and a half feet deep on the ground. No sooner was this packed down and frozen than another drive of snow came till there was a four-foot depth of it on the level. It was easy pick-ing for the light-footed wolves who could run on the top crust and take their way with cattle. Wheat crops went to ruin; cows, hogs, horses died in the fields. Connections between houses, settlements, grain mills, broke down; for days families were cut off, living on parched corn; some died of cold, lacking wood to burn; some died of hunger, lacking corn.

Those who came through alive, in the years after, called themselves "Snowbirds." The Lincoln family had hard days. It was hard on new settlers with no reserve stocks of meat, corn, and wood; young Lincoln made a try at wading through to the Warnick house four miles off, nearly froze his feet, and was laid up at home.

As the winter eased off, the Lincoln family moved southeast a hundred miles to Goose Nest Prairie, in the southern part of Coles County.

CHAPTER 26

EIGHT miles from the new farm was the town of Charleston. Young Lin-coln drove there with an ox team and sold loads of cordwood split with his own ax. One afternoon he was late in selling his wood and decided with dark coming on he wouldn't try to drive his ox team to the farm. Tarlton Miles, the horse doctor, living just outside of Charleston, took him in overnight, and they sat up till midnight talking.

In the morning, Lincoln goaded his steers on out to the farm, drove wedges with a maul, split more cordwood. In the evening, as he lay on a board reading, a stranger came to the house and asked to stay over-night. Tom Lincoln said there were only two beds, one belonged to his son, and it depended on whether his son wanted to sleep with a stranger. The two shared the bed that night. . . . It was a country where the veterinary surgeon took in the ox-driver and the ox-driver took in the stranger.

Over in Cumberland County, which joined Coles, the champion wrestler was Dan Needham. It came to his ears several times that the new tall boy over at Goose Nest could· throw him. "I can fling him three best out of four any day," was Needham's answer. At a house-raising at Wabash Point the two faced each other, each one standing six feet, four inches, each a prairie panther. "Abe, rassle 'im," said Tom Lincoln.

Abe held off; the crowd egged both of them on. They grappled four times and each time Needham went under. Then Needham lost his head, threatened a fist fight, calmed down with hearing Lincoln's drawling banter, and at last put out his hand with a grin and said, "Well, I'll be damned." And they shook hands.

In February, 1831, there came to the neighborhood of John Hanks, when Abe Lincoln was lingering there, a man named Denton Offut, a hard drinker, a hustler, and a talker shrewd with his tongue, easy with promises, a believer in pots of gold at the rainbow end. He would have a flatboat and cargo to go to New Orleans, all ready for Abe Lincoln, John Hanks, and John Johnston, "as soon as the snow should go off," if they would meet him on a Sangamo River branch near the village of Springfield. They were there at the time set but Denton Offut wasn't; they walked to Springfield, asked for Offut, found him drunk at the Buckhorn Tavern, and helped sober him.

Offut hired them at twelve dollars a month, gave them permission to go onto Government timber-land and get out gunwales for the flatboat, while the rest of the needed lumber could come from Kirkpatrick's sawmill, charged to Offut. They slung together a camp outfit and started building, with Lincoln calling himself "chief cook and bottle-washer." A sleight-of-hand performer came along and giving his show asked for an empty hat to take eggs out of. Lincoln offered his hat in a hesitating way, saying he hesitated not so much cut of respect for the hat as for the eggs.

Two men, whose canoe turned over and got away from them were shivering in a tree on a raw April day with the freshet-flooded Sangamo River under them. Lincoln got out across the rampaging waters to the tree, on a log with a rope tied to it; the men in the tree straddled the log and were pulled on shore. People began talking about Lincoln's cool wit.

Thirty days saw the flatboat finished, loaded, and on her way, with Lincoln on deck in blue homespun jeans, jacket, vest, rawhide boots with pantaloons stuffed in, and a felt hat once black but now, as the owner said, "sunburned till it was a combine of colors." On April 19, rounding the curve of the Sangamo at the village of New Salem, the boat stuck on the Cameron milldam, and hung with one third of her slanted downward over the edge of the dam and filling slowly with water, while the cargo of pork-barrels were sliding slowly so as to overweight one end.

She hung there a day while all the people of New Salem came down to look at the river disaster, which Lincoln fixed by unloading the pork barrels into another boat, boring a hole in the end of the flatboat as it hung over the dam, letting the water out, dropping the boat over the dam and reloading. As she headed toward the Mississippi watercourse, New Salem talked about the cool head and ready wit of the long-shanked young man with his pantaloons stuffed in his rawhide boots.

Again Lincoln floated down the Mississippi River, four to six miles an hour, meeting strings of other flatboats, keel-boats, arks, sleds, proud white steamboats flying flags. Stepping off their flatboat at New Orleans, Lincoln and Hanks went nearly a mile, walking on flatboats, to reach shore. Stacks of pork and flour from the West, and piles of cotton bales from the South, stood on the wharves. Some shippers, about one in six, were cursing their luck; on the long haul from north of the Ohio River their pork and flour had spoiled; all they got for the trip was the view of the Mississippi River scenery. In New Orleans, Lincoln saw advertisements of traders offering to "pay the highest prices in cash for good and likely Negroes" or to "attend to the sale and purchase of Negroes on commission." A firm advertised: "We have now on hand, and intend to keep throughout the entire year, a large and well-selected stock of Negroes, consisting of field hands, house servants, mechanics, cooks, seamstresses, washers, ironers, etc., which we can sell and will sell as low or lower than any other house here or in New Orleans; persons wishing to purchase would do well to call on us before making purchases elsewhere, as our fresh and regular arrivals will keep us supplied with a good and general assortment; our terms are liberal; give us a call."

One trader gave notice: "I will at all times pay the highest cash prices for Negroes of every description, and will also attend to the sale of Negroes on commission, having a jail and yard fitted up expressly for boarding them." Another announced: "The undersigned would respectfully state to the public that he has forty-five Negroes now on hand, having this day received a lot of twenty-five direct from Virginia, two or three good cooks, a carriage driver, a good house boy, a fiddler, a fine seamstress, and a likely lot of field men and women; all of whom he will sell at a small profit; he wishes to close out and go on to Virginia after a lot for the fall trade." There were sellers advertising, "For sale—several likely girls from 10 to 18 years old, a woman 24, a very valuable woman 25, with three very likely children," while buyers indicated wants after the manner of one advertising, "Wanted—I want to purchase twenty-five likely Negroes, between the ages of 18 and 25 years, male and female, for which I will pay the highest prices in cash."

An Alabama planter advertised, "Runaway—Alfred, a bright mulatto boy, working on plantation; about 18 years old, pretty well grown, has blue eyes, light flaxen hair, skin disposed to freckle; he will try to pass as free-born." Another Alabama planter gave notice: "One hundred dollars reward for return of a bright mulatto man slave, named Sam; light sandy hair, blue eyes, ruddy complexion, is so white as very easily to pass for a free white man."

Lincoln saw one auction in New Orleans where an octoroon girl was sold, after being pinched, trotted up and down, and handled so the buyer could be satisfied she was sound of wind and limb. After a month's stay he worked his passage, firing a steamboat furnace, up the Mississippi River, stayed a few weeks on his father's farm in Coles County, Illinois, and then spoke the long good-by to home and the family roof.

Saying good-by to his father was easy, but it was not so easy to hug the mother, Sally Bush, and put his long arms around her, and lay his cheeks next to hers and say he was going out into the big world to make a place for himself.

The father laughed his good-by, and not so long after told a visitor: "I s'pose Abe is still fooling hisself with eddication. I tried to stop it, but he has got that fool idea in his head, and it can't be got out. Now I hain't got no eddication, but I get along far better'n ef I had. Take bookkeepin'—why, I'm the best bookkeeper in the world! Look up at that rafter thar. Thar's three straight lines made with a firebrand: ef I sell a peck of meal I draw a black line across, and when they pay, I take a dishcloth and jest rub it out; and that thar's a heap better'n yer eddication." And the visitor who heard this told friends that Thomas Lincoln was "one of the shrewdest ignorant men" he had ever seen.

With his few belongings wrapped in a handkerchief bundle tied to a stick over his shoulder, Abraham was on his way to New Salem.

CHAPTER 27

ABRAHAM LINCOLN, in the spring of the year 1831, is spending a night at the cabin of John Hanks, planning his canoe trip down the Sangamo River to New Salem, where he is going to work on his new job in the store of Denton Offut.

Spring breezes move in the oaks and poplars. The branches of the trees register their forks and angles in flat black shadows over the white flat spread of moon-silver on the ground.

For a moment there flits through his head the memory of the face of an auburn-haired girl, a head with corn-silk hair; he had seen her at New Salem; he would see her again there.

And as Abraham Lincoln stepped out of the cabin door of the Hanks

home that night in 1831, he might have looked up and asked the moon to
tell him about the comings and goings of men and machines, guns and
tools, events and enterprises, the drift of human struggle and history,
over and around the earth.

And the moon might have told him many things that spring night in
the year 1831.

The ships and guns of the white men of western Europe were beginning
to travel world routes. A vast interwoven fabric of international selling,
buying, manufacturing, merchandising, with its circles of operation
around the earth, was starting to develop. Coal and iron, steam and steel,
and new ways to use them, had been found. In Lancashire and West Riding, England, and in Lyons, France, were new cities with miles of smoke-
stacks sending their scrolls of soot against the sky; under them were
roaring power-driven looms, the rattling and clicking spindles and bobbins of machines weaving cloth from American cotton, from Australian
wool. The machines had knuckles and fingers weaving faster than any
man or woman ever had woven by hand; a boy or a woman watching a
machine did the work ten men or twenty used to do. And the ships and
guns of England, France, the Netherlands, had gone out over the earth
and found millions of new customers for the cloths, fabrics, prints, from
these factories, where "the iron man" did the heavy work, the iron man
who neither ate nor drank nor slept nor revolted nor took strong drink
and came late to work.

The human swarms of India, Asia Minor, Egypt, of Tripoli, Tunis, and
Algeria, were on the routes of British, French, and Dutch ships that unloaded the factory goods and took on food products and raw materials
to bring to their home countries. The British dominions in America, Aus-
tralia, New Zealand, were on the regular pathways of the British merchant ships. The bayonets of France in Algiers had established dependable
business relations. At the straits of the Dardanelles, Mohammedan and
Christian soldiers had been fighting till the waters of the Black Sea and
the straits of Constantinople and the Dardanelles were opened for the
international navigation of all merchant ships. Governments were learning
to speak of protectorates, suzerainties, spheres of influence, zones of
understanding.

A new form of world civilization was shaping, founded on the production of merchandise by power-driven machinery and the selling and trading of that merchandise in markets as far off as cargoes could be carried
by sailing vessels—and by the new incoming steamboats. Merchants,
manufacturers, and bankers could now operate with the earth as their
region of action. This was the large fact of history before which it seemed
all other facts bent and crumpled. Old sleeping, mysterious dynasties of
Asia gave way before it and let open their arabesque portals, at the re-

quest or bidding of diplomats, salesmen, or the demands of fleets and squadrons.

Yet it was happening that the millions of new customers for the factory-made goods of Europe were not able to buy all that the new power-driven looms and spindles could turn out. Factories shut their doors and turned workmen out. And one day in Lancashire an army of men out of work broke into the factories and smashed a thousand looms. In Paris a tailor had invented a chain-stitch sewing-machine worked with a treadle, and workmen who hated labor-saving machines had wrecked a new factory with eighty of these sewing-machines in it. At Lyons, France, workmen out of jobs rioted with banners inscribed, "Live working or die fighting." In Germany the rulers were in fear of university students who had organized societies and were taking the word "Liberty" for a password. When a student killed a royal spy named Kotzebue, he was put to death, and in Prussia there were 203 students arrested and 94 condemned to death. In middle and eastern Europe was agitation for the serfs to be set free. One French king was told of as the last to die decently in bed as a sovereign; he pointed at the bed and said the next king of France would not die in that bed. Neither dying nor living was a safe and comfortable thing for the kings of Europe amid the rapid zigzag of events.

Such were a few of the drifts in Europe in the year 1831 and years just before. Thus ran the ferment and the stew of human conditions that made sections of the people of Europe so restless that they looked to see where else over the earth they could go. There was an appeal to them in "land uncultivated to an extent almost incalculable," land at $1.25 an acre, in "no established church, no privileged orders," and in "property on a different tenure." That appeal would hold across several decades, sending millions in the long suffocating voyage across the ocean to make their gamble in the new country. In the history of America across coming decades, that never-ending stream of newcomers to its soil would be a factor in the ever westward moving of frontiers, in the structure of railroads, cities, armies.

As the ships from Europe came into American ports the ten years following the year 1831, they would deliver 600,000 emigrants, four times as many as in the preceding ten years. Factory and farm jobs, railroad and canal construction jobs called them, work in lumber woods, brickyards, dockyards; the first words they learned were "job," "work," "boss," "dollars," "cents," "eat," "sleep." Railroads were to be built; wooden rails covered with iron strips, then iron ways. Thousands of Irishmen hired out with pick, shovel and wheelbarrow. R. W. Emerson wrote in his journal, "The poor Irishman, the wheelbarrow is his country." On the Erie Canal and the Great Lakes route to the north, on the wagon roads to Pittsburgh and the Ohio River route to the south, the human traffic was thicker and heavier, as well as on the newer Cumberland road between the two older routes. There were now about 10,000,000 white people in the United States, and about 2,300,000 colored slaves.

The people lived in three sections or regions, each section with a character of its own in products, land, and people. There was the North with a long belt of factories, shops, and mills running from southern Maine to Chesapeake Bay. There was the South with its cotton, tobacco, rice, and slaves. There was the West with its corn, wheat, pork, furs. In some respects these sections or regions were three separate countries, with different ways of looking at life; their soil, climate, slang, and subtleties of personal communication were different.

And behind that tissue of time called the Future, events were operating, shaping lines of destiny for these three sections or regions of America. First of these events was the coming of the railway. An American-made, horizontal-boiler engine was running on the first stub line called the Baltimore & Ohio Railway. Processes for smelting iron with anthracite coal by use of a hot-air blast were almost ready. The transportation revolution was breaking. Blunt facts stood up: iron production jumped from 54,000 tons in 1810 to 165,000 tons in 1830 and would go to 347,000 tons in 1840. Beyond the little narrow Atlantic states, where the dinky B. & O. engines puffed along fifteen miles an hour and slipped on the uphill drag, there were the Great Plains, where miles were measured by thousands, vast level stretches of territory where the building and running of railroads would be easier and faster than anywhere else in the world.

McCormick, Hussey, and other men were fixing their wits on the making of harvesting machines, so that one farmer alone on a mower would cut as much grain as a gang of field hands with scythe and cradle. Morse was nearly ready to connect the Mississippi Valley with the Atlantic seaboard by instantaneous wire communication. Electricity was to be moved from the laboratory to the workshop and have its horsepower measured and harnessed. These were events sleeping behind that tissue of time called the Future, almost ready to step out into the drama called History.

The South, in the early thirties, was an empire of cotton blossoms, and cotton bales, held in the loose leashes of cotton planters who lived on horseback, accustomed to command. The old-time tobacco and rice planters had closed their silver snuff-boxes, spoken muffled farewells to the power they once held, and acknowledged some new and terrible chapter was in the writing for the South. In some counties in Virginia, half the population had been swept out and away downward into the Cotton Belt; John Randolph said publicly his plantation was going bankrupt; at an auction sale in 1829, the stately white home of Thomas Jefferson was bidden in for $2,500; the speech, the tone of voice, and the human slant of the Declaration of Independence were fading out from approved conversation. As a region the South covered 880,000 square miles; less than one-fourth held in its grip the controlling economic and political element; on a peculiar strip of land, where cotton crops laughed with snow-white harvests, there lived in 1830 about a million and a half people, one in three a negro. The dominant interest each year was the cotton crop; Massachusetts, Connecticut, New York, Great Britain, France sent more and more ships every year for this cotton crop; its bales in 1830 were worth $29,-000,000. On a crisscross neck of land running from lower North Carolina to the Red River counties of Louisiana and Arkansas was rising the cotton civilization. A phenomenon with a star of destiny, the talk of the world, was the South. Pot-luck hunters and rainbow-chasers came from states north, from Britain, Ireland, and continental Europe, hoping a small gamble would bring quick rich returns. Land wore out as the soil was mined and exploited without care or manure; so the worked-out land was left empty or rented to poorer whites, while the big planters turned west and farther west to fresh and virgin soils. Virginia cotton production slumped from 25,000,000 pounds in 1826 to 10,000,000 pounds in 1834; in the same time the cotton crops of Mississippi, far below the Allegheny Mountains, leaped from 20,000,000 to 85,000,000 pounds. The exploitation was decisive, blind, relentless. Superb timber on a million and more acres of land was cut down and burned or the trees girdled, the sap choked and the trunks deadened, to make room for more cotton crops. The covenants of the Federal Government with the Red Indian tribes were torn to scraps of paper while the Cherokee, Choctaw, Creek, and Chickasaw Indian tribes were charged with "an attempt to establish an independent government," and driven off their rich and wide tracts of land, to make room for cotton crops and the cotton civilization of the white man.

Sections of the South outside the Cotton Belt became economic tributaries of it; in parts of Virginia the breeding of negroes for the slave-labor markets farther south had become a recognized live-stock business, selling 6,000 negroes south every year; Alexandria was a loading point for brigs hauling cargoes of black freight to New Orleans; Delaware and Maryland were pouring fresh supplies into the famous barracoons or slave barracks selling and shipping regularly from Washington, D. C.; along the Wilderness Road and through Cumberland Gap moved kaffles or chain gangs headed away from the worn-out cotton lands of Virginia into strips of virgin soil south and west. The ships of smugglers on the high seas and the wagons of legitimate traders and breeders on the inland highways were carrying the fresh labor supplies called for by the big planters as imperative requisites toward larger cotton crops. Mississippi had doubled her negro labor supply in ten years; Alabama had tripled hers. Tax assessors had counted more than two million slaves, taxable at more than a billion dollars. This negro labor supply was the backbone of wealth production, connecting directly with the economic supremacy of the South as shown in its exports of cotton, tobacco, and rice between 1821 and 1830, which were valued at $33,000,000.00 as against a total of only $20,000,000.00 for all other states.

"Slave labor is more productive than free labor," was the argument of Thomas R. Dew, president of a Virginia college, replying before a legislative committee to other Virginians who were asking for a gradual emancipation of slaves. He pointed to the 470,000 slaves of Virginia as worth $94,000,000.00 and nearly equal in value to one-half the assessed value of all the houses and lands of the state, or $206,000,000.00. He respectfully challenged Jefferson's statement, "The whole commerce between master and slave is a perpetual exercise of the most boisterous passions," and countered, "Look to the slaveholding population and you everywhere find them characterized by noble and elevated sentiments; the most cruel masters are those who have been unaccustomed to slavery; it is well known that northern gentlemen who marry southern heiresses are much severer masters than southern gentlemen. The slaves of a good master are his warmest, most constant, and most devoted friends; we have often heard slave-holders affirm that they would sooner rely upon their slaves' fidelity and attachment in the hour of danger, than on any other equal number of individuals." He referred to the population of Virginia as "consisting of three castes, free white, free colored, and slave colored."

In 200 years there had been only three slave insurrections, with less than 100 lives lost, declared Dew, in discussing the Nat Turner insurrection in which negro slaves one summer night killed 60 white persons in Southampton County. It was an action to be traced chiefly to a fanatical leader who heard voices in the air telling him he was sent from Heaven to save the slaves; an eclipse of the moon followed by a green sun were signs the work of emancipation should begin.

Slave labor is superior to free labor in southern climates, it was urged. "The slave districts in China, according to travelers, are determined by latitude and agricultural products; the wheat-growing districts have no slaves, but the rice-, cotton-, and sugar-growing districts situated in warm climates have all of them slaves." The sweeping postulates were stated: "The exclusive owners of property ever have been, ever will and perhaps ever ought to be, the virtual rulers of mankind. It is the order of nature and of God that the being of superior faculties and knowledge, and therefore of superior power, should control and dispose of those who are inferior. It is as much in the order of nature that men should enslave each other as that other animals should prey upon each other."

Circumstances beyond control of the southern states had brought slavery; it was a long age in developing and would take a long age to go; it was rooted so deep that no rash or sudden act could cut it loose. "The original sin of introduction rests not on our heads," declared Dew. "With regard to the assertion that slavery is against the spirit of Christianity, we are ready to admit the general assertion, but deny, most positively, that there is anything in the Old or New Testament to show the master commits any offense in holding slaves. No one can read the New Testament without seeing and admiring that the meek and humble Savior of the world in no instance meddled with the established institutions of mankind; he came to save a fallen world, and not to excite the black passions of men, and array them in deadly hostility against each other; He nowhere encourages insurrection; he nowhere fosters discontent, but exhorts always to implicit obedience and fidelity."

A church association in Georgia had formally decided that when slave husbands and wives were separated by sale, either could marry again as though the other had died; "such separation, among persons situated as our slaves are, is civilly a separation by death, and in the sight of God, it would be so viewed." In North Carolina, to sell or to give a slave any book, the Bible not excepted, was punishable with 39 lashes for a free negro or a $200.00 fine for a white man. The statute urged that "teaching slaves to read and write tends to excite dissatisfaction in their minds, and to produce insurrection and rebellion." Twenty lashes "well laid on" was the penalty for slaves meeting for "religious worship" before sunrise or after sunset in South Carolina; in one year, thirty-five slaves were executed at Charleston, after trial and conviction on a charge of intended insurrection. Any meeting of slaves at any school, day or night, for instruction in reading or writing, was held by the laws of Virginia to be an act of unlawful assembly, punishable with twenty lashes on the back of any slave found in such school. In Louisiana, the penalty for teaching slaves to read and write was one year's imprisonment; in Georgia $500.00 fine and imprisonment.

In South Carolina and Georgia, any person finding more than seven slaves together in the highway without a white person could give each one twenty lashes. In Maryland, for "rambling, riding, or going abroad in the night, or riding horses in the daytime, without leave," a slave could be whipped, have his ears cropped, be branded on the cheek with the letter R, or punished by any method which would not render the slave "unfit for labor."

Prices of slaves fluctuated with the market price of cotton. The coasts of Florida and the bayous of Louisiana were favorite places for the landing of wild Africans, to be later mixed with squads of American-born blacks and sold off singly or in couples. The captain of *La Fortuna*, a 90-ton schooner, brought 217 slaves from the African Gold Coast to Havana, Cuba, sold them for $77,469, itemized a net profit of $41,438.54 to the shipowners for an investment during six months of $3,700.00 in the schooner, and a capital all told amounting to less than $21,000.00. That is, they doubled their money in six months. The *Napoleon*, a Baltimore clipper, earned a profit of $100,000.00 in one trip; she brought to the

Cuban market 250 full-grown men and 100 picked boys and girls; cost per head was $16.00; they sold for an average of $360.00 per head. A first-class ship for carrying from 300 to 400 slaves cost less than $30,-000.00 and earned from $35,000.00 to $100,000.00 each voyage. Three to four voyages soaked the timbers of the vessel with such filth that no crew could sail it; seamen said the odor of a slave ship could be sniffed definitely in the ocean air more than "five miles down wind." The slaves were packed "spoon-fashion" in a space three feet, ten inches high, between decks, the men ironed together, two and two by the ankles, the women and children left unironed.

Cargoes were usually loaded on the west African coast where there were stations or depots to which negro African tribal chiefs brought slaves, captives from defeated tribes, for sale; that is, negroes sold negroes to white men; most often the payment was in rum. In the later days of the trade there were larger lots of children in the cargo; they were easier to handle. Sometimes the negro men and women refused to eat; they were flogged under commands to eat—and to sing and dance. Some tricked the captains into heavy blows, till they knew death was coming; then they smiled quiet mockery at the captains, saying, "Soon we shall be free." Home ports of many of the ships were in New England; at one time Newport alone had 150 ships hauling these oversea cargoes of perishable freight.

For more than 200 years, ships had sailed to the west African coast, shackled their loads of live stock, and hauled them to American harbors. John Rolfe, the white man who married the Indian princess Pocahontas, recorded in his diary one day in 1619 the arrival of a ship in the harbor of Jamestown, "a dutch man of warre that sold us twenty Negars." And since 1619, two centuries past, their increase through importation and birth had gone on till the census takers reckoned two million and more negro slaves in the South.

Most of this negro labor supply was on the large plantations, where the approved unit was a hundred slaves to a thousand acres. On a single plantation might be found coal-black Africans with slant skulls and low foreheads, direct from the jungles, speaking a guttural mumble; men and women of brown or bronze faces, with regular features; some who came evidently from Arabia or northern Africa, with flashes of intelligence and genius from old civilizations; and persons thirty-one thirty-seconds white blood and one thirty-second negro blood, white in color, having manners, skill, and accomplishments, held as slaves.

The bulk of slaves were on the large one- or two-thousand-acre cotton plantations. Yet a slave-owner might be a small farmer raising crops with the help of one or two slaves who worked side by side with him in the fields. Or, the owner of a copper-faced slave might be a copper-faced Indian, as happened in a few instances. Or again the owner might be a free negro;

there were mulattoes and quadroons in New Orleans who owned negro house-slaves. There were nearly 200,000 free negroes in the South; most of them had been given papers of freedom by their masters. Every child of a negro slave-mother was lawfully born as a slave and the property of her owner; there were slaves who knew their owners were their fathers. There were slim and appealing mulatto girls who sold for prices upward of $3,000.00 each. There were free negroes who had earned their freedom, had been arrested and convicted of violations of law, and sold at auction back into slavery. There were free negroes, who had come back asking to live as slaves again, which happened in cases of negroes given freedom on the plantation of John Randolph. There were house negroes who considered themselves superior to field negroes; there were field negroes who had contempt for struggling white farmers, called "po' w'ite trash."

There were negroes who had been jailed and charged with crimes in New York, shackled, put on ships and unloaded at Gulf-coast states; one ship from New York came to New Orleans with 70 such negroes from New York prisons; the brig *Mary Ann* in 1818 took 36 negroes from Perth Amboy, New Jersey, to New Orleans, where a newspaper remarked: "It is probable the greater part of these unfortunate creatures were stolen; negro trading seems to be actively carried on through certain great villains holding their headquarters in New Jersey."

Great Britain, France, and Sweden had an agreement to handle slave-traders as "pirates, felons, and robbers"; they had agreed to search each other's ships. The United States held off from this agreement—and the favorite flag of the slave ships along the coast of Africa was the Stars and Stripes. The American flag was protection against search from any vessels except American cruisers, operating under orders from the Secretary of the Navy at Washington, who was responsible to a President who was a slaveholder.

Thus in the early thirties was weaving the fabric of an empire, a pastoral and agricultural nation, with its foundations resting on three chief conditions: (1) the special fertility of a certain strip of land for cotton crops; (2) the raising of the cotton crop by negro slave labor; (3) the sale of that crop to northern American and to English cotton-mills that sold their finished products in a constantly widening world market. The planters who had control of its destiny, in so far as there was control rather than blind luck and brute hazard, were men of pride, valor, and cunning; they lived on horseback, accustomed to command.

The North was a section of country fumbling and groping toward control of water power, iron, steel, canals, railways, ocean-going boats. Her controlling men sat in office chairs, accustomed to add and subtract, measure and multiply, with maps, statistics, diagrams and designs before their eyes. By one route and another, the money of American regions was streaming toward banks in New York, Philadelphia, and Boston Brickyards were running night and day in order that new factories and mills might rise on the banks of swift-running rivers whose water power would operate woolen and cotton mills. The ten years before 1830 had seen the mills of New England and the Middle States triple their output twice over. The shipping, mercantile, fisheries, and farming interests of New England slipped back from their places of importance to make room for the manufacturing interests, which, with their allied banks, were taking the chief control.

Cotton mills were the industrial phenomenon; each year they called for increasing tens of millions of pounds of cotton from the South; they produced cotton goods worth $2,500,000 in 1820, and their value kept mounting till in 1831 the total was $15,500,000; in the same period the woolen-mill output increased from less than $1,000,000 to more than $11,-000,000. It was a process that shook up culture, religion, and politics in New England and so mixed the currents of its destinies that Daniel Webster wrote, "We are disgraced beyond help or hope; there is a Federal interest, a Democratic interest, a bankrupt interest, an orthodox interest, and a middling interest; but I see no national interest, nor any national feeling in the whole matter." The spinning-wheels and distaffs of millions of homes had become old-fashioned; their place was the garret and attic; spinning was to be done in cotton and woolen mills and clothes were to be cheap.

From thousands of farms the people moved into the industrial cities to go to work, men, women, and children, in the mills. Other thousands of New England farmers were selling out and moving via the Erie Canal over into the Mohawk Valley and western New York, or out still farther west into Ohio, Indiana, Michigan, and Illinois. Some could tell of the New England farmer who called a minister to pray for better crops from the soil; and the minister, after looking over the stony and stingy soil, had said, "This farm doesn't need prayer—what this farm needs is manure!"

Farmers' daughters filled the cotton mills in Lowell, Massachusetts; they started work at five o'clock in the morning and worked till seven o'clock in the evening, with a half-hour off for breakfast, and forty-five minutes off at noon for dinner; they spent fourteen hours a day at the factory and had ten hours a day left in which to sleep and to refresh themselves and to improve their minds and bodies. One girl, operating a single spinning-machine, carrying 3,000 spindles, spun as much cotton cloth as 3,000 girls working by hand a single thread at a time on the old-fashioned spinning-wheel. In fifteen years the price of ordinary cloths for sheeting had dropped from forty cents a yard to eight and one-half cents a yard.

Bells rang at "break of day" in some factory towns; the workers tumbled out of sleep, crept into their clothes and reported at the factory gates in fifteen minutes, when the gates closed. An hour or two later, twenty-five minutes was allowed for breakfast, and at noon twenty-five minutes was again allowed for dinner. The gates were opened at eight o'clock at night to let the workers go back to supper, play, amusements, recreation, education, strong drink, sleep, or whatever they chose till the ringing of the bell again the next morning at "break of day." The Hope factory in Rhode Island ran on this plan. In the Eagle Mill at Griswold, Connecticut, the work-day lasted fifteen hours and ten minutes. At Paterson, New Jersey, women and children began the day's work at half-past four o'clock in the morning. Overseers in some textile mills cracked a cowhide whip over women and children. "The only opportunities allowed to children generally, employed in manufactories, to obtain an education, are on the Sabbath and after half-past eight o'clock of the evening of other days," declared the report of a committee of the newly organized New England Association of Farmers, Mechanics, and Other Workingmen.

In language dark as the early winter dawns in which boys and girls went to work rubbing sleep from their eyes, the association declared its purpose to be "the organization of the whole laboring class," with the express hope "to imbue our offspring with abhorrence for the usurpations of aristocracy, so that they shall dedicate their lives to a completion of the work which their ancestors commenced in their struggle for *national*, and their sires have continued in their contest for *personal*, independence." The first labor paper on the American continent, *The Workingman's Advocate*, had been started in New York by two English workingmen. It was followed by *The Mechanics' Free Press*.

A jury in New York City heard the evidence against striking workingmen charged with "conspiring to raise wages" and awarded a fine of one dollar. The growing wage-earning class was organizing trade associations, and in Philadelphia had formed its first central body of such associations. Strikes were called to raise wages, to bar from work the nonunion men known later as "rats" and "scabs." But most of all the strikes were aimed to get the ten-hour work-day. In politics this labor movement stood against jailing for debt, against banking monopoly, for easier access to public lands, for schools open to all, for the United States mails to run on the Sabbath, for limitation of ownership of land to 160 acres per person, and for "abolition of chattel slavery and of wages slavery."

Thread, yarn, twine, sheeting, shirting, ticking, print cloth, gingham, and bags were leaving North Atlantic states for all parts of the world. They went west on the Erie Canal and the Great Lakes; they were on Ohio River flatboats going west and south; they were loaded on pack horses and mules moving in four parallel columns from Independence, Missouri, for the seventy-day trip to Sante Fe, where they were traded for gold dust, buffalo skins, rugs, Mexican blankets. The South was buying back in finished cloth part of the cotton it raised. Ships leaving North Atlantic ports carried cargoes for South America. The United States had become in 1830 second only to England in the amount of cotton it bought for its humming spindles. In 1831, were reported 795 mills, 1,246,500 spindles and 70,000 mill workers. The industrial and commercial fact of cotton had moved into world history as a reckonable factor. The seeds of a "tree-wool," gathered in India by Englishmen and planted in Bermuda and from there transplanted to South Carolina and Georgia, had spread and grown till they were part of the lives and work of millions of people.

Yet the development was merely in its beginnings. In New York and Pennsylvania, companies were organizing to mine the iron and coal fields. In the coming ten years the railroads and steam boats would want iron and steel for their equipment and rolling-stock, and coal to generate steam power. And with railroads and steamboats connecting the cotton plantations with the cotton mills of America and Europe, and then moving the finished products with higher speed to the world-wide markets, there would be realized another step in the international industrial revolution. Patents on new tools, machines, and devices had more than doubled in ten years; in 1830 there were 544 patents granted. The pilgrim people who came to the North Atlantic coast with Milton and Bunyan in their veins, with Bibles and prayer-books in their hands, were to gain a world name for a figure known as the Inventive Yankee, making breech-loading firearms, air pumps, rock drills, lathes, planing machines, pile drivers, truss frames, harvesters and reapers, sewing machines. Edward Everett issued an essay on "The Inevitable March of Improvement."

Three thousand prisoners were in jail for debt in Massachusetts, 10,000 in New York, 7,000 in Pennsylvania, and 3,000 in Maryland. In one city forty cases were recorded in which the sum total of the debt was $23.40, an average of less than sixty cents for each prisoner.

An industrial civilization was coming over the Middle States and New England. It covered less than 175,000 square miles and held a little more than 6,000,000 people, elements of Dutch blood in New York, Germans and Scotch-Irish in Pennsylvania, Swedes in Delaware and Philadelphia. And there were Irish in New York; they toiled on the Erie Canal; they toiled on canals in Massachusetts.

The proudest, most cohesive unit in the North was New England; she had dialect, religion, law, climate, and regional personality enough to set up as a nation by herself, if there had been enough salt water or steep mountains to isolate her; geography and history were her enemies in that respect; when her shipping and trade were shot to pieces in the War of 1812, and she was ready and set for secession from the Union of states, events shifted,

Log cabin the twenty-year-old Abe Lincoln helped his father build on Goose Nest Prairie in Coles County, Illinois.

From original photograph in the Barrett Collection

The famous Methodist preacher and circuit rider, Peter Cartwright. A Democrat beaten by Lincoln in the run for Congress in 1846. He personally threw scoffers out of church when they interrupted sermons. He once told a cold deacon who had prayed, "Brother, three prayers like that would freeze hell over."

Daguerreotype presented by Mrs. B. C. Keene to Bloomington (Ill.) Historical Society

And so, over New England and the Middle States had sprung up, without forewarning or foretelling, the beginnings of a civilization of power-driven looms, wage-earning labor, of iron, coal, and fast transport. The controlling men sat in office chairs, accustomed to add and subtract, measure and multiply, with maps, statistics, diagrams and designs before their eyes. The fabric and structure of the basic system of life at the North was in high contrast to that of the South. The big word in the South was Chivalry. In the North it was Improvements.

In the West, if there was a big word, it was something like "Freedom" or "Independence," or a slogan, "Hands Off." Its reckonings were under large skies and in spreading numbers. For the West was a stretch of country with the Great Lakes at the north, the Gulf of Mexico to the south, the Allegheny Mountains to the east, and a ragged-edged, shifty frontier on the west, moving its line farther west every year out into the Great Plains and beyond toward the Rocky Mountains. Its controlling physical feature was the Mississippi River waterway system, branching with tireless streams fed by regular rainfalls, into a region covering one and a quarter million square miles.

Pioneers in waves were crossing this stretch of country; there was an element of movers always selling out, packing up, and passing on, some saying, "It's time to move if you can hear your neighbor's shotgun." The early settlers had clung to rivers and timbers; now they were locating on prairie land and learning to farm it. Each wave of settlers made it easier for more to come. The young Frenchman, De Tocqueville, was writing: "This gradual and continuous progress of the European race toward the Rocky Mountains has the solemnity of a providential event; it is like a deluge of men rising unabatedly and daily driven onward by the hand of God!"

The New York millionaire fur-trader, Astor, was buying thousand-acre tracts in Illinois, Missouri, Wisconsin. For De Tocqueville had noted also: "The Valley of the Mississippi is, upon the whole, the most magnificent dwelling-place prepared by God for man's abode; and yet it may be said that at present it is but a mighty desert." Wild horses roamed in grass taller than their heads, occasionally roped and broken by white men. Buffaloes were killed by thousands, the skins sold in St. Louis or New Orleans, the carcasses left on the open plains for the wolves and crows. Little populations were pocketed in corners where European races were intermingled with Indians and negroes. Off southwest Texas was calling; cabins were empty in Kentucky and Tennessee with a scribble on the doors, "Gone to Texas"; a boom was on; men and women slanged each other, "Go to Texas"; six years had seen over 20,000 settlers, rustlers, horsemen, enter Texas. And a restless pioneer breed swarmed overland by wagon, horse, and afoot, across the Allegheny Mountains; in ten years the West had added a million and a half people; its population was one-third of the United States.

Connecting products with market, they took horses, mules, cattle, and hogs across country on foot, sometimes four and five thousand hogs in a drove; the turnpike gate at Cumberland Gap saw live stock worth a million dollars in the year 1828; tobacco and whisky worth another million dollars passed over the Falls of the Ohio at Louisville in one year; aggregates of a million dollars were getting common. Corn, oats, barley, hay were fed to cattle and hogs that walked to market, or the grain was distilled into whisky for concentrated transport. Three thousand wagons were making hauls east from Pittsburgh to traders in Baltimore, Philadelphia, and New York; feeding grounds for live stock had been located on plantations along the Potomac River where cattle were fattened for the eastern markets. Cincinnati had the nickname of "Porkopolis" and was packing hams, bacon, and salt pork. Exports from the West had mounted in 1830 to $17,800,000.

The West had become a granary sending food supplies to the factory and textile-mill towns of New England and the Middle States, to Great Britain and France, as well as corn, horses, and mules to the big cotton planters of the South. It was of immense importance, then, that in the year 1831, for the first time, goods were shipped from the Atlantic seaboard to St. Louis by way of Chicago at one-third lower cost than by the New Orleans route. History was in the reckoning. Cheaper and quicker movement of corn and cattle going east, and of textiles, iron, hardware, and human passengers coming west, would set up new connections west, east, south, and overseas.

Over the earth were many little dramas of personal struggle and hope in that year of 1831. A cadet named Edgar Allan Poe, guilty of "neglect" and "disobedience," had been thrown out of the West Point military academy and was writing poetry, drinking whisky, toiling with black bats in the belfries. A young English doctor named Charles Darwin, just twenty-one years old, was starting on a five-year trip in a ship, the *Beagle;* he was taking along thick pads of writing-paper to put down notes about plants, animals, rocks, weather.

An Englishman, Michael Faraday, had been working in a partnership of international scientists, with facts and principles handed him by the Italian, Alessandro Volta, the Dane, Hans Christian Oersted, the Frenchman, A. M. Ampère, the German, G. S. Ohm, toilers on the borderland of fact and speculation; proud, conjectural fools in the realms of wire, plates, pivoted magnets, currents, circuits, attractions, and repulsions; they had identified, caged, captured, and measured that lightning terror, electrodynamic force; hitherto "electricity" had been a useless, mysterious juice; Faraday was making a dynamo; he was going to harness, drive and use the power of electromagnetism.

Such were a few of the things the white moon in its high riding over the sky might have told Abraham Lincoln that spring night in 1831. He would have listened with an understanding head and heart because he was blood and bone of North, South, and West, because there were in him the branched veins of New England emigrant, Middle State Quaker, Virginia planter, and Kentucky pioneer. As the regions of America grew and struggled, he might understand their growth and struggle.

In ten years there had been other little dramas of personal struggle and hope besides the one of Abraham Lincoln. John Keats, the poet, had died at twenty-five years of age among the ivies, marbles, and lizards of Rome, buried with his own epitaph on the gravestone: "Here lies one whose name was writ in water." In the same year passed out Napoleon with the declaration: "I die in the Apostolical and Roman religion, in the bosom of which I was born; it is my wish that my ashes may repose on the banks of the Seine, in the midst of the French people whom I have loved so well." The next year had seen the poet Shelley drowned in the Mediterranean and his body burned and its ashes placed next to the burial urn of Keats; only the year before he had written of Keats, "I weep for Adonais—he is dead." Two years more and the poet Lord Byron, fighting in Greece and far from home, in so far as he had a home, died of fever; of him Shelley had written, "Space wondered less at the swift and fair creations of God when he grew weary of vacancy, than I at this spirit of an angel in the mortal paradise of a decaying body"; while Symonds, a critic, was to write, "It was his misfortune to be well born, but ill bred." Beethoven, too, stepped out of his mortal frame, having been deaf twelve years so that the finest music he knew was in the inner arrangements of sound and silence known only to his own imagination; an escort of 20,000 music lovers swarmed to his grave the day he was laid away. In London town, the mad, sweet, colossal poet, William Blake, had died; "he wandered up and he wandered down, Ever alone with God."

Out of them all, a little flame blue, from the gray of their ashes. lived on.

Each had sung in his own way that line young Abraham Lincoln had written with a turkey-feather pen at Pigeon Creek: "Time! What an empty vapor 'tis!"

CHAPTER 28

In the summer of the year 1831, Abraham Lincoln, twenty-two years old, floated a canoe down the Sangamon River, going to a new home, laughter and youth in his bones, in his heart a few pennies of dreams, in his head a ragbag of thoughts he could never expect to sell.

New Salem, the town on a hill, to which Abraham Lincoln was shunting his canoe, was a place of promise there in the year 1831, just as all towns in Illinois then were places of promise. New Salem then had a dozen families as its population, just as Chicago in the same year reckoned a dozen families and no more. Both had water transportation, outlets, tributary territory, yet one was to be only a phantom hamlet of memories and ghosts, a wind-swept hilltop kept as cherished haunts are kept.

New Salem stood on a hill, a wrinkle of earth crust, a convulsive knob of rock and sod. The Sangamon River takes a curve as it comes to the foot of that bluff and looks up. It is almost as though the river said, "For such a proud standing hill as this I must make a proud winding curve for it to look at."

Up on the ridge level of that bluff, the buffalo, the wild horse, the wild hog and the Red Indian had competed for occupation a thousand years and more. Herds of shaggy-whiskered buffalo had roamed the Sangamon Valley; deer antlers had been plowed up and arched above doorways where men six feet tall walked under without stooping. Plows had turned up brown and white flint arrowheads of Indian hunters, red men whose learning had included buffalo and snake dances, and a necromancy of animal life unknown to men of the white race. Before the rifle and plow of the white man, the red man in that particular southern region of Illinois had moved off, had, in the words of some who followed, "gone and skedaddled." Yet the red man was still a near enough presence to be spoken of as more than a ghost who had just passed.

At the foot of a bluff where the Sangamon begins its curve, a thousand wagon-loads of gravel had been hauled and packed into the river to make a power-dam and mill-grind. The Rutledges and Camerons who started the mill bought the ridge of land on the bluff above and in 1829 laid out a town, sold lots, put up a log tavern with four rooms, and named the place New Salem.

Farmers came from fifty miles away to have their grain turned into flour and to buy salt, sugar, coffee, handkerchiefs, hardware, and calico prints and bonnets. If people asked, "Has the mud wagon come in?" they referred to the stagecoach driving from Havana to Springfield once a week, and carrying mail to the New Salem post office. The town in its time had a sawmill, fifteen houses, a hundred people, two doctors, a school, a church and Sunday school, a saloon, and a squire and two constables. The Herndon brothers, Rowan and James, kept a store; so did the partnership of Samuel Hill and James McNamar; also one Reuben Radford had a grocery.

And Denton Offut, who had rented the Rutledge and Cameron gristmill, had ordered a stock of goods and was going to open a new store, with A.

Lincoln as clerk in charge. When Offut had seen Lincoln handle his flat-boat on the New Salem mill-dam so masterfully, Offut had told people he would soon have a regular steamboat running up and down the Sangamon with Lincoln as captain; the boat would run the year round, in all weathers, with rollers for shoals and dams, runners for ice; Offut said that with Lincoln in charge, "By thunder, she'd have to go!"

Election Day was on when Lincoln arrived in New Salem and loafed along the main street. At the voting-place they told him a clerk was wanted and asked if he could write. Of course, he might have answered that where he came from in Indiana he used to write letters for the whole township; instead he answered with an up-and-down of careless inflections, "Oh, I guess I can make a few rabbit tracks." So, with a goose quill he sat registering ballots that first day in New Salem; and he felt as much at home with the goose quill as he had felt with the ax, the hoe, the flat-boat oars, and other instruments he had handled.

The voting was by word of mouth. Each voter told the election judges which candidates he wanted to vote for. Then a judge would bawl out the voter's name and his candidates, which names would be written down by the clerks. Lincoln got acquainted with names and faces of nearly all the men in New Salem on his first day there.

Offut's stock for the new store had not come as yet, so when Dr. Nelson, who was leaving New Salem for Texas, said he wanted a pilot to take his flatboat through the channels of the Sangamon to Beardstown on the Illinois River, Lincoln was willing. When he came back from that little job, he said there were times he ran the flatboat three miles off onto the prairies, but always got back to the main channel of the Sangamon. A genius of drollery was recognized by the New Salem folks as having come among them to live with and be one of them. They were already passing along the lizard story, a yarn spun by the newcomer the first day he arrived. He had said it happened in Indiana and was as strange as many other things that had happened in Indiana.

In a meeting-house far and deep in the tall timbers, a preacher was delivering a sermon, wearing old-fashioned baggy pantaloons fastened with one button and no suspenders, while his shirt was fastened at the collar with one button. In a loud voice he announced his text for the day, "I am the Christ, whom I shall represent today." And about that time a little blue lizard ran up under one of the baggy pantaloons. The preacher went ahead with his sermon, slapping his legs. After a while the lizard came so high that the preacher was desperate, and, going on with his sermon, unbuttoned the one button that held his pantaloons; they dropped down and with a kick were off. By this time the lizard had changed his route and circled around under the shirt at the back, and the preacher, repeating his text, "I am the Christ, whom I shall represent today," loosened his one collar button and with one sweeping movement off came the shirt. The congregation sat in the pews dazed and dazzled; everything was still for a minute; then a dignified elderly lady stood up slowly and, pointing a finger toward the pulpit, called out at the top of her voice, "I just want to say that if you represent Jesus Christ, sir, then I'm done with the Bible."

Men were telling of Lincoln and a crew loading Squire Godbey's hogs onto a flatboat down at Blue Banks; the hogs were slippery and stubborn and the crew couldn't chase them on board. The gossip was that Lincoln said, "Sew their eyes shut." And farmers were "argufyin'" as to whether a hog is easier handled when his eyes are sewed shut.

On a lot Offut bought for ten dollars, he and Lincoln built a cabin of logs; this was to be the new store, and Lincoln started boarding at the home of the Reverend John Cameron, whose eleven daughters ran the house.

Offut's goods arrived; Lincoln stacked shelves and corners with salt, sugar, tea, coffee, molasses, butter and eggs, whisky, tobacco, hardware, stoneware, cups and saucers, plates, dishes, calico prints, hats, bonnets, gloves, socks, shoes. Bill Green, the eighteen-year-old son of Squire Bowling Green, was put in as a helper mainly to tell Lincoln which of the customers were good pay. Offut's enthusiasm about his new clerk ran high: "He knows more than any man in the United States. . . . Some day he will be President of the United States. . . . He can outrun, outlift, outwrestle, and throw down any man in Sangamon County."

And the Clary's Grove Boys, just four miles away, began talking about these claims; what they said mostly was, "Is that so?" Bill Clary, who ran a saloon thirty steps north of the Offut store, put up a bet of ten dollars with Offut that Lincoln couldn't throw Jack Armstrong, the Clary's Grove champion.

Sports from fifty miles around came to a level square next to Offut's store to see the match; bets ran high, from money to jackknives and treats of whisky. Armstrong was short and powerful in build with the muscle haunches of a wild steer; his aim from the first was to get in close with his man where he would have the advantage of his thick muscular strength.

Lincoln held him off with long arms, wore down his strength, got him out of breath and out of temper. Armstrong then fouled by stamping on Lincoln's right foot and instep with his boot heel. This exasperated Lincoln so that he lost his temper, lifted Armstrong up by the throat and off the ground, shook him like a rag, and then slammed him to a hard fall, flat on his back.

As Armstrong lay on the ground, a champion in the dust of defeat, his gang from Clary's Grove started to swarm toward Lincoln, with hot Kentucky and Irish epithets on their lips. Lincoln stepped to where his back was against a wall, braced himself, and told the gang he was ready for 'em.

Then Jack Armstrong broke through the front line of the gang, shook Lincoln's hand and told the gang Lincoln was "fair," had won the match, and, "He's the best feller that ever broke into this settlement."

As the Clary's Grove Boys looked Lincoln over they decided he was one of them; he weighed 180 pounds; he was hard as nails; he outran the foot-racers of Sangamon County; he threw the maul and crowbar farthest; he told the lizard story; he saved a flatboat that looked like a wreck on the Cameron mill-dam. Yes, he belonged; even though he didn't drink whisky nor play cards, he belonged. They called on him to judge their horse-races and chicken fights, umpire their matches, and settle disputes. Their homes were open to him. He was adopted.

CHAPTER 29

Counting the money a woman paid for dry goods one day, Lincoln found she had paid six and a quarter cents more than her bill; that night he walked six miles to pay it back. Once, finding he weighed tea with a four-ounce weight instead of an eight, he wrapped up another quarter of a pound of tea, took a long walk and delivered to the woman the full order of tea she had paid for. A loafer used the wrong kind of language when women customers were in the store one day; Lincoln had warned him to stop; he talked back. Lincoln took him in front of the store, threw him on the ground and rubbed smartweed in his face. When trade was slack he split rails for Offut and built a pen to hold a thousand hogs.

The two clerks, Lincoln and young Bill Green, slept together on a narrow cot in the back of the store; "when one turned over, the other had to." When a small gambler tricked Bill, Lincoln told Bill to bet him the best fur hat in the store that he (Lincoln) could lift a barrel of whisky from the floor and hold it while he took a drink from the bunghole. Bill hunted up the gambler, made the bet and won it; Lincoln lifted the barrel off the floor, sat squatting on the floor, rolled the barrel on his knees till the bunghole reached his mouth, drank a mouthful, let the barrel down—and stood up and spat out the whisky.

Wildcat money, "rag money," "shinplasters," came across the counter sometimes. The clerk asked a customer "What kind of money have you?" Once in a while he told about a Mississippi steamboat captain, short of firewood, who steered to a landing-place and offered the man in charge wildcat money for wood; but the owner of the wood said he could only trade "cord for cord," a cord of money for a cord of wood.

Lincoln and John Brewer acted as seconds for Henry Clark and Ben Wilcox when those two settled a dispute with a stand-up and knockdown fight with bare fists. The seconds had washed the blood off the faces and shoulders of the two fighters, when John Brewer, whose head came about as high as Lincoln's elbows, strutted like a bantam rooster up to Lincoln and broke out, "Abe, my man licked yours and I can lick you." Lincoln searched his challenger with a quizzical look and drawled: "I'll fight you, John, if you'll chalk your size on me. And every blow outside counts foul." In the laugh of the crowd even Brewer joined.

Between times, in spare hours, and in watches of the night when sleep came to the town and river, Lincoln toiled and quested for the inner lights of what was known as education and knowledge. Mentor Graham, the schoolmaster, told him there was a grammar at Vaner's house, six miles off; he walked the six miles, brought back the book, burned pine shavings in the blacksmith shop to light a book with a title page saying it held, "English Grammar in Familiar Lectures accompanied by a Compendium embracing a New Sytematick Order of Parsing, a New System of Punctuation, Exercises in False Syntax, and a Key to the Exercises, designed for the Use of Schools and Private Learners. By Samuel Kirkham." As he got farther into the book, he had Bill Green at the store hold it and ask him questions. When Bill asked what adverbs qualify, Lincoln replied, "Adverbs qualify verbs, adjectives and other adverbs." When Bill asked "What is a phrase?" the answer came, "A phrase is an assemblage of words, not constituting an entire proposition, but performing a distinct office in the structure of a sentence or of another phrase."

Geography he studied without knowing he was studying geography. The store had calico prints from Massachusetts, tea from China, coffee from Brazil, hardware and stoneware from New York and Pennsylvania, products and utensils from the hands and machines of men hundreds and thousands of miles away. The feel of other human zones, and a large world to live in, connected with the Offut grocery stock.

A literary and debating society was formed in New Salem, with the educated and accomplished people as members, and all others who wished to "advance" themselves. Lincoln stood up for his first speech one evening. And there was close attention. For they all knew this was a joker, the young husky who brought the lizard story to their town, the lusty buck who grappled Jack Armstrong and slammed him for a fall, the pleasant spinner of yarns. He opened his address in a tone of apology, as though he had been thinking over what he was going to say, but he wasn't sure he could put on the end of his tongue the ideas operating in his head. He went on with facts, traced back and picked up essential facts, and wove them into an argument, apologized again and said he hoped the argument would stand on its own legs and command respect. His hands wandered out of the pockets of his pantaloons and punctuated with loose gestures some of the decisive propositions, after which his hands slowly and easily slid back into the pantaloons pockets.

Then it came to Lincoln through the talk of friends that James Rutledge, the president of the society, was saying there was "more than wit and fun" in Abe's head; he was already a fine speaker; all he lacked was "culture to enable him to reach a high destiny which was in store for him." Lincoln noticed that Mr. Rutledge looked more keenly into his face and was more kindly in manner.

This had a double interest for the young store-clerk, because he had spent afternoon and evenings in the Rutledge tavern, and he had almost trembled and dark waves ran through him as he had looked wholly and surely into the face of the slim girl with corn-silk hair, Ann Rutledge, the eighteen-year-old daughter of James Rutledge.

When all New Salem laughed and wondered at the way he saved his flatboat when it hung over the dam the spring before, he had glimpsed this slim girl with light corn-silk hair, blue-eyed, pink-fair. Since then he had spoken with her as she sat sewing in a hickory splint chair, a quiet soft bud of a woman.

Some mentioned her as "beautiful"; the Clary's Grove Boys said she "wasn't hard to look at." While her two sisters, Nancy and Margaret, helped their mother with the dishes and the baby, Sarah, Ann did the sewing for all the women and showed new stitches to other New Salem girls who came in.

After the first evening in which Lincoln had sat next to her and found that bashful words tumbling from his tongue's end really spelled themselves out into sensible talk, her face, as he went away, kept coming back. So often all else would fade out of his mind and there would be only this riddle of a pink-fair face, a mouth and eyes in a frame of light corn-silk hair. He could ask himself what it meant and search his heart for an answer and no answer would come. A trembling took his body and dark waves ran through him sometimes when she spoke so simple a thing as, "The corn is getting high, isn't it?"

The name "Ann Rutledge" would come to him and he would pronounce it softly to the shadows in the blacksmith shop where he lay burning wood shavings to light the pages of Kirkham's Grammar. He knew the Rutledges branched back out of South Carolina and the Revolutionary War Rutledges, one of whom signed the Declaration of Independence; their names were in high places; her father was a southern gentleman of the old school; and he, Abe Lincoln, was from the Kentucky "Linkerns" who had a hard time to read and write. His heart would be hurting if he hadn't learned long ago to laugh at himself with a horse laugh.

The Cameron girls, where he boarded, tried to tease him about his long legs, long arms, his horsy ways; and he was always ready to admit he "wasn't much to look at." And as the blue spray from one young woman's eyes haunted him, he felt it was enough to have looked into such a face and to have learned that such an earthly frame as that of Ann Rutledge had been raised out of the breathing dust. He could say, and it was easy to say, "It can't happen that a sucker like me can have a gal like her."

During the winter of 1832, as Abe Lincoln took down calico prints from the shelves of the Offut store and measured off as many yards as the women customers asked for, or as he stepped to the whisky barrels and measured out as many quarts or gallons as the men customers asked for, he had warnings that the business of Denton Offut in New Salem was going to pieces. Offut was often filling his personal pocket-flask at his own barrels of pure and unsurpassed Kentucky rye whisky; he was more often loose with his tongue and its descriptions and predictions. Once it was said, "He talks too much with his mouth." As his cash dwindled and his prospects faded, his eyes became more red, his face more bleary and it was harder for his tongue to persuade men of the rainbow empires he saw beyond the horizon; it was said, "Offut is petering out."

CHAPTER 30

THE sawmill, the gristmill, the stores, and the post office of New Salem drew customers from different localities, such as Rock Creek, Clary's Grove, Little Grove, Concord, Sand Ridge, Indian Point, New Market, and Athens. The people mostly traced back to Kentucky and Virginia families, but Yankees from New England, Down-easters from New York, Pennsylvania Dutch, and emigrants from the British Isles and from Germany were sprinkled through. From the east of New Salem came the Smoots, Godbys, Rigginses, Watkinses, Whites, Wilcoxes, Clarks, Straders, Baxters; from the north came the Pantiers, Clarys, Armstrongs, Wagoners; from the west the Berrys, Bones, Greens, Potters, Armstrongs, Clarks, Summerses, Grahams, Gums, Spearses, Conovers, Whites, Joneses; from the south the Tibbses, Wisemans, Hoheimers, Hornbuckles, Purkapiles, Mattlings, Goldbys, Wynns, Cogdals.

They were corn-fed. The grain that came in sacks, slung over horses riding to the mill at New Salem dam, was nearly all corn, seldom wheat or rye. The mill ran all the year, and the people ate corn six days in the week and usually on Sunday. Milk and mush, or milk with corn-bread crumbled in it, was the baby food. For the grown-ups there were corn-dodgers. Two quarts of corn meal were mixed with cold water, a finger of salt thrown in, and into a well-greased skillet the cook put three pones (cakes), giving each pone a pat so as to leave the print of her hand on the bread; the skillet lid was fastened tight and a shovel of coals put on top; then, with the hot charcoal over and under the skillet was put in the fireplace. Sometimes, it was said, the cake came out "so hard that you could knock a Texas steer down with a chunk of it or split a board forty yards off."

On Saturdays young men off the farms came riding in. Horse races, with Abe Lincoln for judge, were run off between the river and Jacob Bale's place. There, too, were the gander pullings. An old tough gander was swung head down from the limb of a tree, with his neck greased slippery. Riders, who paid ten cents for the chance, rode full-speed, and the one who grabbed the gander's neck and pulled the head off, got the bird.

Up the river the boys sometimes took colts to break. They had found that a horse in water over his depth is helpless and will learn to obey. The boys would take one in, several would get onto his back, others would cling to his mane and tail, and by the time they let him come out, he could understand better the language of men speaking to horses.

Some Saturdays, when there were no strangers to pick a fight with, they fought among themselves. A gang of Wolverines from Wolf had taken on drinks in Petersburg one day and were on their horses pulling at each other's shirts, when little Johnny Wiseman called out to Greasy George Miller, "George, you have torn my shirt." "Yes," said George, "and I can tear your hide, too." And the gang got off their horses, formed a ring, and watched Wiseman and Miller fight it out till one had enough.

Between some families there was bitter hate year on year; they called it a "feud" between the families. Once two men met on the New Salem side of the river, spat hate at each other before a crowd of men, and then decided to go alone across the river and fight it out. They crossed over, stripped their clothes, and fought as wolves fight, with claw, tooth, and fang, till men came from over the river, parted them, and made them shake hands. One of the fighters was sick for a year and then died of his wounds and gouges.

And there were people who tried to stop the fighting, horse racing, gambling, and drinking. Through churches, schools, books, temperance societies, and the Government, they tried to correct these habits, and institute industry, thrift, sobriety, and bring into favor the admonition of St. Paul, "Let all things be done decently and in order." As many as fifty men, women, and children on one Sunday were baptized in the Sangamon River. The Methodists, Campbellites, Presbyterians, kept growing; at first the members of a faith met in a dwelling-house; then they had grove camp-meetings, and as they grew in membership they erected churches and sent delegates to state and national conferences, synods, presbyteries.

The most famous of all preachers in southern Illinois then was Peter Cartwright, a Jackson Democrat, a fighting Methodist, a scorner of Baptists, and an enemy of whisky, gambling, jewelry, fine clothes, and higher learning. As he visited along the Sangamon River, he would tell anecdotes. "I recollect once to have come across one of these Latin and Greek scholars, a regular graduate in theology. In order to bring me into contempt in a public company he addressed me in Greek. In my younger days I had learned considerable of German. I listened to him as if I understood it all, and then replied in Dutch. This he knew nothing about, neither did he understand Hebrew. He concluded that I had answered him in Hebrew, and immediately caved in, and stated to the company that I was the first educated Methodist preacher he ever saw."

And taking dinner with the governor of the State of Illinois, Cartwright stopped the serving of victuals by saying, "Hold on, Governor, ask the blessing." The governor said he couldn't, he didn't know how. So Cartwright pronounced the blessing—and afterward rebuked the governor for not being a practicing Christian.

One of the oldest and best loved of the Cumberland Presbyterians was Uncle Jimmy Pantier. He was a faith healer said to have cured cases of snake bite and of the bite of a mad dog; he took the patient into a room, rubbed the wound, mumbled unknown words, and sometimes the patient stood up and walked free from evil. Uncle Jimmy took a front seat at church services and would repeat the sermon as fast as the preacher preached it; he would nod approval or again shake a finger at the preacher and say in an undertone, "You are mistaken," or "That is not so, brother." He had hunted all manner of wild beasts, owned large tracts of land, wore a buckskin fringed shirt, and was a friend and neighbor to all men in the Sangamon River country.

Out around the New Salem neighborhood were men and women, known to everybody. The father of James Short, for instance, was pointed out at the Fourth of July picnics as a soldier who had fought in the Revolutionary War; he had become a wild-turkey hunter, and once in blazing away at fifty had killed sixteen turkeys. Another veteran who had served under the Commander-in-Chief George Washington was Daddy Boger, who lived in Wolf and wove bushel baskets out of white oak splints; he would go to town with a basket under each arm, trade his baskets, rest awhile, and then start home.

Farmers who had taken beef hides to the tanyard would bring hides to Alex Ferguson in New Salem, and give Alex the foot measures of the family; William Sampson, a farmer with a big family, used to come after his shoes with a two-bushel sack and take a dozen pairs home. There was Granny Spears of Clary's Grove, who was so often seen helping at houses where a new baby had come; she had been stolen by Indians when a girl and living with them had heard from them how to use herbs and salves; she was a little dried-up woman whose chin and nose pointed out and curved out till they nearly touched each other.

Uncle Johnny Watkins had a flat stone the size of a dollar, given him by a friend in Pennsylvania. The stone was to cure snake bite. It was laid on the place where the snake had bitten, and clung there soaking the poison out. Then the stone was dropped into sweet milk, which soaked the poison out of the stone, and then again the stone was put on the snake bite; this was kept up till all the poison was drawn out. Some said Uncle Johnny's stone was a sure cure for snake bite; others said corn whisky was better.

Here and there the question was asked, "Who is this Abe Lincoln?" In Menard County one story was told about how Lincoln came to New Salem and what happened. The boys in and around New Salem had sized up Abe, as they called him, and decided to see what stuff he had in him. First, he was to run a foot race with a man from Wolf. "Trot him out," said Abe. Second, he was to wrestle with a man from Little Grove. "All right," said Abe. Third, he must fight a man from Sand Ridge. "Nothing wrong about that," said Abe. The foot-racer from Wolf couldn't pass Abe. The man from Little Grove, short and heavy, stripped for action, ran at Abe like a battering-ram. Abe stepped aside, caught his man by the nape of the neck, threw him heels over head, and gave him a fall that nearly broke the bones. Abe was now getting mad. "Bring on your man from Sand Ridge," he hooted. "I can do him up in three shakes of a sheep's tail, and I can whip the whole pack of you if you give me ten minutes between fights." But a committee from the boys came up, gave him the right hand of fellowship and told him, "You have sand in your craw and we will take you into our crowd."

Thus one story was beginning to be told of how Lincoln had arrived in Illinois and what manner of man he was. Henry Onstott and others were telling the story, just like that.

CHAPTER 31

In the winter of 1832, a steamboat, the *Talisman*, from Cincinnati had started down the Ohio going west, had turned up the Mississippi running north, and in spite of fogs, rain, and floating ice-jams, she had twisted into the channel of the Illinois River and arrived at Beardstown in April.

As a sporting event it was interesting that she came through that far as a winner. As a business event it was important; after she turned into the Sangamon River and unloaded part of a cargo at Springfield, the stores there advertised arrival of goods "direct from the East per steamer *Talisman*." Storekeepers and land-buyers along the Sangamon were excited; if the steamer made all its connections and its plans worked out, then the Sangamon prairie valley would have direct water-route connections with Cincinnati and Pittsburgh; land and business values would go booming. It was a matter aside that the steamer captain, Bogue, had sent a dude captain to command the boat and this deck officer had worried the women of Springfield by bringing along a flashily dressed woman not his wife, and both of them were drunk and loose-tongued at a reception and dance in the county courthouse tendered by the ladies and gentlemen of Springfield.

She steamed up the river past New Salem, and tied up at Bogue's Mill. After the high waters of spring had gone down, making a narrower river and shallower channel, she started on her trip downstream. In charge as pilot the boat officers had put Abe Lincoln; he sat by and listened as the boat was stopped at the New Salem dam and the boat officers quarreled with the dam owners, Cameron and Rutledge, about whether they could tear a hole so as to run the boat through. At last a rip was made through the dam, the boat made the passage downstream, and everybody concerned said it must happen never again.

It was a serio-comic chapter, one of many, in the struggles of western pioneer communities for outlets, transportation, connections with the big outside world, to bring more people to the prairies, and to sell crops and produce to the East in exchange for hardware and nails; there were as yet more houses and wagons held together by wooden pegs and cleats than by iron nails and spikes.

On a ridge the other side of Green's Rocky Branch, a creek south of New Salem, stood a log schoolhouse, where Lincoln occasionally dropped in to sit on a bench and listen to the children reciting their lessons to Mentor Graham, the tall, intellectual, slant-jawed school-teacher. He wanted to find out how much he already knew of what they were teaching in the schools. And he spent hours with Mentor Graham going over points in mathematics, geography, grammar, and correct language. The words "education" and "knowledge" were often on his lips when he talked with thoughtful people; they referred to him as "a learner." He called himself that, "a learner." The gift of asking questions intelligently, listening to the answers, and then pushing quietly on with more questions, until he knew all that could be told to him, or all there was time for—this gift was his. "He could pump a man dry on any subject he was interested in."

In the month of March, 1832, he launched forth into an action that took as much nerve as wrestling Jack Armstrong the year before. He had just passed his twenty-third year, had for the first time in his life read through a grammar, was out of a job, and, except for a few months as a grocery clerk, he still classified as a workingman or a propertyless manual laborer. And he announced that he was going to run for the office of member of the legislature of the state of Illinois, to represent the people of Sangamon County in the chief law-making body of the state. He told friends he didn't expect to be elected; it was understood that James Rutledge and others had told him to make the run; it "would bring him prominently before the people, and in time would do him good." So he took his first big plunge into politics.

In a long speech, later printed as a handbill, he expressed his views about navigation of the Sangamon River and railroad transportation as compared with rivers and canals. Having floated boats and cargoes some four thousand miles in four years, he felt at home in discussing water transportation. A railroad connecting Sangamon County with other parts of Illinois, was, he said, "indeed, a very desirable object," but the cost, $290,000, he pointed out, "forces us to shrink from our pleasing anticipations." Then he analyzed the geography of the Sangamon River, argued for improvements in its channel, and pledged himself to support all measures for such improvements.

He declared, "I think I may say, without the fear of being successfully contradicted, that its navigation may be rendered completely practicable as high as the mouth of the South Fork." Next, he called for a strong law to stop "the practice of loaning money at exorbitant rates of interest," and declared that cases of greatest necessity may arise when the evasion of laws is justifiable. His four closing sentences on this subject were: "A law for this purpose [fixing the limits of usury], I am of the opinion, may be made without materially injuring any class of people. In cases of extreme necessity, there could always be means found to cheat the law; while in all other cases it would have its intended effect. I would favor the passage of a law on this subject which might not very easily be evaded. Let it be such that the labor and difficulty of evading it could only be justified in cases of greatest necessity."

He closed in a manner having the gray glint of his eyes and the loose hang of his long arms, "If the good people in their wisdom shall see fit to keep me in the background, I have been too familiar with disappointments to be very much chagrined."

CHAPTER 32

ONE morning in April, when the redbud was speaking its first pink whispers, and the dandelions scattered butter colors in long handfuls over the upland bull-grass, a rider on a muddy, sweating horse stopped in New Salem and gave out handbills signed by the governor of the state calling for volunteer soldiers to fight Indians. The famous old red man, Black Hawk, had crossed the Mississippi River with the best fighters in the Sac tribe, to have a look at land where they and theirs had planted corn, also a burying-ground at the mouth of the Rock River where their fathers and mothers of far back were buried.

For hundreds of years, the Sac tribe had hunted and fished in the rich prairie valley of the Rock River, and among the rocky hills and bluffs of northwestern Illinois; in the time of the falling leaves and the ghost shapes of the hazes of Indian summer, they had piled harvest corn in their little villages, and told the Great Spirit, Man-ee-do, with songs, dances, and prayers, they were thankful it was a good corn year.

The land of their stories, their corn-planting and harvest, their hunting and fishing places, the burying ground of their fathers who had fought for its possession as against other tribes, had passed from under their feet. In the year 1804, they sold their corner in northwestern Illinois to the United States Government, with the promise on paper, a sheet of writing, saying that they could hunt and could plant corn in Illinois till the lands were surveyed and opened up for settlers.

Then they had taken their horses, women, children, and dogs across the Mississippi River. And now they were saying the white men had broken the written promises; white squatters had come fifty miles past the line of settlement; and more than that, the United States Government could not buy land because land cannot be sold. "My reason teaches me," wrote Black Hawk, "that land cannot be sold. The Great Spirit gave it to his children to live upon. So long as they occupy and cultivate it they have the right to the soil. Nothing can be sold but such things as can be carried away."

Black Hawk was now sixty-seven years old and could look back on forty years as a chief of the Sac tribe. On his blanket was a blood-red hand, the sign that he had killed and scalped an enemy when he was a fifteen-year-old boy. In his time he had straddled his pony and helped other Indian tribes and had joined hands with British soldiers in fighting back the tide of American settlers; he had seen the red man drink the fire water of the white man and then sign papers selling land. Now he felt the Great Spirit, "Man-ee-do! Man-ee-do!" telling him to cross the Mississippi River, scare and scatter the squatters and settlers, and then ambush and kill off all the pale-faced soldiers who came against him.

The voices of his fathers said, "Go." The Fox, Winnebago, Sioux, Kickapoo, and other tribes had sent word they would join him in driving out the palefaces. Already his young men on fast ponies had circled among settlers around Rock Island and along the Rock River, leaving cabins in ashes and white men and women with their scalps torn out. And Black Hawk himself was leading his paint-face warriors, with strings of eagle feathers down their heads and shoulders, with rifles and tomahawks, up the Rock River valley, telling settlers, "We come to plant corn," saying also, "Land cannot be sold." Copper-faced men had tumbled off their horses with the rifle bullets of white men in their vitals; white men had wakened in their cabins at night to hear yells, to see fire and knives and war-axes burn and butcher.

Across all northern Illinois any strange cry in the night sent shivers of terror to the white people in their lonely cabins. Men on horses picked for speed rode to the governor at Springfield and asked for help.

The Washington government, a thousand miles away, was sending the pick of its young regulars to handle the revolt of the Indian chief who would sell land and afterward raise the point that land cannot be sold.

Sons of Alexander Hamilton and Daniel Boone were helping young commanders named Albert Sidney Johnston, Zachary Taylor, and Winfield Scott. The white civilization of firearms, printed books, plows, and power-looms was resolved on a no-compromise war with the redskin civilization of spears, eagle feathers, buffalo dances, and the art and tradition of the ambush.

And now over the rolling prairie and the slopes of timber bottoms along the Rock River, with a measureless blue sky arching over them, the red man and the white man hunted each other, trying to hand crimson death to each other. As they hunted they measured small and were hard to see, each trying to hide from the other till the instant of clash, combat, and death—bipeds stalking each other; only keen eyes could spot the pieces of the action and put together the collective human movement that swerved, struck, faded, came again, and struck, in the reaches of rolling prairie and slopes of timber bottom where the green, rain-washed bushes and trees stood so far, so deep under the arch of a measureless blue sky.

The Indians shaped and reshaped their army as a shadow, came and faded as a phantom, spread out false trails, mocked their enemy with being gone from horizons they had just filled. An ambush was their hope. They tried for it and couldn't get it. The white men had fought Indians before and had solved the theory of warfare by ambush.

By zigzag and crisscross paths, with the Sacs and Foxes the only tribes fighting, Black Hawk was driven north out of Illinois and, in swamp and island battles on Wisconsin rivers, his armies were beaten and his last chance taken.

Black Hawk did not know then that the white men had ambushed him by a white man's way of ambush, that Sioux and Winnebago Indians acting as guides for his army were in the pay of the whites and had led his army on wrong roads. It was these same red men who were paid by the whites to bring him in as a prisoner after he escaped from the battle on the Bad Axe.

And Black Hawk was taken a thousand miles to Washington, where at the White House he met President Andrew Jackson. They faced each other a white chief and red chief; both had killed men and known terrible angers, hard griefs, high dangers, and scars; each was nearly seventy years old; and Black Hawk said to Jackson; "I—am—a man—and you —are—another."

And he explained himself: "I took up the hatchet to avenge injuries which could no longer be borne. Had I borne them longer my people would have said, 'Black Hawk is a squaw; he is too old to be a chief; he is no Sac.' This caused me to raise the war-whoop. I say no more of it; all is known to you."

Abraham Lincoln had two reasons, if no more, for going into the Black Hawk War as a volunteer soldier. His job as a clerk would soon be gone, with no Offut store to clerk in. And he was running for the legislature; a war record, in any kind of war, would count in politics. He enlisted, and Jack Armstrong and the Clary's Grove Boys said they were going to elect him captain of the company. They ran him against a sawmill owner named Kirkpatrick, who had one time cheated Lincoln out of two dollars.

Kirkpatrick had hired Lincoln to move logs, and agreed that because he didn't supply a tool known as a cant hook, he would pay Lincoln an extra two dollars for doing the heavier work without a cant hook. On pay day the two dollars wasn't paid. Now the Clary's Grove boys said, "We'll fix Kirkpatrick."

The two candidates, Lincoln and Kirkpatrick, stood facing the company of recruited soldiers, and each soldier walked out and stood behind the man he wanted for captain. Lincoln's line was twice as long as Kirkpatrick's.

He was now Captain Lincoln, and made a speech thanking the men for the honor, saying the honor was unexpected, the honor was undeserved, but he would do his best to merit the confidence placed in him. After that he appointed Jack Armstrong first sergeant, with plenty of other sergeants and corporals from among the Clary's Grove boys.

But Kirkpatrick, too, was promoted from the ranks, just nine days after the company was enrolled.

On the muster-roll were such names as Obadiah Morgan, Royal Potter, Pleasant Armstrong, Michael Plaster, Isaac Guliher, Robert S. Plunkett, Travice Elmore, Usil Meeker, and Joseph Hoheimer.

Their military unit was officially designated as "Captain Abraham Lincoln's Company of the First Regiment of the Brigade of Mounted Volunteers commanded by Brigadier-General Samuel Whiteside." And though officially they were mounted volunteers, they had no mounts as yet. All were afoot, including Captain Lincoln.

The first military order he gave as captain got the reply, "Go to hell." He knew his company could fight like wildcats but would never understand so-called discipline. Other volunteer companies, also the regular army soldiers and officers, said they were "a hard set of men."

As their captain was drilling them one day with two platoons advancing toward a gate, he couldn't think of the order that would get them endwise, two by two, for passing through the gate. So he commanded, "This company is dismissed for two minutes, when it will fall in again on the other side of the gate." At Henderson River, with horses swimming the stream, it was a camp rule that no firearms should be discharged within fifty yards of the camp. Somebody shot off a pistol inside the camp; the authorities found it was Captain Lincoln; he was arrested, his sword taken away, and he was held under arrest for one day.

At another time his men opened officers' supplies and found a lot of whisky; on the morning after, the captain and his sergeants had a hard time rousing the men out of their blankets; some were dead drunk, others straggled on the march. A court-martial ordered Captain Lincoln to carry a wooden sword two days.

An old Indian rambled into camp one day. The men rushed at him; they were out in an Indian war, to kill Indians. Lincoln jumped to the side of the Indian, showed the men that the old copper-face had a military pass, and said with a hard gleam, "Men, this must not be done; he must not be shot and killed by us." One of the men called Lincoln a coward, as though he were taking advantage of his men as captain. The gleam in his eyes blazed as he stood by the old Indian and quietly told the mob, "If any man thinks I am a coward, let him test it." There was a cry, "Lincoln, you're bigger and heavier than we are," and the answer came like a shot, "You can guard against that—choose your weapons!" And the hot tempers cooled down and came to an understanding that they had an elemental captain who didn't presume on his authority.

The Sangamon County volunteers were part of an army of 1,600 soldiers mobilized at Beardstown, and marched in cold and drizzly weather across muddy roads to Yellow Banks on the Mississippi, then to Dixon on the Rock River. Sometimes the company cooks had nothing to cook and there was growling from the volunteers; one company refused to cross the line out of Illinois toward the north; Colonel Zachary Taylor, in command, made them a speech saying that some of them would probably be congressmen and go to Washington; they were important citizens of Illinois; but he had his orders from Washington to follow Black Hawk and take the Illinois troops along; behind them he had drawn up lines of regular soldiers; ahead of them were the flatboats to cross the river and leave Illinois; they could take their choice. They decided to get into the flatboats and fight Indians rather than the regular soldiers.

About this same time Captain Lincoln went to the regular army officers of his brigade and told them that, representing his men, he had to say that there would be trouble if his men didn't get the same rations and treatment as the regulars. Bill Green remembered Lincoln saying to a regular army officer: "Sir, you forget that we are not under the rules and regulations of the War Department at Washington; we are only volunteers under the orders and regulations of Illinois. Keep in your own sphere and there will be no difficulty, but resistance will hereafter be made to unjust orders. My men must be equal in all particulars—in rations, arms, camps—to the regular army." And this threat of mutiny, voiced by the leader of the Clary's Grove boys, resulted in better treatment, so that no mutiny followed.

Marching from Dixon to the Fox River, the little army camped one night, put its horses to grass, ate bread and fried salt pork, and a short hour after dark was ready for sleep. Suddenly the whole army shook with terror, fire streaked the air, drums and fifes sounded, hoots and yells were on all sides—and running horses. A scare had hit the horses as they cropped the prairie summer grass, some unknown fear, and they had broken in a run across the camp, snorting and cavorting, stepping on corporals and privates stretched out for the night sleep. No enemy Indians were in sight or hearing; but a battle-line was formed, every man clutched his gun—and nothing happened, only they lost a night's sleep.

While they were marching across Knox County, a young white sow joined Lincoln's company as a mascot, marched, swam the creeks, foraged for food, and, when greased by the company cook, slipped loose from those who tried to catch and hold her; she stayed through past Paw Paw Grove to the mouth of the Fox River, where she was butchered to make a Clary's Grove holiday.

While Lincoln's company was quartered near a fort, his men noticed that the officers had plenty of milk from two cows, one stub-tailed. And the men planned to borrow or steal one of the cows, and see what the taste of milk was like. One man rode to a slaughterhouse and came back with a long red cow's tail to match the color of the stub-tailed cow, and it was fastened to the stub-tailed cow, which had been taken from the officers. Then along came the fort commander, saying, "If that cow of yours had a stub tail, I should say it was ours." "But she hasn't got a stub tail, has she?" "No, she certainly has not a stub tail." "Well, she isn't yours then."

The lizard story and all the other stories Lincoln could remember were told around the camp-fires. "That reminds me of a feller down in Indianny," he would open up—and go on. At his hip was the wrestler's handkerchief; champions from neighborhoods in all parts of Illinois tried him out. The Clary's Grove Boys said no man in the army could throw him. This reached the ears of a wrestler named Thompson, who had friends.

A championship match was arranged, and Lincoln's friends bet money, hats, whisky, knives, blankets, and tomahawks. On the day of the match, as the two wrestlers tussled in their first feel-outs of each other, Lincoln turned to his friends and said, "Boys, this is the most powerful man I ever had hold of." For a while Lincoln held him off; then Thompson got the "crotch hoist" on him, and he went under, fairly thrown. The match was for the best two out of three falls.

In the second grapple, Lincoln went to the ground pulling Thompson down with him. It looked like a "dog-fall"; the boys from Clary's Grove swarmed around; an all-round fight seemed next on the program of the day's events, when Lincoln raised his head over the crowd, "Boys"; and in the silence that followed, he said: "Boys, give up your bets. If this man hasn't thrown me fairly, he could."

And his men paid their bets to the last dollar or jackknife or blanket—

but still went on claiming it was a dog-fall wrestle, and Lincoln could throw any man in the army. At a later time Lincoln told friends about Thompson: "I never had been thrown in a wrestling match until the man from that company did it. He could have thrown a grizzly bear."

Near Kellogg's Grove Lincoln helped bury five men killed in a skirmish the day before. This was the nearest to actual war combat that he came. He and his men rode up a little hill as the red light of the morning sun streamed over the five corpses. Telling about it afterward, he said each of the dead men "had a round spot on the top of his head about as big as a dollar, where the redskins had taken his scalp." He said it was frightful, grotesque, "and the red sunlight seemed to paint everything all over."

When his company of volunteers was mustered out, he enlisted again, serving as a private till his term was up. At Whitewater, Wisconsin, his horse was stolen and he walked to Peoria, Illinois, resting his long shanks if a comrade on a horse let him ride a mile.

Crops had gone to waste that year of Indian fighting in northern Illinois; food was scarce; Lincoln and the returning soldiers lived on corn-meal mixed with water baked over a fire in rolls of bark.

They bought a canoe at Peoria, paddled the Illinois River to Havana, sold the canoe, and walked back to good old New Salem, where there was a dry place to sleep.

So, Abe Lincoln had been through an Indian war without killing an Indian, and having saved the life of one Indian. He had seen deep into the heart of the American volunteer soldier; he had fathomed a thousand reasons why men go to war, march in the mud, sleep in cold rain, and kill when the killing is good. In the depths of his own heart there were slow changes at work; a slant of light had opened when he was elected captain; it had made him glad; it had softened and lit up shadows that floated around him sometimes in a big dark room alone with his thoughts, alone with ghosts and faded dreams that went as far back as Nancy Hanks and the lonely grave where they laid her in early winter so long ago; and, if he could be a captain of men who chose him for captain as they were going to war, he might perhaps have two hopes where before he had had only one or none at all; he might perhaps make a less desperate figure at the door of the house where the girl lived with light corn-silk hair framing a pink-fair face.

He had spent long hours talking with a volunteer from Springfield, Major John T. Stuart, who was a lawyer and had told him he could be a lawyer. Reading a tough grammar through hadn't stumped him; maybe reading law would be the same; maybe he would suddenly find himself a lawyer making speeches to the court and jury, just as he suddenly had found himself captain of a company of Sangamon County volunteers going to an Indian war.

Life seemed to be a series of doors that open and shut and with no telling beforehand which door is to be shut with its "No! No!" and which door is to swing open with a "Welcome! I was waiting for you!"

CHAPTER 33

ELECTION DAY was to be August 6, and, after reaching New Salem and washing off the Black Hawk War mud from his rawhide boots, Lincoln started electioneering and kept it up till the ballots were counted. He traveled over Sangamon County with his long frame wrapped in flax and tow-linen pantaloons, a mixed jean coat, claw-hammer style, short in the sleeves, and bobtail, "so short in the tail he could not sit on it"; a straw hat topped the long frame. To the reading and educated public, a small fraction, he gave the arguments in his long address, written in the spring, on Sangamon River navigation, a usury law, and education.

Mixing with the voters known as "the butcher-knife boys," who carried long knives in the belts of their hunting-shirts, he had the lizard story and others to tell, besides all the fresh jokes and horsy adventures by night and day in the Black Hawk War. His first stump speech was at Pappville, when the auctioneers, Poog & Knap, were selling hogs, bulls, and steers to the highest bidders.

As Lincoln stepped on a box, ready to say "Gentlemen and fellow citizens," and make his speech, he saw several fellow citizens on the edge of the crowd planting their fists in each other's faces, rushing and mauling. He noticed one of his own friends getting the worst of it, stepped off the box, shouldered his way to the fight, picked a man by the scruff of the neck and the seat of the breeches, and threw him ten feet for a fall. Then he walked back to his box, stepped up, swept the crowd with his eyes in a cool way as though what had happened sort of happened every day, and then made a speech, which Bill Green recalled afterward in these words:

"Gentlemen and fellow citizens: I presume you all know who I am. I am humble Abraham Lincoln. I have been solicited by many friends to become a candidate for the legislature. My politics are short and sweet, like the old woman's dance. I am in favor of a national bank. I am in favor of the internal-improvements system and a high protective tariff. These are my sentiments and political principles. If elected, I shall be thankful; if not, it will be all the same."

In campaigning among farmers, Lincoln pitched hay at the barns and cradled wheat in the fields to show the gang he was one of 'em; at various crossroads he threw the crowbar and let the local wrestlers try to get the crotch hoist on him. At one town a doctor, who had heard about Lincoln, asked Row Herndon, "Can't the party raise no better material than that?" but after hearing a stump speech from the young candidate, he told Herndon, "He is a take-in, knows more than all of them put together."

On Election Day Lincoln lost, standing seventh from the highest of twelve candidates.

But in his own neighborhood, the New Salem precinct where the poll-books showed 300 votes cast, he got 277 of those votes.

CHAPTER 34

LINCOLN was now out of a job, and had his choice of learning the black-smith trade or going into business. He drifted into business; friends took his promissory notes.

Five stores were running in New Salem, and somehow, after a time, three of the stores, or the wrecks and debts of them, passed into Lincoln's hands.

He and William F. Berry, the son of a Presbyterian minister, bought out the Herndon Brothers and hung up the sign Berry & Lincoln. Also they bought the stock of Reuben Radford's store.

It happened Radford passed threatening words with the Clary's Grove Boys, and one day went away from the store telling his younger brother that if the Clary's Grove Boys came in they should have two drinks apiece and no more. The boys came, took their two drinks, stood the young clerk on his head, helped themselves at the jugs and barrels, wrecked the store, broke the windows, and rode away yelling on their ponies.

When Radford came back and looked the store over, he was dis-couraged and sold the stock to Bill Green, who sold it at a profit to Berry & Lincoln. On top of these stocks, they bought out the little grocery of James Rutledge.

As the store of Berry & Lincoln ran on through the fall and winter, business didn't pick up much, and nobody cared much. Berry was drink-ing and playing poker; Lincoln was reading law and learning Shakespeare and Burns.

Early harvest days came; the oat straw ripened to cream and gold; the farmers bundled the grain in the russet fields. From the Salem hilltop, the prairie off toward Springfield lifted itself in a lazy half-world of har-vest haze; the valley of the Sangamon River loitered off in a long stretch of lazy, dreamy haze.

The tawny and crimson sunsets faded off into purple lines of prairie haze; the harvest moon, in a wash of pumpkin colors, lifted its balloon float over silver prairie haze; in the harvest days the prairie kept its horizons in haze.

For Abraham Lincoln these were haze and horizon days. Mornings and afternoons went by with few customers to bother him. He had never in his life sat so free with so many uninterrupted thoughts, so footloose day after day to turn and look into himself and find the measure of his personal horizons, to let dark, vivid roots take deeper root in their clutch and climb for the sun.

All the insides of him that could be nourished by hard work and steady chores had seen their days in plenty. Now he was having, for once, the days that might nourish by letting him sit still and get at himself, by letting him lean a moment at his door lintels and feel the flow and the slow drive of his deeper channels.

He had a keen, tenacious memory; he could review, with immensity of fact and impression, all the panoramas and sketches of his past years; and on this record he could turn the scrutiny of a developing and sharpening eye of analysis. He was growing as inevitably as summer corn in Illinois loam, when its stalks thicken as it lifts ears heavier with juices, and longer with its dripping tassels of brown silk. Leaning at the porchposts of a store to which fewer customers were coming, he was growing, in silence, as corn grows.

A mover came by, heading west in a covered wagon. He sold Lincoln a barrel. Lincoln afterward explained, "I did not want it, but to oblige him I bought it, and paid him half a dollar for it." Later, emptying rubbish out of the barrel, he found books at the bottom, Blackstone's "Commentaries on the Laws of England."

By accident, by a streak of luck, he was owner of the one famous book that young men studying law had to read first of all; it had sneaked into his hands without his expecting it; he remembered his Springfield lawyer-friend, John T. Stuart, saying the law student should read Blackstone first.

He remembered how he walked barefoot to the courthouse at Booneville down in Indiana and heard a "distinguished" lawyer make a speech to a jury with logic, sarcasm, and tears, and how he wished deep wishes he might some day be a lawyer like that. And now the book, Blackstone's Commentaries, had jumped into his hands out of an empty barrel, as if to say, "Take me and read me; you were made for a lawyer."

So he read Blackstone, the book of lectures delivered by Sir William Blackstone at Oxford, England, in 1753. Laws derive their validity from their conformity to the so-called law of nature or law of God. The objects of law are rights and wrongs. Rights are either rights of persons or rights of things. Wrongs are either public or private. And so on, read Lincoln, on the flat of his back on the grocery-store counter, or under the shade of a tree with his feet up the side of the tree. One morning he sat barefoot on a woodpile, with a book. "What are you reading?" asked Squire Godby. "I ain't reading; I'm studying." "Studying what?" "Law." "Good God Almighty!"

Jack Kelso came with gypsy ways, and Shakespeare and Burns on his tongue. He drew Lincoln to him with talk; they were chums. Lincoln hated fishing, yet he went to the river and spent hours listening while Kelso talked and fished. It was said that when other men in New Salem got drunk they wanted to fight, but Jack Kelso recited Shakespeare and Burns.

They sat along quiet river-banks where the waters were living and the fish bit; they asked: "Who am I? What is a man or a woman? Who is God? Where do we go from here?" Kelso watched his bobber and line, and discussed such things from Shakespeare as a king's skull at the bottom of the sea with pearls grown in its green eyesockets, or a queen haunted by a murder, trying to wash a blood-spot off her hand, moaning, "Out, out, damned spot."

And Lincoln, with his heart drawn to this vagabond who fished and drank corn whisky, went his own way; he couldn't see any sport in fishing nor any health, for him, in whisky. Across the road from the store of Berry & Lincoln was the house of Dr. John Allen, a Presbyterian elder who started the first Sunday school in the village, spoke strong words against negro slavery, and organized the Washingtonian Society, whose members pledged themselves to drink no intoxicating liquors.

He was an earnest, obstinate, quiet man, was Dr. Allen; and he drew Lincoln to him, by the way he practiced his religion. On Sundays, the doctor had his horse tied in front of the church, with large double-pocketed medicine saddlebags in his church pew, ready for any sick call. In sleet or snow of winter or in the sweltering dog-days of late summer, he went when his patients called; but all money collected for Sunday visits was put in a separate fund to be given to the church or to poor or sick people; house servants or hired hands on farms, he charged only for the price of the medicine. Other towns knew him as a skilled physician; doctors in Springfield and Jacksonville called him into consultations. Unless a patient was well off with property, Dr. Allen never sent a bill. His smoke-house cured hams and bacons with which farmers had paid their doctor's bills; ox-teams hauled the cured meat to Beardstown to be sent by flatboat to St. Louis and New Orleans. He was scorned, hated, and laughed at by some settlers along the Sangamon because he never let up on his steady, quiet arguments against slavery and whisky.

Even the Hard-shell Baptist church was not then ready to take a stand against whisky. When Mentor Graham, the schoolmaster, joined the temperance reform movement, the church trustees suspended him. Then, to hold a balance and hand out even justice all around, the trustees suspended another church member who had gone blind drunk. This action puzzled one member, who stood up and took from his pocket a quart bottle half full, which he shook till it bubbled, as he drawled: "Brethering, you have turned one member out beca'se he would not drink, and another beca'se he got drunk, and now I wants to ask a question. How much of this 'ere critter does a man have to drink to remain in full fellership in this church?"

Dr. Allen had a close friend in John Berry, the Cumberland Presbyterian preacher, and father of Lincoln's partner in the firm of Berry & Lincoln. Rev. Mr. Berry's arguments against whisky reached deep into Lincoln's life. At this time he was watching what whisky could do in the case of his business partner, who was physically going to wreck. He could name homes where the children were afraid of the father coming home, where crops had been lost, where the mothers had learned to take comfort from the bottle, and babies were put to sleep with wild corn-juice. Lincoln came to understand why earnest, obstinate men like Dr. Allen and Rev. Mr. Berry should go on as they did, never letting up on their argument against whisky.

Whisky seemed to be making his business partner useless. Lincoln ran the store alone. The name of "Honest Abe" was sticking. One winter morning a farmer, Harvey Ross, asked for a pair of buckskin gloves. Lincoln threw him a pair of gloves and said they were dogskin, good gloves, and 75 cents for the pair. Ross said he never had heard of dogskin gloves; they had always been deerskin. He asked if Lincoln was sure they were dogskin. The answer was: "I'll tell you how I know. Jack Clary's dog killed Tom Watkins's sheep, and Tom Watkins's boy killed the dog; old John Mounts tanned the dogskin, and Sally Spears made the gloves. That's the way I know they're dogskin."

Business dropped off; customers got scarcer. Berry & Lincoln took out a license in March, 1833, to keep a tavern and sell retail liquors. Their license specified that they could sell whisky at 12½ cents a pint, and French brandy, peach and apple brandies, Holland and domestic gins, and wine and rum, at various other prices.

In May, Lincoln was appointed postmaster; no Democrat cared for the office; but Lincoln wanted to read the newspapers. The four-horse "mud-wagon" brought most of the mail; the postmaster carried all the letters in his hat till they were called for. He came to know people always asking for a letter, and acting as though the Government was holding back a letter from them. It was here, a report ran, he met the Irishman who asked, "Is there a letter for me?" "What is the name?" "Oh, begorry, an' ye'll find the name on the letter!" He read the newspapers, kept in touch with St. Louis and Louisville and Cincinnati. "Howdy, Jack?" he would say to Jack Kelso, tell him the news, and then hear Kelso talk about Shakespeare and Burns. Some days he locked up the store for a couple of hours on an afternoon to go down to the river and listen while Kelso fished and talked.

He read in newspapers such oddities as why Lieutenant-governor William Kinney had used the little "i" in his writings; Kinney said that Governor Edwards had used up all the capital "I's," leaving him only the small "i's." And when Kinney ran for governor and his friends were mentioning his humble beginnings, the *Kaskaskia Democrat* queried and replied, "Why should Mr. Kinney be elected governor? Because he plowed in his shirt-tail."

As postmaster of New Salem Lincoln either was too careless or didn't have the heart to force newspaper subscribers to pay postage in advance, as the Government regulations required. And when George Spears sent postage money to Lincoln by a messenger somewhat loaded with corn juice, he wrote a note telling Lincoln he wanted a receipt. Lincoln replied he was "surprised" at the request. "The law requires Newspaper postage to be paid in advance and now that I have waited a full year you choose to wound my feelings by intimating that unless you get a receipt I will probably make you pay again."

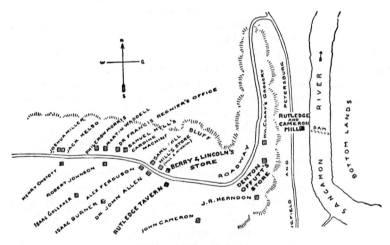

Map of New Salem.

Drawn by J. McCann Davis and loaned by Ida M. Tarbell

CHAPTER 35

MORE and more often it happened the store of Berry & Lincoln was locked for the day; customers went to other stores; Lincoln took jobs splitting fence-rails, worked at the sawmill, harvested hay and oats, and helped out when there was a rush of customers at the store of Samuel Hill. He now saw that honesty and hard work are not enough in order to win respect as a merchant; he didn't have the trader's nose for business; he lacked the gumption to locate where trade had to come and then to use customers so they would come back. The store was a goner. "It winked out."

And Lincoln was reading books about famous ruins of large enterprises, Volney's "The Ruins of Empire" and Gibbon's "The Decline and Fall of the Roman Empire." Also, Thomas Paine's "The Age of Reason." He was out of a job, with debts. Misery and melancholy he had learned to stand against; he could chase them away with a few comic stories told to the boys. But debts—they wouldn't laugh away.

No matter how he forgot himself and laughed through his lean ribs with the ins and outs of new gay stories—after all was over and he was alone, there were the debts. They were little rats, a rat for every dollar, and he could hear them gnawing in the night when he wanted to sleep.

He had one possession: many friends. One of them was John Calhoun, a Jackson Democrat, surveyor of Sangamon County, who sent word he would like to appoint Lincoln his deputy. Lincoln walked twenty miles to Springfield, and fixed the point clear with Calhoun that he could speak as he pleased, and was not tied up politically, if he took the job.

As he walked back to New Salem he saw ahead of him a tough piece of work to husk out; he had to transform his blank ignorance of the science and art of surveying into a thorough working knowledge and skill.

As he hiked along the low hills of prairie overlooking the Sangamon, it happened that Mrs. Calhoun, back in Springfield, was telling her husband she had never seen such an ungodly-looking gawk as the caller that day. He puzzled her. To which her husband offered the reply, "For all that, he is no common man."

With a copy of "The Theory and Practice of Surveying," by Robert Gibson, published in 1814, Lincoln hunted up Mentor Graham, the schoolmaster, and settled down to gain the knack of surveying. Many nights Graham's daughter woke up at midnight, she told friends, and saw Lincoln and her father by the fire, figuring and explaining.

On some nights Lincoln worked alone till daylight. The sleep he took was in short stretches. The work wore him down. Bowling Green and Jack Armstrong told him to take care of himself.

From decimal fractions the book ran on into logarithms, the use of mathematical instruments, trigonometry, operating the chain, circumferentor, surveying by intersections, changing the scale of maps, leveling, and the General Method, also the Pennsylvania Method, for mensuration of areas.

Lincoln was fagged, with sunken cheeks and bleary, red eyes; friends said he looked exactly like a hard drinker on a spree that has lasted two or three weeks.

"You're killing yourself," good people told Lincoln; and among themselves they whispered it was too sad; he would break under the load and come forth shattered.

In six weeks' time, however, Lincoln had mastered his books, the chain, the circumferentor, and Calhoun put him to work on the north end of Sangamon County. The taste of open air and sun healed him as he worked in field and timberland with compass and measurements. Winter came on and his fibers toughened.

In January, 1834, Russel Godbey paid him two buckskins for work done. As there was no other job ahead then, he took them to Hannah Armstrong, the wife of Jack, and while Lincoln rocked the baby's cradle and told the Armstrong children stories to chuckle over, Hannah sewed the buckskins on the inner, lower part of his trousers, "foxed his pants," as the saying was, so that between ankles and knees he would have leather protection in briers and brush. He and Hannah sort of adopted each other; he was one of her boys; she talked to him with snapping lights in her eyes; she reminded him of Sally Bush, though she had a different religion. Jack Armstrong and Jack Kelso went along as helpers on surveying trips; one of the Jacks could tell about all the fights and wrestling matches for years back in that part of Illinois; the other Jack was full of Shakespeare and Burns.

For his surveying Lincoln was paid three dollars a day—when he worked. Yet he saw that even with the best of luck it would be a long time before he could pay the $1,100.00 he was owing. Berry, his store partner, was dead, was through battling with whisky; a Rock Creek farmer rode in one day with the news. And the Trent brothers, who had bought with promissory notes what was left of the Berry & Lincoln store, had gone away without leaving their next address; the few groceries in the store were taken by constables in behalf of creditors. So Lincoln at twenty-four years of age had on his hands the airy wrecks and the cold, real debts of three bankrupt stores.

He could go away from New Salem by night, leaving no future address, as the Trent brothers did, as Offut had done, as many others did on the frontier. Or he could stay and stick it out.

He was sued for ten dollars owing on his horse; a friend let him have the ten dollars; the horse was saved. He was sued again, and his horse, saddle, bridle, surveying instruments were taken away. James Short, a Sand Ridge farmer, heard about it; he liked Lincoln as a serious student, a pleasant joker, and a swift cornhusker; he had told people, when Lincoln worked for him, "He husks two loads of corn to my one."

Short went to the auction, bought in the horse and outfit for $125.00, and gave them back to Lincoln, who said, "Uncle Jimmy, I'll do as much for you sometime." Lincoln had stayed away from the auction, too sad to show up. And when Short came along with his horse, saddle, bridle, compass, and all, it hit him as another surprise in his life.

He noticed these surprises kept coming regularly into his young life. It was a surprise when Gentry asked him to take a flatboat down the

Ohio and Mississippi rivers, when Offut picked him to clerk in a new store, when the Sangamon River boys elected him captain for the Black Hawk War, when James Rutledge and others told him he ought to run for the legislature, when New Salem voted for him and it was nearly unanimous, and again now when Uncle Jimmy Short, without saying anything about it beforehand, came in at the last dark moment with his horse and surveying outfit.

It seemed as though he planned pieces of his life to fit together into personal designs as he wanted. Then shapes and events stepped out of the unknown and kicked his plans into other lines than he expected, and he was left holding a sack, wondering just what it was he wanted.

When dreams came in sleep, he tried to fathom their shapes and reckon out events in the days to come. Beyond the walls and handles of his eyesight and touch, he felt other regions, out and away in the stuff of stars and dreams.

If a blizzard stopped blowing and the wind went down, with the white curve of a snow floor over Salem Hill looking up to a far blue scoop of winter stars blinking white and gold, with loneliness whispering to loneliness, a man might look on it and feel organization and testimony in the movement of the immense, relentless hubs and sprockets on the sky.

CHAPTER 36

As Lincoln boarded round here and there in New Salem, his days and hours were filled with many different occupations besides the work of surveying and politics. As postmaster he was the first in the village to receive and to read the *Sangamo Journal,* published at Springfield, the *Louisville Journal,* the *St. Louis Republican,* and the *Cincinnati Gazette.* He wrote to a firm of publishers: "Your subscriber at this place, John C. Vance, is dead; and no person takes the paper from the office."

He dipped into popular and trashy fiction such as Mrs. Lee Hentz's novels, and stories having such titles as "Cousin Sally Dillard," "Becky Williams' Courtship," "The Down-Easter and the Bull." He was at the barbecue pit when there were roastings, at the ridge south of the old Offut store when there were gander pullings, at the horse races at the west end of the main street, the horses starting or finishing in front of the Berry & Lincoln store. He played marbles with boys and took a hand often at pitching big round flat stones in a game played like quoits or horseshoes.

He worked in cornfields and timbers to earn money needed on top of his surveyor's fees and postmaster's pay. In an off hour one day he took his jackknife and cut on one side of his ax handle "A. Lincoln" and on the other side "New Salem 1834."

He saw Bab McNab's fancy red rooster get scared of another cock it was pitted against and run rings around the pit, till Bab got so disgusted he jumped in, grabbed the bird by the neck, and threw it off into the air so it lit on a pile of fresh-cut saplings. There the rooster stood up,

New Salem, Ills
Nov 3 1835

Messrs

Your subscriber at this place John C Vance, is dead; and no person takes the paper from the office

Respectfully,
A. Lincoln P.M.

Postmaster Lincoln notifies publishers their subscriber is dead and no person takes the paper.

stretched its neck, flapped its wings, and let out a long cock-a-doodle-doo. And Bab McNab yelled, "Yes, you little son of a gun, you're great on dress parade, but you're not worth a damn in a fight." Surveying near Bobtown, Lincoln put up one evening at the McHenry home, Mrs. McHenry being Nancy, a sister of Jack Armstrong. Her three-year-old girl climbed Lincoln's knee; he asked the mother what was the girl's name; the mother said she hadn't been named yet, and Lincoln could name her, if he pleased. He said, "I name you Parthenia Jane."

When called on, and at times without being called on, Lincoln recited for a crowd of men drying their mittens at the fireplace in the store on a winter afternoon, the ballad of "How St. Patrick Came to Be Born on the Seventeenth of March." Two of its verses were:

> On the eighth day of March, as some people say,
> St. Patrick at midnight he first saw the day;
> While others assert 'twas the ninth he was born—
> 'Twas all a mistake—between midnight and morn.

> Some blamed the baby, some blamed the clock;
> Some blamed the doctor, some the crowing cock,
> With all these close questions sure no one could know
> Whether the babe was too fast or the clock was too slow.

One winter morning he saw the boy, Ab Trent, chopping up the logs of an old stable that had been pulled down. Rags wrapped around Ab's feet took the place of shoes; he told Lincoln he was earning a dollar to buy shoes. Lincoln told him to run to the store and warm his feet. And after a while Lincoln came to the store, handed the boy his ax, and told him to collect the dollar and buy shoes; the wood was chopped. And it happened later that Ab, who was a Democrat, told his friends he was going to vote for Abe Lincoln for the legislature.

And when the poll-books showed that Ab Trent had voted against Lincoln, Ab came to Lincoln with tears in his eyes and said his friends got him drunk and he voted against the way he intended.

One of his best friends was the justice of the peace, Bowling Green, who carried a little round paunch of a stomach in front of him, and was nicknamed "Pot." The squire had a smooth, translucent, fair skin, and an original sense of justice. When John Ferguson sued Jack Kelso, claiming a hog, Ferguson put on the stand two witnesses who swore the hog belonged to him, while Kelso swore it was his. Squire Green gave his decision in favor of Kelso, saying: "The two witnesses we have heard have sworn to a damned lie. I know this shote, and I know he belongs to Jack Kelso."

Bowling Green was acquainted with the statutes and Lincoln spent hours in the Green home talking about the statutes. Nancy Green, the squire's wife, cooked hot biscuit smothered in butter and honey, doughnuts, and cookies, to eat with buttermilk, apples, and sweet cider.

Another friend was Dr. Charles Chandler, who was so busy practicing medicine and stocking his farm that he didn't have time to register a Government title to his land over where he had a cabin and horses in Cass County. A stranger named English, buying land tracts for a Philadelphia capitalist, took dinner with Dr. Chandler and made himself at home.

Late in the afternoon, a few hours after English had gone away, word came to Chandler that English was heading for Springfield to register for himself Dr. Chandler's two 80-acre tracts. Dr. Chandler got on a horse, skirmished among neighbors and raised the cash needed to file his land claims, and started about midnight for Springfield.

In the morning he was twelve miles from Springfield and his horse played out. He was afoot leading the nag when Abe Lincoln on a fresh fast horse came along, listened to a few words from the doctor, jumped off his horse, shortened his stirrups, changed saddlebags on the two horses, and cried: "There, doctor, mount my horse, and leave me yours, and don't let any grass grow under his feet on the way. Leave him at Herndon's stables, where I will have yours sometime today and we'll swap back. I want to get you and your pill-bags and the specie into the land office ahead of that shark. No thanks—just go." So Chandler's title to two 80-acre tracts of land was saved.

A case came up before Squire Berry at Concord one afternoon which Lincoln heard about, so that he left his surveying and acted as the lawyer for a girl in a bastardy case. Several elderly women whom he knew were put on the witness stand and felt awkward and flustered till Lincoln put them at ease by calling them "Aunt Polly" or "Aunt Sally" and the given names their homefolks used. In his address to the court, Lincoln's speech likened a man's character in such a case to a piece of white cloth, which, though it became soiled, yet could be washed and hung out in the sun, and by the aid of water, sun, and air would become white again; whereas the character of the girl, who was no more to blame, and in most instances not nearly so much to blame as the man, was like a broken and shattered bottle or glass vase, which could not be restored or made whole again.

Surveying the town of Petersburg, he laid out one street crooked. If he had run it straight and regular, the house of a Jemima Elmore and her family would have been in the street. She was the widow of an old friend who had been a private in Lincoln's company during the Black Hawk War and was farming on a little tract of land with her children.

In those New Salem days of Abraham Lincoln there were some who said he would be a great man, maybe governor of the state, anyhow a great lawyer. And there were others who looked on him as an athlete, an ordinary man, and a homely, awkward joker who felt sad sometimes and showed it.

When he kept store he often held an open book in his hand, reading five or ten minutes, closing the book to wait on a customer or to tell a story, then opening the book and reading in spite of the babblings of the men drying their mittens by the fire. He was seen walking the main street of New Salem reading a book, and, if attracted by a page or paragraph, shuffling slowly to a standstill, pausing for contemplation.

And whereas in former days in Indiana he had hunted company, hungry for human talk and thought of any kind, he found himself now drifting away from people; days came oftener when he wanted hours alone to think his way through the circles and meshes around him. It was noticed among men that he had two shifting moods, the one of the rollicking, droll story and the one when he lapsed into a gravity beyond any bystander to penetrate.

At one time, while storekeeping, he slept on the counter of the store because the Rutledge tavern was overcrowded. He wore flax and tow-linen pantaloons, no vest, no coat, and one suspender, a calico shirt, tan brogans, blue yarn socks, and a straw hat bound round with no string or band.

The Onstotts took over the Rutledge tavern and had Lincoln for a boarder a year or two. And one of the Onstotts said Lincoln never drank liquor of any kind, never smoked nor chewed tobacco, and the nearest he came to swearing was when, excited, one time he had blurted out, "By Jing!" That was his behavior in the Onstott tavern. He didn't fish or shoot. Though he was the champion wrestler and crowbar thrower, one of his favorite sports was playing marbles with boys.

One morning Lincoln asked Mentor Graham, the school-teacher, "Graham, what do you think of the anger of the Lord?" to which Graham replied, "I believe the Lord never was angry and never will be; His loving-kindness endures forever; He never changes." Lincoln then brought out a manuscript, carefully written, arguing that God never gets excited, mad, or angry. It quoted from the Bible, "As in Adam all men die, even so in Christ shall all be made alive," and defended the idea of universal salvation.

At that time it was preached from nearly all pulpits that the earth is flat, and below the earth is a pit of fire and brimstone into which an angry God will cast sinners. Against this doctrine of eternal punishment by a God of wrath Lincoln directed the argument of his manuscript. To friends he quoted the line from Burns's "Holy Willie's Prayer": "What! Send one to heaven and ten to hell?" And he had a clear memory of an old man named Glenn over in Indiana who used to say, "When I do good, I feel good; when I do bad, I feel bad."

His voice was tenor in pitch, and managed tunes in a reciting, sing-song tone. A drinking song titled "Legacy" having an old Irish air with verses by Thomas Moore, was a favorite with groups who heard him substitute his own words "old gray" for the regular words "red grape" in the hymn. The lines were:

> When in death I shall calm recline,
>   Oh, bear my heart to my mistress dear.
> Tell her it lived on smiles and wine,
>   Of brightest hue while it lingered here.

Bid her not shed one tear of sorrow
To sully a heart so brilliant and light;
But balmy drops of the red grape borrow,
To bathe the relict from morn till night.

Jack and Hannah Armstrong, out at Clary's Grove, took him in two and three weeks at a time when he needed a place to eat and sleep. Hannah said, "Abe would come out to our house, drink milk, eat mush, corn-bread and butter, bring the children candy, and rock the cradle while I got him something to eat. I foxed his pants, made his shirts. He would tell stories, joke people, boys and girls at parties. He would nurse babies —do anything to accommodate anybody."

Jack once nailed up a man in a barrel and set the barrel rolling from the top of Salem Hill to the river bank three hundred yards down; and once he nailed up two men, the barrel ran crooked, jumped off an embankment and nearly killed the two men inside. Another time, as he was nailing up old man Jordan, a hard drinker, he explained to Abe Lincoln, "Old man Jordan *agreed* to be rolled down the hill for a gallon of whisky."

Sometimes, Lincoln could tease or coax Jack into another line of fun. When a stranger backed up to a woodpile, took a club and knocked Jack to the ground, there seemed to be a mean fight on hand between the two men. Jack told Lincoln he had called the man a liar and a coward, and Lincoln asked, "If you were a stranger in a strange place and a man called you a liar and a coward, what would you do?" "Whip him, by God!" "Then this man has done no more to you than you would have done to him," Lincoln explained. And Jack insisted on the stranger having a drink with him.

A little frontier drama took place one day which A. Y. Ellis told about in this way: "I remember of seeing Mr. Lincoln out of temper and laughing at the same time. It was at New Salem. The boys were having a jollification after an election. They had a large fire made of shavings and hemp stalks; and some of the boys made a bet with a fellow I shall call 'Ike,' that he couldn't run his bobtail pony through the fire. Ike took them up, and trotted his pony back about one hundred yards, to give him a good start, as he said. The boys all formed a line on either side, to make way for Ike and his pony. Presently here he come, full tilt, with his hat off; and just as he reached the blazing fire, Ike raised in his saddle for the jump straight ahead; but pony was not of the same opinion, so he flew the track, and pitched poor Ike into the flames. Lincoln saw it and ran to help, saying, 'You have carried this thing far enough.' I could see he was mad, though he could not help laughing himself. The poor fellow was considerably scorched about the head and face. Jack Armstrong took him to the doctor, who shaved his head to fix him up, and put salve on the burn. I think Lincoln was a little mad at Armstrong, and Jack himself was very sorry for it. Jack gave Ike next morning a dram, his breakfast, and a skin cap, and sent him home."

Ellis kept a store where Lincoln helped out on busy days. "He always disliked to wait on the ladies," said Ellis. "He preferred trading with the men and boys, as he used to say. He was a very shy man of ladies. On one occasion, when we boarded at the same log tavern, there came an old lady and her son and three stylish daughters, from the state of Virginia, and stopped there for two or three weeks; and during their stay, I do not remember of Mr. Lincoln ever eating at the same table when they did. I thought it was on account of his awkward appearance and his wearing apparel."

When Ellis was asked about the first time he saw Lincoln, he said, "I was out collecting back tax for General James D. Henry. I went from the tavern down to Jacob Bale's old mill, and then I first saw Lincoln. He was sitting on a saw log talking to Jack and Rial Armstrong and a man by the name of Hoheimer. I shook hands with the Armstrongs and Hoheimer, and was conversing with them a few minutes, when we were joined by my old friend, George Warburton, pretty tight as usual; and he asked me to tell him the old story about Ben Johnson and Mrs. Dale's blue dye, and so on, which I did. And then Jack Armstrong said, 'Lincoln, tell Ellis the story about Governor Sichner, his city-bred son, and his nigger Bob,' which he did, with several others, by Jack's calling for them. I found out then that Lincoln was a cousin of Charley Hanks of Island Grove. I told him I knew his uncle, old Billy Hanks, who lived up on the North Fork of the Sangamon River. He was a very sensible old man; he was father to Mrs. Dillon on Spring Creek; and Charley, Billy, and John were his sons; they were all low-flung, could neither read nor write."

CHAPTER 37

THE Rutledge family was serious, pious, though they lived in a tavern, where travelers and strangers ate and talked around a big table, and gathered afterward around the big fireplace with talk not always serious nor pious. In the big loft of the cabin they had stowed away a dozen sleepers of a night. The Rutledges were not isolated people. They had plenty of company. Yet they were earnest, sober, a little somber.

They sang from a book, "The Missouri Harmony," published by Morgan and Sanxay in Cincinnati, "a collection of psalm and hymn tunes, and anthems, from eminent authors: with an introduction to the grounds and rudiments of music," and a supplement of "admired tunes and choice pieces of sacred music."

Lincoln and Ann Rutledge could read the learned admonition: "There should not be any noise indulged while singing (except the music) as it destroys entirely the beauty of the harmony, and renders the performance (especially to learners) very difficult; and if it is designedly promoted, is nothing less than a proof of disrespect in the singers to the exercise, to themselves who occasion it, and to the Author of our existence."

The human family has a heavy load, "hills of guilt" to carry, during tedious rounds of sluggish years, said the lines of songs. Man is a pilgrim across scorching sands, longing for a cooling stream; a wandering sheep in a howling wilderness, seeking rivers of salvation and pleasant fields of paradise. Shaped in a case of clay, man lives in a babel of loose tongues till the case falls off him, the captive is free, and he is ready to go to hell or to Zion. "In the worship of my God I'll spend my breath," ran one line, and a couplet:

> The Jewish wintry state is gone,
> The mists are fled, the spring comes on.

There was a promise in the tone of Abe Lincoln telling Ann Rutledge of one attribute of God. It was sung:

> While the lamp holds out to burn,
> The vilest sinner may return.

Englishmen who knew the sea and had been fascinated in contemplating the sea, had written the hymn, "Judgment," of how on the Last Day,

> The earth was from her center tossed
> And mountains in the ocean lost,
> Torn piecemeal by the roaring tide.

Flashes of eloquence jutted forth, as in the line, "Teach me some melodious sonnet, sung by flaming tongues above." Many of the pieces were occupied with the fact that man's life is a short and momentary breath in the world of flesh.

> Death, like an overflowing stream,
> Sweeps us away; our life's a dream,
> An empty tale, a morning flow'r,
> Cut down and withered in an hour.

Beauty, youth, wealth are phantoms of folly. They become ripe corn that an inevitable later phantom cuts down with a sickle. "Let us live so in youth that we blush not in age." The body is feeble, wanders, faints, dies, is released from this vale of tears. "Vain, delusive world, adieu!" So soon will death disrobe us all.

There was occasional jubilation, joy over moments to come when life was over on earth, when the scroll of time was rolled and the region of the timeless, the eternal, was entered. Many a line in "The Missouri Harmony" songbook had the testimony of hands strengthened for living through reverence and humility toward the regions of the invisible, the inscrutable. "Through faith, the glorious telescope, I viewed the worlds above," ran one extravagant metaphor. And there was something to think about in the line, "Not to our worthless names is glory due."

There were lines singing of world illusions, of the dissolving of strong frameworks, of proud men to be "light as a puff of empty air," of the "dear sov'reign whirl of seasons," the melting phantasmagoria of the years. Of these the meditative Lincoln was kith and kin.

CHAPTER 38

When the Illinois legislature met at Vandalia in 1834, one of the sitting members was Abraham Lincoln. He was twenty-five years old, holding his first elective political office, and drawing three dollars a day pay, with privileges of ink, quills, and stationery. The four highest candidates from Sangamon County in the voting had stood: Dawson, 1,390; Lincoln, 1,376; Carpenter, 1,170; Stuart, 1,164. On being elected Lincoln went to a friend, Coleman Smoot, who was farming near New Salem, and asked Smoot, "Did you vote for me?" and on Smoot answering "Yes," he said, "I want to buy some clothes and fix up a little, and I want you to loan me $200.00." Therefore he sat at his desk in the state capitol wearing bran-new blue jeans.

He was now away from New Salem and Ann Rutledge. And the girl Ann Rutledge had been engaged to marry John McNeil, the storekeeper and farmer who had come to New Salem and in five years acquired property worth $12,000.00. In money and looks McNeil was considered a "good catch"; and he and Ann Rutledge were known as betrothed, when McNeil started on a trip East. In a short time, as soon as he could visit his father and relatives in New York, he would come back and claim his bride. This was the promise and understanding.

And it was known to Lincoln, who had helped McNeil on deeds to land holdings, that McNeil's real name was McNamar. This was the name put in the deeds. He said he had come West taking another name in order that he might make his fortune without interference from his family back East. He had, for convenience, kept his name off election poll books, and never voted.

McNamar had been away for months and sent few letters, writing from Ohio that he was delayed by an attack of fever, writing again from New York that his father had died and he could not come West till the estate was settled. Thus letters came, with excuses, from far off. Whisperers talked about it in New Salem. Had his love died down? Or was a truthful love to be expected from a man who would live under a false name?

Days were going hard for the little heart under the face framed in auburn hair over in New Salem, as Lincoln had his thoughts at his desk in the capitol at Vandalia. She had sung to him, clear-voiced, a hymn he liked with a line, "Vain man, thy fond pursuits forbear."

He introduced a bill limiting the jurisdiction of justices of the peace; he introduced a bill to authorize Samuel Musick to build a toll bridge across Salt Creek; he moved to change the rules so that it should not be in order to offer amendments to any bill after the third reading; he offered a resolution relating to a state revenue to be derived from the sale of public lands; he moved to take from the table a report submitted by his committee on public accounts. And he had his thoughts. The line had been sung for him clear-voiced, "Vain man, thy fond pursuits forbear."

Back to New Salem he came in the spring of 1835. And there was refuge for Ann Rutledge, with her hand in a long-fingered hand whose bones told of understanding and a quiet security. She had written McNamar that she expected release from her pledge to him. And no answer had come; letters had stopped coming. Her way was clear. In the fall she was to go to a young ladies' academy in Jacksonville; and Abraham Lincoln, poor in goods and deep in debts, was to get from under his poverty; and they were to marry. They would believe in the days to come; for the present time they had understanding and security.

The cry and the answer of one yellowhammer to another, the wing flash of one bluejay on a home flight to another, the drowsy dreaming of grass and grain coming up with its early green over the moist rolling prairie, these were to be felt that spring together, with the whisper, "Always together."

He was twenty-six, she was twenty-two; the earth was their footstool; the sky was a sheaf of blue dreams; the rise of the blood-gold rim of a full moon in the evening was almost too much to live, see, and remember.

CHAPTER 39

JAMES RUTLEDGE had sold his New Salem tavern to the Onstotts, and taken his family to a farm near Sand Ridge. Lincoln rode back and forth between New Salem and the Rutledge farm when he paid Ann a call. They were talking over their plans. Ann was proud of Lincoln, and believed he had a future and would make a name as a great man. In her father's tavern at New Salem she had heard men say Abe Lincoln was considerable of a thinker and a politician; he had a way with people; he had an independent mind and yet he wanted to learn. He would go far and she would go with him; she would be to him what other women had been to other men in days gone by, women who were the wives of Rutledges, among whom there had been a signer of the Declaration of Independence, a governor, judges of courts, and other holders of high place.

For a time Ann worked at the farm of James Short and Lincoln rode over there to see her. He could laugh with her over Parthenia Hill, who had married a man who once wanted to marry Ann, saying, "Ann isn't beautiful—to begin with she has red hair."

She and Lincoln talked over the plan for her to go in the following autumn to the Jacksonville Female Academy, while he would register in the Illinois College at Jacksonville. A brother of Bill Green was a student there, some of the school-teachers around Sangamon County had been Illinois College students, and Ann's own brother David was studying there in that spring of 1835. Out of his companionship with Ann Rutledge, Lincoln had taken seriously to plans for a college education. He would have to leave college to sit in legislative sessions, but that could be arranged.

He was a witness to the wedding of William Taylor and Emaline Johnson in May, signed their "Bans of Matrimony," and believed that with luck he would in another year be married himself.

In the summer of 1835, the brother of Lincoln's betrothed woman wrote three letters, all on one sheet of paper, and saved postage by having a fellow-student carry the three-in-one letter from Jacksonville to the Rutledge farm near Sand Ridge. This letter of young David Rutledge to his father explained that the carrier of the letter, Mr. Blood, should be invited to stay all night free of cost; also that an editor, Brooks, could not pay money owing to James Rutledge and therefore David had subscribed for the editor's paper; and furthermore that David had planned to come home, but that the college wouldn't pay him back his tuition money for the term, and therefore he was staying on.

The letters were quaint, as in David addressing Anna Rutledge as "Valued Sister," and in closing each of the letters with the formal expression, "I add nomore," the word "nomore" being used then in letters, speeches, and sermons as one word, with the accent on the second syllable. Also in the missive, the ideals of courtesy and the aspirations for higher life, among the Rutledges, were reflected. The letter to the father read:

COLLEGE HILL, July 27, 1835.

DEAR FATHER:—

The passing of Mr. Blood from this place to that affords me an opportunity of writing you a few lines. I have thus far enjoyed good health, and the students generally are well. I have not collected anything of Brooks, except that I agreed to take his paper as I thought that would be better than nothing at all, though he says he could pay the order in about two months. L. M. Greene is up at home at this time trying to get a school, and I had concluded to quit this place and go to him untill the commencement of the next term, but I could not get off without paying for the whole term, therefore I concluded to stay here.

If Mr. Blood calls on you to stay all night, please to entertain him free of cost, as he is one of my fellow students and I believe him to be a good religious young man. I add nomore, but remain yours with respect until death.

D. H. RUTLEDGE.

To James Rutledge.

The second letter was to James Kittridge about school-teaching on Sand Ridge, the letter closing: "I want intelligence to come the next mail concerning it. I add nomore." Then came advice and hopes for his sister, in the following letter:

To Anna Rutledge:

Valued Sister. So far as I can understand Miss Graves will teach another school in the Diamond Grove. I am glad to hear that you have a notion of coming to school, and I earnestly recommend to you that you would spare no time from improving your education and mind. Remember that Time is worth more than all gold therefore throw away none of your golden moments. I add nomore, but &c.

D. H. RUTLEDGE.

Anna Rutledge.

And Ann might have remarked to herself that some of the golden moments of that year had been snatched and counted, and measured over again in memories afterward.

CHAPTER 40

AUGUST of that summer came. Corn and grass, fed by rich rains in May and June, stood up stunted of growth, for want of more rain. The red berries on the honeysuckles refused to be glad. The swallows and martins came fewer.

To the homes of the settlers came chills and fever of malaria. Lincoln had been down, and up, and down again with aching bones, taking large spoons of Peruvian bark, boneset tea, jalap, and calomel. One and another of his friends had died; for some, he had helped nail together the burial boxes.

Ann Rutledge lay fever-burned. Days passed; help arrived and was helpless. Moans came from her for the one man of her thoughts. They sent for him. He rode out from New Salem to the Sand Ridge farm. They let him in; they left the two together and alone a last hour in the log house, with slants of light on her face from an open clapboard door. It was two days later that death came.

There was what they called a funeral, a decent burial of the body in the Concord burying ground seven miles away. And Lincoln sat for hours with no words for those who asked him to speak to them. They went away from him knowing he would be alone whether they stayed or went away.

A week after the burial of Ann Rutledge, Bill Green found him rambling in the woods along the Sangamon River, mumbling sentences Bill couldn't make out. They watched him and tried to keep him safe among friends at New Salem. And he rambled darkly and idly past their circle to the burying ground seven miles away, where he lay with an arm across the one grave.

"Vain man, thy fond pursuits forbear." As the autumn weeks passed, and the scarlet runners sent out signals across the honey locust and the sycamore tree where they had sat together on the Salem hilltop, and the sunsets flamed earlier in the shortening afternoons, the watchers saw a man struggling on a brink; he needed help. Dr. Allen said rest would help. They took him to the home of Bowling and Nancy Green, at the foot of a bluff climbed by oak-timber growths. A few days he helped in the field at cornhusking; most of the time Nancy had him cutting wood, picking apples, digging potatoes, doing light chores around the house, once holding the yarn for her as she spun.

In the evenings it was useless to try to talk with him. They asked their questions and then had to go away. He sat by the fire one night as the flames licked up the cordwood and swept up the chimney to pass out into a driving storm-wind. The blowing weather woke some sort of lights in him and he went to the door and looked out into a night of fierce tumbling wind and black horizons. And he came back saying, "I can't bear to think of her out there alone." And he clenched his hands, mumbling, "The rain and the storm shan't beat on her grave."

Slowly, as the weeks passed, an old-time order of control came back to him—only it was said that the shadows of a burning he had been through were fixed in the depths of his eyes, and he was a changed man keeping to himself the gray mystery of the change.

CHAPTER 41

AGAIN Lincoln was in Vandalia as a lawmaker, and, his term over, again he was back surveying in Sangamon County. On June 13, 1836, he had announced himself as a candidate again, declaring he was for internal improvements, that he would vote for Hugh L. White, the Tennessee Whig, for President in November, and declaring that women ought to have the vote. "I go for admitting all whites to the right of suffrage who pay taxes or bear arms (by no means excluding females)."

Bob Allen, a Democratic candidate, came through New Salem and sort of allowed he could tell a few things about Abe Lincoln and Ninian W. Edwards, only it wouldn't be fair to tell 'em.

Lincoln wrote him: "I am told that during my absence last week you stated publicly that you were in possession of a fact or facts, which if known to the public would entirely destroy the prospects of N. W. Edwards and myself at the ensuing election, but that through favor to us you would forbear to divulge them. No one has needed favors more than I, and generally few have been less unwilling to accept them, but in this case favor to me would be injustice to the public, and therefore I must beg your pardon for declining it. That I once had the confidence of the people of Sangamon County is sufficiently evident; and if I have done anything, either by design or misadventure, which if known would subject me to a forfeiture of that confidence, he that knows of that thing and conceals it, is a traitor to his country's interest. I find myself wholly unable to form any conjecture of what fact or facts, real or supposed, you spoke; but my opinion of your veracity will not permit me for a moment to doubt that you at least believed what you said. I am flattered with the personal regard you manifested for me; but I hope that on mature reflection you will view the public interest as a paramount consideration and therefore let the worst come. I assure you that the candid statement of fact on your part, however low it may sink me, shall never break the ties of personal friendship between us. I wish an answer to this, and you are at liberty to publish both if you choose."

No reply came from Allen; Lincoln's mention of "personal friendship" between himself and Allen was sarcasm; his friends alluded to Allen as "a bag of wind."

On the stump in Springfield, speaking in the courthouse, Lincoln was challenged by George Forquer, a lawyer who had switched from Whig to Democrat and after the switch was named by the Democratic administration at Washington as register of the land-office. Forquer had just finished building a frame house, the finest in Springfield, and put up a lightning-rod on it. Farmers and their wives hitched the horses at the public square and went to have a look at Forquer's lightning-rod before buying calico, sugar and coffee, or harness buckles; it was the first lightning-rod in that part of Illinois. Forquer was a prominent citizen.

The crowd was starting to leave after a speech by Lincoln. Forquer took the platform and said the young man who had just spoken was sailing too high and would have to be "taken down"; and he was sorry the task devolved on him. Then he made what Josh Speed called "a slasher-gaff speech," while Lincoln stood by with folded arms and measuring eyes.

When Forquer quit speaking, Lincoln stepped up quietly, apologized, offered his argument and closed as follows: "Mr. Forquer commenced his speech by announcing that the young man would have to be taken down. It is for you, fellow citizens, not for me, to say whether I am up or down. The gentleman has seen fit to allude to my being a young man; but he forgets that I am older in years than I am in the tricks and trades of politicians. I desire to live, and I desire place and distinction; but I would rather die now than, like the gentleman, live to see the day that I would change my politics for an office worth $3,000.00 a year, and then feel compelled to erect a lightning-rod to protect a guilty conscience from an offended God."

As a speech it held the audience screwed to the benches, and earned a reputation for Lincoln as a hard man to handle when he was stumping for the legislature. His friends carried him from the courthouse on their shoulders. There was a new feeling for him about being carried on men's shoulders. It was like wrestling, but different.

Once he rode to a meeting with a Democratic candidate in a rig that belonged to the Democrat. At the meeting he told the farmers: "I am too poor to own a carriage, but my friend has generously invited me to ride with him. I want you to vote for me if you will; but, if not, then vote for my opponent, for he is a fine man."

The Whigs took Sangamon County away from the Democrats, by an average majority of four hundred votes, Lincoln in the lead. The famous "Long Nine" went to Vandalia, nine Whigs averaging six feet in height and over 200 pounds weight. They were for big schemes "commensurate with the wants of the people," a railroad from Galena to the mouth of the Ohio River, running the north-and-south length of the state; a railroad from Alton to Shawneetown; from Alton to Mt. Carmel; from Alton to the eastern state line, running the east and west breadth of the state; from Quincy to the Wabash River; from Bloomington to Pekin; from Peoria to Warsaw; in all about 1,350 miles of railroad. They would spend $100,000.00 to improve the Rock River; $4,000,000.00 to complete the Illinois and Michigan Canal; $250,000.00 for the Western Mail Route.

Altogether, the scheme would cost $12,000,000.00. Lincoln was among the leaders arguing for it. They would sell bonds to raise the $12,000,-000.00; they would raise the money in the same way Lincoln and Berry bought their stores in New Salem, by promises on paper. The bonds would sell like hot cakes; the Rothschilds and the Baring Brothers over in London would snap up the bargains.

The scheme won out in the legislature. And the legislature was in close touch with the people of the state, who as a mass were silent and had their silence taken for consent. The Black Hawk War had put $4,000,-000.00 in circulation. Land speculators and real-estate dealers were busy; on open prairies many towns and cities were laid out in lots; men joked each other that soon no land would be left for farming.

The governor of the state had officially declared: "Under the blessing of a bountiful Providence, Illinois is fast ascending in the scale of importance and will in a short time take her station among the first States in the Union; the steadiness and grandeur of her outward march, will however, in a great degree, depend on her future legislation."

A boom was on, overloaded and sure to collapse. It was the pioneer stock, taking its chances, believing in the future, and believing that future would come sooner if boomed.

That Lincoln, who could not finance himself, should show no ability in financing the state of Illinois in a vast economic project was to have been expected. And yet he had a vision of himself at this time as a constructive statesman, pushing through plans in Illinois for transportation ways, schools, and education. He told his friend, Joshua Speed, at Springfield that he aimed at being called "the De Witt Clinton of Illinois," achieving for his state what a constructive statesman had done for New York in getting the Erie Canal built and in bringing school improvements.

Lincoln led the "Long Nine" in finding the votes in the legislature to pass a bill moving the capital of the state from Vandalia to Springfield. Other counties besides Sangamon were hustling for the location; it went to Springfield mainly because of the patient and skilled manipulation of Lincoln. A few members voted for the bill because they liked Lincoln, but most of the voters came through trades, deals, "log-rolling." "You scratch my back and I'll scratch yours."

And yet as a manipulator, trading, fixing, coaxing, Lincoln operated by a code of his own. An all-night session was held by the members favoring Springfield for the state capital; and Lincoln was told of a block of votes he could have if he would give his vote for a certain measure that he considered against his principles; the members went home at daybreak without having brought him their way.

A second meeting was called; again they tried to ride down Lincoln's objections; midnight came, the candles burned low, all were tired. Lincoln began speaking amid silence, seriously and with feeling, telling why he couldn't in such a case trade his vote.

As old man Henderson remembered the speech, it ended: "You may burn my body to ashes, and scatter them to the winds of heaven; you may drag my soul down to the regions of darkness and despair to be tormented forever; but you will never get me to support a measure which I believe to be wrong, although by doing so I may accomplish that which I believe to be right."

After the bill passed and Springfield was named as the future capital city of the state, the Democrats charged the Sangamon County Whigs with "bargain and corruption." At an extra session General L. D. Ewing, who favored Vandalia, declared the Springfield crowd had "sold out to the internal improvements men." Lincoln then delivered a speech that bristled with keen thrusts. "He tore the hide off Ewing." And Ewing, who was an army general and a proud man, was ready for a duel. Friends stepped between and saved bloodshed.

With drawling and whimsical good nature, Lincoln opened his discussion of a resolution offered by Linder to investigate the state bank, saying: "It is not without a considerable degree of apprehension that I venture to cross the track of the gentleman from Coles [Mr. Linder]. Indeed, I do not believe I could muster a sufficiency of courage to come in contact with that gentleman, were it not for the fact that he, some days since, most graciously condescended to assure us that he would never be found wasting ammunition on small game. . . . Whenever I shall have occasion to allude to that gentleman I shall endeavor to adopt that kind of court language which I understand to be due to decided superiority. In one faculty, at least, there can be no dispute of the gentleman's superiority over me, and most other men; and that is, the faculty of entangling a subject so that neither himself, nor any other man, can find head or tail to it. . . . In the present case, if any gentlemen whose money is a burden to them choose to lead off a dance, I am decidedly opposed to the people's money being used to pay the fiddler. No one can doubt that the examination proposed must cost the State some ten or twelve thousand dollars; and all this to settle a question in which the people have no interest, and about which they care nothing. These capitalists generally act harmoniously and in concert to fleece the people; and now that they have got into a quarrel with themselves, we are called upon to appropriate the people's money to settle the quarrel."

Then he filed the declaration: "Mr. Chairman, this work is exclusively the work of politicians; a set of men who have interests aside from the interests of the people, and who, to say the most of them, are, taken as a mass, at least one long step removed from honest men. I say this with the greater freedom because, being a politician myself, none can regard it as personal."

He was now meeting men of importance from all parts of Illinois; they came from towns and counties wanting appropriations, from banks, railroads, contractors, seeking legislation for special interests. Lincoln, the story-teller, the whimsical, good-natured philosopher, was asked to their game suppers and banquets. It cost $600.00 to pay for the supper, wines, cigars, whisky, and damages, at a party given by the newly elected United States Senator, John M. Robinson.

Attending the party was a brother of William Cullen Bryant, the New York poet, one John Bryant, sent from Princeton to help legislation for Bureau County. He wrote that after the company had got noisy and mellow on rye and corn-juice, "Mr. Douglas and General Shields, to the consternation of the host and intense merriment of the guests, climbed up on the table at one end, encircled each other's waists, and, to the tune of a rollicking song, pirouetted down the whole length of the table, shouting, singing, and kicking dishes, glasses, and everything right and left, helter-skelter."

The Douglas referred to was a short, thick-set, blue-eyed man whose full name was Stephen Arnold Douglas, a young lawyer from Vermont.

Neither he nor Lincoln took any special notice of each other, except that Lincoln remarked to others that Douglas was "the least man I have ever seen."

After a day of legislative sessions, committee meetings, conferences, study of bills and measures, and a game supper, Lincoln enjoyed sitting in a hotel room with friendly souls, sitting with his knees up to his chin, drawling out stories, talking about how they were beating the Democrats, emphasizing a good point by drawing his knees again up to his chin and letting both feet down on the floor with a slam.

Newton Walker had brought his fiddle from Lewistown. Lincoln would go over to where Walker was boarding and ask him for a tune. Then Lincoln would tell a story, and it would be a story and a tune till late hours. Walker said, "When he grew weary of telling stories he would ask me to give him a tune, which I never refused to do."

Each of several taverns in Vandalia called itself a "House of Entertainment." Willis & Maddox issued a card "to respectfully inform the public" they were located two doors from the post office, and, "They will serve up at any hour of the day or the night Fried Ham, Turkeys, Grouse, or Prairie Chicken, Partridges, Venison, Pigs' Feet, Tripe, Sausages, Oysters, Mackerel, Herrings, and Crackers: Coffee, Tea, and Soups, together with many other nicknacks unmentionable; Hot Punch, Egg Nogg &c. at any time: all of which will be afforded with great goodwill and on the most accomodating terms. They have also on hand and for sale Best Teas, Loaf and Brown Sugars, Tobacco, Oranges, Lemons, Figs; Lobsters, Olives, Mushrooms, Walnut and Tomato Pickles, Ketchups, Rochelle, Cherry, Champaign, Cogniac, Peach, American and other Brandies; Claret, Teneriffe, Sherry, Dry, Brown, Port, Malaga and Madeira Wines; Seidlitz and Soda Powders; Fire Crackers, &c., &c."

There were yarns, true to fact, told among people then, to pass the time. One was about Governor Duncan, who had a misunderstanding with the Jackson administration and switched his politics from Democrat to Whig. One plain old henchman came to him and spoke the regrets: "You was young, poor, friendless; we put you into high office and enabled you to make a fortune. You was like a poor colt. We caught you up out of the thicket, fed you on the best, combed the burrs out of your mane and tail, and made a fine horse of you. And now you have strayed away from your owners."

Among politicians there was a tradition of a legislature which passed a law forbidding small bulls to roam at large. Owners of such small stray bulls would get heavy fines, under the law. The small farmers rose in anger, claiming that the law was all in favor of the rich farmers who had only big bulls, and the law let the big bulls roam as they pleased. At the next election the small farmers revolted and threw out of office every politician who had voted against small bulls.

Quaint tales out of green, moist solitudes passed around. One was of James Lemon, an old-time Baptist preacher and farmer in Monroe County, who made his own horse-collars, of straw or corn-husks plaited together. While breaking stubble, with his wild son helping, he left the harness on the beam of the plow at dinner-time. The son hid the horse-collar, so as to have a longer rest at dinner in the hours his father would plait a new horse-collar of corn-husks. But when, after dinner, the old man saw the horse-collar gone, he pulled off his leather breeches, stuffed the pant-legs with stubble, straddled them across the neck of the horse for a collar, and so plowed the rest of the afternoon, "as bare-legged as when he came into the world."

There was William Meharry, herding cattle in Champaign County. He rode horseback, snapping off rattlesnake heads with a long cattle whip, sometimes killing twenty-five in a day.

There was talk of farmers like Andrew McCorkle, not far from Springfield, who was afraid the railroads would scare his cows so they wouldn't give milk.

There had been weather to talk about one rainy day in December of 1836, when soft mud turned hard in an hour, and Washington Crowder, riding to Springfield, froze to his saddle and had to be carried into a house, saddle and all, to be thawed out.

And it was told of various communities that a mob went to the house of a man and took him away and hanged him to a tree. It was a dark night and when morning came they saw they had hanged the wrong man. And they went and told the widow, "The laugh is on us."

The end of the legislative session at Vandalia came on March 6, 1837, and the "Long Nine," with their long legs and 200 pounds weight apiece, started home on their horses, with the exception of Lincoln, whose horse had been stolen, leaving him without cash to buy another. As Lincoln walked, the others pointed to the size of his feet; when he shivered, "Boys, I'm cold," another noticed, "No wonder—there's so much of you on the ground."

Arrived at Springfield, the "Long Nine" sat down to a game supper while spokesmen for Springfield expressed gratitude to those who had arranged to move the state capital from Vandalia to their own city. One toast ran, "Abraham Lincoln: he has fulfilled the expectations of his friends, and disappointed the hopes of his enemies," and Lincoln offered the toast, "All our friends: they are too numerous to mention now individually, while there is no one of them who is not too dear to be forgotten or neglected."

On the way to New Salem he stopped at the village of Athens, the home of his colleague, Robert L. Wilson of the "Long Nine." At a banquet he was toasted, "Abraham Lincoln: one of nature's noblemen." And Wilson gave people this size-up of Lincoln, "He was as much at home in the legislature as at New Salem; he had a quaint and peculiar way, all his own, of treating a subject, and he frequently startled us. He seemed to be a born politician. We followed his lead; but he followed nobody's lead. It may almost be said that he did our thinking for us. He inspired respect, although he was careless and negligent. We would ride while he would walk, but we recognized him as a master in logic. He was poverty itself, but independent. He seemed to glide along in life without any friction or effort. "

Wilson had spent many hours with Lincoln during the years they were together in the legislature, and with Athens and Wilson's home so near New Salem they had seen a good deal of each other in action. When Wilson had occasion to tell later what he knew about Lincoln, he said: "I made a canvass through Sand Ridge; Mr. Lincoln accompanied me, and we called at nearly every house. At that time it was the custom to keep whisky in the house. The subject was always mentioned, but with the remark to Mr. Lincoln, 'You never drink, but maybe your friend would like to take a little.' "

"In a conversation about that time," Wilson said, "Lincoln told me that although he appeared to enjoy life rapturously, still he was the victim of terrible melancholy. He sought company, and indulged in fun and hilarity without restraint or stint as to time; but, when by himself, he told me that he was so overcome by mental depression that he never dared carry a knife in his pocket; and as long as I was intimately acquainted with him, previous to his commencement of the practice of law, he never carried a pocketknife."

When people talked about Lincoln, it was nearly always about one or more of these five things: (1) how long, tall, quick, strong, or awkward in looks he was; (2) how he told stories and jokes, how he was comical or pleasant or kindly; (3) how he could be silent, melancholy, sad; (4) how he was ready to learn and looking for chances to learn; (5) how he was ready to help a friend, a stranger, or even a dumb animal in distress.

Henry E. Dummer, a lawyer in Springfield, remarked: "Lincoln used to come to our office—Stuart's and mine—in Springfield from New Salem and borrow law books. Sometimes he walked but generally rode. He was the most uncouth-looking young man I ever saw. He seemed to have but little to say, seemed to feel timid, with a tinge of sadness visible in the countenance, but when he did talk all this disappeared for the time, and he demonstrated that he was both strong and acute. He surprised us more and more at every visit."

CHAPTER 42

DURING the winter at Vandalia, Lincoln had written a drawling and half-bashful love letter to the daughter of a rich farmer in Green County,

Kentucky. She was Miss Mary Owens, one year older than Lincoln, with a head of dark curly hair, large blue eyes, standing five feet five inches high, and, on her first visit to New Salem three years before, weighing about one hundred and fifty pounds.

Her sister, Mrs. Bennet Able, was anxious for the two to get married. But Mary Owens held off; she had been trained in Kentucky schools for refined young ladies; she dressed in what one of the Greens called "the finest trimmings I ever saw"; and she took note in the case of Lincoln, "His training had been different from mine; there was not congeniality; he was deficient in those little links which make up a woman's happiness."

Once when a party were riding to Uncle Billy Green's, they came to a branch of the creek which was a bad crossing. Miss Owens noticed the other men helping their partners, while Lincoln rode ahead of her without looking back. "You are a nice fellow!" she remarked when she caught up with him. "I suppose you did not care whether my neck was broken or not." And he had laughed back a defense that was a compliment, telling her he knew she was plenty smart enough to take care of herself.

She climbed a steep hill with Lincoln and Mrs. Bowling Green. And Lincoln kept on joking and talking to her, not once offering to help carry the fat baby Mrs. Green had in her arms. It seemed to Miss Owens to be "neglect" on Lincoln's part.

She was puzzled by him; in some things he was so soft-hearted; he told her he saw "a hog mired down" one day when he was crossing a prairie and, as he had a new suit of blue jeans on and was "fixed up" in his best clothes, he said to himself he would pass by and pass on without looking again at the struggling shote in the mud. But after he had passed on, the hog haunted him and seemed to be saying, "There, now my last hope is gone," and he had turned around, gone back, and got the hog loose from the mire. It was puzzling to Miss Owens's ideas about chivalry that a man could be so thoughtful about a hog in that way and at another time be so abstracted and lost in his own feelings that he couldn't stay alongside his woman partner when riding across a dangerous creek.

They had parted without any particular understanding except that they were good friends. She had gone home to Green County, Kentucky, and talked with her father, of whom she said, "Few persons placed a higher estimate on education than he did." And if she told her father about Lincoln's personal speech she included such information as the fact that Lincoln said "ain't" as often as "isn't" and that sometimes his pronunciation of "such" sounded like "sich."

Lincoln, at Vandalia, making laws for the commonwealth of Illinois, one cold, lonesome winter night, wrote her a letter which he called dry and stupid, which he said he was ashamed to send. The letter read:

VANDALIA, December 13, 1836.

MARY:

I have been sick ever since my arrival, or I should have written sooner. It is but little difference, however, as I have very little even yet to write. And more, the longer I can avoid the mortification of looking in the post-office for your letter and not finding it, the better. You see I am mad about that old letter yet. I don't like very well to risk you again. I'll try you once more, anyhow.

The new State House is not yet finished, and consequently the legislature is doing little or nothing. The governor delivered an inflammatory political message, and it is expected there will be some sparring between the parties about it as soon as the two Houses get to business. Taylor delivered up his petition for the new county to one of our members this morning. I am told he despairs of its success, on account of all the members from Morgan County opposing it. There are names enough on the petition, I think, to justify the members from our county in going for it; but if the new members from Morgan oppose it, which they say they will, the chances will be bad.

Our chance to take the seat of government to Springfield is better than I expected. An internal-improvement convention was held here since we met, which recommended a loan of several millions of dollars, on the faith of the State, to construct railroads. Some of the legislature are for it, and some against it; which has the majority I cannot tell. There is great strife and struggling for the office of the United States Senator here at this time. It is probable we shall ease their pains in a few days. The opposition men have no candidate of their own, and consequently they will smile as complacently at the angry snarls of the contending Van Buren candidates and their respective friends as the Christian does at Satan's rage. You recollect that I mentioned at the outset of this letter that I had been unwell. That is the fact, though I believe I am about well now; but that, with other things I cannot account for, have conspired, and have gotten my spirits so low that I feel I would rather be any place in the world than here. I really cannot endure the thought of staying here ten weeks. Write back as soon as you get this, and, if possible, say something that will please me, for really I have not been pleased since I left you. This letter is so dry and stupid that I am ashamed to send it, but with my present feelings I cannot do any better.

Give my best respects to Mr. and Mrs. Able and family.

Your friend,
LINCOLN.

CHAPTER 43

ONE day in March of that year of 1837, Lincoln visited the home of Bowling and Nancy Green at the foot of the bluff with its timber of oak-growth climbing. And he and Squire Bowling Green talked about politics —and about Lincoln going to Springfield to be a lawyer, practicing law in the law firm of Stuart & Lincoln. Like all lawyers, he had been certified to the supreme court as having good moral character; he was licensed to write his name, "Abraham Lincoln, Attorney-at-Law."

So he was leaving the town of the hilltop at the curve of the Sangamon River, with its memories of the flatboat stuck on the dam, of the trip as pilot on the *Talisman*, of the Offut store that petered out, of the Black Hawk War and the boys that stepped to the front and elected him a captain, the wrestling match with Jack Armstrong, the horse races and rooster fights of the boys from Clary's Grove and Wolf Creek and Sand Ridge, the mastery of Kirkham's Grammar and surveying, the store of Berry & Lincoln that winked out and left him struggling under debts it would take years to pay off, the winning of the girl with the wavy corn-silk hair and the folding of her hands and the taking her away, shadows speaking in thin whispers.

Men talked about John McNamar, the first betrothed of Ann Rutledge, coming back, buying more land to raise more corn to feed more hogs to buy more land, how quick McNamar was at figuring fractions and decimals, how sharp he was at reading mortgages and deeds, and one woman saying he was cold as the multiplication table.

James Rutledge had died the same year as his daughter Ann. The new owner of the farm at Sand Ridge was John McNamar, and he told the Widow Rutledge she would have to move; he couldn't use promises or hopes and would have to have rent money. And the daughters had told friends, "Mother is having a hard time. We're turned out, moving to Iowa, to begin all over again."

One morning Lincoln saddled a horse borrowed from Bowling Green, threw across its back saddlebags containing his copies of Blackstone and a change of underwear, and started on the twenty-mile ride to Springfield. On this ride his thoughts were different from the time when he moved from Kentucky up into Indiana at eight years of age, and again when he moved from Indiana to Illinois at twenty-one. Now he was twenty-eight years old; he had talked with men on main-traveled roads, everlastingly asking questions; he had read newspapers and heard public speakers; he was watching civilization.

In the legislature that winter just passed, he had done a thing as independent as the way he wore his hat. He had stood almost alone against the whole legislature; he had found only one other man to stand with him.

Over the nation the question had come up whether the slavery of the negro race under the white race was right or wrong, and whether any man or woman, believing it wrong, should be free to say so.

Forty peculiar and solemn men and women meeting in a house in Philadelphia four years previous had organized the American Antislavery Society, calling on the free states to remove slavery "by moral and political action, as prescribed in the Constitution of the United States," and announcing, "With entire confidence in the overruling justice of God, we plant ourselves upon the Declaration of Independence and the truths of divine revelation as upon the everlasting rock. We shall organize anti-slavery societies, if possible, in every city, town, and village in the land. We shall send forth agents to lift up the voice of remonstrance, of warning, of entreaty, and of rebuke. We shall circulate unsparingly and extensively antislavery tracts and periodicals."

In the southern states it was no longer lawful to speak against slavery; any person found guilty of an agitation that might cause an insurrection of slaves would be hanged, in accordance with the statutes. Governor Lumpkin and the legislature of the state of Georgia offered $5,000.00 for the person of one Boston agitator to be brought to Georgia for trial. The three million negro workers in the southern states were property, live stock valued by tax assessors at more than one thousand million dollars; in the Senate at Washington Henry Clay had named the total slave property value as twelve hundred million dollars; the cotton belt was spreading westward, adding thousands of acres every month.

The *Richmond Whig* of Virginia urged: "The people of the North must go to hanging these fanatics if they would not lose the benefit of the Southern trade, and they will do it. Depend upon it, the Northern people will never sacrifice their present lucrative trade with the South, so long as the hanging of a few thousands will prevent it." The New York *Courier and Enquirer* declared, "They (the Abolitionists) have no right to demand protection of the people they insult. Ought not, we ask, our city authorities to make them understand this—to tell them that they prosecute their treasonable and beastly designs at their own peril?"

President Jackson had told Congress: "I would respectfully suggest the propriety of passing such a law as will prohibit under severe penalties, the circulation in the Southern States, through the mail, of incendiary publications intended to instigate the slaves to insurrection." The *Augusta Chronicle* of Georgia offered the prophecy: "We do firmly believe that, if the Southern States do not quickly unite, and declare to the North, if the question of slavery be longer discussed in any shape, they will instantly secede from the Union, that the question must be settled, and very soon, by the sword, as the only possible means of self-preservation." Riots in Philadelphia lasted three nights, ending with forty-four houses smashed, a colored Presbyterian church battered, one negro beaten to death, another drowned in the Schuylkill River.

In Boston an agitator who came to a meeting of the Female Antislavery Society had his clothes torn off, was dragged at a rope's end through the streets, and, after being rescued by the police, had to borrow coat, hat, and pantaloons to go to jail for further safety from those hunting him, who were respectable, well-to-do citizens of Boston. When Miss Prudence Crandall opened a school for negro children at Canterbury, Connecticut, she was sent to jail for violation of the state law forbidding the teaching of colored children from other states. At Concord, New Hampshire, an academy was wrecked where colored children were being taught reading and writing.

The meek, mild, soft-spoken little Quaker, Benjamin Lundy, editing a paper with the meek, mild, soft-spoken title, "The Genius of Universal Emancipation," was beaten by a Baltimore mob. And James Gillespie Birney, Kentucky-born and raised, a brilliant young lawyer who had been an Alabama planter and had given all his slaves freedom papers, couldn't get a paper printed nor hire a hall for a speech in Owensville, Kentucky; the *Philanthropist*, which he was publishing in Cincinnati, was refused delivery by postmasters in the states South. He had traveled southwest and met dreams of southern empire while listening to planters talking about the big land stretches west of the Mississippi River and how to make them slave territory. He wrote: "There will be no cessation of conflict until slavery shall be exterminated or liberty destroyed. Liberty and slavery cannot live in juxtaposition." And while Birney and his group tried to bring gradual emancipation by lawful and constitutional methods, the Garrison group demanded immediate emancipation by moral suasion and Christian wisdom, or somehow otherwise, maintaining that the United States Constitution in its silent assent to slavery was "a compact with Hell."

From week to week the Abolitionist papers published articles and items about mobs North and South, about auctioneers of slaves calling for bids near the steps of the Capitol in Washington, the tactics of John Quincy Adams in Congress against the so-called "Gag Rule," a resolution passed by Congress providing that all petitions relating to slavery should be laid on the table without being referred to a committee or printed. Events were splitting the churches into northern and southern divisions.

Far down in Texas men of southern kin were fighting, the Alamo garrison of 187 men dying to the last man in trying to hold out against a Mexican army of 5,000; it was part of the march of the South, or the southern planters, to wider regions, more cotton-planted land. Sam Houston's men took victory from a Mexican army at San Jacinto and won independence for Texas; planters had come; slave ships had arrived at the coast line of Texas direct from Africa; a woman wrote of fresh arrivals, shipwrecked near Galveston Bay: "As soon as the beeves were skinned the negroes acted like dogs, they were so hungry; they laughed and chattered like monkeys; they did not understand a word of English; all the men and boys in the neighborhood came to see the wild Africans."

So, windy and clamorous forces blew across America. The future held unknown cross-paths. While the hot blood of the South tingled to the sneers and curses of the Abolitionists, and while the South was now openly phrasing its defense of slavery as an inevitable institution and a necessary practice, there had not yet come a clear vision of a southern empire. The nearest to that was the attempt of South Carolina to break out of the Union of states in 1832; medals were struck reading, "John C. Calhoun, First President of the Southern Confederacy"; the flag was ready, a palmetto tree coiled with a rattlesnake, "Don't tread on me"; arrangements for troops, and defense operations were under way; Governor Hayne proclaimed: "I recognize no allegiance as paramount to that which the citizens of South Carolina owe to the State of their birth or their adoption. If the sacred soil of Carolina should be polluted by the footsteps of an invader, or be stained with the blood of her citizens, shed in her defense, I trust in Almighty God that no son of hers, native or adopted, who has been nourished at her bosom, or been cherished by her bounty, will be found raising a parricidal arm against our common mother."

This, while President Andrew Jackson publicly appealed: "To say that any State may at pleasure secede from the Union, is to say that the United States are not a nation. Fellow-citizens of my native State, let me not only admonish you, as the First Magistrate of our common country, not to incur the penalty of its laws, but use the influence that a father would over his children whom he saw rushing to a certain ruin. In that paternal language, with that paternal feeling, let me tell you, my countrymen, that you are deluded by men who are either deceived themselves or wish to deceive you."

And privately, Jackson said to a go-between from South Carolina: "Tell them, if one South Carolina finger be raised in defiance of this Government, that I shall come down there; and once I'm there, I'll hang the first man I lay hands on to the first tree I can reach."

As that small yet significant storm died down, Andrew Jackson wrote to his friend, the Rev. A. J. Crawford of Georgia, "Haman's gallows ought to be the fate of all such ambitious men who would involve the country in a civil war. . . . The tariff, it is now well known, was a mere pretext, and disunion and a Southern confederacy the real object. The next pretext will be the negro or slavery question."

By the ballots of voters North and South, a New York Tammany Democrat, Martin Van Buren, took office as President of the nation on March 4, 1837, telling the country he was an "inflexible and uncompromising opponent of every attempt on the part of Congress to abolish slavery in the District of Columbia against the wishes of the slaveholding states."

From the Government at Washington and the national church organizations on down to business partnerships and families, the slavery question was beginning to split the country in two. At one far end was the Abolitionist agitator who wanted to take away a billion dollars' worth of property from the Southerners; and at the other far end was the Southerner who cried, "The people of the North must go to hanging these fanatics."

At two far opposite ends of an issue were passionate, reckless, stubborn men whose grandfathers had fought side by side in open combat to over-throw by violent revolution the government of the British Empire over the American colonies.

Aggravations between people South and North were getting worse. Across the northern states had been organized "The Underground Rail-way," a series of routes from the slave states across the free states and over the line into Canada. An antislavery man would keep a runaway slave in his house, cellar, or barn, and drive him to the next house or tell him the way. Officers of the law and slave owners came North with warrants hunt-ing their runaway property; Illinois was seeing them often. Also there were bogus slave hunters scattered through southern Illinois; they kid-naped free negroes, took them to St. Louis or across the Ohio River into Kentucky and sold them.

Wagons from Tennessee and Kentucky drove across southern Illinois with movers who called out from the wagon seat that they were driving to Missouri, where a man "had a right to own a nigger if he wanted to." Hostile feeling developed between Illinois and Missouri people; the Mis-sourians called Illinois land a suckhole and its people "Suckers" while the Illinoisans let it pass by alluding to Missouri residents as "Pukes."

In St. Louis a negro, McIntosh, killed a deputy sheriff, and a large mob took and burned him one night and the next morning boys threw stones to see who could hit the skull most often. At the trial of the mob leaders before Judge Lawless, he charged the jury: "If the destruction of the murderer was the act of congregated thousands, seized upon and im-pelled by that mysterious, metaphysical, and almost electric frenzy which, in all ages and nations, has hurried on infatuated multitudes to deeds of death and destruction—then I say the case transcends your jurisdiction —it is beyond the reach of human law."

A young Presbyterian minister, Elijah P. Lovejoy, a halfway Aboli-tionist editing a paper in St. Louis, had written: "Today a public meeting declares you shall not discuss slavery. Tomorrow another meeting decides it is against the peace of society that property be discussed. The next day a decree is issued speaking against distilleries, dramshops, or drunken-ness. And so on. The truth is, if you give ground a single inch, there is no stopping place. I deem it, therefore, my duty to take my stand upon the Constitution, and declare my fixed determination to maintain this ground."

The editorial which discussed Judge Lawless, was answered by a mob that smashed his press and threw his type out of the window. Lovejoy got the press repaired, decided to move up the river to Alton, Illinois, loaded the press on a boat, and was met at Alton by a mob that threw the press into the river.

Events slowly changed Lovejoy to an "immediate emancipationist"; he wrote: "As well might a lady think to bail out the Atlantic Ocean with her thimble, as the Colonization Society to remove slavery by colonizing the slaves in Africa."

These drifts were known to Abraham Lincoln, as he had spent the past winter months in Vandalia. He knew the legislature was mostly of southern blood and point of view. In the first legislature in which he had served there were 58 members from Kentucky and Tennessee or south of the Ohio River, 19 from the middle Atlantic states, and only 4 from New England. He knew that there was this crimson kinship of life blood between populations in southern Illinois, Indiana, Ohio, and in states south of the Ohio River; and that beyond blood kinship there were the closely interlocking interests of the southern planters buying immense quantities of pork, corn, and produce from the northern frontier states, and the New England power-loom mills buying increasing millions of bales of cotton each year.

Legislatures of four southern states were asking that states North "effectually suppress all associations purporting to be abolition societies"; governors of New York and Massachusetts had asked their legislatures to take such action; a mass meeting of 1,800 of the wealthiest, influential citizens of Boston had declared the Abolitionists to be dangerous meddlers; the years were short and few since John Randolph of Virginia had pronounced slavery "a volcano in full operation."

Amid this welter, Lincoln could understand his fellow members of the legislature when they passed resolutions declaring: "We highly disapprove of the formation of Abolition Societies; . . . the right of property in slaves is sacred to the slaveholding States by the Federal Constitution, and . . . they cannot be deprived of that right without their consent. . . ."

Lincoln voted against these resolutions, and was joined by only one other member. Dan Stone and he recorded a protest spread on the Journal of Proceedings as follows:

Resolutions upon the subject of domestic slavery having passed both branches of the General Assembly at its present session, the undersigned hereby protest against the passage of the same.

They believe that the institution of slavery is founded on both injustice and bad policy, but that the promulgation of abolition doctrines tends rather to increase than abate its evils.

They believe that the Congress of the United States has no power under the Constitution to interfere with the institution of slavery in the different States.

They believe that the Congress of the United States has the power under the Constitution to abolish slavery in the District of Columbia, but that the power ought not to be exercised unless at the request of the people of the district.

The difference between these opinions and those contained in the resolutions is their reason for entering this protest.

Just five weeks before filing this protest, Lincoln had delivered an address before the Young Men's Lyceum at Springfield, taking as his subject "The Perpetuation of Our Political Institutions." He had spoken windy sentences such as: "Shall we expect some transatlantic military giant to step the ocean and crush us at a blow? Never! All the armies of Europe, Asia, and Africa combined, with all the treasure of the earth (our own excepted) in their military chest, with a Bonaparte for a commander, could not by force take a drink from the Ohio or make a track on the Blue Ridge in a trial of a thousand years."

With this he connected the solemn, quiet murmur: "At what point then is the approach of danger to be expected? I answer, If it ever reach us it must spring up amongst us; it cannot come from abroad. If destruction be our lot we must ourselves be its author and finisher. As a nation of freemen we must live through all time or die by suicide."

He went on: "Accounts of outrages committed by mobs form the everyday news of the times, from New England to Louisiana. In Mississippi they first commenced by hanging the regular gamblers—a set of men certainly not following for a livelihood a very useful or honest occupation, but one which, so far from being forbidden by the laws, was actually licensed by an act of the legislature passed but a single year before. Next, negroes suspected of conspiring to raise an insurrection were caught up and hanged in all parts of the state; then, white men supposed to be leagued with the negroes; and finally strangers from neighboring states, going thither on business, were in many instances subjected to the same fate. Thus went on this process of hanging, from gamblers to negroes, from negroes to white citizens, and from these to strangers, till dead men were seen literally dangling from the boughs of trees upon every roadside, and in numbers that were almost sufficient to rival the native Spanish moss of the country as a drapery of the forest.

"When men take it into their heads today to hang gamblers or burn murderers, they should recollect that in the confusion usually attending such transactions they will be as likely to hang or burn some one who is neither a gambler nor a murderer as one who is, and that, acting upon the example they set, the mob of tomorrow may, and probably will, hang or burn some of them by the very same mistake. And not only so; the innocent, those who have ever set their faces against violations of law in every shape, alike with the guilty fall victims to the ravages of mob law; and thus it goes on, step by step, till all the walls erected for the defense of the persons and property of individuals are trodden down and disregarded. . . .

"Good men, who love tranquillity, who desire to abide by the laws and enjoy their benefits, who would gladly spill their blood in the defense of their country, become tired and disgusted with a government that offers them no protection. . . . Whenever the vicious portion of population shall be permitted to gather in bands of hundreds and thousands, and burn churches, ravage and rob provision stores, throw printing-presses into rivers, shoot editors, and hang and burn obnoxious persons at pleasure and with impunity, depend upon it, this government cannot last."

He touched on the topic of human glory, how men of ambition spring up, with towering genius. "It thirsts and burns for distinction," he said, "and if possible, it will have it whether at the expense of emancipating slaves or enslaving freemen. Is it unreasonable, then, to expect that some man possessed of the loftiest genius, coupled with ambition to push it to its utmost stretch, will at some time spring up among us? And when such a one does, it will require the people to be united with each other, attached to the government and laws, and generally intelligent, to successfully frustrate his designs."

Sprinkled through the address were sentences imitating the famous orator, Daniel Webster of Massachusetts, and the other famous orator, Henry Clay of Kentucky, besides still other famous orators of that day. He closed in a manner modeled on Webster, saying: "Upon these let the proud fabric of freedom rest, as the rock of its basis; and as truly as has been said of the only greater institution, 'The gates of hell shall not prevail against it.'"

An honest poetry of his own heart, an inevitable, mournful rhythm from the shadows of his own melancholy, stood forth in a passage where he had spoken of "the generation just gone to rest" and how near that generation was to the passionate, fighting men who accomplished the American Revolution. Each scarred and mutilated form that lived through the Revolution was himself a living history. "But those histories are gone. They can be read no more forever. They were a fortress of strength; but what invading foeman could never do, the silent artillery of time has done—the leveling of its walls. They are gone. They were a forest of giant oaks; but the all-restless hurricane has swept over them, and left only here and there a lonely trunk, despoiled of its verdure, shorn of its foliage, unshading and unshaded, to murmur in a few more gentle breezes, and to combat with its mutilated limbs a few more ruder storms, then to sink and be no more."

He was growing, young Abraham Lincoln. He was a learner, calling himself, and called by others, "a learner always."

As he rode with his long legs straddling a borrowed horse that day in March, 1837, toward Springfield, where his name would be put on a lawyer's shingle, he had seven dollars in cash in his pockets, and he was more than a thousand dollars in debt.

On certain March days in Illinois, the sky is a ragbag of whimsies. It may whisper of spring to come with soft slants of sun, while baby pearl-shell clouds dimple and drift, and then let blusters of wind blow up followed with flurries of snow, a little sleet, a drizzle of rain, then sunshine again and baby pearl-shell clouds dimpling and drifting.

CHAPTER 44

SPRINGFIELD with its 1,500 inhabitants in 1837 was the big town of Sangamon County, selling to the 18,000 people of the county a large part of their supplies, tools, groceries, handling grain, pork, beef, and produce, with stores, churches, schools, banks, newspapers, courts, lawyers, offices of government, taverns, saloons, places of entertainment. It was a city, its people ready to say there was no more wilderness in that part of the country; the land had been surveyed and allotted.

The farm women who came to town wore shoes where they used to go barefooted; the men had changed from moccasins to rawhide boots and shoes. Farmers no longer spent time killing deer, tanning the hide and making leather breeches to tie at the ankles: it was cheaper and quicker to raise corn and buy pantaloons which had come from Massachusetts over the Ohio or the Mississippi River or the Great Lakes. Stores advertised "velvets, silk, satin, and Marseilles vestings, fine calf boots, seal and morocco pumps, for gentlemen," and for ladies "silks, bareges, crepe lisse, lace veils, thread lace, Thibet shawls, lace handkerchiefs, fine prunella shoes."

Carriages held men riding in top-boots and ruffled silk shirts, and women in silks and laces. It was civilization which Abraham Lincoln, twenty-eight years old, saw as he rode into Springfield that March day in 1837—to be a lawyer. Its people were mostly from Kentucky, coming by horse, wagon, and boat across country not yet cleared of wolves, wildcats, and horse thieves. And there were in Sangamon County 78 free negroes, 20 registered indentured servants, and 6 slaves.

The centre of the town was a public square, with the courthouse, jail, stores, churches, banks, harness-makers, and blacksmiths lined about the square. The streets and sidewalks were plain black Illinois soil underfoot, except for gravel here and there for dry footing in rain or snow, and stones and sticks for street crossings.

Lincoln pulled in his horse at the general store of Joshua Speed. He asked the price of bedclothes for a single bedstead, which Speed figured at $17.00. "Cheap as it is, I have not the money to pay," he told Speed. "But if you will credit me until Christmas, and my experiment as a lawyer here is a success, I will pay you then. If I fail in that I will probably never pay you at all." Speed said afterward: "The tone of his voice was so melancholy that I felt for him. I looked up at him and thought that I never saw so gloomy and melancholy a face in my life." Speed offered to share his own big double bed upstairs over the store. Lincoln took his saddlebags upstairs, came down with his face lit up and said, "Well, Speed, I'm moved."

His meals he had arranged to take with Bill Butler, one of the "Long Nine," who said Lincoln could put his feet under the table at the Butler home as long as he wanted to; they wouldn't worry about the board bill. He joined Stuart, and their professional card read, "J. T. Stuart and A. Lincoln, Attorneys and Counsellors at Law, will practice conjointly, in the Courts of this Judicial Circuit—Office No. 4 Hoffman's Row, upstairs. Springfield, April 12, 1837."

In his new copy of Webster's dictionary, he wrote, to see how it would look, on the flyleaf, "A. Lincoln, Esq., Attorney and Counselor-at-Law."

The county courtroom was on the lower floor of a two-story building in Hoffman's Row. Upstairs, over the courtroom, was the law office of the new firm of Stuart & Lincoln: a little room with a few loose boards for bookshelves, an old wood stove, a table, a chair, a bench, a buffalo robe, and a small bed.

Stuart was running for Congress, so Lincoln handled all of the law practice in range of his ability. His first case was one he had helped work on during the previous year, defending David Wooldridge, in a suit brought by James P. Hawthorn. Hawthorn claimed Wooldridge was to furnish him two yoke of oxen to break up twenty acres of prairie sod-ground; also he claimed Wooldridge was to allow him to raise a crop of corn or wheat on a certain piece of ground; and Wooldridge had failed him in both cases.

Furthermore, Hawthorn claimed damages because Wooldridge struck, beat, bruised, and knocked him (Hawthorn) down; plucked, pulled, and tore large quantities of hair from his head. Also because with a stick and his fists he struck Hawthorn many violent blows and strokes on or about the face, head, breast, back, shoulders, hips, legs, and divers other parts of the body, and because he had with violence forced, pushed, thrust, and gouged his fingers into Hawthorn's eyes.

Such were the allegations on assumpsit and trespass vi et armis, including also replevin action demanding return of a black and white yoke of steers, one black cow and calf, and one prairie plow. Lincoln's first move was to bring up a board bill for eight months which Hawthorn owed Wooldridge, amounting at $1.50 a week to $45.75. Also, for the same eight months, he had used a wagon and team for which he should pay $90.00 besides a cash loan of $100.00. The case never came to trial. Peacemakers settled it out of court. The plaintiff and defendant divided the court costs.

Between law cases he kept up his political fences, writing such letters as this to John Bennett at Petersburg:

SPRINGFIELD, August 5, 1837.

DEAR SIR:

Mr. Edwards tells me you wish to know whether the act to which your town incorporation provision was attached, passed into a law. It did. You can organize under the general incorporation law as soon as you choose.

I also tacked a provision on to a fellow's bill to authorize a relocation of the road from Salem down to your town; but I am not certain whether or not the bill passed; neither do I suppose I can ascertain before the laws will be published. If it is a law, Bowling Green, Bennet Abell, and yourself are appointed to make the change.

No news. No excitement except a little about the election of Monday next. I suppose, of course, our friend, Dr. Henry, stands no chance in your "diggings."

Your friend and humble servant,

A. LINCOLN.

Mrs. Joseph Anderson, a widow, came into the office of Stuart & Lincoln, to ask if they could help her. She had come to Springfield to sell ten acres of land left by her husband, but she found that General James Adams claimed the ten acres had been signed over to him by her husband for a debt he owed General Adams as a lawyer. Lincoln worked on the case, searched the records, and then published a handbill opening with the statement: "It is well known to most of you, that there is existing at this time, considerable excitement in regard to Gen. Adams's titles to certain tracts of land, and the manner in which he acquired them."

He then went into a tissue of facts to show that Adams had falsified documents in order to swindle "a widow woman" out of ten acres of land. General Adams wrote a reply which filled six newspaper columns, and Lincoln returned with a one-column answer analyzing affidavits offered by Adams, saying they were "all false as hell," and adding: "In conclusion I will only say that I have a character to defend as well as Gen. Adams, but I disdain to whine about it as he does."

When Adams again filled six newspaper columns with his defense, Lincoln commented: "Let it be remembered that when he first came to this country he attempted to impose himself upon the community as a lawyer, and actually carried the attempt so far, as to induce a man who was under a charge of murder to entrust the defense of his life in his hands, and finally took his money and got him hanged. Is this the man that is to raise a breeze in his favor by abusing lawyers? If he is not himself a lawyer, it is for the lack of sense, and not of inclination. If he is not a lawyer, he *is* a liar, for he proclaimed himself a lawyer, and got a man hanged by depending on him."

His scorn of Adams was put into a clear lingo. "It is true I have no children nor *kitchen boys;* and if I had, I should scorn to lug them in to make affidavits for me."

He declared further newspaper argument closed. "Farewell, General. I will see you again at Court, if not before—when and where we will settle the question whether you or the widow shall have the land."

In the trial he won for Mrs. Anderson her ten acres of land, shortly after which an editorial supposed to have been written by Lincoln was published in the *Sangamo Journal*, containing a copy of an indictment found against Gen. Adams in Oswego County, New York, in 1818, the crime charged being forgery of a deed. "A person of evil name and fame and of a wicked disposition," was the *Journal's* allusion to Adams, who at the August election had been chosen probate justice of the peace.

The affair with General Adams was taken by some people as a noisy rumpus that could have been conducted more decently by Lincoln, while others held it as a sign that chivalry was alive, even if it came in drab blue jeans, with a grin.

Veiled accusations were published in the *Illinois Republican*, a Democratic newspaper, that Lincoln's friend, Dr. A. G. Henry, the acting commissioner in charge of the construction work on the new Statehouse, was hornswoggling the taxpayers; a committee of Whigs marched on the editorial rooms of the newspaper; warnings and threats were exchanged; it was said that among the Democratic leaders who got their hair mussed was Stephen A. Douglas, reported to be the writer of the unsigned articles attacking Dr. Henry.

Lincoln helped organize a mass meeting where he offered a resolution pointing at Dr. Henry as being accused of "squandering uselessly and wastefully the public money" appropriated for the Statehouse. Therefore, said Lincoln's resolution, a committee of seven should be appointed to investigate whether the work under Dr. Henry was "progressing in the most economical and judicious manner." The committee was appointed and did its duty in a report vindicating the Whig commissioner, Lincoln's friend.

The young politician and philosopher could look out from the Stuart & Lincoln office window on the main street and the public square, with freedom to read what could be read in the passers-by, the forms and faces, the doctors going to a birth, the hearse leading a burial party, children going to school, the town drunkard dragged by the town constable, bankers, landowners, squatters, carpenters, well-diggers, washerwomen, Kentuckians, Virginians, Yankees, French-Canadians, Pennsylvania Dutch, Irish, and Germans—passers-by.

Past the window of the law office came farmers hauling corn, wheat, potatoes, and turnips, in wagons; the axles creaked; husky voices bawled at the yokes of steers while the whip thongs lashed and cracked.

Droves of hogs came past, in muddy weather wallowing over their knees, the hair of their flanks spattered, their curls of tails flipping as they grunted onward to sale and slaughter.

And there were horses, and men riding and driving who loved horses. It was a horse country. They too were passers-by—roans, grays, whites, black horses with white stockings, sorrels with a sorrel forelock down a white face, bays with a white star in the forehead.

In a letter to Levi Davis, Esq., of Vandalia, Lincoln wrote one April day, "We have generally in this Country, Peace, Health, and Plenty, and no News."

CHAPTER 45

One day Lincoln had dipped a pen in an ink-bottle and written the words, "State of Illinois, Sangamon County and Circuit—of the July term of the Sangamon Circuit Court in the Year of Our Lord One Thousand Eight Hundred and Thirty-Nine." And he had since dipped his pen and written the same words, changing only the date, dozens of times, and he knew if he lived he would write them thousands of times. He could almost write those words in his sleep. Likewise with the form he scratched off, reading, "I do hereby enter myself as security for costs in this cause, and acknowledge myself bound to pay, or cause to be paid, all costs which may accrue in this action either to the opposite party or to any of the officers of this court in pursuance of the laws of this state." He could repeat that, almost, backward.

Money came to his hands, fees, of which half must go to Stuart. He wrote a memorandum, such as "I have received five dollars from Deed of Macon, five from Lewis Keeling, five from Andrew Finley, one half of which belongs to Stuart and has not been entered on the books."

"Safety" was the anxious key word in one letter. "I am unwilling to make any conveyance until I see the assignments and original certificate. If Mr. Underhill will bring that certificate I will do all an honorable man should do. It is not money, but safety, I desire." And closing the letter he repeated, "If Mr. Underhill will come and bring the certificate I will do all in safety I can."

A caller came one day, representing the United States Government and its Post Office Department. The caller wanted to ask about a certain number of dollars and cents that had come into the hands of Lincoln as postmaster at New Salem. Lincoln stepped to a corner of the office, dug out a sack and counted the money in it, the exact amount asked for by the inspector, who took the money, gave a receipt, and went away satisfied.

His grocery days were an advantage to Lincoln in the case where the Hickox brothers had sold flour to the defendant as "good, merchantable, superfine flour," against which Lincoln pleaded that "twenty barrels were *not* at the time of sale, good, merchantable, superfine flour, but, on the contrary, greatly inferior in quality."

In one of his first murder cases, tried in Hancock County, Lincoln failed to save William Fraim, who was convicted on April 25, 1839, and, by court order, hanged by the neck till dead, just twenty-three days later.

Murderers, horse thieves, scandalmongers, and slanderers came at various times and poured out their stories amid the walls of the Stuart & Lincoln law office. There came bothered and puzzled people.

George Stockton walked in one day and told how a cooking-stove was spoiled a hundred dollars' worth, he guessed; and Lincoln brought suit against Tolby for that amount of damages to "a cooking-stove." But he had many quiet hours when there was little business, because there was little crime. In the office record of expenses he made an entry, "Lincoln paid for wood . . . $.50," and "Lincoln paid for saw . . . $2.25." If not busy at law practice, he was sawing wood.

A boatload of corn coming down the Sangamon River ran onto a fish-trap dam, and sprang a leak so that the corn was wet. On being unloaded the corn got rained on and further damaged. Lincoln brought suit for the owners of the boat and the corn against the fish-trappers for obstructing the navigation of the Sangamon River and unlawfully damaging the boat and the corn as property.

One hot summer day Harvey Ross came; in order to prove ownership of his farm at Macomb he had to have the testimony from a witness near Springfield. Court had closed for six months, Lincoln explained, but they would go out to Judge Thomas's farm a mile east and see what he could do. Lincoln took off his coat, laid it on a chair, and with a bundle of papers in one hand and a red handkerchief for wiping sweat off, in the other hand, he and the witness walked out to the Thomas farm, asking the way and taking the short cuts.

The judge's wife said the judge had gone to the north part of the farm, where he had a tenant house, to help his men put up a corncrib. If they went the main road it would be a half-mile, but if they cut across the cornfield it would be only a quarter-mile, Mrs. Thomas said; and on Lincoln asking her to show them the path she came out of the house and pointed to where the short cut led across the cornfield from their barn.

They struck out Indian-file, Lincoln with a bundle of papers in one hand and a red handkerchief in the other, till they came to where the judge and his men were raising logs to make a corn-crib and hogpen. Lincoln put the case to the judge, who looked over the papers, swore in the witness, and, with pen and ink from the tenant house, signed the documents.

All were in shirt-sleeves, and Lincoln remarked it was a kind of shirt-sleeve court they were holding. "Yes," laughed the judge, "a shirt-sleeve court in a cornfield."

The main business being over, Lincoln asked the judge if he didn't want some help in rolling up the logs. The judge guessed two of them were pretty heavy and he could stand a little help. So Lincoln and Ross pitched in and helped, and when Ross offered to pay the judge for his services the judge said he guessed the helping with the logs was pay enough.

On the road back to Springfield Lincoln could have told Ross some of the stories passing among lawyers and judges, of the man, for instance, charged with sheep-killing, who was asked by the court, "Are you guilty or not guilty?" And the man wouldn't answer. The court kept at him, and at last said, "You must do something—what do you do?" The man answered, "I stands mute," and, pushed further, would only answer, "I stands mute." On trial the case was decided against him, but he was told he could carry it higher up to the Court of Errors. And he murmured, "If this here ain't a court of errors, I'd like to know where you kin find one!"

In the case of a defendant charged with mistreating a livery-stable horse, a witness testified, "When his company rides fast he rides fast, and when his company rides slow he rides slow." "I want to know," said the important lawyer for the other side, "how he rides when he is alone. "W-e-l-l," said the witness, a slow talker, "I—never—was—with—him—when—he—was—alone; so—I don't know."

And there was a case told among lawyers of a defendant, losing, who stood up and called the court unjust, corrupt, and false. He was fined ten dollars for contempt of court, and handed the clerk a twenty-dollar bill. "I can't change this," said the clerk. "Never mind about the other ten dollars," came the hot reply, "I'll take it out in contempt!"

CHAPTER 46

ONE day early in May, when the stir of new grass was green over the prairie, and lazy winds came in the jack-oak brush and among the prongs of the oak and the shagbark in their spring coat of leaves, Lincoln took his pen and wrote a quaint letter out of an odd, lonely heart. It was another letter to Miss Mary Owens down in Green County, Kentucky. She would have to be poor and show her poverty, if she married him. He was willing to marry, if she so wished. His advice would be not to marry. The letter read:

SPRINGFIELD, May 7, 1837.

MISS MARY S. OWENS.

Friend Mary: I have commenced two letters to send you before this, both of which displeased me before I got half done, and so I tore them up. The first I thought was not serious enough, and the second was on the other extreme. I shall send this, turn out as it may.

This thing of living in Springfield is rather a dull business, after all; at least it is so to me. I am quite as lonesome here as I ever was anywhere in my life. I have been spoken to by but one woman since I have been here, and should not have been by her if she could have avoided it. I've never been to church yet, and probably shall not be soon. I stay away because I am conscious I should not know how to behave myself.

I am often thinking of what we said about your coming to live at Springfield. I am afraid you would not be satisfied. There is a great deal of flourishing about in carriages here, which it would be your doom to see without sharing it. You would have to be poor, without the means of hiding your poverty. Do you believe you could bear that patiently? Whatever woman may cast her lot with mine, should any ever do so, it is my intention to do all in my power to make her happy and contented; and there is nothing I can imagine that would make me more unhappy than to fail in the effort. I know I should be much happier with you than the way I am, provided I saw no signs of discontent in you. What you have said to me may have been in the way of jest, or I may have misunderstood it. If so, then let it be forgotten; if otherwise, I much wish you would think seriously before you decide. What I have said I will most positively abide by, provided you wish it. My opinion is that you had better not do it. You have not been accustomed to hardship, and it may be more severe than you now imagine. I know you are capable of thinking correctly on any subject, and if you deliberate maturely upon this before you decide, then I am willing to abide your decision.

You must write me a good long letter after you get this. You have nothing else to do, and though it might not seem interesting to you after you had written it, it would be a good deal of company to me in this "busy wilderness." Tell your sister I don't want to hear any more about selling out and moving. That gives me the "hypo" whenever I think of it.

Yours, etc.,

LINCOLN.

Mary Owens came on a visit to her sister near New Salem that summer. She and Lincoln saw each other and talked and came to no understanding. After they parted, and on the day that they parted, Lincoln wrote her another letter. It read:

SPRINGFIELD, August 16, 1837.

FRIEND MARY: You will no doubt think it rather strange that I should write you a letter on the same day on which we parted, and I can only account for it by supposing that seeing you lately makes me think of you more than usual; while at our late meeting we had but few expressions of thoughts. You must know that I cannot see you or think of you with entire indifference; and yet it may be that you are mistaken in regard to what my real feelings toward you are. If I knew you were not, I should not trouble you with this letter. Perhaps any other man would know enough without further information; but I consider it my peculiar right to plead ignorance, and your bounden duty to allow the plea. I want in all cases to do right, and most particularly so in all cases with women. I want at this particular time, more than anything else, to do right with you; and if I knew it would be doing right, as I rather suspect it would, to let you alone, I would do it. And for the purpose of making the matter as plain as possible, I now say that you can now drop the subject, dismiss your thoughts (if you ever had any) from me forever, and leave this letter unanswered, without calling forth one accusing murmur from me. And I will even go further, and say that if it will add anything to your comfort or peace of mind to do so, it is my sincere wish that you should. Do not understand by this that I wish to cut your acquaintance. I mean no such thing. What I do wish is that our further acquaintance shall depend upon yourself. If such further acquaintance would contribute nothing to your happiness, I am sure it would not to mine. If you feel yourself in any degree bound to me, I am now willing to release you, provided you wish it; while, on the other hand, I am willing and even anxious to bind you faster, if I can be convinced that it will, in any considerable degree, add to your happiness. This, indeed, is the whole question with me. Nothing would make me more miserable than to believe you miserable—nothing more happy than to know you were so.

In what I have now said, I think I cannot be misunderstood, and to make myself understood is the only object of this letter.

If it suits you best to not answer this, farewell. A long life and a merry one attend you. But if you conclude to write back, speak as plainly as I do. There can be neither harm nor danger in saying to me anything you think, just in the manner you think it.

My respects to your sister.

Your friend,

LINCOLN.

And the months passed by till the first day of April came in the next year. And the comedy of man, woman, and destiny, the fact that marriages are often accidents, was lighting up his brain as his imagination reviewed events. He wrote a letter filled with the chuckles and oddities of a story-teller telling a story with the laugh on himself. Among his men acquaintances and friends there was not one he could pour out the story to.

He chose a woman, Mrs. O. H. Browning, the wife of a fellow member of the legislature, to hear his confessions that he had vanity, that he had stupidity, that he had made a fool of himself, that he believed he had had a narrow escape from a marriage that would have been a comic. The letter:

SPRINGFIELD, April 1, 1838.

DEAR MADAM:—

Without apologizing for being egotistical, I shall make the history of so much of my life as has elapsed since I saw you the subject of this letter. And, by the way, I now discover that, in order to give a full and intelligible account of the things I have done and suffered since I saw you, I shall necessarily have to relate some that happened before.

It was, then, in the autumn of 1836 that a married lady of my acquaintance and who was a great friend of mine, being about to pay a visit to her father and other relatives residing in Kentucky, proposed to me that on her return she would bring a sister of hers with her on condition that I would engage to become her brother-in-law with all convenient despatch. I, of course, accepted the proposal, for you know I could not have done otherwise, had I really been averse to it; but privately, between you and me, I was most confoundedly well pleased with the project. I had seen the said sister some three years before, thought her intelligent and agreeable, and saw no good objection to plodding life through hand in hand with her. Time passed on, the lady took her journey sure enough. This stomached me a little; for it appeared to me that her coming so readily showed that she was a trifle too willing; but, on reflection, it occurred to me that she might have been prevailed on by her married sister to come, without anything concerning me ever having been mentioned to her; and so I concluded that, if no other objection presented itself, I would consent to waive this. All this occurred to me on hearing of her arrival in the neighborhood; for, be it remembered, I had not yet seen her, except about three years previous, as above mentioned. In a few days we had an interview; and, although I had seen her before, she did not look as my imagination had pictured her. I knew she was over-size, but she now appeared a fair match for Falstaff. I knew she was called an "old maid," and I felt no doubt of the truth of at least half of the appellation; but now, when I beheld her, I could not for my life avoid thinking of my mother; and this, not from withered features, for her skin was too full of fat to permit of its contracting into wrinkles, but from her want of teeth, weather-beaten appearance in general, and from a kind of notion that ran in my head that nothing could have commenced at the size of infancy and reached her present bulk in less than thirty-five or forty years; and, in short, I was not at all pleased with her. But what could I do? I had told her sister I would take her for better or for worse; and I made a point of honor and conscience in all things to stick to my word, especially if others had been induced to act on it, which in this case I had no doubt they had; for I was now fairly convinced that no other man on earth would have her, and hence the conclusion that they were bent on holding me to my bargain. "Well," thought I, "I have said it, and, be the consequences what they may, it shall not be my fault if I fail to do it." At once I determined to consider her my wife; and, this done, all my powers of discovery were put to work in search of perfections in her which might be fairly set off against her defects. I tried to imagine her handsome, which, but for her unfortunate corpulency, was actually true. Exclusive of this, no woman that I have ever seen has a finer face. I also tried to convince myself that the mind was much more to be valued than the person; and in this she was not inferior, as I could discover, to any with whom I had been acquainted.

Shortly after this, without coming to any positive understanding with her, I set out for Vandalia, when and where you first saw me. During my stay there I had letters from her which did not change my opinion of either her intellect or intention, but on the contrary confirmed it in both.

All this while, although I was fixed, "firm as the surge-repelling rock," in my resolution, I found I was continually repenting the rashness which had led me to make it. Through life I have been in no bondage, either real or imaginary, from the thraldom of which I so much desired to be free. After my return home I saw nothing to change my opinions of her in any particular. She was the same, and so was I. I now spent my time in planning how I might get along through life after my contemplated change of circumstances should have taken place, and how I might procrastinate the evil day for a time, which I really dreaded as much, perhaps more, than an Irishman does the halter.

After all my suffering upon this deeply interesting subject, here I am, wholly, unexpectedly, completely, out of the "scrape"; and now I want to know if you can guess how I got out of it—out, clear, in every sense of the term; no violation of word, honor, or conscience. I don't believe you can guess, and so I might as well tell you at once. As the lawyer says, it was done in the manner following, to-wit: After I had delayed the matter as long as I thought I could in honor do (which, by the way, had brought me round into the last fall), I concluded I might as well bring it to a consummation without further delay; and so I mustered my resolution, and made the proposal to her direct; but, shocking to relate, she answered, No. At first I supposed she did it through an affectation of modesty, which I thought but ill became her under the peculiar circumstances of her case; but on my renewal of the charge, I found she repelled it with greater firmness than before. I tried it again and again, but with the same success, or rather with the same want of success.

I finally was forced to give it up; at which I very unexpectedly found myself mortified almost beyond endurance. I was mortified, it seemed to me, in a hundred different ways. My vanity was deeply wounded by the reflection that I had been too stupid to discover her intentions, and at the same time never doubting that I understood them perfectly; and also that she, whom I had taught myself to believe nobody else would have, had actually rejected me with all my fancied greatness. And, to cap the whole, I then for the first time began to suspect that I was really a little in love with her. But let it all go. I'll try and outlive it. Others have been made fools of by the girls; but this can never with truth be said of me. I most emphatically, in this instance, made a fool of myself. I have now come to the conclusion never again to think of marrying, and for this reason: I can never be satisfied with any one who would be blockhead enough to have me.

When you receive this, write me a long yarn about something to amuse me Give my respects to Mr. Browning.

Your sincere friend,
A. LINCOLN.

And a few months later when Mrs. Bennet Able of New Salem, Illinois, visited her sister Mary Owens in Green County, Kentucky, Miss Owens told neighbors that Abe Lincoln said to Mrs. Able in Springfield, "Tell your sister that I think she was a great fool, because she did not stay here, and marry me."

And when one of the Greens at New Salem was asked later to write a letter telling what he knew about Miss Owens and especially her looks, he wrote: "Bill, I am getting old; I have seen too much trouble to give a lifelike picture of this woman. I won't try it. None of the poets or romance writers has ever given to us a picture of a heroine so beautiful as a good description of Miss Owens in 1836 would be."

CHAPTER 47

A school for young ladies in Springfield was announcing that besides ordinary branches of education and training in "intellectual and moral science," it would conduct "a class in Mezzotint painting." A store was offering on sale "cloth, comb, tooth, hair and nail brushes." Civilization and culture were stirring in Illinois. The Alton Literary Society met in the courthouse in that city and debated the question, "Was Brutus justified in killing Cæsar?"

Lincoln read newspapers, skirmished through exchanges in the *Sangamo Journal* office. He could read there in the year 1839 that the Northern Cross Railroad would pay cash for timber to make the grade from Springfield to Meredosia. Shipments of rifles had arrived in Illinois, "all lengths and sizes, mounted with brass, silver, and gold, single and double barrel, with shotguns to fit the same stock, some very fine in mahogany and leather cases."

Orchards were being planted with new kinds of apple trees, Winter Sweets, Red Streaks, Red Russets, Yellow Hearts, Rainbows. One January day the *Journal* announced, "Our farmers can now be supplied with Ruta Baga seed at Mr. Canedy's Drug Store. Now is the time to sow it. Select a piece of clean land, harrow in the seed well, keep the land clear of weeds, and thin the plants to six inches apart. The drill culture is better, but is more troublesome."

One, and often two, columns in a newspaper had the heading "Estrays," and told of lost horses, sorrels, bays, dapple bays, some "blaze-faced," some with saddle-marks or spots and scars, or "bit in the ear," or long-tailed or switch-tailed or with "a snip on the nose." Lincoln, on losing his horse, advertised:

Strayed or Stolen: From a stable in Springfield on Wednesday, 18th inst., a large bay horse, star in his forehead, plainly marked with harness; supposed to be eight years old; had been shod all around, but is believed to have lost some of his shoes, and trots and paces. Any person who will take up said horse and leave information at the Journal office or with the subscriber, shall be liberally paid for their trouble. A. Lincoln.

One week in November of 1839, Lincoln saw two editorials which he read carefully more than once or twice in the *Illinois State Register*, the Democratic newspaper of Springfield. The articles were about him, aimed straight at him. It was the first time any attempt had been made through the public prints to improve his manners. His personal behavior was publicly discussed and he was advised how he should so act that he would appear to better advantage and win more general approval. He looked on the public platform like a clown, but in so looking he was a good deal of an actor, a sort of comedian, not a real clown, but one playing a part—thus the *State Register* pictured him.

Lincoln had spoken in the courthouse as a candidate for presidential elector on a Tuesday evening, in reply to Stephen A. Douglas, and the *State Register* commented:

"Mr. Lincoln's argument was truly ingenious. He has, however, a sort of *assumed clownishness* in his manner which does not become him, and which does not truly belong to him. It is *assumed*—assumed for effect. Mr. Lincoln will sometimes make his language correspond with this clownish manner, and he can thus frequently raise a loud laugh among his Whig hearers; but this entire game of buffoonery convinces the *mind* of no man, and is utterly lost on the majority of his audience. We seriously advise Mr. Lincoln to correct this clownish fault before it grows upon him."

In Tuesday's debating, Douglas was the loser, the *Register* acknowledged. "The main object of calling in Mr. Lincoln was to raise up Cyrus Walker, a Whig, who had been actually demolished by Mr. Douglas in the afternoon. Lincoln made out to get Walker rather unsteadily on his legs again and between the two Whig speakers, our Democratic 'little giant,' as Walker called him, had a rough time of it. Lincoln misrepresented Douglas, as was apparent to every man present. This brought a *warm* rejoinder from Mr. Douglas. Mr. Walker then rose, complained of Mr. D. for his *warmth* and went on for an hour starting new points. Thus a concerted plot of 'two pluck one' began to show itself."

On the Wednesday night following, Douglas argued against the United States Bank, and it seemed to the *State Register:* "There was a profound silence upon his conclusion and a settled gloom covered the Whigs. They saw how utterly hopeless must be the attempt to answer. Mr. Lincoln was, however, again put forward; but he commenced with embarrassment and continued without making the slightest impression. The Mr. Lincoln of Wednesday night was not the Mr. Lincoln of Tuesday. He could only meet the arguments of Mr. Douglas by relating stale anecdotes and old stories, and left the stump literally whipped off of it, even in the estimation of his own friends." Then, after declaring Lincoln and Walker were without measures or principles to advocate, the editorial closed, "The *men* are smart enough, but the *cause* they have espoused is rotten to the core."

The second editorial had the heading, "Mr. Lincoln and the Register," and opened: "On last Wednesday night, Mr. Lincoln, in the course of his reply to Mr. Douglas, traveled out of his way to attack the veracity of the editors of this paper. Under the rule agreed upon by a committee, governing the discussion, Mr. Lincoln could not be replied to by either of the editors of this paper. This Mr. Lincoln knew, and he has lowered himself in our estimation by his conduct on that occasion. He asserted that he did not advise the running of John Bennett for the Legislature, but was in favor of Bowling Green; and that the editors of the *Register* had lied in making such a statement. Mr. Lincoln said further that we had no *authority* for making the statement; and that having no authority even had we published the truth, we were still *liars!* Such was the language of the man selected by the Whig party to be an elector of the high office of President of the United States. To the indecorous language of Mr. Lincoln we make no reply."

Then followed the publication of an anonymous letter, which the *Register* said was written by "a highly respectable citizen of Petersburg." The letter set forth that two good candidates had been turned down by Lincoln and two other Whig bosses, who had handed the nomination to John Bennett, "a Nullifier, also a thorough aristocrat, an advocate for taking the election of Justices and Constables from the people."

The same letter had been published two weeks previous in the *Register,* and, neither Lincoln nor any other Whigs replying to it, the *Register* assumed it was true. "Before and since, we have heard several of the friends of Mr. Lincoln admit, on the streets, and undertake to justify, this party arrangement. Mr. Lincoln's allowing two weeks to pass by with the accusation resting on him, and making no effort to relieve himself from it, gave the public the right to look upon the accusation as true."

Also in the same issue of the *Register,* Lincoln could turn a page and read an advertisement of a sort common in all newspapers then. Usually such advertisements were scattered among the lost-horses and strayed-cattle notices. One read:

$50 Reward. Ran away from the subscriber, living in Lewis County, Mo., four miles from Tully, a slave named Charles, about 20 years of age, five feet six or seven inches high, well made, free spoken among whites, and pleasant in conversation, had a white speck in the ball of eye, a scar at the extremity of the left eyebrow, also a scar on the right wrist, and one between the neck and collar-bone; had also scars on his back.

Then followed particulars about the payment of the reward for the delivery of the property.

CHAPTER 48

Looking out through the little windowpanes of the law office overlooking the main street and the public square where the new capitol building was to stand, listening at the street corners in summer and at the circles around wood stoves in the grocery stores in winter, Lincoln came to know the haunts and tabernacles of politics, their passions and hatreds, their stormy laughter.

Once more Lincoln carried an election to the legislature, also stumping for his law partner John T. Stuart, who was elected to Congress. Two years later, in 1840, he and Stuart were again elected to the same offices.

Talk ran that he deserved a nomination to Congress for his efforts in behalf of the Whig party; he was pushed by his party for speaker of the house in the legislature.

Besides wit and personality, a man had to have bulldog courage and "a constitution like a horse" to stand up in the game. When Stuart was running against Steve Douglas for Congress in 1838 the two struck, grappled, and "fought like wildcats" back and forth over the floor of Herndon's grocery till each was too tired to hit another blow. When Stuart came to, he ordered a barrel of whisky for the crowd.

Lincoln, a while later, sending news to Stuart in Washington, wrote: "Yesterday Douglas, having chosen to consider himself insulted by something in the *Journal*, undertook to cane Francis [the editor] in the street. Francis caught him by the hair and jammed him back against a market-cart, where the matter ended by Francis being pulled away from him. The whole affair was so ludicrous that Francis and everybody else, Douglas excepted, have been laughing about it ever since."

The Whigs rented the courthouse for a campaign meeting one day, and Edward D. Baker, speaking on the issues of the day, led up to the point where he declared that wherever there was a land office, there was a Democratic newspaper to defend its corruption. Democrats in the audience yelled, "Pull him down."

A riot was starting when Lincoln, who had been listening to the speech through a trapdoor looking from his office down into the courtroom, came dangling down with his long legs through the hole in the ceiling. He helped bring order by saying: "Hold on, gentlemen. This is a land of free speech. Baker has a right to speak, and if you take him off the stand you'll have to take me, too."

When a railroad contractor, Reuben Radford, brought in a construction gang to man the polls for the Democratic ticket one election day, Lincoln heard about it and went to the polling-place on a slow trot. In warning Radford, he remarked, "Radford, you'll spoil and blow if you live much longer." He told Speed in the evening that he wanted to hit Radford but couldn't get a chance. "I intended just to knock him down and leave him kicking."

At a political meeting in Springfield he replied to an attack on the "Long Nine" by Jesse B. Thomas; it was a furious and directly personal handling he gave Thomas, with jabs of sarcasm and a mimicking of Thomas; Springfield called it a "terrible skinning," and it was alluded to as "the skinning of Thomas." The crowd had "egged him on" with yell and cheers so that Lincoln gave Thomas a worse skinning than he intended; he went to Thomas's office and said he was sorry; he told friends he wasn't proud of the performance.

James Matheny joined Lincoln, Evan Butler, and Noah Rickard, one evening, in dragging a man to the courthouse pump where they stripped him of his shirt, tied him to the pump, and gave the man's wife a switch and told her, "Light in." The man was a shoemaker who had been getting drunk regularly and always when drunk brutally beating his wife. Lincoln had warned him that if he beat his wife again he would have to take a beating himself. Matheny said the wife had to be encouraged to lay on with the switch—and after that night he and Lincoln didn't hear anything more about the shoemaker beating his wife.

When Colonel Dick Taylor, known also as "Ruffled Shirt" Taylor, on account of his wearing ruffled silk shirts, got sarcastic about the Whigs being elegant and wearing fine clothes while pleading for the plain people, Lincoln, who was debating with Taylor, listened coolly, but after a while slipped to the side of Taylor, and tore open a coat buttoned up close. A bulge of ruffled silk flew out, and there came to sight a colored velvet vest and a watch-chain with gold seals.

The audience roared, heard Taylor through, and then later heard Lincoln say, as Ninian Edwards recalled it: "While Colonel Taylor was making these charges against the Whigs over the country, riding in fine carriages, wearing ruffled shirts, kid gloves, massive gold chains with large gold seals, and flourishing a heavy gold-headed cane, I was a poor boy, hired on a flatboat at eight dollars a month, and had only one pair of breeches to my back, and they were buckskin. Now, if you know the nature of buckskin when wet and dried by the sun, it will shrink; and my breeches kept shrinking until they left several inches of my legs bare between the tops of my socks and the lower part of my breeches; and whilst I was growing taller they were becoming shorter, and so much tighter that they left a blue streak around my legs that can be seen to this day. If you call this aristocracy I plead guilty to the charge."

While Stuart was in Washington, Lincoln handled the law practice and kept track of politics. Out of the silences of the little law office, he sent letters to Stuart about the many errands he was running from day to day and the items of news, the twists of life he had his eyes and ears bent toward. Two of the letters to Stuart read:

SPRINGFIELD, November 14, 1839.

DEAR STUART:

I have been to the secretary's office within the last hour, and find things precisely as you left them. No new arrivals of returns on either side. Douglas has not been here since you left. A report is in circulation that he has abandoned the idea of going to Washington, though the report does not come in a very authentic form, so far as I can learn. Though, by the way, speaking of authenticity, you know that if we had heard Douglas say that he had abandoned the contest, it would not be very authentic. There is no news here. Noah, I still think, will be elected very easily. I am afraid of our race for representative. Dr. Knapp has become a candidate, and I fear the few votes he will get will be taken from us. Also some one has been tampering with old

Esquire Wicoff, and induced him to send in his name to be announced as a candidate. Francis refused to announce him without seeing him, and now I suppose there is going to be a fuss about it. I have been so busy that I have not seen Mrs. Stuart since you left, though I understand she wrote you by today's mail, which will inform you more about her than I could. The very moment a Speaker is elected, write me who he is.

Your friend as ever,
A. LINCOLN.

SPRINGFIELD, December 23, 1839.

DEAR STUART:

Dr. Henry will write you all the political news. I write this about some little matters of business. You recollect you told me you had drawn the Chicago Masack money, and sent it to the claimants. A d—d hawk-billed Yankee is here besetting me at every turn I take, saying that Robert Kinzie never received the eighty dollars to which he was entitled. Can you tell me anything about the matter? Again, old Mr. Wright, who lives up South Fork somewhere, is teasing me continually about some deeds which he says he left with you, but which I can find nothing of. Can you tell me where they are? The legislature is in session and has suffered the bank to forfeit its charter without benefit of clergy. There seems to be little disposition to resuscitate it.

Whenever a letter comes from you to Mrs. S——, I carry it to her, and then I see Betty; she is a tolerable nice "fellow" now. Maybe I will write again when I get more time.

Your friend, as ever,

A. LINCOLN.

P.S. The Democratic giant is here, but he is not now worth talking about.

He closed one letter to Stuart with a reference to "Ruffled Shirt Taylor" delivering a speech which William May answered. "The way May let the wind out of him was a perfect wonder; neither you nor I ever saw a crowd in this country so near all on one side, and all feeling so good." To this letter was the postscript: "Japh Bell has come out for Harrison. Ain't that a caution?"

His first published speech in pamphlet form was coming off the printing-presses early in 1840 and he wrote Stuart: "Well, I made a big speech which is in progress of printing in pamphlet form. To enlighten you and the rest of the world, I shall send you a copy when it is finished." The speech was one of a series of discussions of issues of the day, each speaker taking an entire evening, the general public invited to attend, in the hall of the House of Representatives in Springfield.

The smallest audience of the season came to hear Lincoln, and he alluded to that fact and let it stand in the published pamphlet, which opened:

"Fellow citizens: It is peculiarly embarrassing for me to attempt a continuance of the discussion, on this evening, which has been conducted in this hall on several previous ones. It is so because on each of those evenings there was a much fuller attendance than now, without any reason for its being so, except the greater interest the community feel in the speakers who addressed them then than they do in him who is to do so now. I am, indeed, apprehensive that the few who have attended have done so more to spare me mortification than in the hope of being interested in anything I may be able to say. This circumstance casts a damp upon my spirits, which I am sure I shall be unable to overcome during the evening."

From this mournful beginning, the thirty-year-old orator swept out into a speech that ranged across many fierce issues of the hour. Not only was he the strong young man who could take an ax handle and go to the polls and alone open a way through a gang blocking passage to the voting-place; not only was he the athlete they had seen take two fighting men and throw them apart as though they were two kittens. He was impressionable, with soft spots, with tremulous pools of changing lights. Though he stood up loose-jointed and comic with appeals in street-corner slang, and dialect from the public square hitching-posts, yet at moments he was as strange and far-off as the last dark sands of a red sunset, solemn as naked facts of death or hunger.

He declared ten years of Democratic administration had cost more money than the first twenty-seven years of the country's government, including the cost of the War of 1812. "The large sums foolishly, not to say corruptly, thrown away, constitute one of the just causes of complaint against the Administration. The agents of the Government in connection with the Florida (Indian) war needed a certain steamboat; the owner proposed to sell it for $10,000.00; the agents refused to give that sum, but hired the boat at $100.00 per day, and kept it at that hire till it amounted to $92,000.00. The contract for carrying the mail upon a certain route had expired, and of course was to be let again. The old contractor offered to take it for $300.00 a year. One James Reeside bid $99.00, and received the contract. On examination, it was discovered that Reeside had received for the service on this route, which he had contracted to render for less than $100.00, the enormous sum of $1,999.00. This is but a single case. Many similar ones, covering some ten or twenty pages of a large volume, are given."

He took up discussion of the subtreasury plan proposed by the Democrats, declaring it "less safe" than the national bank plan of the Whigs. "By the subtreasury scheme the public money is to be kept between the times of its disbursement, by treasurers of the mint, custom-house officers, land officers, and some new officers to be appointed. Has a year passed since the organization of the Government, that numerous defalcations have not occurred among this class of officers? Look at Swartout with his $1,200,000, Price with his $75,000, Harris with his $109,000, Linn with his $55,000, together with some twenty-five hundred lesser lights."

With however much care selections of bank officers might be made, there would be some unfaithful and dishonest. "The experience of the whole world, in all bygone times, proves this true. The Saviour of the world chose twelve disciples, and even one of that small number, selected by superhuman wisdom, turned out to be a traitor and a devil. And it may not be improper here to add that Judas carried the bag—was the subtreasurer of the Saviour and his disciples."

He took the instance of a subtreasurer having in his hands $100,000 of public money. "His duty says, 'You ought to pay this money over,' but his interest says, 'You ought to run away with this sum and be a nabob the balance of your life.' And who that knows anything of human nature doubts that in many instances interest will prevail over duty, and that the subtreasurer will prefer opulent knavery in a foreign land to honest poverty at home?"

He inquired whether a penitentiary department annexed to the subtreasury was not itself an admission that they expected public money to be stolen. "Why build the cage if they expect to catch no birds? But as to the question how effectual the penitentiary will be in preventing defalcations, how effectual have penitentiaries heretofore been in preventing the crimes they were established to suppress? Has not confinement in them long been the legal penalty of larceny, forgery, robbery, and many other crimes, in almost all the states? And yet are not those crimes committed weekly, daily—nay, and even hourly—in every one of those states? Again, the gallows has long been the penalty of murder, and yet we scarcely open a newspaper that does not relate a new case of that crime. If, then, the penitentiary has ever heretofore failed to prevent larceny, forgery, and robbery, and the gallows and halter have likewise failed to prevent murder, by what process of reasoning, I ask, is it that we are to conclude the penitentiary will hereafter prevent the stealing of public money? But our opponents seem to think they answer the charge that the money will be stolen fully if they can show that they will bring offenders to punishment. Not so. Will the punishment of the thief bring back the stolen money? No more so than the hanging of a murderer restores his victim to life. What is the object desired? Certainly not the greatest number of thieves we can catch, but that the money may not be stolen. If, then, any plan can be devised for depositing the public treasure where it will never be stolen, never embezzled, is not that the plan to be adopted? Turn, then, to a national bank."

Toward the end of his speech, thirty-year-old Abraham Lincoln spoke like a man watching a crazy and cruel horizon. "Many free countries have lost their liberty; and ours may lose hers; but if she shall, be it my proudest plume, not that I was the last to desert, but that I never deserted her. I know that the great volcano in Washington, aroused and directed by the evil spirit that reigns there is belching forth the lava of political corruption in a current broad and deep, which is sweeping with frightful velocity over the whole length and breadth of the land, bidding fair to leave unscathed no green spot nor living thing; while on its bosom are riding, like demons on the waves of hell, the imps of that evil spirit, and fiendishly taunting all those who dare to resist its destroying course with the hopelessness of their effort; and knowing this, I cannot deny that all may be swept away. Broken by it I, too, may be; bow to it I never will."

The allusions to imps, lava, waves of hell, and fiendish taunts, concerned a town seventy miles from Springfield, where a wild drama had been acted out two years before. A young man in the town of Alton told men he must speak what he believed ought to be spoken And the men to whom he so spoke answered that if he did speak what he believed ought to be spoken, they would kill him. He had brought a printing-press up from St. Louis, intending through the columns of his weekly newspaper to speak what he believed ought to be spoken; they threw his printing-press into the Mississippi River. He brought another printing-press to Alton; they wrecked it. And a third time he brought a printing-press to Alton, and they circled by night with torches and guns around the warehouse where he had the printing-office, and they set the warehouse on fire, and they shot him and killed him. And over the Illinois prairies and from the frontier to the eastern coast of America there was discussion about whether this young man, Elijah P. Lovejoy, was right or wrong in saying, against repeated warnings, that he must speak what he believed ought to be spoken.

In Springfield, as Abraham Lincoln read the newspapers, the picture of what happened at Alton shocked him. That was his own word for it; he was shocked. Feet on the office table, gazing across the public square, he sat huddled with his thoughts.

When a bill came up in the legislature to throw off to the territory of Wisconsin the fourteen northern counties of the State of Illinois, he fought to defeat it. He wanted Illinois to have Chicago, a port on one of the Great Lakes within its borders, connecting the West with the East. If the measure had won, it would have left Illinois depending on the Ohio and Mississippi rivers for water transportation, with its main economic outlets toward the South, with its future tied closer to the South. The bill was beaten by 70 votes to 11.

At Page Eaton's carpenter shop one afternoon he stopped and talked. Page Eaton allowed that everybody said Lincoln would never make a good lawyer because he was too honest. And as Eaton told it: "Lincoln said he had a notion to quit studying law and learn carpentering. He thought there was more need of carpenters out here than lawyers."

CHAPTER 49

AMONG the men with whom Lincoln was mixing in company day by day in his Springfield life as he passed thirty years of age, there were future congressmen, governors, senators, judges. He was watching masters in the game of politics and law. He saw the young Stephen A. Douglas move from job to job; Douglas had been state's attorney, member of the Illinois legislature, had become register of the land office at Springfield, and was always mentioned for congressman.

Watching his fellow citizens, he learned more ways and habits of politics than are told of in the books. After trying a case in the courthouse, gossiping on street corners a few minutes and stopping in at two or three stores, and then going to his office and reading the latest newspapers, he could put his feet on the office table, tilt back his chair, and look out over the moving shadows of the public square with enough history and philosophy to supply him for hours of thought, surmise, deduction, suspicion, mystery.

The spinning of weaves and webs was going on, schemers winding back and forth trying to piece together their schemes. In order to live and stand up and be one of the men among men in that frontier town and state in the years around 1840, a man had to know schemers, had to know how to spot a scheme when he saw one coming, and how to meet scheme with scheme. It was not only Abe Lincoln's honesty that had put him in the front among leaders of the Whig party, nor only that he had personality and was a vote-getter on the stump and at electioneering; it was also that he was a schemer: he had a long head and could gun for game far off. He was peering at Stephen A. Douglas, the register of the land office, just as he had peered at unknown lights moving in shallows of the Mississippi River as he drew near in a flatboat.

A young man lit up with wild human enthusiasms had begun clerking in the Speed store, and sleeping upstairs in the big room with Speed and Lincoln. He was William H. Herndon, whose father had taken him out of Illinois College at Jacksonville when the killing of Lovejoy started Abolition bonfires among its professors and students. He had been with Lincoln on one or two stumping trips, and had first seen Lincoln as he was riding horseback along the Sangamon River at the time Lincoln piloted the *Talisman* over the broken dam at New Salem. Young Herndon was thinking of studying law. Between these two men, Lincoln nine years the older, there was a trust and understanding not common among men. They belonged with Speed to a club of young men who met and read their writings to each other; Lincoln once entertained them with rhymes about the mistakes of men and women toward each other, one reading:

> Whatever spiteful fools may say,
> Each jealous ranting yelper,
> No woman ever went astray,
> Without a man to help her.

Interest in politics, the science of government, and the destiny of the human race was so keen at this time that the young Democrats and Whigs had a debating tournament that ran eight days straight, Sunday excepted, four speakers to a side, each speaker taking an evening. Lincoln's night to speak came last, and, as the listeners to politics and the science of government had their ears full of discussions by that time, Lincoln had the smallest audience of all.

The future held the thoughts of the young men. What with railroads coming West, the border would move, the Great Plains fill up with settlers, the frontier would shift from the Mississippi River to the Rocky Mountains, and after that to the Pacific Coast.

Peoria ran stages daily to Springfield, three times a week to Galena, Ottawa, and Rushville, and twice a week to Oquawka. The name "O-quaw-ka" was mentioned by people as a place where white men had a town; it was not an Indian tribe nor a bird or rabbit. Seven steamers made trips between Peoria, St. Louis, and Pittsburgh; another ran between St. Louis and the Rock River. History and destiny were in the air; the name of Stone's Landing was changed to Napoleon; the name of Goose Run to Columbus River.

The land was now all surveyed; fences were coming; if timber for rail-fencing was not handy, there was the Osage orange hedge which with a few years' growth would keep cows in a pasture and out of a cornfield on the prairie farms. Land speculators now held the larger part of the land in Illinois. By 1837, there had been issued 17,075 patents for 2,831,840 acres of land; in 1839 were recorded 1,132,872 land sales. The wilderness was passing into the hands of landlords and speculators. Romulus Riggs, who lived in Philadelphia and gave his daughter the name of "Illinois," offered 226 quarter-sections of land for sale at prices from $5.00 to $40.00 an acre; of his total holdings he wished to sell 42,560 acres.

In state and national politics, the western public lands became an issue. Martin Van Buren, the New York Tammany Democrat who was picked by Andrew Jackson to follow him in the White House, was beaten in the wild campaign of 1840 partly because of his record of having voted against western internal improvements, against the Cumberland Road, the Illinois and Michigan Canal grant, and the reduction of the price of public lands. William Henry Harrison, the first Whig and the first northern man from west of the Allegheny Mountains, entered the White House.

The campaign and the election filled the Illinois Whigs with enthusiasm; some predicted their party had come to stay, that the Democratic party was hitting a slump that would mean its death.

One of Lincoln's early speeches in the campaign was in Alton, where it was announced by large handbills declaring:

ATTENTION! THE PEOPLE!!

A. Lincoln, Esq'r., of Sangamon County,
one of the Electoral Candidates, will Address
the People this Evening!! At Early Candlelighting,
at the   ☞   Old Court Room   ☞   (Riley's
Building). By request of Many Citizens.
Thursday April 9th, 1840.

In this campaign Lincoln did more stumping than in any previous campaign. He was matched against Douglas in many debates. He took up the nickname by which Whigs referred to all Democrats—"Locofocos" or "Locos." At a meeting of New York Democrats two factions were trying to control the meeting. One gang turned off the gas-lights, and in the darkness the other gang, who had come prepared, took the new friction matches, called "Locofoco," from their pockets, struck their matches and lighted the room and ran the meeting.

Lincoln spoke from a wagon at a big conclave of Whigs in Springfield in June, which was attended by 15,000 people, some from as far as Chicago. "They came in carriages and wagons, on horseback and on foot. They came with log cabins drawn on wheels by oxen, and with coons, coonskins, and hard cider. They came with music and banners, thousands from long distances." Among the Whig orators were Fletcher Webster, a son of Daniel Webster, E. D. Baker, John J. Hardin, the Rev. John Hogan, and Ben Bond, a son of Shadrach Bond.

One man who heard Lincoln make this wagon speech at the big Springfield powwow, wrote about it afterward:

"The questions involved were not such as enlisted and engaged Lincoln's best thoughts. At times he discussed the questions in a logical way, but much time was devoted to telling stories to illustrate some phase of his argument, though more often the telling of these stories was resorted to for the purpose of rendering his opponents ridiculous. In that kind of oratory he had no equal in the state. One story he told on that occasion was full of salient points, and well illustrated the argument he was making. It was not an impure story, yet it was not one it would be seemly to publish; but rendered, as it was, in his inimitable way, it contained nothing that was offensive to a refined taste."

In the audience that Lincoln spoke to were delegates from Chicago; they had been hauled by fourteen teams; it took them three weeks to make the trip. One log cabin on wheels had been hauled by thirty yoke of oxen; it had a hickory tree growing by a cabin, with live coons in the tree, and a barrel of hard cider on tap by the cabin door. The Chicago delegates were flying a petticoat, a Democratic symbol of Harrison as a warrior; they had torn it away from Democrats on the way from Chicago. There was singing:

> Without a why or a wherefore
> We'll go for Harrison therefore.

A large handbill got out by the Whigs, with Lincoln's name printed among other Whig electors, was headed "To the Friends of the Na-

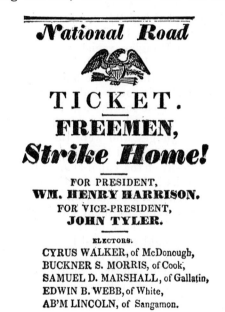

National Road

TICKET.
FREEMEN,
Strike Home!

FOR PRESIDENT,
WM. HENRY HARRISON.
FOR VICE-PRESIDENT,
JOHN TYLER.

ELECTORS.
CYRUS WALKER, of McDonough,
BUCKNER S. MORRIS, of Cook,
SAMUEL D. MARSHALL, of Gallatin,
EDWIN B. WEBB, of White,
AB'M LINCOLN, of Sangamon.

From a Whig campaign sheet in 1841. In the Barrett Collection.

tional Road." The slogan "Freemen, Strike Home!" stood in large type. In smaller type were such accusations as, "The scows, pile-drivers, hammers, &c. &c. used in constructing the harbor at Chicago, and which is now unfinished, have been sold by order of government for $201—having cost more than $6,000." Van Buren and the Democrats were blamed for the failure to build the Cumberland Road on through the West, while the pledge was offered, "Elect Harrison and the National Road is saved."

Banker, merchant, mechanic, and farmer toasted Harrison in mugs of hard cider. A Galena rally had 2,846 men and 340 women; at Carlinville were 3,000. Illinois voted for Harrison. A. Lincoln as one of the electoral

college cast his vote for the first northern and western man to be sent
to the White House. It was a famous campaign proving that sometimes
the American democracy goes on a rampage and shows that it has swift
and terrific power, even though it is not sure what to do with that power.

Among Illinois Whigs there were regrets. They carried their national
ticket, but lost the state to the Democrats. This put a new color on a
case they were interested in. Months earlier they had charged the Democrats with fraud in voting; thousands of Irish workmen in the canal zone
had started a test action before a circuit judge who ruled that foreign-
born inhabitants must be naturalized before they could vote. The Democrats took the case to the Supreme Court, knowing that if they lost the
case they would lose thousands of votes.

Then came the newly elected legislature into session, with a Democratic
majority holding power through the ballots of the canal-zone workers.
This was the hour Stephen Douglas, register of the land office, seized; he
wrote a draft of a bill; he made a speech in the rotunda of the capitol
asking the legislature to pass the bill; the bill passed and became law; it
threw out of office four circuit-court judges, set up five new supreme
court judgeships, and arranged for the legislature to appoint nine new
judges, who would be the supreme court of the state besides doing the
work of the circuit-court judges who were thrown out. The bill passed
the senate by a vote of 22 to 17, and the house by a vote of 45 to 40. By
this move the Democrats saved the canal-zone vote for their party, appointed Democrats as clerks in half the counties of the state as provided
in the bill, and placed Stephen A. Douglas, who could no longer be register
of the land office under a Whig national administration, on the bench
as a supreme court judge. The reply of the Whig party to this reform
of the judiciary was a calm address issued by a committee of which Lincoln was a member, entitled, "Appeal to the People of the State of Illinois," declaring "that the independence of the judiciary has been destroyed, that hereafter our courts will be independent of the people, and
entirely dependent on the legislature; that our rights of property and liberty of conscience can no longer be regarded as safe from the encroach-
ments of unconstitutional legislation."

During this session of the legislature there were bitter feelings between
the Whigs and Democrats. The voting was often close. Once when the
Democrats wanted a quorum and the Whigs didn't, the Democrats locked
the door of the house so as to keep the quorum in. Lincoln, Joe Gillespie,
and another Whig raised a window and jumped out and hid.

It was a time in which the Democrats had many sneering and furious
ways of saying that the Whigs were too respectable, while the Whigs on
the other hand had many proud, cool ways of saying that the Democrats
were not respectable enough.

CHAPTER 50

IN the early days of Illinois there was a man named Ninian Edwards who stood foremost among politicians, land speculators, and citizens of wealth and influence. He had been born in Maryland in the opening year of the American Revolution, and was taken as a child along the Wilderness Road through Cumberland Gap to Lexington, Kentucky, where he grew up and became a lawyer, a circuit judge, and a judge of the court of appeals. He left his bench as chief justice of the courts of Kentucky to take a commission from President Madison and to journey west and north into Illinois, of which newly carved territory he was the newly appointed governor, and its first United States senator in 1818. He later was Ambassador to Mexico, resigned, and for years, then, Illinois politics was torn with "war on Ninian Edwards." He fought through scandalous campaigns when personal and political enemies charged him with embezzlement. He was master of connecting webs between banking, land speculation, and politics.

Elected governor of the state in 1826, he lived as one of its powerful and substantial citizens, holding land in blocks of thousands of acres and snapping up many tracts of land delinquent in tax payments. He died in 1833, with reminiscences of years when his wife helped him tie their horses close to the house at night because so many horse thieves prowled the country, years when he was organizing companies of riflemen and building stockade forts from the Missouri to the Wabash River.

Ninian W. Edwards, the son of Ninian Edwards, lived in Springfield, was one of the "Long Nine." was of the same age as Abraham Lincoln, and the two had campaigned and electioneered together over Sangamon County. The Edwards house stood two stories high and was big enough to hold within its walls a dozen prairie-farmer cabins. Its walls and chimneys were of brick, with porches running the lengths of two sides of the house; a large one-story kitchen stretched flat to the rear of the house; its tall windows went higher than a tall man's arms would reach.

Green blinds opened out from the second-story windows. Brocades of wooden scrollwork embellished the eaves; an ornamented railing guarded the margins of the second-story portico.

Lincoln was a signer of one printed invitation to a cotillion ball at the Edwards house. He joined three other Springfield men in a written request sent to the wife of a Quincy member of the legislature, Lincoln writing:

To THE HONORABLE MRS. BROWNING:
We, the undersigned, respectfully represent to your honoress that we are in great need of your society in the town of Springfield and therefore humbly pray that your honoress will repair forthwith to the seat of Government bringing in your train all ladies in general who may be at your command and all Mrs. Browning's sisters in particular.

This was the same Mrs. Browning to whom he had written the long letter about his love affair with Miss Mary Owens—and Mrs. Browning, when she met Lincoln in Springfield, spoke to him as though the letter was one of his jokes, just a prank of his strange, whimsical mind, as though in a gay, story-telling mood he had invented, made up out of his head, an adventure to have a laugh over.

He had played "muggins," sitting opposite a young woman, looking her in the eye, touching the plate in his lap when she touched hers, and finally winning the game by not once taking his eyes from hers, and by always repeating each motion she made in touching her face with her fingers or thumbs. But when they led him to a mirror he saw his face streaked black; the plate put in his lap for the game had been sooted over a candle flame.

It seemed as though Lincoln at this time was looking for a woman. And yet there were things operating against him in the getting of a woman from among those who had come his way and met his fancy. He was backward, perhaps bashful, about telling any one woman truly how he felt about all women, that they had a harder path in life than men, that he felt sacred and mysterious urges living in the bodies of women, which he didn't feel about men, that there were soft mystic confusions about the behavior of women that upset him; and without showing that he was upset he would talk politics or science or the latest news, whatever it might be, or drift into droll and dry humors, that would puzzle women.

In the matter of compliments, for instance, he was not at home with women. Among men, he could find compliments to speak. Picking a man's point of pride or interest and then saying something that was true and that pleased the man in connection with that pride or interest, was an act of his every day. With women, however, he did not have this gift of finding a high pride or interest about which he could make a winning and honest compliment.

"Lincoln goes out when they take him but he isn't much for society," one Springfield woman noticed. "I don't think he can be called bashful. He is never embarrassed that I see, and he seems to enjoy the ladies' company. But he does not *go* much, as some of the young men do."

There was Miss Sarah Rickard, sixteen years old, staying at Bill Butler's house where Lincoln took his meals. He gave her presents, was her escort at parties, lectures, entertainments; they saw a home-talent dramatization of "The Babes in the Wood," and attended together the first theatre performance with regulation stage and curtain in Springfield. To her, he pointed out that, her name being Sarah, and the Sarah of Bible times having become the wife of Abraham, it was written that she, Sarah Rickard, was foreordained to marry him, Abraham Lincoln.

Then came an older sister, telling Sarah she was too young to think about marrying. And at the time Lincoln's interest in her was growing

keener, she sent him away, remarking afterward, "I found I was beginning to like him; but you know his peculiar manner and general deportment would not be likely to fascinate a young lady entering the society
world."

He was odd; he did have a "peculiar manner"; he was homely, ironical,
kindly, simple, whimsical, adroit, with a lean and fierce physical strength
kept under fine control. And yet it was never said of him by those close
to him, as was said of his father before him, "He had a way with women."

It seemed as though Miss Mary Owens and Miss Sarah Rickard both
spoke of him as rather a strange apparition, an aloof and removed creature who mounted barriers or slipped through fine meshes where they
could neither see nor feel barriers or meshes, while on the other hand he
might drawl a slow earthy mother-wit about cheap common things, of all
doorsteps and kitchens, somewhat like a farmer or a carpenter, too common and familiar for the woman in quest of romance with roses, moonlight—and compliments.

He was a paradox, so easy to see through with his funny street-corner
stories, and so baffling when his face settled into granitic calm and there
came into the depths of his eyes the shadows of a burning he had been
through, and he was a changed man keeping to himself the gray mystery of the change.

It was this Lincoln who was going to parties at the two-story brick
house of the Edwards' across the street from the new state capitol. It
was this Lincoln—who seemed to be looking for a woman. His name had
been on the printed invitations to a cotillion ball at the Edwards mansion.

CHAPTER 51

AND now there came to the house of Ninian W. Edwards in 1840 a young
woman from Lexington, Kentucky. This was her second visit. She had
been there three years before on a short visit. Now she had come to stay.
She was Miss Mary Todd, and was a younger sister of the wife of Ninian
W. Edwards, Elizabeth.

They were the granddaughters of Todds who had fought with Washington through the American Revolution. Their father, Robert Smith
Todd, had been a captain in the War of 1812, had served in both houses
of the legislature in Kentucky, and was president of the Bank of Kentucky in Lexington.

Miss Mary Todd was twenty-two years old, plump, swift, beaming, with
ready answers slipping from a sharp tongue, in the year that Springfield,
and Abraham Lincoln, became acquainted with her. She had her gifts, a
smooth soft skin, soft brown hair, and flashing clear blue eyes. With her
somewhat short figure sheathed in a gown of white with black stripes, cut

low at the neck and giving free play to her swift neck muscles, her skirt fluffed out in a slightly balloonish hoop, shod in modish ballroom slippers, she was a centre of likes and dislikes among those who came to the house where her sister was mistress.

Though her tongue and its sarcasm that came so quickly and so often, brought dislikes and hates, there was a shine and a bubbling, a foaming over of vitality, that won friends. For Lincoln, as he came to know her, she was lighted with magnets.

She was the first aggressively brilliant feminine creature his friends ever knew of who crossed his path and waylaid him with resources known to an accomplished and vital woman. She haunted him and held his attentions by the use of age-old fascinations, difficult of analysis by man because they move in a world of intuitive half-lights, swift gestures, and shaded intonations, lies, white lies, and lies shifting a medium course between lies and white lies. He could keep his head and outguess lights, shoals, and sand-bars of the Ohio and Mississippi rivers and take a flatboat through; with Mary Todd he lost his head. His experience was rich with rivers, starved with women; as one woman remarked, he didn't *go* as much as other young men for "ladies company."

Besides the charm that attached to Mary Todd in her smooth soft skin, soft brown hair, swift movement of neck muscles, flying glimpses of slippers, she was a triumph of cultivation: she had what were known as accomplishments; she had gone to the schools where the accomplishments were taught, and she had all that the most aristocratic schools of Kentucky could implant. She spoke and read the French language, had partaken often of dinners in which only talk in French was permitted, had read French classics of literature in the original.

Conversation, manners, belles-lettres, the piano and approved classical music, were taught in the schools she attended. How to be polite and suave while not stiff nor garrulous, how to mingle the sprightly and the reserved, how to conform in the stiff points of etiquette while maintaining a superior ease in the precise and the punctilious, these were subjects of instruction in which she had been tempered and drilled, coaxed, reminded, and told, from the time she wore bibs till she first stepped into a low-cut ballroom gown. The one word "nice" and the two words "nice people" were words almost born to her with her tongue.

She had kept a native and bottom fibre of strength and will; she had left her home in Kentucky and taken up a new home in Illinois because of a dispute with her stepmother. She was impetuous, picked the ridiculous angle, the weak point of any one she disliked and spoke it with thrust of phrase. In her first Springfield days Bill Herndon danced a waltz with her, and finding her the most amazingly smooth and easy waltzer he had ever danced with, he told her she seemed to glide through the waltz with the ease of a serpent. She drew back, flashed her eyes, retorted, "Mr.

Herndon, comparison to a serpent is rather severe irony, especially to a newcomer," bowed with accomplished dignity, and was gone. She could be hurt, just like that, when no one wanted to hurt her.

Far from ordinary was Miss Mary Todd; she was vivid, perhaps too vivid, ebullient, combative, too quick to "fly off the handle." She was in her element, moving in a swirl, delirious and inevitable when hot, stinging words were flying off her tongue, out of her lips. It connected directly with the fear and trembling that took her when a thunderstorm with zigzags of lightning came over the sky. Her temper colored her; she could shine with radiance at a gift, a word, an arrival, a surprise, an achievement of a little cherished design, at winning a withheld consent. A shaft of wanted happiness could strike deep in her.

The modish woman at a "levee" in Springfield then often wore eight or twelve starched petticoats with an overskirt of "changeable silk." There might be several "illusion skirts" worn over white satin. Mary Todd was read, informed and versed in apparel and appearance. She hummed gay little ditties putting on a flowered bonnet and tying a double-bow knot under her chin. A satisfying rose or ostrich plume in her hair was a psalm.

She embodied a thousand cunning, contradictory proverbs men have spoken about woman as a wildcat and as a sweet angel. She was vivid, perhaps too vivid. From far back in her forerunners of proud, passionate people had come this drag and lift that mixed in her personality, this paradoxical burden and balloon of personality. Her mother had died when she was a child. Visiting at Walnut Hills near Lexington, she was with a party of girls in a room when an alarm came that Indians were near. The other girls scampered under beds, into closets, but Mary Todd, finding no place to hide, stood in the centre of the room crying, "Hide me, O my Saviour, hide."

Style was instinctive with her; fashion was of her desires; when she was a girl and hoop skirts were worn by women, she toiled by candlelight till late in the night basting a hoop skirt with weeping willow twigs, starting for Sunday school the next day with a girl chum, both wearing white dresses stretched tight over silly, homemade hoops; their aunt saw them and called: "What frights you are! Take those things off and then go to Sunday school." While offhand observers spoke of her as having "bounce" and "spunk," it was an understanding among her friends that she had what they chose to call "ambition" and was "an ambitious woman." She was intense with the quality Kentuckians refer to in their horses as "high-strung."

Mary Todd was decisive. She and Mercy Levering once went out in muddy weather, taking along an armful of shingles. On Fifth Street they laid shingles ahead to step on while crossing. When they came back they saw the shingles wouldn't hold them up out of the mud. Hart, the drayman, came along with his two-wheeled sloping dray. Mary Todd called to him to give them a lift. He gee-hawed over next to the sidewalk and backed up. Mary Todd climbed on. But Mercy Levering didn't; she was afraid of how she would look and still more of what people would say. And as Mary Todd was driven to the Edwards' house, windows flew up and heads popped out to see, as Dr. E. H. Merryman put it in verses later, "this lady gay in silken coat and feathers white, a-riding on a dray."

There was "go" to her, an urge sending her toward place, power, station, "high degree." She cared deeply for all objects representative of class, the acclaim of prizes, blue ribbons, distinction. Again, like certain fast horses of the blue-grass country, she "chafed at the bit" if the restraints of life, the leashes put on the frail, mortal limbs and hours of woman, were too much and too many; or again she was full of the lust of being vividly and proudly alive for the gaze of others; her stride and attitude was that of the horse champing, the hoofs wanting to go, to be a winner known to grandstands, vast amphitheatres of spectators. She was a crucible of forces, of a blood with flame in its currents, a brain with far contrasts, with explosions sometimes that shook the entire physical framework, the entire retort that held the pathos of her fate; her tears could flow from sacs that had containers of the strength of salt tears; her laughter could dimple in wreaths running to the core of her; she was born to impulses that rode her before she could ride them. And yet after excesses of temper had worn her to a babbling and moaning exhaustion, she could rise and stand up to battle again for a purpose definitely formed.

The Todds traced back to Scottish Covenanters who fought the king and the established church of England; among Covenanters sentenced to transportation to the American colonies were two Todds; their vital and stubborn blood ran in Mary Todd. She was of a Presbyterian line crossed with Episcopalian. Her telling a Kentucky friend, before leaving for Illinois, that she was going to be the wife of some future President of the United States, may have been a piece of idle gossip or the evidence of a hope for distinction.

Society life, the social drama and its gleaming mirrors and garnished promenades, called to her; life should be a series of ceremonial occasions —interspersed with sleep, forethought, and preparations for ceremonial occasions. In the phrasing of a breakfast greeting, in the tuck of a napkin corner and the disposition of its folded triangles as related to knife, fork, plate, in the employment of a spoon for the conveyance of hot soup or the negotiation of a fork of green peas, in the buckling of a slipper or the knotting of a satin sash, there was a correct style; and superior persons were known by their use of the correct style; beyond their portals was the human rabble shading off into the incorrect, the common, the ignorant, the vulgar, the dirty, the indecent, and the perfectly disgusting.

During her first year in Springfield both Abraham Lincoln and Stephen A. Douglas took their turns at being entertained by Mary Todd in the big parlor of the Edwards house, took their turns at escorting her to parties and balls; she was asked which of the two she intended to have for her husband, and answered, "The one that has the best chance of being President."

In the Edwards circle they believed there were clues to her character in a remark she passed at a party around a fireside one evening. A young woman married to a rich man far along in years was asked, "Why did you marry such a dried-up husband, such a withered-up old buck?" Her answer was, "He had lots of horses and gold." And the quick-tongued Mary Todd said in surprise: "Is that true? *I* would rather marry a good man, a man of mind, with bright prospects for fame and power, than to marry all the horses, gold, and bones in the world."

CHAPTER 52

ALONG in the year 1840 Lincoln and Mary Todd plighted their troth and were engaged to be married. Ninian W. Edwards and his wife had argued she was throwing herself away; it wasn't a match; she and Lincoln came from different classes in society. And her stubborn Covenanter blood rose; she knew her own mind and spoke it: Lincoln had a future; he was her man more than any other man she had met.

The months passed. Lincoln, the solitary, the melancholy, was busy, lost, abstracted; he couldn't go to all the parties, dances, concerts Mary Todd was going to; she flared with jealousy and went with other men. She accused him; tears; misunderstandings; they made up, fell out, made up again. The wedding was set for New Year's Day, 1841. In the kitchen of the Edwards house the wedding cakes were put in the oven.

And then something happened. The bride was ready. The groom didn't come. It was a phantom wedding, mentioned in hushes. There was gossip and dispute about whether the wedding had been set for that date at all.

On the day set for the wedding, Lincoln took his seat and answered roll-call in the legislature, and during two months was absent from his seat only seven days. He toiled with the Whigs on an "Appeal to the People of the State of Illinois," on circulars and protests trying to rouse public opinion against the Democrats. He wrote letters, tried law cases.

And yet, as he walked the streets of Springfield, he was a haunted man. He had torn himself away from a woman; she had stood ready and waiting; his word had been pledged; he had failed to meet her; he had sent word he didn't love her and there could only be pain and misery in a marriage where the man knew he didn't love her. And was he sure he didn't love her? If he did love her it was a terrible wrong to leave her with arms ɔpen, waiting for him; and even if he could be sure he didn't love her, the tears and the storms of her heart came because he had been blind and foolish and gone farther than he should have in telling her he loved her.

Once he had written it all out in a letter, how he had made a mistake in telling her he loved her, and Speed had read the letter and thrown it into a fire, saying words may be forgotten but letters are a permanent record. And Speed had told him: "If you have the courage of manhood, go see Mary yourself; tell her if you do not love her, tell her so, tell her you will not marry her." And he had gone from the Speed store saying he would be careful not to say much and would leave Mary as soon as he had told her. And he was gone an hour, two hours.

It was past eleven o'clock that night when he came back and said to Speed: "When I told Mary I did not love her, she burst into tears and, almost springing from her chair and wringing her hands as if in agony, said something about the deceiver being himself deceived. It was too much for me. I found the tears trickling down my own cheeks. I caught her in my arms and kissed her."

Speed told him he was a fool; he had renewed the engagement; and he said: "Well, if I'm in again, so be it. It's done, and I shall abide by it." Then the wedding date had been set, the wedding cakes baked. And he couldn't go.

So now he walked the streets of Springfield; he brooded, looking out of the windows of the second-story law office; he went to Dr. Henry's office; he took Dr. Henry's advice and wrote a long statement of his case for a doctor in Cincinnati. And the doctor answered that in this kind of case he could do nothing without first a personal interview. He wrote his partner Stuart: "I am now the most miserable man living. If what I feel were equally distributed to the whole human family, there would not be one cheerful face on the earth."

He was seeing Dr. Henry often, and wrote Stuart, "Whether I shall ever be better, I cannot tell; I awfully forebode I shall not. To remain as I am is impossible; I must die or be better, it appears to me. The matter you speak of on my account you may attend to as you say, unless you shall hear of my condition forbidding it. I say this because I fear I shall be unable to attend to any business here, and a change of scene might help me. If I could be myself, I would rather remain at home with Judge Logan. I can write no more." He wrote to the *Sangamo Journal* meditations entitled "Suicide."

He begged Stuart to go the limit in Washington toward the appointment of Dr. Henry as postmaster at Springfield. "You know I desired Dr. Henry to have that place when you left; I now desire it more than ever—I have within the last few days been making a most discreditable exhibition of myself in the way of hypochondriasm, and thereby got an impression that Dr. Henry is necessary to my existence—Unless he gets that place he leaves Springfield."

He further urged the merits of Dr. Henry, added that nearly all the Whig members of the Legislature besides other Whigs, favored the doctor for Postmaster. He declared, "My heart is very much set upon it," and ended the painful letter, "Pardon me for not writing more; I have not sufficient composure to write a long letter."

The legislature adjourned. Josh Speed was selling his store and going back to his folks in Kentucky. Lincoln traveled to Kentucky a little later.

As the redbud, the honeysuckle and the clambering springtime roses of Kentucky came out, the lost Lincoln struggled to come back. He told Speed one day that he had done nothing to make any human being remember that he had lived, that what he wished to live for was to connect his name with the events of his day and generation and to link his name with something that would be to the interest of his fellow men.

Slowly, he came back. A sweet and serene old woman, Joshua Speed's mother, talked with him, gave him a mother's care, and made him a present of an Oxford Bible.

In June he was in Springfield handling the cases of two clients accused of murder; excitement ran high and hangings were expected; but the man supposed to have been killed turned up alive. And Lincoln ended a long letter to Speed with the remark, "Hart, the little drayman that hauled Molly [Mary Todd] home once, said it was too *damned* bad to have so much trouble, and no hanging after all."

Writing to Speed's sister three months later from Bloomington, on the court circuit, he informed her:

Do you remember my going to the city, while I was in Kentucky, to have a tooth extracted, and making a failure of it? Well, that same old tooth got to paining me so much that about a week since I had it torn out, bringing with it a bit of the jaw-bone, the consequence of which is that I can neither talk nor eat. I am literally subsisting on savory remembrances—that is, being unable to eat, I am living upon the remembrance of the delicious dishes of peaches and cream we used to have at your house. When we left, Miss Fanny Henning was owing you a visit, as I understand it. Has she paid it yet? If she has, are you not convinced that she is one of the sweetest girls in the world? There is but one thing about her, so far as I could perceive, that I would have otherwise than it is—that is, something of a tendency to melancholy. This is a misfortune, not a fault. Is little Siss Eliza Davis at your house yet? If she is, kiss her o'er and o'er again for me. Tell your mother that I have not got her "present," an Oxford Bible, with me, but I intend to read it regularly when I return home. I doubt not that it is really, as she says, the best cure for the blues, could one but take it according to the truth.

A child was a natural belonging in the big arms of Lincoln. He could be free and familiar, lavish with compliments, mockery and cajolery, when among children or with any child. The kiss of a snuggling child for him, and his kiss for a snuggling child, this was homelike. The likes of little Siss Eliza Davis did him good.

Anything walking on two legs or four could have a corner in his lonesome heart. In his letter to Miss Speed, he sketched a steamboat scene that met his eyes traveling from Louisville to St. Louis:

A fine example was presented on board the boat for contemplating the effect of condition upon human happiness. A gentleman had purchased twelve negroes in different parts of Kentucky, and was taking them to a farm in the South. They were chained six and six together. A small iron clevis was around the left wrist of each, and this fastened to the main chain by a shorter one, at a convenient distance from the others, so that the negroes were strung together precisely like so many fish upon a trot line. In this condition they were being separated forever from the scenes of their childhood, their friends, their fathers and mothers, and brothers and sisters, and going into perpetual slavery, where the lash of the master is proverbially more ruthless and unrelenting than any other where; and yet amid all these distressing circumstances, as we would think them, they were the most cheerful and apparently happy creatures on board. One whose offense for which he had been sold was an over-fondness for his wife, played the fiddle almost continually, and the others danced, sang, cracked jokes, and played various games with cards from day to day. How true it is that God tempers the wind to the shorn lamb, or in other words, that he renders the worst of human conditions tolerable, while he permits the best to be nothing better than tolerable.

CHAPTER 53

Joshua Speed was a deep-chested man of large sockets, with broad measurement between the ears. A streak of lavender ran through him; he had spots soft as May violets. And he and Abraham Lincoln told each other their secrets about women. Lincoln too had tough physical shanks and large sockets, also a streak of lavender, and spots soft as May violets.

"I do not feel my own sorrows more keenly than I do yours," Lincoln wrote Speed in one letter. And again: "You know my desire to befriend you is everlasting."

The wedding-day of Speed and Fanny Henning had been set; and he was afraid he didn't love her; it was wearing him down; the date of the wedding loomed ahead of him as the hour for a sickly affair; he wrote Lincoln he was sick.

And Lincoln wrote a letter analyzing Speed, telling him what was wrong with his physical and mental system. It was a letter as tender as loving hands swathing a feverish forehead, yet direct and logical in its facing of immediate, practical facts. It was a letter showing that the misery of Abraham Lincoln in the unlucky endings of his love affairs with

Ann Rutledge and with Mary Todd, must have been a deep-rooted, tangled, and baffling misery.

"You are naturally of a nervous temperament," he told Speed. "And this I say from what I have seen of you personally, and what you have told me concerning your mother at various times, and concerning your brother William at the time his wife died." Besides this general cause, he gave three special reasons for Speed's condition. "The first special cause is your exposure to bad weather on your journey, which my experience clearly proves to be very severe on defective nerves. The second is the absence of all business and conversation of friends, which might divert your mind, give it occasional rest from the intensity of thought which will sometimes wear the sweetest idea threadbare and turn it to the bitterness of death. The third is the rapid and near approach of that crisis on which all your thoughts and feelings concentrate."

Lincoln's broodings over the mysteries of personality, and the connections of a man's behavior with the juices and currents of his body, his ideas about his own shattered physical system at the time he had wandered mumbling and friends had taken care of him, were indicated in his telling Speed: "If, as I expect, you will at some time be agonized and distressed, let me, who have reason to speak with judgment on such a subject, beseech you to ascribe it to the causes I have mentioned, and not to some false and ruinous suggestion of the Devil. The general cause—nervous debility, which is the key and conductor of all the particular ones, and without which they would be utterly harmless,—though it does pertain to you, does not pertain to one in a thousand. It is out of this that the painful difference between you and the mass of the world springs." That is, Lincoln believed that he and his friend had exceptional and sensitive personalities. "Though it does pertain to you, it does not pertain to one in a thousand."

Their births, the loins and tissues of their fathers and mothers, accident, fate, providence, had given these two men streaks of lavender, spots soft as May violets. "It is out of this that the painful difference between you and the mass of the world springs." And Lincoln was writing in part a personal confession in telling Speed: "I know what the painful point with you is at all times when you are unhappy; it is an apprehension that you do not love her as you should. What nonsense! How came you to court her? Was it because you thought she deserved it, and that you had given her reason to expect it? If it was for that, why did not the same reason make you court at least twenty others of whom you can think, and to whom it would apply with greater force than to her? Did you court her for her wealth? Why, you know she had none. But you say you reasoned yourself into it. What do you mean by that? Was it not that you found yourself unable to reason yourself out of it? Did you not think and partly form the purpose of courting her the first time you ever saw her or heard of her?" Reason had little to do with it at that early stage. "There was nothing at that time for reason to work upon. Whether she was moral, amiable, sensible, or even of good character, you did not, nor could then know, except, perhaps, you might infer the last from the company you found her in. All you then did or could know of her was her personal appearance and deportment; and these, if they impress at all, impress the heart, and not the head.

"Say candidly, were not those heavenly black eyes the whole basis of all your early reasoning on the subject? Did you not go and take me all the way to Lexington and back, for no other purpose but to get to see her again? What earthly consideration would you take to find her scouting and despising you, and giving herself up to another? But of this you have no apprehension; and therefore you cannot bring it home to your feelings. I shall be so anxious about you that I shall want you to write by every mail."

Thus ended a letter which had begun, "My dear Speed: Feeling, as you know I do, the deepest solicitude for the success of the enterprise you are engaged in, I adopt this as the last method I can adopt to aid you, in case (which God forbid!) you shall need any aid."

A few days before Speed's wedding, Lincoln wrote a letter to the bridegroom. "I assure you I was not much hurt by what you wrote me of your excessively bad feeling at the time you wrote. Not that I am less capable of sympathizing with you now than ever, but because I hope and believe that your present anxiety and distress about her health and her life must and will forever banish those horrid doubts which I know you sometimes felt as to the truth of your affection for her. If they can once and forever be removed (and I almost feel a presentiment that the Almighty has sent your present affliction expressly for that object) surely nothing can come in their stead to fill their immeasurable measure of misery. The death scenes of those we love are surely painful enough; but these we are prepared for and expect to see; they happen to all and all know they must happen. Should she, as you fear, be destined to an early grave, it is indeed a great consolation to know that she is so well prepared to meet it. Her religion, which you once disliked so much, I will venture you now prize most highly."

Lincoln hoped Speed's melancholy forebodings as to Fanny's early death were not well founded. "I even hope that ere this reaches you she will have returned with improved and still improving health, and that you will have met her, and forgotten the sorrows of the past in the enjoyment of the present. I would say more if I could, but it seems to me that I have said enough. It really appears to me that you yourself ought to rejoice, and not sorrow, at this indubitable evidence of your undying affection for her. Why, Speed, if you did not love her, although you might not wish her death, you would most certainly be resigned to it. Perhaps this point is no longer a question with you, and my pertinacious dwelling on it is a rude intrusion upon your feelings.

"You know the hell I have suffered on that point, and how tender I am upon it. You know I do not mean wrong. I have been quite clear of 'hypo' [hypochondria] since you left; even better than I was along in the fall.

"I have seen Sarah [Rickard] but once. She seemed very cheerful, and so I said nothing to her about what we spoke of. Old Uncle Billy Herndon is dead, and it is said this evening that Uncle Ben Ferguson will not live. This, I believe, is all the news, and enough at that unless it were better. Write me immediately on the receipt of this."

Speed's wedding-day came; the knot was tied. And in a few days he read lines from Lincoln at Springfield: "When this shall reach you, you will have been Fanny's husband several days. You will hereafter be on ground that I have never occupied, and consequently, if advice were needed, I might advise wrong. I do fondly hope, however, that you will never again need any comfort from abroad. But should I be mistaken in this, should excessive pleasure still be accompanied with a painful counterpart at times, still let me urge you, as I have ever done, to remember, in the depth and even agony of despondency, that very shortly you are to feel well again. I am now fully convinced that you love her as ardently as you are capable of loving. Your ever being happy in her presence and your intense anxiety about her health, would place this beyond dispute in my mind.

"I incline to think it probable that your nerves will fail you occasionally for a while; but once you get them firmly guarded now, that trouble is over forever. I think, if I were you, in case my mind were not exactly right, I would avoid being idle. I would immediately engage in some business, or go to making preparations for it, which would be the same thing. If you went through the ceremony calmly, or even with sufficient composure not to excite alarm in any present, you are safe beyond question, and in two or three months, to say the most, will be the happiest of men."

Thus messages went back and forth. "If I were you, in case my mind were not exactly right, I would avoid being idle," wrote Lincoln.

One had undertaken to marry a woman, and was smitten with such fear that he didn't love her, that on the fixed wedding day he wandered alone and there was no wedding. And he was writing from Illinois to a cherished friend down across the Wabash and Ohio rivers, how to take care of himself so that he would be on hand when the wedding-bells rang. "I know the painful point with you is an apprehension that you do not love her as you should. . . . You know the hell I have suffered on that point, and how tender I am upon it." A postscript to one letter read, "I have been quite a man since you left."

And when the single man received a letter from his just married friend, he wrote: "Yours of the 16th instant, announcing that Miss Fanny and you are 'no more twain, but one flesh,' reached me this morning. I have no way of telling you how much happiness I wish you both, though I believe you can conceive it. I feel somewhat jealous of both of you now; you will be so exclusively concerned for one another, that I shall be forgotten entirely. . . .

"I regret to learn that you have resolved not to return to Illinois. I shall be very lonesome without you. How miserable things seem to be arranged in this world! If we have no friends, we have no pleasure; and if we have them, we are sure to lose them, and be doubly pained by the loss. I did hope she and you would make your home here; but I own I have no right to insist. You owe obligations to her ten thousand times more sacred than you can owe to others, and in that light let them be respected and observed. It is natural that she should desire to remain with her relatives and friends. As to friends, however, she could not need them anywhere; she would have them in abundance here."

In closing he asked his friend to write often, and added the postscript: "Poor Easthouse is gone at last. He died awhile before day this morning. They say he was very loath to die." A few dots indicated an unfinished thought at the end of the sentence, "They say he was very loath to die."

CHAPTER 54

By wagon and river routes, breweries in St. Louis and Chicago were sending to towns in southern and central Illinois stocks of ale, pale ale, extra pale ale, lager beer, porter, and brown stout. Kentucky distilleries were shipping many grades of rye and corn whisky. Up the Mississippi River from New Orleans came cargoes of liquors and liqueurs, wet goods as varied as Scotch whisky, Holland gin, French brandy and rum, Madeira wine, port, Teneriffe, dry and sweet wines, Malaga, claret, and other light and heavy alcoholics.

A crusade against heavy drinking was carried on by the Washington Society, thus named in the belief that General George Washington was a drinking man but knew when to stop—in fact, was a temperance man. In districts of other states than Illinois, sensational campaigns had been carried on against strong drink. The Springfield *Journal* reported in 1841: "Whisky is quoted at Dayton, Ohio, at twelve cents a gallon. The Washingtonian cause is flourishing there. Eight thousand have signed the Temperance pledge in Cincinnati, a fact which has had some effect in lowering the price of whisky."

Among the leading advocates of temperance in Springfield was Abraham Lincoln. So far in the forefront was he, at this time, as an enemy of strong drink, that he was chosen as the orator of the day at a large important gathering of Washington societies. The Springfield *Journal* on February 14 announced the "celebration" to be held on the 22d of the month, as follows:

The Washington Society of Springfield, and other invited societies, will meet at the Methodist Church at 10 o'clock A.M. The procession will be formed by Col. B. S. Clement, chief marshal, between 11 and 12 o'clock, and will proceed through several of the principal streets of the city, to the Second Presbyterian Church, where an address will be delivered by A. Lincoln, Esq., and several appropriate airs, prepared for the occasion, will be sung by the choir—and such other services as are proper for the occasion. The order of the procession will be as follows: First, Chief Marshal; Second, Sangamon Guards; Third, Committee of Arrangements; Fourth, President and Orator; Fifth, Vice-President, Secretary and Treasurer; Sixth, Invited Societies; Seventh, Springfield Society. Seats will be reserved for the ladies at the Second Church. By order, etc., William Porter, Secretary, Committee of Arrangements.

Under such auspices, and after riding around the public square in a carriage as "the orator of the day," Lincoln faced his audience with an address on "Charity in Temperance Reform." He took notice of the "new and splendid" success of the temperance cause, and then went on to analyze some points in temperance reform that didn't quite satisfy him. "The warfare hitherto waged against the demon intemperance has somehow or other been erroneous. Either the champions engaged or the tactics they have adopted have not been the most proper. These champions for the most part have been preachers, lawyers, and hired agents. They are supposed to have no sympathy of feeling or interest with those very persons whom it is their object to convince and persuade."

Then he pictured the reformed drunkard as the best of all temperance crusaders. "When one who has long been known as a victim of intemperance appears before his neighbors 'clothed and in his right mind,' a redeemed specimen of long-lost humanity, and stands up, with tears of joy trembling in his eyes, to tell of the miseries once endured, now to be endured no more forever; of his once naked and starving children, now clad and fed comfortably; of a wife long weighted down with woe, weeping, and a broken heart, now restored to health; and how easily it is all done, once it is resolved to be done; how simple his language!—there is a logic and an eloquence in it that few with human feelings can resist. They cannot say he is vain of hearing himself speak, for his whole demeanor shows he would gladly avoid speaking at all; they cannot say he speaks for pay, for he received none and asked for none. In my judgment, it is to the battles of this new class of champions that our late success is greatly, perhaps chiefly, owing."

Men selling liquor, and men drinking it, were blamed too much. Denunciation of dram-sellers and dram-drinkers was "both impolitic and unjust." And why? "Because it is not much in the nature of man to be driven to anything; still less to be driven about that which is exclusively his own business; and least of all where such driving is to be submitted to at the expense of pecuniary interest or burning appetite."

"When the dram-seller and drinker were incessantly told—not in accents of entreaty and persuasion, diffidently addressed by erring man to an erring brother, but in the thundering tones of anathema and denunciation with which the lordly judge often groups together all the crimes of the felon's life, and thrusts them in his face just ere he passes sentence of death—that they were the authors of all the vice and misery and crime in the land; that they were the manufacturers and material of all the thieves and robbers and murderers that infest the earth, that their houses were the workshops of the devil; and that their person should be shunned by all the good and virtuous, as moral pestilences—I say, when they were told all this, and in this way, it is not wonderful that they were slow, very slow, to acknowledge the truth of such denunciations."

He quoted the maxim, "A drop of honey catches more flies than a gallon of gall," and urged: "If you would win a man to your cause, first convince him that you are his sincere friend . . . Assume to dictate to his judgment, or to command his action, or to mark him as one to be shunned and despised, and he will retreat within himself, close all the avenues to his head and his heart; and though your cause be naked truth itself, transformed to the heaviest lance, harder than steel, you shall no more be able to pierce him than to penetrate the hard shell of a tortoise with a rye straw."

He sketched the history of liquor-making and liquor-drinking. "The practice of drinking is just as old as the world itself. When all of us of maturity first opened our eyes upon the stage of existence, we found intoxicating liquor recognized by everybody, used by everybody, repudiated by nobody. It commonly entered into the first draught of the infant and the last draught of the dying man."

The sideboard of the parson and the ragged pocket of the houseless loafer both held whisky. "Physicians prescribed it in this, that, and the other disease; government provided it for soldiers and sailors; and to have a rolling or raising, a husking or 'hoedown' anywhere about without it was positively insufferable."

Everywhere it was a respectable article of manufacture and merchandise. The making of it was regarded as honorable. "He who would make most was the most enterprising and respectable. Large and small manufactories of it were everywhere erected, in which all the earthly good of their owners were invested. Wagons drew it from town to town; boats bore it from clime to clime, and the winds wafted it from nation to nation; and merchants bought and sold it, by wholesale and retail, with precisely the same feelings on the part of the seller, buyer, and bystander as are felt at the selling and buying of plows, beef, bacon, or any other of the real necessaries of life."

"Even then it was known and acknowledged that many were greatly injured by it," Lincoln declared. "But none seemed to think the injury arose from the use of a bad thing, but from the abuse of a very good thing. The victims of it were to be pitied and compassionated, just as are the heirs of consumption and other hereditary diseases. Their failing was treated as a misfortune, and not as a crime, or even as a disgrace. If, then, what I have been saying is true, is it wonderful that some should think and act now as all thought and acted twenty years ago? and is it just to assail, condemn, or despise them for doing so? The universal sense of mankind on any subject is an argument, or at least an influence, not easily overcome."

It was as though he had been speaking with the voice of the Tom Lincoln who hauled four hundred gallons of whisky from the Knob Creek farm in Kentucky up to the Pigeon Creek farm in Indiana. He spoke next with the voice of the Abe Lincoln who on a freezing night near Gentryville had lugged on his shoulders the snoring drunkard picked from a ditch alongside the road.

"Another error, as it seems to me, into which the old reformers fell, was the position that all habitual drunkards were utterly incorrigible and therefore must be turned adrift and damned without remedy. . . . There is in this something so . . . uncharitable, so cold-blooded and feelingless, that it never did, nor ever can, enlist the enthusiasm of a popular cause. We could not love the man who taught it—we could not hear him with patience. The heart could not throw open its portals to it, the generous man could not adopt it—it could not mix with his blood. It looked . . . like throwing fathers and brothers overboard to lighten the boat for our security."

Were the benefits of temperance to be only for the next generation, for posterity? "Posterity has done nothing for us; we shall do very little for it unless we are made to think we are at the same time doing something for ourselves. There is something ludicrous in promises of good or threats of evil a great way off. 'Better lay down that spade you are stealing, Paddy; if you don't you'll pay for it at the day of judgment.' 'Be the powers, if ye'll credit me so long I'll take another jist.' "

Out in the audience Lincoln could see his law partner, Bill Herndon, a hard drinker when he drank, and Lincoln offered the opinion: "If we take habitual drunkards as a class, their heads and their hearts will bear an advantageous comparison with those of any other class. There seems ever to have been a proneness in the brilliant and warm-blooded to fall into this vice—the demon of intemperance ever seems to have delighted in sucking the blood of genius and of generosity."

At the close of the address, he showed he was not yet free from the influence of the famous orator Daniel Webster, and other famous orators who furnished the examples for the rising young orators. "Happy day when—all appetites controlled, all poisons subdued, all matter subjected —mind, all-conquering mind, shall live and move, the monarch of the world. Glorious consummation! Hail, fall of fury! Reign of reason, all hail!"

That he ranged far in his guesses and his hopes was seen in his declaration: "Whether or not the world would be vastly benefited by a total and final banishment from it of all intoxicating drinks seems to me not now an open question. Three-fourths of mankind confess the affirmative with their tongues, and, I believe, all the rest acknowledge it in their hearts . . . When there shall be neither a slave nor a drunkard on earth—how proud the title of that land which may truly claim to be the birthplace and the cradle of those revolutions that shall have ended in that victory. How nobly distinguished that people who shall have planted and nurtured to maturity both the political and moral freedom of their species."

In the audience to which Lincoln spoke there were many reformed drunkards, men who had been familiar figures in the doorways of the town's dramshops. The tone of Lincoln's address was keyed to these men; he didn't drink; but he did wish to say, "In my judgment such of us as have never fallen victims have been spared more from the absence of appetite than from any mental or moral superiority over those who have."

And young Bill Herndon standing at the door of the Presbyterian church, as the people passed out, said he heard remarks showing there were people not at all pleased with the address. Herndon said he caught one remark, "It's a shame that he should be permitted to abuse us so in the house of the Lord."

Writing to Speed about the address, Lincoln said: "You will see by the last *Sangamo Journal* that I made a temperance speech which I claim that you and Fanny shall read as an act of charity to me; for I cannot learn that anybody else has read it, or is likely to. Fortunately it is not very long, and I shall deem it a sufficient compliance with my request if one of you listens while the other reads it."

On the same Washington's birthday anniversary on which he made his speech, he gave advice to George E. Pickett, who was starting East to be a West Point cadet:

"Deceit and falsehood, especially if you have got a bad memory, is the *worst* enemy a fellow can have.

"Now, boy, on your march, don't you go and forget the old maxim that 'one drop of honey catches more flies than a half-gallon of gall.' Load your musket with this maxim, and smoke it in your pipe."

CHAPTER 55

A WEEK or so after Joshua Speed's wedding day, he wrote to Lincoln saying that "something indescribably horrible and alarming" haunted him. And Lincoln, in answering Speed's letter, said he was ready to swear it was not the fault of the woman Speed had married.

He went further and ventured the guess that both he and Speed had been dreaming dreams. "I now have no doubt that it is the peculiar misfortune of both you and me to dream dreams of Elysium far exceeding all that anything earthly can realize."

And Lincoln recalled an old saying of his father: "If you make a bad bargain, hug it all the tighter." The single man wrote to his married friend this letter:

SPRINGFIELD, February 25, 1842.

DEAR SPEED:

I received yours of the 12th written the day you went down to William's place, some days since, but delayed answering it till I should receive the promised one of the 16th, which came last night. I opened the letter with intense anxiety and trepidation; so much so, that, although it turned out better than I expected, I have hardly yet, at a distance of ten hours, become calm.

I tell you, Speed, our forebodings (for which you and I are peculiar) are all the worst sort of nonsense. I fancied, from the time I received your letter of Saturday, that the one of Wednesday was never to come; and yet it did come, and what is more, it is perfectly clear, both from its tone and handwriting, that you were much happier, or, if you think the term preferable, less miserable, when you wrote it than when you wrote the last one before. You had so obviously improved at the very time I so much fancied you would have grown worse.

You say that something indescribably horrible and alarming still haunts you. You will not say that three months from now, I will venture. When your nerves once get steady now, the whole trouble will be over forever. Nor should you become impatient at their being even very slow in becoming steady. Again you say, you much fear that that Elysium of which you have dreamed so much is never to be realized. Well, if it shall not, I dare swear it will not be the fault of her who is now your wife. I now have no doubt that it is the peculiar misfortune of both you and me to dream dreams of Elysium far exceeding all that anything earthly can realize.

Far short of your dreams as you may be, no woman could do more to realize them than that same black-eyed Fanny. If you could but contemplate her through my imagination, it would appear ridiculous to you that any one should for a moment think of being unhappy with her. My old father used to have a saying, "If you make a bad bargain, hug it all the tighter"; and it occurs to me that if the bargain you have just closed can possibly be called a bad one, it is certainly the most pleasant one for applying that maxim to which my fancy can by any effort picture.

I write another letter, inclosing this, which you can show her, if she desires it. I do this because she would think strangely, perhaps, should you tell her that you received no letters from me, or, telling her you do, refuse to let her see them. I close this, entertaining the confident hope that every successive letter I shall have from you (which I here pray may not be few, nor far between) may show you possessing a more steady hand and cheerful heart than the last preceding it.

As ever, your friend,

LINCOLN.

A month passed and Lincoln had news from Speed that the marriage bells rang merrily. Speed wrote that he was far happier than he ever expected to be. To which Lincoln replied: "I know you too well to suppose your expectations were not, at least sometimes, extravagant, and if the reality exceeds them all, I say, Enough, dear Lord. I am not going beyond the truth when I tell you that the short space it took me to read your last letter gave me more pleasure than the total sum of all I have enjoyed since the fatal 1st of January, 1841."

Then he referred to Mary Todd for the first time in his letters to Speed, explaining why a piece of gladness could not live long with him. "Since then [the fatal 1st of January, 1841] it seems to me I should have been entirely happy, but for the never-absent idea that there is one still unhappy whom I have contributed to make so. That still kills my soul. I cannot but reproach myself for even wishing to be happy while she is otherwise. She accompanied a large party on the railroad cars to Jacksonville last Monday, and on her return spoke, so that I heard of it, of having enjoyed the trip exceedingly. God be praised for that."

As far as seventeen-year-old Sarah Rickard was concerned, his mind was easy; from her came no reproaches nor news of unhappiness. He wrote Speed: "One thing I can tell you which I know you will be glad to hear, and that is that I have seen Sarah [Rickard] and scrutinized her feelings as well as I could, and am fully convinced she is far happier now than she has been for the past fifteen months."

A flower had come with the Speed letter. "The sweet violet you inclosed came safely to hand, but it was so dry, and mashed so flat, that it crumbled to dust at the first attempt to handle it. The juice that mashed out of it stained a place in the letter, which I mean to preserve and cherish for the sake of her who procured it to be sent. My renewed good wishes to her in particular, and generally to all such of your relations who know me."

Three months later there came to Lincoln thanks and thanks from Speed for what he had done to bring and to keep them together. He wrote to Speed: "You make a kind acknowledgment of your obligations to me for your present happiness. I am pleased with that acknowledgment. But a thousand times more am I pleased to know that you enjoy a degree of happiness worthy of an ackowledgment. The truth is, I am not sure there was any merit with me in the part I took in your difficulty; I was drawn into it by a fate. If I would I could not have done less than I did.

"I always was superstitious; I believe God made me one of the instruments of bringing your Fanny and you together, which union I have no doubt he had foreordained. Whatever he designs he will do for me yet. 'Stand still and see the salvation of the Lord,' is my text just now. If, as you say, you have told Fanny all, I should have no objection to her seeing this letter, but for its reference to our friend here; let her seeing it depend upon whether she has ever known anything of my affairs; and if she has not, do not let her."

His reference to "our friend here" meant Mary Todd. Lincoln was now sure he had made a mistake first of all in not taking Speed's advice to break off his engagement with Mary Todd; and his second mistake was in not going through and keeping his resolve to marry her. "As to my having been displeased with your advice, surely you know better than that. I know you do, and therefore will not labor to convince you. True, that subject is painful to me; but it is not your silence, or the silence of all the world, that can make me forget it. I acknowledged the correctness of your advice too; but before I resolve to do the one thing or the other, I must gain my confidence in my own ability to keep my resolves when they are made.

"In that ability you know I once prided myself as the only or chief gem of my character; that gem I lost—how and where you know too well. I have not yet regained it; and until I do, I cannot trust myself in any matter of much importance. I believe now that had you understood my case at the time as well as I understood yours afterward, by the aid you would have given me I should have sailed through clear, but that does not now afford me sufficient confidence to begin that or the like of that again."

Such was the frank and pitiless self-revelation he did not wish Fanny Henning Speed to see unless she knew everything else along with it. He closed his letter, "My respect and esteem to all your friends there, and, by your permission, my love to your Fanny."

And in one sentence he had sketched himself, "I am so poor and make so little headway in the world, that I drop back in a month of idleness as much as I gain in a year's sowing."

One June evening he ended a letter to Speed, "Nothing new here. . . . I have not seen Sarah since my last trip, and I am going out there as soon as I mail this letter."

CHAPTER 56

MRS. SIMEON FRANCIS, wife of the editor of the *Sangamo Journal*, often invited a list of guests and entertained them in the parlor of the Francis house. She believed with her husband that Abraham Lincoln had a famous career ahead of him. Also she believed her friend Mary Todd to be a rare, accomplished, brilliant woman. In her eyes Lincoln and Miss Todd were a match; she would play her part as a matchmaker.

She invited Lincoln to a party in her parlor, brought the two of them together and said, "Be friends again." It was said that she told neither of the couple beforehand about her plan to have them meet again; it was said the meeting came to each of them as a surprise, and that neither Lincoln nor Miss Todd had any suspicions or advance information of the plan to bring them together to be told, "Be friends again."

Whatever of fate or woman-wit was at work, it did happen that they were friends again. But they didn't tell the world so. They had done that before. For a while their quiet meetings in the parlor of the Francis house were known only to Mrs. Francis.

Not even Mrs. Ninian Edwards knew what was going on till weeks had passed. Mrs. Edwards said later: "I asked Mary why she was so secretive about it. She said evasively that after all that had occurred, it was best to keep the courtship from all eyes and ears. Men and women and the whole world were uncertain and slippery."

Julia Jayne, a friend of Mary Todd, joined the quiet little parties in the Francis house. One day they read together an article written to be printed in the *Sangamo Journal*. It was a Whig attack on the state auditor of accounts, James Shields, who had issued an order that certain paper money, of which the people had more than they had of silver or gold money, would not be taken by the state government for taxes. Besides being a political attack on Shields as an official, it was a personal lampoon hitting at Shields's manners and clothes and struts in Springfield society.

Miss Todd and Miss Jayne told Lincoln to go ahead and have the article printed. It was written in the lingo of backwoods farmers, alluded to the state officials as "High Comb'd Cocks," asked whether Shields's $2,400 a year would be paid in paper money or silver, mentioned the penitentiary, and declared: "Shields is a fool as well as a liar. With him truth is out of the question; and as for getting a good, bright, passable lie out of him, you might as well try to strike fire from a cake of tallow." This, however, was only a beginning. There was this swift, marvelous cartoon:

If I was deaf and blind, I could tell him [Shields] by the smell. I seed him when I was down in Springfield last winter. They had a sort of gatherin' there one night among the grandees, they called a fair. All the gals about town was there, and all the handsome widows and married women, finickin' about trying to look like gals, tied as tight in the middle, and puffed out at both ends, like bundles of fodder that hadn't been stacked yet, but wanted stackin' pretty bad. And then they had tables all around the house kivered over with caps and pincushions and ten thousand such little knickknacks, tryin' to sell 'em to the fellows that were bowin' and scrapin' and kungeerin' about 'em. They wouldn't let no Democrats in for fear they'd disgust the ladies, or scare the little gals, or dirty the floor.

I looked in at the window and there was this same fellow Shields floatin' about on the air, without heft or earthly substances, just like a lock of cat fur where cats had been fighting. He was paying his money to this one, and that one, and t'other one, and sufferin' great loss because it wasn't silver instead of State paper; and the sweet distress he seemed to be in,—his very features, in the ecstatic agony of his soul, spoke audibly and distinctly, "Dear girls, it is distressing, but I cannot marry you all. Too well I know how much you suffer; but do, do remember, it is not my fault that I am so handsome and so interesting." As this last was expressed by a most exquisite contortion of his face, he seized hold of one of their hands, and squeezed, and held on to it about a quarter of an hour. "Oh, my good fellow!" says I to myself, "if that was one of our Democratic gals in the Lost Townships, the way you'd get a brass pin let into you would be about up to the head."

The article ended with declaring that if some change for the better did not come in state government, the taxpayers would not have a cow left to milk, "or a calf's tail to wring."

The name "Rebecca" was signed. It was followed by a second article also signed "Rebecca," this written by Miss Todd and Miss Jayne. Parts of it read: "Now I want you to tell Mr. S—— that, rather than fight, I'll make any apology; and if he wants personal satisfaction, let him only come here, and he may squeeze my hand. Jeff tells me the way these fire-eaters do is to give the challenged party choice of weapons, etc., which bein' the case, I'll tell you in confidence that I never fights with anything but broomsticks or hot water or a shivelful of coals or some such things; the former of which, being somewhat like a shillalah, may not be very objectionable to him. I will give him choice, however, in one thing, and that is, whether, when we fight, I shall wear breeches or he petticoats, for, I presume that change is sufficient to place us on an equality."

Shields was a bachelor, thirty-two years old, had been a lawyer ten years, and was born in Dungannon, County of Tyrone, Ireland. As a boy of fifteen in Ireland, he had challenged a veteran of Napoleonic wars to a duel. But when it came to the shooting the pistols wouldn't go off, the deadly enemies shook hands, and the veteran had taught Shields the French language as Shields later taught it when a school-teacher in Kaskaskia, Illinois. He asked the *Sangamo Journal* editor who wrote the articles and was told Lincoln took all the responsibility for them. Then Shields wrote Lincoln: "Whilst abstaining from giving provocation, I have become the object of slander, vituperation, and personal abuse. I will take the liberty of requiring a full, positive, and absolute retraction of all offensive allusions used by you in these offensive communications, in relation to my private character and standing as a man, as an apology for the insults conveyed in them. This may prevent consequences which no one will regret more than myself. Your ob't servant."

Lincoln's seconds notified Shields' seconds that the duel would be fought with cavalry broadswords, across a plank ten feet long and nine to twelve inches broad, within three miles of Alton, on the Missouri side of the Mississippi River. By horse and buggy, and by an old horse-ferry, the two parties traveled on September 22 to a sand-bar in the Mississippi River, located in the state of Missouri and beyond the reach of the Illinois laws against dueling.

Riding in a rowboat to the sandbar, Lincoln said he was reminded of the time a Kentuckian enlisted for the War of 1812. The sweetheart of the soldier told him she was embroidering a bullet pouch and belt for him to wear in battle and she would stitch in the words, "Victory or Death." He asked her, "Ain't that rayther too strong? S'pose you put 'Victory or Be Crippled'!"

Lincoln took a seat on a log and practiced swings and swishes in the air with his cavalry broadsword, while friends, lawyers, seconds on both sides, held a long confab. After the main long confabs there were shorter confabs with Lincoln and with Shields. Then a statement was issued declaring that although Mr. Lincoln was the writer of the article signed "Rebecca" in the *Sangamo Journal* of September 2, "yet he had no intention of injuring the personal or private character or standing of Mr. Shields as a gentleman or a man, and that Mr. Lincoln did not think, nor does he now think, that said article could produce such an effect; and had Mr. Lincoln anticipated such an effect, he would have forborne to write it; said article was written solely for political effect, and not to gratify any personal pique against Mr. Shields, for he had none and knew of no cause for any."

A crowd waiting on the Alton levee saw the ferryboat come near the shore with what seemed to be a man in blood-soaked clothes in the bottom of the boat. As the boat tied up they saw it was a log covered with a red shirt. The duel had become a joke. Lincoln and Shields came off the boat together, in easy and pleasant chat.

The weapon with which Lincoln was to have fought Shields was a good deal like the ax he had handled so many years as boy and young man. He told Bill Herndon: "I did not intend to hurt Shields unless I did so clearly in self-defense. If it had been necessary I could have split him from the crown of his head to the end of his backbone."

One man who made the trip to the sand-bar was asked how Lincoln behaved. He said: "I watched Lincoln closely while he sat on his log waiting the signal to fight. His face was serious. I never knew him to go so long without making a joke. He reached over and picked up one of the swords, which he drew from its scabbard. Then he felt along the edge of the weapon with his thumb, like a barber feels of the edge of his razor, raised himself to his full height, stretched out his long arms and clipped off a twig from above his head with the sword. There wasn't another man of us who could have reached anywhere near that twig, and the absurdity of that long-reaching fellow fighting with cavalry sabers with Shields, who could walk under his arm, came pretty near making me howl with laughter. After Lincoln had cut off the twig he returned the sword to the scabbard with a sigh and sat down, but I detected the gleam in his eye, which was always the forerunner of one of his yarns, and fully expected him to tell a side-splitter there in the shadow of the grave—Shields's grave."

The *Alton Telegraph and Democratic Review*, in an editorial said of the two chief figures:

Both of them are lawyers—both have been to the legislature of this state and aided in the construction of laws for the protection of society. Why, therefore, they should be permitted to escape punishment, we are at a loss to conjecture. We are astonished to hear that large numbers of our citizens crossed the river to witness a scene of cold-blooded assassination between two of their fellow-beings. It was no less disgraceful than the conduct of those who were to have been actors in the drama. Hereafter we hope the citizens of Springfield will select some other point than Alton.

Lincoln wrote to Josh Speed:

You have heard of my duel with Shields, and I have now to inform you that the dueling business still rages in this city. Day before yesterday Shields challenged Butler, who accepted, and proposed fighting next morning at sunrise in Bob Allen's meadow, one hundred yards' distance, with rifles. To this Whitesides, Shields's second, said "No," because of the law. Thus ended duel No. 2. Yesterday Whitesides chose to consider himself insulted by Dr. Merryman, so sent him a kind of quasi-challenge, inviting him to meet him at the Planter's House in St. Louis on the next Friday to settle their difficulty. Merryman made me his friend, and sent Whitesides a note, inquiring to know if he meant his note as a challenge, and if so, that he would, according to the law in such case made and provided, prescribe the terms of the meeting. Whitesides returned for answer that if Merryman would meet him at the Planter's House as desired, he would challenge him. Merryman replied in a note that he denied Whitesides's right to dictate time and place, but that he (Merryman) would waive the question of time, and meet him at Louisiana, Missouri. Upon my presenting this note to Whitesides and stating verbally its contents, he declined receiving it, saying he had business in St. Louis, and it was as near as Louisiana. Merryman then directed me to notify Whitesides that he should publish the correspondence between them, with such comments as he thought fit. This I did. Thus it stood at bedtime last night. This morning Whitesides, by his friend Shields, is praying for a new trial, on the ground that he was mistaken in Merryman's proposition to meet him at Louisiana, Missouri, thinking it was the State of Louisiana. This Merryman hoots at, and is preparing his publication; while the town is in a ferment, and a street fight somewhat anticipated.

And a story arose, and was told as true to fact by many friends of Lincoln, that a pompous and punctilious challenger had come to him from Shields and told him that honor would have to be satisfied by mortal and bloody combat in the medieval manner, saying, "As the challenged party you will have the choice of weapons—what will your weapons be?" Lincoln's reply was, "How about cow-dung at five paces?"

CHAPTER 57

THE year after Lincoln's broken engagement with Mary Todd and the months in which he was writing letters to nerve Speed up to get married in the year 1842, were times filled with a good deal of action for Lincoln. It was said of him in this time, "He went crazy as a loon."

Yet there were friends of his who knew that at this very time he was plunged deep in stretches of work that made him forget his troubles. The same medicine that he prescribed for the nervous debility of Joshua Speed and the melancholy of Fanny Henning, he was giving himself in big doses. Activity, occupation, were good for whatever ailed them, he had said, and he kept his grip on himself by doses of activity, occupation.

In the summer of 1841, he went into law partnership with Stephen T. Logan, and he learned law from Logan. Though Logan had frowsy hair, wore cotton shirts and heavy shoes, and never put on a necktie, he was one of the most neat, scrupulous, particular, and exact lawyers in Illinois when it came to preparing cases, writing letters, and filing documents. In law practice Logan knew how to be thorough, how to make results come from being thorough. From him Lincoln learned; the word "thorough" became important among his words.

He argued before the supreme court in the widely known case of Bailey vs. Cromwell. Cromwell had sold Bailey a negro girl, saying the girl was a slave. Bailey had given a note promising to pay cash for the slave. Lincoln argued, in part, that the girl was a free person until she was proven to be a slave, and, if she was not proven a slave, then she could not be sold nor bought and no cash could be exchanged between two men buying and selling her. The supreme court took practically the same view, and Lincoln won his case.

He did law work for a Rock Creek quarryman, Isaac Cogdal, and meeting Cogdal a few weeks afterward on the Statehouse steps, he saw the quarryman had one arm off. Besides losing his arm he was losing his business, Cogdal said. Lincoln took out his pocketbook and handed Cogdal the note Cogdal had signed promising to pay a fee for law work Lincoln had done. It didn't look just right for him to take the note, Cogdal was trying to say. "If you had the money, I wouldn't take it," blurted Lincoln, hurrying away.

Over in Tazewell County he met a crooked lawyer. An old farmer named Case sold a breaking plow and three yoke of oxen. Two boys named Snow signed notes promising to pay for the plow and oxen. But since signing the notes they had come of age. They admitted on the witness stand they were using the plow and oxen to break prairie, and that they had signed the notes. Their lawyer pleaded they were infants or minors when the notes were signed and therefore they could not be held to pay. Lincoln's speech to the jury stripped the other lawyer of his pretensions.

"Gentlemen," he said, "these boys never would have tried to cheat old farmer Case out of these oxen and that plow, but for the advice of counsel. It was bad advice, bad in morals and bad in law. The law never sanctions cheating, and a lawyer must be very smart to twist it so that it will seem to do so. The judge will tell you what your own sense of justice has already told you, that these Snow boys, if they were mean enough to plead the baby act, when they came to be men should have taken the oxen and plow back. They cannot go back on their contract, and also keep what the note was given for." The jury, without leaving their seats, gave a verdict for old farmer Case.

Between law cases he could think about newspaper items such as one in 1842, reading:

Mr. Adams presents to the Senate (Jan. 24) a petition signed by citizens of Haverhill, Mass., *for the adoption of measures peaceably to dissolve the Union,* and moves its reference to a select committee with instructions to report the reasons why the prayers should not be granted; Mr. Gilmer offers a resolution of censure upon Mr. Adams for presenting such a petition; Mr. Marshall offers a substitute declaring Mr. Adams' action the deepest indignity to the House and the people; violent debate ensues ten days, the resolution is laid on the table, reception of the petition is refused.

When Martin Van Buren stopped overnight in the town of Rochester, Illinois, a Springfield party took along Lincoln to help in a night of entertainment for the former President. The two main tavern performers that evening were Lincoln and Van Buren. Lincoln opened his big ragbag of memories of life in Illinois, Indiana, and Kentucky, while Van Buren told about New York ways and New York lawyers as far back as Hamilton and Burr. Lincoln, of course, had a thousand funny, pointed anecdotes such as the one of the farmer who moved so often that when he was going to move again, the chickens could tell it and walked up and lay down to have their feet tied; his father's story of the man who was asked for a warrantee bill of a horse he was selling and he guaranteed him "sound of skin and skeleton and free from faults and faculties"; and so on. Van Buren said his sides were sore from laughing.

Lincoln might have told of a judge who, trying to be kindly, asked a convicted murderer, politically allied to him, "When would you like to be hung?" Or of the lawyer jabbing at a hostile witness who had one large ear, with the remark, "If he bit off the other ear he would look more like a man than a jackass." Or of the old man with whiskers so long it was said of him when he traveled, "His whiskers arrive a day in advance." Or of Abraham Bale, the tall and powerful-voiced preacher from Kentucky, who was baptizing new converts in the Sangamon River just below Salem Hill; as Bale was leading a sister out into the water, her husband, watching the ceremony from the bank, called out: "Hold on, Bale! Hold on, Bale! Don't you drown her. I wouldn't take the best cow and calf in Menard County for her."

He could have told Van Buren how Bill Engle, the Campbellite preacher from Sugar Grove, and Fog Atchison of Petersburg, took to jolly bragging about which raised the fatter sheep; and Engle got the laugh on Atchison by saying: "I tell you, Mr. Atchison, I have the fattest sheep. An ox hooked one the other day and we rendered it up. It was all tallow and its tail made a tallow candle."

But one day there came news that hurt Lincoln. Bowling Green was dead. In the house over at New Salem, at the foot of the bluff with the timber of oak growth climbing up, lay the body of his friend, teacher, companion, with the life gone. This was the place where Nancy and Bowling Green had nursed him back to health, coaxed his mind to come back and live and be strong. There Nancy had prepared for him hot biscuits smothered in honey. And he had lain on their cellar door in the sunshine of cool autumn days reading Blackstone's Commentaries.

He rode out to the Green home; he stayed till the day of the funeral. Though he was not a Freemason, word came to him that the Masons, who were to conduct the funeral, wished him to make some remarks on the character and life of Bowling Green.

On the day of the burial the Masons in white aprons gathered in the Green cabin, the chaplain carrying the open Bible, the tyler his drawn sword and other regalia of the Masonic brotherhood. The master of ceremonies finally called Lincoln to the head of the coffin.

For a few moments Lincoln stood looking down at the still, white, round face of Bowling Green. He began to tremble, and there were struggles the length of his long, bony frame. He slowly turned and looked around; the room was filled with faces; in the doorways and at the windows were living faces looking at him, the faces of old New Salem and Clary's Grove and Sand Ridge and Wolf Creek friends.

A few words came off his lips, broken and choked words. Tears filled his eyes and ran down his cheeks; he gripped his hat, slowly lifted a handkerchief to his face, and smothered his face in the handkerchief. Then he turned to Nancy Green, who stood up from her chair and took the arm he offered her.

He stood with the widow, and slowly the tears came to an end and the struggles in the length of his long, bony frame came to an end. He looked toward the pallbearers; his hands calmly motioned them to take charge.

The lid was screwed on to the coffin, and Lincoln, with Nancy Green on his right arm, and his left hand in the hand of her granddaughter, followed the burial party to a corner of the farm where Bowling Green was laid away near the cabin he had built.

CHAPTER 58

At the meetings of Lincoln and Mary Todd in the Francis home, Miss Todd made it clear to him that if another date should be fixed for a wedding, it should not be set so far in the future as it was the time before. Lincoln agreed with her.

Early in October he wrote to his friend Speed, as a single man to a trusted married friend, asking for information:

You have now been the husband of a lovely woman nearly eight months. You are happier now than the day you married her. Returning elasticity of spirits is manifested in your letters. But I want to ask you a close question, "Are you in feeling as well as judgment glad that you are married as you are?" From anybody but me this would be an impudent question, not to be tolerated; but I know you will pardon it in me. Please answer it quickly as I am impatient to know.

A few weeks later, on the morning of November 4, 1842, Lincoln came to the room of his friend James Matheny, before Matheny was out of bed. And to Matheny under the quilts he said, "I am going to be married to-day."

On the street that day he met Ninian W. Edwards and told Edwards that he and Mary were going to be married that evening. And Edwards gave notice, "Mary is my ward, and she must be married at my house."

And when Edwards asked Mary Todd if what he had heard was true, and she told him it was true, they all started to make the big Edwards house ready—as best they could on such short notice—for a wedding of one of the Edwardses. Mrs. Edwards sent for her sister Frances, to bake a cake. The big house was swept and garnished—as well as possible on such short notice.

Lincoln watched carefully a plain gold ring he carried, on the inside band of which the jeweler Chatterton had engraved the words, "Love is eternal."

And he had a fleeting thought or two of his old honest, tried, rugged friend John Hanks of cornfield and flatboat days. He had written Hanks a week or so before:

Dear John:

I am to be married on the 4th of next month to Miss Todd. I hope you will come over. Be sure to be on deck by early candlelight.

Yours,

A. Lincoln.

At the Edwards house that evening, the Reverend Charles Dresser in canonical robes performed the ring ceremony of the Episcopal Church for the groom, thirty-three years old, and the bride, twenty-three years old. Behind Lincoln stood a supreme court judge, Thomas C. Brown, fat, bluff, blunt, and an able lawyer not accustomed to weddings. As Lincoln placed the ring on the bride's finger and repeated the form, "With this ring I thee endow with all my goods, chattels, lands, and tenements," the supreme court judge blurted out in a suppressed tone that everybody heard, "God Almighty, Lincoln, the statute fixes all that." The minister kept a straight face, became serious, and then pronounced Abraham Lincoln and Mary Todd man and wife in the sight of God and man.

Afterward came talk about the wedding, the bride, the groom. Jim Matheny said Lincoln had "looked as if he was going to slaughter." It was told at the Butler house where Lincoln roomed that, as he was dressing, Bill Butler's boy came in and wanted to know, "Where are you going?" Lincoln's answer being, "To hell, I suppose."

Mrs. Edwards said: "I am sure there had been no 'time fixed' for any wedding; no preparations had ever been made until the day that Mr. Lincoln met Mr. Edwards on the street and told him that he and Mary were going to be married that evening. The wedding guests were few; it was not much more than a family gathering. The entertainment was simple but in beautiful taste; the bride had neither veil nor flowers in her hair. There had been no elaborate trousseau for the bride, nor even a handsome wedding-gown; nor was it a gay wedding."

The bride's sister, Mrs. Frances Wallace, said: "The same morning they told Mrs. Edwards they were going to be married that night, she was terribly disappointed, for she could not get up a dinner in that short time. They asked me if I would help. So I worked all day. I never worked harder in my life, and in the evening we had a very nice little supper, but not what we would have had if they had given Mrs. Edwards time. Mr. Lincoln and Mary may have had a lovers' quarrel, for all I know. But I saw him the night he was married and he was not distracted with grief or anything else. He was cheerful as he ever had been, for all we could see. He acted just as he always had in company. No, no one stood up for him. Just he and Mary stood up alone, and Mr. Dresser married them. Mr. Herndon says that Mrs. Lincoln wore a white silk dress, but I know she never had a white silk dress. After I was married I gave her my white satin dress and told her to wear it till it got soiled but then to give it back

The forty-year-old congressman, A. Lincoln.   He writes Joshua Speed, "Being elected to Congress . . . has not pleased me as much as I expected."

Original photograph loaned by H. W. Fay of Springfield. Ill.

The Bronze Lincoln.

to me, for I wanted to keep all things like that—my wedding dress, you know. She was not married in the white satin. It was too soiled. She may have been married in a white Swiss muslin but I think it was not a white dress at all. I think it was delaine or something of that kind."

The Springfield *Journal*, in a corner of its third page on Nov. 11, 1842, had the item:

MARRIED—In this city on the 4th instant, at the residence of N. W. Edwards, Esq., by Rev. C. Dresser, ABRAHAM LINCOLN, Esq., to Miss MARY TODD, daughter of Robert Todd, Esq., of Lexington, Ky.

And Lincoln, in his law office five days after the wedding, sent a letter to Marshall at Shawneetown. He began the letter, "Dear Sam: Yours of the 10th Oct. enclosing five dollars was taken from the office in my absence by Judge Logan who neglected to hand it to me till about a week ago, and just an hour before I took a wife. Your other of the 3d Inst., is also received."

Then he discussed two law cases, and ended the letter: "Nothing new here, except my marrying, which, to me, is a matter of profound wonder."

In January the new husband wrote Speed: "Mary is very well and continues her old sentiments of friendship for you. How the marriage life goes with us I will tell you when I see you here." And in July: "We shall look with impatience for your visit this fall. Your Fanny cannot be more anxious to see my Molly [Mrs. Lincoln] than the latter is to see her, nor so much as I am—Don't fail to come—We are but two, as yet—"

CHAPTER 59

MORE than four years had gone by since William Trailor was in jail in Springfield, charged with murder, and men around the public square were growling about "the rope" for Trailor. Then Lincoln had helped turn up, alive and healthy, the man who was supposed to have been killed, having stood by his client during false accusations and threats of lynching. And the years passed and Trailor couldn't or wouldn't pay the fee of his lawyer and best friend in the hours a noose was knotted for his neck. And Trailor died a peaceable, homelike death—without having paid his lawyer, his valued counsel. And Lincoln sued the estate of William Trailor, and collected $100.00.

Cash of many kinds came into his hands. He wrote one client, "Walters has paid me $703.25 (in gold) for you." Or again, "We send you enclosed two one hundred dollar Missouri bills." Or, "He paid me $74 State Bank paper, $42 Shawneetown paper and $2.59 cents silver."

"We foreclosed on Walter's house and lots and sold them and bought them in your name," he wrote Joshua Speed.

Then among involved angles of the transaction for Speed, which included a secret contract, "It was sold for about $1,200, the amount of Van's debt, but although you are the ostensible purchaser, we have a secret contract with Van that he is the purchaser for so much of the purchase money as is over and above what will pay you."

Law practice, however, didn't have the charm for Lincoln in 1844 that he found in politics. He spent days studying the tariff issue, delivered hour-and-a-half speeches, and took such a leadership as a protective-tariff advocate in Springfield that the *State Register* referred to him as "the great Goliah of the Junto."

So earnestly did he consider himself the mouthpiece and exponent of the protective tariff that he kept up a running combat of argument against the opposition—took on all comers as he did in wrestling days. The *State Register*, a Democratic organ, told its readers on March 22 that a free-trade speech by Judge Caverly, a Democratic presidential elector, "so disturbed Mr. Lincoln that he promised to forfeit his 'ears' and his 'legs' if he did not demonstrate that protected articles have been cheaper since the 1842 tariff than before."

The ways of Lincoln as a "mixer" in politics were in a letter he wrote Alden Hall of Pekin:

SPRINGFIELD, Feby. 14, 1843.

FRIEND HALL:

Your county and ours are almost sure to be placed in the same congressional district—I would like to be its Representative; still circumstances may happen to prevent my even being a candidate— If, however, there are any Whigs in Tazewell who would as soon I should represent them as any other person, I would be glad they would not cast me aside until they see and hear farther what turn things take.

Do not suppose, Esq., that in addressing this letter to you, I assume that you will be for or against all other Whigs; I only mean, that I know you to be my personal friend, a good Whig, and an Honorable man, to whom I may, without fear, communicate a fact which I wish my particular friend (if I have any) to know.

There is nothing new here now worth telling.

Your friend as ever,

A. LINCOLN.

Sam Marshall wrote from Shawneetown complaining that Lincoln was careless about the Shawneetown bank cases and others. Lincoln explained that he had misplaced the letter about the bank cases and forgotten all about it. "The truth is, when I received your letter, I glanced it over, stuck it away, postponed consideration of the cases mentioned, and forgot them altogether."

In the case of Gatewood *vs.* Wood and Wood, he wrote to Marshall:

"We would have failed entirely to get into court but for an agreement with Mr. Eddy, which saved us. By the agreement we altered the record

Lincoln as a "mixer" in politics stands forth vividly in this letter to Alden Hall. Four months after his wedding he is actively hunting political support that might make him a congressman. He writes of his congressional district, "I would like to be its Representative," and indicates, "Circumstances may prevent my even being a candidate." And he assures the fellow party worker in a neighboring county, "I know you to be my personal friend, a good Whig, and an honorable man."

From the Original in the
Possession of Mrs. W. Halsted Vander Poel.

so as to make it appear that it had been sent to the circuit court, also agreeing that at the next term of court, all the papers and orders are to be altered then accordingly *nunc pro tunc*."

To beat the opposition in a case that honestly interested him, Lincoln would ambush the enemy with any trick or device within the law. In the Dorman-Lane case, for instance, he believed certain rascals were trying to take a piece of land away from a hard-working couple of young people who were getting a start at farming. He wrote Sam Marshall, his partner in that case, in 1845: "I think we can plead limitations on them, so that it will stick for good and all. Don't speak of this, lest they hear it, and take the alarm."

When the first baby came to the clients in that case, it was a boy whom they named Samuel Marshall. And they promised that if the second baby was a boy they would name it Abraham Lincoln.

CHAPTER 60

LINCOLN didn't forget the *State Register* warning about his "assumed clownishness." Herndon cautioned him; he carried jokes too far in public; it came too easy for him to slip out of his usual dignity, do a swift monkeyshine, and be back in his own face and character before men knew he was mimicking. On the stump and in courtrooms or hotel loafing rooms, he could be pointedly funny when feeling that way. He described weddings and funerals where the expected dignity of events was upset, incidents dealing with fiddlers, teamsters, mules, coons, skunks. One of his important proverbs was remembered from his father, "Every man must skin his own skunk."

He used words natural to farmers shucking corn in a cold November wind or carpenters putting the adze to oak rafters. He spoke of parts and members of the body in the words of common, hard-handed men, and often seemed to have some definite philosophy of human meekness, the frailty of mortal clay, the pride that goeth before a fall, the dignity whose assumptions suffer and wither in the catching of a greased pig.

When he had finished a story, he may have shocked or annoyed men who called themselves polite and who desired to be known as men of good taste, but other thoughtful men said there was always a point or a lesson or some genius of whim or nonsense connecting with the final strands of the tale or anecdote.

In the repertoire of characters he mimicked were circuit-riding preachers who snorted hellfire, Quakers, Irishmen, Germans, men of struts, and a stutterer who whistled between stutters. He could do a sketch of the drug-store man Diller irritated by little Judge Logan sitting in the store and whittling the chairs; Diller ordered Judge Logan out of the store; and the leader of the Sangamon County bar walked out in a huff saying he would never come back—though later he did.

He might compare the squabbling of politics and the howling of hostile factions to cats wailing with pain and spitting at each other at night outside the hotel rooms. In the morning perhaps the alley would be full of dead cats—so the sounds indicated. But in the morning the cats were at peace, with assured futures.

One hot day in July Lincoln drove his horse and one-seated gig from Bloomington to Tremont with Swett, a 200-pound man on one side of him, and Judge Davis, a 300-pound man on the other side. At Tremont he threw the livery-stable man the reins, calling out, "Put up that horse and let me get out of here quick." And he added a remark often recalled in that livery-stable, and often told among cronies of Swett. He mocked coarsely in a swift comic exclamation at his misery in a long drive on a hot day sitting between two sweating, odorous, large men.

One day in a courthouse on the Eighth Circuit, Lincoln rattled off a lingo changing the letters of words so that "cotton patch" became "potten catch" and "jackass" became "jassack." A dozen other words were given tricky twists. Some were strictly barnyard and tavern words—to be found published perhaps only in unexpurgated prints of Shakespeare and Burns. The court clerk asked Lincoln to write out a copy of it. And for many years that court clerk took special care of the scrap of paper on which Lincoln had scribbled a piece of nonsense.

Usher Linder said he noticed that Abe Lincoln and Abe's uncle Mordecai were a good deal alike as story-tellers. "No one took offense at Uncle Mord's stories. I heard him tell a bevy of fashionable girls that he knew a very large woman who had a husband so small that in the night she often mistook him for the baby, and that one night she picked him up and was singing to him a soothing lullaby when he awoke and told her that the baby was on the other side of the bed." Once when Linder was telling about Mordecai, Lincoln remarked, "Linder, I have often said that Uncle Mord ran off with all the talents of the family."

It was a horsey country of horsey men. A thirty- or forty-mile drive was counted an easy day. They spoke of one-horse towns, one-horse lawyers and one-horse doctors—even of one-horse horse doctors. They tied their horses to hitching posts half-chewed away by horse teeth. They brushed off horse hair from their clothes after a drive. They carried feed bags of oats. They spliced broken tugs with rope to last till they reached a harness shop.

CHAPTER 61

THERE were in 1846 in Springfield old settlers who remembered the Van Noy hanging twenty years previous in a hollow just south of where the new Statehouse was built. Van Noy stood in a wagon under the gallows, while the noose was put around his neck; the wagon drove off from under him and left his feet walking on air. These old settlers could tell about

Nathan Cromwell, who went with his good-looking wife to the home of a man who had said something to or about Mrs. Cromwell; and he pointed a pistol at the man's heart and made him get down on his knees and beg Mrs. Cromwell's pardon.

And there was a man whose name had been forgotten, though what happened to him was remembered. He had been drinking all day and on a cold winter night started to go home along the St. Louis road. A couple of rods south of the Masters cornfield, later the intersection of Grand Avenue and Second Street, he fell or was thrown from his horse, and in the morning was frozen stiff; Dr. Merryman was called and pronounced the man dead.

Only twenty years had passed since the first regular shoemaker, Jabez Capps, had located his shop and store on the north side of Jefferson Street between First and Second. The first harness-maker, Thomas Strawbridge, had come twenty-two years before. On the south side of Jefferson Street, near Second, stood a building that the old settlers pointed out as the first two-story brick store in Springfield; P. C. Canedy had opened his stock of books and drugs there sixteen years before. What had become northwest Jefferson and Second streets, a busy central corner of Springfield, was twenty-four years previous a piece of John Kelley's cornfield; on that spot had stood a log-cabin courthouse, the first county seat of Sangamon County. Away from it had swept the rolling prairie, a mile east and west, a half-mile north and south, bordered on the north by heavy timber and on the south by growths of pin oak, elm, cherry, and hackberry, with fringes of plum, crabapple, and haw trees, besides hazelbrush and blackberry bushes, festoons of grapevines and winding strawberry runners.

In the heavy timber that had once stood between First and Third streets, boys used to gather pawpaws and dig ginseng and turkey peas. One of those boys, Zimri Enos, could recollect how his father loved big oxen and drove them with only a hazel stick for a goad, and how in the winter of the deep snow, 1831, his two big yoke of oxen plowed through snow that horses couldn't travel and brought from the timbers loads of wood for people whose cabin fires had gone out.

So early the town of Springfield was beginning, as a town, to have a memory.

It was only twenty-five years since, in the log-cabin courthouse then at Jefferson and Second streets, John Kelley was allowed by the county commissioner the sum of $42.50 due him by contract for building the courthouse, and $5.00 for "extras." At the same time the county was divided into four districts, and overseers for the poor were appointed, two for each district, with three trustees appointed by the county court to supervise the overseers of the poor. Then Robert Hamilton was allowed $84.75

for building the county jail, which the sheriff, John Taylor, found to be a "no-account jail" and so told the county commissioners.

Since that time there had come a new courthouse, built of brick, in the middle of the public square, with a hip roof and cupola; it had cost $6,841.00, and was knocked down and carried off to make way for the new capitol, costing $240,000.00, nearly twice as much as was first estimated. And it was one of the settled memories of Springfield that the lawyer and politician, Lincoln, had log-rolled through the legislature the bill that located the capitol in Springfield. Besides Hoffman's Row, where Lincoln's office with Herndon was located, there was Chicken Row, a string of one-story shops and stores on another side of the square. But Hoffman's Row and Chicken Row were new. They were not of Springfield's past, to which the memories of old settlers ran.

They could recall how a near-by town named Sangamo, on a bluff of the river where Lincoln had built the Offut flatboat, had nearly won a decision from the county commissioners for the location of the county seat; and the commissioners had also come near to selecting for the county seat a town laid out by William S. Hamilton, a young lawyer who was the son of the famous Alexander Hamilton, and who had vanished after his plans were rejected. It was then that Elisha and John Kelley from North Carolina had named the town Calhoun, after the South Carolina senator, and it was so called until named after Spring Creek.

Along with some of the early settlers had come their slaves. The Kirkpatricks brought their colored boy, Titus, Colonel Thomas Cox his two girls, Nance and Dice, Daniel Curtwright his boy, Major, George Forquer, his boy, Smith. And Colonel Cox, who had come twenty-three years before, as Register of the Land Office, appointed by President Monroe, had bought out the Kelleys, put up a mill and distillery, and a hewn-log house with a hall and a brick chimney. Then debt and drink broke him, the law turned him out of house and home and he and his wife and two children took shelter in a deserted log cabin a mile and a half from town. First they had sold Nance and Dice, and the circuit-court clerk entered on the records that, on July 12, 1827, John Taylor bought at public auction the person, Nance, for $151.00, and the person, Dice, for $150.00, and the court commission was $15.40.

It was a later time that Erastus Wright came from Fort Clark to live in Springfield where he traded eighty acres of land for a tame elk that he rode and drove to harness like a horse.

CHAPTER 62

THE thirty-seven-year-old son of Thomas Lincoln and Nancy Hanks Lincoln had changed with a changing western world. His feet had worn deerskin moccasins as a boy; they were put into rawhide boots when he was full-grown; now he had them in dressed calf leather. His head-cover was a coonskin cap when he was a boy, and all men and boys wore the raccoon tail as a high headpiece; floating down the Mississippi to New Orleans he wore a black felt hat from an eastern factory and it held the post-office mail of New Salem; now he was a prominent politician and lawyer wearing a tall, stiff, silk hat known as a "stovepipe," also called a "plug hat."

In this "stovepipe" hat he carried letters, newspaper clippings, deeds, mortgages, checks, receipts. Once he apologized to a client for not replying to a letter; he had bought a new hat and in cleaning out the old hat he missed this particular letter. The silk stovepipe hat was nearly a foot high, with a brim only an inch or so in width; it was a high, lean, longish hat and it made Lincoln look higher, leaner, more longish.

As he had gone along farther in law practice and politics, he had taken more care of his looks. His first partner, John T. Stuart, was one of the handsomest figures and best-dressed men in Springfield; and Lincoln had to take Stuart's place once in a courthouse near Springfield, handling a case for a client; when Lincoln introduced himself as the man sent by Stuart to take Stuart's place, the client, an Englishman accustomed to wigs and gowns in a courtroom, refused to take Lincoln as his lawyer, snorted with disgust, and hired another lawyer.

And though Lincoln had begun wearing broadcloth and white shirts with a white collar and black silk cravat, and a suggestion of sideburns coming down three-fourths the length of his ears, he was still known as one of the carelessly dressed men of Springfield, along with Stephen Logan, who wore unbleached cotton shirts and had sat two years as a circuit-court judge wearing an unbleached cotton shirt with no cravat or stock.

The loose bones of Lincoln were hard to fit with neat clothes; and, once on, they were hard to keep neat; trousers go baggy at the knees of a story-teller who has the habit, at the end of a story, where the main laugh comes in, of putting his arms around his knees, raising his knees to his chin, and rocking to and fro. Those who spoke of his looks often mentioned his trousers creeping to the ankles and higher; his rumpled hair, his wrinkled vest. When he wasn't away making speeches, electioneering or practicing law on the circuit, he cut kindling wood, tended to the cord-wood for the stoves in the house, milked the cow, gave her a few forks of hay and changed her straw bedding every day.

He analyzed the tariff, the national banks, the public lands, and the annexation of Texas, while pailing a cow. One evening he went to where his cow was pastured with other cows, and as he told it: "I found the calves all together and away from the cows, and I didn't know my calf well enough to distinguish her from the others. Still, I picked out one that I thought was mine. Presently that identical calf went and sucked my cow, and then I knew it was mine."

He looked like a farmer, it was often said; he seemed to have come from prairies and barns rather than city streets and barber shops; and in his own way he admitted and acknowledged it; he told voters from the stump that it was only a few years since he had worn buckskin breeches and they shrank in the rain and crept to his knees leaving the skin blue and bare. The very words that came off his lips in tangled important discussions among lawyers had a wilderness air and a log-cabin smack. The way he pronounced the word "idea" was more like "idee," the word "really" more like a drawled Kentucky "ra-a-ly."

As he strode or shambled into a gathering of men, he stood out as a special figure for men to look at; it was a little as though he had come farther on harder roads and therefore had longer legs for the traveling; and a little as though he had been where life is stripped to its naked facts and it would be useless for him to try to put on certain pretenses of civilization. He could be immensely solemn, tenderly grave, quizzically humorous, and flatly comic. Some of the range of his feeling, the gamut of the solemn and comic, was registered in the angles of his body, in the sweeping lengths of extra long arms and legs, in the panther slouch of running and throwing muscles, in the wiry, rawbone frame that seemed to have been at home once handling an ax in tall timber, with the silent silhouette of an eagle watching.

Standing, Lincoln loomed tall with his six feet, four inches of height; sitting in a chair he looked no taller than other men, except that his knees rose higher than the level of the seat of the chair. Seated on a low chair or bench he seemed to be crouching. The shoulders were stooped and rounded, the head bent forward and turned downward; shirt-collars were a loose fit; an Adam's apple stood out on a scrawny neck; his voice was a tenor that carried song-tunes poorly but had clear and appealing modulations in his speeches; in rare moments of excitement it rose to a startling and unforgettable falsetto tone that carried every syllable with unmistakable meaning. In the stoop of his shoulders and the forward bend of his head there was a grace and familiarity so that it was easy for shorter people to look up into his face and talk with him.

The mouth and eyes, and the facial muscles running back from the mouth and eyes, masked a thousand shades of meaning. In hours of melancholy, when poisons of dejection dragged him, the underlip and its muscles drooped; his friends felt either that he then was a sick man with a disorder of bile and secretions or else that his thoughts roamed in farther and darker caverns than ordinary men ventured into. Ordinarily there was a fresh, gracious calm; it was a grave, sad calm, perhaps gloomy, but strong with foundations resting on substrata of granite; a mouth shaped with depths of hope that its fixed resolves would be kept and held. And between this solemn mouth of Lincoln and at the other end of the gamut, his comic mouth, there was the play of a thousand shades of meaning. Besides being tragedian, he was comedian. Across the mask of his dark gravity could come a light-ray of the quizzical, the puzzled. This could spread into the beginning of a smile and then spread farther into wrinkles and wreaths of laughter that lit the whole face into a glow; and it was of the quality of his highest laughter that it traveled through his whole frame, currents of it vitalizing his toes.

A fine chiseling of lines on the upper lip seemed to be some continuation of the bridge of the nose, forming a feature that ended in a dimple at the point of the chin. The nose was large; if it had been a trifle larger he would have been called big-nosed; it was a nose for breathing deep sustained breaths of air, a strong shapely nose, granitic with resolve and patience. Two deepening wrinkles started from the sides of the right and left nostrils and ran down the outer rims of the upper lip; farther out on the two cheeks were deepening wrinkles that had been long crude dimples when he was a boy; hours of toil, pain, and laughter were deepening these wrinkles. From the sides of the nose, angular cheek-bones branched right and left toward the large ears, forming a base for magnificently constructed eye-sockets. Bushy black eyebrows shaded the sockets where the eyeballs rested with gray transformers of action, thought, laughter. Shaded into the gray of his eyes was a tinting of hazel. In his eyes as nowhere else was registered the shifting light of his moods; their language ran from rapid twinkles of darting hazel that won the hearts of children on to a fixed baffling gray that the shrewdest lawyers and politicians could not read, to find there an intention he wanted to hide.

The thatch of coarse hair on the head was black when seen from a distance, but close up it had a brownish, rough, sandy tint. He had been known to comb it, parting it far on the right side, and slicking it down so that it looked groomed by a somewhat particular man; but most of the time it was loose and rumpled. The comb might have parted it either on the far right or on the far left side; he wasn't particular.

It was natural that Abraham Lincoln was many things to many people; some believed him a cunning, designing lawyer and politician who coldly figured all his moves in advance; some believed him a sad, odd, awkward man trying to find a niche in life where his hacked-out frame could have peace and comfort; some believed him a superb human struggler with solemn and comic echoes and values far off and beyond the leashes and bones that held him to earth and law and politics.

In his own mind he did not divide people into good people and bad people. As he walked from his own home close to the cornfields near the city limits of Springfield and met people on his way to the courthouse and the post office, and as he watched the two-legged figures on their many errands or, forgetting their errands, moving around the public square, he saw good mixed in the bad and bad mixed in the good.

In his own mind he made the note: "The true rule in determining to embrace or reject anything, is not whether it have any evil in it, but whether it have more of evil than of good. There are few things wholly evil or wholly good. Almost everything is an inseparable compound of the two; so that our best judgment of the preponderance between them is continually demanded."

CHAPTER 63

THERE are certain old poems, old stories, old books, clocks, and jack-knives, old rose and lavender keepsakes with musk and dusk in them, with a sunset smoke loitering in the faded shine of their walnut and mahogany stain and embellishment.

And we learn them by heart; we memorize their lines and outlines, and put them away in the chests and the attics of our memories, keeping them as keepsakes, taking them out and handling them, reciting their feel and rhythm, scanning their lines, and then putting them back till the next time they will be wanted, for they will always be wanted again.

Abraham Lincoln had such an old keepsake, a rhymed poem with stanzas having for him the sweet pathos of a slow, quaint tune hummed by a young woman to the auburn western sky of a late winter twilight. It spun out and carried further the hymn line, "Vain man, thy fond pursuits forbear."

It came from an old country across the sea and was written like an air from an old-fashioned spinet with its rosewood touched with a yellow tarnish. It was put together like some old melodrama that measures out life so that we want to cry as we look at it.

In the year he ran for Congress Lincoln sent William Johnston a copy of the poem, and later wrote him, "You ask me who is the author of the piece I sent you, and you do so ask me as to indicate a slight suspicion that I myself am the author. Beyond all question, I am not the author. I would give all I am worth, and go in debt, to be able to write so fine a piece as I think that is. Neither do I know who is the author." The poem read:

> Oh, why should the spirit of mortal be proud?
> Like a swift-fleeting meteor, a fast-flying cloud,
> A flash of the lightning, a break of the wave,
> He passes from life to his rest in the grave.
>
> The leaves of the oak and the willow shall fade,
> Be scattered around, and together be laid;
> And the young and the old, the low and the high,
> Shall molder to dust, and together shall lie.

The infant a mother attended and loved;
The mother that infant's affection who proved;
The husband, that mother and infant who blessed:
Each, all, are away to their dwelling of rest.

The maid on whose cheek, on whose brow, in whose eye,
Shone beauty and pleasure—her triumphs are by;
And the memory of those who loved her and praised,
Are alike from the minds of the living erased.

The hand of the king that the sceptre hath borne,
The brow of the priest that the mitre hath worn,
The eye of the sage, and the heart of the brave,
Are hidden and lost in the depths of the grave.

The peasant, whose lot was to sow and to reap,
The herdsman, who climbed with his goats up the steep,
The beggar, who wandered in search of his bread,
Have faded away like the grass that we tread.

The saint, who enjoyed the communion of Heaven,
The sinner, who dared to remain unforgiven,
The wise and the foolish, the guilty and just,
Have quietly mingled their bones in the dust.

So the multitude goes—like the flower or the weed
That withers away to let others succeed;
So the multitude comes—even those we behold,
To repeat every tale that has often been told.

For we are the same that our fathers have been;
We see the same sights that our fathers have seen;
We drink the same stream, we feel the same sun,
And run the same course that our fathers have run.

The thoughts we are thinking, our fathers would think;
From the death we are shrinking, our fathers would shrink;
To the life we are clinging, they also would cling—
But it speeds from us all like a bird on the wing.

They loved—but the story we cannot unfold;
They scorned—but the heart of the haughty is cold;
They grieved—but no wail from their slumber will come;
They joyed—but the tongue of their gladness is dumb.

They died—aye, they died—we things that are now,
That walk on the turf that lies over their brow,
And make in their dwellings a transient abode,
Meet the things that they met on their pilgrimage road

Yea, hope and despondency, pleasure and pain,
Are mingled together in sunshine and rain;
And the smile and the tear, the song and the dirge,
Still follow each other, like surge upon surge.

'Tis the wink of an eye—'tis the draught of a breath—
From the blossom of health to the paleness of death,
From the gilded saloon to the bier and the shroud
Oh, why should the spirit of mortal be proud?

Such was one of the keepsakes of his heart—written by a young Scotchman, William Knox, who died when he was thirty-six years old in Edinburgh in 1836. And a young Scotchman, Jason Duncan, had first shown it to Lincoln in New Salem days.

In the letter to Johnston, explaining that beyond all question he was not the author of the poem, he also wrote: "In the fall of 1844, thinking I might aid some to carry the State of Indiana for Mr. Clay, I went into the neighborhood in that State in which I was raised, where my mother and only sister were buried, and from which I had been absent about fifteen years. That part of the country is, within itself, as unpoetical as any spot of the earth; but still, seeing it and its objects and inhabitants aroused feelings in me which were certainly poetry; though whether my expression of those feelings is poetry is quite another question. When I got to writing, the change of subject divided the thing into four little divisions or cantos, the first only of which I send you now, and may send the others hereafter." The enclosure read:

My childhood's home I see again,
    And sadden with the view;
And still, as memory crowds my brain,
    There's pleasure in it too.

O Memory! thou midway world
    'Twixt earth and paradise,
Where things decayed and loved ones lost
    In dreamy shadows rise,

And, freed from all that's earthly vile,
    Seen hallowed, pure, and bright,
Like scenes in some enchanted isle
    All bathed in liquid light.

As dusky mountains please the eye
    When twilight chases day;
As bugle-notes, that, passing by,
    In distance die away;

As leaving some grand waterfall,
  We, lingering, list its roar—
So memory will hallow all
  We've known, but know no more.

Near twenty years have passed away
  Since here I bid farewell
To woods and fields, and scenes of play,
  And playmates loved so well.

Where many were, but few remain
  Of old familiar things;
But seeing them, to mind again
  The lost and absent brings.

The friends I left that parting day,
  How changed, as time has sped!
Young childhood grown, strong manhood gray,
  And half of all are dead.

I hear the loved survivors tell,
  How naught from death could save,
Till every sound appears a knell,
  And every spot a grave.

I range the fields with pensive tread,
  And pace the hollow rooms,
And feel (companion of the dead)
  I'm living in the tombs.

Five months later he again wrote Johnston, the letter reading:

FRIEND JOHNSTON: You remember when I wrote you from Tremont last spring, sending you a little canto of what I called poetry, I promised to bore you with another sometime. I now fulfill the promise. The subject of the present one is an insane man; his name is Matthew Gentry. He is three years older than I, and when we were boys we went to school together. He was rather a bright lad, and the son of the rich man of a very poor neighborhood. At the age of nineteen he unaccountably became furiously mad, from which condition he gradually settled down into harmless insanity. When, as I told you in my other letter, I visited my old home in the fall of 1844, I found him still lingering in this wretched condition. In my poetizing mood, I could not forget the impression his case made upon me. Here is the result:

But here's an object more of dread
  Than aught the grave contains—
A human form with reason fled,
  While wretched life remains.

When terror spread, and neighbors ran
   Your dangerous strength to bind,
And soon, a howling, crazy man,
   Your limbs were fast confined:

How then you strove and shrieked aloud,
   Your bones and sinews bared;
And fiendish on the gazing crowd
   With burning eyeballs glared;

And begged and swore, and wept and prayed,
   With maniac laughter joined!
How fearful were these signs displayed
   By pangs that killed the mind!

And when at length the drear and long
   Time soothed thy fiercer woes,
How plaintively thy mournful song
   Upon the still night rose!

I've heard it oft as if I dreamed,
   Far distant, sweet and lone,
The funeral dirge it ever seemed
   Of reason dead and gone.

To drink its strains I've stole away,
   All stealthily and still,
Ere yet the rising god of day
   Had streaked the eastern hill.

Air held her breath; trees with the spell
   Seemed sorrowing angels round,
Whose swelling tears in dewdrops fell
   Upon the listening ground.

But this is past, and naught remains
   That raised thee o'er the brute;
Thy piercing shrieks and soothing strain
   Are like, forever mute.

Now fare thee well! More thou the cause
   Than subject now of woe.
All mental pangs by time's kind laws
   Hast lost the power to know.

O death! thou awe-inspiring prince
   That keepst the world in fear,
Why dost thou tear more blest ones hence,
   And leave him lingering here?

If I should ever send another, the subject will be a "Bear Hunt."

Yours as ever,

A. LINCOLN.

Yet a short time later he did send Johnston twenty-two verses of a piece he called "The Bear Hunt," mixing the backwoodsman's slang with picked pet words from stylish English poets. Three verses get the bear running, nine verses have the bear chased, four have him fighting and dying, then six verses draw a moral and lesson. The piece read:

A wild bear chase didst never see?
Then hast thou lived in vain—
Thy richest bump of glorious glee
Lies desert in thy brain.

When first my father settled here,
'Twas then the frontier line;
The panther's scream filled night with fear
And bears preyed on the swine.

But woe for bruin's short-lived fun
When rose the squealing cry;
Now man and horse, with dog and gun
For vengeance at him fly.

A sound of danger strikes his ear;
He gives the breeze a snuff;
Away he bounds, with little fear,
And seeks the tangled *rough*.

On press his foes, and reach the ground
Where's left his half-munched meal;
The dogs, in circles, scent around
And find his fresh made trail.

With instant cry, away they dash,
And men as fast pursue;
O'er logs they leap, through water splash
And shout the brisk halloo.

Now to elude the eager pack
Bear shuns the open ground,
Through matted vines he shapes his track,
And runs it, round and round.

The tall, fleet cur, with deep-mouthed voice
Now speeds him, as the wind;
While half-grown pup, and short-legged fice
Are yelping far behind.

Abraham Lincoln of Illinois (left) and Alexander Stephens of Georgia (right). They were Whig congressmen together, and Lincoln once wrote Stephens, "This is the longest letter I ever wrote in my life." One weighed 180 pounds, the other 90 pounds. Jefferson Davis called Stephens "the little pale star from Georgia." *See* pages 377, 378.

The lawyer Abraham Lincoln (lower) and the Matamora Courthouse (upper left) and the Petersburg Courthouse (upper right).

And fresh recruits are dropping in
  To join the merry corps;
With yelp and yell, a mingled din—
  The woods are in a roar—

And round, and round the chase now goes,
  The world's alive with fun;
Nick Carter's horse his rider throws,
  And Mose Hills drops his gun.

Now, sorely pressed, bear glances back,
  And lolls his tired tongue,
When as, to force him from his track
  An ambush on him sprung.

Across the glade he sweeps for flight,
  And fully is in view—
The dogs, new fired by the sight
  Their cry and speed renew.

The foremost ones now reach his rear;
  He turns, they dash away,
And circling now the wrathful bear
  They have him full at bay.

At top of speed the horsemen come,
  All screaming in a row—
'Whoop!' 'Take him, Tiger!' 'Seize him, Drum!'
  Bang—bang! the rifles go!

And furious now, the dogs he tears,
  And crushes in his ire—
Wheels right and left, and upward rears,
  With eyes of burning fire.

But leaden death is at his heart—
  Vain all the strength he plies,
And, spouting blood from every part,
  He reels, and sinks, and dies!

And now a dinsome clamor rose,—
  'But who should have his skin?'
Who first draws blood, each hunter knows
  This prize must always win.

But, who did this, and how to trace
  What's true from what's a lie,—
Like lawyers in a murder case
  They stoutly *argufy.*

Aforesaid fice, of blustering mood,
  Behind, and quite forgot,
Just now emerging from the wood
  Arrives upon the spot,

With grinning teeth, and up-turned hair
  Brim full of spunk and wrath,
He growls, and seizes on dead bear
  And shakes for life and death—

And swells, as if his skin would tear,
  And growls, and shakes again,
And swears, as plain as dog can swear
  That he has won the skin!

Conceited whelp! we laugh at thee,
  Nor mind that not a few
Of pompous, two-legged dogs there be
  Conceited quite as you.

And from then on there seemed to be no more exercises of this kind. Lincoln quit his doggerel habit, writing to Johnston: "I am not at all displeased with your proposal to publish the poetry, or doggerel, or whatever else it may be called, which I sent you. I consent that it may be done. Whether the prefatory remarks in my letter shall be published with the verses, I leave entirely to your discretion; but let names be suppressed by all means. I have not sufficient hope of the verses attracting any favorable notice to tempt me to risk being ridiculed for having written them."

The mood of melancholy running through his verses could drop off him like a cloak, while he lighted with a quizzical look on his face. When his children were born, he chuckled. Even before the first one was born, in the months when the stork was promising to come, he joked Speed about the glad event coming. Speed first heard of the coming event from Bill Butler and so wrote Lincoln, who replied: "In relation to the 'coming events' about which Butler wrote you, I had not heard one word before I got your letter; but I have so much confidence in the judgment of a Butler on such a subject that I incline to think there may be some reality in it. What day does Butler appoint?"

And he countered: "By the way, how do 'events' of the same sort come on in your family? Are you possessing houses and lands, and oxen and asses, and menservants and maidservants, and begetting sons and daughters?" And he closed with, "Mary joins in sending love to your Fanny and you."

When the second boy came, he sketched the two of them and the family life for Speed. "We have another boy. He is very much such a child as Bob was at his age, rather of a longer order. Bob is 'short and low,' and I expect always will be. He talks very plainly,—almost as plainly as anybody. He is quite smart enough. I sometimes fear that he is one of the

A wild-bear chase, didst never see?
  Then hast thou lived in vain—
Thy richest bump of glorious glee,
  Lies desert in thy brain.

And furious now, the dogs he tears,
  And crushes in his ire—
Wheels right and left, and upward rears,
  With eyes of flaming fire—

But leaden death is at his heart,
  Vain all the strength he plies.
And, spouting blood from every part,
  He reels, and sinks, and dies—

And now a dinsome clamor rose,
  'Bout who should have his skin;
Who first draws blood, each hunter knows,
  His prize must always win—

But who did this, and how to trace
  What's true from what's a lie.
Like lawyers, in a murder case
  They stoutly argufy—

Lincoln writes doggerel, "The Bear Hunt."

From the original manuscript.

little rare-ripe sort that are smarter at about five years than ever after. He has a great deal of that sort of mischief that is the offspring of such animal spirits. Since I began this letter, a messenger came to tell me Bob was lost; but by the time I reached the house his mother had found him, and had whipped him, and by now, very likely, he is run away again. Mary has read your letter, and wishes to be remembered to Mrs. Speed and you, in which I most sincerely join her."

CHAPTER 64

LINCOLN and his law-partner, Stephen T. Logan, both had hopes of going to Congress; they didn't get along smoothly. Lincoln had left the partnership with regrets, for Logan was one of the foremost lawyers of the state and well started on a paying business. Logan had come to Illinois from Kentucky, a short sliver of a man, with a wrinkled, pinched face and tight lips. His head carried a thicket of frowsy hair, his voice rasped— yet he commanded attention when he spoke. He had been a circuit judge two years. That he should have picked Lincoln for a junior partner testifies that Lincoln had unusual ability or character of some sort. And that Lincoln should tell Usher F. Linder that he had an ambition to become as good a lawyer as Stephen T. Logan testified that Logan was far out of the ordinary as lawyers go.

During the two years they met so often and worked together in the same law office on the same cases, Lincoln had chances to dig through and get at that magic or whatever it was that made some people believe Logan could take apart and put together again that colossal box of devices called government. Logan knew how to be a lawyer so that people had fear and respect for lawyers; Lincoln had his chance to watch Logan every day, close up, to see how Logan did it. He was sorry to break with Logan. But one day something happened between him and Logan, so that he went to young William H. Herndon, who had read the law books in the office of Logan & Lincoln on the invitation of Lincoln, and had been admitted to the bar.

He asked Herndon to be his partner; Herndon didn't believe his ears; he said, "Mr. Lincoln, don't laugh at me." "Billy, I can trust you if you can trust me." They shook hands, opened an office, and hung out the shingle "Lincoln & Herndon." Lincoln was nine years the older; for ten years he had been seeing Herndon, off and on, watching the boy grow up to a young man. He knew that when a mob killed Lovejoy at Alton, the president of Illinois College at Jacksonville was with Lovejoy, and the college, faculty and students were blazing with Abolitionist ideas. Archer Herndon, the father of William, heard about it and said he wasn't going to have his boy grow up "a damned Abolitionist pup," and ordered him home to Springfield where he had clerked in Josh Speed's store; he and Speed and Lincoln slept in the same big room over the store and some nights talked each other to sleep.

Once Lincoln had asked Herndon as to slavery, "What tells you the thing must be rooted out?" The answer, "I feel it in my *bones*." And Lincoln sometimes mentioned issues, public questions, that had stood the test of "Bill Herndon's bone philosophy." They had an upstairs back-room office. There came the Abolitionist newspapers week by week stirring up Herndon, with the news of what the American Anti-slavery Society was doing, and the latest actions of the Liberty party. Though slight as a political organization, it had savagely swept Henry Clay out of the political reckoning in 1844, when Polk defeated Clay with the narrow popular majority of 38,801 and the Liberty party candidate got 62,270 votes which could have made Clay President.

For young Herndon there was far, passionate magic in words such as liberty, equality, brotherhood, justice, humanity. For him there was reality, driving and terrific, back of the phrase, "the cause of humanity." Sometimes the whole world of human struggle divided itself for him into two causes, the "high and noble cause," and the "low and degraded cause." Enthusiasms lighted torches in him and flung banners; a human cause must have bonfires of elation and faith. His father, Archer Herndon, was born in Virginia from Herndons who were in the Old Dominion as early as 1654, grew up in Kentucky, married, and moved to Illinois, arriving in 1821 in Sangamon County driving a one-mule cart, with the mother holding the two-year-old baby Billy. They stayed four years on a prairie farm five miles from Springfield and then moved to Springfield.

Herndon pictured the moving: "The whole way was clear bog; father made a small board cart, into which he threw the chickens, the little pigs, and the young children. He and I and mother walked beside the cart, which had two wheels. We skipped from hill to hill; and when the wheels of the cart stuck or floundered, we lifted them out of the mud and balanced them somehow on one of the hummocks. We reached Springfield at last. We had to build our log cabin on the edge of a ridge, while we labored to subdue the muck. The marks of bear's claws were deep in the trees right round us. Ten years later I killed a hundred snakes in three-quarters of a mile, so you may guess what it was then. There they all were: rattlesnakes, vipers, adders, and copperheads." "And what sort of a snake is the copperhead?" was asked. His answer was: "A mean thing. A rattlesnake rattles, a viper hisses, an adder spits, a black snake whistles, a water snake blows, but a copperhead just sneaks."

And he could go on with memories. "At nightfall we laid green logs in parallel rows, set them on fire, and drove the cattle between them. Then whichever way the wind blew, we could keep off the gallinippers, mosquitoes with stings three-quarters of an inch long. The dumb beasts knew what it meant and we never had to drive them again. They went in of themselves. Words cannot tell this life. The prairies of Illinois are watered with the tears, and enriched by the graves, of her women. The first generation lived on mush and pork. Fencing was too costly. No gardens could stand the herds of cattle, a thousand strong, which might come swooping over any minute. Just as our corn was ripe, the bears would strip the ears; just as the pumpkins grew golden, herds of deer would hollow out the gourds. As we got more land there was no transportation to carry away the crops."

Herndon was intense, sensitive, varied as his father and grandfather. His grandfather in Virginia had given slaves their freedom; his father in Illinois had stood fast with those who fought to make Illinois a slave state; a brother of his grandfather had married the youngest sister of Patrick Henry; his father had kept a store, had fought politically with those who tried to call a convention to change Illinois from a free to a slave state, and had put up the first regular tavern in Springfield. The son grew up in a tavern, had a tavern eye for judging people, and took pride in the way he could size up men by looking in their eyes. He was of medium height, rather rawboned, with particularly high cheek-bones, dark eyes set far back in the sockets, and the careless shock of hair on his head was a peculiar black, a sort of blue-black. He had picked up tavern learning, the names of drinks men called for, the talk of men who talk about cards, horse races, chicken fights, women. Yet he was full of torches, banners, bonfires, lighted for what he called the cause of freedom, justice, humanity.

As he and his senior law partner looked from the office window to the state capitol with its massive enigmatic walls, they had a good deal to talk about when there was time. And in their talk, one was always "Mr. Lincoln" and the other plain "Billy."

CHAPTER 65

ONCE in late summer, after showers had soaked the earth and sent the corn higher, Lincoln passed a cornfield a block from his home, meeting young Alexander Black, who noticed Lincoln had his head bowed forward, his chin at his breast, wrapped in thought. "He will pass by me without speaking," said young Alexander to himself. But as they met Lincoln's face lighted, he nodded his head, beckoned with a hand toward the field, and said, "This rain makes the corn laugh."

Toward the courthouse and the public square there were city lots where corn was growing; off toward the country were cornfields. The panorama of the ways of growing corn was before their eyes from the front yard and the back yard of the Eighth Street home.

Always, as the seasons passed from year to year, that panorama of corn was one of the immense facts. In the spring they saw the sweet, black loam turned over and laid in furrows, with a shine and a gleam on the strips of stiff dirt curved with a steel plow curve as they lay waiting for the seed kernels. As the weeks passed, the silk of this corn ran out of the opening where the ends of the husk wrappers met; and the sun tanned the cornsilk with darkening copper and maroon. The weeks came when the green corn was full-grown; the stand of the corn would hide a tall man if it was a good corn year. The ripened ears, the corn crop of the season, were ready for the shucking.

Then men came and tore off the ears, stripped the husks, and threw the red, white, and gold ears into wagons. It was harvest time. The stalks were cut close to the roots, piled, tied, shaped into patient, mysterious dummies that waited by dawn and noon till they were hauled away. The stumps of the stalks stood bare, marking the rows where the corn crop had grown.

The corn kernels had been shelled off cobs and saved as meal for men, and fodder for cattle, hogs, horses, chickens; they were the year's guarantee against hunger; they stood off famine and gave man a permit to live another year. Harvest time had come and gone. Afterward came the months when snow blew across the fields, and covered the stumps, and the fields were white and lonely.

CHAPTER 66

Two farmers, Samuel Wycoff and Dennis Forrest, came to see Lincoln one day. Each owned a quarter-section of land in Township Fourteen North of Range Six, West, in Sangamon County. They had a dispute concerning a small strip of land, each claiming it. And they agreed in writing to submit their dispute "to the arbitrament of Abraham Lincoln."

Two weeks later Lincoln handed the two farmers, who had come to him instead of a court, his decision, reading: "In pursuance of agreement, having fully heard the evidence, I decide that the land in dispute between Wycoff and Forrest belongs to said Wycoff, and that the old United States Surveyor's line, beginning at the West end thereof, and running thence Easterly as marked through the timber by said U. S. Surveyor, so far as the timber extends, and continuing the same course as so marked, the proper distance to reach the East side of the lands of said Wycoff and Forrest above described, shall hereafter be the dividing line between the said lands of the parties."

Once a jury picked by the Menard County sheriff got filled up with men of whom Lincoln said: "I would like to throw the whole panel out, for I know every single one of them; but I can't object to a man among them." It was a murder case, with Lincoln called in as a prosecutor. Two brothers named Denton had got into a dispute with a brother-in-law named Brown. They fought with axes; Brown was killed; the Dentons were the only witnesses.

During the trial, which lasted a week, Lincoln felt sure the jury wouldn't convict; he left the questioning of witnesses and the final plea to the jury with another prosecutor. And, as it happened, the jury freed the Dentons. Lincoln had sensed from the first that it would be uphill work to convict with that particular jury—and Lincoln never made much of a record when called in as a prosecutor.

Fine points in justice came before him. He pressed a claim of John Warner against John Calhoun, who had been his chief when he was a surveyor; he questioned Calhoun as to transfers and assignments of property. Then there was the case of Nancy Green, who had loaned $200.00 and got a note for it, but couldn't collect. She put it in Lincoln's hands. He had to collect it from Mentor Graham, the New Salem schoolmaster who had helped Lincoln learn the science of surveying and had loaned Lincoln books. Lincoln sued Graham, won the suit, but didn't force immediate payment. What he asked was that the schoolmaster should do his best to pay the woman. This was the second suit Lincoln won for Nancy Green, the first being a dissolution of her marriage-bond with Aaron Green.

He took a case to the supreme court, and wrote Marshall, his Shawnee-town friend: "At the request of Mr. Eddy, I got the judgment reversed. This was no business of yours, and I now only ask, as a favor of you, that if Mr. Eddy is well, you say to him I would like to have the little fee in the case, if convenient."

In the divorce case of Samuel Rogers *vs.* Polly Rogers, Lincoln represented the husband and advised that no charge of adultery be made. In the development of the case he filed an affidavit: "A. Lincoln being first duly sworn says that he was employed as counsel in the case of Samuel Rogers *vs.* Polly Rogers for a Divorce; that he, the affiant, drew up the complainant's bill; that said complainant at that time told this affiant that he could prove that the said defendant had been guilty of adultery with one William Short while she was living with said complainant; but that affiant advised said complainant not to make the charge in his bill as there was other sufficient grounds upon which to obtain a divorce, to-wit, absence of more than two years." In effect, Lincoln was ready to help his client get a divorce, but was not willing to make an unnecessary public record against the woman in the case.

In the same year Thomas McKibben came to Lincoln down in Coles County. Jonathan Hart had called McKibben a horse thief. Lincoln brought court action against Hart for slander, demanding $2,000.00 damages. The case was tried; McKibben was awarded $200.00; Lincoln was paid a fee of $35.00. And old Thomas Lincoln, the father of Abraham Lincoln, living in his log cabin out from Charleston, came in to town and was handed the $35.00, as required by Abraham Lincoln, who had left instructions with the clerk of the court thus to deliver the money to his father and get a receipt.

In Lincoln's Springfield office was an account book marked "Day Book of Lincoln & Herndon," in one place, and in another "Lincoln & Herndon's Fee Book." The fees in 180 cases for the year 1846 were entered, mostly by Lincoln; one fee was $2.50; two were $3.00; in 64 cases the charge was $5.00; in five, $7.00; in 63, $10.00; in five, $50.00; in one, $100.00; and in the remainder from $15.00 to $25.00. One entry read, "Scott *vs.* Busher (for Def't). To attending case in Menard Cir. Court if it ends where it is. Paid $20." Another case, tried before a justice of the peace, was recorded, "Negro *vs.* Robert Smith (for Deft.) To attending case of Negro Bob. J. P. $5.00."

His reputation was spreading as a man and lawyer of whom people said, "He'll be fair and square." He couldn't talk just to be talking. At a political meeting, where an orator was speechifying splendiferously with arms uplifted, and with a voice bawling and ranting neither fact nor argument, Lincoln turned to friends and said in an undertone, "Cut his galluses and let him go up!"

Lincoln couldn't talk against time if there was nothing to talk about. His quitting-time, for speaking, came earlier than for other lawyers. With nothing to say, he was dumb. In a criminal case he tried with Usher F. Linder, the two of them agreed that in the strategy of the case each should make the longest speech possible, and go on talking till he was used up. And, as Linder told it afterward, Lincoln's performance ran out of wind at the end of an hour, while he, Linder, rambled on in a three-hour speech to the jury.

A doctor at Matamora, Robert C. Lamson, said that he had learned from Lincoln, who had stayed overnight at his house several times, that it was a healthy habit to tell other people all he positively knew about one thing or a few things, and to say nothing at all about things he wasn't sure of. Of a patient doomed to pass away, Lamson used to remark, "He's got the can't-help-its," a phrase he said he had picked up from hearing Lincoln use it.

Homely phrasings of Lincoln often lingered and were repeated. The lawyer Bagby at Pekin told Lincoln of a lawsuit with a highly educated minister as the important witness. And the minister had an extra-fine sense of the distinctions and definitions of words. Bagby found the witness would not testify positively to things which Bagby knew that the witness knew. "I think so" and "I believe so" were the answers. Finally Bagby asked, "What do you mean by the expression 'I think'?" The witness answered at once, "That, sir, is the knowledge I have of my recollection of things of which I am not positively certain." He was then asked, "What do you mean by the expression, 'I believe'?" To which he just as smoothly answered, "That is the faith I have in the existence of objects of which I have a distinct recollection." Which made Lincoln chuckle, "He came out of the same hole he went in at."

Passions, deaths, reputations, the incessant and shifting forces of life, the stuff of the plays of Shakespeare and the books of Boccaccio and Rabelais, plain tales of life's surprises, put the stain of their designs on the parchments of Lincoln's law practice. Among his clients were descendants of Cain and Abel, of David and Bathsheba, of prodigal sons, of virgins who brought oil or came empty-handed.

CHAPTER 67

In the year 1843 a man named Robert Matson came from his home in Bourbon County, Kentucky, and bought a large tract of land in Coles County, Illinois, not many miles from the cabin of Thomas Lincoln in that county. Matson started farming his land, naming it Black Grove farm, bringing with him his slaves from Kentucky to plant and gather the crops. When the harvests were over he took the negroes back to Kentucky, working his Illinois land with a different gang of slaves each year.

One free negro, Anthony Bryant, stayed in Illinois from year to year, acting as foreman or overseer for Matson, studying the Bible at odd times, learning to spell his way slowly through some of the chapters. In the year 1847 Bryant's slave wife and four children were brought from Kentucky, and put to work on the Matson farm.

Matson's housekeeper, Mary Corbin, who was more than a housekeeper to him, one day exploded with anger and spoke terrible words to Jane Bryant, the wife of Anthony. "You're going back to Kentucky," shrieked Mary Corbin, "and you're going to be sold way down South in the cotton fields."

Anthony Bryant heard what seemed to be a death sentence on his wife, and drove as fast as horseflesh would let him to the village of Oakland, two miles away. There he talked to Hiram Rutherford, a young doctor from Pennsylvania, and Gideon M. Ashmore, from the Duck River country of Tennessee. And in the middle of that night Anthony Bryant, his wife and one child, on horseback, and three children on foot, arrived at the Ashmore home in Oakland. They stayed at the Ashmore home several days while Robert Matson and his friend, Joseph Dean, argued and threatened. Then Matson went before William Gilman, justice of the peace, swore that the negro woman and her children were his property, and they were arrested and locked up in the county jail at Charleston.

Squire Gilman heard the arguments of Orlando B. Ficklin for the negroes, and of Usher F. Linder for Matson. The squire decided he didn't have authority on the question of freedom or slavery for the negroes, and turned the prisoners back into the hands of the sheriff. After the Bryant woman and her children had spent forty-eight days in jail, the sheriff, A. G. Mitchell, put into the hands of lawyers a bill to be collected from Matson. The main item read, "To keeping and dieting five negroes forty-eight days at 37 cents per day, $107.30."

Next, Matson was arrested and convicted, the charge being that he had lived unlawfully with Mary Corbin, a woman not his wife. After that Matson brought an action against Rutherford and Ashmore, claiming damages for the unlawful seizure and holding of his property, negro slaves.

The main action came when Matson went into circuit court, demanding the release of his property on grounds of habeas corpus and calling for $2,500.00 damages from Rutherford, valuing the slaves at $500.00 apiece. When the summons in the case was served on Rutherford he rode to Charleston, found Abraham Lincoln sitting tilted in a chair on the tavern veranda, interrupted as Lincoln had finished telling one story and was going to start on another, and they went to one side for a talk.

As Rutherford told his troubles, he noticed Lincoln growing sober, sad, looking far off, shaking his head in a sorry way. "At length, and with apparent reluctance, Lincoln answered that he could not defend me, because he had already been counselled with in Matson's interest," said Rutherford, later. "This was a grievous disappointment and irritated me into expressions more or less bitter in tone. He seemed to feel this, and endeavored in his plausible way to reconcile me to the proposition that, as a lawyer, he must represent and be faithful to those who counsel with and employ him. I appeared not to be convinced, retorting that 'my money was as good as any one's else.' Although thoroughly in earnest I presume I was a little hasty."

A few hours later Lincoln sent a message to Rutherford, and followed the first message quickly with a second. "The interview and my quick temper," said Rutherford, "made a deep impression on Mr. Lincoln, I am sure, because he dispatched a messenger to me with the information that he had sent for the man who had approached him in Matson's behalf, and if they came to no more decisive terms than at first he would probably be able to represent me. In a very brief time this was followed by another message, that he could now easily and consistently free himself from Matson and was, therefore, in a position if I employed him to conduct my defense. But it was too late; my pride was up, and I plainly indicated a disinclination to avail myself of his offer. Instead, I employed Charles H. Constable, a lawyer who had emigrated to Illinois from Maryland, a classical scholar, fluent and ready in debate, and of commanding physical presence. Ashmore made terms with Orlando B. Ficklin, a Kentuckian, who had won renown as a lawyer."

The case came to trial before Judges Willson and Treat, of the supreme court of the state, with Lincoln and Usher F. Linder as counsel for Matson. Farm hands went on the witness stand for Matson and swore he had told them at the time he brought the slaves to his Illinois land that he didn't intend to keep them there permanently.

It seemed as though Matson's lawyers expected to win by showing that Matson had no plans for permanently locating slaves in Illinois. And yet, when Lincoln presented his statements for Matson, they sounded like a searching inquiry into the cold facts and the elemental justice of the case, rather than an argument for a plaintiff. A Coles County lawyer, D. F. McIntyre, got the impression that Lincoln was clumsy at handling the case in favor of his client. He made no attack on the defense, no attempt to batter down the points of the opposition, and practically gave his case away by the outright admission that if the Kentucky slave owner had brought his slaves to Illinois for the purpose of working them and using them as slaves on the Coles County farm, the negroes were thereby entitled to freedom. McIntyre noted that Lincoln said the whole case turned on one point. "Were these negroes passing over and crossing the State, and thus, as the law contemplates, *in transitu*, or were they actually located by consent of their master? If only crossing the State, that act did not free them, but if located, even indefinitely, by the consent of their owner and master, their emancipation logically followed. It is, therefore, of the highest importance to ascertain the true purpose and intent of Matson in placing these negroes on the Black Grove farm."

McIntyre noted further: "When Mr. Lincoln arose to make the closing argument, all eyes were fixed upon him. Every person in the court room was curious to hear what reasons he could or would assign, in behalf of this slave holder, to induce the court to send this mother and her four children back into lives of slavery. But strange to say Lincoln did not once touch upon the question of the right of Matson to take the negroes back to Kentucky. His main contention was that the question of the right of the negroes to their freedom could only be determined by a regular habeas corpus proceeding."

Judge Willson leaned forward over the bar and asked: "Mr. Lincoln, your objection is simply to the form of the action by which, or in which this question should be tried, is it not?" "Yes, sir."

Then came the high point of the day for Lincoln. Judge Willson asked: "Now, if this case was being tried on issue joined in a habeas corpus, and it appeared there, as it does here, that this slave owner had brought this mother and her children, voluntarily, from the State of Kentucky, and had settled them down on his farm in this State, do you think, as a matter of law, that they did not thereby become free?" And Lincoln answered, "No, sir, I am not prepared to deny that they did."

Linder then argued, for Matson, that slaves were chattel property, the

Federal Constitution protected such property, and it could not lawfully
be taken from him. But the court decree on October 17, 1847, declared
Jane Bryant and her four children "are discharged from the custody as
well of the Sheriff as of Robert Matson and all persons claiming them as
slaves, and they shall be and remain free from all servitude whatever to
any person or persons from henceforward and forever."

And Matson quietly slipped away toward the Wabash River, quit the
county, and without paying Lincoln his fee. Rutherford saw Lincoln leave
Charleston for the next county on the circuit. "As he threw across the
animal's back his saddlebags, filled with soiled linen and crumpled court
papers, and struck out across the prairie, he gave no sign of any regret
because, as a lawyer, he had upheld the cause of the strong against the
weak." Thus spoke Rutherford, who had put up the barriers after Lincoln had gone the limit trying to break into the case on the side he preferred.

As Lincoln straddled his gray mare and rode in the October prairie
haze, he might have recalled the remark he once made to a lawyer who had
asked him to go in on a case he didn't believe in, and he had said: "You'll
have to get some other fellow to win this case for you. I couldn't do it.
All the while I'd be talking to that jury I'd be thinking, 'Lincoln, you're
a liar,' and I believe I should forget myself and say it out loud."

CHAPTER 68

FOUR years after his marriage to Mary Todd, Lincoln was thirty-seven
years old, and getting ready to leave Springfield to go to Washington,
D.C., to sit, vote, and speak as the one and only Whig congressman
elected from the state of Illinois. He had become what was called a public
man.

Mary Todd had borne him two children, the first in 1843 named Robert
Todd, the second in 1846 named Edward Baker. She, the daughter of a
Kentucky bank president, had married him with all his debts; they had
started their married life as two boarders and roomers at four dollars a
week in the Globe Tavern. Though he was still not out of debt, and still
paying installments on the old debts from New Salem days when his
grocery store winked out into bankruptcy, they had bought a house and
lot on Eighth and Jackson streets, a few blocks from the public square,
with a story-and-a-half frame house on it.

His run for congressman was against Peter Cartwright, an old-fashioned circuit rider, famous as an evangelist and exhorter and a Jackson
Democrat. Years before little Abe Lincoln had helped his father at chopping logs for their cabin near Little Pigeon Creek, in Indiana, Cartwright
had rode the Salt River circuit with Bible and rifle; if a sinner came in

drunk and interrupted the sermon Cartwright jumped from the pulpit and personally threw him out; a deacon spoke a cold, precise, correct prayer and Cartwright had to say, "Brother, three prayers like that would freeze hell over"; he had a contempt for Yankees and snorted that they were "imps who eat oysters." When a presiding elder at a church meeting in Tennessee whispered to Cartwright, pointing out a visitor, "That's Andrew Jackson," the reply was: "And who's Andrew Jackson? If he's a sinner God'll damn him the same as he would a Guinea nigger."

Cartwright was twenty-four years older than Lincoln, and, besides his own children and grandchildren, he could count on political support from a big personal acquaintance including not only church members who believed in his religious faith but also sinners who admired the swift, clean way he could throw disturbers out of church. The people farther east with their mansions, elegance, and fashions, New York with its dancers from Paris, roused sarcasm from him; he was proud of the human stuff of Kentucky and Illinois; the Democrats picked him as the one man who had the best chance of taking the Springfield district away from the Whigs.

Cartwright's men spread reports during the campaign that Lincoln's wife was a high-toned Episcopalian, that Lincoln in a temperance speech in Springfield had said that drunkards are as good as Christians and church members, that Lincoln was a "deist" who believed in God but did not accept Christ and the doctrines of atonement and punishment, that Lincoln said, "Christ was a bastard." Lincoln made speeches and electioneered personally over the district, wrote many letters, and near the end of the campaign was sure he would win. Months earlier a Democratic friend said that he did not like to vote against his party but he would vote for Lincoln if Lincoln told him the vote was needed. A few days before election Lincoln told him, "I have got the preacher, and I don't want your vote."

In spite of warnings he went anyhow to a religious meeting where Cartwright was to preach. In due time Cartwright said, "All who desire to lead a new life, to give their hearts to God, and go to heaven, will stand," and a sprinkling of men, women, and children stood up. Then the preacher exhorted, "All who do not wish to go to hell will stand." All stood up— except Lincoln. Then said Cartwright in his gravest voice, "I observe that many responded to the first invitation to give their hearts to God and go to heaven. And I further observe that all of you save one indicated that you did not desire to go to hell. The sole exception is Mr. Lincoln, who did not respond to either invitation. May I inquire of you, Mr. Lincoln, where you are going?"

And Lincoln slowly rose and slowly spoke. "I came here as a respectful listener. I did not know that I was to be singled out by Brother Cartwright. I believe in treating religious matters with due solemnity. I admit that the questions propounded by Brother Cartwright are of great importance. I did not feel called upon to answer as the rest did. Brother Cartwright asks me directly where I am going. I desire to reply with equal directness: I am going to Congress." The meeting broke up.

Two years before this campaign Lincoln had met charges somewhat like those of Cartwright's supporters. At that time he was seeking nomination for Congress and the friends of Edward D. Baker brought several points against him. He wrote to a friend: "It would astonish if not amuse the older citizens to learn that I (a strange, friendless, uneducated, penniless boy, working on a flatboat at ten dollars a month) have been put down here as the candidate of pride, wealth, and aristocratic family distinction. Yet so, chiefly, it was. Baker is a Campbellite, and therefore, as I suppose, got all that church. My wife has some relations in the Presbyterian churches and some with the Episcopalian churches, and therefore, wherever it would tell, I was set down as either one or the other, while it was everywhere contended that no Christian ought to go for me, because I belonged to no church, was suspected of being a deist, and had talked about fighting a duel." He and Baker were good personal friends and he made it clear that Baker had nothing to do with the politics of personal misrepresentation.

One day the campaign tale again was told to him in a store in Springfield that he belonged to a proud family and his aristocratic relatives came to visit him. And A. Y. Ellis said he heard Lincoln explain: "That sounds strange to me because I do not remember of but one who ever came to see me, and while he was in town he was accused of stealing a jew's-harp."

He wrote letters; he sat at a desk, dipped a quill pen into an ink bottle and wrote to editors, politicians, voters, precinct workers. And there was a deadly accuracy to his letters; he put things in an exact way that what he meant could be clearly understood; if it was a promise he made it as specific as possible, telling just what he could do and what he couldn't do in filling the promise; if it was a compliment what there was to it was all there, entirely sincere, standing up under the test of repeated reading.

As he would finish a sentence or a paragraph he read it out loud usually to see how it would sound; the sound of words helped him see more clearly just what he was saying. Often he wrote in a pinched, crabbed, labored style, bringing in details of fact, and citing arrays of facts, but when the letter was finished all the crabbed details massed together into a smooth, compact surface that made a truthful letter, a letter that he could stand by afterward.

Ink bottles were emptied and filled again as he wrote piles of letters, with his eye on a seat in Congress. "I have written to three or four of the most active Whigs in each precinct of the county," he wrote a friend in Marshall County.

The man he had had to beat for the nomination was Hardin. And he had only compliments for Hardin in a letter to B. F. James: "Hardin is a man of desperate energy and perseverance, and one that never backs out; and, I fear, to think otherwise is to be deceived in the character of our adversary." He reckoned the counties for and against his nomination: "I can possibly get Cass, but I do not think I will. Morgan and Scott are beyond my reach; Menard is safe to me; Mason neck and neck; Logan is mine. I suppose Tazewell is safe. Keep your eyes continually on Woodford and Marshall. Let no opportunity of making a mark escape. When they shall be safe, all will be safe, I think." A newspaper said he should be nominated for governor; he let it be understood he wished to be mentioned for governor if the mention would help him go to Congress; the goal was Congress.

A movement against Lincoln was on foot in a town; he wrote the editor of the paper there, "I want you to let nothing prevent your getting an article in your paper of this week." He could appeal frankly, "If your feelings toward me are the same as when I saw you (which I have no reason to doubt), I wish you would let nothing appear in your paper which may operate against me. You understand. Matters stand just as they did when I saw you."

The blunt little sentence crept in often, "You understand." Some letters ended, "Confidential, of course," or "Don't speak of this, lest they hear of it," or "For your eye only." There were times to travel in soft shoes. "It is my intention to take a quiet trip through the towns and neighborhoods of Logan County, Delevan, Tremont, and on to and through the upper counties. Don't speak of this, or let it relax any of your vigilance. When I shall reach Tremont, we will talk everything over at large."

A direct personal appeal was phrased, "I now wish to say to you that if it be consistent with your feelings, you would set a few stakes for me." No personal feelings against Hardin must be permitted. "I do not certainly know, but I strongly suspect that General Hardin wishes to run again. I know of no argument to give me a preference over him, unless it be 'Turn about is fair play.'" And again, to another: "It is my intention to give him [Hardin] the trial, unless clouds should rise, which are not yet discernible. This determination you need not, however, as yet, announce in your paper, at least as not coming from me. In doing this, let nothing be said against Hardin. Nothing deserves to be said against him. Let the pith of the whole argument be, 'Turn about is fair play.'"

If a man had promised not to take sides in a fight, he wanted that man to stay put. "Now tell me, is Morris going it openly? You remember you wrote me that he would be neutral." And in fixing up political fences it would be worth while to know who was trying to tear the fences down. "Nathan said that some man, who he could not remember, had said lately that Menard County was going to decide the contest and that that made the contest very doubtful. Do you know who that was? Don't fail to write me instantly on receiving, telling me all—particularly the names of those who are going strong against me."

There must be harmony, joint purpose; a regiment of political workers facing an enemy must not fight among themselves. "Previous to General Hardin's withdrawal some of his friends and some of mine had become a little warm; and I felt, and meant to say, that for them now to meet face to face and converse together was the best way to efface any remnant of unpleasant feeling, if any such existed. I did not suppose that General Hardin's friends were in any greater need of having their feelings corrected than mine were. Since I saw you at Jacksonville, I have had no more suspicion of the Whigs of Morgan than of those of any other part of the District. I write this only to try to remove any impression that I distrust you and the other Whigs of your county." In politics there are insinuations published in newspapers not worth answering. "So far as this communication may relate to the convention, I prefer that your paper let it 'stink and die' unnoticed." He took on debaters as carelessly as in the Black Hawk War he took on wrestlers. "If alive and well I am sure to be with you on the 22d. I will meet the trio of mighty adversaries you mention, in the best manner I can."

Besides keeping track of neighborhood politics, the hundreds of names of men for and against him, he was following national drifts with an eye for the big facts. In a Whig circular of which he was the chief writer, he discussed the tariff and national banking and public lands, and, arguing against low prices for state and Government lands, said: "By the time one of the original new States (Ohio, for example) becomes populous and gets weight in Congress, the public lands in her limits are so nearly sold out that in every point material to this question she becomes an old State. She does not wish the price reduced, because there is none left for her citizens to buy."

Chairmen at political meetings introduced him as an Illinois man known from Galena at the north to Cairo in the south, from the Mississippi River on the west to the Wabash on the east.

He had campaigned in Indiana for Henry Clay for President, and when he made his speech in Gentryville, his old employer, Josiah Crawford, was in a front seat, proud of the boy that had husked corn in his fields. Crawford noticed Lincoln didn't use books nor read statistics in his speech; he wanted to know, "Where's your books, Abe?" And Abe laughed, "It's my stuckout lip." They smiled, remembering the days and nights when the boy pushed out his underlip while tussling with a book to get at its meanings.

He had gone to Kentucky and talked with Henry Clay, and grasped Henry Clay's hand, and he had found Henry Clay a little different from what he had expected, colder, stiffer, more precise, farther from the people than he had imagined.

He had seen the word "roorback" come into the American language. The Whigs used a story that James K. Polk, the Democratic nominee for President in 1844, had marched a gang of slaves South to be sold, each slave branded "J.K.P.," saying the story came from a travel book written by Baron von Roorback.

Lincoln was going to Washington to sit, to speak, and to vote under the big white dome, the only Whig congressman from a state in a rough triangle between Lake Michigan, the Mississippi River, and the Wabash. His letters, appeals, speeches, conversations, and explanations had gone to the eyes and ears of thousands of people; he had poured himself out tirelessly to be a congressman. He had written to Richard Thomas of the town of Virginia, "If you should hear any one say that Lincoln don't want to go to Congress, I wish you, as a personal friend of mine, would tell him that you have reason to believe him mistaken. The truth is, I would like to go very much."

He was now what was called a public man; he was trying to read the mind and the feelings of the public, to look under surface currents and find the deep important drifts, and to connect public opinion and feeling with politics. He was reading faces, voices, and whispers; he listened for insinuations, pretensions, truths, in the little changes to be seen and heard in the faces, voices, whispers, he met. He was trying to learn how to tell what men want to live for and what they are willing to die for, by what was spoken in faces, voices, whispers.

While his campaign for Congress was on, some Whig friends clubbed together and raised $200.00 and handed it to him for personal campaign expenses. After the election he handed them back $199.25, saying he had spent only 75 cents in the campaign. "I did not need the money. I made the canvass on my own horse; my entertainment, being at the houses of friends, cost me nothing; and my only outlay was 75 cents for a barrel of cider, which some farmhands insisted I should treat to." The count of ballots had given Lincoln 6,340 votes, Cartwright 4,829, and Walcott (Abolitionist) 249.

He had been elected to Congress and was to go to the halls where Clay, Webster, Calhoun had spoken and reached the ears of the nation; after hundreds of speeches and letters, after thousands of handshakes, after scheming and waiting and struggling, he had become a congressman; and he wrote Josh Speed, "Being elected to Congress, though I am very grateful to our friends for having done it, has not pleased me as much as I expected."

CHAPTER 69

NEARLY a year had passed between the time of Lincoln's election to Congress and his going to Washington. He watched and waited. War began with Mexico. Rifle companies of young men who had drilled regularly, and marched in processions on the Fourth of July, were offering themselves for service; of 8,370 volunteers in Illinois only 3,720 could be taken; they went down the Mississippi, across the Gulf to Texas, and on into Mexico; they were writing letters back home about occasional deer-meat and wild grapes as a change from rations of pork and beans; they were writing about plantations, sugar cane, cypress trees, Spanish moss, prickly pear and cholla, tarantulas and Texans.

Edward D. Baker had raised a regiment, received a commission as colonel, and gone to Mexico. John J. Hardin, whose seat in Congress Lincoln was to take, was killed while leading his regiment in a charge at the battle of Buena Vista. The third and fourth regiments of Illinois volunteers distinguished themselves in the campaign against the City of Mexico and in the Battle of Cerro Gordo. James Shields, challenger of Lincoln to a duel, received wounds at Cerro Gordo. Two of the three Illinois colonels at Buena Vista were killed.

In Washington the young congressman, Stephen A. Douglas, spoke for aggressive war against Mexico. John Quincy Adams wrote of Douglas in his diary, "In the midst of his roaring, to save himself from choking, he stript off and cast away his cravat, unbuttoned his waistcoat, and had the air and aspect of a half-naked pugilist." Douglas quoted from General Andrew Jackson, "The wanton character of some of the outrages upon the persons and property of our citizens, upon the officers and flag of the United States, independent of recent insults to this Government, would justify, in the eyes of nations, immediate war." For himself Douglas said: "Aside from the insults to our flag, the indignity to the nation, and the injury to our commerce, it is estimated that not less than ten millions of dollars are due our citizens for these and many other outrages which Mexico has committed within the last fifteen years. When pressed by our Government for adjustment and remuneration, she has resorted to all manner of expedients to procrastinate and delay. She has made treaties acknowledging the justice of our claims, and then refused to ratify them on the most frivolous pretexts. Gentlemen have the hardihood to tell us that the President has unwisely and unnecessarily precipitated the country into an unjust and unholy war. They express great sympathy for Mexico, profess to regard her as an injured and persecuted nation—the victim of American injustice and aggression. They have no sympathy for the widows and orphans whose husbands and fathers have been robbed and murdered by the Mexican authorities; no sympathy with our own countrymen who have dragged out miserable lives within the walls of her dungeons, without crime and without trial; no indignation at the outrages upon our commerce and shipping, and the insults to our national flag, no resentment at the violation of treaties and the invasion of our territory. I despair of ever seeing my country again in the right, if they are to be the oracles."

Douglas quoted Frederick the Great, "Take possession first and negotiate afterward," and declared: "That is precisely what President Polk has done. He has taken possession and proposed to negotiate."

And while the Whigs politically had stood against the declaration of war, calling it a fight for a land grab, they took the position that the war having been started and the nation committed to it, the thing to do was to fight it through with no stint of sacrifice. This was the position of General Zachary Taylor, a Whig in politics, who commanded the American army in its expedition across the Rio Grande and into northern Mexico to the Battle of Buena Vista. It was also the position of such Whigs as Colonel Baker and Colonel Hardin, who was killed. Sons of the famous Whigs, Daniel Webster and Henry Clay, died in field service on Mexican soil.

Lincoln watched events, collected facts and data, worked on the policies he would stand for in Congress. He noticed that dinners, barbecues, brass bands, fireworks, cannon salutes, speeches of welcome met the returning soldiers; five thousand people gathered in Springfield for the home greeting. Returning officers received high appointments; in Menard County five returned volunteers were elected to the offices of judge of probate, clerk of the county commissioner's court, assessor, treasurer, and recorder.

Lincoln wrote to O. H. Browning of Quincy about law and politics in which they were interested. "Don't fret yourself about trouble you give me; when I get tired I'll tell you. I am glad you sent this letter, because it reminds me to write the result of your two cases of Moore *vs.* Brown and God knows who all."

After reporting the news of lawsuits, he told Browning what he expected the then assembling constitutional convention might do. "Indeed, indeed, I do not know what they are doing in the convention. Some things I have fears for. I am not easy about the Courts. I am satisfied with them as they are, but shall not care much if the judges are made elective by the People, and their term of office limited. I fear, however, something more, and as I think, much worse than all this, to wit, 'A Puppy Court,' that is, a Judge in each county, with civil jurisdiction in all cases up to a thousand dollars, and criminal in all cases not capital. 'A Migratory Supreme Court' and salaries so low as to exclude all respectable talent. From these—may God preserve us. As to what I and everybody else are doing, I am preparing to go to the Chicago River & Harbor Convention, and everybody is doing pretty much what everybody is always doing."

In Chicago he stood on the shore of Lake Michigan and looked across its stretch of blue water rising to meet the sky. It was the largest mass

of fresh water he had ever looked on; he had known large rivers; a vast
inland fresh-water sea was new to him. He learned that Chicago had installed a slaughterhouse where they killed 130 cattle a day and exported
to the English market. A fast-settling north country was hauling its
produce to Chicago; in one year when other points were paying 40 and
50 cents a bushel for wheat, the Chicago market was paying 87 cents
and $1.00 a bushel; farmers and wheat-buyers were hauling wheat to
Chicago from as far as 250 miles away; lines of 10 and 20 wagons headed
for Chicago were common; one line of 80 wagons loaded with wheat had
been counted; in Ottawa one year a firm advertised for 50 teams to haul
wheat to Chicago.

Delegates came to the River and Harbor Convention from all the
northern states; seven from Connecticut; 28 from Massachusetts; 27
from Pennsylvania. From Missouri came 45, from South Carolina one.
Daniel Webster, Henry Clay, and other famous national leaders sent
letters of hope that the convention would bring internal improvements.

Here Lincoln met Horace Greeley, editor of the *New York Tribune*,
and Thurlow Weed, boss of the Whig party in New York. Greeley wrote
for his paper: "In the afternoon Hon. Abraham Lincoln, a tall specimen
of an Illinoisan, just elected to Congress from the only Whig district in
the state, was called out, and spoke briefly and happily." The *Chicago
Journal* told its readers: "Abraham Lincoln, the only Whig representative to Congress from this State, we are happy to see in attendance upon
the Convention. This is his first visit to the commercial emporium of the
State, and we have no doubt his first visit will impress him more deeply,
if possible, and inspire a higher zeal for the great interest of river-and-
harbor improvements. We expect much from him as a representative in
Congress, and we have no doubt our expectations will be more than
realized, for never was reliance placed in a nobler heart and a sounder
judgment. We know the banner he bears will never be soiled." The convention, run by Whigs, went on record in favor of more river and harbor
improvement, and against the Democratic President James K. Polk, for
his failure to help lake harbors with Government money.

The question of the tariff would be sure to come up in Congress, and
Lincoln was putting down on paper his thoughts as they came to him
about the protective tariff which the Whig party favored. "Iron, and
everything made of iron, can be produced in sufficient abundance, and
with as little labor, in the United States as anywhere else in the world;
therefore all labor done in bringing iron and its fabrics from a foreign
country to the United States is useless labor. The same precisely may be
said of cotton, wool, and of their fabrics, as well as many other articles."
He made note of certain naked first principles which were the starting-
points for a system of economics:

"If at any time all labor should cease, and all existing provisions be equally divided among the people, at the end of a single year there could scarcely be one human being left alive; all would have perished by want of subsistence. So, again, if upon such division all that sort of labor which produces provisions should cease, and each individual should take up so much of his share as he could, and carry it continually around his habitation, although in this carrying the amount of labor going on might be as great as ever so long as it could last, at the end of the year the result would be precisely the same—that is, none would be left living. The first of these propositions shows that universal idleness would speedily result in universal ruin; and the second shows that useless labor is, in this respect, the same as idleness. I submit, then, whether it does not follow that partial idleness and partial useless labor would, in the proportion of their extent, in like manner result in partial ruin; whether, if all should subsist upon the labor that one-half should perform, it would not result in very scanty allowance to the whole.

"In the early days of our race the Almighty said to the first of our race, 'In the sweat of thy face shalt thou eat bread'; and since then, if we except the light and the air of heaven, no good thing has been or can be enjoyed by us without having first cost labor. And inasmuch as most good things are produced by labor, it follows that all such things of right belong to those whose labor has produced them. But it has so happened, in all ages of the world, that some have labored, and others have without labor enjoyed a large proportion of the fruits. This is wrong and should not continue. To secure to each laborer the whole product of his labor, or as nearly as possible, is a worthy object of any good government.

"The habits of our whole species fall into three great classes—useful labor, useless labor, and idleness. Of these the first only is meritorious, and to it all the products of labor rightfully belong; but the two latter, while they exist, are heavy pensioners upon the first, robbing it of a large portion of its just rights. The only remedy for this is to, so far as possible, drive useless labor and idleness out of existence."

CHAPTER 70

By stage and by steamboat Lincoln traveled East, crossed the Allegheny mountain range, rested his eyes on the Potomac River, on the slopes where George Washington had lived most of his years, and gazed up the broad pathway of Pennsylvania Avenue connecting the White House where President James K. Polk lived and the Capitol with its mystic white curves amid which the Congress of the United States was to sit in deliberation on laws, measures, and events, and the name of Abraham Lincoln was to be called in the roll-calls.

Here he stood for the first time at the hub of the wheel of government, the central point from which the armies and navies of the United States, the post offices and postmasters, the public lands, the rivers and harbors, the seacoasts and the lighthouses, the customs officials, ambassadors, consuls, expeditions, and commanders, were controlled, advised, dismissed, appointed, pensioned, paid in currency.

Here came ambassadors from Europe, Asia, South America, Mexico, with their wives, servants, uniforms, appropriate apparel, trunks, portfolios, diplomatic missions, phrases, conventions, precedents. Republics, kings, queens, czars, ameers, pashas, and shahs had told these representatives what to look for and what to say in Washington.

Here were the stage and footlights where Jackson, Clay, Calhoun, Webster, and John Quincy Adams had spoken their lines so many years. Jackson, the most passionate and forthright of all, Calhoun offering merciless logic, Webster polished oratorical periods, Clay many sentences varying the styles of all, and John Quincy Adams offering the queries of the perplexed, honest philosopher. Jackson had gone; the footlights were out for him; soon another and another was to go; in a few years the stage would be dark for a little row of players who had put their impress on every large issue and event in the Government for thirty years and more. After them were to come other players; they would have lines to speak on a fiercely lighted stage.

On the halfway line between the states of the North and of the South they had placed and laid out this city; it was built on something resembling an oath that the states North and South belonged together and should meet at a halfway point; and since the year it was platted into streets the human streams had coursed over the crest of the Allegheny Mountains, beyond to the Mississippi River, out to the Rocky Mountains, and now were threshing out the news of the Mexican War and of gold in California and of the Frémont exploring expeditions; so that soon, it was seen, the little city with the big white dome on the Potomac River would be the gathering place of men from states at distances staggeringly beyond anything in the dreams and plans of those who placed and laid out the city.

This was the one planned city in America, with its spaces and outlooks measured by design rather than accident; with an architecture and a layout of streets deliberate and free-handed; in the mystic shadows of the Capitol walls rested some mystery of the republic, something that people a thousand miles from the Potomac River believed in and were ready to die and make sacrifices for.

Here were libraries, museums, documents, gardens. Here were dialects from Louisiana to Maine, from the Carolinas to Minnesota; the soft southern drawl, the Yankee nasal twang, the slow western slang. Here were more boarders and roomers, ready to pack and go on short notice, than in any other city in the world. Here Abraham Lincoln and his family were to board and room for two years beginning in December of 1847.

CHAPTER 71

THE Lincoln family, with the two boys, Bob and Ed, one four years old, the other eighteen months old, rented lodgings on Capitol Hill, to live in a city ten times the size of Springfield, Illinois. By the banks of the Potomac, and not the Sangamon, Abraham Lincoln was to spend his thirty-ninth birthday anniversary and round out his fortieth year. He had become a legislative member of the Washington government, which spent sixty million dollars a year; he and two hundred other men were to decide on what the sixty million would be spent for; he was a law-maker of the American republic.

Into his hands came a 509-page book, embroidered with gilt scrolls, gilt edges, the gilt title "The Constitution" on the back, and on the front cover in gilt letters:

HON. ABRAHAM LINCOLN
REP^{E.} U.S. ILL.

The printer of the book, W. Hickey of Philadelphia, took the first eight pages of the book and filled them with testimonials in ornamental scroll type telling what an excellent book he had assembled and printed. The language throughout the book was splendiferous, and in the style Eighth Circuit lawyers in Illinois called "orgmathorial." Of the Constitution it declared, "Esto Perpetua!!!" three exclamation points being necessary to carry the enthusiasm.

As in Springfield, Illinois, so it was in the national capital: nearly all the lawmakers were lawyers. Already acquainted with many through newspapers and published speeches, Lincoln studied them further as they sat at their desks or rambled through the lobbies, the House post office, the Capitol grounds. He found men, such as Alexander Stephens of Georgia, Andrew Johnson of Tennessee, Joshua Giddings of Ohio, who like himself had come up from cabins of poverty. He took the measure of such aristocrats as Robert C. Winthrop of Boston, Speaker of the House; he searched the gentle, thoughtful face of Horace Mann, full of hope for a universal free school system; he joked the six Democrats from Illinois, who were keeping their eyes on the record of the one Whig from their state.

He sat at breakfasts in the home of Daniel Webster where William, a negro he had freed, and Daphne, a slave negro woman not yet freed, were servants, though the fact of Daniel Webster of Massachusetts having neglected to free the negro woman, Daphne, whom he owned, was a carefully kept secret; he scrutinized the cherubic, bland face of Horace Greeley, with pink skin fresh as that of a farm hand just come from milking, and a little round forehead contemplative of public abuses to be corrected by righteous citizens.

Horace Greeley often would point to an "abuse" and announce, "We propose to attack this abuse." He spread on the front page of the *New York Tribune* one morning the mileage charges of congressmen, "showing the amount of miles charged and mileage pocketed by each member at the last Session. In the case of Abraham Lincoln, for instance, the official distance from Washington by the shortest mail-route to Springfield was 780 miles but Lincoln had charged the government for travel by a route of 1,626 miles, and collected $1,300.80, which the *Tribune* figured was $676.80 in "excess of mileage over what it would have been if the distance had been computed by the most direct mail-route." The Lincoln mileage account, like that of nearly all members of Congress from the West, assumed that the way to travel from the West was to go to Chicago and take a steamboat and ride on the Great Lakes to Buffalo. The law provided payment for mileage by "the usually traveled road," and the *Tribune* declared: "The usually traveled road for a great many Members of the last Congress was an exceedingly crooked one, even for politicians. The wrong, as respects their cases, is not in them but in the *law*." Greeley urged: "If the People will only give a little thought to this subject, they will do themselves a service, for I am confident the Mileage abuse is the parent of many others. Let every man do a little, and soon 'the crooked shall be made straight.' "

Lincoln had his money bothers. He accepted from Senator Stephen A. Douglas on December 21, 1847, a note to Messrs. Corcoran and Riggs, reading, "Pay to A. Lincoln or order one hundred and sixty-seven dollars and charge same to my account."

At the mess table in Mrs. Spriggs's boarding-house, where Lincoln took his meals, he ate with four Pennsylvania congressmen, Patrick Thompson of Mississippi, Elisha Embree of Indiana, Joshua Giddings, and others. As the Mississippi and Ohio members between helpings of victuals clashed over the slavery issue, Lincoln sometimes interrupted and steered the discussion into a good-natured channel. At Caspari's bowling alley, near Mrs. Spriggs's place, he tried for ten-strikes with his long right arm and told yarns between plays and games.

In the House of Representatives post office Lincoln was at home in a corner where story-tellers met. After listening to others during the Christmas holidays he had let go a few reminiscences of the Black Hawk War.

"By New Year's he was recognized as the champion story-teller of the Capitol,' wrote a newspaper man. "His favorite seat was at the left of the open fireplace, tilted back in his chair, with his long legs reaching over to the chimney jamb. He never told a story twice, but appeared to have an endless repertoire always ready, like the successive charges of a magazine gun."

He might have told stories like an old Illinois favorite of his, one that he told in the legislature when a good law was proposed and a member spoke against it; it was unconstitutional. The member had shaggy, overhanging eyebrows, wore spectacles, and wanted his fellow members to understand he had keen eyes for any points not constitutional. Lincoln said the debate reminded him of an old fellow on the Wabash River who had shaggy, overhanging eyebrows and wore spectacles. One morning this old fellow was looking up a tree near his cabin and thought he saw a squirrel sitting on a high branch. Getting his rifle, he fired one load, reloaded, fired again, but couldn't hit the squirrel. He asked a boy, "Don't you see that squirrel, humped up about halfway up the tree?" "No, I don't," said the boy, and, looking keenly into his father's face, he broke out: "I see your squirrel! You've been shooting at a louse on your eyebrow!"

Lincoln had anecdotes such as one about John T. Stuart, the Whig, and Stephen A. Douglas, the Democrat, stumping Sangamon County and arriving late one night at a tavern. The landlord showed them two beds, each with a man sleeping in it. Douglas asked the landlord their politics. One was a Whig and the other a Democrat, the landlord told them. And Douglas said, "Stuart, you sleep with the Whig and I'll sleep with the Democrat." Or he could tell of the Kentucky magistrate who was tired of hearing two lawyers wrangling after he had given his decision. He admonished them, "If the court is right—and she think she air—why, then, you air wrong, and she knows you is—shut up."

There were anecdotes such as the one concerning Robert Owen, the Indiana congressman from the Ohio and Wabash River district. After a campaign debate with an opponent, Owen heard two farmers talking, "Did you hear Owen talk?" asked one. "Yes," said the other, "I hearn him." "Now, ain't he a hoss?" was next asked. And the answer was, "Well, yes; they're both blooded nags. They make a very pretty race." It was Owen who told a farmer in Posey County that he hesitated about running for the legislature because, having been born in England, he was an adopted American citizen and his foreign birth would be brought up against him. The Posey County farmer replied: "Well, it oughtn't to. A man isn't a horse, if he was born in a stable."

It was a time when pigs roamed the streets of Washington sniffing for food. In saloons and taverns were lithographs showing President Tyler at a steamboat dock. His secretary was calling: "Captain, hold on there,

Ex-President Tyler is coming. Hold on!" And the captain, a Henry Clay Whig, pulled the engine bell, looked scornfully at the Tyler party, and yelled: "Ex-President Tyler be dashed! Let him stay!" And there was the grog ration in the navy to talk about. It was said two congressmen voted to cut down the ration, and then said to each other, "Now we can go out and have a drink."

CHAPTER 72

At the time Lincoln swore his oath and took his seat as congressman the war with Mexico was nearly over. American armies in Mexico were clinching their hold on that country. The Government in Washington spent $27,000,000 and the lives of 27,000 soldiers. Mexico was beaten. The question of the day was: "What next? What price shall we force Mexico to pay us for what the war has cost us?"

One answer to this question came from a man who stood up on crutches in the Senate; he was six feet high, lean of build, with wide gray-blue eyes, a thin shrewd nose, bushy eyebrows, proud, independent, positive. He had been shot in the foot at the Battle of Buena Vista and stayed in the saddle with his bleeding foot till the battle was won; his father and uncles had served in Revolutionary War armies from 1776 to Yorktown; three of his older brothers had fought in the War of 1812, two of them being officially commended for gallantry at the Battle of New Orleans; he himself had graduated from the West Point military academy and served twelve years in the regular army of the United States; he had been in Illinois and Wisconsin through the Black Hawk War.

His name was Jefferson Davis; he had been colonel of the Mississippi Rifles, a crack regiment of young aristocrats from Mississippi; he was a cotton planter with several thousand acres at Biloxi, Mississippi; the governor of Mississippi had appointed him United States senator to fill a vacancy. Now he was asking Congress to vote money to send ten regiments of soldiers to garrison the cities and provinces of Mexico and to hold that territory till the Washington government decided what to do with it.

In a speech on March 17, 1848, Senator Davis told the Senate: "I hold that in a just war we conquered the larger portion of Mexico and that to it we have a title which has been regarded as valid ever since man existed in a social condition—the title of conquest. It seems to me that that question is now, how much shall we keep, how much shall we give up, and that Mexico cedes nothing."

Yucatan should be annexed, or England would take it, Davis believed. Furthermore, if the American advance to the isthmus was resisted by

Britain, he would make war on Britain; also, if Britain set foot in Cuba, America should interfere. He was a fighting man, sensitive, proud, independent, positive.

The Ten Regiments bill passed the Senate by a vote of 29 to 19; it went to the House; there it never came to a vote; it was pigeonholed by the Committee on Military Affairs; Whigs controlled the House.

South and North the politicians hesitated, straddled. There was confusion. Congressman Lincoln stood up and pointed at James K. Polk, the head of the government, calling him "a bewildered, confounded, and miserably perplexed man." Only five southern states had voted solidly for the Ten Regiments bill. In the other southern states there was opposition to the taking of all Mexico and the annexation of it to the United States. John C. Calhoun, the Senator from South Carolina, along with senators from Tennessee and Georgia, voted against ten regiments of regulars to garrison Mexico; they saw danger in the scheme. In the North, however, Senator Benton of Missouri was for it; so was Senator Lewis Cass of Michigan. In short, the South was not solid in favor of the dream of the "fire eater" for national expansion southward; yet there were northern politicians who spoke and voted the wish of the big cotton planters on every important bill. The Senate, controlled by the planters through the Democratic party, voted for the Ten Regiments; the House, controlled by Whigs less under the thumb of the planters, pigeonholed the Ten Regiments. The two leading members of the House committee on military affairs, which did the pigeonholing, were Robert Toombs and Howell Cobb of Georgia. Yet though Toombs and Calhoun, both from cotton states, opposed the Ten Regiments bill, they were bitter political enemies; when Calhoun had started a movement for the organization of a separate southern party, with an eye toward secession from the Union, Toombs and other Whigs had got inside of the movement and broken it up.

On all bills and measures hitting at slavery, the South voted solid. On the matter of secession from the Union as an advantage to the South and the slavery institution, southern congressmen were not solid. There were members such as Robert Toombs and Alexander Stephens of Georgia, who believed that slavery would have a better chance with the southern states in the Union than out. They called the extremists "fire eaters," and "ultras."

What seemed to be architectural statesmanship sometimes traced into spitework or the backwashes of cunning politics. Congressman Brinkerhoff wanted offices for friends back home, and, not getting what he wanted from President Polk, set out to knife the Administration. He wrote a proviso to ride with the appropriations bill, and took it to Judge David Wilmot, a quiet member from Pennsylvania. Wilmot looked it over, inquired about the meaning of it, and said he guessed he would introduce it, since he was asked. Thus came into Congress a little piece of writing that called up storms of debate. It provided that any new territory that came into the United States from the Mexican War treaty should be free and not slave territory. Onto one bill after another it was put as an amendment. Voted down, it came back. Lincoln spoke "Aye" for the Wilmot Proviso so many times he couldn't exactly remember how many; he guessed it was "about forty times," at least.

Tom Corwin of Ohio had killed himself politically when he broke out in the Senate one day with the declaration: "Were I a Mexican, as I am an American, I would say to the invader: 'We will welcome you with bloody hands to hospitable graves.'" Stephen A. Douglas had held to his original stand that President Polk had properly done what Frederick the Great had done in Silesia, by the rule, "Take possession first and negotiate afterward."

There seemed to be in the air the beginnings of a realization of an ocean-bound republic, with the territory from the Atlantic to the Pacific coasts in the hands of the United States. It was a carrying further of the thought of General Jackson years before that Texas must be annexed; more and more western territory must be taken into the Union, or there would be alliances formed that would make war for the control of western America.

For many of the free-riding and free-shooting men of the Southwest, who lived in the saddle, the Mexican War was a grand adventure across a grand piece of country. They felt in their way something of the size of the adventure as told by a British officer writing in the *Montreal Gazette:*

From the 42d degree of latitude, and Santa Fe to Vera Cruz, a line, say of 2,500 miles, is now covered by American troops or ships of war, and though so immensely long, all perfectly safe in its rear, and resting upon supplies. The American government has, in a short time, established a grander base of operations (in extent) than has ever been seen in modern warfare.

To Lincoln his own way was clear; there were no zigzags in the course of his thinking about the war. His public speeches and his confidential letters to Herndon back home fitted together in all parts, pieces, corners, and dovetails.

Behind the war he saw politics. He believed one motive back of the war was that Polk and the Democratic party wanted to take away public attention from the backdown of the Democratic party on the Oregon boundary; they had said they would take all land up to the "fifty-four-forty" or they would fight Great Britain; the slogan had been "fifty-four-forty, or fight"; they had backed down; and in order to cover up they started a war where they were sure they could win, and the winnings looked good. That was the big reason. Next to that was another reason; the Democrats knew that the war would win more territory into which the southern planters could spread out with cotton, slave labor, and the politics of cotton and slavery.

He saw at a desk in the Senate chamber the spare figure of John C. Calhoun, with a face carved by merciless events, a time-worn forehead with the relentless thoughts back of it: "People do not understand liberty or majorities. The will of the majority is the will of a rabble. Progressive democracy is incompatible with liberty. Those who study after this fashion are yet in the horn-book, the A B C of governments. Democracy is leveling—this is inconsistent with true liberty. Anarchy is more to be dreaded than despotic power. It is the worst tyranny. The best government is that which draws least from the people, and is scarcely felt, except to execute justice, and to protect the people from animal violation of law."

With his power slipping from him, the eye of Calhoun was on Jefferson Davis as the one to follow in his own independent paths of southern leadership. When President Polk had sent Colonel Davis a commission as brigadier general of volunteers, Davis had sent back the commission with the message to the President that states only had the power to grant such a commission. In the summer of 1848, Davis had told the Senate: "If folly and fanaticism and pride and hate and corruption of the day are to destroy the peace and prosperity of the Union, let the sections part like the patriarchs of old, and let peace and good will subsist among their descendants. Let no wounds be inflicted which time may not heal. Let the flag of our Union be folded up entire, the thirteen stripes recording the original size of our family, untorn by the unholy struggle of civil war."

Davis was offering the counsel to the people of Mississippi: "The generation which avoids its responsibility sows the wind and leaves the whirlwind as the harvest to its children; let us get together and build manufactories, enter upon industrial pursuits, and prepare for our own self-sustenance." Of slavery he told his people: "If slavery be a sin, it is not yours. It is a common-law right and property in the service of man; its origin was divine decree—the curse upon the graceless son of Noah."

Yet Davis was not sure that the states North might develop a cheaper labor that would push labor out of the states South. "Leave the country to the south and west open," he urged, "and speculation may see in the distant future slavery pressed by a cheaper labor to the tropical regions." Yet he also believed the development might take still another course; he noted that laws of the states of Ohio, Indiana, and Illinois forbade free negroes from entering those states; the next development might be the extension of slavery into those states.

CHAPTER 73

LINCOLN sat as a member of the congressional committee on post offices, and, in bringing in a report on post-office matters, he started to tell the House that all the Whigs in committee voted for the report, and all the Democrats, except one. He was interrupted; didn't he know it was out of order to tell on the floor what happened in the committee-room?

"He then observed," said the House minutes, "that if he had been out of order in what he said, he took it all back as far as he could. He had no desire, he could assure gentlemen, ever to be out of order—though he never could keep long in order."

As to making speeches on the floor of the House, Lincoln wrote back to Herndon at the Springfield law office: "By way of getting the hang of the House, I made a little speech two or three days ago on a post-office question of no general interest. I find speaking here and elsewhere about the same thing. I was about as badly scared, and no worse, as I am when I speak in the court." This was a try-out; a more thorough effort was to come. "As you are all so anxious for me to distinguish myself I have concluded to do so before long."

Getting the floor of the House on January 12, 1848, he defended the vote of his party given a few days previous "declaring that the war with Mexico was unnecessarily and unconstitutionally commenced by the President." He spoke of his impression of how he and others believed they ought to behave while their country was engaged in a war they considered unjustly commenced. "When the war began, it was my opinion that all those who because of knowing too little, or because of knowing too much, could not conscientiously oppose the conduct of the President in the beginning of it should nevertheless, as good citizens and patriots, remain silent on that point, at least till the war should be ended."

Now he was forced to break silence; the President was telling the country, continually, that votes of the Whigs for supplies to the soldiers in the field were an indorsement of the President's conduct of the war. Then too, the President was holding back documents and information to which the public was entitled.

Lincoln had earlier introduced resolutions and demands that the President should locate the exact "spot" where the war began. He now accused the President of marching an American army out of proven American territory into land not established as American soil, and there shedding the first blood of the war. The President was attempting "to prove by telling the truth what he could not prove by telling the whole truth."

Back in Illinois were political enemies murmuring that Lincoln was revealed as a Benedict Arnold in his "spot" resolutions. He now wanted the folks back home to see him pressing the President for the documents of the war, all of them. "Let the President answer the interrogatories I proposed. Let him answer fully, fairly, and candidly. Let him answer with facts and not with arguments. Let him remember he sits where Washington sat, and so remembering, let him answer as Washington would answer. As a nation should not, and the Almighty will not, be evaded, so let him attempt no evasion—no equivocation. And if, so answering, he can show that the soil was ours where the first blood of the war was shed—then I am with him."

And if the President refused to answer or set up pretenses that there was nothing to answer? "Then I shall be fully convinced of what I more than suspect already—that he is deeply conscious of being in the wrong; that he feels the blood of this war, like the blood of Abel crying to Heaven against him."

He dramatized James K. Polk. "Originally having some strong motive to involve the two countries in a war, and trusting to escape scrutiny by fixing the public gaze upon the exceeding brightness of military glory—that attractive rainbow that rises in showers of blood—that serpent's eye that charms to destroy—he plunged into it, and has swept on and on till, disappointed in his calculations of the ease with which Mexico might be subdued, he now finds himself he knows not where.

"How like the half-insane mumbling of a fever-dream is the whole war part of his late message! At one time telling us that Mexico has nothing whatever that we can get but territory; at another showing us how we can support the war by levying contributions on Mexico.

"The President is in no wise satisfied with his own positions. First he takes up one, and in attempting to argue us into it he argues himself out of it, then seizes another and goes through the same process, and then, confused at being able to think of nothing new, he snatches up the old one again. His mind, taxed beyond its power, is running hither and thither, like some tortured creature on a burning surface, finding no position on which it can settle down and be at ease. . . .

"He knows not where he is. He is a bewildered, confounded, and miserably perplexed man. God grant he may be able to show there is not something about his conscience more painful than all his mental perplexity."

If Lincoln could have known what had happened in the White House, he would have known that, behind its closed doors, two men saw President Polk every day and did their best to push him into taking all of Mexico. The two men were James Buchanan of Pennsylvania, Secretary of State, and Robert J. Walker of Mississippi, Secretary of the Treasury.

For months the President hesitated; he was precisely what Lincoln had characterized him, a bewildered, confounded, and miserably perplexed man. Of Walker the President noted in his diary, "He was for taking all of Mexico"; of Buchanan the notation was similar. Finally, he wrote in his diary, after endless advice to seize the whole territory of the Mexican nation: "I replied that I was not prepared to go to that extent, and furthermore, that I did not desire that anything I said should be so obscure as to give rise to doubt or discussion as to what my true meaning was; that I had in my last message declared that I did not contemplate the conquest of Mexico."

In rehearsing the start of the Mexican War, Lincoln for the first time told in public his views about revolutions and the rights of peoples to revolutionize. His declarations had a breath of the smoky days of Washington, Jefferson, and the American Revolution. "Any people anywhere being inclined and having the power have the right to rise up and shake off the existing government, and form a new one that suits them better. This is a most valuable, a most sacred right—a right which we hope and believe is to liberate the world. Nor is this right confined to cases in which the whole people of an existing government may choose to exercise it.

"Any portion of such people that can may revolutionize and make their own of so much of the territory as they inhabit. More than this, a majority of any portion of such people may revolutionize, putting down a minority, intermingled with or near about them, who may oppose this movement. Such minority was precisely the case of the Tories of our own revolution. It is a quality of revolutions not to go by old lines or old laws; but to break up both, and make new ones."

All of Mexico, including Texas, he pointed out, had revolutionized against Spain, after which Texas revolutionized against Mexico, raising the question of just how far the boundary-line ran that was fixed by the Texas revolution. So far as Lincoln could learn, the "spot" where the first blood of the war was shed was outside the Texas line and over in Mexican territory. It, the spot, was located between two rivers on a strip of land over which the United States government did—or did not—exercise jurisdiction. And Lincoln was trying to get President Polk to tell just how far the jurisdiction of the United States was exercised over that strip of land—-if at all.

He voted for all supplies for soldiers, for every help to the fighting men in the field, yet also for every possible measure that would lay blame on President Polk and the administration. He hoped the folks back home would understand from his speeches how he looked at the war. But the folks back home refused to understand.

Even Bill Herndon couldn't see it. He wrote Herndon:

You fear that you and I disagree about the war. I regret this . . . because if you misunderstand I fear other good friends may also. I will stake my life that if you had been in my place you would have voted just as I did. Would you have voted what you felt and knew to be a lie? I know you would not. Would you have gone out of the House—skulked the vote? I expect not. If you had skulked one vote you would have had to skulk many more before the end of the session. No man can be silent if he would. You are compelled to speak; and your only alternative is to tell the truth or a lie. I cannot doubt which you would do.

He named Whig congressmen, who had been officers through some of the fiercest fighting in Mexico; they were voting to condemn the war, the administration and the conduct of the President. He closed the letter to Herndon:

I do not mean this letter for the public, but for you. Before it reaches you, you will have seen and read my pamphlet speech, and perhaps been scared anew by it. After you get over your scare, read it over again, sentence by sentence, and tell me honestly what you think of it.

What bothered Herndon and others back home was a resolution maneuvered through Congress by the Whigs, voicing thanks to the officers of the Mexican War—with a stinger for the Polk administration. It added to the thanks the words, "in a war unnecessarily and unconstitutionally begun by the President of the United States." The vote was 82 to 81.

In a second letter to Herndon, Lincoln explained that the President of the United States is the same as a king, in power, if he can do what President Polk had done in commencing the Mexican War:

Allow the President to invade a neighboring nation whenever he shall deem it necessary to repel an invasion, and you allow him to do so whenever he may choose to say he deems it necessary for such purpose, and you allow him to make war at pleasure. Study to see if you can fix any limit to his power in this respect. If today he should choose to say he thinks it necessary to invade Canada to prevent the British from invading us, how could you stop him? You may say to him, "I see no probability of the British invading us"; but he will say to you, "Be silent: I see it, if you don't."

The Constitution gave the war-making powers to Congress, as Lincoln understood it, by this reasoning:

Kings had always been involving and impoverishing their people in wars, pretending generally, if not always, that the good of the people was the object. This our convention understood to be the most oppressive of all kingly oppressions, and they resolved to so frame the Constitution that no one man should hold the power of bringing this oppression upon us. But your view destroys the whole matter, and places our President where kings have always stood.

His guess was correct that if Herndon was misunderstanding there would be others misunderstanding. The *Belleville Advocate* for March 2 came along with a report of a meeting in Clark County of patriotic Whigs and Democrats who adopted this declaration: "Resolved, That Abe Lincoln, the author of the 'spotty' resolutions in Congress, against his own country, may they long be remembered by his constituents, but may they cease to remember him, except to rebuke him—they have done much for him, but he has done nothing for them, save in the part they have taken in their country's cause." The *Illinois State Register* was telling its readers of newspapers and public meetings that declared Lincoln to be "a second Benedict Arnold."

To Rev. J. M. Peck, Lincoln wrote a letter. The minister had spoken at a Belleville celebration of the battle of Buena Vista, saying, after an exhibit of facts, "In view of all the facts, the conviction to my mind is irresistible that the Government of the United States committed no aggression on Mexico." To him Lincoln wrote: "Not in view of all the facts. There are facts which you have kept out of view." And he went on:

It is a fact that the United States army in marching to the Rio Grande marched into a peaceful Mexican settlement, and frightened the inhabitants away from their homes and their growing crops. It is a fact that Fort Brown, opposite Matamoras, was built by that army within a Mexican cotton-field, on which at the time the army reached it a young cotton crop was growing, and which crop was wholly destroyed and the field itself greatly and permanently injured by ditches, embankments, and the like. It is a fact that when the Mexicans captured Captain Thornton and his command, they found and captured them within another Mexican field.

Now I wish to bring these facts to your notice, and to ascertain what is the result of your reflections on them. If you deny that they are facts, I think I can furnish proof which shall convince you that you are mistaken. If you admit that they are facts, then I shall be obliged for a reference to any law of language, law of States, law of nations, law of morals, law of religions, any law, human or divine, in which an authority can be found for saying those facts constitute "no aggression." Possibly you consider those acts too small for notice. Would you venture to so consider them had they been committed by any nation on earth against the humblest of our people? I know you would not. Then I ask, is the precept, "Whatsoever ye would that men should do to you, do ye even so to them" obsolete? of no force? of no application? I shall be pleased if you can find leisure to write me.

Lincoln went to the State Department, sleuthing for facts, trying to satisfy himself that the treaty signed between Mexico and the Republic of Texas had been copied correctly from the original for its publication in the newspaper *Niles Register*. And what he learned at the State Department indicated that President Polk had never sent to that department for its official copy of the treaty, and that the President had based his statements about the document from reading the copy of it published in *Niles Register*.

So Lincoln told Congress, with a shade of a quizzical tone, "If any one should suppose that *Niles Register* is a curious repository of so mighty a document as a solemn treaty between nations, I can only say that I learned to a tolerable degree of certainty, by inquiry at the State Department, that the President himself never saw it anywhere else."

One evening at the library of the Supreme Court, after digging in many books and documents, he drew out volumes to read in his room at Mrs. Spriggs's boarding-house. The library was going to close for the night. And he took his books, piled them on a table, pulled a large bandana out of his hip pocket, tied it around the books, ran a stick through the knots, slung the stick over his shoulder, and walked out of the library of the Supreme Court in the way natural to him, in the way he carried his earthly belongings from his canoe on the Sangamon River up into the town of New Salem when he was going to clerk in Offut's store. Over his shoulder was a short circular blue cloak he had bought since he came to Washington.

Thus he walked to his Capitol Hill lodging, where he untied the knots of his handkerchief bundle, read his books, took a brass key from his vest pocket and wound his watch, put his boot-heel into a boot-jack and pulled off his boots, blew out the candlelights and crept into a warm yellow flannel nightshirt that came down halfway between his knees and ankles. Then he slept the sleep of a man who had been searching Washington dissatisfied with mere claims, looking for the foundations of claims.

He may have dreamed of old Tom Lincoln writing for money and pleading, "I haven't a thing I could sell."

And there was a sweetness in Tom writing, "The Old Woman is well."

CHAPTER 74

One morning in February of 1848 a man sat at his desk in the House of Representatives writing a piece of poetry. He was an old man; he had been born in 1767, or seven years before the Revolutionary War commenced with the firing of shots at Lexington; and he was a very practical man, even though on this morning, as the House was called to order for business, he was writing a piece of poetry.

A resolution was introduced expressing thanks to the generals of the Mexican War for their brave conduct and skilled strategy; the clerk had read, "Resolved by the House, That"—when there was a cry and a stir and the members of the House looked toward the old man; he had stood up as if he might speak once more from the floor where he had spoken hundreds of times; he clutched his desk with groping, convulsive fingers, then he sank back into his chair with a slump; a friend and two doctors carried him to a sofa and he was taken first into the rotunda and then into the Speaker's room. Mustard poultices were placed on his chest and back; he was rubbed and given a friction treatment.

About an hour afterward he spoke a few words. "This is the last of earth, but I am content." His wife, relatives, and friends stood by his side; one was Henry Clay of Kentucky, who held the old man's hand and looked into the old man's face, while tears came into his eyes. At the funeral services in Washington one Representative from each state was in attendance; they escorted the body to Faneuil Hall in Boston; the body was laid in a grave in Quincy, Massachusetts.

This was the end of John Quincy Adams, his life, career, and works. For seventeen years he had been a member of Congress; during eight of those years he had fought against the "gag rule" by which Congress voted against any petitions relating to slavery being received; each year the majority against him was less until the gag rule was beaten; he had been President of the United States from 1825 to 1829, and before that was Secretary of State under President Monroe and had more of a hand in writing the Monroe Doctrine than did Monroe; earlier yet he had been in London and Paris at work with Henry Clay and Albert Gallatin on the treaty that ended the War of 1812.

This same John Quincy Adams saw Napoleon come back to Paris from Elba; he was in Russia representing President Madison at the time the armies of Napoleon were burned out of Moscow and sent reeling and harried back toward France; before that he had been a professor of rhetoric and oratory at Harvard University; he had come to Harvard after serving as United States Senator from Massachusetts and helping President Jefferson make the Louisiana Purchase; Washington had appointed him Minister to Portugal, after which his father, President John Adams, sent him to Berlin; before his graduation from Harvard he had served as a secretary to the American commissioners who negotiated the treaty of peace that ended the Revolutionary War in 1782; the year before that he was with the American envoy to Russia, following university studies at Paris and Leipzig.

A sweet, lovable man who had led a clean life full of hard work, steady habits, many dangers, furious enemies, such was John Quincy Adams. Most of the days of his life he got out of bed and put on his clothes before half-past four in the morning, and then read one or two chapters in the Bible. When in Washington he took a swim every morning, summer and winter, in the Potomac River. He was a little undersized, wore delicate sideburns, had a mouth with the peace of God on it, and spoke often as though his body was a rented house and John Quincy Adams would step out of the tenement and live on. His last words there in February of 1848 fitted him. "This is the last of earth, but I am content."

One day four years before he died, John Quincy Adams of Massachusetts wrote four little verses to another congressman, Alexander Stephens of Georgia, the wizened, wry, dry member, weighing less than a hundred pounds, known to Jefferson Davis as "the little pale star from Georgia."

The verses were titled "To Alexander H. Stephens, Esq., of Georgia," and two of them read:

We meet as strangers in this hall,
But when our task of duty's done,
We blend the common good of all
And melt the multitude in one.

As strangers in this hall we met;
But now with one united heart,
Whate'er of life awaits us yet,
In cordial friendship let us part.

He drew men to him, this Alexander Stephens; in his black eyes, set deep in a large-boned, homely head, there was a smolder by which men knew he would play politics only so far, after which a personal sincerity must be considered. He stood up one day to speak on the Mexican War and declared: "All wars, to be just, must have some distinct and legitimate objects to be accomplished. . . . One of the strangest . . . circumstances attending this war is, that though it has lasted upwards of eight months, at a cost of many millions of dollars, and the sacrifice of many valuable lives, both in battle and by the diseases of the camp, no man can tell for what object it is prosecuted. And it is to be doubted whether any man, save the President and his Cabinet, knows the real and secret designs that provoked its existence. To suppress inquiry, and silence all opposition to conduct so monstrous, an executive ukase has been sent forth, strongly intimating, if not clearly threatening, the charge of treason, against all who may dare to call in question the wisdom or propriety of his measures.

"It is to be seen," said Stephens, "whether the free people of this country have so soon forgotten the principles of their ancestors as to be so easily awed by the arrogance of power. For a very little further interference with the freedom of discussion, Charles X, of France, lost his throne; and for a very little greater stretch of royal prerogative, Charles I, of England, lost his head. There are some things more to be dreaded than the loss of a throne, or even the loss of a head—amongst which may be named the anathema of a nation's curse, and the infamy that usually follows it."

And it happened that on February 2, 1848, while sitting at his desk in the House of Representatives, Abraham Lincoln wrote a note to his law partner, Herndon, saying: "I just take up my pen to say that Mr. Stephens, of Georgia, a little slim, pale-faced, consumptive man, with a voice like Logan's, has just concluded the best speech, of an hour's length, I ever heard. My old, withered, dry eyes are full of tears yet. If he writes it out anything like he delivered it, our people shall see a good many copies of it."

Washington, Feb. 2. 1848

Dear William

I just take up my pen to say, that Mr. Stephens of Georgia, a little slim, pale-faced, consumptive man, with a voice like Logan's, has just concluded the very best speech, of an hour's length, I ever heard. My old, withered, dry eyes, are full of tears yet. If he writes it out any thing like he delivered it, our people shall see a good many copies of it—

Yours truly
A. Lincoln

To W. H. Herndon

Lincoln of Illinois and Stephens of Georgia were Whig Allies and personal friends. Stephens said, "I was as intimate with Mr. Lincoln as with any other man, except perhaps Mr. Toombs." The letter above is a slightly reduced facsimile from the original in the Barrett collection.

CHAPTER 75

LINCOLN got "the hang of the House," as he called it, and made speeches on internal improvements, public roads, rivers, harbors, canals, saying in one speech that so far as he could see there was the same wrangling in state legislatures and in counties and towns as there was in the national Congress, over improvements. "One man is offended because a road passes over his land, and another is offended because it does not pass over his; one is dissatisfied because the bridge for which he is taxed crosses the river on a different road from that which leads from his house to the town; another cannot bear that the county should be got in debt for these same roads and bridges; while not a few struggle hard to have roads located over their lands, and then stoutly refuse to let them be opened until they are first paid the damages."

As a first step toward fair dealing out of the nation's money for needed improvements among the states, Lincoln suggested statistical information to guide congressmen, saying he did not see much force in one member's objection "to counting all the pigs and chickens in the land." Though the speech was mainly constructive and practical, it was lighted with the observation: "An honest laborer digs coal at about seventy cents a day, while the President digs abstractions at about seventy dollars a day. The coal is clearly worth more than the abstractions."

Mainly, the speech was coaxing, advisory, conciliatory, hoping to get practical work done. "Difficulty though there be, let us meet and encounter it. Determine that the thing can and shall be done, and then we shall find the way. Let each contribute his mite in the way of suggestion." He was voicing the wishes of the Chicago river and harbor convention. To pay for canals with canal tolls and tonnage duties, before canals were dug, was like the Irishman and his new boots. "I shall niver git 'em on till I wear 'em a day or two, and stretch 'em a little."

Often during the first half of the year 1848, Lincoln was rushed with work. He wrote Archibald Williams a letter about politics, closing: "Excuse this short letter. I have so many to write that I cannot devote much time to any one. Yours, as ever." And to Richard Thomas: "Excuse the shortness of this letter; I am really very much hurried. Yours, as ever." And again to Thomas, "In great haste, yours as ever."

Tacked on to some of his letters were the abrupt, odd postscripts of a quizzical man of affairs. To one: "Taylorism seems to be going right, for which I am glad. Keep the ball rolling." To Andrew McCallen: "Don't pay postage on letters to me. I am entitled to them free." To Samuel Marshall, at Shawneetown, Illinois, after short news about a law case, "As to the matter of your lost horse, I will look into it, & do something if I can."

And to his old friend Richard Thomas he had to explain he had no influence with President Polk. "As to Mr. Graham's application for a Lieutenancy, I have already submitted it to the President in the best way I could think of it to give it success. I wrote him about it; and do not know anything more that I can do for him. You know I can have no intimacy with the President, which might give me personal influence over him."

In replying to Rev. Henry Slicer, who had written to ask why he was excluded from the funeral services of John Quincy Adams, Lincoln wrote that he had not been consulted, knew nothing about it, and, "So entirely ignorant was I, in relation to your having been excluded from the funeral services of Mr. Adams, that, until I received your letter, I should have given it as my recollection, that you actually did participate in those services." He advised E. B. Washburne on a political campaign matter, "Make Baker help about it. He is a good man to raise a breeze."

Lincoln turned out dozens of letters a day, "fixing his political fences." He ordered *The Battery*, a Whig campaign paper, sent to S. A. Hurlbut at Belvidere, Illinois, and wrote: "If it strikes you as giving promise of being a good campaign paper, please get as many subscribers as you can and send them on—I have put you down for one copy, the subscription for which I will pay myself if you are not satisfied with it."

Back in Sangamon and other counties of his district were Whigs who wanted to be officers in the army. They wrote Lincoln to get them commissions from the Democratic Administration. He wrote to the Springfield postmaster: "The thing that perplexes me more than most anything else, are the cases of Whigs calling on me to get them appointments to places in the army, from the President. There are two great obstacles in the way which they do not understand—first, the President has no such appointments to give—and secondly, if he had, he could hardly be expected to give them to Whigs, at the solicitation of a Whig member of Congress."

One February day in 1848, a scandal arose from an affair at Mrs. Spriggs's boarding-house. The negro servant in the house had been buying his freedom at a price of $300.00; he had paid all but $60.00 when, one day, two white men came to the house, knocked him down, tied and gagged him, took him to a slave jail, and had him sent to New Orleans for sale. Joshua Giddings of Ohio asked for a hearing by Congress to get at the facts; he was voted down by 98 to 88.

Giddings and Lincoln enjoyed each other's company. Lincoln was not radical in Giddings's way. But both the men had streaks of stubborn and personal quality. Each was meek about picking a fight. Giddings had made a speech in Congress a few years previously, taking a violent stand against slavery. A southern member had lurched against Giddings, shoved Giddings out of an aisle, and thrust a right hand into a vest pocket as if he might have a bowie knife there. Giddings inquired, "Did you push me?" "I did." "Intentionally?" "Yes." "For the purpose of insult?" "Yes." "Well, sir, we are in the habit of leaving men who wantonly insult others to the contempt of public opinion." At that point, friends from North and South interfered.

CHAPTER 76

ALEXANDER STEPHENS in telling about friendships in the Thirtieth Congress said, "I was as intimate with Mr. Lincoln as with any other man except perhaps Mr. Toombs." They had comradeship; scrawls of personal tragedy, pinches of hunger and fate, were on their two faces; yet they had depths of clean laughter together.

Whereas men looked up toward Lincoln's head and asked, "How's the weather up there?" Stephens said, "Men address me familiarly as 'my son'; such often happens to me." Each felt it uphill work to act the part of a Great Man. Stephens once wrote in a diary: "I believe I shall never be worth anything, and the thought is death to my soul. I am too boyish, unmanful, trifling, simple in my manners and address."

Both were uneasy amid women, Stephens once writing in his diary after examining drawings of ancient statues: "With the Gladiator and Venus I am delighted. Pity but some of our fashionable belles would take a lesson from this form of true grace, the Venus; they would change their present disgusting waspish shape."

Both had stories mocking at their dignity as lawyers. Stephens used to pass a shoe-shop in Crawfordsville, Georgia, and heard a voice, "Who is that little fellow that walks so fast by here every day?" and a replying sarcastic voice, "Why, *that's* a *lawyer!*" And he had visited a farmer uncle in Pennsylvania who asked at family dinner, "What business do you follow, Alex?" "I am a lawyer, Uncle." Then silence, broken by the uncle's husky voice, "Alex, don't you have to tell lies?"

Stephens, Lincoln and the five other Whigs, in the winter of 1847-48 organized the Taylor Club, with members nicknamed the Young Indians. They saw that the Whig war hero, who had protested against leading his troops onto Mexican soil and starting a war of invasion, and then had obeyed orders and gone in and fought as a wildcat from hell, would make a candidate the Democrats couldn't keep from getting into the White House. How to get Taylor nominated was the high point with the Young Indians.

CHAPTER 77

LINCOLN went to Philadelphia in June as a delegate to the national convention of the Whig party and helped nominate General Zachary Taylor, the hero of the Mexican War, for president. He wrote to Illinois: "Taylor's nomination takes the Locos (Democrats) on the blind side. It turns the war thunder against them. The war is now to them the gallows of Haman, which they built for us, and on which they are doomed to be hanged themselves." And he analyzed: "One unmistakable sign [of victory] is that all the odds and ends are with us—Barnburners, Native Americans, Tyler men, disappointed office-seeking Locofocos, and the Lord knows what." The nickname "Barnburners" had been given discontented Democrats who had drawn out and formed a new organization they called the Free Soil party; they were named after the farmer who burned his barn to drive the rats out.

The Whig nomination of General Zachary Taylor had peculiar angles; he was nicknamed "Old Rough and Ready"; and he had spoken positively, before the war commenced, his view that a war was not called for; it was only when direct orders to move reached him that he took his troops to where the first blood was shed. He kept quiet on the slavery issue, and it was said that a letter to him from a southern planter read:

SIR:

I have worked hard and been frugal all my life, and the results of my industry have mainly taken the form of slaves, of whom I own about a hundred. Before I vote for President, I want to be sure that the candidate I support will not so act as to divest me of my property.

To which General Taylor, who had a plantation in Louisiana, replied:

SIR:

I have the honor to inform you that I too have been all my life industrious and frugal, and that the fruits thereof are mainly invested in slaves, of whom I own *three* hundred.

Yours,

One day in July, Lincoln stood up on the floor and began remarks that carried him striding back and forth up the aisle of the house. It was a stump speech that had the champing of a campaign war-horse in it, with a sniffing of defiance and contempt for the enemy, and a snorting of challenge for the opposition to come on and do battle. It was the kind of horseplay that veteran stump speakers use to send the farmers home refreshed and perhaps convinced. He lammed and lambasted General Lewis Cass, of Michigan, the Democratic nominee for President. It was rough-and-tumble, meant to "raise a breeze."

Lincoln pictured the Democrats' use of General Jackson's nickname, "Old Hickory." "Hickory poles and hickory brooms your never-ending emblems, even now your campaign paper here is proclaiming that Cass and Butler are of 'Hickory stripe.' Like a horde of hungry ticks you have stuck to the tail of the Hermitage lion to the end of his life; and you are still sticking to it, and drawing a loathsome sustenance from it, after he is dead.

"A fellow once advertised that he had made a discovery by which he could make a new man out of an old one, and have enough of the stuff left to make a yellow dog. Just such a discovery has General Jackson's popularity been to you. You not only twice made President of him out of it, but you have had enough of the stuff left to make Presidents out of several comparatively small men since; and it is your chief reliance now to make still another."

Then came pointed mockery and the bubbling jokes that across southern Illinois had given the name of Abe Lincoln a special tang. The Democrats were trying to make a heroic military figure out of their presidential candidate, General Cass, who had been a volunteer aid to General Harrison at the battle of the Thames, and had held a command during an Indian war. So Lincoln pitched in: "Mr. Speaker, old horses and military coat-tails, or tails of any sort are not figures of speech such as I would be the first to introduce into discussions here; but as the gentleman from Georgia has thought fit to introduce them, he and you are welcome to all you have made or can make by them. If you have any more old horses, trot them out; any more tails, just cock them and come at us. I repeat, I would not introduce this mode of discussion here; but I wish gentlemen on the other side to understand that the use of degrading figures is a game at which they may not find themselves able to take all the winnings. ('We give it up!') Aye, you give it up, and well you may. The point—the power to hurt—of all figures consists in the truthfulness of their application. They are weapons which hit you, but miss us.

"But in my hurry I was very near closing this subject of military tails before I was done with it. There is one entire article of the sort I have not discussed yet—I mean the military tail you Democrats are now engaged in dovetailing into the great Michigander [General Cass]. Yes, sir; all his biographies have him in hand, tying him to a military tail like so many mischievous boys tying a dog to a bladder of beans. True, the material they have is very limited, but they drive at it with might and main. He invaded Canada without resistance, and he outvaded it without pursuit. As he did both under orders, I suppose there was to him neither credit nor discredit in them; but they constitute a large part of the tail. He was volunteer aid to General Harrison on the day of the battle of the Thames; and as you said in 1840 Harrison was picking huckleberries two miles off while the battle was fought, I suppose it is a just conclusion with you to say Cass was aiding Harrison to pick huckleberries.

"By the way, Mr. Speaker, did you know I am a military hero? Yes, sir; in the days of the Black Hawk War I fought, bled, and came away. If General Cass went ahead of me in picking huckleberries, I guess I surpassed him in charges upon the wild onions. If he saw any live, fighting

Indians it was more than I did; but I had a good many bloody struggles with the mosquitoes, and although I never fainted from the loss of blood, I can truly say I was often very hungry. Mr. Speaker, if ever I should conclude to doff whatever our Democratic friends may suppose there is of black-cockade federalism about me, and therefore they shall take me up as their candidate for the Presidency, I protest they shall not make fun of me, as they have of General Cass, by attempting to write me into a military hero."

Next he took up General Cass's record while governor of the Territory of Michigan, to show that the governor drew $1,500.00 a year for office rent and clerk hire as Superintendent of Indian Affairs without really having a separate office or hired clerk. Then he passed to the matter of General Cass during nine years drawing ten rations a day from the Government at $730.00 a year. And further: "At eating, his capacities are shown to be wonderful. From October, 1821, to May, 1822, he ate ten rations a day in Michigan, ten rations a day here in Washington, and near five dollars' worth a day on the road between the two places! There is an important discovery in his example—the art of being paid for what one eats, instead of having to pay for it. Hereafter, if any nice young man should owe a bill which he cannot pay in any other way, he can just board it out.

"Mr. Speaker, we have all heard of the animal standing in doubt between two stacks of hay and starving to death. The like of that would never happen to General Cass. Place the stacks a thousand miles apart, he would stand stock-still midway between them, and eat them both at once, and the green grass along the line would be apt to suffer some, too, at the same time. By all means, make him President, gentlemen. He will feed you bounteously—if—if there is any left after he shall have helped himself."

The moment came when he had only three minutes left and had to close. He spoke of splits and breaks in the Democratic party ranks, and wound up: "I have heard some things from New York; and if they are true, one might well say of your party there, as a drunken fellow once said when he heard the reading of an indictment for hog-stealing. The clerk read on till he got to and through the words, 'did steal, take, and carry away ten boars, ten sows, ten shoats, and ten pigs,' at which he exclaimed, 'Well, by golly, that is the most equally divided gang of hogs I ever did hear of!' If there is any other gang of hogs more equally divided than the Democrats of New York are about this time, I have not heard of it."

The *Baltimore American* said the speaker kept the House roaring. "He would commence a point in his speech far up one of the aisles, and keep on talking, gesticulating, and walking until he would find himself, at the end of a paragraph, down in the center of the area in front of the clerk's desk. He would then go back and take another *head*, and *work down* again. And so on." The paper hit off Lincoln as "a very able, acute, uncouth, honest, upright man, and a tremendous wag withal."

Lincoln had his personal ways, his own methods of playing politics. A first element to line up, in his plans, was the young men, especially the shrewd, wild boys such as those who were his never-failing guards in Sangamon County, at Clary's Grove, Sand Ridge, and Wolf Creek.

He wrote to Herndon: "As to the young men, you must not wait to be brought forward by the older men. For instance, do you suppose that I should ever have got into notice if I had waited to be hunted up and pushed forward by older men? You young men get together and form a 'Rough and Ready Club' and have regular meetings and speeches. Take in everybody you can get. As you go along gather up all the shrewd, wild boys about town, whether just of age or a little under age,—Chris Logan, Reddick Ridgely, Lewis Zwizler, and hundreds such. Let every one play the part he can play best,—some speak, some sing, and all 'holler.' Your meetings will be of evenings; the older men, and the women, will go to hear you; so that it will not only contribute to the election of 'Old Zach,' but will be an interesting pastime, and improving to the intellectual faculties of all engaged. Don't fail to do this."

Then he went on to write a line and speak in a tone he didn't use often. "This makes me a little impatient," he told Herndon. The last letter from Herndon had asked for all the speeches made in Congress about General Taylor, the Mexican War, and campaign issues. He explained: "I have regularly sent you the 'Congressional Globe' and 'Appendix,' and you cannot have examined them, or you would have discovered that they contain every speech made by every man in both houses of Congress, on every subject during the session. Can I send any more? Can I send speeches that nobody has made?"

Lincoln was trying to figure out what had happened back home. The Whig newspapers were not publishing the speeches of Whig congressmen as they should. "With the exception of my own little speech which was published in two of the then five, now four, Whig papers, I do not remember having seen a single speech or even extract from one, in any single one of those papers."

And he was trying to figure where Herndon had been keeping himself; he knew Herndon was a widely read scholar and lost himself in books sometimes, and, too, that Herndon was a hard drinker when he drank and lost himself at the taverns sometimes. He wrote: "You ask how Congress came to declare that war had existed by the act of Mexico. Is it possible you don't understand that yet? You have at least twenty speeches in your possession that fully explain it."

And he wrote wearily, "I will, however, try it once more," and launched off into a complete statement unraveling in a simple way what went on in

Congress, how the Whigs were forced to vote that war existed by act of Mexico or else vote against money and supplies for the soldiers in the field. "They did not want to vote against sending help to General Taylor, and therefore they voted for both together. Is there any difficulty in understanding this? Even my little speech shows how this was."

Then from the young partner and friend at Springfield came a bitter letter. And the older man at Washington wrote that he was young once— but now he was no longer young. "Your letter is exceedingly painful to me; and I cannot but think there is some mistake in your impression of the motives of the old men. I suppose I am now one of the old men; and I declare, on my veracity, which I think is good with you, that nothing could afford me more satisfaction than to learn that you and others of my young friends are doing battle in the contest, and endearing themselves to the people, and taking a stand far above any I have ever been able to reach in their admiration. I cannot conceive that other old men feel differently. Of course I cannot demonstrate what I say; but I was young once, and I am sure I was never ungenerously thrust back. I hardly know what to say. The way for a young man to rise is to improve himself every way he can, never suspecting that anybody wishes to hinder him.

"Allow me to assure you that suspicion and jealousy never did help any man in any situation. There may sometimes be ungenerous attempts to keep a young man down; and they will succeed, too, if he allows his mind to be diverted from its true channel to brood over the attempted injury. Cast about, and see if this feeling has not injured every person you have ever known to fall into it."

They were two fine friends. The older man tried to reach across the Alleghenies and the plains and tell it. "In what I have said, I am sure you will suspect nothing but sincere friendship. I would save you from a fatal error. You have been a laborious, studious young man. You are far better informed on almost all subjects than I have ever been. You cannot fail in any laudable object, unless you allow your mind to be improperly directed. I have somewhat the advantage of you in the world's experience, merely by being older; and it is this that induces me to advise."

Yes, Lincoln was growing older. He wrote notes, memoranda, on what he thought General Taylor ought to say as presidential candidate. "Were I President, I" should do so and so, on the tariff, the national debt, a national bank. And, "In the final treaty of peace [with Mexico], we shall probably be under the necessity of taking some territory; but it is my desire that we shall not acquire any extending so far south as to enlarge and aggravate the distracting question of slavery."

Back pay was due Joseph Ferguson, who had died in Mexican War service. The father of the soldier was writing from Springfield to Lincoln, "I am very much in want of the money and would be glad to have you call and obtain it immediately and forward the same to me without delay." And Lincoln made calls at the War Department in Washington until the matter was adjusted.

Sometimes his past, of the days before he was born, interested him. A Shenandoah Valley congressman mentioned the Lincolns of Rockingham County, Virginia. It was there his grandfather, Abraham Lincoln, had lived. He wrote to one David Lincoln, at Sparta, Virginia, and was told that the Lincolns of Virginia had come from Berks County, Pennsylvania. Several letters passed between the congressman and David Lincoln about their kinfolk. But later, in writing to a Jesse Lincoln in Tennessee, Abraham referred to David of Virginia, saying, "I forget, if he informed me, which of my grandfather's brothers was his father." He was interested in his genealogy, but not enthusiastic. On Christmas Eve of 1848, he sent his father twenty dollars, as asked for, and wrote a letter with kindly, sly digs at the poor excuses offered by Tom Lincoln in asking for the money.

CHAPTER 78

LINCOLN delivered a speech in Congress on July 27 of 1848 in which he outlined a portrait or sketched a cartoon of another politician. Yet in his very caricature of another man there was a report of himself, a revelation of what he would rather quit politics than to be and do. In fact, he knew he was slipping in popularity and influence at home because of his refusal to be obedient to public opinion on the Mexican War issue.

He analyzed the wiggling weasel course of General Lewis Cass, the Democratic presidential candidate, on the Wilmot Proviso. In 1846 General Cass was for the Proviso at once; in March, 1847, he was still for it, but not just then; in December, 1847, he was against it altogether. "This is a true index to the whole man," declared Lincoln. "When the question was raised in 1846, he was in a blustering hurry to take ground for it. He sought to be in advance, to avoid the uninteresting position of a mere follower; but soon he began to see glimpses of the great Democratic ox-gad waving in his face, and to hear indistinctly a voice saying: 'Back! Back, sir, back a little!' He shakes his head and bats his eyes and blunders back to his position of March, 1847; but still the gad waves, and the voice grows more distinct and sharper still, 'Back, sir! Back, I say!' —and back he goes to the position of December, 1847, at which the gad is still, and the voice soothingly says: 'So! Stand at that.'"

The style of the speech was "scathing and withering," a newspaper commented. Lincoln wasn't always humble. He could be cutting and scornful.

CHAPTER 79

LINCOLN had decided after a short stay of his wife in Washington that it would be best for her to return to Springfield, which she did. When again she wished to go East she wrote to him asking him about it as though in such a case it was for her to ask and for him to advise or decide.

He signs his letters to her, "Affectionately" or "Most Affectionately," and the name "A. Lincoln." She signs her letters, "Truly yours," and initials and dash, "M. L——." His salutation is "My Dear Wife" or "Dear Mary," and hers "My Dear Husband."

He wrote her he hated to sit down and direct documents back to Illinois voters, and he hated to be in an old boarding-house room by himself. While she was there he had thought she hindered him in attending business, but since then, having nothing but business, no variety, the daily routine had grown tasteless.

All of the boarders with whom she was on decided good terms, he wrote, sent their love to her, while the others of the house were saying nothing. He has been shopping in the stores of Washington, as she asked, but cannot find a pair of plaid stockings of any sort to fit "Eddy's dear little feet."

He wished her to enjoy herself in every possible way, he wrote, but as to her open intimacy with a certain Wickliffe family he asked if there were not danger of her wounding the feelings of her own good father.

One letter Lincoln wrote to his wife that year, read, in full, as follows:

WASHINGTON, July 2, 1848.

My dear wife:

Your letter of last sunday came last night— On that day (sunday) I wrote the principal part of a letter to you, but did not finish it, or send it till tuesday, when I had provided a draft for $100 which I sent in it— It is now probable that on that day (tuesday) you started to Shelbyville; so that when the money reaches Lexington, you will not be there— Before leaving, did you make any provision about letters that might come to Lexington for you? Write me whether you got the draft, if you shall not have already done so, when this reaches you— Give my kindest regards to your uncle John, and all the family— Thinking of them reminds me that I saw your acquaintance, Newton, of Arkansas, at the Philadelphia Convention— We had but a single interview, and that was so brief, and in so great a multitude of strange faces, that I am quite sure I should not recognize him, if I were to meet him again— He was a sort of Trinity, three in one, having the right, in his own person, to cast the three votes of Arkansas— Two or three days ago I sent your uncle John, and a few of our other friends each a copy of the speech I mentioned in my last letter; but I did not send any to you, thinking you would be on the road here, before it would reach you— I send you one now— Last wednesday, P. H. Hood & Co. dunned me for a little bill of $5—38 cents, and Walter Harper

& Co. another for $8—50 cents, for goods which they say you bought— I hesitated to pay them, because my recollection is that you told me when you went away, there was nothing left unpaid— Mention in your next letter whether they are right—

Mrs. Richardson is still here; and what is more, has a baby—so Richardson says, and he ought to know— I believe Mary Hewett has left here and gone to Boston— I met her on the street about fifteen or twenty days ago, and she, told me she was going soon— I have seen nothing of her since—

The music in the Capitol grounds on saturdays, or, rather, the interest in it, is dwindling down to nothing— Yesterday evening the attendance was rather thin— Our two girls, whom you remember seeing first at Canisis, at the exhibition of the Ethiopian Serenaders, and whose peculiarities were the wearing of black fur bonnets, and never being seen in close company with other ladies, were at the music yesterday— One of them was attended by their brother, and the other had a member of Congress in tow— He went home with her; and if I were to guess, I would say, he went away a somewhat altered man—most likely in his pockets, and in some other particular— The fellow looked conscious of guilt, although I believe he was unconscious that everybody around knew who it was that had caught him—

I have had no letter from home, since I wrote you before, except short business letters, which have no interest for you—

By the way, you do not intend to do without a girl, because the one you had has left you? Get another as soon as you can to take charge of the dear codgers— Father expected to see you all sooner; but let it pass; stay as long as you please and come when you please— Kiss and love the dear rascals—

Affectionately
A. Lincoln.

A letter dated "Lexington, May —, '48," arrives one day from Mrs. Lincoln; he may think old age has set its seal upon her: "in few or none of my letters, I can remember the day of the month. I must confess it is one of my peculiarities; I feel wearied and tired enough to know, that this Saturday night, our babies are asleep, and as Aunt Maria B. is coming in for me tomorrow morning, I think the chances will be rather dull that I should answer your last letter tomorrow."

She gives news from her sister Frances at Springfield. Willie is recovering from another spell of sickness. As to Springfield, she reports it "as dull as usual."

Then the family Kentucky news, "Eddie has recovered from his spell of sickness." Bobby came across a kitten, brought it to the house, Eddie spied it, fed it with bread, was delighted over it. "In the midst of his happiness Ma came in, she you must know dislikes the whole cat race, I thought in a very unfeeling manner, she ordered the servant near, to throw it out, which of course, was done, Ed—screaming and protesting loudly against the proceeding, she never appeared to mind his screams, which were long & loud, I assure you."

She sketches her mother. " 'Tis unusual for her nowadays, to do any-thing quite so striking, she is very obliging & accommodating, but if she thought any of us were on her hands again, I believe she would be worse than ever—In the next moment she appeared again in a good humor, I know she did not intend to offend me—By the way she has just sent up a glass of ice cream, for which this warm evening, I am duly grateful."

Then the wife in Kentucky writes to her husband in Washington wish-ing he and she were together. She wants to go East, join him, and visit eastern cities "sightseeing." Her uncle, James Parker of Mississippi, is to travel East to put his eldest daughter in school in Philadelphia. Why shouldn't she travel with her uncle and meet her husband in Washington?

"I believe it would be a good chance to pack up and accompany them," she writes. "You know I am so fond of sightseeing, & I did not get to New York or Boston, or travel the lake route—But perhaps dear husband can-not do without his wife next winter, and must needs take her with him again—I expect you would cry aloud against it."

She darts from topic to topic. "How much, I wish instead of writing, we were together this evening, I feel very sad away from you—Ma and myself rode out to Mr. Bell's splendid place this afternoon, to return a call, the house and grounds are magnificent, Frances would have died of their rare exotics—It is growing late, these summer eves are short, I ex-pect my long scrawls, for truly such they are, weary you greatly."

Then came more news or chat, and, "I must bid you good-night—Do not fear the children have forgotten you, I was only jesting—Even E— eyes brighten at the mention of your name—My love to all."

CHAPTER 80

EARLY in September of 1848 Lincoln stumped New England for the na-tional Whig ticket. He rode into new territory, and saw the factories, mills, shops, foundries, that made the middle Atlantic states and New England rich and powerful; regions that were almost nations by them-selves; the white faces of thousands of wage-workers. He was a man immensely and intensely impressed by facts that spread before his eye-sight; he could analyze, deduce, synthesize facts that came within ear-shot; he would pick up facts and play with them, turn them over in his mind, and make them pay out with results beyond facts.

As committees of Whigs escorted him, they felt, often, here was a sober, sad man from far west, with a strangeness they could not solve. As he loosened and lightened, they felt they knew him; he was so warmly and simply human; then he would lapse to the sober, sad face again, the slouching, angular shoulders that drooped. In Boston he saw Faneuil Hall and at Cambridge, near the walls of Harvard University, he delivered a speech. At Lowell, he spoke, and saw there the incessant move-ment of its thousands of power looms and spindles translating raw cotton fabrics to be moved on the new steam cars and the new steamships into far home and world markets.

At Worcester, he was introduced by an ex-governor of the state, Levi Lincoln; the two of them traced back to a Samuel Lincoln who had come two hundred years before to Hingham, Massachusetts; Abraham said to Levi, "I *hope* we both belong, as the Scotch say, to the same clan; but I *know* one thing, and that is, that we are both good Whigs." He told the State Whig convention at Worcester that in speaking "this side of the mountains" he felt modest and referred to his home people looking on his auditors as "instructed and wise."

The new Free Soil party reminded him of the Yankee peddler who offered for sale a pair of pantaloons "large enough for any man, and small enough for any boy." As to slavery, he believed the people of Illinois agreed with the people of Massachusetts, except perhaps that they did not keep so constantly thinking about it.

The *Boston Advertiser* noted: "Mr. Lincoln has a very tall and thin figure, with an intellectual face, showing a searching mind, and a cool judgment. He spoke in a clear, cool, and very eloquent manner, for an hour and a half, carrying the audience with him, only interrupted by warm and frequent applause." At Cambridge a reporter sized him up as "a capital specimen of a Sucker Whig, six feet at least in his stockings." There were halls where his head almost scraped the ceiling. "They were struck with his height, as he arose in the low-studded hall."

A young Whig, George H. Monroe, and others, called at the Tremont House in Boston to take Lincoln to Dedham for a day speech. "He was as sober a man in point of expression as I ever saw," said Monroe, telling about it later. "In the cars he scarcely said a word to one of us. He seemed uneasy. . . . I should say the atmosphere of Boston was not con-genial to him. We took him to one of the most elegant houses in the town of Dedham, and here he seemed still less . . . at home. The thing began to look rather blue for us. When we went over to the hall it was not much better. It was a small hall and only about half full; for Mr. Lincoln had not spoken in Boston yet, and there was nothing in his name particularly to attract. But at last he arose to speak, and almost instantly there was a change.

"His indifferent manner vanished as soon as he opened his mouth. He went right to work. He wore a black alpaca sack, and he turned up the sleeves of this, and then the cuffs of his shirt. Next he loosened his neck-tie, and soon after he took it off altogether. All the time he was gaining upon his audience. He soon had it as by a spell. I never saw men more delighted. His style was the most familiar and offhand possible. His eye had lighted up and changed the whole expression of his countenance. He began to bubble out with humor. But the chief charm of his address lay in the homely way he made his points. There was no attempt at eloquence or finish of style. But, for plain pungency of humor, it would have been difficult to surpass his speech. The speech . . . ended in a half-hour. The bell that called to the steam cars sounded. Mr. Lincoln instantly stopped. 'I am engaged to speak at Cambridge tonight and I must leave.' The whole audience seemed to rise in protest. 'Go on! Finish it!' was heard on every hand. One gentleman arose and pledged to take his horse and carry him across country. But Mr. Lincoln was inexorable."

That evening Lincoln spoke at Tremont Temple, following the speech of William H. Seward, Governor of New York, and in a few weeks to be elected United States senator. The Whig newspaper, *The Atlas*, the next morning printed a column of Seward's speech and itemized Lincoln's as "powerful and convincing, and cheered to the echo."

Lincoln told Seward at their hotel that night, "I reckon you are right. We have got to deal with this slavery question, and got to give much more attention to it."

He left Boston on the steam cars one Saturday morning, and from the windows as he traveled he saw the walls of the cotton mills, with their power-driven looms, their miles of spindles, with their bobbin boys and girls.

At Albany he stopped off and talked with Thurlow Weed, the Whig boss of New York; they went out and visited Millard Fillmore, the Whig candidate for Vice President. He rode on the Erie Canal to Buffalo, visited Niagara Falls, went down Lake Erie, and overland to Chicago and Springfield.

After visiting his family, his law partner, and friends, he turned his law-office corner into a shop where he whittled on a wooden model of a steamboat with "expansible buoyant chambers," "sliding spars," and ropes and pulleys. It was an invention, he told Herndon, and was going to work a revolution in steamboat navigation. On the way from Niagara Falls, the steamboat he was on got stuck on a sand-bar; the captain ordered barrels, boxes, and empty casks forced under the vessel; they lifted the vessel off the sand-bar with their "expansible buoyant chambers." So Lincoln finished off a model, and wrote a description of its workings, all to be patented.

Between times, he and Herndon talked about Niagara Falls. "What made the deepest impression on you?" asked Herndon. The answer: "The thing that struck me most forcibly when I saw the Falls was, where in the world did all the water come from." And he wrote notes for a lecture: how the geologist can prove by the wearing back of the Niagara plunge that the world is at least fourteen thousand years old; how Niagara calls up the past. "When Columbus first sought this continent—when Christ suffered on the Cross—when Moses led Israel through the Red Sea—nay, even when Adam first came from the hand of his Maker; then, as now, Niagara was roaring here." In the autumn weeks before Election Day, Lincoln stumped Illinois for the national and state Whig ticket, helping to make General Taylor President. His stand on the Mexican War he sometimes tried to make clear by saying the United States was like the farmer who said, as to wanting more land: "I ain't greedy; I only want what jines mine." Stephen T. Logan, running for Lincoln's seat in Congress, lost the race to a Democrat who was a Mexican War veteran.

CHAPTER 81

BACK home in Springfield, Lincoln had to help decide which Whigs should have plums. The Springfield postmaster, J. R. Diller, had done his best to defeat Lincoln's plans, and Lincoln recalled how five years previously he had got the postmastership for Diller. He had written a letter on December 16, 1844, to Congressman Hardin, reading:

DEAR JOHN J.:
You perhaps know of the great scramble going on here about our Post Office. Upon general principles, you know this would be no concern of the Whigs, but in this particular case, if it be in your power to do anything, you may thereby do a favor to some of your friends here, without disobliging any of them, so far as I believe—The man we wish appointed is J. R. Diller—The reason is that Major Spotwood's family, now comparatively destitute, will be *favoured* by it—I write this by an understanding with Diller himself who has seen its contents.

And having thus helped put Diller into office, Lincoln later found it necessary to ask politely that Diller be put out. This he did in a letter to the Postmaster General, recommending Abner Y. Ellis for the office, and declaring: "J. R. Diller, the present incumbent, I cannot say has failed in the proper discharge of any of the duties of the office. He, however, has been an active partisan in opposition to us."

Lincoln went to Washington, sat as a congressman who had failed of reëlection, introduced resolutions to abolish the slave trade in the District of Columbia, watched the hungry office-hunters come swarming in on President Taylor, tried and failed to land a high diplomatic appointment for Ned Baker, delivered a few remarks on the public lands, looked on the riotous whirl of the President's inauguration ball, had his hat stolen and walked Washington streets bareheaded at three o'clock in the morning, said good-by here and there—and came home to Springfield, through as a congressman.

Then during four or five months he carried on a campaign of letter-writing and conferences aimed at getting for himself or for some other

Illinois man the appointment of Commissioner of the General Land Office at Washington, salary $3,000 a year. Finally the politics of the affair seemed to narrow down to where Lincoln personally would have to go after the office or it would be lost to the Whigs of southern Illinois.

Early in June he was writing friends: "Would you as soon I should have the General Land Office as any other Illinoisan? If you would, write me to that effect at Washington, where I shall be soon. No time to lose."

Later in June he was in Washington wearing a linen duster, carrying a carpetbag, offering President Taylor eleven reasons why he should be named for the land-office job.

The appointment went to Justin Butterfield, who had marshaled northern Illinois and Chicago influence, besides that of Daniel Webster. And from then on, for months and years, Cyrus W. Edwards of Illinois refused to speak to Lincoln because he believed he himself should have had the land office, and Lincoln's handling of the affair had lost it to him. "To lose the friendship of Mr. Edwards by the effort for him," wrote Lincoln, "would oppress me very much, were I not sustained by the utmost consciousness of rectitude."

Lincoln's decision then was to stay in Springfield and practice law. During the spring he had been busy, as a leading Whig, in recommending Whigs to be appointed by the Taylor administration to various offices. Toward the end of July he wrote to John M. Clayton, the Secretary of State, that President Taylor's policy of throwing all responsibility for appointments on departments was having a bad effect.

The appointments need be no better than they have been, but the public must be brought to understand, that they are the *President's* appointments. He must occasionally say, or seem to say, "by the Eternal," "I take the responsibility." Those phrases were the "Samson's locks" of Gen. Jackson, and we dare not disregard the lessons of experience.

Your Ob't Sev't.

The months passed by and 3,400 Democratic office-holders were turned out and 3,400 Whigs put in their places. Shady claims of former years were brought up; the Secretary of War, Crawford, was paid, as his share of one claim, the sum of $115,000.00. President Taylor, sixty-four years old, walked the streets of Washington alone enjoying the weather; or he rode on "Old Whitey," the horse that went through the Mexican War with him; his wife, who didn't like leaving the Louisiana plantation to go to Washington, spent most of her time knitting in the White House; gas was installed to light the White House; new furniture and carpets were put in; when the President was introduced to a dozen young women in white dresses at a party one evening, he smiled slowly. "I have been so long among Indians and Mexicans that I hardly know how to behave myself, surrounded by so many lovely women."

Sam Houston came on from Texas as senator, wearing a vest made from a panther skin, and during Senate sessions sat whittling sticks of soft pine-wood supplied by the sergeant-at-arms.

The months passed and General Taylor sat in the hot sun near the Washington Monument and listened to two Fourth of July orations for nearly three hours; he drank ice-water, he went home to the White House and ate from a basket of cherries; he drank goblets of iced milk; he disobeyed his doctor and ate more cherries and iced milk; he had stood against all the ravages of Mexico and wild life in the Southwest; but he could not stand civilization. He said, "In two days I shall be a dead man." His mind was clear to the last and he murmured, "I have endeavored to do my duty."

Henry Clay had come back as senator from Kentucky, seventy-three years old; he had wept over his loss of the Presidency; he had seen two Whigs, who had beaten him for the nomination, die in office. He went to balls and parties, kissed the pretty girls as he chose, and played cards in his room at the National Hotel, always with a glass of toddy standing by, made from Kentucky Bourbon County whisky.

And out in Illinois Abraham Lincoln was settling down and straightening out his desk and papers in the law office with Bill Herndon. He was asking no nominations.

CHAPTER 82

ON the same front page of the *Illinois State Journal*, where Abraham Lincoln and W. H. Herndon announced, in 1849, they were "attornies and counselors-at-law," was the statement of J. H. Adams, at the Sign of the Big Hat, "He is determined to sell hats at the lowest prices." Adams enumerated fresh arrivals of hats, viz., beaver, fine brush, Angola drab, nutria, smooth cassimere, fashionable pearl, otter, moleskin, plush, Spanish shape, muskrat of French style, and round-crown Russia, also wool hats of all colors. Adams, however, was not alone in meeting the hat needs of Sangamon County. The New Hat Store was opening with hats "which will favorably compare with those made in St. Louis or any other city, fine moleskin hats, silk hats, fine Russia, and Rough and Ready Hats, warranted to stand hard service."

Adams lived by and for hats, and sometimes looked like a hat of a man, while John G. Ives led a quiet tick-tock, tick-tock existence, and looked like a clock of a man. Ives informed Springfield that "having been engaged in this city over eight years, in the repairing of clocks and watches, I feel confident I can give satisfaction to all who may favor me with their custom." Those having any disorder of the body were told that Birchall & Owen's drug-store kept Dr. Keeler's Panace which would cure all ills, including "constitutional debility, mercurial and hereditary predispositions, etc."

The saddle-maker, Amos Camp, said his motto was "Live and let live." Lowery, Lamb & Co. were selling a plow they said was "the best plough in the country for breaking up stubble and foul ground, as it is almost impossible to choke it." R. F. Ruth, the harness-maker, had put in a stock of saddles, saddlebags, carpetbags, carriage whips, and silver- and brass-mounted carriage and buggy harness, besides an assortment of horse collars, blind bridles, backbands, bellybands, long and short tugs.

Arrivals were announced of steel pens, Havana cigars, feather beds, india-rubber shoes, coal stoves, Russia parlor-stoves with self-regulators, silk fans, music boxes, eight-day brass clocks, silver candlesticks, ladies' buskins, bootees, slippers, chameleon silks, satin de chine, ladies' work-boxes, earrings, card cases, bracelets, Boston butter-crackers, new-style side and hanging lard-lamps, silk-fringed Thibet shawls, French merinoes, plaid lustres, drab modes. And at Hickox Brothers were 100 muffs for ladies, misses and children at fifty cents to fifteen dollars.

Rev. N. H. Hall, D.D., of Lexington, Kentucky, published a notice as to the day and hours he would preach in the First Presbyterian church, "God willing." Watson's saloon announced, "Oysters, sardines and other 'fixens' can be had at all hours except Sundays and Sunday nights." D. Barnes advertised, "Wanted, 10,000 deer skins—The highest price paid in cash for deer skins."

During the agitation for laying plank pavements around the public square of Springfield, and on the streets leading from the main hotels to the railroad depots, it was told that a traveling man one muddy week during spring rains, was saluted by another traveling man, "Didn't I see you yesterday morning sitting on a box in the middle of the street?" "No," was the reply, "I was sitting on top of the Chenery House bus."

Civilization was creeping in. Year by year, with no violence, but with slow, steady accretions, as an organic growth, civilization was rooting itself. Lincoln strolled hither and yon, on his shoulders the scrawny blue military cape he had bought in Washington when he was a member of the Congress of the United States. He saw cow pastures his feet had worn paths on, filled with lumber frame cottages; fences hedged the old paths. He saw city lots where a log cabin had stood and the dishes inside were pewter; in their stead had come a brick house with a pantry and little fan-shaped ice-cream dishes tinted with gold and blue violets.

"Who is bound for California?" queried a want ad, saying, "All persons who feel interested in the California Expedition will meet in the courthouse Saturday evening at early candlelight."

Lincoln was a spectator and a philosopher as he rambled and saw his fellow townsmen making out as well as they could with life. It interested him when a man such as John Hutchinson, the undertaker, opened a line of cabinet furniture, and announced: "He also continues the undertaking, as heretofore, and is proprietor of the new burying ground, which is laid off in small lots, suitable for families. Also half lots and graves for one person. Coffins of every size and quality ready made, and as cheap as can be had in the city of the same quality; and hearse-gentle horse and careful driver furnished as heretofore."

Yet Lincoln's life was not held down to the humdrum of Springfield. He had law cases in towns out on the Eighth Circuit. On the day before Christmas of 1849, he was in Cincinnati, Ohio, writing a letter to Peter Hitchcock, chief justice of the supreme court of Ohio, at Columbus. Either that day or the next Lincoln expected to get the brief of the other side in the case, and then go on to Columbus, for the hearing. He was associated with T. D. Lincoln of Cincinnati. Their client was Linus Logan, whose steamboat, *Mail*, was rammed by the steamboat, *Clipper*, on the Ohio River. Lincoln's client had won a verdict of $3,760.00 in a lower court. In the hearing before the supreme court at Columbus, this verdict was sustained.

CHAPTER 83

THE little frame house which was the Lincoln home on the corner of Eighth and Jackson streets in Springfield was painted white, with green blinds, and white chimneys. Under the care of Mary Todd Lincoln, who was spick and span about such things, it was a clean, snug-looking place. There the ex-congressman, back from Washington, settled down to law practice, shoveled snow from the front door to the street, from the back door to the barn and the outhouses.

As he put the currycomb to the horse and slicked axle grease on his buggy wheels, he could think about little Stephen A. Douglas, the short, thick-chested, blue-eyed man who had been a common struggler with the rest of them in Springfield a few years back, now sitting in conferences with Clay, Calhoun, and Webster at Washington, a defender of the memory of Andrew Jackson, and fast taking place as a national leader of the Democratic party.

It seemed only yesterday that Simeon Francis caught Douglas by the hair and jammed him against a hayrack on the public square. And James Shields, whom he had met on a sand-bar in the Mississippi River and was ready to cleave in two with a cavalry broadsword, was Douglas's colleague from Illinois in the Senate. The mayor of Springfield was John Calhoun, his old friend who had started him as a surveyor. They were all Democrats. Among Whigs luck was the other way; his old law partners were practicing law; Stuart had been in Congress and never got back; Stephen T. Logan, the little thin-lipped, sharp-voiced, bushy-haired man who had tried hard to be elected, had not reached Congress but had stayed at home and become known as one of the ablest lawyers in Illinois.

Quaint statistical facts stood in plain garb in the newspaper columns; puppets with prophetic fingers. Eighty thousand cords of wood were burned yearly in the railroad locomotives of the country; but coal had been tried out and coal mines were opening up. In April of 1848, when the telegraph lines from New York had reached as far as Niles, Michigan, the *Tribune* of Chicago notified its readers that perhaps in two weeks Chicago would have telegraphic connection with New York, Boston, and Washington. "When that takes place, look to the *Tribune* for late news."

The slavery question seemed to be settled by the Omnibus bill. Five negroes were in jail down on the public square; they were fugitive slaves, and, according to the law, would go back to their owners. And yet, though the slavery question did seem settled, there were more quiet men here and there who were helping to pass on runaway negroes, up from Jacksonville, Springfield, Bloomington, on up to Galesburg, Princeton, Chicago and so to Canada, where the British law prohibiting slave ownership made them safe.

The northern part of Illinois had been filling up with settlers. Towns such as Princeton and Galesburg were like little pieces of New England, more Yankee than some towns in New England which had filled their factories with newcomers from Europe. Irish and Germans were swarming into Chicago by thousands. At Bishop Hill was a settlement where the women wove rag-carpets and wore black kerchiefs around their heads, knotted under the chins; it was a spot as humanly Swedish as Sweden. Yes, Illinois was changing. What was ahead in politics, no man could tell. The one sure thing was that the people from Kentucky, Tennessee, and Virginia and the Carolinas, who had controlled Illinois, were to be out-numbered and outvoted at some time in the near future.

Up in Bureau County was Owen Lovejoy, brother of Elijah; over in Ohio was Joshua Giddings; Edward D. Baker had gone to California and was lighting the Sacramento Valley with his oratorical torch.

New men, new issues, were coming. The writing of the history of the country would have to be with new names.

Over the breakfast and supper table at the Lincoln home, the woman of the house told him her hopes that he would move onward and upward to a high place where his name would shine. He knew that fame, name, and high place would please her more than anything else. When he made a move in politics he usually knew her view of it; she told him her views, and plainly. She read, she talked with people of influence, she gave him her judgment. She told him when she was pleased, when she wasn't.

He believed in dreams and tried to read his dreams for their connections with his future. She believed in signs; she told him about signs, portents. Both were superstitious. Both had hopes.

As the ex-congressman and prominent Whig leader shoveled snow, he had thoughts and hopes.

News came one day as he was trying a case over in Bloomington. The Whig administration at Washington had a message for the leading Whig in Illinois. Was he willing to take an appointment as governor of the Territory of Oregon? Lincoln made a quick answer. Whether he would go depended on what he heard from his wife. Her decision was "No." She was willing to live in Washington as the wife of the general land-commissioner, but she did not care to live in a pioneer country separated by weeks of wagon travel from the settled regions of the country.

Illinois itself then had enough silent places. The plumes of smoke from the breakfast and supper fires of the cabins along the Sangamon were lonely enough. The corn-fed population of the Midwest frontier was only beginning to learn how to raise corn, and fatten and market cattle and hogs. The corn belt was young. It had yet to learn how to fill the food bunkers of cities and armies.

CHAPTER 84

LINCOLN studied and worked on law cases as never before in his life. For five years politics was a side issue. He said he was out of politics. He traveled on the Eighth Judicial Circuit with a court that moved across fourteen counties, staying two days to two weeks in each county seat among "a very litigious people."

From September till Christmas and from February till June, he was away from his Springfield home, handling all kinds of law cases, driving a buggy across the prairie of fourteen counties in all kinds of weather. It was his way of earning a living, keeping bread and butter in the home pantry at Springfield. He dropped into a way of life that kept him in close touch with people, their homes, kitchens, barns, fields, their churches, schools, hotels, saloons, their places for working and worshiping and loafing.

For the first time he held in his arms the white still body of a child of his own; he could call the name of Eddie to his boy and the boy had no ears to hear nor breath to answer.

This was his own kith and kin, who had come out of silence and gone back to silence, back where Nancy Hanks had gone the year he helped his father peg together a plank coffin.

He tried to pierce through into the regions of that silence and find replies to questions that surged in him.

On the day Eddie was buried, a funeral sermon was pronounced by Rev. James Smith of the First Presbyterian Church, and a friendship developed between the Lincoln family and the Reverend Mr. Smith. The minister had been a wild boy in his young days in Scotland, had been a scoffer at religion, and had been a preacher in Kentucky; he could tell a story—he and Lincoln were good company.

The Lincolns rented a pew in the church. Mrs. Lincoln took the sacrament, and joined in membership. Reverend Mr. Smith presented Lincoln with a copy of his book, "The Christian's Defence," a reply to infidels and atheists; it argued that the creation of the world as told in the Book of Genesis, the fall of man in the Garden of Eden, the flood which ended with Noah's Ark on Mount Ararat were true events, that the books of the Old Testament are not forgeries, that a number of profane authors testify to the truth of the New Testament evangels, that only an atheist can deny divine inspiration; the divine authority of the Scriptures is proved from prophecy and its fulfilment.

Lincoln read "The Christian's Defence," said he was interested, later attended revival meetings held in the First Presbyterian Church, and said he was interested. But when asked to join the church he said he "couldn't quite see it."

To his law partner he remarked: "There are no accidents in my philosophy. Every effect must have its cause. The past is the cause of the present, and the present will be the cause of the future. All these are links in the endless chain stretching from the Infinite to the finite." The *Edinburgh Review* was on their office table periodically, and in Herndon's library Lincoln read as he chose, from volumes by Locke, Kant, Fichte, Herbert Spencer; the sermons and essays of Theodore Parker and Ralph Waldo Emerson; Thomas Paine's "The Age of Reason" and "Common Sense"; Gregg's "Creed of Christendom"; Volney's "The Ruins of Empires"; Feuerbach's "Essence of Christianity"; McNaught on "Inspiration."

Lincoln read some of these, and read carefully a second time "Vestiges of the Natural History of Creation," by Robert Chambers, a Scotchman who said his book was "the first attempt to connect the natural sciences with the history of creation." The rock layers over the earth hold the bones of animals and plants showing that the world was millions of years in the making, that God practiced at making many other animals before at last he made man, according to Chambers's book. It interested Lincoln; six or eight years before, he had read a copy borrowed of James W. Keys; now he read again carefully the sixth and revised edition in Herndon's library. Many ministers were telling their congregations the book was a bad book, was against the teachings of the Bible; other ministers were saying it was a book worth reading.

Close friends of Lincoln, such as his law partner Herndon, and Matheny, who stood as best man at his wedding, had a notion Lincoln was a sort of infidel. They said Lincoln told them he did not believe the Bible was the revelation of God, and in a little book he wrote in New Salem he tried to prove Jesus was not the Son of God. "Lincoln did tell me that he did write a little book on infidelity—I got it from Lincoln's mouth," said Matheny. "An infidel, a theist, a fatalist," was Herndon's notion.

And yet Lincoln read the Bible closely, knew it from cover to cover, was familiar with its stories and its poetry, quoted from it in his talks to juries, in political campaigns, in his speeches, and in his letters. There were evangelical Christian church members who felt he was a solemn, earnest, religious man.

Still others, like Jesse W. Fell at Bloomington, felt that he held a good deal the same views as the famous heterodox New England preachers, Theodore Parker and William Ellery Channing. When Fell talked with enthusiasm about Channing's sermons, Lincoln showed such a keen interest that Fell asked Lincoln if he would like to have a complete collection of the sermons. So Fell bought a special edition for Lincoln, who put it in his little library where it kept company with "Exercises in the Syntax of the Greek Language," by Rev. William Nielson, D.D.

On page 34 was a sentence reading in Greek, "Ye have loved me, and have believed that I came forth from God," with the words "from God" crossed with a pen and the words "from nature" scribbled in Lincoln's handwriting.

When word came that his father down on the Coles County farm was dying, Lincoln wrote a letter to John D. Johnston, the stepson at the farm.

I feel sure you have not failed to use my name, if necessary, to procure a doctor, or anything else for father in his sickness. My business is such that I could hardly leave home now, if it was not as it is, that my own wife is sick-a-bed. (It is a case of baby-sickness, and I suppose is not dangerous.) I sincerely hope father may recover his health, but at all events, tell him to remember to call upon and confide in our great and good merciful Maker, who will not turn away from him in any extremity. He notes the fall of a sparrow, and numbers the hairs of our heads, and He will not forget the dying man who puts his trust in Him. Say to him that if we could meet now it is doubtful whether it would not be more painful than pleasant, but that if it be his lot to go now, he will soon have a joyous meeting with many loved ones gone before, and where the rest of us, through the help of God, hope ere long to join them.

When death was close by, and there was a murmur out of deep rivers, and the moan of a long wind out of a cavern of dark stars, Lincoln often used Bible language.

The young printer, Gilbert J. Greene, drove out with him from Springfield one time to a farmhouse where a woman was dying. Lincoln was to draw up her last will and testament. After the paper was signed and witnessed, as the young printer remembered what happened, the woman asked, "Mr. Lincoln, won't you read a few verses out of the Bible for me?"

A Bible was brought; but, instead of taking it, the lawyer began reciting from memory the psalm, "Though I walk through the valley of the shadow of death I will fear no evil, for thou art with me; thy rod and thy staff they comfort me." And again, without taking the Bible, he repeated such verses as, "Let not your heart be troubled; ye believe in God, believe also in me," and "In my Father's house are many mansions; if it were not so I would have told you. I go to prepare a place for you."

He had told Mrs. Rankin, over near New Salem, that before he learned to read as a boy he had heard his mother saying over certain Bible verses day by day as she worked. He had learned these verses by heart; the tones of his mother's voice were in them; and sometimes, as he read these verses, he seemed to hear the voice of Nancy Hanks speaking them. This he told Mrs. Rankin one day when a Sunday-school convention was being held at Petersburg and the question was discussed as to the age at which children were morally responsible and prepared to be taught the Bible.

Mrs. Rankin was a friend of the preacher, Peter Cartwright, who ran for Congress against Lincoln; in her house Cartwright was called "Uncle Peter." And she had heard that Cartwright claimed Lincoln was no Christian and that Lincoln had said, "Christ was a bastard." Yet Lincoln was also a friend of the family. At her house he had borrowed books; there they had reached out kindly hands when he was groping and trying to pierce the silence into which Ann Rutledge had faded. So one evening Mrs. Rankin told him she knew the Cartwright charges against him were false; and yet—there was the question of what his religion really was.

The raising of the question made Lincoln restless; he stood up, crossed the room, rested an elbow on the fireplace mantel, and ran his hand through his hair. He said slowly that he could not discuss the character and religion of Jesus Christ in stump speeches. "That is no place for it."

He mentioned "shadows and questionings" that came to him at New Salem. "There came into my life sad events and a loss that you were close to; and you knew a great deal about how hard they were for me, for you were, at the time, a mutual friend. Those days of trouble found me tossed amid a sea of questionings. They piled big around me. Through all I groped my way until I found a stronger and higher grasp of thought, one that reached beyond this life with a clearness and satisfaction I had never known before. The Scriptures unfolded before me with a deeper and more logical appeal, through these new experiences, than anything else I could find to turn to, or ever before had found in them. I do not claim that all my doubts were removed then, or since that time have been swept away. They are not.

"Probably it is to be my lot to go on in a twilight, feeling and reasoning my way through life, as questioning, doubting Thomas did. But in my poor, maimed, withered way, I bear with me as I go on a seeking spirit of desire for a faith that was with him of the olden time, who, in his need, as I in mine, exclaimed, 'Help thou my unbelief.' "

He had by now slowed down from his first restless feeling; he left the fireplace and took his chair again. "I do not see that I am more astray— though perhaps in a different direction—than many others whose points of view differ widely from each other in the sectarian denominations. They all claim to be Christians, and interpret their several creeds as infallible ones. I doubt the possibility, or propriety, of settling the religion of Jesus Christ in the models of man-made creeds and dogmas.

"It was a spirit in the life that He laid stress on and taught, if I read aright. I know I see it to be so with me. The fundamental truths reported in the four gospels as from the lips of Jesus Christ, and that I first heard from the lips of my mother, are settled and fixed moral precepts with me. I have concluded to dismiss from my mind the debatable wrangles that once perplexed me with distractions that stirred up, but never absolutely settled anything. I have tossed them aside with the doubtful differences which divide denominations. I have ceased to follow such discussions or be interested in them. I cannot without mental reservations assent to long and complicated creeds and catechisms.

"If the church would ask simply for assent to the Savior's statement of the substance of the law: 'Thou shalt love the Lord thy God with all thy heart, and with all thy soul, and with all thy mind, and thy neighbor as thyself,'—that church would I gladly unite with."

That was the way Mrs. Rankin remembered Lincoln talking about his religion that evening. She was sure that if she didn't remember all his words exactly as he spoke them she did get his thought clear, because he spoke his words in a slow manner and meant his words to be so clear that his thoughts would be remembered afterward.

Some who knew him in his home town said he was careless about church, never went inside of a church. Others, such as his friend, James C. Conkling, had other views. Of Lincoln's taking the pulpit and giving an address before the Springfield Bible Society, Conkling said: "When he had finished, he came down and slid into the seat with me. He was somewhat puzzled to understand why he had been selected to talk about the Bible. He whispered to me, 'I don't know why on earth they got me to make this kind of a speech unless it was to milk the Gentiles.' "

For the Kickapoo Indian, Johnny Kongapod, Lincoln used an epitaph that had the breath of his religion in it:

> Here lies poor Johnny Kongapod;
> Have mercy on him, gracious God.
> As he would do if he was God
> And you were Johnny Kongapod.

He was troubled about man, about God, about his country. Driving to

Petersburg one day with Herndon, the year after he came back from Washington, he broke out: "How hard, oh, how hard it is to die and leave one's country no better than if one had never lived for it! The world is dead to hope, deaf to its own death struggle, made known by a universal cry, What is to be done? Is anything to be done? Who can do anything? And how is it to be done? Do you ever think of these things?"

And he was trying to live up to the pieces of advice which he boxed in with a lead pencil in his book of exercises in Greek syntax:

> Deliberate slowly, but execute promptly, the things which have appeared unto thee proper to be done.
> Love, not the immoderate acquisition, but the moderate enjoyment, of present good.

CHAPTER 85

"The great Calhoun is dead," mourned South Carolina and her neighbors in 1850. "The great Henry Clay is dead," cried other mourners in 1852; and in that same year was heard the cry, "The great Daniel Webster is dead."

All three had been congressman, senator, Secretary of State; all three had missed the Presidency by narrow margins of whimsical ballots. They had spoken yes and no on the War of 1812, on the Mexican War, and they were dying as the country was blundering along with grave problems they had failed to solve.

In their places were rising new young leaders to play with public opinion. Moving toward a chief place in the Democratic party was young Stephen A. Douglas. The names of Seward of New York, Sumner of Massachusetts, Chase of Ohio, Greeley of the *Tribune,* were beginning to count.

Among the Abolitionists rose young Wendell Phillips, aristocratic, handsome, ironical, scathing, bitter not only with the bitterness of a man in anguish over slaves chained, flogged, bought and sold, but bitter with some added tincture of a man gnashing and jeering at a whole humanity of chattels and puppets. He invented a form of oratory staccato with sneers and javelins. There were hours when he seemed to be a personally foiled creature who was able to make people think his own frustrations were the frustrations of the dreams of democracy. Eggs kept overlong in storage crossed the air and broke on his face as he was speaking from a platform; he wiped the smear from his face and smiled, "They are fresh." He embodied proud yearnings and gifts of contempt.

Far to the south lived Jefferson Davis, the choice of Calhoun for southern leadership; six feet high, loose-jointed, a West Pointer who walked militarily erect, with a springy step, his war-wounded foot healed. He had for his body servant the black man called Pemberton, who had been with him in the Black Hawk War and again was with him through the Mexican War when the southerners of the Mississippi Rifles had their own slave servants along. From his cotton plantation and slave quarters at Biloxi, Mississippi, he could look out on the Gulf of Mexico. His home soil was swept by tropic breezes from a salt gulf whose warm waters touched Mexico, Yucatan, Cuba, Haiti; the breath of his home outlook in winter was different from that of bleak and frozen New England and that of the Northwest where blizzards piled their snowdrifts up to the latches of the cabin doors of the settlers.

Often Davis could vision the so-called Union of states as two sections or confederacies with two cultures, fated to separate. When it seemed that California was going to be let into the Union as a free state there were mass meetings in all parts of Mississippi; as Davis left for Washington he believed the state of Mississippi would draw out of the Union and be joined by other states.

In Illinois was the potential Abraham Lincoln trying a law case in Chicago, and called on to deliver the address at memorial exercises for General Zachary Taylor. He spoke mournfully and quoted seven stanzas from the star poem of the album of his memory, "Oh, Why Should the Spirit of Mortal Be Proud?" In Taylor's character he noted two traits, "absence of excitement and absence of fear."

When Henry Clay, foremost of Whigs, died in 1852, Lincoln was named to deliver a fifty-minute speech of eulogy at a memorial meeting in the statehouse in Springfield. As he searched among papers, speeches, and books, he found less material than he expected. He tried to put his hand on a model eulogy that Henry Clay had spoken about some other great man. But except for a few lines on the death of John Calhoun, it seemed that Clay never had eulogized anybody.

Lincoln had a feeling that Henry Clay had been rather cold, hard, selfish, with personal ambitions that had helped wreck the Whig party. But this, of course, couldn't be put into a speech. Neither could he put into a speech his own picture of Henry Clay's manipulation of the famous compromise measures in Congress. Lincoln mentally noted, but not for the eulogy: "When Clay wanted to carry an important measure, he drew it up in such a way as to embody his own idea as nearly as he could, and at the same time not be offensive to those whose aid was indispensable—he then presented it to the strong men whose help he must have or whose opposition he must stifle, and who were of strong wills, and either argued them into its support, or made such concessions and modifications as they insisted on, or added palatable features to suit them, and thus got a powerful force enlisted in behalf of his measure:—then he visited the members of feeble wills and simply bullied them into its support without yielding one iota to them." This, too, could not be put into a speech of eulogy.

In the address, as given, he noted that Clay was born in 1777 and grew up with the country; when Clay got his start in politics the Union of states was holding together; when he quit, the Union was holding together; Clay must have had something to do with it. "Mr. Clay's predominant sentiment, from first to last, was a deep devotion to the cause of human liberty." And, "Our country is prosperous and powerful; but could it have been quite all it has been, and is, and is to be, without Henry Clay?"

He referred to "Mr. Clay's eloquence," saying: "All his efforts were for practical effect. He never spoke merely to be heard. He never delivered a Fourth of July oration, or a eulogy on an occasion like this."

One little chapter in the life of Clay fascinated Lincoln. That had to do with an hour when Clay forgot himself and tore loose a speech that was so wild, bold, and free that the reporters dropped their pencils and the language of it was never written down. This lost speech lived in the memories of men as the best speech Clay ever made.

A speech that Lincoln's best friends were sorry about was delivered this year—a reply to remarks of Stephen A. Douglas in Richmond, Virginia. Douglas was four years younger than Lincoln, had come as a Vermont Yankee to Illinois about the same time as Lincoln, and had fought his way to high Democratic leadership.

A streak of jealousy ran through Lincoln's opening remarks to the Scott Club of Springfield. "This speech [that of Douglas at Richmond] has been published with high commendations in at least one of the Democratic papers in this state, and I suppose it has been and will be in most of the others. When I first saw it and read it I was reminded of old times, when Judge Douglas was not so much greater a man than all the rest of us, as he is now—of the Harrison campaign twelve years ago, when I used to hear and try to answer many of his speeches; and believing that the Richmond speech, though marked with the same species of 'shirks and quirks' as the old ones, was not marked with any greater ability, I was seized with a strange inclination to attempt an answer to it; and this inclination it was that prompted me to seek the privilege of addressing you on this occasion."

He took up Douglas's statement that Providence had saved the country from one military administration by the timely removal of General Taylor, and closed his speech: "Let us stand by our candidate [General

Scott] as faithfully as he has always stood by our country, and I much doubt if we do not perceive a slight abatement in Judge Douglas's confidence in Providence, as well as in the people. I suspect that confidence is not more firmly fixed with the judge than it was with the old woman whose horse ran away with her in a buggy. She said she 'trusted in Providence till the britchin' broke,' and then she didn't know 'what on airth to do.' The chance is, the judge will see the 'britchin' broke'; and then he can at his leisure bewail the fate of Locofocoism as the victim of misplaced confidence."

Election Day came in that year of 1852. The Whig party went to pieces. General Winfield Scott, the hero of Vera Cruz, was snowed under, carried only four states, and the Democrats sent to the White House the young Colonel Franklin Pierce, handsome, well educated, conciliatory, the hero of a campaign book written by Nathaniel Hawthorne, author of "The Scarlet Letter," a great writer of books who earned his living as a custom-house official.

CHAPTER 86

WHEN Robert Todd, the bank president and cotton-yarn manufacturer, died at his home in Lexington, Kentucky, in 1849, Abraham Lincoln had spent some days in Lexington attending to the division of the estate in behalf of his wife, Mary Todd Lincoln, the second eldest daughter of Robert Todd. Four years later a suit was filed against Lincoln charging that he had collected money in Illinois for Robert Todd.

"I find it difficult to suppress my indignation towards those who have got up this claim against me," Lincoln wrote his lawyer at Lexington. He pushed for action to show when he had collected money, from whom, where they lived, and when. He wrote long letters to his lawyer with particular instructions, and traced the cause of the suit back to the bad feeling held by Levi O. Todd against his three sisters who lived in Springfield. Levi Todd asserted that his father had let the sisters have money freely—and there was money owing the estate.

"This matter harasses my feelings a good deal," Lincoln again wrote his lawyer, again with special instructions. At the trial it was proven that another lawyer in Illinois had made the collections referred to in the suit.

The record cleared Lincoln completely, and he wrote his lawyer, "I expect and desire you to be paid a separate fee for your attention to that suit; and to authorize you to retain what you shall deem reasonable on that account, out of any money of mine which is or may come into your hands. If nothing further for me is, or is likely to be in your hands, write me and I will forward you the amount."

Another money matter to look after was down on the Coles County farm where Sally Bush Lincoln, his stepmother, was living. Her son, John D. Johnston, wrote asking for eighty dollars. Lincoln replied: "Your request for eighty dollars I do not think it best to comply with now." He had husked corn in Indiana with John D. Johnston and knew Johnston's ways. He wrote advice: "You are not lazy, and still you are an idler. I doubt whether, since I saw you, you have done a good whole day's work in any one day. This habit of uselessly wasting time is the whole difficulty; it is vastly important to you, and still more so to your children that you should break the habit."

He promised he would give Johnston one other dollar for every dollar Johnston went to work and earned. "If you hire yourself at ten dollars a month, from me you will get ten more, making twenty dollars a month for your work. In this I do not mean you shall go off to St. Louis, or the lead mines, or the gold mines of California, but I mean for you to go at it for the best wages you can get in Coles County. You say you would almost give your place in heaven for seventy or eighty dollars. Then you value your place in heaven very cheap, for I am sure you can, with the offer I make, get the seventy or eighty dollars for four or five months' work."

On a trip to Coles County, Lincoln found out that Johnston was anxious to sell the land he lived on and move to Missouri. He wrote to Johnston:

Such a notion is utterly foolish. What can you do in Missouri better than here? Is the land any richer? Can you there, any more than here, raise corn and wheat and oats without work? Will anybody there, any more than here, do your work for you? If you intend to go to work, there is no better place than right where you are; if you do not intend to go to work, you cannot get along anywhere.

Squirming and crawling about from place to place can do no good. You have raised no crop this year; and what you really want is to sell the land, get the money, and spend it. Part with the land you have, and my life upon it, you will never after own a spot big enough to bury you in. Half you will get for the land you will spend in moving to Missouri, and the other half you will eat, drink, and wear out, and no foot of land will be bought. Now, I feel it my duty to have no hand in such a piece of foolery. I feel that it is so even on your own account, and particularly on mother's account.

The eastern forty acres I intend to keep for mother while she lives; if you will not cultivate it, it will rent for enough to support her—at least it will rent for something. Her dower in the other two forties she can let you have, and no thanks to me. I do not write in any unkindness. Your thousand pretenses for not getting along are all nonsense; they deceive nobody but yourself. Go to work is the only cure for your case.

Thus a stepson to the son of his stepmother. In all the letters of Lincoln to John D. Johnston there shines far back the feeling of love and care for Sally Bush Lincoln. It was she who tried to tell what there was between her and young Abe in saying, "His mind and mine, what little **I** had, seemed to run together."

CHAPTER 87

IN the little white house with the green blinds and the white chimneys at Eighth and Jackson streets, Mary Todd Lincoln had in ten years' time borne four children. In the winter of 1850 came William Wallace; in the spring of 1853 came Thomas, nicknamed Tad.

At the cradles of these babies, at the grave of one who had died, the mother and father had stood together. For these little ones who came, pink, soft, and helpless, lying on their backs and kicking their heels toward the ceiling, Lincoln was thankful.

To handle them, tickle them, and talk their goo-goo talk, and watch them grow, had an appeal for his sense both of the solemn and of the ridiculous. Kittens he had always liked; where other men enjoyed hunting and fishing, he found sport in petting kittens. And babies, particularly his own babies, were sacred keepsakes loaned out of a silence.

As the years had passed, the two who had so suddenly and independently married came to understand that each was strong and each was weak. Habits held him that it was useless for her to try to break. If he chose to lie on the front-room carpet, on the small of his back, reading, she knew that was his way. Likewise if he came to the table in his shirt-sleeves and ate his meat and potatoes absently, with his eyes and his thoughts far off, that too was his way.

She tried to stop him from answering the ring of the front-door bell; the servant should answer the bell. But he would go to the front door and ask the callers what was wanted. Once two fine ladies wanted Mrs. Lincoln; he looked the house over and came back to ask the callers in, drawling pleasantly, "She'll be down soon as she gets her trotting harness on."

And when his wife wrangled with the iceman claiming an overcharge or when she screamed at John Mendonsa that she would pay only ten cents a quart for berries, that they were not worth fifteen cents, he spoke quietly to her as "Mary," and did his best to straighten things with the iceman or the berry-picker. Mary had sewed her own clothes, had sewed clothes for the children; he let her manage the house.

Young Chevalier Henry Haynie came to the law office asking money for a new hose cart for the volunteer fire company. And he told Haynie and a committee: "Boys, when I go home to supper—Mrs. Lincoln is always in a fine, good humor then—I'll say to her, over the toast: 'My dear, there is a subscription paper being handed round to raise money to buy a new hose cart. The committee called on me this afternoon, and I told them to wait until I consulted my home partner. Don't you think I had better subscribe fifty dollars?' Then she will look up quickly and exclaim: 'Will you never learn, never learn? You are always too liberal, too generous. Fifty dollars! No, indeed; we can't afford it. Twenty-five's quite reasonable enough.' "

And he chuckled: "Bless her dear soul, she'll never find out how I got the better of her; and if she does, she'll forgive me. Come around tomorrow, boys, and get your twenty-five dollars."

A workman caring for the Lincoln yard went to Lincoln's office to ask about cutting down a tree. "What did Mrs. Lincoln say?" was Lincoln's question. "She said yes." "Then, in God's name, cut it down to the roots."

There were friends and relatives of Mrs. Lincoln who felt sorry for her. One said: "Mrs. Lincoln comes of the best stock, and was raised like a lady. Her husband was the opposite, in origin, in education, in breeding, in everything; and it is therefore quite natural that she should complain if he answers the doorbell himself instead of sending the servant to do so. Neither is she to be condemned if she raises 'merry war' because he persists in using his own knife in the butter, instead of the silver-handled one intended for that purpose."

Among servant girls in Springfield Mrs. Lincoln had a reputation of being hard to get along with. A girl named Maria came; she would stay a few days, maybe a month, said the other girls. But she stayed two years. Lincoln had arranged to pay her a dollar a week extra, Mrs. Lincoln knowing nothing about the extra dollar.

"The madame and I began to understand each other," said Maria. "More than once, when she happened to be out of the room, Mr. Lincoln, with a merry twinkle in his eye, patted me on the shoulder, urging, 'Stay with her, Maria, stay with her.' "

When John Bradford bought a new carriage and invited Mrs. Lincoln to join him and his family for a drive in the country, he said she came out of the house nervous and wrought up and he had a suspicion she had been in a wrangle with a new servant girl, for just as she settled back in her seat she exclaimed with a sigh: "Well, one thing is certain: if Mr. Lincoln should happen to die, his spirit will never find me living outside the boundaries of a slave state."

A law student, Gibson W. Harris, in the office of Lincoln and Herndon, often ran errands out to the Lincoln home. Twice, when Lincoln was away on the circuit, he was Mrs. Lincoln's escort at a ball. He remarked: "I found her to be a good dancer; she was bright, witty, and accomplished. The sportive nickname she gave me was Mr. Mister. Mr. Lincoln showed great consideration for his wife. She was unusually timid and nervous during a storm. If the clouds gathered and the thunder rolled, he knew its effect on his wife and would at once hasten home to remain there with her till the skies cleared and the storm was safely over."

In many important matters Lincoln trusted her judgment. Herndon noted: "She was an excellent judge of human nature, a better reader of men's motives than her husband and quick to detect those who had designs upon and sought to use him. She was, in a good sense, a stimulant. . . . She kept him from lagging, was constantly prodding him to keep up the struggle. She . . . wanted to be a leader in society. . . . Realizing that Lincoln's rise in the world would elevate and strengthen her, she strove in every way to promote his fortunes, to keep him moving, and thereby win the world's applause."

She wrote to him one spring when he was in Washington that her headaches were gone; he wrote back the news was good considering it was the first spring since they were acquainted that she had been free from headaches.

He asked her to get weighed and report to him how many pounds she had put on. And he could joke her, "I am afraid you will get so well and fat and young as to be wanting to marry again."

Having bought a set of shirt-bosom studs, he wrote her they were set in gold—modest, pretty, little ones—only costing fifty cents apiece or $1.50 for the set of three.

On leaving home he would beg her not to let the children forget father. Once when away he had a dream about bad luck happening to Bobby, and called it a foolish dream, but couldn't rid himself of its impression till a letter from home said Bobby was safe and well.

Living next door to the Lincolns, and watching their ups and downs, was a shoemaker, James Gourley. When the Lincoln cow went dry, Lincoln stepped over to Gourley's for milk.

"He used to come to our house with his feet in a pair of loose slippers, wearing an old, faded pair of trousers fastened with one suspender," was Gourley's impression. "Our rooms were low, and one day he said, 'Jim, you'll have to lift your loft a little higher; I can't straighten out under it very well.' To my wife, who was short, he used to say that little people had advantages; they required 'less wood and wool to make them comfortable.' I think the Lincolns agreed moderately well. As a rule Mr. Lincoln yielded to his wife—in fact, almost any other man, had he known the woman as I did, would have done the same thing. She was gifted with an unusually high temper and that invariably got the better of her. She was very excitable and when wrought up had hallucinations.

"I remember once when her husband was away from home she conceived the notion that some rough characters had designs on her and the hired girl. She had worked herself up to a furious pitch, weeping and wailing loud enough to be heard by the neighbors, and even asked me to spend the night at her house guarding the premises and thus protect her and her girl. Of course I expressed a willingness to do whatever she asked, although I knew the whole thing was imaginary. This was not the only time her demonstrations were loud enough to be heard by some of her neighbors.

"If she became excited or troublesome, as she sometimes did when Mr. Lincoln was at home, it was interesting to know what he would do. At first, he would apparently pay no attention to her. Frequently he would laugh at her, which is a risky thing to do in the face of an infuriated wife; but generally, if her impatience continued, he would pick up one of the children and deliberately leave home as if to take a walk. After he had gone, the storm usually subsided, but sometimes it would break out again when he returned.

"Notwithstanding her unfortunate temper and her peculiarities generally, I never thought Mrs. Lincoln was as bad as some people here in Springfield represented her. The truth is, she had more than one redeeming trait. She and I rarely differed—in fact, we were good friends. Although I do not believe she could plead justification for many of the things she did, yet, when I hear her criticized by some people, I cannot but recall what she once said to me about her husband, which was that, if he had been at home as much as he ought, she could have been happier and loved him more."

Harriet Hanks, a daughter of Dennis, stayed at the Lincoln house a year and a half, going to school in Springfield, and leaving because she couldn't get along with Mrs. Lincoln. "I often heard Mr. Lincoln say he could eat corn cakes as fast as two women could make them," said Harriet. "He seldom ever wore his coat in the house, and went to the table in his shirt-sleeves, which annoyed his wife, who loved to put on style. One day he undertook to correct his child and his wife was determined that he should not, and attempted to take it from him; but in this she failed. She tried tongue-lashing, but met with the same fate, for Mr. Lincoln corrected the child, as a father ought to, in the face of his wife's anger, and that too without changing his countenance or making any reply to her."

So there was talk about Mrs. Lincoln over Springfield. She economized in the kitchen in order to have fine clothes; she had a terrible temper and tongue; so the talk ran. That her husband had married her a thousand dollars in debt, that he charged low fees as a lawyer and was careless about money, and that she had managed the household so well that her husband trusted her and let her have her own way in all the household economy, didn't get into the gossip. That she was often sorry, full of regret, after a bad burst of temper, didn't get into the gossip.

She had borne four children for the man she had chosen for a husband at a time when she had a wide range of choices, when an elegant marriage in her own class was planned for her. She had chosen one of the loneliest, strangest men in the world—for a husband. She had chosen him deliberately, calling him back when over and again he tried to slip away. She sewed clothes for herself and her children. She read and spoke French, keeping on with her studies.

While he was away six months of the year, she kept up connections socially that were of value politically. There were others saying, as young Gibson Harris said, "I found her to be a good dancer; bright, witty, accomplished." She had soft brown hair, clear blue eyes that swept with laughter or scorn. She liked fixing herself up, making herself pretty.

As Lincoln sat across from her at the breakfast table, he could see on her hand the plain gold ring he had once placed there—on the inside of it the words Chatterton, the jeweler, had engraved, "Love is eternal."

He had bought that ring only a little while after he had written his Kentucky chum, Joshua Speed, that his father used to say, "If you make a bad bargain, hug it all the tighter."

CHAPTER 88

As Lincoln walked the streets of Springfield and as he rode the circuit of twelve counties, living in hotels and courthouses, he met people shaken and stirred by slavery; they had read a book; the book had set their hearts on fire with hate; they hated the South, the people of the South; it was a hate that made them hate their own country, its laws, its flag: they believed their own country guilty of a crime worse than the crimes of any other country in any other time.

They had read a book; men couldn't pitch hay or fix a wagon, women couldn't wash dishes or knit baby-shirts, without thinking of the book, its terrible pages, and the terrible story. They moaned the word "Terrible!" to each other; a few could only be silent and pray to God. The book was a personal book with a personal story for its origin.

In the year 1849 there was living at Walnut Hills, just a little outside of Cincinnati, a woman who was thirty-eight years old and the mother of six children, all living. She worked hard, and for thirteen years had done most of the sewing and washing for the family; she had put together the house furniture and varnished it, made her own pillows, pillowcases, bedspreads, quilts, and mattresses. When a neighbor found her laying cloth on the floor and cutting a dress for herself, the neighbor asked if she had a pattern to go by, getting the answer, "I guess I know my own shape."

She cut and sewed her husband's coats; and besides was a cobbler, cutting leather soles and nailing leather heels onto uppers she had cut and sewed so as to lace the shoes up behind. Her husband read the Greek, Hebrew, Latin, and Arabic languages, and was Bible professor in the Lane Theological Seminary at Walnut Hills. Only that year he had told her:

"There is no woman like you in this wide world. Who else has so much enterprise with so little extravagance; so much tongue with so little scold; so much sweetness with so little softness?" And she had answered, "If you were not already my dearly loved husband, I should certainly fall in love with you."

As to growing old and taking care of six children, she wrote to a school-days friend:

I like to grow old and have six children and cares endless. I wish you could see me with my flock all around me. They sum up my cares, and were they gone I should ask myself, What now remains to be done? They are my work, over which I fear and tremble.

She was born and raised in Connecticut, reading in the "New England Primer":

Young pious Ruth
Left all for truth.

And such rhymes as:

Young Obadias,
David, Josias,
All were pious.

Her father was a Congregational minister and read aloud to his children from Milton's poem, "Paradise Lost." Sometimes she cried and sometimes her father cried when he read about how Beelzebub was thrown out of heaven and then began gathering together the lost angels thrown out with him, and how Beelzebub broke into tears as he tried to rally them. "Thrice he essay'd, and thrice, in spite of scorn, Tears, such as angels weep, burst forth." On Sunday nights after services, when the children begged him, the father took down his violin and played, "Go to the Devil and Shake Yourself."

She read Sir Walter Scott's novel, "Ivanhoe," seven times as a girl, and learned by heart and recited many scenes from that book. At thirteen she was translating the Latin poet, Ovid, into English, and the next year was teaching the Latin classic, Virgil, in the Hartford Female Seminary, also studying French and Italian and drawing and painting.

Life was grave, serious, as she heard her father preach a sermon on the text, "I call you not servants, but friends," and plead, "Come, then, and trust your soul to this faithful Friend." Into her eyes came tears, and she answered, "I will," and sat through sacramental service. On the same day she had gone to her father's study corner in the attic of their house and crept into his arms, whispering, "Father, I have given myself to Jesus and He has taken me." And the father held her, and his tears fell on her hair. And he said: "Is it so? Then a new flower has blossomed in the Kingdom this day."

Then had come the moving to Cincinnati, a stopover in New York, which city she said would "kill her dead" if she stayed; it was "an agreeable delirium." And in the years of bearing her children and taking care of her husband, whose health was delicate, and doing many kinds of housework she found time to write articles that magazines printed and paid for. One book of her sketches had been published. She broke down, and went to a water cure in Vermont for six months, and came home with aches in her eyes so that for six months she could not stand daylight, and lived in darkened rooms. It was then she wrote a school-days' friend, "I like to grow old and have six children and cares endless."

There was a tracery of curves in her face, lines of pansy edging. She was a little trim woman, with blue-gray eyes full of changes, often dreamy, with ringlets of dark-brown hair clinging to the temples of her forehead, and quick little hands that illustrated her words or spoke for her without words.

As a seventeen-year-old girl teaching in her sister's female seminary in Hartford, she had said, "Where persons are determined to be anything, they will be!" The word "determination" had specific value for her. It was determination that set her father's face toward locating in the West in the Ohio River country. He said he had thought seriously of "consecrating all my children to God in that region who are willing to go." He had a vision of schools, churches, libraries, colleges, culture, and religion working a development of national spirit in the West. "If we gain the West, all is safe; if we lose it, all is lost. This is not with me a transient flash of feeling, but a feeling as if the great battle is to be fought out in the valley of the Mississippi, and as if it may be the will of God that I shall be employed to arouse and help marshal the host for the conflict. These are only my thoughts, but they are deep, and yet withal, my ways are committed to God."

The father and the daughter had solemn depths. When the books of the British poet, Byron, were published, the father had preached a sermon about the wasted life of the poet, and the daughter had read and been astonished by "The Corsair." She was only eleven years old when she asked what the line meant, "One I never loved enough to hate," and was told, "Oh, child, it's one of Byron's expressions."

When her father told her one day, "My dear, Byron is dead—gone!" the daughter was silent. So was the father a minute or two; then he added: "Oh, I am sorry that Byron is dead. I did hope that he would live to do something for Christ. What a harp he might have swept!"

And the girl went up a slope called Chestnut Hill where there was a strawberry field. She had a basket and meant to pick the red ripe berries. Instead she lay on her back among daisies, looked up into a blue sky, and wondered where Byron had gone and how it was with his soul.

Yes, there was a tracery of curves in her face, lines of pansy edges. In the Hartford school, when girls had asked if they could just once be allowed to do this or that, she answered them: "Allow you? I have not the power; you can do so if you think best." And she wrote her sister, "The force of moral influence seems equal to that of authority, and even stronger." One girl liked animals, bugs, things that creep, weave, fly, swim, and had under her desk cover a little menagerie of spiders, tumble-bugs, frogs; it was against the rules; the teacher made a new rule, that she and this girl should share the fun and the learning to be had from the little zoölogical garden hidden under the desk cover.

And so the year 1849 had come and she saw with it a pestilence of cholera come to Cincinnati; on a single day there were 120 deaths. She buried one of her own children. She got along as best she could with her curly-headed twins and the three other little ones, while her husband was off at Brattleboro, Vermont, seeking health.

Then her husband came back and again took up biblical exegesis in the Lane Theological Seminary, and the old threads of life were taken up. Standing at the front door of her Walnut Hills home, she could see a flaring in the sky over Cincinnati sometimes where a house was burning. And she knew again that a mob was at work. At the foot of the hills ran the Ohio River, the border line on one side of which negroes were property and the other side not.

Back and forth across this line she had seen the anger and the hate of men flame and spit and with the years going by it was getting worse. Down in the big town had been James G. Birney, who had given freedom papers to his slaves on an Alabama plantation and had published a weekly journal, *The Philanthropist*, in a fireproof building. Her brother, an editor on the *Cincinnati Journal*, was keeping loaded revolvers handy. Another brother had been a collector for a New Orleans commission house and told her about life in that city and in the Red River district. He told of seeing a slave mother leap from the deck of a Mississippi River steamboat, with a girl child who was to be sold. She had driven on a stormy night along Mill Creek to the farmhouse of the Quaker, John Vanzandt, with a negro girl who didn't have freedom papers, and whose lawful owner was hunting his property. She had crossed the Ohio River, visited with friends at a Kentucky plantation, and seen the slave system under the kindlier and more intelligent masters and overseers.

A call came for her husband at Bowdoin College, Maine. The family moved. The mother stayed ten days in Boston at the home of a brother; there the Abolitionist organization and propaganda was shaping into a sort of religious crusade; it had leaped into a fiercer stride with the passage at Washington of a law requiring all people North to help slave hunters from the South in the capture of runaway property.

All the smoldering fire in the woman, which had been softened and kept down when she lived on the Ohio River, shot up into blazing desires for sacrifice, even martyrdom. "I feel as if I should be willing to sink with it, were all this sin and misery to sink in the sea." A brother, a brother's wife, told her to use her pen. It roused her determination—one of her keywords was "determination." "I will write something—I will if I live."

She went to Bowdoin, wrote her brother's wife that a new-born baby was holding her back. "As long as the baby sleeps with me nights I cannot do anything, but I will do it at last. I will do that thing if I live."

One Sabbath at church a chapter of a book started to write itself as she sat listening to the sermon. She wrote it and read it to her children and the tears ran down their faces; the father came in; he cried too.

Then, while caring for her six children, and with a feeling that she was in her way helping to ransom countless unborn children, writing furiously out of her mother-heart, she wrote the chapters and they were sent with the ink hardly dry to *The National Era* for publication under the title, "Uncle Tom's Cabin, or Life Among the Lowly."

They were published as a book in 1852; eight power presses were soon printing copies of it; the sales reached more than 300,000; letters and poems came to her from Whittier, Holmes, Longfellow, and many others; from England came letters of praise from Dickens, Macaulay, Kingsley, Lord Carlisle, the Earl of Shaftesbury; in Great Britain were sold 150,-000 copies in a year; in Paris a dramatization of the book was produced in eight acts to an overflow audience that sat till half-past one in the morning for the final curtain-drop; translations came out in France, Germany, Denmark, Sweden; in Italy editions of "Il Zio Tom" were sold in all cities; in Wales appeared "Caban F' Ewythr Twm." Another year saw translations into Armenian, Russian, Bengalese, Persian, Japanese, and Chinese.

A check for $10,000.00 arrived four months after the publication of the book. The author and her husband went on their first sea voyage; she wrote to her children that the ocean was a "restless, babbling giant." She returned from Europe to write "A Key to Uncle Tom's Cabin; presenting the Original Facts and Documents upon which the Story is Founded, together with Corroborative Statements, verifying the Truth of the Work."

A lone little woman, with a houseful of children to take care of, with the grass not yet grown over one baby's grave, with her breasts hardly dry from the nursing of a new baby, had written a book timed with the same hours that the antislavery movement was gathering an ever fiercer stride and voice, becoming a terrible, irreconcilable crusade, chanting of eyes that saw the glory of the coming of the Lord, of a just God to come and trample out the vintage where the grapes of wrath were stored.

In the flow of her story of slavery, she had seldom paused to deal with some of its peculiar growths. It would have interfered with the swift movement of her drama to notice that in certain southern states the laws permitted free negroes to own slaves; and by inheritance, gift, and purchase 4,500 free negroes were in 1830 recorded as owning slaves, and in a number of cases free negroes controlled large plantations. Slaves of negroes were in some cases the children of a free father who had purchased his wife; if the free negro husband of the slave woman did not buy her freedom, as many husbands failed to do, the children of the marriage were born slaves and were the lawful property of the father. Some husbands held off from buying freedom for their wives; an unsatisfactory wife could be sold; a negro shoemaker in Charleston, South Carolina, bought his wife for $700.00, and, finding her hard to please, sold her a few months later for $750.00. A negro Baptist minister in St. Louis was recorded in 1836 as the owner of twenty slaves. Samuel Gibson, a Mississippi free negro, in 1844 took six slaves he owned to Cincinnati, and gave them freedom papers.

Little Harriet Beecher Stowe had set out to register in the bosoms of millions of other Christians her own shame of Christian civilization in America, and her own cry for martyrdom. A picture of a slave society was what she tried to make in a large panoramic structure, and it had become mixed with a great personal ideal of the Christ Man. Her hero, Uncle Tom, was a black Christ. He embodied all the implications of the saying, "The meek shall inherit the earth." He did what he was told to do; his word was trusted by his master; he could suffer grimly and humbly in his belief that Heaven, a world after this one, would take him in and put right all wrongs. He did what he was told to do until he was told to tell which way runaway slaves had run; then, bleeding from whip thongs, his skin and flesh welted and pounded, he died moaning forgiveness to the master who had ordered another obedient negro to beat him to death. It was the story of Judea located south of the Ohio River, with a whipping-post for a Cross, slave owners for Pharisees, ministers and politicians for hypocrites and Pilates, and a cotton plantation for the scene of a Passion Play.

By the device of dramatizing a black Christ, she led millions of people to believe there were two countries with two cultures in the United States; in one humanity was desecrated; in the other it was held sacred. She became the prophetess of a passionately emotional point of view that south of the Ohio River was a widespread and terrible wrong, while north of the Ohio River nothing so much was wrong; only in the South was there a vicious and brutal control by exploiters over producers; in the North was no comparable cruelty, mismanagement of the common welfare, and ignorant wastage of the lives of a lower class existing chiefly for the ease and profit of an upper class.

Yet while Mrs. Stowe read the first manuscript sheets of her book to her weeping husband and children, a committee of the legislature of Massachusetts was circulating a report prepared the year before on conditions in that New England state. The report was dry, factual, painstakingly accurate, crabbedly truthful, as even in tone as the accents of a surgeon reporting a pulse-beat or a definite condition of a particular anatomical area; that is, the report was in method the opposite of "Uncle Tom's Cabin." In the industrial belt of the northern states were some 4,000,000 wage laborers, most of them held in a control analyzed in the Massachusetts committee report; it declared:

The Legislature, with the intention of promoting the manufacturing interest, has by its action interfered with and destroyed the natural relations as existing between the class of employers and the class of employees. That natural equality of condition, which ought to exist between the two classes, does not practically exist between the corporations and the great mass of laborers in their employment.

These immense artificial persons, with far larger powers than are possessed by individuals, are not chastened and restrained in their dealings with the laborers, by human sympathy and direct personal responsibility to conscience and to the bar of public opinion.

The transactions between the corporations and the laborers are conducted by agents, who are hired to so manage, as to make the most profits for the stockholders; and the stockholders, throwing all responsibility upon the corporations, receive their dividends with a high opinion of the fidelity and efficiency of these several agents, high and low, who have managed profitably, but they know nothing of the hardships endured by the laborers, whose work has produced all they thus receive. The larger corporations employing large numbers of laborers, all act substantially in concert, in dealing with laborers, and avoid all competition in overbidding for labor.

They are thus enabled to fix inexorably, without consultation with the laboring class, all the terms and conditions of labor. The will of the corporations thus becomes law, and declares how many hours the laborers shall work, and how much shall be their compensation. From the decision of these powerful employers, large masses of the laboring people have practically no escape. Circumstances practically compel them to submit to the offered terms. Many of them must do so, or have no work at all; and to some, this is equivalent to having no honest means of support.

The power of the corporations, thus exercised in determining the conditions of labor of large numbers of the laboring classes, not only oppresses those whom they employ, but also exerts a powerful influence to depress the condition and prolong the hours of labor of every branch of industrial pursuit.

The report suggested as a first step a shorter workday.

Thousands of women and girls, 8,000 in one city, were tending the looms and bobbins of New England mills, working twelve to fourteen hours a day, and the report noted:

Instead of the female operatives being nearly all New England girls, as was formerly the case, large numbers of them are now foreigners. The infusion of foreigners has been rapid, and is going on at a constantly increasing rate. In a few years, an entire modification and depression of the state of society in and about manufacturing places will be wrought by this cause.

By the present system of working, no sufficient time is allowed between working and sleeping, for the improvement of the mental faculties. Their working twelve hours or more, per day, in the noxious air of the factories, tends to deaden mental vigor, although it may not quench the intellectual fire once lighted.

Far different results must be anticipated for the future when there is taken into consideration the rapid influx of foreigners, which is fast changing the character of the factory population. If this change continues to go on, there will be gathered into the manufacturing places a strictly manufacturing population permanently bound by circumstances to factory employments, similar in character to the factory population of England. Then, the evils of excessive hours of labor will become manifest in the depressed tone of the moral and intellectual character of the mass of operatives, and also in their deteriorated physical condition.

One evil result of devoting so much time to labor is the increased competition of labor. Prolonging the hours of labor decreases, in some degree, its wages. In Massachusetts, there is always a surplus of labor unemployed. Those, therefore, who are out of employment through the effects of the excess of the hours of labor, go into the labor market and underbid those who are at work, and thus the general rate of wages is reduced.

And far out among the farmers near the frontier, Lincoln was writing in a notebook some of the points that stood out big for him as he looked at the relations of Man and Master, the upper and lower classes of America.

He could see two sorts of inequality, "the British aristocratic sort" and "the domestic slavery sort." Neither was as good as "a society of equals" where every man had a chance.

He had heard southern men declare slaves were better off in the South than hired laborers in the North. Yet he would argue, "There is no permanent class of hired laborers amongst us. Twenty-five years ago I was a hired laborer. The hired laborer of today labors on his own account today, and will hire others to labor for him tomorrow."

He set up the indictment, "Although volume upon volume is written to prove slavery a good thing, we never hear of the man who wishes to take the good of it by being a slave himself."

And he writhed as a man under the weight of some heavy conundrum of history in writing, "As labor is the common burden of our race, so the effort of some to shift their share of the burden onto the shoulders of others is the great durable curse of the race."

CHAPTER 89

THE Northwest and the South were paying their large debts in New York. While the centre of politics was Washington, the money centre of the country was New York. Canals, railroads, steamboats, crop transfers were handled through the nation's financial capital at the lower end of Manhattan Island. Affairs of size in cash outlay waited on word from New York. The streams of cash from the Mississippi and Gulf regions led to New York and the East. Nearly two-thirds of the banking capital of the country was in the East; per capita circulation in the East was $16.50 as against $6.60 for the country as a whole.

In a small eastern area of 200,000 square miles were factories, mills, stores, shipping-lines, railways, and banks that earned yearly returns equal usually to the total of capital invested. The bulk of the banking profits of the country was in the control of eastern banks. The list of bank presidents in New York City showed an interesting percentage of them as having accumulated $100,000 to $500,000 in New England or the middle eastern states, and then moving to New York, the American vortex of cash and credit. A new bank was started for every month in the year in New York City in 1851. And in the two years following fifteen more banks opened their doors.

Among large fortunes were some out of the "African trade." A book published for bankers and merchants, "Wealth and Biography of the Wealthy Citizens of New York," rated Peter Harmony as worth $1,500,-000. "The ship, *Warsaw*, sold in 1844, made him $90,000 in one voyage round Cape Horn. Some of his ships to Africa brought out cargoes, it is said, that paid a profit equal to the difference in price between negroes in Africa and Cuba."

Whisky, cotton, and real estate had brought Stephen Whitney ten million dollars. "He was born in Connecticut, and began life as a poor boy by retailing liquor, and finally dealt in the article by the wholesale. The great impetus to his fortune, however, was given by several heavy but fortunate speculations in cotton. His investments in real estate doubled his fortune."

William P. Furniss, a millionaire, "made all his money in the South, and is now a broker in Wall Street." John Suydam's estate of $700,000 came from cotton speculation. "Mercantile business south, at Mobile" was the source of Jonathan Hunt's million. Samuel Packard, $500,000, was plainly "a rich cotton planter, resident in New York," while Isaac Packard got his $250,000 from "negro plantations in Cuba," and Mauran Oroondates came by his $500,000 "in the southern trade, and by the steam-ferry at Havana."

Little pieces of land on Manhattan Island had doubled, and kept doubling, in price. Henry Brevoort's father left him an eleven-acre farm, and when Ninth and Tenth streets cut across Fifth Avenue where the cows were once pastured, Brevoort had become a millionaire. Peter G. Stuyvesant, of the ancient Knickerbockers, was rated at $4,000,000, mostly real estate. The estate of Stephen Van Rensselaer also came to $4,000,-000, and was divided between two sons, "one of whom owns Albany County, and the other Van Rensselaer County."

Iron, coal, hardware, drugs were the sources of fortunes invested mainly in real estate. Anson G. Phelps, worth $1,000,000, owned Pennsylvania iron mines, a part of Missouri mountain, "altogether perhaps a half-million acres," and had "contracts to supply the Federal Government with nearly all the copper used for the national vessels."

Sometimes the little book published for the information of bankers and merchants came close to impertinence. It rated Morgan Lewis at $700,000 and declared, "He acquired his estate by marrying a Livingston of wealth." And there was the odd item about Thatcher T. Payne, brother of John Howard Payne, author of the song, "Home, Sweet Home." He was "of a family part Jew from the east end of Long Island, not far from Montauk," and his $100,000 came "through marriage with a wealthy widow." Benjamin L. Swan had $500,000. "His firm was peculiarly lucky in commercial arrangements during the late Mexican War."

The name of Vanderbilt was looming. Cornelius, rated at $1,200,000, had only begun on transportation and finance that would bring him tens of millions. In Daniel Drew, president of the Erie Railroad, was an example of a financier performing a vital and important public service and charging for the service a price unknown to the public. He had millions; just how many he did not tell, if he knew. He had organized and reorganized the Erie and was one of the first adepts in railroad accounting. The estimated construction cost of connecting New York and Lake Erie was $2,000,000. But when built it had cost $15,000,000. And the total capital obligations were $26,000,000. Thus at last a rail line ran between the seaboard and the Great Lakes.

The railroad and the telegraph speeded up trade, sent the volume of business higher, and initiated the piling up of such personal fortunes as the New World had not seen before. Millionaires were getting common. "With princely fortunes accumulating on the one hand, and the stream of black poverty [from Europe] pouring in on the other," said the *New York Tribune*, "contrasts of conditions are springing up as hideous as those of the old world."

John Jacob Astor was rated as high as $50,000,000 and as low as $25,000,000. "He has, by the sole aid of his own industry, accumulated a fortune scarcely second to that of any individual on the globe, and has executed projects that will perpetuate his name to the latest age." At eighteen years of age he had left his home in Baden, Germany, "resolved to be honest and industrious, and never to gamble." He clerked in a fur store, went into the fur business for himself, and built trade till he **was** able to send sixty men to locate a fort and trading-post, Astoria, on the Columbia River.

Next he had a chain of forts and posts in the northern Pacific Coast wilderness, trading hardware, knickknacks and rum to Indians and white trappers for furs later shipped to China and traded for teas, silks, nankeens. "His ships now ploughed every sea."

Two-thirds of his profits year by year went into real estate and first mortgages. "In case of foreclosure, which has often happened, he has bought the property in at much less than its real value. . . . Mr. Astor has vast tracts of land in Missouri, Wisconsin, Iowa, and other parts of the West. . . . His income must be $2,000,000 a year, or $4 a minute. . . . It has been remarked of him that Mr. Astor was **capable of com-** manding an army of 500,000 men. . . . During active life. **he resided in** a large house in the lower part of Broadway, and lived in a style of princely magnificence, attended by servants from some of the various nations with which he traded, among them some from the Empire of the Celestials. His house was furnished with the richest plate, and his apart- ments adorned with works of art, among which was a Cupid by Mignard."

Thus was America growing. Thus life was arranging itself at the financial capital of America. New York had a nickname. It was known among Americans as the Front Door.

Emerson, the Concord preacher, saw war, revolution, violence, breeding in the antagonisms of bold, powerful men. "Vast property, gigantic in- terests, family connections, webs of party, cover the land with a network that immensely multiplies the dangers of war."

CHAPTER 90

As Lincoln traveled over the fourteen counties of the Eighth Judicial Circuit six months of the year, making his home in Springfield, with occasional trips north and south in the state, there was a feel of change in the air. He had seen the frontier pass from Illinois and move west of the Mississippi. He had floated past St. Louis, a town of 5,000 people, and had seen it grow to 74,000 in twenty years. He had watched Spring- field with less than a thousand people grow to 4,500; its citizens had voted for no license to saloons. He had seen cholera arrive in Springfield and the mayor ordering a day of prayers against the plague.

The public square that Lincoln saw just before turning up the stair- way to his law office was sketched by the *Journal* when it urged: Our streets and alleys should be cleaned everywhere, especially in and around the neighborhood of the square. The brickbats, trash, old hats, old boots, and shoes, rags, bones, manure and many other things which grace our streets, should be hauled off, and hog holes filled up."

The town council had passed an ordinance to stop the running at large of hogs in the streets; the council had repealed the ordinance, and finally settled the matter by a law providing that no hogs should run at large in the streets of the capital city of Illinois unless the said hogs had rings in their noses.

The hog-raisers of the state in 1850 counted 1,915,907 hogs. Travelers from Chicago said cows ambled along the sidewalks of that city as freely as the people, while residents of Quincy had their saying that geese filled the streets and as scavengers were superior to hogs.

Besides Springfield, the cities of Quincy and Rockford had voted no license to saloons. The slogan, "The saloon must go," was heard. A petition with 26,000 signers asked the legislature in 1853 for a state-wide vote on liquor-selling in Illinois; the legislature refused. Nearly all the Whig newspapers were for temperance, and had nicknamed the Democratic party the "Whisky party"; at the far southern point of Egypt, the Cairo *Weekly Times and Delta* declared, "The use of intoxicating drinks seems more natural than the use of water."

In 1855, the question went to a vote; the proposed prohibition law, modeled on the one in force in Maine, was beaten by a majority of 14,447 votes. In Chicago and in the canal and railroad zones, with the largest number of foreign-born voters, the balloting was heaviest against the proposed law.

Lincoln was asked if he were a temperance man. He replied: "I am not a temperance man, but I am temperate to this extent: I don't drink."

The temperance movement had its main strength among the New Englanders who had filled up northern counties of the state. Raiding squads with axes knocked holes in whisky barrels and destroyed liquor stocks in the smaller towns; such raids were not attempted in Chicago, where 800 saloons were licensed.

In the air, strung on poles, were "lightning wires"; a telegraph operator in Pekin told Lincoln all he could tell about electric currents and the Morse alphabet; the telegraph connected Chicago, Springfield, and St. Louis. Within two years a network of wires joined all parts of Illinois in a system controlled by Judge John D. Caton, called "the telegraph king of the West." The *Journal* and the *Register* at Springfield announced they would have telegraphic news; if the President at Washington issued a message they would publish it as it came over the lightning wires; likewise with steamboat explosions, train robberies, muiders. Eight newspapers were published daily in Illinois in 1850; they increased in four years to twenty; also in the state were 118 weekly publications. Chicago had seven daily newspapers, fifteen weeklies, and six monthly and other periodicals. In the southern part of the state the publications were fewer;

the *Southern Illinois Advocate* of Shawneetown was the only newspaper in ten counties; its principles and aims were unlimited—"universal liberty abroad, and an ocean-bound republic at home."

The West was beginning to feel its oats and lift its voice. The *Gem of the Prairie,* the weekly magazine of the *Chicago Tribune,* declared: "The West must have a literature peculiarly its own. It is here that the great problem of human destiny will be worked out on a grander scale than was ever before attempted or conceived."

When southern representatives in Congress spoke threats of leaving the Union, at the time California was admitted as a free-soil state and the South felt itself losing ground politically, Texas was reported to be making ready to defy the Federal Government by force of arms. The *Alton Telegraph* voiced the opinion, "The great and patriotic West has become strong enough to strangle the monster of disunion the moment it shall venture to raise its head."

This, while Senator Douglas was telling the country from the floor of the Senate: "There is a power in this nation greater than either the North or the South—a growing, increasing, swelling power, that will be able to speak the law to this nation, and to execute the law as spoken. That power is the country known as the great West—the Valley of the Mississippi, one and indivisible from the Gulf to the Great Lakes, and stretching on the one side and the other, to the extreme sources of the Ohio and the Missouri—from the Alleghenies to the Rocky Mountains. There, sir, is the hope of this nation—the resting-place of the power that is not only to control, but to save the Union. This is the mission of the great Mississippi Valley, the heart and soul of the nation and continent."

And while Douglas was openly telling the country this sentiment, his right-hand man in the House of Representatives was secretly writing Governor French of Illinois that if Texas defied the Federal Government, it would be the signal for the whole South to draw out of the Union; and therefore he advised strengthening the state militia, warning the governor: "I would prepare for this storm—I would provide against portentous violence. This, as a citizen of Illinois and a lover of the Union, I call upon you to do."

The human inflow from Europe came before Lincoln's eyes. He saw Germans, Irish, and English by tens of thousands come into the state. Fourteen steamboats, ice-locked in the Mississippi River near Cairo in the winter of 1854, were loaded with 2,000 German and Irish immigrants. Up at Nauvoo, where the Mormon colony had moved out and crossed the Great Plains and the Rocky Mountains, to settle at the Great Salt Lake in the midst of the Great American Desert, had come a group of French Communists. Near Athens in Sangamon County was a settlement of Norwegians; north of Springfield was a huddle of Portuguese.

The Germans outnumbered all others; Lincoln carried a German grammar and studied the language in a night class. He wrote "nix com raus" in letters. A Turnverein was organized in Springfield in 1851.

In Bureau and Sangamon counties were Fourier phalanxes, experiments aimed at making perfect model human corners on earth, planned somewhat after Brook Farm, the famous phalanx in New England started by Albert Brisbane and having Horace Greeley, Charles A. Dana, and Nathaniel Hawthorne among its members.

Many new organizations were started; societies, unions, lodges, churches. Some were ancient, tested, filling deep human wants; others were new, fantastic, untried. And it seemed that Lincoln didn't belong to any organization, new or old, secret or open, except the Whig party, the state bar, and the American Colonization Society.

CHAPTER 91

LATE in the afternoon of an autumn day in 1850 Abraham Lincoln is riding in the rattletrap buggy which he drives from one courthouse to another across the fourteen counties of the Eighth Judicial Circuit. He has spoken only occasionally to "Old Buck," his horse; the head and the haunches, the hair and the ribs of "Old Buck," are familiar to him; he has curried and cleaned this horse; the ears of "Old Buck" have a language for him; he knows the places where the tugs and collar have worn the hair off and left the horsehide.

On this drive, however, he has spoken hardly at all to "Old Buck"; he is lost in one of the dark moods that come to him; the rattle of the buggy, the jog of the horse, the flutter and flip of the blackbirds picking up corn and wheat in the fields, the rumble of wagons, axles and wheels, the far sounds of cow bells and grunting hogs and sudden zigzags of scared grouse in the pasture grass—to these he is lost.

The smell of the moist loam is in the air; one or two frosts of a passing week have whitened the ground, gone into mist under the morning sunshine; and there is in the air a faint memory of these frosts, as well as a ghostly recollection of the marching, majestic panoramas of the laughing corn, their stalks and tassels, their ears with a shine of yellow and of red gold.

The time is the coming of evening when all the revealed shapes of daylight take on the rags or the silks of mist and dark and form themselves into fine or comic apparitions not seen in daylight; it is the time when men of dreams or mathematics, or both, have to be keener and more elusive with the outlines of their reveries or the statements of their theorems. Circling the horizon levels is gray haze, the first hint of Indian summer.

The red ball of the sun performs the final arc of its day and drops below the prairie line. While the lamplighters of the cities of men are doing their daily work, the sprinklers of the stars are doing their daily stint up in the spans of the evening sky. Up the sky has come a little silver sliver of an early moon, a basket-shaped baby moon; as mist wraps around it in moments it might be a shining papoose cover.

To these little moving fire-spots on the sky, the life of a man or a nation of men is put down in two easy almanac dates, telling of a coming and of a going away. "Mortal man with feet of clay, Gone tomorrow, here today." Ten years slip into a man's life and slip out, each year "a swift-fleeting meteor, a fast-flying cloud," each year "a flash of the lightning, a break of the wave."

In the ten years now just ahead in the life of Abraham Lincoln, the human procession marches, toils, fights, laughs, sings, scrambles, dances, prays, its supreme wonder the simple fact of birth, speech, song, its supreme majesty the plain fact of death, silence, night. Behind that filmy tissue called The Future, events are operating, facts toiling to their ends, shaping destiny, history.

In the ten years between 1850 and 1860, the country grows; its 23,-000,000 people become 31,000,000. The United States has 2,000,000 more people than Great Britain. The United States becomes one of the Powers of the World. And it is only beginning to grow. A secretary in Washington figures that in forty years more the country will have a hundred million people.

A legend spreads. Henry Clay on his last ride from Washington to Kentucky steps out of a stage, goes back a few paces, leans over and puts his ear to the ground as if listening. "What are you listening for, Mr. Clay?" the driver asks. "I was listening to the tread of unnumbered thousands of feet that are to come this way westward."

In ten years the ships at the ports of the country unload 2,600,000 people from overseas. In one year come 400,000. The East grows 21 per cent, the South 28 per cent, the Northwest 77 per cent, in population. Little towns peep up on the prairies where there used to be only gophers and jack rabbits. Cities swell from little towns. The country grows.

The peopling of America with labor supplies, for the operation of her factories and mills, for the breaking of her prairies and the raising of crops and building of towns on these prairies, goes on directly connected with events in Europe. Into America come men, women, and children who saw the dark year of 1848 in Europe, when the barricades and battalions of revolution arose from London to Moscow, from Prussia on the north to Sicily on the south.

In England the speeches, pamphlets, and street meetings of the Chartist movement scare the government into passing a law making seditious speeches an act of felony. The habeas corpus act is suspended in Ireland.

No less than 17,000 constables are sworn in to keep the peace in London when a crowd of a half-million persons is to gather on Kensington Common. One agitator cries: "If a few hundreds do fall on each side, they will only be the casualties in a mighty movement."

Police and troops with guns are mounted on public buildings; military arrangements are put into the hands of none less than the conqueror of Napoleon, the Duke of Wellington. Street traffic is ordered suspended out of fear that wagons may be used for street barricades as in Paris revolts. A proclamation is issued, warning the people against assembling for disorderly purposes.

The mammoth mass action assembly planned for Kensington Common collapses. Feargus O'Connor, the chief organizer of the movement, broken with grief, loses his mind and spends years in the quiet of an asylum.

The British government employs its guns not only to keep order among its home-born people; in far Afghanistan 30,000 Sikhs with sixty guns, screened by a thick jungle, slaughter 2,500 British officers and men in the opening of a campaign that ends with British batteries, bayonets, and cavalry in control of the disputed region. In South Africa, a fourth war with the wild Kafir tribes ends with the British flag flying over the Orange River territory; Boer settlers in near-by territory are declared to be under a British protectorate.

And though the white men of the north are thus bringing civilization to the jungles of Africa and Asia, that civilization has not yet learned how to guard itself from the filth of cholera; in London a thousand persons a day die from the plague and a total of 50,000 die in England and Wales.

The search goes on for markets, more people and territory where the products of the British power looms can be sold; a British steamship meeting a fleet of Chinese pirates shoots to pieces thirteen of the junks. The ports of Burma are blockaded; up the terraces of the Great Pagoda at Rangoon go the British bayonets hoisting their banner over the golden dome of the final sacred Pagoda. A fifth war is fought with the wild Kafir tribes, and martial law proclaimed throughout Cape Colony in South Africa.

When the Czar of Russia tries to get footholds on the Black Sea and control of Constantinople, the British army and navy join with allied European forces and fight a war in the Crimea. The famous Light Brigade charges. "All in the valley of Death rode the six hundred." They are of England's strong arm keeping the routes clear and the connections open for the trading vessels carrying the cargoes from the power looms of Manchester and Lancaster and West Riding.

And these wide-flung actions are little chapters in the new development of world trade in world markets, wider and fresher markets being wanted because of the immense output from the new machines, the power-driven looms taking more and more millions of pounds of cotton from the southern American states and more and more millions of bushels of corn from far western America to feed the growing populations. As at times the mills slow down and men are out of jobs, and as land becomes scarcer in proportion tc the population, there is an added attraction in the call of America and its prairies where land is cheap, and the black soil sometimes six feet deep.

Europe has grim memories of 1848; civilization was shaken into wild pieces of hunger and hate. The French February revolution spread to every corner of Europe. King, emperor, czar, and sultan loaned each other money, guns, armies. Thousands of barricaded workmen took power and possession over the cities of Paris and Vienna, held those cities for weeks and were shot down and their revolutions blown off the map by superior guns and fighting forces.

So far did the revolutions go in the old feudal governments of Prussia and Austria that Prince William left Berlin for London, leaving placards saying that his palace was the property of the nation; the Austrian Prince Metternich, chased out of Vienna, told a friend in London, "I have sometimes ruled Europe, but Austria never."

As the news of the barricades in Paris reached Czar Nicholas in Russia, he had mobilized his armies and ordered a manifesto written, closing with the words from Isaiah, "Listen, ye heathen, and submit, for with us is God." In Italy and Hungary governments changed hands like chess pieces; Garibaldi, Mazzini, Kossuth became famous names.

And republics set up for a few days or weeks by the revolutionists were tumbled over. In France, Louis Napoleon, a whiskered nephew of Napoleon the First, took a crown as Emperor.

Such events set the faces of hundreds of thousands of homeless, landless, propertyless peasants and city workmen toward America. In England, Ireland, Germany, France, and Italy, they sell their pigs and chickens, they scrape and save, they borrow money from relatives and friends in Europe or America, pack their belongings in sacks, bundles, and handkerchiefs, and cross the "big pond," wondering how much of what they hear they will find to be true in America, the wonder country, where across thousand-mile prairies the plow and harrow had not yet put teeth into the rich black soil. It can hardly be true. They will see.

By war and by treaty there has come on the map of the United States, Texas, and the open spaces to be shaped into the states of California, New Mexico, Arizona, Utah, Nevada, Oregon, Washington, Montana, and parts of Colorado, Wyoming, and Kansas.

A homestead bill comes before Congress; the bill says any free white citizen who settles on 160 acres and farms it five years shall have it free of cost; the bill is changed; he must pay for the land; a sliding scale of prices is fixed.

For ten years argument goes on about what shall be done with millions of acres of public lands. The Government owns the land; the Government says who shall next own it. In the twenty years between 1840 and 1860, the Government lets go of 269,406,415 acres; it sells 68,752,-889; it gives away the rest; it gives a single railroad 2,500,000 acres, and the railroad in seven years sells half this land for $14,000,000.

In Washington, congressmen, senators and Cabinet officials squabble about what shall be done with the public lands, millions of acres Northwest and Southwest. There are land speculators, business interests, powerful in Washington, who for reasons of their own do not want free land for actual settlers. A few senators such as Stephen A. Douglas, and congressmen such as John Wentworth and William Richardson of Illinois, Andrew Johnson of Tennessee, try to get a free homestead law. They fail.

Philosophers, farmers, and mechanics, calling themselves an Industrial Congress, meet in Chicago, and declare "the free land proviso would everywhere, on the cotton plantations of the South, and in the cotton factories of the North, unite all lovers of freedom and humanity, against all haters of freedom and humanity, and would strip the question of all prejudices resulting from sectional and partial agitation." They put the blame for bad feeling between the North and the South not only on the planters and landlords of the South, but also on forces in the North, which they name as "Factory Lords, Landlords, Bankers, Speculators, and Usurers." For a simple, honest homestead law, the country waits. A movement with the slogan, "Vote yourself a farm," rises and disappears.

Free-land bills keep coming up in Congress; it is argued by Andrew Johnson of Tennessee that the poor whites trying to farm stony corners on the slopes of the Allegheny Mountains ought to have a chance to break west and settle on free land; a Virginia congressman pooh-poohs the idea that every man has a right to land; a radical from Pennsylvania says the eastern manufacturers are afraid of western free land because it would take men from the factories and send wages higher; another congressman says it is the big landholders North and South who are stopping the passage of a free-land bill.

An embryo—a tugging, unborn baby—of a giant industrial and transportation civilization takes form and grows. The organism of society breaks the cords and bonds tying it to handicraft production and the organic structure resting on feudal land-ownership; the society functioning its production and distribution of the means of life through capital and capitalists, issues definitely from its birth folds. It is the end of feudal society: the knickerbockers, silk stockings, and silver snuffboxes are gone, in America and Europe; the pantaloons, the Prince Albert coat, the stovepipe hat, the Havana cigar have arrived.

The transcontinental railroad, the iron-built, ocean-going steamship, the power-driven factory—the financiers and rulers of these are to be the rulers of an earth ruled by the white race. Europe connects coal and steel areas with factory cities by railways. Russia runs a rail line from St. Petersburg to Moscow. Into northern Africa, into fringes of Asia, the rail paths go; among tombs of the Pharaohs and amid walled altars of China, the whistle of the locomotive is heard. The society resting on land-ownership gives way to the new civilization operating through control of finance, industry, and transportation.

Of railroads men had said, "They begin anywhere and end anywhere." Between cities, rivers, and lakes and canals there were connecting short lines, stub roads for local service. Then the Erie Railroad puts a line through from a station near New York City across Pennsylvania to Dunkirk on Lake Erie; the Atlantic Ocean and the Great Lakes are connected now by rail to the north. The Baltimore & Ohio line pushes on through to St. Louis; the seaboard and the Mississippi Valley are joined by steel rails. Twenty-one thousand miles of rails are laid. Total railroad mileage grows from nine to thirty thousand.

Gradually between the seaboard and the Mississippi River there comes a net of lines with cars hauling the pork and grain of the West to the factory towns of the East, to the holds of vessels sailing to the factory cities of Europe; the cars come back loaded with sewing machines, churns, scissors, saws, steel tools.

The American threshing machine, which Cyrus H. McCormick has been perfecting for twenty years, goes into a competition with the threshing machines of other nations. The London *Times* pokes fun at the McCormick machine—before the test. In the race the American machine cleans 740 litres of wheat while the English machine cleans 410, and while six threshers with the flails of Bible times clean 60 litres. The official report of the Fair says, "The triumph of the American reapers worked a new era in agriculture."

Man toils, thinks, sweats for new tools, so that one farmer will be able to do the work of ten. New reaping and threshing machinery comes on the farms. Fewer wheat and oat harvests rot in the fields. Single-handed, a farmer can gather the crop on a quarter-section of land. Grain drills, corn planters, wagons and buggies with springs under the boxes and seats are bought by the farmers. The new churns, the new sewing machines, help the farmer's wife.

Over in England a man works on improving artillery; he is trying to make guns stronger and cheaper; his name is Bessemer; he invents a way to force a blast of air through molten cast iron, resulting in a hard steel that he can sell $100 a ton cheaper than other steel of the same quality. The Bessemer process comes to America, where a man named Kelly is experimenting with that same process. Everything made of steel becomes cheaper. Steam fire-engines, gas-lighting systems, the Hoe revolving cylinder-press, vulcanized rubber, photography, the use of anesthesia, these arrive.

In London they build a big palace of iron and glass and hold an international exhibition of the products of inventive, dextrous Man. In New York, too, they hold an exhibition in the Crystal Palace. More and more is heard of discoveries, inventions, products, improvements, conveniences.

The white man has spread his ships around the earth. Once the earth was wilderness. Now it is to be civilization. White men say so. England begins building all her ocean-going ships of iron.

In the Middle West, there is keen interest in Stephen A. Douglas's plan for a railroad the length of the state of Illinois. He is asking the Federal Government to make land grants along the railroad route. Congress refuses.

Douglas then lays the plan before southern interests, proposing that they shall have a railroad connecting with the Illinois Central, running to the Gulf, with Federal land grants for the southern states. This bill passes. The Illinois Central gets 2,500,000 acres of land free without cost, and in seven years receives $14,000,000 from its land sales, and has sold only half its holdings.

Asa Whitney is heard of. He is a merchant, lays up a fortune in New York, sails to China, comes back with a feel for distances. From city to city he goes holding mass meetings, calling for a coast-to-coast railway across America: let the Federal Government give public lands thirty miles wide along such a railroad from Lake Michigan to the Pacific. Public meetings pass resolutions in favor of his plan; so do legislatures; but nothing is done; it is all talk. He spends his fortune trying to get a Pacific railroad built; his money is gone; he runs a milk-wagon in Washington, D. C. He wanted to finish the work of Columbus and have a straight passage around the world westward from Europe to Asia; he sells milk at the doors of congressmen and senators in Washington. Asa Whitney: he is a crank, perhaps a man of vision, born a little early. His epitaph might be "He tried to finish what Columbus started."

California is a place to talk about, to guess and wonder about. There in a week ten men shake gravel through hand screens and shake out a million dollars of gold nuggets; the San Francisco city council adjourns without setting a date when it will meet again, churches close their doors, newspapers stop printing, ships lie in harbor with no sailors; cooks and soldiers run away from the military forts and leave the officers to do their own cooking; there is a free-for-all rush to the gold diggings; a spade sells for $1,000.00.

The wild times tame down; the first big gold rush is over; gunmen, thieves, and crooks take hold of the government of California and San Francisco; they own or control governors, mayors, judges; 2,500 private citizens organize a committee, hold military drill, set up courts; and, defying the regular, legal government, they hang and deport murderers, firebugs, thieves, and make property and life safer. The Committee of

Vigilantes, they call themselves. It is a little revolution in the name of safety for property and life.

Across the Great Plains stretching east from the foothills of the Rocky Mountains toward the Mississippi River, move wagon trains; a traveler counts 459 wagons in ten miles along the Platte River. They are moving across vast empty prairies. Between the Arkansas River on the south and the Canadian border far to the north is the land not settled, not really opened for settlement, not peaceably organized and humanly made ready for settlement.

A territory of Kansas is organized, but there is civil war in this territory; riders from Missouri, a slave state, get on their horses with rifles and ride over into Kansas and battle with Abolitionists from New England. It is a taunt hurled from the anti-slavery platforms of New England that shipments of boxes marked "Books" are sent to Kansas, the boxes incasing rifles. In the settlement at Osawatomie is a quiet, stubborn man with his family; morning and night they have Bible reading and prayers. The enemy kill two of his sons; he steals horses from the enemy and kills sons of theirs; it is war. The man's name is John Brown.

Over in Clay County, Missouri, are two boys growing up, Frank and Jesse James; they are learning to ride and shoot, to be reckless about life; the enemy burn their house, shoot their mother in the arm so the arm has to be cut off; it is war.

Into Kansas come men from many parts of the country: John Calhoun, who used to be county surveyor of Sangamon County in Illinois, becomes Governor of Kansas. There comes Robert J. Walker; he controlled politics in the Democratic party in the state of Mississippi twenty years back; he was the first to put Jefferson Davis into politics; he was Secretary of the Treasury under President Polk; he came within an inch of getting President Polk to annex all Mexico to the United States; he is Governor of Kansas when the slavery men let the people vote on a state constitution, with a joker in it so that the people can't vote slavery out; he meets his friend, Stephen A. Douglas, at a conference in Chicago; they tell the country the Kansas election is crooked. There are months in which the whole country talks about the latest news from Kansas.

In the South are to be found all the imaginable conditions that lie between the two extremes of plantations managed by owners who are efficient, kindly, decent, thoughtful, and plantations and jail yards and auctions managed by hard, hopeless plantation owners and slave traders and breeders. On one plantation the owner issues printed instructions, going into full details on how "The overseer shall see that the negroes are properly clothed and well fed; he shall lay off a garden of at least six acres, cultivate it as part of his crop, and give the negroes as many vegetables as may be necessary. The negroes shall not be worked in the rain, or kept out after night. Sick negroes are to receive particular attention. When the negro shall die, an hour shall be set apart by the overseer for his burial; and at that hour all business shall cease, and every negro who is on the plantation, who is able to do so, shall attend the burial. Humanity on the part of the overseer, and unqualified obedience on the part of the negro, are, under all circumstances, indispensable. Whipping, when necessary, shall be in moderation, and never done in a passion; and the driver shall in no instance inflict punishment except in the presence of the overseer, and each negro man will be permitted to keep his own axe, and shall have it forthcoming when required by the overseer. No other tool shall be taken by any negro without permission from the overseer."

In the North are to be found all the imaginable conditions that lie between the two extremes of factories and mills managed by owners who are efficient, kindly, decent, thoughtful, and factories and mills operated by hard, hopeless owners. The Hamilton Manufacturing Company in Massachusetts issues "Public Factory Rules," proclaiming: "All persons in the employ of the Hamilton Manufacturing Company are to observe the regulations of the room where they are employed. They are not to be absent from work without the consent of the overseer, except in cases of sickness, and then they are to send word as to the cause of their absence. They are to board in one of the houses of the company and give information at the counting-room where they board, when they begin, or, whenever they change their boarding-place; and are to observe the regulations of their boarding-house. Those intending to leave the employ of the company are to give at least two weeks' notice thereof to their overseer. All persons entering into the employment of the company are considered as engaged for twelve months, and those who leave sooner, or do not comply with all the regulations, will not be entitled to a regular discharge. The company will not employ any one who is habitually absent from public worship on the Sabbath, or known to be guilty of immorality."

Peace societies organize; they aim to stop war; they circulate Charles Sumner's oration on "The True Grandeur of Nations"; he says, "There is no war which is honorable, no peace which is dishonorable." However, the National Convention of Reformers, headed by Parke Godwin, raises a point and asks a question: "The Peace Societies are built upon a noble foundation of justice and philanthropy, but must not expect success in establishing permanent peace, or its parent, justice, in the intercourse of nations, established upon the right of conquest. Why shall not the laws, which create motives in all men to obtain from all their fellow citizens, by cunning, or any force not expressly forbidden in the law, all their lands, houses, goods, wares and merchandise, also stimulate nations to foreign conquest and warlike aggression?"

The first undersea telegraph messages are sent; Washington and London exchange words. And the breech-loading rifle arrives; man shoots bullets quicker and oftener.

Wendell Phillips, the aristocratic young lawyer who dropped law practice to become an Abolitionist agitator, says the churches are slow in their duty, hurling the taunt: "The theatres in many of our large cities bring out, night after night, all the radical doctrines and all the startling scenes of 'Uncle Tom.' They preach immediate emancipation, and slaves shoot their hunters with applause. The theatre, bowing to its audience, has preached immediate emancipation, and given us the whole of 'Uncle Tom'; while the pulpit is either silent or hostile." Yet in hundreds of communities, it is the church people who carry on the antislavery organizations, hide runaway negroes in barns, cellars, wagons, and man the stations of the Underground Railroad; in a little church built of walnut wood in Galesburg, Illinois, they hide negroes in the steeple.

Frederick Douglass, the escaped mulatto slave, edits a paper, the *North Star;* always the runaway slaves, sleeping by day, heading north by night, try to follow the north star. Says Frederick Douglass, "Prejudice against free colored people has shown itself nowhere so invincible as among mechanics of the north." In Virginia, white mechanics go on a strike because negroes have been put to work alongside of them to learn skilled mechanical labor. The *Charleston Mercury* editorially hopes the white strikers will be crushed; interference and rebellion from white workmen has the same spirit as that of a black slave insurrection.

Civil war in Kansas comes near to spreading out over the whole country in 1856. Fifteen hundred miles from Kansas people make sacrifices in order that Kansas shall not be a slave territory. Emerson, in far-off Massachusetts, says, "We must learn to do with less, live in a smaller tenement, sell our apple-trees, our acres, our pleasant houses."

The faith of Emerson in the Government is gone. "I think the towns should hold town meetings, and resolve themselves into Committees of Safety, go into permanent sessions, adjourning from week to week, from month to month. I wish we could send the Sergeant-at-arms to stop every American who is about to leave the country. Send home every one who is abroad, lest they should find no country to return to. Come home and stay at home, while there is a country to save." As his eyes sweep the years ahead of the nation, he cries, "The hour is coming when the strongest will not be strong enough."

On a late afternoon of an autumn day in the year 1850 Abraham Lincoln, sitting in his rattletrap buggy, might have been lost still deeper in his thoughts if he could have snatched the film of tissue off the Future and read events to operate in the ten years to come.

CHAPTER 92

Young Bill Green, who had clerked in the Berry & Lincoln store, slept in the same bed with Lincoln and held Kirkham's Grammar while Lincoln recited, was in northern Illinois in 1852, and met some families of movers at Princeton. One was the Carr family, who had come from the Mohawk Valley to Chicago by boat, and were going by wagon to the little log city of Galesburg in Knox County, where the Rev. George Gale and a company from Whitesboro, New York, had plans for churches, schools, colleges, religion, culture, and freedom, in the new prairie region.

Clark E. Carr, the boy of the family, listened with sharp ears to the talk of Bill Green. He was the same Bill Green who was on a witness stand one time when John T. Stuart asked him who were the principal citizens of New Salem, Green answering: "There are no principal citizens; every man in New Salem neighborhood is a principal citizen."

He had a Tennessee skill in telling stories, and the Carrs told him he was the best at spinning yarns that they had ever heard. He replied: "I ain't a primin' to a curi's young feller who used to keep a grocery down whar I live. He kin make a cat laugh. I've seen the whole neighborhood turn out to hear him tell stories. They ain't all jest the kind fer women to listen to, but they's always a pint to 'em. He's a great big feller, with a big mouth, and he kinder acts it all out, smilin' and laffin'. I never seed a real clown, but he'd make one. But I've seen him when he was the solumest man in ten states. When he kem back from runnin' a flatboat to New Orleans, ef anybody said anything about niggers he would git so solum, an' tell about a nigger auction he seed in New Orleans—how they sold a fambly, the man to one planter and his wife to another an' passeled the childern out among the highes' bidders, an' he thought it was awful. I've seen him turn pale," Green went on, "when talkin' about this auction, and seem to take sick to his stomick, and then begin to cuss and take on; and I've heard him say he'd ruther tend sawmill all his life than to sell niggers, an' he'd ruther do all the work on a plantation hisself than to buy a nigger boy or girl from its mammy. I never once heerd him swar excep' when talkin' o' that nigger auction."

Mr. Carr interrupted. "He must be an Abolitionist." "Ab'litionist! Ab'litionist!" cried Green. "You bet he ain't. He's a true loyal man, who loves his country. No, he's no Ab'litionist."

And what had become of this young man? "Wal," Green went on, "he went an' larned law, made speeches, run fer the legislatur, set up in Springfield, an' got to Congriss. But he's only a kind of a jackleg lawyer —an' as fer Congriss, he couldn't git 'lected ag'in, an' now he's kind o' played out."

And his name? Green went on: "He's as good a feller as ever lived;

but he's kinder common—sorter jes' like everybody, no better no worse, jes' a good feller. Thar's another feller in that country who beats him— Dick Yates of Jacksonville. He's a feller who can beat anybody as a talker. He is thet eloquent thet he'll make you fergit your own name. Talk about the American Eagle an' the Star-Spangled Banner! He can jes' lift you off your feet, an' make you soar an' yell an' hurrah, an' swing yer hat, an' holler—think ye're Patrick Henry, an' George Washington, an' Andrew Jackson, an' Henry Clay, an' Bunker Hill an' everything. I've seen him make people hold their breaths, an' wipe their eyes, an' blow their noses, jes' by his talk. He'll be Pres'dent some day!"

But what was the name of the first young man who could make a cat laugh? "Abe Linkern."

And in further sketching "Abe Linkern," Green wanted them to know: "He is curi'est feller I ever seed! He could ask more questions than a Philadelphia lawyer could answer. Thar never kem a man inter the neighborhood, but he'd find out jes' the things he knowed. He'd make friends with him by tellin' him stories an' then he'd pump him I've seen him pump a down-East Yankee 'bout Boston till he knowed more 'bout Boston, an' Plymouth Rock, and Bunker Hill than the Boston feller hisself. When he heerd of a grammar-book he walked six miles to git it, an' when he got through with it he knowed more grammar than the schoolmaster, Mentor Graham."

Arriving in Knox County, young Carr heard Colonel Finch, the leading Whig politician, say: "I've seen Abe Lincoln go into a caucus or convention, and jist git up and talk kind of honest-like, with no fuss, but jist plain sense, windin' up with a story square to the point, and carry the whole outfit, bag and baggage, along with him."

And one day in Galesburg as the boy, Clark E. Carr, was looking away down East Main Street toward the Knoxville Road, he heard a horn blow and saw a big rockaway stagecoach make the turn into Main Street, four horses breaking into a run, the driver half standing, and cracking a whip, while pigs and chickens in the road scattered, and women ran out of the kitchens and waved handkerchiefs and dish-cloths.

As the stage came to a standstill in front of the one-story log post-office on the southeast corner of the public square, a tall stranger was among those who stepped out. Colonel Finch was ready to greet him but another man put himself between Finch, put his hand out to the stranger and blurted, "Abe Lincoln, by God!" "Yes, governor, here I am," said Lincoln, shaking hands with the Honorable William McMurtry, lieutenant governor of the state, a Democrat, and a farmer on Henderson Creek, north of Galesburg. "I'm glad to see you and to be in Knox County. How are you, Colonel Finch? I hear you are keeping those rascally Democrats level here in Knox! How are you, Squire?"

And shaking hands with everybody, even young Clark E. Carr, he swept the gathering with a glance, and said with a wreath of a smile: "That's a good story we had on the governor. You see, an Irishman had a bill before the legislature for some imaginary service he had performed on the canal, which the governor here squelched in the senate. The Irishman's account of it was that his bill had passed the house and he was watching it from the gallery of the senate; that it finally came up, and 'jist as it was about to pass, a big nayger named McMurtry got up and motioned that my bill be laid under the table till the Fourth of July; and that killed it sure.' " After that everybody walked into what was called the "bar-room" of the tavern, though no liquor was sold; it was a church and college town; a block from the tavern was to be erected the First Church, of solid walnut.

"Lincoln, how can you keep out of politics?" asked O. H. Browning, a Quincy lawyer with the blood and manners of a Kentucky gentleman. "Nothing going on in politics that I care about. I am trying to become a lawyer," was the reply. And it was suggested that the Missouri Compromise line between slave and free states might be wiped out. "We cannot tell what men will do," said Browning. "Well," was Lincoln's answer, "if anybody should attempt such an outrage while I live, I think I'd want to take a hand in politics again."

When he had gone, Browning remarked that Lincoln was "always a learner," and in that respect was the most notable man he had ever seen. "I have known him for ten years, and every time I meet him I find him much improved. He is now about forty years old. I knew him at thirty, and every time I have seen him I have observed extraordinary improvement. Most young men have finished their education, as they say, at twenty-five; but Lincoln is always a learner. If he keeps out of politics, he will in ten years stand at the head of the profession in this state."

Four miles south of Galesburg, on the Seminary Street road, lived a farmer, Daniel Green Burner, who was born in New Salem, had seen Lincoln go off to the Black Hawk War and had lived there when Lincoln was keeping a grocery store. He told people, when asked, that Lincoln sold whisky in the New Salem store but never drank any himself and never used tobacco. "He would swear under strong provocations, but this was not often. I don't think he made any pretensions to special goodness. The community was raw and green and he was one of us. Lincoln was as full of fun as a dog is of fleas, yet he had no part in the tricks of the Clary's Grove gang. They had queer notions of fun. Once they called up an old man with a wooden leg and made him a prisoner. They then built a fire around the wooden leg, and held the man there till the wooden leg was burnt off."

Burner could run on with recollections. "I have seen Lincoln place a cup of water between his heels, and then folding his arms, bend his tall form backward until he could grip the edge of the cup between his teeth and then straighten himself up, without spilling the water. He would back up against a wall and stretch out his arms; I never saw a man with so great a stretch. He did little things like that to please people.

"Lincoln was the strongest man I ever knew. In the grocery I often saw him pick up a forty-four-gallon barrel of whisky, place it on the counter, and then lower it on the other side. And while Lincoln was full of fun and life, I never saw him dance and he courted no girls. The four years I knew him in New Salem I never saw him with a girl. He did not go to others for his amusement, but if they wanted fun they came to him, and they found him full of it. . . . There was singing school, but Lincoln couldn't sing any more than a crow. So he did not go often."

Thus, in odd corners of Illinois men were telling each other what Abe Lincoln was and wasn't.

Across the state of Illinois, in the towns where Lincoln practiced law for a living, men gained different impressions of him. This and that man had his own little individual portrait of Lincoln. He could, paradoxically, make a cat laugh, and also be the solemnest man in ten states. He was always a learner. It was of a piece with the mental sketch formed by the Quaker, Ira Haworth, who saw Lincoln in Danville and noted, "Lincoln doesn't show at first all that is in him," or the swift characterization in the remark of Leonard Swett, who often tried cases with and against him. "You can never tell what Lincoln is going to do till he does it."

Other lawyers could not say beforehand just when Lincoln would switch the management of his case and be off on a trail not noticed before. He would speak to a jury and give away one point after another. "Yes, we admit this," and "Yes, we admit that." And it would look as though the case were slipping away, when suddenly he would come down with unexpected power on the weakest point of the opposition and bring up his own strongest point. Once, during a criminal trial, a colleague, Amzi McWilliams, whispered to other attorneys, as Lincoln was speaking, "Lincoln will pitch in heavy now, for he has hid."

In silence and in ways covered from the eyes of other men, he struggled, grew, learned, in the years just after he came home from Congress and Washington. The boy who had lain awake nights and wrestled to unravel the big words "in-de-pend-ence" and "pre-des-ti-na-tion" had become a grown man who wrestled to unravel the ways of putting simple words together so that many could understand the ideas and feelings he wanted them to understand. He said, "I am never easy when I am handling a thought, till I have bounded it north, bounded it south, bounded it east, and bounded it west."

He bought a book on logic and studied the science of explanations, how to analyze the absolutely true and the relatively true, the proximate causes and the remote causes, how to untangle fallacies and take them apart piece by piece and show mistakes in reasoning. He heard the word "demonstrate" and said to himself: "What do I do when I demonstrate. more than when I reason or prove? How does demonstration differ from other proof?" He looked in Noah Webster's dictionary and learned that demonstration is "proof beyond the possibility of doubt."

The definition didn't satisfy him; he went to all the dictionaries and books of reference he could find for the meaning of the word "demonstrate" and in the end said to himself that their definitions meant about as much to him as the color blue when explained to a blind man. He said to himself, "Lincoln, you can never make a lawyer of yourself until you understand what 'demonstrate' means."

He bought "The Elements of Euclid," a book twenty-three centuries old. It went into his carpetbag as he went out on the circuit. At night, when with other lawyers, two in a bed, eight and ten in a hotel room, he read Euclid by the light of a candle after others had dropped off to sleep.

Herndon and Lincoln had the same bed one night, and Herndon noticed his partner's legs pushing their feet out beyond the footboard of the bed, as he held Euclid close to the candlelight and learned to demonstrate such propositions as: "In equal circles, equal angles stand on equal arcs, whether they be at the centres or circumferences," and "Equal parallelograms which have one angle of the one equal to one angle of the other, have their sides about the equal angles reciprocally proportional; and parallelograms which have one angle of the one equal to one angle of the other, and their sides about the equal angles reciprocally proportional, are equal to one another."

"In this troublesome world we are never quite satisfied," he remarked once. Dreaminess filtered through him. He planned a speech in Congress; a week passed without his getting a chance to make the speech; and he commented, "Now my interest in the subject has passed too."

One night in Danville at the McCormick House, the ladies' parlor was turned into a bedroom for Judge David Davis, who had a bed to himself, and Lincoln and his fellow lawyer, Henry C. Whitney, who slept two in a bed. In the morning a thing happened that Whitney later told in this way:

"I was awakened early, before daylight, by my companion sitting up in bed, his figure dimly visible by the ghostly firelight, and talking the wildest and most incoherent nonsense all to himself. A stranger to Lincoln would have supposed he had suddenly gone insane. Of course, I knew Lincoln and his idiosyncrasies, and felt no alarm, so I listened and laughed. After he had gone on in this way for, say, five minutes, while I was awake, and I know not how long *before* I was awake, he sprang out of bed, hurriedly washed, and jumped into his clothes, put some wood on the fire and then sat in front of it, moodily, dejectedly, in a most sombre and gloomy spell, till the breakfast bell rang, when he started as if from sleep, and went with us to breakfast. Neither Davis nor I spoke to him; we knew this trait; it was not remarkable for Lincoln, although this time to which I refer was a radical manifestation of it, a proof that 'true wit to madness, sure, is oft allied.' "

John T. Stuart had remarked to Whitney that Lincoln was a hopeless victim of melancholy. "Look at him now," said Stuart, in a McLean County courthouse. "I turned a little," said Whitney, "and saw Lincoln sitting alone in a corner of the bar, remote from any one, wrapped in abstraction and gloom. . . . I watched him for some time. He seemed to be pursuing in his mind some specific painful subject, regularly and systematically through various sinuosities, and his sad face would assume, at times, deeper phases of grief. No relief came till he was roused by the adjournment of court, when he emerged from his cave of gloom, like one awakened from sleep."

He was spending more and more time by himself. Books, newspapers, his own thoughts, kept him alone in his room on evenings when the other lawyers on the circuit had all gone to a party and returned to find Lincoln asleep. If he went to a concert, lecture, or negro minstrel show, he would as soon go alone.

The habit stuck to him of reading out loud to himself whatever he wanted particularly to remember, and of reading out loud as he wrote. The proverb about "wits gone a-wool-gathering," he applied to some of his own moods. Whitney noticed him often during a court session "with his mind completely withdrawn from the busy scene before his eyes, as abstracted as if he were in absolute and unbroken solitude." Whitney noticed also: "Lincoln had no method, system, or order in his exterior affairs; no library, clerk, no *index rerum*, no diary. When he wanted to preserve a memorandum, he noted it down on a card and stuck it in a drawer or in his vest pocket or his hat. While outside of his mind all was anarchy and confusion, inside all was symmetry and method. His mind was his workshop; he needed no office, no pen, ink and paper; he could perform his chief labor by self-introspection." For his important business matters he had an envelope marked, "When you can't find it anywhere else, look in this."

The branches and crotches of trees interested him more in the wintertime, stripped of leaves and naked in design, than in the summer, when covered; he searched for basic anatomy of structure.

Finding Herndon reading a new book, "The Annual of Science," he glanced through it and commented that the book was on the right track because it took account of failures as well as successes in its field. "Too often we read only of successful experiments in science and philosophy, whereas if the history of failure and defeat was included there would be a saving of brain-work as well as time. The evidence of defeat, the recital of what was not as well as what cannot be done serves to put the scientist or philosopher on his guard—sets him to thinking on the right line."

These remarks were prophetic, in their way, for Herndon found Lincoln had arrived earlier than usual one morning at the office. Spread before him on his desk were sheets of paper covered with figures and equations, plenty of blank paper, a compass, rule, pencils, bottles of ink of different colors. He hardly turned his head as Herndon came in. He covered sheet after sheet of paper with more figures, signs, symbols. As he left for the courthouse later in the day he told Herndon he was trying to square the circle.

He was gone only a short time, came back and spent the rest of the day trying to square the circle, and the next day again toiled on the famous problem that has immemorially baffled mathematicians. After a two days' struggle, worn down physically and mentally, he gave up trying to square the circle.

He was trying to organize his mind and life so that he could not accuse himself, as he had accused President Polk, of being "a bewildered, confounded, and miserably perplexed man." He wanted to be simple as the alphabet, definite as the numbers used in arithmetic, sure as the axioms or common notions that are the starting-points of Euclid. Had he trusted too much to his feelings, and not reasoned, proved, and demonstrated his propositions clearly enough in his own mind before speaking them during his term in Congress? He wasn't sure. Hadn't he made a sort of fool of himself, and made his friends sorry for him, when he spoke before the Scott Club in Springfield in reply to the Richmond speech of Judge Douglas? He wasn't sure.

He would see if he could be as simple as the alphabet, as definite as numbers, as sure as a demonstrated proposition in Euclid. He scribbled notes trying to be as absolute as mathematics.

"If A can prove, however conclusively, that he may, of right, enslave B, why may not B snatch the same argument, and prove equally that he may enslave A? . . . You say A is white, and B is black. It is *color*, then: the lighter, having the right to enslave the darker? . . . Take care. By this rule, you are to be slave to the first man you meet with a fairer skin than your own. . . . You do not mean *color* exactly? You mean the whites are *intellectually* the superiors of the blacks, and therefore have the right to enslave them? . . . Take care again. By this rule, you are to be slave to the first man you meet, with an intellect superior to your own. . . . But, say you, it is a question of *interest;* and, if you can make it your interest, you have the right to enslave another? . . . Very well. And if he can make it his interest, he has the right to enslave you."

Into these notes he put the high human hopes spoken by the men who made the American Revolution. One note read:

"The ant who has toiled and dragged a crumb to his nest will furiously defend the fruit of his labor against whatever robber assails him. So plain that the most dumb and stupid slave that ever toiled for a master does constantly know that he is wronged. So plain that no one, high or low, ever does mistake it, except in a plainly selfish way; for although volume upon volume is written to prove slavery a very good thing, we never hear of the man who wishes to take the good of it by being a slave himself.

"Most governments have been based, practically, on the denial of the equal rights of men, as I have, in part, stated them; ours began by affirming those rights. They said, some men are too ignorant and vicious to share in government. Possibly so, said we; and, by your system, you would always keep them ignorant and vicious. We proposed to give all a chance; and we expected the weak to grow stronger, the ignorant wiser, and all better and happier together. We made the experiment, and the fruit is before us. Look at it, think of it. Look at it in its aggregate grandeur, of extent of country, and numbers of population—of ship, and steamboat, and railroad."

Though Lincoln was an entertainer, and when he arrived in Bloomington, Knoxville, or Pekin, men passed around the word that he had come to town and was retailing stories and jokes at a certain store or harness shop, he had his moods. A young man in Bloomington took special notice of these moods. His name was Jonathan Birch and he was licensed to practice law on an examination given him by Lincoln. Birch noticed that an hour or two after Lincoln had been in the court clerk's office, and entertained a crowd, and himself shaken with laughter as he drew his knees up to his chin at the end of a story, he might be seen in the same office or in some law office near by in a changed mood.

Birch noted: "His chair would be leaning back against the wall, his feet drawn up and resting on the front rounds so that his knees and chair were about on a level; his hat tipped slightly forward as if to shield his face; his eyes no longer sparkling with fun or merriment, but sad and downcast, and his hands clasped around his knees. There, drawn up within himself, he would sit for hours at a time. No one ever thought of breaking the spell by speech; he had thrown about him a barrier no one dared break through."

Glimpses of the ways by which history works with the individual— what a little and willing piece of sacrifice a man must be for the sake of his highest purpose—these came to him. "He visited no public places seeking applause; but quietly, as the earth in its orbit, he was always at his post," Lincoln had spoken of Zachary Taylor, murmuring the text, "He that humbleth himself shall be exalted."

To develop an illuminated, mysterious personality, and to be an elusive and dark player on the stage of destiny, is a dream of achievement lightly carried by a man of whom it is said, "He can make a cat laugh." Yet when such a dream does develop in such a man he is hard to follow even when he most explains himself.

The inside changes that began to work in Abraham Lincoln in the four or five years after he came back from Washington had their connection with the changes developing in the heart and mind of the country. He was ready to be the tongue and voice of those changes. As he walked with his long, easy stride, with a head bowed till the chin rested on his collar-bone, with a sober face and eyes of deepening mystery, he was already carrying a load, already in the toils, almost ready to cry, "I shall never be glad again." He was lawyer, politician, a good neighbor and story-teller, a live, companionable man; these belonged to his rôle. He was to be a mind, a spirit, a tongue and voice.

Out of the silent working of his inner life came forces no one outside of himself could know; they were his secret, his personality and purpose, beside which all other facts of his comings and goings were insignificant. He became a seer and sayer; he took responsibility personally; he solved, resolved, and answered terrible questions; or he said, with out-and-out honesty and a desperate toss of his head, that he had no answer, no man could form the answer; only history and the future could bring the answer.

True, he had ambitions; goals beckoned and banners called; but he would wreck and sink the ambition that interfered with his life and personality. "He could make a cat laugh."

In the speeches he was now ready to make, with the American nation for an audience, there would be reason and passion rising so overwhelmingly out of them that some men and women would know they came from other regions than those of personal ambition. He was in the toils of something else than personal ambition. He was beginning to see what a little and willing piece of sacrifice a man must be for the sake of a dark fame.

CHAPTER 93

In the Whig Almanac of 1854 Lincoln could read of strange contrasts in the kaleidoscope of history that year. Old Josiah Quincy had stood before the Whig State Convention in Boston that summer and told his fellow Whigs: "Slaveholders have multiplied their black cattle by the million; and are every day increasing their numbers, and extending their cattle field into the wilderness. Are we bound to be their field drivers and poundkeepers?" And Quincy answered that "common law" might require obedience but there was no "moral obligation" to obey the Fugitive Slave Law.

He sketched a scene, did old Josiah Quincy. "We have seen our Court-house in chains, two battalions of dragoons, eight companies of artillery, twelve companies of infantry, the whole constabulary force of the city police, the entire disposable marine of the United States, with its artillery loaded for action, all marching in support of a Prætorian band, consisting of 120 friends and associates of the United States Marshal, with loaded pistols and drawn swords, and in military costume and array—for what purpose? To escort and conduct a poor trembling slave from a Boston Courthouse to the fetters and lash of his master! This display of military force the mayor of this city officially declared to be necessary."

In the same Whig Almanac of that year was the speech of Victor Hugo, a Frenchman exiled from France, speaking at the funeral of Jean Bosquet, also a Frenchman exiled from France. And Hugo had said in April: "We have seen him, an inflexible exile, waste away among us, a yearning for home gnawing at his heart. The earth will soon cover him, his soul gone to the hopes of the tomb. Let him sleep here, this republican. Let the republic know that men will perish rather than forsake her. Let him sleep, this patriot, in the land of the stranger."

Hugo spoke of the sword, the ax, and scaffolds, the gallows removing revolutionaries. He looked to the future for "the deliverance of every nation, the enfranchisement of all mankind." He ended: "Friends, our sufferings give us a claim on Providence; God owes us a reward. Let us then cherish a manly faith and make our sacrifice with gladness. Oppressed of all nations, offer up your wounds. Poles, offer your misery; Hungarians offer your gibbet; Italians, offer your cross; heroic transported brothers of Cayenne, of Africa, offer your chains; exiles, offer your proscription; and thou, O martyr! offer thy death to the liberty of the human race! *Vive la république!*"

Thus the reprints of the Whig Almanac, published by the *New York Tribune,* then the most powerful and widely read newspaper in the country.

Such were a few glints. Men with a scorn of ease in life or ease in death were talking and talking, refusing to give up a dream that man is the most improbable of animals, kissing farewell to mother and home as though errands called, as though the drums of change on change drum eternally, and to live high is to follow those mystic drums.

Lincoln saw and heard. Dreams ran deep in him. He too wanted to look beyond his day and have men murmur of him, mention his name as one with a little streak of honest glory. He had so spoken to Josh Speed, once, and ten years later to Bill Herndon.

That want still lived in him, lived far under in him, in the deeper blue pools of him. It was one of his secrets as he touched elbows with people in Diller's drug store, in Canedy's, and mixed with men in shirt-sleeves around the public square in Springfield. On guard he had his horse sense, mathematics, and an eye for the comic.

CHAPTER 94

AROUND the public square of Springfield every day in 1854 came "movers." They drove in covered wagons, heading west for homesteads. They were pioneers. But to speak of them as "pioneers" was considered highfalutin. They were movers.

A Peoria newspaper that year counted 1,473 wagons in one month, movers going to Iowa. Twelve thousand emigrants arrived on railroad trains at Chicago in one week of that year. Three hundred houses were built in Davenport in a year. Though a building boom was on in Bloomington, its hotels sometimes could not accommodate all comers, and Lincoln one evening in that city went canvassing among private houses for a furnished room.

"How's things?" was a query. "Booming," was a reply. Flush times were on. Those incessant westbound wagons were a sign.

Cyrus H. McCormick, the farm-reaper man, had come up from Virginia, with letters of introduction from Stephen A. Douglas; McCormick located in Chicago, having decided it was to be the farm-machinery centre of the world. He said: "I made and sold 1,558 machines in 1854 with less than one-half of one per cent of returned machines. Three-fourths of these were combined reaping and mowing machines. I shall manufacture as near 3,000 machines for 1855 as I can."

That year the Illinois Central made the grade from Chicago to Galena. Six new states for the Union would be carved out in the Northwest, newspapers were saying. On the Great Plains north of the Missouri River, east of the Rockies, and west of the Great Lakes would come fifteen million people in forty years.

Millions of dollars were passing in money orders from America to Europe, the poor people of a new country trying to help the poorer people of the old countries. Edward Everett, of the Department of State, said on December 1, 1851, that official inquiry showed, "The emigrants to the United States, from Ireland alone, besides having subsisted themselves, have sent back to their kindred, for the last three years, nearly five million dollars each year."

In that flush year and those boom times, the Midwest prairie state of Illinois was holding its annual state fair in Springfield, in the harvest month of October.

Shorthorn cattle were feeding in sheds where farmers by hundreds passed through, discussing whether it would pay to try to raise these high-class, high-bred cattle instead of scrubs without pedigree. A shorthorn bull drew particular attention; he had crossed the Atlantic Ocean and the Great Lakes on steamboats; his owner had a tent near by with tables, chairs, whisky, cigars, where farmers could sit and take cheer while they talked about the bull; some of the farmers had heard a caretaker ɒf the bull say: "Thet bull's wuth his weight in gold. Ever sence he left old England, Queen Victoree's been cryin' her eyes out on account o' the loss o' thet calf, fer he was jist a calf then. Now you kin go up and down these sheds and see what a fambly he's got. All the gold in Californy couldn't buy his childern and grandchildern."

There was keen interest in the farmers named as receiving blue ribbons for the long yellow or golden red ears of corn they had raised. To walk around among these exhibits, to see the horse races where runners, trotters, and pacers with Kentucky and Tennessee pedigrees competed on a mile track, and then to listen to the political speakers discussing "purrins-a-pulls" and "the Const-ti-too-shun"—this made a holiday for the farmers and city people who came.

For many a young couple who came riding on a farm workhorse, the young man in front holding the bridle, the young woman behind him, the two straddling a blanket on the horse's back—it was one of the high holidays of the year. They went home to talk for a year about what they had seen at the state fair in Springfield.

The hero of the holiday came, Stephen A. Douglas, formerly of Springfield, once land commissioner, then supreme-court judge, later a congressman, and then United States senator from Illinois, at forty-one years of age a national leader of the Democratic party and the nearest of any man in Congress to filling the shoes of Clay, Calhoun, or Webster as an orator and parliamentary whip. He had been an active official in the Masonic order; he had carried the bulk of the Irish Catholic vote of the State; a large block of votes in both church and saloon elements were with him.

Blue-eyed, magnetic, chin drawn in, with a lionlike head, pivoting, elusive, with a face that drew men as Napoleon at Austerlitz or Nelson at Trafalgar, he was the most daring and forthright personal political force that had held the American stage since Andrew Jackson stepped off. His hero was Jackson; he was known as the foremost "whole-hog Jackson man." He was spokesman for what he called Young America as against what he called Old Fogyism.

Though he stood a short five feet, two inches, his head was shapely, balanced, large, and with its big shock of a black pompadour swept back in curly waves, and his deep bass voice dramatically calling for an ocean-to-ocean American republic, he was a figure that captured the imaginations of people and led them as Napoleon led; they were willing to go anywhere he said, without asking why; he embodied drama, politics, and a picturesque conduct of life; men wondered about him, tried to solve his personality and had no sooner done so to their satisfaction than he was on the stage in a new rôle with a new play.

He had come close to taking the Democratic nomination for President; Caleb Cushing and the wheelhorses who pulled the nomination for Franklin Pierce were not yet sure that blind luck had not been the chief factor. To be decisive, to be positive, to win men his way by grand acting, was the sport of Douglas's life; political life was to his nostrils what the military was to Napoleon; he had an instinct for the grand manner, the sweeping and absolute jerk of the head or the defiant brandish of clenched fists or the contemplative and majestic pause of the man who knows how and can tell.

When he was leaving for Europe, with his sister managing his Washington house, she told him, "I don't know how to entertain senators and such big men." He asked, "You never have been afraid of me, have you?" "Of course not; I'm older than you and I've managed you." "Well, then, they say I'm the biggest toad in the puddle, and you needn't be afraid of them."

While telling the United States Senate what was right and wrong with the country, he could at times double his fists and shake them at imaginary enemies in the name of the Constitution and Andrew Jackson. He spoke the dedicatory oration for the Jackson equestrian statue in Washington, himself of a piece with the horse rearing on its hind legs with forefeet in the air. "He lashed himself into such a heat," wrote an observer, "that if his body had been made of combustible matter, it would have burnt out."

When the city council of Chicago in 1850 voted with only two dissenting members that the Fugitive Slave Law was cruel, unjust, unconstitutional, and that the city police should not be required to help arrest fugitive slaves, Douglas went to a mass meeting in Chicago where he was hissed to begin with, but in the end his arguments won a vote for the repudiation of the action of the city council. When his bill in Congress for Federal land grants to the proposed Illinois Central Railroad was beaten by southern votes, he won those votes solidly by routing the proposed railroad through southern territory with similar land grants. On his head in that year of 1854 had fallen such a storm of epithets and ridicule as probably no other public man in American history had known.

As the representative friend of Chicago business interests allied with New York and Boston interests, he had set out to open the vast stretch of territory west of Iowa to the Pacific Ocean and make it ready for transportation and trade tributary to Chicago. Toward the south in St. Louis other business interests planned a "National Central Highway" from that city to San Francisco; the plans of Jefferson Davis, the Secretary of War, favored a railway to the Pacific with Memphis as its eastern terminus. The slavery question, land grants, Indian tribal reservations, railroad routes, territorial government for Nebraska, were snarled in what seemed to be a hopeless tangle.

Douglas cut through the tangle and won support for a bill which would make two territories, Nebraska on the north, Kansas on the south, in each of which the ballots of its voters would decide whether it should be free or slave territory. "They could vote slavery up or down" under the principle of "popular sovereignty," also called "squatter sovereignty." Southern votes in Congress came to this measure, with its provision that the Missouri Compromise was expressly repealed.

He had accepted from Senator Dixon of Kentucky a rider to his territorial bill; it was the only way to get required southern support. Dixon quoted Douglas as saying, "By God, sir, you are right, and I will incorporate it in my bill, though I know it will raise a hell of a storm."

On his way from Washington to Illinois, Douglas had looked from car windows to see the burning of dummies rigged out to look like himself, labeled with his name; in Ohio women had presented him with thirty pieces of silver; newspapers declared his middle name of Arnold derived from Benedict Arnold. In Chicago on a Saturday night a crowd had yelled "meow" and "boo" at him for two hours while he tried to explain his Missouri Compromise Bill; he was howled down.

The mob sang, "We won't go home till morning, we won't go home till morning." Douglas faced it, and, "The spirit of a dictator flashed out from his eye, curled upon his lip, and mingled its cold irony in every tone of his voice and every gesture of his body," according to the Chicago *Daily Democratic Press*. At midnight he looked at his watch, shook a fist at the crowd, and shouted, "It is now Sunday morning—I'll go to church, and you may go to hell!"

The opening up of the territory west of the Missouri River for settlement and transportation and trade tributary to Chicago had come at a higher price than he expected.

So he was the central figure of attraction at the state fair. Thousands who hated his face and the very breath of him wanted a look at him. Other thousands who loved him and would go to war and bloody battles for his sake, who would answer his call as the boys of France answered the call of Napoleon, were ready to stand in the frosty night air of mid-October to hear him deliver a speech.

He registered at the Chenery House in Springfield on arriving; a brass band, men with torches, and a street black with people serenaded the senator; there were calls for "the Judge," "Judge Douglas," the "Little Giant"; he came out on the porch of the Chenery House, torches were held up so that the people could see his face; around him stood Lieutenant Governor McMurtry, John A. McClernand, Sam Buckmaster, John A. Logan, William R. Morrison.

And how should a United States senator, accused of wrong, speak to his home people when they came with a brass band and torches to serenade him? Douglas knew how. He should speak slowly, measuredly, distinctly. Each word should come forth from his lips as a piece of money from a deep casket. So he spoke, "Neither—to legislate—slavery—into—a territory—nor to exclude it—therefrom—but—to leave—the peo-ple—perfectly free—to form—and regulate—their—domestic institutions—in their own way—subject—only—to the—Constitution—of—the United States: that is—all—there is—of the Nebraska Bill. That is 'popular sovereignty'—upon which—I am to speak—tomorrow at the Statehouse." This was the voice in which he spoke for them, for Illinois, in Washington, the national capital.

Then he became a little familiar, as befitted a speech to the home people; the words came faster, as the torches flickered and the black mass of people in the street listened amid huge shadows. "I have come home, as I have done so many times before, to give an account of my stewardship. I know the Democrats of Illinois. I know they always do their duty. I know, Democrats, that you will stand by me as you have always done. I am not afraid that you will be led off by those renegades from the party, Trumbull, Palmer, Judd, and Cook, who have formed an unholy alliance to turn the glorious old Democratic party over to the black Abolitionists. Democrats of Illinois, will you permit it?" And the street shook with voices en masse: "No! no! never! never!"

Between the torches his blue eyes flashed, his lips trembled. "I tell you the time has not yet come when a handful of traitors in our camp can turn the great State of Illinois, with all her glorious history and traditions, into a negro-worshiping, negro-equality community. Illinois has always been, and always will be, true to the Constitution and the Union." And he gracefully wished them good night; the torches, the brass band, the crowd, vanished; the street was empty.

On the afternoon of the next day Douglas spoke for nearly three hours in the Statehouse. Had not the Missouri Compromise been practically wiped out by the Omnibus Bill of 1850? Was not the real question whether the people should rule, whether the voters in a Territory should control their own affairs? If the people of Kansas and Nebraska were able to govern themselves, they were able to govern a few miserable negroes. The crowd enjoyed it; cries came, "That's so!" "Hit 'em again," and, the speech over, three ringing cheers were given for the "Little Giant."

Lincoln had a seat up front; he whispered occasionally in the ears of friends, and they chuckled and grinned. He walked down the main aisle at Douglas's elbow, joking the senator. It was only a few years back that Douglas had loaned Lincoln a hundred dollars and Lincoln had signed a note and later paid it. They had argued on the stump, in courtrooms, churches, grocery stores. To a pretty young woman Abolitionist who told Douglas she didn't like the speech, Lincoln said: "Don't bother, young lady. We'll hang the judge's hide on the fence tomorrow."

When the young woman later insisted to Lincoln that he had no business laughing and joking during such a brutal speech, Lincoln answered that maybe he ought to feel a little guilty. As to the slaveholder's way of looking at slavery, it didn't hurt him so very much. "I have heard it all my life," he said, "and as the boy said about skinning eels, it don't hurt 'em so very much; it has always been done, they're used to it." Dick Oglesby hinted to the young woman that she had been unfair to Lincoln: "He knows how to manage us sapsuckers; just let him alone."

There had been a saying around courthouses, "With a good case Lincoln is the best lawyer in the state, but in a bad case Douglas is the best lawyer the state ever produced."

The next afternoon Lincoln stood before the same crowd that Douglas had spoken to. Judge Douglas had arrived at the Statehouse in an open carriage, standing with his hat in his hand bowing to a crowd that cheered him. In the carriage also were the governor of the state, Joel A. Matteson, and Douglas's colleague in the United States Senate, General James T. Shields, who had one time gone with Lincoln to a sand-bar in the Mississippi River to fight a duel. Douglas took a seat on the platform.

Lincoln came in, pushing and squirming his way to the platform where he was to reply to Douglas's speech of the day before. After being introduced, he questioned whether he was just the man who should be selected to reply to the senator, mentioned the world-wide fame of Senator Douglas, the high position in the United States Senate and the power Douglas held as a debater. He was going to discuss the Missouri Compromise, presenting his own connected view of it, and in that sense his remarks would not be specifically an answer to Judge Douglas, though the main points of Judge Douglas's address would receive respectful attention. "I do not propose to question the patriotism or to assail the motives of any man or class of men, but rather to confine myself strictly to the naked merits of the question." With these apologies and explanations out of the way he was set for his main speech.

He began with a short history of the United States and slavery. He dug back into beginnings and traced out the growth of slavery: "Wherever slavery is it has been first introduced without law. The oldest laws we find concerning it are not laws introducing it, but regulating it as an already existing thing."

He gave five burning reasons for hating it as a "monstrous injustice." And he added: "Let me say I think I have no prejudice against the southern people. They are just what we would be in their situation. If slavery did not now exist among them, they would not introduce it. If it did now exist among us, we should not instantly give it up. This I believe of the masses North and South. Doubtless there are individuals on both sides who would not hold slaves under any circumstances, and others who would gladly introduce slavery anew if it were out of existence.

"We know that some southern men do free their slaves, go North and become tiptop Abolitionists, while some northern ones go South and become most cruel slave-masters. When southern people tell us they are no

Stephen A. Douglas and his wife, Adele Cutts Douglas

Lincoln and his kin, Joseph Hanks and his wife, who farmed
near Quincy, Illinois, where their young relative several times
visited them and saluted "Uncle Joe."

Joshua Speed, the only man to whom Lincoln wrote long letters
on the perplexities of love and marriage. "We are dreaming
dreams," he wrote Speed eventually, as though both sought more
than could be realized in life.

more responsible for the origin of slavery than we are, I acknowledge the fact. When it is said that the institution exists, and that it is very difficult to get rid of in any satisfactory way, I can understand and appreciate the saying. I surely will not blame them for not doing what I should not know how to do myself."

Was this oratory? debating? The man, Abraham Lincoln, was speaking to thousands of people as if he and another man were driving in a buggy across the prairie, exchanging their thoughts. He was saying that if all earthly power were given him he wouldn't know what to do as to slavery.

There were not ships and money to send the slaves anywhere else; and when shipped anywhere else outside of America they might all die. "What then? Free them all, and keep them among us as underlings? Is it quite certain that this betters their condition? I think I would not hold one in slavery at any rate, yet the point is not clear enough for me to denounce people upon.

"What next? Free them, and make them politically and socially our equals? My own feelings will not admit of this, and if mine would, we well know that those of the great mass of the whites will not. Whether this feeling accords with justice and sound judgment is not the sole question, if indeed it is any part of it. A universal feeling, whether well or ill founded, cannot be safely disregarded. We cannot then make them equals. It does seem to me that systems of gradual emancipation might be adopted, but for their tardiness in this I will not undertake to judge our brethren of the South."

And yet, while he could not say what should be done about slavery where it was already established and operating, he was sure it would be wrong to let it spread North. "Inasmuch as you do not object to my taking my hog to Nebraska, therefore I must not object to your taking your slave. Now, I admit that this is perfectly logical, if there is no difference between hogs and negroes."

The South had joined the North in making the law that classified African slave traders as pirates and provided hanging as the punishment. "If you did not feel that it was wrong, why did you join in providing that men should be hung for it? The practice was no more than bringing wild negroes from Africa to such as would buy them. But you never thought of hanging men for catching and selling wild horses, wild buffaloes, or wild bears."

The speaker at times was in a way lost from his audience, as though language had not been invented for what he was trying to say. He referred to the man whose business was to operate "a sort of negro livery stable," buying and selling slaves. "He watches your necessities, and crawls up to buy your slave, at a speculating price. If you cannot help it, you sell to him; but if you can help it, you drive him from your door. You despise him utterly. You do not recognize him as a friend, or even as an honest

man. Your children must not play with his; they may rollick freely with
the little negroes, but not with the slave dealer's children. If you are
obliged to deal with him, you try to get through the job without so much
as touching him, instinctively shrinking from the snaky contact. If he
grows rich and retires from business, you still remember him, and still
keep up the ban of nonintercourse upon him and his family. Now why
is this? You do not so treat the man who deals in corn, cotton, or tobacco."

Over the country were 433,643 free black men, at $500.00 a head worth
over $200,000,000.00. "How comes this vast amount of property to be
running about without owners? We do not see free horses or free cattle
running at large. How is this? All these free blacks are the descendants of
slaves or have been slaves themselves; and they would be slaves now but
for something which has operated on their white owners. What is that
something? Is there any mistaking it? In all these cases it is your sense
of justice and human sympathy continually telling you that the poor
negro has some natural right to himself—that those who deny it and
make mere merchandise of him deserve kickings, contempt, and death. And
now why will you ask us to deny the humanity of the slave, and estimate
him as only the equal of the hog? Why ask us to do what you will not
do yourselves? Why ask us to do for nothing what two hundred millions
of dollars could not induce you to do?"

He drew a line between his position and that of the Abolitionists. "Let
it not be said I am contending for the establishment of political and social
equality between the whites and blacks. I have already said the contrary."

He reasoned that the application of what Douglas called "the sacred
right of self-government" depended on whether a negro was a man. "If
he is not a man, in that case he who is a man may as a matter of self-
government do just what he pleases with him. But if the negro is a man,
is it not to that extent a total destruction of self-government to say that
he too shall not govern himself? When the white man governs himself,
that is self-government; but when he governs himself and also governs
another man, that is more than self-government—that is despotism. If
the negro is a man, why, then my ancient faith teaches me that 'all men
are created equal,' and that there can be no moral right in connection
with one man's making a slave of another. What I do say is that no man
is good enough to govern another man without that other's consent. I say
this is the leading principle, the sheet anchor of American republicanism."

He referred to bowie knives and six-shooters ruling the border between
Missouri and Kansas, with "never a glimpse of the ballot box," analyzed
the Nebraska Bill to show that while the people were supposed to decide
the slavery question for themselves, no time or place or manner of voting
was named in the bill. "Could there be a more apt invention to bring about
collision and violence on the slavery question than this Nebraska project

is? I do not charge or believe that such was intended by Congress; but if they had literally formed a ring and placed champions within it to fight out the controversy, the fight could be no more likely to come off than it is. And if this fight should begin, is it likely to take a very peaceful, Union-saving turn? Will not the first drop of blood so shed be the real knell of the Union?"

And what should be done first of all? "The Missouri Compromise ought to be restored. For the sake of the Union, it ought to be restored. We ought to elect a House of Representatives which will vote its restoration." If it should not be restored, what would the country see? "The South flushed with triumph and tempted to excess; the North, betrayed as they believe, brooding on wrong and burning for revenge. One side will provoke, the other resent. The one will taunt, the other defy. Already a few in the North defy all constitutional restraints, resist the execution of the Fugitive Slave Law, and even menace the institution of slavery in the states where it exists. Already a few in the South claim the constitutional right to take and to hold slaves in the free states—demand the revival of the slave trade—and demand a treaty with Great Britain by which fugitive slaves may be reclaimed from Canada."

The speech was three hours long. Through most of it Lincoln spoke as though he were not debating, trying to beat and crush an opponent, but rather as though he were examining his own mind, his own facts and views, his own propositions and the demonstrations of them.

And again he was no philosopher at all; he was a sad, lost man chanting a rhythm of the sad and lost. "Little by little, but steadily as man's march to the grave, we have been giving up the old for the new faith. Near eighty years ago we began by declaring that all men are created equal; but now from that beginning we have run down to the other declaration that for some men to enslave others is a 'sacred right of self-government.' These principles cannot stand together. They are as opposite as God and Mammon; whoever holds to the one must despise the other."

He pointed to "the liberal party throughout the world," watching slavery "fatally violating the noblest political system the world ever saw." And he intimated his knowledge of the movement on foot to extend slavery from the black race to certain lower grades of white labor, in saying: "Is there no danger to liberty itself in discarding the earliest practice and first precept of our ancient faith? In our greed-chase to make profit of the negro, let us beware lest we 'cancel and tear to pieces' even the white man's charter of freedom."

He stood among neighbors, in his shirt-sleeves, on a warm October day. The words came slow, hesitating, to begin with, and he spoke often in the tang of his childhood speech. "Just" sounded a little like "jist," and "such" suspiciously like "sich." As his body loosened and swayed to the cadence of his address, and the thoughts unfolded, drops of sweat stood out on his forehead; he was speaking not only with his tongue but with every blood-drop of his body.

A scholarly man said: "His manner was impassioned and he seemed transfigured; his listeners felt that he believed every word he said, and that, like Martin Luther, he would go to the stake rather than abate one jot or tittle of it." A farmer said: "I don't keer fur them great orators. I want to hear jist a plain common feller like the rest on us, thet I kin foller an' know where he's drivin'. Abe Linkern fills the bill."

And the *Springfield Journal* account, written by Bill Herndon: "Lincoln quivered with feeling and emotion. The whole house was as still as death. And the house approved the glorious triumph of truth by loud and continued huzzas. Women waved their white handkerchiefs in token of woman's silent but heartfelt assent. Douglas felt the sting. He frequently interrupted Mr. Lincoln. The Nebraska Bill was shivered, and like a tree of the forest, was torn and rent asunder by the hot bolts of truth. It was a proud day for Mr. Lincoln. His friends will never forget it."

The speech came to an end. The crowd that heard it scattered out of the Statehouse to their homes. But in Peoria twelve days later, Lincoln gave the same speech again to a crowd of thousands and then went home to Springfield and wrote it out for publication.

Now among many politicians and people in Illinois it was seen there was one man in the state who could grapple and hold his own with Stephen A. Douglas. Among Whig and anti-Nebraska politicians it was recognized that a mind was among them that could strip a political issue to what he called its "naked merits." And among thousands of plain people was an instinct, perhaps a hope, that this voice was their voice.

Douglas came to Lincoln after the Peoria speech and told him that he (Lincoln) had been more troublesome than all the opposition he had met in the United States Senate; he made the offer that he would go home and speak no more during the campaign if Lincoln would do the same. Lincoln took the offer. And one friend said, "This was certainly running Douglas into his hole and making him holler 'Enough.'"

CHAPTER 95

WHILE Lincoln was away from Springfield he was put on the Whig ticket as a candidate for the legislature, without being asked about it. Mrs. Lincoln went to Simeon Francis, editor of the *State Journal*, and had his name taken off. On Lincoln getting back to Springfield, William Jayne, who had put his name on the ticket, went to see him.

"I went to get his consent to run," said Jayne later. "This was at his house. He was the saddest man I ever saw, the gloomiest. He walked up and down the floor, almost crying; and to all my persuasions to let his name stand in the paper, he said: 'No, I can't. You don't know all. I say you don't begin to know one-half, and that's enough.' "

Yet Jayne went away and again put Lincoln's name on the ticket, where it stayed; and he was elected to the legislature—and resigned—having other plans.

Six weeks after the Peoria speech Lincoln was sending out letters in the tone of one written to Joseph Gillespie, who had become a leading lawyer for the Alton Railroad. "I have really got it into my head to try to be United States senator, and, if I could have your support, my chances would be reasonably good. But I know, and acknowledge, that you have as just claims to the place as I have; and therefore I cannot ask you to yield to me, if you are thinking of becoming a candidate yourself. If, however, you are not, then I should like to be remembered affectionately by you . . . We shall have difficulty to unite our forces. Please write me, and let this be confidential."

Three months later he sat in the Statehouse watching an election for United States senator. He got 47 votes. Three more would have elected him. The balloting went on, his vote slumped to 15.

Of those who left him, he wrote to a friend: "One notable instance was Mr. Strunk of Kankakee. At the beginning of the session he came a volunteer to tell me he was for me and would walk a hundred miles to elect me; but lo! it was not long before he leaked it out that he was going for me the first few ballots and then for Governor Matteson."

The minute came when Lincoln saw that if he held his 15 loyal votes, Matteson, a Douglas and Nebraska Democrat, would be elected. Lincoln let his votes go to Lyman Trumbull, Anti-Nebraska bolter from the Democratic party. Trumbull was elected.

Lincoln wrote to a friend: "I regret my defeat moderately, but I am not nervous about it. I could have headed off every combination, had it not been for Matteson's double game—and his defeat now gives me more pleasure than my own gives me pain. On the whole, it is perhaps as well for our general cause that Trumbull is elected. The Nebraska men confess that they hate it worse than anything that could have happened. It is a great consolation to see them worse whipped than I am."

Jim Matheny and a few other friends of Lincoln were sore about his being beaten for the senatorship. Democrats began quoting Matheny as having said in a speech: "In the most perfidious manner, they refused to elect Mr. Lincoln; and the mean, low-lived, sneaking Trumbull succeeded, by pledging all that was required by any party, in thrusting Lincoln aside and foisting himself, an excrescence from the rotten bowels of the Democracy, into the United States Senate; and thus it has ever been, that an honest man makes a bad bargain when he conspires or contracts with rogues."

From Lincoln, however, came no whisper nor murmur against Trumbull. At a reception to the new senator in the Edwards house in Spring-field, he and Mrs. Lincoln came to be counted present. Asked if he was disappointed, he smiled, stepped over to Trumbull, and, shaking hands, said, "Not too disappointed to congratulate my friend Trumbull."

Mrs. Lincoln greeted Mrs. Trumbull, who had been Miss Julia Jayne. They were the two women who had helped write the "Rebecca" letters that had led Lincoln into the duel with Shields.

A newspaper man noted Lincoln's face as "overspread with sadness," yet the sorrow dropped as the face "lighted up with a winning smile, keen intelligence, genuine kindness of heart, and the promise of true friend-ship."

CHAPTER 96

JOSHUA SPEED, the one-time chum of Lincoln, wrote from his Kentucky home in May asking Lincoln, "Where do you stand now in politics?" And Lincoln, busy with law and politics, didn't answer for three months.

Then he wrote: "I think I am a Whig; but others say there are no Whigs, and that I am an Abolitionist. I now do no more than oppose the extension of slavery. I am not a Know-Nothing; that is certain. How could I be? How can any one who abhors the oppression of negroes be in favor of degrading classes of white people? Our progress in degeneracy appears to me to be pretty rapid. As a nation we began by declaring, 'All men are created equal.' We now practically read it, 'All men are cre-ated equal, except negroes.' When the Know-Nothings get control, it will read, 'All men are created equal except negroes, foreigners and Catholics.' When it comes to this I shall prefer emigrating to some country where they make no pretense of loving liberty—to Russia, for instance, where despotism can be taken pure, and without the alloy of hypocrisy."

Violence instead of law or intelligence was operating over the country; the word "violence" came oftener than any other in his letter to Speed. The Nebraska Bill was violence all through. "The Nebraska Law I look upon not as a law, but as a violence from the beginning. I say it was con-ceived in violence, is maintained in violence, and is being executed in violence. I say it was conceived in violence, because the destruction of the Missouri Compromise, under the circumstances, was nothing less than violence. It was passed in violence, because it could not have passed at all but for the votes of many members in violence of the known will of their constituents. It is maintained in violence, because the elections since clearly demand its repeal; and the demand is openly disregarded."

Of Andrew Reeder, an antislavery free-state governor of Kansas, who had been driven from office by armed men, he commented, "Poor Reeder is the only public man who has been silly enough to believe that anything like fairness was ever intended."

In writing to Speed, Lincoln knew he was searching the mind and heart of an honest man and a southern slaveholder with a tested, clean heart. "You say that sooner than yield your legal right to the slave, especially at the bidding of those who are not themselves interested, you would see the Union dissolved. I am not aware that any one is bidding you yield that right: very certainly I am not. I leave that matter entirely to yourself. I also acknowledge your rights and my obligations under the Constitution in regard to your slaves. I confess I hate to see the poor creatures hunted down and caught and carried back to their stripes and unrequited toil; but I bite my lip and keep quiet."

He reminded Speed of the time on an Ohio River steamboat when they saw a dozen slaves shackled together with irons. "That sight was a continual torment to me, and I see something like it every time I touch the Ohio or any other slave border. It is not fair for you to assume that I have no interest in a thing which has, and continually exercises, the power to make me miserable. You ought rather to appreciate how much the great body of the northern people do crucify their feelings, in order to maintain their loyalty to the Constitution and the Union."

He presented his facts and deduced, "The slave breeders and slave traders are a small, odious, and detested class among you; and yet in politics they dictate the course of all of you, and are as completely your masters as you are the master of your negroes."

It was a letter with tears and soft cries in it. He was writing to the one man with whom he had exchanged his secrets about women. The Speeds had sent him violets from their honeymoon.

He ended the letter: "My kindest regards to Mrs. Speed. On the leading subject of this letter, I have more of her sympathy than I have of yours; and yet let me say I am, Your friend forever." And as he mailed that letter to Speed he knew he had let his feelings go more freely than he dared to when speaking in public in Illinois.

His plain ways of living and talking carried over into his politics. Often at the Sangamon County courthouse, the lawyers had seen him arrive and greet them: "Ain't ye glad to see me? Ain't ye glad I come?"

Though commanding higher pay as a lawyer, he was driving his own cow from pasture and milking her, cutting wood and carrying it into the house, shoveling the snow off his sidewalks. It was natural he should explain to Joe Gillespie that social snobbery was involved in the slavery question.

He had asked a Kentuckian why it was becoming more respectable than it used to be to own slaves. The Kentuckian answered: "You might have any amount of land, money in your pocket, or bank stock, and while traveling around, nobody would be any wiser; but if you had a darky trudging at your heels, everybody would see him and know you owned a slave. It is the most glittering property in the world. If a young man goes courting, the only inquiry is how many negroes he or she owns. Slave ownership betokens not only the possession of wealth, but indicates the gentleman of leisure, who is above labor and scorns labor." Lincoln also noted there were 600,000 white people in Kentucky who did not own slaves, as against 33,000 who did; and political conventions were controlled by the slave owners.

He was asked to subscribe money for the defense of free-state Kansas; he subscribed with a proviso, "Twenty-five dollars to be paid whenever Judge Logan would decide it was necessary to enable the people of Kansas to defend themselves against any force coming against them from without the Territory, and not by authority of the United States." Logan made no decision.

To the same Abolitionists who wanted to shoot their way to a free-state Kansas, he had said: "I believe in the providence of the most men, the largest purse, and the longest cannon. You would rebel against the Government, and redden your hands in blood. If you are in the minority, as you are, you can't succeed. When they have the most men, the longest purse, and the biggest cannon, you can't succeed. If you have the majority, as some of you say you have, you can succeed with the ballot, throwing away the bullet. Let there be peace.

"In a democracy, where the majority rule by the ballot through the forms of law, these physical rebellions and bloody resistances are radically wrong, unconstitutional, and are treason. Our own Declaration of Independence says that governments long established, for trivial causes should not be resisted. Revolutionize through the ballot box."

Bill Herndon was one of this Abolitionist group and he said that this talk from Lincoln steered their efforts into other channels, and, "It saved many of us from follies, if not our necks from the halter."

Polly, a free negro woman working in Springfield, came to the Lincoln & Herndon law office one day. Her boy had been hired as a steamboat hand down the Mississippi, and, arriving in New Orleans without his freedom papers, had been put in jail. Lincoln and Herndon went to the governor of Illinois, who said he could do nothing, and wrote to the governor of Louisiana, who said he could take no action. The two lawyers headed a subscription-list and raised the cash that bought the negro boy's freedom. And Herndon said Lincoln had told the governor of Illinois, "By God, governor, I'll make the ground in this country too hot for the foot of a slave, whether you release this boy or not."

Once, between law cases in a courthouse, he had argued with a Chicago lawyer that the slavery question would split the nation. And the two lawyers had beds in the same room at the hotel, and that night sat up in their nightshirts arguing. "At last we went to sleep," said the Chicago lawyer afterward; "and early in the morning I woke up and there was Lincoln half sitting up in bed. 'Dickey,' he said, 'I tell you this nation cannot exist half slave and half free.' " To which the Chicago lawyer answered, "Oh, Lincoln, go to sleep."

CHAPTER 97

IN the year 1856, on the Missouri and Kansas border, two hundred men, women, and children were shot, stabbed, or burned to death in the fighting between free- and slave-state settlers and guerrillas. The cost of the fighting, counting crops burned and cattle and horses stolen or killed, amounted to two million dollars.

In the month of May, as the first state convention to organize the Republican party of the state of Illinois was meeting in Bloomington, the town of Lawrence, Kansas, had been entered by riding and shooting men who burned the "Free State" hotel and wrecked two printing offices. The *Herald of Freedom* had published an editorial, calling: "Come one, come all, slaveocrats and nullifiers; we have rifles enough, and bullets enough, to send you all to your (and Judas's) own place. If you're coming, why don't you come along?" The governor of Kansas had been arrested in Missouri, his house had been set on fire, and himself chained on a prairie, a jail being lacking.

A Massachusetts senator had said of a South Carolina senator that every time he opened his mouth "a blunder flew out," and a nephew of the South Carolina senator had walked into the United States Senate chamber and broken a cane over the head of the Massachusetts senator and beaten his victim near to death.

While these issues were in the air, the dissatisfied political elements of Illinois, as of other states, were holding conventions to organize state parties and get up a national organization. Of the delegates who came to Bloomington about one-fourth were regularly elected and the others had appointed themselves. All stripes of political belief outside of the Democratic party were represented: Whigs, bolting anti-Nebraska Democrats, Free-Soilers, Know-Nothings, Abolitionists. Some who came were afraid that wild-eyed radicals would control.

As Lincoln and Henry C. Whitney walked to the Alton depot to see who would come as delegates from Chicago, Lincoln stopped in at a jewelry store and bought his first pair of spectacles; he was forty-seven years old and kind of needed spectacles, he told Whitney.

Seeing Norman B. Judd, a conservative politically, and an attorney for the Rock Island Railroad, arrive, Lincoln remarked to Whitney: "That's the best sign yet; Judd is here and he's a trimmer."

The convention met in Major's Hall, upstairs over Humphrey's Cheap Store, near the Courthouse Square, adopted a platform denouncing the Democratic administration, declared Congress had power to stop the extension of slavery and should use that power, and nominated for governor Colonel William H. Bissell, who while a member of Congress had clashed with Jefferson Davis, the Secretary of War, over the conduct of Illinois troops during the Mexican War, and when challenged by Davis to a duel had chosen as weapons "muskets loaded with ball and buckshot."

Then came speeches to dedicate the new party and forecast its life and work. After several delegates had loosed their oratory, there were calls for Lincoln. He stood up. There were cries, "Take the platform," which he did.

He looked the convention in the eye and reminded it, "We can hardly be called delegates strictly, inasmuch as, properly speaking, we represent nobody but ourselves."

He observed, "We are in a trying time," which they all knew very well; then suddenly came the thrust, "Unless popular opinion makes itself felt very strongly, and a change is made in our present course, blood will flow on account of Nebraska and brother's hand will be raised against brother." And the delegates sat up and put their elbows on the backs of benches in front of them. It was a sober man speaking. "We must not promise what we ought not, lest we be called on to perform what we cannot. We must not be led by excitement and passion to do that which our sober judgments would not approve in our cooler moments."

He noted that the delegates had been collected from many different elements. Yet they were agreed. "Slavery must be kept out of Kansas." The Nebraska Act was usurpation; it would result in making slavery national. "We are in a fair way to see this land of boasted freedom converted into a land of slavery in fact."

A terribly alive man stood before them. By this time Joseph Medill, of the *Chicago Tribune*, and the other newspaper writers had felt their pencils slip away; they were going to listen, somebody else would get the report of the speech. Herndon and Whitney had started to take notes, and forgotten they had pencils. Listeners moved up closer to the speaker. "I read once in a law book, 'A slave is a human being who is legally not a *person* but a *thing*.' And if the safeguards to liberty are broken down, as is now attempted, when they have made *things* of all the free negroes, how long, think you, before they will begin to make *things* of poor white men?"

He summarized the history of the United States to show that freedom and equality, sacred to the men of the American Revolution, had become words it was fashionable to sneer at. "Suppose Kansas comes in as a slave state, and all the 'border ruffians' have barbecues about it, and free-state men come trailing back to the dishonored North, like whipped dogs with their tails between their legs, is it not evident that this is no more the 'land of the free'? And if we let it go so, we won't dare to say 'home of the brave' out loud." Monstrous crimes were being committed in the name of slavery by persons collectively which they would not dare commit as individuals. The slave power came dangerously near taking Illinois in 1824; it did get Missouri in 1821. By violence, craft, intimidation, it was making steady advances. "But as sure as God reigns and school children read, that black foul lie can never be consecrated into God's hallowed truth."

He rehearsed the panorama of current events. "The repeal of the sacred Missouri Compromise has installed the weapons of violence: the bludgeon, the incendiary torch, the death-dealing rifle, the bristling cannon—the weapons of kingcraft, of the Inquisition, of ignorance, of barbarism, of oppression. We see its fruit in the dying bed of the heroic Sumner; in the ruins of the 'Free State' Hotel; in the smoking embers of the *Herald of Freedom;* in the free-state governor of Kansas chained to a stake on freedom's soil like a horse thief, for the crime of freedom.

"We see it in Christian statesmen, and Christian newspapers, and Christian pulpits applauding the cowardly act of a low bully, who crawled upon his victim behind his back and dealt the deadly blow. We note our political demoralization in the catchwords that are coming into such common use; on the one hand, 'freedom shriekers,' and sometimes 'freedom screechers'; and on the other hand 'border ruffians,' and that fully deserved. And the significance of catchwords cannot pass unheeded, for they constitute a sign of the times."

Should force be met with force? He could not say. "The time may yet come, and if we are true to ourselves may never come. Do not mistake that the ballot is stronger than the bullet."

Applause came regularly. He was saying what the convention wanted said. He was telling why the Republican party was organized. As the applause roared and lingered, the orator walked slowly toward the back of the platform, took a fresh start and worked toward the front. To Bill Herndon and others he seemed taller than ever before in his life. "He's been baptized," said Herndon.

The speech came to its climax with the declaration that no matter what was to happen, "We will say to the southern disunionists, We won't go out of the Union and you shan't," and the caution and threat: "There is both a power and a magic in popular opinion. To that let us now appeal; and while, in all probability, no resort to force will be needed, our moderation and forbearance will stand us in good stead when, if ever, we must make an appeal to battle and to the God of Hosts." The delegates applauded, stamped, cheered, waved handkerchiefs, threw hats in the air, and ran riot. He was their tongue and voice.

And after it was all over Whitney did the best he could at making notes of the speech, and as he walked with Lincoln to Judge Davis's house afterward, he told Lincoln that Jesse K. DuBois had burst out to him, "Whitney, that is the greatest speech ever made in Illinois, and it puts Lincoln on the track for the Presidency." And Lincoln walked for half a minute with stooped shoulders, not saying a word. Then, said Whitney, "He straightened up and immediately made a remark about some commonplace subject having no relation to the subject we had been considering."

They stopped a minute at the Courthouse Square to listen to Andrew H. Reeder, the ex-governor of Kansas, delivering a three-hour speech on outrages and infamies of Kansas. "He would have to do a great deal to overcome my prejudice against him," said Lincoln. It was the man he had referred to in writing to Speed, "Poor Reeder is the only public man who has been silly enough to believe that anything like fairness was ever intended."

The next morning, at the Illinois Central depot waiting for the Springfield train, delegates wrung Lincoln's hand, and William Hopkins of Grundy burst out, "Lincoln, I never swear, but that was the damnedest best speech I ever heard." And Herndon told people: "The smothered flame broke out; Lincoln stood before the throne of the Eternal Right, in the presence of his God, and unburdened his penitential and fired soul. If Mr. Lincoln was six feet, four inches high usually, at Bloomington he was seven feet."

Speaking for the Democrats who were joining the Republican party, the Chicago *Democratic Press*, edited by "Long John" Wentworth, commented: "Abraham Lincoln made the speech of the occasion. For an hour and a half he held the assemblage spellbound by the power of his argument, the intense irony of his invective, the brilliancy of his eloquence." And the editor went on, "I shall not mar any of its fine proportions by attempting even a synopsis of it." He suggested, "Mr. Lincoln must write it out and let it go before all the people." This was advice Lincoln also heard from others. And he refused to follow the advice. The speech was too full of passion, could be twisted too many ways to please the opposition. He would let it be a memory.

Five days later posters were up in Springfield announcing a Republican mass meeting to be held in the courthouse to ratify. The courthouse was lighted, windows shone at seven o'clock. Bells rang. Into the courtroom came three men who waited for a crowd that failed to come.

Lincoln took the Speaker's stand and said: "Gentlemen, this meeting is larger than I knew it would be. I knew that Herndon and myself would come, but I did not know that any one else would be here; and yet another has come—you, John Pain. These are sad times and seem out of joint. All seems dead, dead, dead; but the age is not yet dead; it liveth as surely as our Maker liveth. Under all this seeming want of life and motion, the world does move, nevertheless. Be hopeful. Let us adjourn and appeal to the people."

They stepped out of the courthouse into a June night of stars, with measured and peaceful constellations arching over the steel blue vault of the sky.

The streets leading to the near-by prairies smelled of loam with the push of new grass in it. And from puddles and ditches along the prairie roads the shrilling of the frogs lifted a song of young summer.

The tiniest sort of corn leaves were coming up in rows in a field near the corner of Eighth and Jackson streets. "The age is not dead; it liveth as surely as our Maker liveth. Be hopeful."

CHAPTER 98

WHEN Lincoln and his wife started housekeeping at the corner house on Eighth and Jackson streets, they could look from their kitchen windows away from the town and out onto cornfields. Since then the prairie had been filling up with houses between them and the tracks of the Great Western Railroad, later known as the Wabash. As Lincoln went to drive up his cow for milking, he could rest his gaze on cottages standing where he once had seen patches of cabbages and onions. He was living in town instead of on the edge of town. Hundreds of other towns in the north-western states were edging farther out into the cornfields. A pavement of wooden planks had been laid around the public square in Springfield. The new gas company was laying pipes and had hired Lincoln to certify title to the gas-works city lot.

The Alton Railroad and the Rock Island had spanned the spaces between Chicago and the Mississippi River so that barbecue orators, discussing progress, sang it as a proud fact that now the iron horse that sipped his morning draught from the crystal waters of Lake Michigan slaked his evening thirst on the banks of the majestic "Father of Waters." On passenger trains it happened occasionally in zero weather that the hose from the water tank to the engine boiler froze, and an hour or two, or an afternoon, would be lost while the fireman and engineer thawed out the hose; also the railroads had not learned to be particular about fences along the right of way, and cows often got caught under the locomotive wheels and spoiled the time tables for a day.

These delays in transportation were familiar to Lincoln, along with many other phases of the transportation revolution. Lawyer friends of his, such as O. H. Browning of Quincy, were addressing gatherings of farmers in schoolhouses and courtrooms, collecting subscriptions to stock payments for the building of railroads to come. Farmers and storekeepers, as well as speculators and big landowners, saw romance, civilization, and big winnings in iron trails that would be carriers of a commerce for constantly increasing populations. Railroads, new settlers, new farm machinery, were sending farm lands higher in price every year. Corn shellers, revolving horse-rakes, a cob and corn crusher, threshing machines, revolving churns, windmills, wheat drills, refrigerators, were advertised in the *Bloomington Pantagraph* in the fall of 1856.

Leading lawyers took cases for and against railroads. Norman B. Judd, the Republican leader in Chicago, was an attorney for the Rock Island Railroad; Joe Gillespie was with the Alton; Browning took cases for the Burlington; Stephen A. Douglas was the particular friend of the Illinois Central. And Abraham Lincoln's reputation as a lawyer went up several notches because of a famous decision he had won for the Illinois Central.

When the Illinois Central got its charter, the legislature provided that it should be free from payment of all taxes, and instead should pay seven per cent of its gross earnings into the state treasury. By this act all counties were stopped from assessing and taxing the railroad. But it happened in 1853 that McLean County decided to assess and tax the Illinois Central Railroad property as it did any other property. Lincoln wrote a letter to T. R. Webber, a McLean County official, saying if they wanted to be sure to have him on their side there was no time to lose. "The company are offering to engage me for them. You have the first right to my services, if you choose to secure me a fee something near such as I can get from the other side." It was understood that if McLean County could win the case, then all the other counties through which the railroad line ran would also have the power to assess and tax the corporation's property.

Lincoln described the issue as involving "the largest law question that can now be got up in the state," adding, "and therefore in justice to myself, I cannot afford, if I can help it, to miss a fee altogether." This letter was dated September 12, 1853. Having given his McLean County friends first chance at retaining his services, he wrote three weeks later to Mason Brayman, counsel for the Illinois Central Railroad: "Neither the county of McLean nor any one on its behalf has yet made any engagement with me in relation to its suit with the Illinois Central Railroad on the subject of taxation. I am now free to make an engagement for the road, and if you think of it you may 'count me in.' Please write me on receipt of this."

As the case came to trial in the McLean circuit court, Lincoln represented the railroad corporation and had against him his old law partners, John T. Stuart and Stephen T. Logan. His case was beaten in the circuit court; the decision was that the railroad must pay a tax in every county through which it passed. The cost in taxes would mount into millions and bankrupt the corporation. Lincoln appealed to the supreme court, argued the case twice, and in December, 1855, won a decision reversing the lower court.

He presented his bill to the Illinois Central Railroad corporation at their Chicago office. The bill was for $2,000.00. The official handling the bill looked at it and said, "Why, this is as much as a first-class lawyer would have charged!" adding that it was "as much as Daniel Webster himself would have charged." And Lincoln was paid a fee of $200.00.

When he got back on the circuit and told the other lawyers, they didn't know whether to laugh or cry at this treatment of a lawyer by a corporation that had been saved millions of dollars through Lincoln's victory in court Lincoln started a suit against the Illinois Central for a fee of $5,000.00. The case was called, the lawyer for the railroad didn't show up; Lincoln was awarded his $5,000.00 one morning; in the afternoon the railroad lawyer arrived and begged Lincoln for a retrial. Lincoln said he was willing, the case was called, and Lincoln read a statement signed by six of the highest-priced lawyers in Illinois that the sum of $5,000.00 for the services rendered in the case "is not unreasonable." Before the jury went out he told them he had been paid $200.00 by the railroad and they should make the verdict for $4,800.00. Which they did.

Thirty-eight days went by and the railroad company failed to pay the $4,800.00 fee. An execution was issued directing the sheriff to seize property of the railroad. Then the fee was paid. And high officers of the railroad stated, "The payment of so large a fee to a western lawyer would embarrass the general counsel with the board of directors in New York."

Lincoln deposited the $4,800.00 in the Springfield Marine Bank, and later, in handing Herndon half of the fee, he pushed it toward his partner, then held it back an instant, and said with a smile, "Billy, it seems to me it will be bad taste on your part to keep saying severe things I have heard from you about railroads and other corporations. Instead of criticizing them, you and I ought to thank God for letting this one fall into our hands." And Herndon wrote, "We both thanked the Lord for letting the Illinois Central fall into our hands."

No bad feeling developed, however, between Lincoln and the Illinois Central Railroad. Five months after he had forced them by court action to pay him the fee he asked for, he met John M. Douglas, the Illinois Central lawyer, and gave him a letter to carry to Jesse K. Dubois, a neighbor of Lincoln in Springfield, a Republican, holding the office of state auditor. The letter:

BLOOMINGTON, Dec. 21, 1857.

DEAR DUBOIS:

J. M. Douglas of the I. C. R. R. Co. is here and will carry this letter. He says they have a large sum (near $90,000) which they will pay into the treasury now, if they have an assurance that they shall not be sued before Jany. 1860—otherwise not. I really wish you would consent to this. Douglas says they *cannot* pay more and I believe him. I do not write this as a lawyer seeking an advantage for a client; but only as a friend, only urging you to do what I think I would do if I were in your situation. I mean this as private and confidential only, but I feel a good deal of anxiety about it.

Yours, as ever,

A. LINCOLN.

He was called on to decide disputes between railroad companies. J. F. Joy, the Illinois Central Railroad official, telegraphed to him from Chicago once: "Can you come here immediately and act as arbitrator in the crossing case between the Illinois Central and Northern Indiana R. R. Companies if you should be appointed? Answer and say yes if possible."

When his annual pass on the Alton Railroad was used up, he wrote the superintendent, Richard P. Morgan: "Says John to Tom, 'Here's your old rotten wheelbarrow. I've broke it usin' on it. I wish you would mend it, 'case I shall want to borrow it this afternoon.' Acting on this as a precedent, I say, 'Here's your old "chalked hat." I wish you would take it and send me a new one, 'case I shall want to use it by the 1st of March.' "

He had become a responsible lawyer, trusted with important affairs of property. The McLean County Bank retained him to bring suit against the City of Bloomington. In Springfield, the Gas Works asked him to make certain their title to the two city lots on which they were located, which Lincoln did, later sending the Gas Works a bill for $500.00.

He had influence among judges and lawyers; not only was he a power in politics so that he counted in putting judges on the bench and taking them off; he was also an attorney who had personal qualities and social attractions that gave him influence. He was asked by a caller in his office one day to use his influence in a certain legal quarter; he was offered $500.00 if he would use his influence.

Herndon heard the offer made, and said later: "I heard him refuse the $500.00 over and over again. I went out and left them together. I suppose Lincoln got tired of refusing, for he finally took the money; but he never offered any of it to me; and it was noticeable that whenever he took money in this way, he never seemed to consider it his own or mine. In this case, he gave the money to the Germans in the town, who wanted to buy themselves a press. A few days after, he said to me in the coolest way, 'Herndon, I gave the Germans $250.00 of yours the other day.' 'I am glad you did, Mr. Lincoln,' I answered. Of course I could not say I was glad he took it."

When he traveled from Springfield to Chicago he sometimes took a long way around, he didn't have a pass on the direct route. Henry C. Whitney took a midnight train at Champaign once, and found Lincoln on board. "He explained to me that he was going to Chicago," said Whitney, "and he had passes on the Illinois Central and the Great West-

Lincoln is trying a law case and watching politics in Chicago in
1854 and sits for this portrait at 12 North Wells Street.

*From original photograph presented to the Chicago
Historical Society by George Schneider*

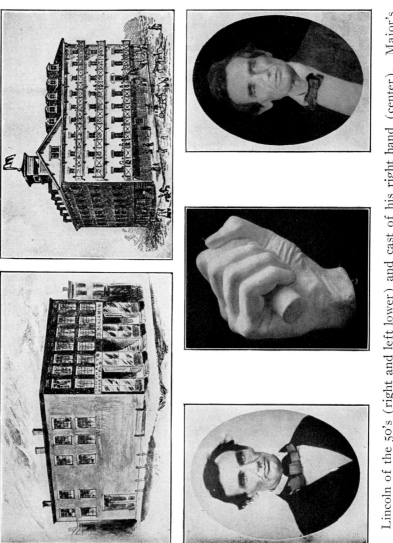

Lincoln of the 50's (right and left lower) and cast of his right hand (center). Major's Hall, Bloomington (upper left), where Lincoln delivered the stormy "Lost Speech." Pike House, Bloomington (upper right), where Lincoln made campaign speeches from a veranda and witnessed campaign street fights.

ern, both; he could get to Chicago by the circuitous route free, while he had no pass by the direct route."

In the famous Rock Island Bridge case Lincoln figured as the apostle of the march of civilization. Against threats of lawsuits and injunctions, the Rock Island Railroad had built a bridge 1,582 feet long, across the Mississippi River, from Rock Island on the Illinois side across to Davenport on the Iowa side.

But—the bridge had enemies. There were men who hated the bridge. They swore vengeance against the bridge. They had a contempt for railroads, and especially any railroad that ran over a river where their boats ran. The cargoes of the world should be carried by steamboats, they believed; yet somehow the bridge arose and crossed the river without being shattered by the steamboatmen riding on their proud, white side-wheelers.

The bridge was built, even though the Chamber of Commerce of St. Louis voted, at the time the cornerstone of the bridge pier was laid, that a bridge across the Mississippi River was "unconstitutional, an obstruction to navigation, dangerous, and that it was the duty of every western state, river city, and town to take immediate action to prevent the erection of such a structure." Threats to force removal of the bridge were heard in congressional committee rooms in Washington. The effort persisted at Washington "to abolish the Rock Island bridge nuisance."

Then, on May 6, 1856, came the steamboat *Effie Afton*. She rammed into a pier of the Rock Island Railroad bridge, took fire, and burned to a total loss, while part of the bridge burned and tumbled into the river. And steamboatmen up and down the Mississippi had a jubilee, shouted the news; there was ringing of bells and blowing of whistles on all boats in view of the burning, sagging truss of the bridge.

Then the owners of the *Effie Afton* sued the bridge company for damages. And Norman B. Judd, general counsel of the Rock Island Railroad, and one of the Bloomington convention organizers of the Republican party, called on Abraham Lincoln to represent the company in the hearing before the District Court of the United States for the Northern District of Illinois, holding sessions in what was known as the "Saloon Building" at the southeast corner of Clark and Lake streets in Chicago, with Judge McLean presiding.

Engineers, pilots, boat owners, river men, bridge builders, were called as witnesses. Lincoln had made himself so familiar with the figures, measurements, distances, facts in the case, that sometimes there was laughter as he rambled around the room looking abstracted, but occasionally turning suddenly to correct a witness on a matter of feet or inches or the span of a truss. Once he sat down by a big box stove, surrounded with cuspidors, and whittled, seemingly lost to the world. An instant came when he straightened up, walked toward a witness and demanded that the original notes as to certain measurements be produced. The witness was shown to be mistaken; it had its effect on the jury. Lincoln went back to whittling by the big box stove, seemingly lost to the world.

In his argument Lincoln plainly felt the call of all the old romance of the Mississippi River and its boat life. He began with pointing out that St. Louis might wish that the Rock Island bridge should not stand, that with the bridge gone a larger volume of Iowa products would have to be shipped by way of St. Louis. Meetings held in St. Louis so indicated. He pointed to the great channel of the Mississippi flowing "from where it never freezes to where it never thaws"; it would not be pleasing to block up such a channel.

Yet there was a growing travel from east to west that had to be considered; it was as important as the Mississippi traffic. It was growing larger and larger, this east-to-west traffic, building up new country with a rapidity never before seen in the history of the world. In his own memory he had seen Illinois grow from almost empty spaces to a population of a million and a half; there were Iowa and other rising communities in the Northwest. "This current of travel has its rights as well as that of north and south." Across the burned bridge the railroad had hauled 12,586 freight cars and 74,179 passengers in eleven months. During four months of the year the river could not be navigated. But the bridge and the railroad could be used. "This bridge must be treated with respect in this court and is not to be kicked about with contempt."

The opposing counsel, Judge Wead, had alluded even to a dissolution of the Union of states. "The proper mode for all parties in this affair is 'to live and let live,' and then we will find a cessation of this trouble about the bridge."

The suggestion had been made that a suspension bridge, having no piers, for steamboats to ram, might solve the difficulty. How so? "A suspension bridge cannot be built so high but that the chimneys of the boats will grow up till they cannot pass. The steamboat men will take pains to make them grow."

He analyzed the angles of the piers, the curve of the river, the depth of the channel, the velocity of the current, and showed the final smash of the boat was "in the splash door aft the wheel." And he proved to general satisfaction that the pilot ran his boat as though the river had no bridge with piers standing in it, and the starboard wheel were not working. But the main drive of his argument was that one man had as good a right to cross a river as another had to sail up or down it.

He asked if the products of the boundless, fertile country lying west of the Mississippi must for all time be forced to stop on its western bank, be unloaded from the cars and loaded on a boat, and after passage across the river be reloaded into cars on the other side. Civilization in the region to the west was at issue.

With a whimsical sarcasm, he touched on the testimony that the boat had "smelled a bar," remarking, "For several days we were entertained with depositions about boats 'smelling a bar.' Why, then, did the *Afton*, after she had come up smelling so close to the long pier, sheer off so strangely? When she had got to the centre of the very nose she was smelling, she seemed suddenly to have lost her sense of smell and to have flanked over to the short pier."

The jury listened two days. The speaker came to a pause. He knew that in handling a jury there is a certain moment when it is an advantage to quit talking. He said: "Gentlemen, I have not exhausted my stock of information, and there are more things I could suggest regarding this case, but as I have doubtless used up my time I presume I had better close."

The jury were locked up; when they came out they had agreed to disagree; their action was generally taken as a victory for railroads, bridges, and Chicago, as against steamboats, rivers, and St. Louis.

As he practiced law and earned from two to three thousand dollars a year, he saw other lawyers adding farm after farm to their possessions. Land was the favorite and general form for the material riches of rich men. Among the men with whom he mixed and joked and worked in his daily life were those who owned more land than they could walk across in a week. Stephen T. Logan, the little frowzy-headed lawyer with whom he had once been in partnership, was adding farm to farm. Judge David Davis had ten thousand acres in Iowa, besides his Illinois farms; he was worth a million dollars, people said. The judge had entered tracts of land in Champaign County and sold sections of them. When notes on these lands were not paid and were overdue, he gave them to Henry C. Whitney, who brought suits for payment.

And Whitney told what happened, in this manner: "At a convenient season, when it came time to adjourn court, he did not adjourn, but remained on the bench till everybody filed out, except the clerk and the sheriff, he busying himself reading some court papers. Then I arose and called up the case of 'Davis vs. Smith.' 'Well,' said the Judge nonchalantly, 'what is wanted?' 'Default on a note.' 'Has the defendant been served in time and no appearance?' asked he. 'Yes, your Honor, all is regular.' 'Mr. Sheriff, call John Smith.' 'Jaw Smy—Jaw Smy—Jaw Smy,' said the sheriff perfunctorily. No answer. 'Judgment by default; clerk assess damages,' said the Judge, and went on with his reading a decent length of time, and then formally adjourned court."

"There was no prearrangement at all about this. I instinctively knew what the judge wanted and how he wanted it done; and he instinctively knew how to play his part, and how I would play mine; and no one in all Champaign County knew that the judge had really rendered judgment in his own case, but himself, the clerk, sheriff, and myself. Could he not have accomplished it thus—he must necessarily have brought another judge there to enter these formal judgments or sent them to another circuit by change of venue. As there was no inherent wrong in this, the judge didn't care for its appearance—provided it could be done in the sly way it was."

One day a check for $500.00 came into Lincoln's hands, the largest retaining fee that he had ever handled for himself as a lawyer. He was hired for a law case that interested him from start to finish. It sent his imagination back to the day when he went to the fields and harvested grain with scythe and cradle, when he had formed calluses on the insides of his hands from holding the scythe handle. Since that time the reaper had come; in Chicago was Cyrus H. McCormick, with his big shops for making a reaping machine; in Rockford was John M. Manny with his shops, also for making a reaping machine. And McCormick was bringing court action against Manny, claiming that Manny's patents were not lawful and valid, and that they infringed on the McCormick rights. If McCormick could win his case he would stop the Manny factory at Rockford and get $400,000.00 as damages. His lawyers were E. N. Dickerson and Reverdy Johnson, while Manny had George Harding, Edwin M. Stanton, and Abraham Lincoln.

Testimony had been taken in Cincinnati and sent on to Lincoln at Springfield for him to read. He was expected to go on to Cincinnati later and make a famous argument before Judge McLean, the same Federal judge before whom the Rock Island bridge case had been tried, with victory for Lincoln's client. His colleague, Stanton, had also figured in a bridge case, the finest steamer on the Ohio River having smashed into the Wheeling suspension bridge in order to show that the bridge stood in the way of free navigation.

A serious man was this Stanton; at his father's knee he had sworn an oath to fight slavery till death; he had toiled through Kenyon College in Ohio and practiced law before he was of legal age; he had swallowed poison while defending a client in a murder trial so as to describe its effects and save his client from hanging, which he did; at his bedside he kept the ashes of his firstborn child in an urn. He was a man strict in language, dress, duty. When his eyes lighted on Lincoln at the Burnett House in Cincinnati, wearing heavy boots, loose clothes, farmer-looking, he used language which sounded like a question, "Where did that long-armed baboon come from?" And he described Lincoln as wearing a linen duster with splotches like "a map of the continent," and was quoted as saying he wouldn't associate with "such a damned, gawky, long-armed ape as that."

Up and down the courtroom walked Lincoln as the testimony was being taken, stopping to listen now and then, resuming his walk, thinking it all over as though he were in his own law office at home. In his coat pocket he had a manuscript of his argument; it was packed with the cunning and attraction he felt about man and machinery, farming and civilization.

The moment came when Stanton told the court that only two arguments would be made for the defense whether he, Stanton, spoke or not. He suggested to Lincoln that he should speak. Lincoln answered, "No, you speak." Stanton replied, "I will," and picking up his hat said he would go and prepare his speech.

Thus Lincoln was frozen out, and his carefully planned speech was not delivered. He sent the manuscript to Harding, with the request that Harding should not show it to Stanton. And Harding, it was said in Cincinnati, threw it into a waste basket without reading it.

A young representative of the Manny company, Ralph Emerson, had come on from Rockford, Illinois, and struck up an acquaintance with Lincoln. They took long walks of evenings. Emerson told Lincoln that the study of law interested him; he had read a little and believed he might choose it for a life work. He wanted to ask a question. "Mr. Lincoln, is it possible for a man to practice law and always do by others as he would be done by?"

Lincoln's chin dropped lower into his bosom as they walked the grade of a long Cincinnati hill in the quiet of evening haze and the peace of hours after sundown. When Lincoln spoke at last he had no answer to the young man's question. And the young man decided that the lack of an answer was in itself one; he decided not to be a lawyer, and said afterward, "That walk turned the course of my life."

Lincoln visited the courts in Cincinnati and enjoyed watching Bellamy Storer, a judge in Room No. 1 of the Superior Court. Storer had careless manners and direct methods; it was said he could "mingle in the same hour the gravity of the judge and the jest of the clown." Lincoln took it all in, and remarked: "I wish we had that judge in Illinois. I think he would share with me the fatherhood of the legal jokes of the Illinois bar."

On leaving Cincinnati he told young Emerson that he was going back to Illinois to study law; eastern lawyers seemed to be coming West for practice. "They have got as far as Cincinnati now; they will soon be in Illinois. I will be ready for them."

Back in Springfield he divided the $2,000.00 fee, half and half, with Herndon, said he had been "roughly handled by that man Stanton," and discussed Judge McLean, classifying the judge as "an old granny." Getting specific, he said of the judge, "If you were to point your finger at him and a darning needle at the same time, he never would know which was the sharper."

Often Lincoln used his inborn sense of the comic to strip the opposition of dignity. In one case his client was a rich man who had beaten an editor with a stick; the editor sued for $10,000.00 damages. The opposition lawyer roused the jury and people who crowded the courtroom to high excitement; many faces were wet with tears. It was Lincoln's turn to speak. And Abram Bergen, who was young and was thinking of studying law, was wondering what Lincoln would do. His impression was: "Lincoln dragged his feet off the table, on the top of which they had been resting, set them on the floor, gradually lifted up and straightened out his length of legs and body, and took off his coat. While removing his coat it was noticed by all present that his eyes were intently fixed on something on the table before him. He picked up the object, a paper, scrutinized it closely, and, without uttering a word, indulged in a long, loud laugh, accompanied by his wonderfully grotesque facial expression. It was magnetic; the whole audience grinned.

"Then he laid the paper down slowly, took off his cravat, again picked up the paper, re-examined it, and repeated the laugh. It was contagious. He then deliberately removed his vest, showing his one yarn suspender, took up the paper, again looked at it curiously, and again indulged in his peculiar laugh. Its effect was absolutely irresistible; the judge, jury, and whole audience joined in the merriment, and this before Lincoln had spoken a single word.

"When the laughter had subsided, he apologized to the court for his seemingly rude behavior and explained that the amount of damages claimed was at first written $1,000.00. He supposed the plaintiff afterward had taken a second look and concluded that the wounds to his honor were worth an additional $9,000.00. He immediately and fully admitted that the plaintiff was entitled to some amount, told a funny story, and specially urged the jury to agree on some amount. The verdict was for a few hundred dollars and was entirely satisfactory to Lincoln's client."

A witness said his name was J. Parker Green. Lincoln cross-examined: Why J. Parker Green?—What did the J. stand for?—John?—Well, why didn't the witness call himself John P. Green?—That was his name, wasn't it?—Well, what was the reason he didn't wish to be known by his right name?—Did J. Parker Green have anything to conceal; and, if not, why did J. Parker Green part his name in that way? As he rang the changes on the name and shifted the tones of his voice in pronouncing the name, he took all dignity away from the witness; it was so ridiculous that boys in the street that day were calling at each other, "J. Parker Green." A Bloomington lawyer, Adlai Stevenson, said: "There was something in Lincoln's way of intoning his questions which made me suspicious of the witness, and I was never able to rid my mind of the absurd impression that there was something not quite right about J. Parker Green. He was discredited and the defendant went free."

In three big cases, involving railroad taxes, a railroad bridge over a great river, and a farmer's reaping-machine patent, he had dug deep in the philosophy of changing civilizations, and the technical engineering as well as the economic structure of the society in which he was living.

The county seat of Logan County had been given his name. Three settlers there had received early information that a railroad was to cross their county and had bought a big tract of land where they guessed the county seat might be located. Lincoln drew up the papers for incorporating the town.

And when he asked them what the name of the new town was to be he was told to call it Lincoln. He warned them, "You better not do that, for I never knew anything named Lincoln that amounted to much." Then he wrote in the name of Lincoln, and it was so spelled out on the maps and the railroad time tables.

CHAPTER 99

THE Quincy lawyer, O. H. Browning, kept a diary. Three July days he once noted in his diary as having cool weather. On Monday he wrote: "Attending court. Commenced trial of Williamson, formerly postmaster at Lacon, who is indicted for robbing the mail. I am assisting Lincoln at his request. Rain in afternoon." On Tuesday: "Argued case against Williamson. The evidence was very strong, almost conclusive. I was so discouraged that I wished to decline a speech, but at the persuasion of Lincoln I addressed the jury for something over two hours. The case was given to them at 4 P.M. and they are yet out at 9. The defendant is a young man, who lost a leg in the Mexican War, and does not look to be very bright, a total stranger to me, and I believe him to be guilty, but wish him acquitted. My sympathies are awakened. I am sorry for the poor devil." And on Wednesday: "Jury found Williamson guilty. Will yet try to arrest the judgment but have not much hope. Weather much cooler."

Browning knew, and so did other lawyers in Illinois, that hidden under his brick-dust coloring Lincoln had queer soft spots and his feelings ran out into understanding of blunderers and stumblers; he spoke their languages and stories.

Lincoln defended an old farmer who had taken a bunch of sheep "on shares," fattened them with his year's crop through the winter, and in the spring, when they all died, couldn't pay the sheep owner for them. The sheep owner sued for the money. The first trial was a mistrial; the second trial was lost, and the costs and damages stripped the old man of nearly all his property. At seventy he was starting west to hunt cheap land and make a new home. As he shook hands with the old man and spoke good-by, Lincoln's eyes were wet and he had to hold back tears.

Lincoln had brought suit one year against Frink & Walker, whose stagecoach between Rushville and Frederick had tipped over on one side, cutting and bruising passengers. And two years later he had brought suit against the Great Western Railway Company in behalf of a brakeman, Jasper Harris, who had, as Lincoln's brief recited, "his right foot, ankle, leg and thigh, while in the services of said company, so greatly torn, crushed and broken that amputation of his said right limb above the knee was necessary."

A woman client of Lincoln's had him survey and lay off into lots a piece of land she owned near the Springfield city limits. He found that by some mistake the woman had become owner of three more acres of land than she was entitled to, and Charles Matheny, the former owner, was the loser of the three acres. Lincoln notified her she ought to pay the heirs of Matheny the money owed them at the price per acre first agreed on. The woman couldn't see it; Lincoln wrote her again; the Matheny heirs were poor and needed the money, he told her. And again he wrote explaining to the woman what seemed to him plain justice. One day the woman sent him payment in full and he hunted up the heirs and shared them out their money.

One lawyer who often talked, walked, and slept in the same bed with Lincoln was Henry C. Whitney of Urbana. To Whitney it seemed that Lincoln, when he had taken a case, wanted to win, like most lawyers— only there were tricks and twists he wouldn't use.

"In a clear case of dishonesty, he would hedge in some way so as not himself to partake of the dishonesty; in a doubtful case of dishonesty, he would give his client the benefit of the doubt," was Whitney's impression. And he told of a murder case in which Lincoln "hedged" after getting into it. Leonard Swett and Whitney had spoken for the defence, and believed they would get a verdict of acquittal. Then Lincoln spoke to the jury, took up the facts and the evidence, and was all of a sudden making arguments and admissions that spoiled the case for the prisoner at the bar. The jury came in with a verdict that sent the client to the penitentiary for three years.

And the case got to working in Lincoln's mind. Somehow he hadn't done just right. Having helped get the man in the penitentiary, he worked to get him out, and in a year handed him a pardon from the governor of the state.

He was of the frontier, had grown up with it, and seen its line shift west. He understood the frontier scorn and hate for a horse thief. In the case in Edgar County of George W. A. Albin versus Thomas Badine, in slander, he briefed the slanderous remarks: "1st. Albin stole Brady's horse out of my pasture last night. He is a horse thief and that is what he came here for. 2nd. Albin stole that horse last night out of my pasture; and he is a horse thief, and I know that was his business here. 3d. He is a horse thief and I always believed his business was horse stealing, and that is what brought him here. 4th. Albin stole Brady's horse out of my pasture last night, and it is not the first horse he has stolen. He is a horse thief and follows that business. 5th. You stole that horse out of my pasture, and it is not the first one you have stole. 6th. You know you stole that horse, and it is not the first horse you have stole, and I believe you follow the business. 7th. You are a horse thief and you came here for that business—and I believe you came here for nothing else. You are a horse thief. 8th. He is a damn'd little thief, his business is horse stealing and I can prove it."

The home of Lincoln's friend and colleague, Whitney, was in Urbana, and Lincoln came one summer day in 1856 to Urbana to speak at a public meeting in a church. Calling Whitney to one side, he whispered: "There is a boy in your jail I want to see, but I don't want any one beside yourself to know it. I wish you would speak to the jailer."

The boy was a cripple, had stolen a watch from an old man named Green in Urbana, and was under a charge of stealing a gun in Charleston; also the boy was the son of Lincoln's step-brother, John D. Johnston, and so a grandson of Sally Bush Lincoln. "I'm going to help him out of these two cases," said Lincoln, "but that's the last; after that, if he wants to continue his thieving, I shall do nothing for him."

The jail was a rough log cabin, with a one-foot-square hole through which prisoners talked with callers. And Whitney told later what happened: "The prisoner heard us and set up a hypocritical wailing and thrust out toward us a very dirty Bible which Lincoln took and turned over the leaves mechanically. He then said, 'Where were you going, Tom?' The latter attempted to reply, but his wailing made it incoherent, so Lincoln cut it short by saying: 'Now, Tom, do what they tell you—behave yourself—don't talk to any one, and when court closes I will be here and see what I can do for you. Now stop crying and behave yourself.' And with a few more words we left. Lincoln was very sad; I never saw him more so."

"At the fall term of the court, Amzi McWilliams, the prosecuting attorney, agreed with us that if the Greens would come into court and state that they did not desire to press the case further he would file a *nolle pros.* That same evening Lincoln and others were to speak in a church, and at my suggestion Lincoln and I left the meeting and made our way to the house where the Greens lived. They were a venerable old couple, and we found them seated in their humble kitchen greatly astonished at our visit. I introduced Lincoln, who explained his position and wishes in the matter in a homely, plain way, and the good old couple assented. The next day they came into court, willing that the boy should be released, which was promptly done."

Once it happened that Lincoln classified himself as a sort of detective.

There came to Springfield an Englishman who had been in St. Louis, passing himself off as a nobleman and buying land and cattle without settling his debts. Claims against him had been put in the hands of the Springfield banker, Jacob Bunn, whose brother, John, sat up with Lincoln nearly all of one summer night in front of the hotel where the confidence man was staying. Noticing that he was closely watched, the Englishman took Lincoln to one side and said he could pay a thousand dollars if that would wipe out the claims against him. Lincoln took the offer to Bunn, who agreed to the settlement, the money was paid, and the Englishman went his way with no one at his heels.

Bunn asked Lincoln what the fee would be. Lincoln answered he had been more of a detective than a lawyer in the case; if some time in the future he felt he had a fee coming he would ask Bunn for it.

And Bunn had nearly forgotten all about the fee, when one morning, as he was eating breakfast, Lincoln came in and asked for a hundred-dollar fee in the case. Bunn said he would be glad to pay the fee but wished to know why Lincoln had let the matter go so long, and why the fee should be collected in the middle of a morning breakfast.

And as Bunn told it later, "Lincoln's answer was that he needed the money, not for himself, but for another who was in trouble and needed his help. Three of his friends had spent the night in a spree, had broken in almost the entire front of a grocery or saloon; they were in the sheriff's office and would be placed in jail unless some one should settle for the damage done. In a few moments I secured the money and turned it over to him. He seemed more or less relieved, and hurriedly left to interview the sheriff and release his friends. I did not press him for names, but learned that two of his friends were the sons of wealthy parents and the third was his law partner. Lincoln was poorer than any of them, and yet he seemed to regard it his duty to crawl out of his bed before daybreak to their rescue. I doubt if another man in Springfield would have done it. No wonder Lincoln sometimes thanked God he was not born a woman!"

In the town of Danville, Lincoln's law partner there, Ward Hill Lamon, brought the case of a girl named Scott, who was, as they said, "not in her right mind." She had $10,000 in property, mostly cash, and a schemer had struck up an acquaintance with her and asked her to marry him. Her brother wanted a conservator appointed by the court to take care of her and her property, and had agreed with Lamon to pay a fee of $250.00 when the case was won. On trial it took Lincoln and Lamon only twenty minutes to win their case, and Lamon was paid $250.00. Lincoln was sore and hurt, forced Lamon to give back to Miss Scott one-half of the $250.00.

Judge Davis said, in the wheezing whisper of a man weighing 300 pounds, "Lincoln, you are impoverishing this bar by your picayune charges of fees, and the lawyers have reason to complain of you." Other lawyers murmured approval. Lincoln stuck to the point: "That money comes out of the pocket of a poor, demented girl, and I would rather starve than swindle her in this manner." In the evening at the hotel, the lawyers held a mock court and fined him; he paid the fine, rehearsed a new line of funny stories, and stuck to his original point that he wouldn't belong to a law firm that could be styled "Catch 'em and Cheat 'em."

The spitework of human tongues, the lashing and snarling of hate that hunts for stinging names to fasten on other people, this came before him in his work, for review and analysis. A dark-complexioned Portuguese named Dungey married a woman named Spencer, whose brother called Dungey a "negro." As it was a crime under Illinois laws then for a white man to marry a negro, the words were slanderous, and Dungey had Lincoln bring a slander suit. Lincoln's brief recited that Spencer, referring to Dungey as "Black Bill," "in the presence of divers good citizens falsely and maliciously spoke and uttered of and concerning the plaintiff, these false, scandalous, malicious, and defamatory words: 'Black Bill (meaning the plaintiff) is a negro and it will be easily proved if called for.' "

In addressing the jury, he mentioned Spencer as having called Dungey a "nigger," and argued: "Gentlemen of the jury, my client is not a negro, though it is no crime to be a negro—no crime to be borne with a black skin. But my client is not a negro. His skin may not be as white as ours, but I say he is not a negro, though he may be a Moor." Not only had Spencer called Dungey a "nigger" but he had followed it up with adding "a nigger married to a white woman."

"And," said Lincoln, "if the malice of the defendant had rested satisfied with speaking the words once or twice, or even thrice, my client would have borne it in silence; but when he went from house to house, *gabbling*, yes, *gabbling* about it, then it was that my client determined to bring this suit." The jury gave a verdict of $600.00 for the Portuguese, who on the advice of Lincoln cut the amount $400.00.

The verdict also required Spencer to pay Lincoln's fee and the court costs; Lincoln asked two other lawyers what he should charge; they told him he would have to fix the fee; he asked, "Well, gentlemen, don't you think I have honestly earned twenty-five dollars?" They could hardly believe their ears; for Lincoln had handled the case through two terms of court, had fought hard in court two days of trial, and the opposition had to pay the bill. They expected a sum more like a hundred dollars; the charge was twenty-five.

Lincoln and Leonard Swett took the defense of Father Chiniquiy, a French Catholic priest in Kankakee County, who was accused by one of his parishioners, Peter Spink, of falsely accusing Spink of perjury. Father Chiniquiy said he could prove his case; he would contest to the last. So a change of venue was taken to Champaign County, where there came to the courthouse in Urbana hundreds of principals, lawyers, witnesses, onlookers, with camp outfits, musicians, parrots, dogs, and changes of clothing. The hotels of Urbana were filled and the overflow slept in tents. The trial dragged on for weeks, and finally the jury went out, and came back unable to agree on a verdict.

Again, at the next term of court, the case was to be called. Hundreds of people had again arrived with camp outfits, musicians, parrots, dogs, and changes of clothing, to hear the testimony and gossip. Lincoln had between-times been at work on a peaceable settlement, and as the gossips and onlookers were getting ready to hear again all the ins and outs of the scandal, he brought into court a paper that wiped the case off the books. It read: "Peter Spink *vs.* Charles Chiniquiy. This day came the parties and the defendant denies that he has ever charged, or believed the plaintiff to be guilty of perjury; that whatever he has said from which such a charge could be inferred, he said on the information of others, protesting his own disbelief in the charge; and that he now disclaims any belief in the truth of said charge against said plaintiff." And they split the court costs and paid their lawyers and everybody went home.

There came a day when Lincoln dropped all his big law cases, dropped all big political affairs then stirring, and threw himself with all he had into the defense of a young man charged with murder, a young man who had grown up since the days at Clary's Grove when he was a baby and Lincoln rocked him in a cradle. As the years passed by, Jack and Hannah Armstrong had moved from Clary's Grove over into Mason County, where they had located on a bluff of the Sangamon River near the mouth of Salt Creek. And Jack Armstrong had died and they had buried him back in Menard County, in Old Concord graveyard where Ann Rutledge had been buried, and where Abe Lincoln had sat alone through long hours. The death of Jack Armstrong had come sooner because a little before he died one of his twin sons, William, nicknamed "Duff" Armstrong, had got into a terrible scrape that many people were talking about; many were saying there had been too much reckless fighting and too many killings, and it might be a good time for a hanging.

At a place called Virgin Grove, not far from the Armstrong home, a camp meeting religious revival had been held; and because it was against the law to sell whisky inside of one mile of a camp meeting, a saloon keeper from Chandlerville had prepared a shack just a little over a mile from the camp-meeting grounds. The bar was made of rough lumber, and poles and brush formed the sides and roof.

And to this place came the wild boy, Duff Armstrong, buying whisky of the bartender, Thomas Steel. For two or three days he was a steady customer, and one evening he was stretched out on a dry-goods box sleeping off the whisky he had taken, when a man named Metzker came in, grabbed Duff Armstrong by the feet and dragged him off the box. Armstrong got up and swore at Metzker, who answered, "Don't be a damn fool; come on and have a drink."

They stood up to the bar and each poured out a glass of whisky. As Armstrong lifted his glass to his lips and started to drink, Metzker threw the whisky from his glass into Armstrong's face and eyes. Armstrong wiped the whisky off his face with his shirt-sleeves, and as soon as his eyes could see and he could make out Metzker, he drove a blow into Metzker's face, knocked him down, and was going to stamp his boots on Metzker when the bartender, Thomas Steel, stepped in and kept Armstrong off.

As feelings cooled down, Armstrong lay down again on the dry-goods box, and went to sleep. Then in came Jim Norris, a friend of Armstrong, took a few drinks, and a fight started between him and Metzker. The bartender stepped between them, gave Metzker a present of a pint of whisky to go home. And they loaded Metzker onto his horse, started him for home, but he fell off the horse and had to be helped on again.

At the house of Ed Ormie, three miles away, where Metzker was staying, they noticed he acted queer the next morning, but he had looked a good deal the same, other times before, when sobering up. This time he was sick five days and then died. A coroner's jury and the doctors decided he had died from a blow over the eye caused by a blunt instrument. A house painter named Charles Allen from Petersburg swore that he saw the fight between Armstrong and Metzker, that it was between ten and eleven o'clock at night, and, by the light of a moon shining nearly straight over them, he saw Armstrong hit Metzker with a sling shot and throw the sling shot away and he, Allen, picked it up. Jim Norris and Duff Armstrong were arrested. And Jack Armstrong, with whom Abe Lincoln had wrestled on the level green next to Offut's store twenty-six years before, told Hannah, "Sell everything you have and clear Duff."

Then Jim Norris who had killed a man, gone to trial and won acquittal a year or two previous, was put on trial, convicted, and sent to the penitentiary for eight years. And the two lawyers defending Duff took a change of venue to Beardstown, and it was there Lincoln told Hannah Armstrong he remembered all her old-time kindness to him and his services were free to her as long as he should live. The two defending lawyers were glad to have the help of Lincoln. And the trial began.

First was the picking of a jury; Lincoln aimed to have young men on the jury; young, hot blood would understand other young, hot blood better, perhaps; the average age of the jurymen, as finally picked, was twenty-three years. Then came the witnesses. With each one Lincoln tried to find some ground of old acquaintance. "Your name?" he asked one. "William Killian." "Bill Killian. . . . Tell me, are you a son of old Jake Killian?" "Yes, sir." "Well, you are a smart boy if you take after your dad."

Of the witnesses, the one that seemed to make out that **Duff Armstrong** was a murderer was Allen, the house painter, who said he saw Armstrong by the light of a moon nearly overhead, on a clear night, hit Metzker with a sling shot. Against him was a witness, Nelson Watkins of Menard County, who testified that he had been to camp meeting the day after the fight, that he had with him a sling shot, and that he had thrown it away because it was too heavy and bothersome to carry. He had made the sling shot himself, he testified; he had put an eggshell into the ground, filled it with lead, poured melted zinc over the lead, but the two metals wouldn't stick; then he had cut a cover from a calfskin bootleg, sewed it together with a squirrel-skin string, using a crooked awl to make the holes; and he had then cut a strip from a groundhog skin that he had tanned, and fixed it so it would fasten to his wrist.

Lincoln took out his knife, cut the string with which the cover was sewed, showed it to be squirrel-skin, and then took out the inside metals and showed they were of two different sorts that did not stick together. He had shown that the sling shot which Allen testified he had picked up was identical with one that Watkins testified he had made and thrown away. Meantime, he had sent out for an almanac, and when the moment came he set the courtroom into a buzz of excitement, laughter, whispering, by showing that, instead of the moon being in the sky at "about where the sun is at ten o'clock in the morning," as the leading witness testified, a popular, well-known family almanac for 1857 showed that on the night of August 29, 1857, the moon had set and gone down out of sight at three minutes before midnight, or exactly 11:57 P.M. The almanac raised the question whether there was enough light by which a murder could be competently and materially witnessed.

In his speech to the jury, Lincoln told them he knew the Armstrongs; he knew whether the Armstrongs were good people or bad people; the wild boy, Duff Armstrong, he had held in his arms when Duff was a baby; he had rocked the baby in the cradle at the pioneer home at Clary's Grove; he was sure in his mind and heart about whether Duff Armstrong ought to be hanged or locked in a prison; he could tell good citizens from bad citizens and if there was anything he was certain of, it was that the Armstrong people were good people; they were plain people; they worked for a living; they made their mistakes; but they were kindly, lovely people and belonged with the salt of the earth. He had told the mother of Duff, "Aunt Hannah, your son will be free before sundown." And so it happened. As the jury had filed out to vote a verdict, one of the jurymen winked an eye at Duff, so he afterwards told it.

Stories started later that Lincoln had played a trick, rubbed out numbers and put in other numbers in the almanac, or he had used an almanac for the wrong year, or he had pasted a bogus page into a good almanac, so as to prove his own case. But when men went and hunted up almanacs for the night of August 29, 1857, they found that all the almanacs had the moon setting at three minutes before midnight, so that a murder at eleven o'clock couldn't have had much light from the sky for a witness to see by.

CHAPTER 100

LINCOLN was careless and easy-going sometimes about collecting money owed to him by clients. Occasionally when money to be paid him was mentioned to him, he didn't seem to be listening. But when he was short of cash he would try to collect by mail, through writing a letter such as one to David A. Smith. He had touched on other matters between him and Smith, and then finished the letter: "One other little matter. I am short of funds and intended to ask Col. Dunlap for my fee in the case in the United States court, but he left sooner than I expected. He is in no default with me, for he once mentioned the subject to me, and I passed it by. But I now need the money and I will take it as a favor if you will show him this note and get him to send it to me. We never agreed on the amount; but I claim $50—which I suppose neither he or you will think unreasonable."

Among the lawyers and among the people along the circuit of courthouses that Lincoln traveled, he was known as odd in his ways; they joined in the feeling of Dennis Hanks, "There's suthin' peculiarsome about him." John W. Bunn, the wholesale grocer, was asked by a Chicago firm to have a local attorney help them in an attachment suit involving several thousand dollars; Lincoln won the suit and charged $25.00; the Chicago firm wrote Bunn, "We asked you to get the best lawyer in Springfield, and it certainly looks as if you had secured one of the cheapest."

He wrote Abraham Bale that a "difficulty" about a wheat sale ought to be settled out of court. "I sincerely hope you will settle it. I think you can if you *will*." The other party, wrote Lincoln, "I have always found a fair man in his dealings." He made his client the offer: "If you settle, I will charge nothing for what I have done, and thank you to boot. By settling, you will more likely get your money sooner, and with much less trouble and expense."

A lease on a valuable hotel property in Quincy was handled by Lincoln for George P. Floyd, who mailed a check for $25.00, to which Lincoln replied: "You must think I am a high-priced man. You are too liberal with your money. Fifteen dollars is enough for the job. I send you a receipt for fifteen dollars and return to you a ten-dollar bill." In coöperation with a Chicago lawyer he saved a farm in Brown County for Isaac Hawley, a Springfield man, and Hawley had $50.00 ready to pay a fee; Lincoln smiled into Hawley's face and drawled, "Well, Isaac, I think I will charge you about ten dollars." To another client he said, "I will charge you $25.00, and if you think that is too much I will make it less."

He wrote free advice to a farmer in Woodford County. "If fraud can be proved, the sale will be set aside. This is all that can be done. Any lawyer will know how to do it."

A woman gave him a check to push a real-estate claim in court; he found the claim no good and told the woman on her next visit to his office that there was no action; she thanked him, took her papers and was going, when Lincoln said, "Wait—here is the check you gave me." A district school-library committee, along with the state superintendent of public instruction, met him on the courthouse steps with a green bag in his hand; he drew up a contract for them with a New York publisher's representative, and on their mentioning a fee he said he couldn't take pay for legal services on a question of public interest.

In notes for a law lecture, he wrote: "The matter of fees is important, far beyond the mere question of bread and butter involved. Properly attended to, fuller justice is done both to lawyer and client. An exorbitant fee should never be claimed. As a general rule never take your whole fee in advance. Then you will feel that you are working for something and you are sure to do your work faithfully and well."

In the case of clients far off, he would take the fee as early as possible, however, for he once wrote James S. Irwin: "Whatever fees we earn at a distance, if not paid before, we have noticed, we never hear of after the work is done. We, therefore, are growing a little sensitive on that point."

When he believed it necessary, and for reasons of his own, wished to hurry up the collection of a claim, he could act as in a letter to Henry Dummer, saying, "While I was at Beardstown, I forgot to tell you that William Butler says if you will give him charge, and full discretion, of a claim in your hands, against George G. Grubb, late of Springfield, now of Chicago, he knows how, and can and will make something out of it for you."

Sitting as a judge in Tazewell County, he heard two farmers testify against each other. Trowbridge had let a corner of his farm lands to Hartsfeller, who had raised a small crop of corn and cribbed it on the same land he raised it on. And Trowbridge had fenced his farm, turned his cattle in, and they had got to Hartsfeller's corn. Their stories told, Lincoln turned a keen eye on each of them, and said to the defendant, Trowbridge, "And you say you went over and fenced the corn after you asked him not to crib it on your land?" "Yes, sir." "Trowbridge, you have won your case."

He had been known to call himself a "jack-leg lawyer," just pegging along, or a "mast-fed" lawyer, referring to hogs fed on "mast" or acorns and other wild foods picked up by hogs let loose to get up their own living in field and timberland. In the Dungey case, when opposing lawyers had the case thrown out of court because Lincoln had not drawn up his papers in a technically correct way, he leaned across the trial table, shook a long bony finger at them, and grinned, "Now, by jing, I'll beat you boys!" Which he did.

In the case of Samuel Short, living near Taylorville, Lincoln cleared him of charges of maliciously and feloniously firing a shotgun at boys stealing watermelons on Short's farm; Short didn't pay his fee and Lincoln collected it through a suit in the court of a justice of the peace. Ending a letter that notified a client his case was won, he wrote, "As the Dutch justice said when he married folks, 'Now vere ish my hundred dollars?'" There was a personal tang or smack in slight things he did. A man asked him for advice on a point of law and he told the man he'd have to look it up; meeting the man again, he gave him the advice wanted on that particular point of law; but when the man wished to know what the fee would be Lincoln answered that there would be no fee because it was a point he ought to have known without looking it up.

On Herndon asking him why he was so prompt in always paying Herndon half of the fees, the answer was: "Well, Billy, there are three reasons: first, unless I did so I might forget I had collected the money; secondly, I explain to you how and from whom I received the money, so that you will not be required to dun the man who paid it; thirdly, if I were to die you would have no evidence that I had your money."

Three or four cases were talked about among other lawyers, in which Lincoln had gone in as counsel for the defense, and as the evidence developed, he said to a colleague: "The man is guilty. You defend him; I can't. If I try to speak the jury will see that I think he is guilty, and convict him." Asked to help a litigant named Harris in a suit, his reply was, "Tell Harris it's no use to waste money on me in that case; he'll get beat." When a rapscallion claimed money was owing him and hired Lincoln to prove it, the opposition lawyer brought in a receipt showing the money had been paid. Lincoln left the courtroom and was sitting in the hotel office with his feet on the stove when word came that he was wanted at court. "Tell the judge," he said, "that I can't come; I have to wash my hands." Joe Gillespie said, "I often listened to Lincoln when I thought he would certainly state his case out of court."

A client complained to Whitney about the way he and Lincoln had managed a case; Whitney tried to get Lincoln to smooth it over with the client, Lincoln's answer being, "Let him howl." Usually he was calm, bland, easy-going with other lawyers; but sometimes he wasn't; Amzi McWilliams, handling a witness on Lincoln's side of a case, called out, "Oh! No! No!! No!!!" which brought Lincoln to undoubling out of a chair with a slow yelling of, "Oh! Yes! Yes!! Yes!!!" putting a stop to the bulldozing of the witness. To a young lawyer he whispered, as the jury was filing out to vote on the case of a slippery client, "Better try and get your money now; if the jury comes in with a verdict for him, you won't get anything."

Another time he undoubled out of a chair when an opposition lawyer had told a jury, "You have been listening for the last hour to an actor, who knows well how to play the rôle of seeming, for effect"; Lincoln was solemn, cool, wrathy, and eying the other lawyer, said, "You have known me for years, and *you know* that not a word of that language can be truthfully applied to me." And part of what the other lawyer said was, "I take it all back, Mr. Lincoln."

A letter from Pekin asked about a land-title case, putting the question, "What is lacking to perfect a title on the part of the defendants?" Lincoln's reply stated: "The trouble with this deed was, that the plaintiff proved it to be a forgery; and I see no way in which the defendants can ever succeed unless they can somehow prove that the deed is not a forgery. This is the whole story. The case cannot be gained by much talking."

A Spoon River client was notified though he had justice and the law on his side he might not win the case. "This position of theirs seems absurd to me; and I found several authorities against it; but they find one *for it,* and, worse than all, the Judge intimates that he is with them."

The widow of a Revolutionary War soldier told Lincoln that a pension agent named Wright had got her a payment from the Federal Government amounting to $400.00—and had kept half of it for himself as a commission. Lincoln told Herndon, "I am going to skin Wright and get that money back." He brought suit and put the tottering widow on the witness stand, where she told her story through her tears.

He told the jury, as Herndon recalled the speech: "She was not always thus. She was once a beautiful young woman. Her step was as elastic, her face as fair, and her voice as sweet as any that rang in the mountains of old Virginia. But now she is poor and defenseless. Out here on the prairies of Illinois, many hundreds of miles from the scenes of her childhood, she appeals to us, who enjoy the privileges achieved for us by the patriots of the Revolution, for our sympathetic aid and manly protection. All I ask is, shall we befriend her?" He pictured the sufferings of the soldiers of the Revolutionary War, and scored the defendant with fierce adjectives.

Some of the jurymen wept. The verdict gave the widow the full amount of money Wright had taken from her. Lincoln paid her hotel bill, bought her a railroad ticket back home, and later sent her the full amount of pension money—with no charge for lawyer's fees. Herndon had picked up Lincoln's notes for his speech to the jury. They read: "No contract.— No professional services.—Unreasonable charge.—Money retained by Def't not given by Pl'ff.—Revolutionary War.—Describe Valley Forge Privations.—Ice.—Soldiers' bleeding feet.—Pl'ff's husband.—Soldier leaving home for army.—Skin Def't.—Close."

E. J. Rice, a judge, made several rulings against Lincoln one morning in a murder trial, and he told Herndon at dinner, "I have determined to crowd the court to the wall." And as the trial went on that afternoon he gradually got the judge puzzled and lost. He read authorities to show that the great jurists and the lessons of the past were against the judge. He hurled facts and questions fast from point to point, insulting the judge and making the court look ridiculous, while keeping clear of remarks that would lay him open to fine or reprimand for contempt of court. He was contemptuous of the court in manner, voice, insinuation, and allegation, without being technically guilty of contempt of court. It was a superb performance, as Bill Herndon saw it. "Figuratively speaking, he peeled the court from head to foot," said Herndon. "The judge reversed his decision in Lincoln's favor. His client was acquitted of murder, and he swept the field. I shall never forget the scene."

Fifteen women came into court in Clinton; they had knocked in the heads of the whisky-barrels of a saloon in a near-by town, and were indicted for trespass. One woman called on Lincoln to help their lawyer, and he argued, "In this case I would change the order of indictment and have it read The State *vs.* Mr. Whisky instead of The State *vs.* The Ladies." He mentioned the Boston Tea Party, said the saloon keeper had neither feared God nor regarded man, gave some of his own observations on the ruinous effects of whisky on men and families. And the court dismissed the women, saying if they were to be fined he would let them know.

An odd case was put into his hands by Abraham Brokaw of Bloomington, who had sued a neighbor and had a debt collected by the sheriff, who went bankrupt; and Brokaw couldn't get his money. And so Brokaw put his case into the hands of Stephen A. Douglas, who sued the sheriff's bondsmen and collected the debt; but Brokaw couldn't get his money from Douglas.

Then he hired Lincoln to collect from Douglas. And Lincoln sent the claim to "Long John" Wentworth, the Chicago congressman and editor, who pushed the claim in Washington; and Douglas sniffed and almost snorted; but he paid Brokaw, who remarked to friends: "What do you suppose Lincoln charged me? Exactly three dollars and fifty cents for collecting nearly six hundred dollars." And Lincoln, asked about this low fee, replied: "I had no trouble with it. I sent it to my friend in Washington, and was only out the postage."

Though he made fifty speeches and traveled far, paying his own expenses in one campaign, he was surprised when a committee of Republicans in Champaign County called on him at his hotel and handed him $35.00. As he held the money, he asked, "What will I do with it?" looking puzzled and sheepish. "Put it in your pocket and keep it there," he was told. Which he did—but with a laughing demurrer, "Don't you fellows do that again."

A rich newcomer to Springfield wanted Lincoln to bring suit against an unlucky, crack-brained lawyer who owed him two dollars and a half; Lincoln advised him to hold off; he said he would go to some other lawyer who was more willing. So Lincoln took the case, collected a ten-dollar fee in advance, entered suit, hunted up the defendant and handed him half of the ten dollars and told him to show up in court and pay the debt. Which was done. And all litigants and the lawyer were satisfied.

A horse thief in the Champaign County jail told his local lawyer, William D. Somers, that he wanted Lincoln to help in the defense. When Lincoln and Somers arrived at the jail they found their client talking with his wife, who was in a delicate condition of health, as Lincoln noticed. When the client handed Lincoln ten dollars and said that was all the money he had, Lincoln looked at the woman again, and asked: "How about your wife? Won't she need this?" The answer was, "She'll get along somehow," which didn't satisfy Lincoln. He handed the woman five dollars, and divided the other five with Somers.

As Lincoln and Whitney stood near the courthouse in Decatur and he pointed to the exact place where he had driven into the town twenty-six years before with an all-wood ox-wagon and four yoke of steers, Whitney asked him if he expected then to be a lawyer. "No, I didn't know I had sense enough to be a lawyer."

Reading authorities in court once he suddenly read one against himself, and, drawing up his shoulders and half laughing, finished reading it, first saying: "There, may it please the court, I reckon I've scratched up a snake; but as I'm in for it, guess I'll read it through." On Whitney's asking him about a mixed point in law, he threw his head back, looked at the ceiling, and chuckled, "Damfino." Helping Whitney in a railroad case, when Whitney was worried about points the opposition was making, Lincoln told him, "All that is very easily answered." And when his time came, Whitney said, "He blew away what seemed to me almost an unanswerable argument as easily as a beer drinker blows off the froth from his foaming tankard."

Yet he had to take his losses at law practice; once he traveled all around the circuit, all his cases were for defendants, and he was beaten every time; so he told Bunn, the banker, in Springfield. And he told himself that people had said, without disturbing his self-respect, "Well, he isn't lawyer enough to hurt him."

In the parlor or barroom of a hotel, there was no telling of an evening whether he would spin yarns or conduct philosophic inquiries. "I have heard Lincoln," said Joe Gillespie, "descant upon the problem whether a ball discharged from a gun in a horizontal position would be longer in reaching the ground than one dropped at the instant of discharge from the muzzle."

As he spoke to juries, men felt that he believed what he had once said to the Washingtonian Temperance Society in Springfield: "There are few things wholly evil or wholly good; almost everything is an inseparable compound of the two." Once in Springfield he was one of five lawyers defending a woman and a man accused of murdering the woman's husband by poison. A handsome young man sat next to the woman, showed an interest in her, frisked around the courtroom, got law books and pointed out pages to Lincoln and other lawyers for the defense. And Usher F. Linder, an assistant prosecutor, began his speech to the jury after Lincoln and three other lawyers had spoken for the defense. Pointing his finger at the handsome young man who had sat next to the accused woman, Linder said, "Gentlemen of the jury, if you wanted any additional evidence of this man's guilt, it would only be necessary for you to recur to his boldness and impudence on this trial." He directed his index finger straight at the face of the young man and cried, "You can see guilt written all over his countenance." And the handsome young man arose and said with warm feeling: "General Linder, you are mistaken; I am not the criminal. My name is Rosette; I am a lawyer, and one of the counsel for the defendants."

Lincoln came to know in whispered consultation and public cross-examination the minds and hearts of a quarreling, chaffering, suspicious, murderous, loving, lavish, paradoxical humanity.

Lincoln defended a man who had thirty-five indictments against him for obstruction of the public highway. He took to the supreme court of the state a case involving a dispute over the payment of three dollars in a hog sale. He became versed in the questions whether a saloon license can be transferred, whether damages can be collected from a farmer who starts a prairie fire that spreads to other farms, whether the divorced wife of a man can compel him to give her custody of her children, and to supply her the means for support of the children; these were causes in which Lincoln argued before the state supreme court. He also argued before that tribunal in cases involving wills, mortgages, notes, land titles, railroad condemnation proceedings, breaches of contract, validity of patents, ejectments, personal injury. A merchant set fire to his stock of goods, collected the insurance, bought a new stock, and was sued by the insurance company for the possession of the new stock. A man and his wife were put off a railroad train because they refused to pay excess cash fare, claiming that the station agent had no tickets to their point of destination; they sued the railroad company. A man named Banet sued the Alton & Sangamon Railroad Company because after he had subscribed for stock in their road they changed its route and ran the line of it twelve miles distant from his real-estate holdings in New Berlin.

Such were a few of the human causes, disputes, and actions in which Lincoln versed himself thoroughly, carrying his arguments up to the highest court in the state, and winning more than half of his cases there.

His memory was indexed and cross-indexed with tangled human causes.

CHAPTER 101

As the years passed there were stories of different kinds that got started about the lawyer and politician, Abe Lincoln, helping pigs that were in trouble. He would be riding along on horseback or in a buggy and see a pig caught under a fence or a gate or mired in mud, and he couldn't ride past without stopping and helping the pig; one story had it that he saw a sow eating one of her own pigs and he got out of his buggy and took a club and beat the sow till she let go of her young one. Or a chickadee had fallen out of its nest in a hollow tree and he had to lift it back into its nest before he could ride on. Or a girl's doll had been knocked down and tramped on, and Lincoln picked it up, whisked the dust off and handed it to the girl, saying with a shine on his face: "There! Now your doll's all right."

These stories seemed to connect with an eager interest in all things moving and alive around him, the growing crops, boys fighting, shirts on a clothesline in the wind, watermelon time, hot cornbread, talk about apple parings, quiltings, shucking-bees, the camp meetings where the ransomed sang to the lost and there was the warning, "You're hangin' to the hinges of time by a hair."

Sometimes the circuit lawyers drove across the prairie on trails through sloughs where the mud was up to the hubs, or across creeks swollen by rains, through sleet and snow, with mittens soaked wet and the leather reins slippery. In zero weather they often broke the ice in the pitchers of the hotel room to wash their faces in the morning. There were winter nights when they piled the cordwood on the fire and talked. There were days when for miles along the road the farmers, with the reins slung over their backs and shoulders, had their hands on the plow-handles, calling to the horses, and sending the steel plowshares into the ground, turning over the soil into long shining black furrows. There were Indian summer days when a smoke haze filled the horizons; the earth seemed to rest and take soft breaths.

On such a day Lincoln and Leonard Sweet were on a fifty-mile drive from De Witt County to Champaign. Tall brown grass swayed in the wind; across far lengths of grass there was a quiver of waves as though wind were running across water; here and there a bluejay flitted in a redhaw tree and sent a screech to his mate; under the haw tree was a sprinkle of red dots, the recurring autumn spatter of red haws; a brown deer scampered out of a stand of hazel brush; and the sleepy Indian summer haze filled the horizons.

And on Swett's asking him to tell where he came from as a boy and how he grew up, Lincoln told of the events that came to his mind, the dirt-floor cabin in Kentucky, the selling out and the going to Indiana. "It was pretty pinching times at first in Indiana, getting the cabin built, and the timber cleared for crops." The mother, Nancy Hanks, and the step-mother, Sally Bush, were both good to him. Then at Anderson Creek he had earned a half-dollar, taking a passenger off a boat from midstream to the bank of the Ohio; and afterward, as he played on a flatboat, the half-dollar slipped away into the river. "I can see the quivering and shin-ing of that half-dollar yet, as it went down the stream and sunk from my sight forever." And then . . . New Orleans, Illinois, New Orleans again, New Salem, the Black Hawk War, election as captain, and with a smile, "I can't tell you how much the idea of being the captain of that company pleased me." Then storekeeping, the legislature, four dollars a day, law practice, Springfield, Washington.

And Swett, the shrewd lawyer, said the story as Lincoln told it was full of chuckles, with sometimes high laughter that interrupted the whistle of the quail in the dun cat-tails. He wasn't sorry for himself, this Lincoln of Kentucky, Indiana, Illinois; he had had a swift, rich life full of action; hunger and struggle had been good for him; he had no regrets worth men-tioning to Swett; he wouldn't mind living it all over again; so it seemed to Swett, who was sharp at reading men's minds.

On a thirty-six-mile drive from Urbana to Danville there were songs and stories all the way, as Whitney told it. "We had no hesitation in stop-ping at a farmhouse and ordering them to kill and cook a chicken for dinner. By dark we reached Danville. Lamon would have whisky in his office for the drinking ones, and those who indulged in petty gambling would get by themselves and play till late in the night. Lincoln, Davis, and a few local wits would spend the evening in Davis's room, talking politics, wisdom, and fun. We who stopped at the hotel would all breakfast to-gether and frequently go out in the woods and hold court. The feelings were those of a great fraternity in the bar, and if we desired to restrict our circle it was no trouble for Davis to freeze out any disagreeable per-sons. Lincoln was fond of going all by himself to any little show or con-cert. I have known him to slip away and spend the entire evening at a little magic-lantern show intended for children. He had the appearance of a rough, intelligent farmer, and his rude, homemade buggy and rawboned horse enforced this belief."

On the same thirty-six-mile drive one October night, there were Lin-coln, Swett and his wife, and Whitney in a two-seated carriage; dark had come on as they rode into a river-bottom road in heavy timber with deep ditches alongside; and the horses and hubs plugged through mud. The driver stopped the horses; some one would have to go ahead and pilot; he didn't want to tip over as one of Frink & Walker's stages had done. Whitney jumped out, Lincoln after him; they rolled up their trousers, and arm in arm went ahead, calling back every minute or so. Lincoln sang,

"Mortal man with face of clay, Here tomorrow, gone today," and other verses that he made up. They drove into Danville later laughing at October night weather and autumn mud.

As the lawyers on the circuit slept six and eight in a room, one of them, Lawrence Weldon, noticed that Lincoln was out of his bed earlier than the others, and usually would poke among the charcoals of the fire, stir up a warmth of flame, and then sit with long thoughts, sometimes talking to himself. Once, on such a morning, in the town of Lincoln, Weldon heard him say over the quaint keepsake of his memory, the poem, "Oh, Why Should the Spirit of Mortal Be Proud?" The verses wouldn't have sounded the same, wouldn't have been so solemn and musical if somebody else said them, Weldon believed—they seemed to fit Lincoln. It was the same Weldon who came to Lincoln in a courtroom with a document he wanted explained, and Lincoln was trying to connect his suspenders to his trousers at a point where a button had come off; he told Weldon, "Wait till I fix this plug of my gallus and I'll pitch into that like a dog at a root." The range of the serious and comic ran wide and far in him.

Speaking from a platform in front of the Menard County courthouse, he was interrupted three times by a call of "Howdy, Abe!" and then located his old friend, James Pantier, hunter, trapper, faith healer, sawmill owner, and farmer. He stooped over and shook hands, saying, "Why, how are you, Uncle Jimmy?" and, still holding hands, he led Pantier up on the platform and put him in his own chair where Pantier in his blue jeans shirt with buckskin lacings sat between two lawyers in "biled" shirts.

The old hunter sat twisting his hat; wind and weather had worn the brim off it; he saw Lincoln's stovepipe hat under the chair, half full of letters, papers, notes; there he shoved his hat; it was out of his restless fingers. Yet he had forgotten something; he couldn't keep quiet; he leaned forward, hands on his knees and elbows out, and called: "Abe! Abe! I forgot to ax you about how Mary and the babies were." And Lincoln turned from his speech and said in a low voice: "All well when I left them at Springfield yesterday morning, Uncle Jimmy; all very well, thank you."

Members of the American or Know-Nothing party called on him and he asked them: "Who are the native Americans? Do they not wear the breechclout and carry the tomahawk? We pushed them from their homes, and now turn on others not fortunate enough to come over so early as we or our forefathers." And he drifted into a little anecdote of an Irishman named Pat who had asked, "Mr. Lincoln, what do yez think of these Know-Nothings?" After telling Pat his views, he asked Pat why he had not been born in America. To which Pat answered, "Faith, I wanted to, but me mother wouldn't let me."

He kept odd happenings in his mind and would tell about them. "As I was going up the path to the house of Dave Lowry in Pekin, some boys were playing marbles near the walk. I stopped and put my hand on the head of Mr. Lowry's boy and said, 'My boy, you're playing marbles!' The boy looked up and replied, 'Any damn fool ought to see that.'"

Often when he was supposed to look and act important, he simply couldn't fill the part or he wouldn't try. He was so easy, so quietly gay and careless, that respectable people found him hard to analyze. The state supreme court, for instance, had appointed Lincoln a member of a committee to examine young law students. When Jonathan Birch came to the hotel in Bloomington to be examined by Lincoln for admission to the bar, Lincoln asked three or four questions about contracts and other law branches. And then, as Birch told it: "He asked nothing more. Sitting on the edge of the bed he began to entertain me with recollections, many of them vivid and racy, of his start in the profession." Birch couldn't figure out whether it was a real examination or a joke. But Lincoln gave him a note to Judge Logan, another member of the examining committee, and he took the note to Logan, and without any more questions was given a certificate to practice law. The note from Lincoln read:

My Dear Judge:
The bearer of this is a young man who thinks he can be a lawyer. Examine him if you want to. I have done so and am satisfied. He's a good deal smarter than he looks to be. Yours,
Lincoln.

Driving cross-country, he stopped at the house of Jack and Hannah Armstrong for a midday lunch. Hannah put a quart bowl of buttermilk before him, and the bowl slipped from his hands and spilled over the table and his clothes; Hannah was telling him not to mind it in the least, it would be all right in a minute, such things do happen. And he took the towel she handed him, slowly wiped the milk off his clothes, put the towel over his knees, and leaning back said, "Well, Aunt Hannah, if you don't mind it, neither will I."

Having told a Peoria audience that he was willing Judge Douglas should have an hour to reply to his speech, he noted, "By giving him the close, I felt confident that you would stay for the fun of hearing him skin me." At the Springfield state fair Judge Douglas rose while Lincoln was speaking, and, denying an allegation by Lincoln said: "No, sir! I will tell you what was the origin of the Nebraska Bill. It was this, sir! God created man, and placed before him both good and evil, and left him free to choose for himself. That was the origin of the Nebraska Bill." And Lincoln, with a lurking smile in the corners of his mouth, replied, "Well, then, I think it is a great honor to Judge Douglas that he was the first man to discover that fact." And laughter came from the audience.

A lawyer in a hog case used much showy language mixed with the word "pigs"; he had to say "pigs" because that was the specific property involved; Lincoln remarked, "He must ape Demosthenes, even if the subject is only pigs." Of T. Lyle Dickey, he commented, "He can draw such fine distinctions, where I can't see any distinction, yet I have no doubt a distinction does exist."

Whitney at Danville once complained to Lincoln that he was getting hardly any law business. Lincoln said: "You have as much business here as I used to have; I listened to a French street peddler's antics here half a day once, simply because I hadn't a particle of business."

Tricks of mind and tongue as between Lincoln and others were noted by Whitney: "No one could ever use the term 'facsimile' in Lincoln's presence without his adding 'sick family'; if any one used the expression 'idem sonans,' in common use as a law term, he would always say 'id sons,' and Davis, if there, would add, 'Seth Post,'" all of which meant that Captain Post of Decatur used the term improperly in that way. A leader of the proslavery party in Kansas was H. Clay Pate, a vain popinjay who used to get his name in the papers; and whenever Lincoln heard his name mentioned, he would echo, "H. Mud Pate." At Pekin, Lincoln was attorney for the winning side in a case that had been appealed, continued, and again appealed so many times that the record looked like a long one as the judge started to read it. He stopped reading and asked, "What does this mean, Mr. Lincoln?" "Harassment, your Honor," was the short reply.

In a dispute between William Butcher and John M. Gipps as to which of the two was the owner of a piano and a colt named Sampson, Lincoln represented Butcher. One paragraph of Lincoln's brief read, "To the fifth interrogatory, he says he did not tell Mr. Gipps and his wife or either of them that he was too smart to leave that evidence on the said Book, and that he did not put his thumb to the side of his nose, and significantly extend the fingers of the same hand, indicating his shrewdness on that subject."

Lincoln carried to the supreme court, at the October term of 1853, a case involving "a scrub male hog." The defendant, his client, lost $3.00 The report of the case read in part: "The defendant proved that he went to plaintiff's house, and the plaintiff not being at home, he told his wife that he had come for his hog. She answered that he had better not take the hog until her husband came home. He returned next day and demanded the hog. when plaintiff answered he did not believe the hog was his. . . . Plaintiff had been heard hallooing to the dogs of the witness to worry the hog, and afterwards the hog was found dead."

The decision of the supreme court was emphatically against Lincoln and his client. "We are forced to the conclusion that plaintiff had been trespassed upon by the hog for two or three years, and had repeatedly tried, without success, either to drive the hog away, or to keep him either in, or outside his cornfields. The hog had been unmarked and ownerless for years, and plaintiff had at last determined to fatten him for a tenant's use, supposing him to have been left by a former tenant. The proofs are so convincing to us, that there is no room for argument, or application of principles of law."

He enjoyed, in certain moods, language stripped naked. A rich lawyer and taxpayer of Bloomington, named Gridley, in a misdemeanor case, discussed the ways and conduct of his home-city government, where there were high taxes. "He used language which would have reflected a brilliant carnation lustre on the pages of the Decameron or Rabelais," Whitney noted. "Lincoln was entranced by reason of the wit and extreme radicalism of the language used. He would turn to me and whisper, every few moments, 'Don't he *dew* that well?' That sort of thing suited Lincoln, but I never heard coarser language in a court in session."

He picked his companions by what they could do for him at the time he wanted something done, Whitney also noted. "As a constant habit he chose as his opponent at billiards a bibulous lawyer of no merit save the negative one of playing billiards as awkwardly and badly as Lincoln himself; it was a strange but not unfamiliar sight to see these two men, who had nothing else in common, playing billiards in an obscure place, sometimes for hours together." And Whitney also wished to note that billiards was the only "non-utilitarian thing" that he ever knew Lincoln to indulge in. However, he had written rhymed verse and learned that he was more skilled in other forms of writing. The young man, Gibson W. Harris, whom Mrs. Lincoln called, "Mr. Mister," arranging books and papers in the office one day, found two or three quires of letter paper stitched together in book form, filled with verses in the Lincoln handwriting. When the manuscript was shown to Lincoln, he took it, asked, "Where did you find it?" and, rolling it up, put it in his coat pocket, and it was never heard of again from Lincoln. There was doggerel such as "The Bear Hunt" which he didn't care to have people read.

There was about Whitney a little of the same streak of lavender, soft spots of sentiment, that Lincoln had met in Josh Speed. He talked freely of many wise, shrewd, gay, nonsensical things to Whitney between times on the circuit. To him Lincoln once wrote, "How miserably things seem to be arranged in this world! If we have no friends we have no pleasure, and if we have them we are sure to lose them and be doubly pained by the loss." As Whitney was leaving Bloomington one day he stepped carefully into a courtroom, hoping to say a quiet good-by to Lincoln, who that day was presiding over the court in place of Judge Davis. Lincoln saw his friend and the look on his friend's face, and he dropped court proceedings and said so that all heard, as he reached over and shook hands, "Great good luck to you! Great good luck to you, Whitney!"

He had taken to the supreme court a case for an orphan, Rebecca Daimwood, who had been cheated out of a piece of land by her guardian, John Lane. While the supreme court was considering the case she had married a young farmer, William Dorman. And they were poor in worldly goods. Lincoln won their case, and the newly married couple came to him asking what he was going to charge them. They had heard about lawyers; he might want as much as the little piece of land was worth. And he told them all he would ask would be their thanks; they might take his services as a wedding present. This was the Dorman and Lane case about which Lincoln wrote to Samuel Marshall, the lawyer handling it at Shawneetown, when Lincoln ended his letter, "Nothing new here except my marriage, which to me is a matter of profound wonder." He had some extra and special feeling about Rebecca Daimwood and William Dorman getting married; they could have his fee for a wedding present.

When he rode the circuit and likewise when he was at home in Springfield there were little things that interested him, but they were different from the little things that interested a good many other people. He could enjoy watching a duck trying to teach its little one to swim; he played marbles with boys when a grown man, enjoyed holding kittens in his hands. He talked over with Herndon his own theory as to why, when he was kicked by a horse in Indiana and woke to his senses, he finished the sentence he had started to say just as the horse kicked him. The general run of small gossip and community chatter didn't interest him. Herndon noticed: "He didn't care who succeeded to the presidency of this or that association; who made the most money; who was going to Philadelphia, when and for what, and what were the costs of such a trip; who got to be street inspector or alley commissioner." And Whitney noticed: "It would have been considered absurd to propose him for chairman of a meeting or convention. Immersed in politics as he was, he never presided over a caucus or political meeting."

Others said, and he said it himself: he had no money sense. Davis, Logan, Bunn, Fell, and other friends whom he saw often were getting hold of farms and thousand-acre tracts of land. Investments, speculations, and schemes for developing property beckoned and whispered to others, but not to him. His field was law, for the earning of a living, and politics, for other reasons. At hotels he took what was offered him with no complaint. He told Joe Gillespie he never felt easy when a waiter or a flunky was around; he could look a murderer in the eye on the witness stand, and be comfortable, but a hotel clerk made him feel sort of useless. When he did drop in at a meeting of Republican editors in Decatur once, he said he was a sort of interloper, and told of a woman on horseback meeting a man riding a horse on a narrow trail or pass. The woman stopped her horse, looked the man over, and broke out, "Well, for the land's sake, you are the homeliest man I ever saw!" The man replied, "Yes, ma'am, but I can't help that," and the woman again, "No, I suppose not, but you might stay at home."

When Judge Davis appointed him to hold court one day, he heard the evidence brought by a clothing merchant trying to collect $28.00 for a suit of clothes sold to the minor son of a rich farmer; the real question was whether the son needed the clothes, having bought them without his father's permission; Lincoln ruled that the suit of clothes was not necessary, saying, "I have never in my life worn a suit costing $28.00."

To a New York firm that wrote asking him about the financial standing of a Springfield man, he replied:

> Yours of the 10th received. First of all, he has a wife and a baby; together they ought to be worth $500,000 to any man. Secondly, he has an office in which there is a table worth $1.50 and three chairs worth, say, $1. Last of all, there is in one corner a large rat-hole, which will bear looking into.
>
> Respectfully,
> A. Lincoln.

One of his boys pronounced the word "gentleman" with the "g" hard, as in "gas"; and Lincoln told friends about it as if it pleased him to have the dignity of the word "gentleman" mussed up. Several times before posing for an ambrotype he ran his fingers through his hair to rumple it properly; often on the stump or during jury speeches his hands wandered over the top of his head and put the hair into disorder. Always, it was noticed, the linen he wore was clean; his barbers didn't let the sign of a beard start; he blacked his own boots. As to shirts and shaves he was clean and neat; as to haircuts, grammar, and technicalities, he wasn't so particular; in many jury arguments and in his "Missouri Compromise Speech" in Springfield, he wiped the sweat off his face with a red silk handkerchief. In the 1856 campaign, going from town to town, he would formally meet a wagonload of pretty girls in white dresses, one for each state in the Union. And he had to end his little speech to them by saying, "I also thank you for your present of this beautiful basket of flowers." He didn't enjoy this part of campaigning, he told Whitney; it pleased the young people, so he went through with it.

He took the case of a woman who was injured on a defective city sidewalk in Alton. As the mayor of Alton, Joseph Brown, later told the affair: "A lady by the name of Mrs. McReady came to Alton on one of the Keokuk packets to give Shakespearean lectures, arriving at 2 o'clock in the morning, and, as luck would have it, she stepped on an old cellar door in front of Johnny Roe's grocery and one leg went part way through the door so that it sprained her ankle and laid her up at the Franklin House for some time. She put in a claim against the city for damages, but the city refused to allow anything, and the result was, as she was permanently lamed, she sued for $5,000.00 in the United States court at Springfield, and engaged Mr. Lincoln as her attorney."

The mayor of Alton went to Lincoln at Springfield and they negotiated. Lincoln: "Mr. Brown, I don't like to take this suit against your town; can't we compromise it in some way?" Brown: "I don't see how we can, as we don't think the city is liable for an injury done to the lady by a man having bad cellar doors." Lincoln: "But the city is liable for its sidewalks, and I feel sure we can get judgment; I think it is best to compromise if we can. How much will you give the lady? She is lamed for life with a stiff ankle." Brown: "I can't make any offer; we have no money." Lincoln: "Will you give her $3,000.00?" Brown: "No, there isn't that much money in the town." They compromised at $1,500.00, Brown asking, "If we give the $1,500.00, are we to have the damaged limb?" Lincoln replying, "I will go over and ask," coming back later to tell Brown, "If you are an unmarried man, and as you are pretty good-looking, you can have the entire woman!" Brown declared later, "We compromised, but I did not accept the lady's marriage offer."

He carried a worn copy of Shakespeare, and sometimes read out loud to a roomful of lawyers in a hotel "The Earthquake Story" from "The Flush Times in Alabama." He read Joe Miller's joke book and repeated some of the jokes on the circuit, though he had a thousand fresher ones of his own; they seemed to sprout by the waysides of his travel. Some of his stories were only for picked and particular listeners, as in the case of one with a line, "If the court understand *herself* and she think she do." When Ward Lamon had a large section of the rear of his trousers torn out in scuffling in front of the courthouse, and was later acting as counsel in a case that same day, a paper was passed around among the lawyers asking contributions for the repair of the trousers; Lincoln wrote, "I can contribute nothing to the end in view."

Of old man Krone at the Macon House in Decatur, he had a tale of a man riding up one night and asking, "Landlord, can I stay here tonight?" And the old man gazed off into the sky, rubbed his chin thoughtfully, and gave no answer. On the rider again asking his question and getting no answer, he rode on into the next county, came back the next day, and again pulled in on his horse and was going to ask the landlord if he could stay that night, when the landlord spoke and said, "I reckon so"—in reply to the question of the day before. And there was the anecdote of John Moore, south of Blooming Grove, driving a yoke of red steers to Bloomington one Saturday, starting home with a jug, and emptying the jug into himself; when he drove through a piece of timber one of the wheels of the cart hit a stump and threw the pole out of the ring of the yoke. The steers ran away; Moore slept till morning in the cart, and when he awoke and looked around, he said: "If my name is John Moore, I've lost a pair of steers; if my name ain't John Moore, I've found a cart."

As Richard Oglesby, who had visited England, was once telling how he saw the British queen at a reception, how the queen looked, what she wore, how she spoke and carried herself, Lincoln put in a question, asking Oglesby with a grave face, "Are we to infer that you have a speaking acquaintance with Queen Victoria?"

A touch of Æsop, the fable maker, was in him. "If three pigeons sit on a fence and you shoot and kill one of them, how many will be left?" he asked. The answer was, "Two, of course." To which Lincoln responded, "No, there won't, for the other two will fly away." And to illustrate a point, he told this one: "A man on foot, with his clothes in a bundle, coming to a stream which he must ford, made elaborate preparations by stripping off his garments, adding them to his bundle, and, tying all to the top of a stick, which enabled him to raise the bundle high over his head to keep them dry during the crossing. He then fearlessly waded in and carefully made his way across the rippling stream, and found it in no place up to his ankles." In a law case having to do with hogs breaking through a fence and damaging crops, he told a story about a fence that was so crooked that whenever a hog went through a hole in that crooked fence, it always came out on the same side from which it started.

And it was told that once when Lincoln heard a farmer bragging too big about the size of a hay crop that year, he said that he had helped to raise hay one year, and when it came harvest time, "We stacked all we could outdoors, and then we put the rest of it in the barn." On a paper written by a lawyer, with too many words and pages, he remarked, "It's like the lazy preacher that used to write long sermons, and the explanation was, he got to writin' and was too lazy to stop."

He sat with his client, Charles Hoyt, on buffalo robes in the Blackhawk store on River Street in Aurora, and talked for hours about their case. Later he had it in such shape that he cautioned Hoyt, "Make no movement about costs till after next term, lest this should stir them up to reinstate the cases." Then finally he wrote: "Our case is decided against us. Very sorry but there is no help. I do not think I could ever have argued the case better than I did. I did nothing else but prepare to argue and argue the case from Friday morning to Monday evening. Very sorry for the result, but I do not think it could have been prevented."

A little dried-up old man wearing a red blouse used to come regularly the first day of court in Urbana, and Lincoln and he would sit out in the courtyard; the old man thought he had a claim on some real estate; Lincoln listened; the old man had hopes; at the next term of court he would come again in his red blouse with his face lit up; he had a title to property; they would go to law and make his title clear; Lincoln listened; they met again and over again, the old man talking about his claims, his hopes —till there was a term of court when he couldn't come, when he was through with claims and hopes on earth. Lincoln somehow felt a kinship to this little old man in a red blouse.

His own failures as storekeeper and inventor probably were vivid to him when a client Hildreth sued Alexander Edmunds of Mount Pulaski. Hildreth gave Edmunds $2,000 worth of land for the county rights to sell a "Horological Cradle." Lincoln's bill declared "the said Edmunds professed to have invented an horological cradle which was to be rocked by machinery, with a weight running on one or more pulleys; the cradle constituting the pendulum, and which, being wound up, would rock itself until it run down, and so save the continual labor to mothers and nurses, of rocking the cradle." The higher court held that Edmunds did not patent a principle for a self-rocking cradle; he had merely patented a design for a cradle, the specifications being for an "ornamental design, in the shape or configuration of horological cradles, and of ornamental designs to be worked thereon."

The decree of Judge David Davis in the lower court that Edmunds should convey the $2,000 piece of land back to Hildreth was reversed by the upper court, and Lincoln had to comfort his client. While working on the case Lincoln set up a specimen "horological cradle" in his office, and explained its workings to visitors. When Bunn, the banker, asked how to stop the contraption when in motion, Lincoln laughed, "There's the rub, and I reckon I'll have to answer you as I did the judge who asked the same question: the thing's like some of the glib and interesting talkers you and I know; when it gets going it doesn't know when to stop."

At the old Macon House in Decatur, he helped unload and screw into place the first piano to arrive in central Illinois. It had come by steamer down the Ohio River, up the Wabash to Crawfordsville, Indiana, and by wagon to Decatur. At dinner that day in the Macon House, Mother Krone told the diners, "Men, if you can't get your teeth through this beef you will have to fall back on the sausage." Jane Martin led in a program of musical numbers that evening for the judge and members of the bar of the Eighth Circuit. And she later told of that program: "For show pieces, I played the 'Battle of Prague' and the 'Carnival of Venice,' then followed with 'Washington's March,' 'Come Haste to the Wedding,' and 'Woodup Quick Step,' to convince the audience I did know a tune or two. For tragedy, I sang Henry Russell's 'Maniac' and 'The Ship on Fire,' and then made their blood run cold with the wild wail of 'The Irish Mother's Lament.' For comic, we sang 'The Widdy McGee' and 'I Won't be a Nun,' topping off with 'Old Dan Tucker,' 'Lucy Long,' and 'Jim Crow,' the crowd joining in the chorus. These were followed by more serious music. Mr. Brown and Mr. Swett joined me in the duet 'Moonlight, Music, Love, and Flowers,' 'Rocked in the Cradle of the Deep,' 'Pilgrim Fathers,' 'Bonaparte's Grave,' and 'Kathleen Mavourneen.' Each and all met with applause. As a finale, I sang 'He Doeth All Things Well,' after which Mr. Lincoln, in a very grave manner, thanked me for the evening's entertainment, and said, 'Don't let us spoil that song by any other music tonight.' "

High pretensions didn't wear easy with Lincoln; he wrote to Owen Lovejoy, "As to my personal movements this summer and fall, I am quite busy trying to pick up my lost crumbs of last year." To a long letter from

Whitney as to whether he would undertake a certain case, he returned papers with the message, "Count me in."

A pithy or quizzical wisdom ran through many of his letters, often in the closing sentence. "Let all be so quiet that the adversary shall not be notified," he wrote before an election. A lengthy epistle ended, "As to an extra session of the legislature, I should know no better how to bring that about than to lift myself over a fence by the straps of my boots." To one law student, "Always bear in mind that your own resolution to succeed is more important than any other one thing"; to another, "Work, work, work, is the main thing." And again before an election, "If we can head off the fraudulent votes we shall carry the day." After showing that certain political results would surely come in a three-cornered contest, he added, "This is as plain as adding up the weight of three small hogs."

Wishing good cheer to Galesburg Republicans, he wrote, "Stand by the *cause*, and the cause will carry you through." The keynote of some letters was, "I am not complaining—I only wish a fair understanding." And of course he gave himself often the same warning he sent a friend, "I must repeat that I think the thing did not originate in malice to you, or to any one, and that the best way all round is to now forget it."

In his copy of Bacon he could read that to win power is to get a foothold where the standing is slippery. "All rising to great place is by a winding stair."

CHAPTER 102

Up in the northwest corner of Illinois is a rocky country where there are lead mines, and the city of Galena sits among high, hard bluffs. In the year 1856 a man named Grant had a wholesale leather store there, the largest in the Northwest; in Kentucky he had a tannery; and living near St. Louis he had a son named Ulysses Simpson Grant, who was farming, teaming, raising hay, grubbing stumps and hauling wood to sell in St. Louis, a quiet man who was a Democrat in politics and was going to vote for Buchanan for President; he believed in Stephen A. Douglas more than any one else at Washington, and he had a feeling that Douglas was mainly right in charging Republicans with being disunionists.

This was the charge that Abraham Lincoln answered in a speech at Galena that year. He asked the opposition to show where the Republicans in their platforms, speeches, conventions, had spoken in favor of dissolving the Union. He pointed to the physical force apparatus that would stop disunion. "With the purse and sword, the army and navy and treasury in our hands and at our command, you could not do it. This government would be very weak indeed if a majority with a disciplined army and navy and a well-filled treasury could not preserve itself when attacked by an unarmed, undisciplined, unorganized minority." His farther thoughts had ranged seriously around the overthrow of the Government.

The Galena neighborhood had always piled up its majorities for Douglas and the Democratic ticket, and he warned them: "All this talk about the dissolution of the Union is humbug, nothing but folly. We do not want to dissolve the Union; you shall not."

This was the summer that saw the first national ticket of the Republican party put in the field, with John C. Frémont and William L. Dayton as candidates for President and Vice President. And though he was so closely following national politics and writing confidential letters of advice as to a presidential candidate, it happened that when the newspapers arrived in Urbana with the information that a person named Lincoln had stood second highest in the balloting for vice-presidential candidate of the Republican party, receiving 110 votes as against 259 for Dayton, the nominee, and getting the total votes of the Illinois and Indiana delegations, Lincoln, the circuit lawyer at Urbana, laughed it off to Judge Davis and Henry C. Whitney, saying carelessly to his excited friends: "I reckon that ain't me; there's another great man in Massachusetts named Lincoln and I reckon it's him."

In the campaign that followed, Lincoln delivered more than fifty speeches north and south in the state; he traveled by railroad, stage, buggy, and wagon; when committees met him and escorted him to the hall or courthouse or the grove where the steer was over the fire for a barbecue, he was easy to pick out as the speaker of the day; at the end of his long body and head was a long stovepipe hat that made him look longer; a lengthy linen duster made him look still lengthier; with a little satchel in one hand and a faded brownish green umbrella in the other, he looked as though he came from somewhere and was going somewhere.

On the platform he asked what was the question between the two parties headed by Buchanan and Frémont, answering: "Simply this, Shall slavery be allowed to extend into United States territories now legally free? Buchanan says it shall, and Frémont says it shall not. That is the naked issue and the whole of it." After everything could be said, his advice to the voter was: "If he shall really think that slavery ought to be extended, let him go to Buchanan; if he think it ought not, let him go to Frémont."

He pointed to the slavery issue as not so much a sectional question as a property matter. "The slaves of the South, at a moderate estimate, are worth a thousand million of dollars."

Then he went into political history. Not in twelve years had there been a southern President or candidates for President from the South. He pointed to the southern politicians, saying, "Give us the measures and you take the men." In the South were candidates for the Presidency, but, "See how it works. If a southern man aspires to be President, they choke him down constantly, in order that the glittering prize of the Presidency may be held up on southern terms to the greedy eyes of northern ambition. With this they tempt us and break in upon us."

He named the northern politicians, Douglas, Pierce, Cass, Buchanan, who had fished for southern indorsement for the Presidency. He asked simple questions in short simple words as to slavery being sectional. "Who can help it? Either side can help it; but how? Simply by yielding to the other side; there is no other way; in the whole range of possibility there is no other way. Then, which side shall yield? To this, again, there can be but one answer—the side which is in the wrong."

Lincoln was out to build up the Republican party, and elect the state ticket and put Illinois on the map as a Republican stronghold. The tone of the campaign in many districts was indicated during one week of politics in Bloomington. A Democratic paper, *The Flag,* gave an account of a Democratic meeting which was interrupted by the passing of a wagon carrying a Frémont and Dayton banner. *The Flag* account said: "The rowdies that were posted on the outside of the crowd raised a shout for Frémont, and a rowdyish rabble started for the wagon. By the interference of some Democrats, together with Messrs. Lincoln and Swett, they were prevented from entering the ground. So they contented themselves with shouting and otherwise disturbing the meeting. To the honor and credit of our Republican friends in Bloomington, we will state that this disgraceful, ungentlemanly, and cowardly attempt to interrupt a public meeting, originated in the low, grovelling, and contemptible brain of a certain doctor of Cheney's Grove, followed by a gang of lesser lights, including a certain not very high-toned doctor of this city, with other rowdies picked up on their way whose names we might mention, and *may* take occasion to do so yet; but will forbear for the present."

On the same evening Lincoln spoke upstairs over Humphrey's Cheap Store, in Major's Hall. The *Weekly Pantagraph* said: "Tuesday evening, last week, while the Democrats were listening to their speakers in front of the Pike House, Mr. Lincoln had a crowded roomful at Major's Hall, who listened with intense interest to a most masterly speech, in which he tore the daytime speeches of the Bucks at their great meeting into ribbons." On the night following, the Republicans had a meeting at the courthouse, with speeches in German; and the night after that Leonard Swett spoke in Major's Hall, supported by a Glee Club consisting of two ladies and three gentlemen; so the *Pantagraph* informed its readers.

A surprisingly radical antislavery sentiment had developed in the northern central part of the state, where Lincoln's colleague, Swett, was beaten for the congressional nomination by an outspoken Abolitionist, Owen Lovejoy. "It turned me blind," Lincoln wrote Whitney, "when I first heard Swett was beaten and Lovejoy nominated; but, after much reflection, I really believe it is best to let it stand. This, of course, I wish to be confidential." He had spoken at a large Fourth of July mass meeting in a picnic grove at Princeton, but had not correctly gauged the Lovejoy organization.

In Petersburg, only two miles from his old New Salem hilltop, he met opposition. He had surveyed the town, made the first map of it, walked on its location when it was empty prairie; and posters announcing that the Hon. Abraham Lincoln would discuss issues of the day at a Republican campaign meeting had been torn down, put up again, and once more torn down. The little Republican committee that escorted him from the Springfield stagecoach to the platform in front of the Menard House were lost amid the swarming Democrats; rushes were made toward a banner reading, "Free Speech, Free Soil, Free Kansas, and Frémont."

At last Lincoln and the little committee managed to squeeze their way up on the platform while the crowd hooted, called boo and meeow; whistles, tin horns, and cow bells added to the racket. Lincoln had taken off his linen duster, handed his stovepipe hat to a member of the committee, moved to the front of the platform, and stood there without saying a word. The howling and hooting went on; there were cheers for Buchanan, for Fillmore, the Free Soil candidate, curses for Abolitionists.

In the crowd was young Henry Rankin, and he photographed Lincoln in his memory that day, and said later: "Nearly half an hour passed. He stood there all that while motionless as a statue. The only change I noticed was that at times he folded both arms across his chest, then releasing them, one hand clasped the lapel of his coat and the other arm hung by his side, the hand of that opening and then clutching. These were the only movements of Lincoln visible to those who stood by. Then a partial lull came, and he began in his lowest outdoor voice to address the assembly. Gradually the tumult near him grew less, then a desire to know what he was saying changed to shouts of 'Louder, louder.' He paused a brief moment—turned from right to left in a masterful glance over the excited people around the platform—and then raised his long left arm above his head, moving slowly his large hand up and down, as if for the first time asking silence." In less than half an hour the muttering and the chatter had died down; he spoke for two hours.

And young Rankin explained part of the situation there that day by saying: "The clergy of Petersburg and vicinity were nearly all from the South, and strong advocates of the alleged Biblical authority for slavery. Lincoln had met most of them while living in Salem, or at court terms in Petersburg. They were all present that day, and in the latter part of his speech, Lincoln addressed his remarks directly to them. "We will suppose the Reverend Dr. Ross has a slave named Sambo, and the question is: 'Is it the will of God that Sambo shall remain a slave, or be set free?' The Almighty gives no audible answer to the question, and His Revelation, the Bible, gives none—or, at most, none but such as admits of a squabble as to its meaning. No one thinks of asking Sambo's opinion on it. So at last it comes to this—that Dr. Ross is to decide the question; and while he considers it, he sits in the shade, with gloves on his hands, and subsists on the bread that Sambo is earning in the burning sun. If he decides that God wills Sambo to be free, he thereby has to walk out of the shade, throw off his gloves, and delve for his bread. Will Dr. Ross be actuated by the most perfect impartiality which has ever been considered most favorable to a correct decision?"

Then from a voice of easy, familiar talk he changed to a high moving wail and cried: "When I see strong hands sowing, reaping, and threshing wheat into bread, I cannot refrain from wishing and believing that those hands, some way, in God's good time, shall own the mouth they feed!"

The gold of October leaves was on the trees; the tawny glow of autumn harvest time was on the air. He had come and he had spoken; he had known well as he rode along the Sangamon River that morning, as the stagecoach turned at the lovely curve of the stream at Salem and he saw yellow slopes his feet had often wandered over—he had known well he would not change the mind and feeling of Menard County people for that year; what he was counting on was a later time.

Back in his Springfield law office he said to his law partner: "Billy, I never felt so full of just what a crowd ought to hear, and never had a crowd more competent, from the common-sense standpoint, if I could just get them still for half an hour as an entering wedge. I gave them my best. I dropped some things among voters in Menard that will stay. I soaked that crowd full of political facts they can't get away from."

CHAPTER 103

THAT year of 1856 saw bonfires for the new Republican party of Illinois; they had hitched together a combination of Abolitionists led by Lovejoy, old-line Whigs led by Lincoln, Yates, and others, bolting Democrats led by Palmer, Judd and others. And in November they found they had put in their man for governor, and taken away from the Democrats all the state offices. The presidential electors and the legislature were held by the Democrats. The Republicans took over the Statehouse; Bill Herndon was appointed bank examiner; Lincoln had a desk in a quiet corner for writing letters when he pleased.

Lincoln spoke at a Republican banquet in Chicago in December and pointed at the national election just past in which the President was elected by no majority at all. "Those who voted for Buchanan," he said, "are in a minority of the whole people by about four hundred thousand votes—one full tenth of all the votes." He raised the point, "The majority may not choose to remain permanently rebuked by that minority." He urged the Free Soil party men to let their organization go and stand with the Republicans. "The human heart is with us; God is with us," he said as he closed, asking for a renewal of the declaration that "all men are created equal."

It was a campaign during which Lincoln's old Georgia friend, Stephens, wrote a letter saying, "I understand that the Republicans have spent $500,000 on Pennsylvania," and the *New York Times* and the *Evening Post* reported that $150,000.00 was sent into Pennsylvania from the slaveholding states; that August Belmont of New York had contributed $50,000.00; and that other Wall Street bankers and brokers, afraid of the rumblings of disunion, disorder, and damage to business from disunion, raised still another hundred thousand dollars.

"Very nearly $500,000" was spent by the Democrats, the *New York Times* estimated, while the Republican expenses were somewhat less. Facts enough were published and generally known to show that moving behind the political contest in Pennsylvania were business and property interests to which a victory in that state was worth money.

Five months after the people had by their ballots spoken more decisively than ever before against slavery extension into new territory, with a majority of 400,000 votes against slavery extension, there came from the Supreme Court at Washington a decision that Congress did not have power to prohibit slavery in the Territories; a slave was property and if a slave owner took that property into a Territory, where the United States Constitution was the high law, the law of that Territory could not take away from him his property.

A defense of this decision was made by Senator Douglas in a speech in Springfield in June; he said: "The courts are tribunals prescribed by the Constitution and created by the authority of the people to determine, expound, and enforce the law. Hence, whoever resists the final decision of the highest judicial tribunal aims a deadly blow at our whole republican system of government."

Lincoln replied, first quoting from a message of President Jackson, disregarding a Supreme Court bank decision. "Again and again," said Lincoln, "have I heard Judge Douglas denounce that bank decision and applaud General Jackson for disregarding it."

And, having eaten many meals with judges and having slept in the same hotel bedrooms with judges, and having himself on a few occasions sat on the bench by appointment during the absence of a judge for a day or two, Lincoln ventured to say, "Judicial decisions are of greater or less authority as precedents according to circumstances. That this should be so accords both with common sense and the customary understanding of the legal profession."

He pointed to the fact that the Supreme Court had often overruled its own decisions, and said, "We shall do what we can to have it overrule this."

Then he went into the history of court decisions and state laws regulating slaves. It had not been so far back that state legislatures had the unquestioned power to abolish slavery. "Now it is becoming quite fashionable to withhold that power."

There had been days when the Declaration of Independence was held sacred. "But now, to aid in making the bondage of the negro universal and eternal, it is assailed and sneered at and construed, and hawked at and torn, till, if its framers could rise from their graves, they could not at all recognize it."

As to the slave, and the operation of law, civilization, the schools, colleges, churches, fine arts and men of learning and women of culture, and their ways of thought and action toward the slave, Lincoln delivered himself of a swift and terrible verbal cartoon, a sardonically sketched poem.

Of the chattel slave, he said: "All the powers of earth seem rapidly combining against him. Mammon is after him, ambition follows, philosophy follows, and the theology of the day is fast joining the cry. They have him in his prison house; they have searched his person, and left no prying instrument with him. One after another they have closed the heavy iron doors upon him; and now they have him, as it were, bolted in with a lock of a hundred keys, which can never be unlocked without the concurrence of every key—the keys in the hands of a hundred different men, and they scattered to a hundred different and distant places; and they stand musing as to what invention, in all the dominions of mind and matter, can be produced to make the impossibility of his escape more complete than it is."

From this he advanced to challenge Judge Douglas's argument that Republicans who insisted that the Declaration of Independence included all, black as well as white men, were so insisting "only because they want to vote, and eat, and sleep, and marry with negroes!"

And he mixed logic and human passion in declaring: "I protest against the counterfeit logic which concludes that, because I do not want a black woman for a slave, I must necessarily want her for a wife. I need not have her for either. I can just leave her alone. In some respects she certainly is not my equal; but in her natural right to eat the bread she earns with her own hands without asking leave of any one else, she is my equal, and the equal of all others."

Did the men who wrote the Declaration of Independence mean to say that all men are equal in all respects, equal in color, size, intellect, moral development, social capacity? No, hardly that. Then what did they mean? "They meant to set up a standard maxim for free society, which should be familiar to all and revered by all. The assertion that 'all men are created equal' was of no practical use in effecting our separation from Great Britain; and it was placed in the Declaration, not for that, but for future use. Its authors meant it to be—as, thank God, it is now proving itself—a stumbling-block to those who in after times might seek to turn a free people back into the hateful paths of despotism. They knew the proneness of prosperity to breed tyrants, and they meant when such should reappear in this fair land and commence their vocation, they should find left for them at least one hard nut to crack."

He took up Judge Douglas's argument that the Declaration of Independence referred to the white race alone, in which Douglas said: "When they declared all men to have been created equal, they were speaking of British subjects on this continent being equal to British subjects born and residing in Great Britain; the Declaration was adopted for the purpose of justifying the colonists in the eyes of the civilized world in withdrawing their allegiance from the British crown."

To which Lincoln replied, "Why, according to this, not only negroes but white people outside of Great Britain and America were not spoken of in that instrument. The English, Irish, and Scotch, along with white Americans, were included, to be sure, but the French, Germans, and other white people of the world are all gone to pot along with the judge's inferior races! I had thought the Declaration promised something better than the condition of British subjects; but no, it only meant that we should be equal to them in their own oppressed and unequal condition. According to that, it gave no promise that, having kicked off the king and lords of Great Britain, we should not at once be saddled with a king and lords of our own."

And he came to the matter of Judge Douglas being horrified at the mixing of blood by the white and black races. He too would be horrified. "Agreed for once—a thousand times agreed. There are white men enough to marry all the white women, and black men enough to marry all the black women; and so let them be married."

But—he wished to note there were 405,751 mulattoes in the United States in 1850. "Nearly all have sprung from black slaves and white masters."

He quoted statistics, and argued that the Supreme Court by its decision in degrading black people was promoting race amalgamation. "Could we have had our way, the chances of these black girls ever mixing their blood with that of white people would have been diminished at least to the extent that it could not have been without their consent. But Judge Douglas is delighted to have them decided to be slaves, and not human enough to have a hearing, even if they were free, and thus left subject to the forced concubinage of their masters, and liable to become the mothers of mulattoes in spite of themselves; the very state of case that produces nine-tenths of all the mulattoes—all the mixing of blood in the nation."

The speech had leaps of ironic humor; it laid the blame for slavery on the love of money, and closed: "The plainest print cannot be read through a gold eagle; and it will be ever hard to find many men who will send a slave to Liberia, and pay his passage, while they can send him to a new country—Kansas, for instance—and sell him for fifteen hundred dollars, and the rise."

And because Illinois and the Northwest and Lincoln were becoming more important nationally, the *New York Times* printed the speech in full.

CHAPTER 104

LINCOLN had become known as one of the active, practical politicians of central and southern Illinois. "I was dabbling in politics, and of course neglecting business," he wrote as an excuse to one client.

He was a party man; the other wheel horses knew him. He kept in close touch with the machinery of the party organization, often holding conferences and exchanging information and advice with other party leaders in the country and state. Caucuses in his own ward, city, county, and congressional district, for the election of delegates to conventions, were watched over by him. He spent hours many a day figuring, tabulating and estimating as to ballots, candidates, tickets.

He was a veteran of politics, familiar with the devices, traps, exploits. He had seen voting by word of mouth at the polls change to marking ballots with a pencil or pen and ink. He had a speaking acquaintance with hundreds of precinct and county workers who were ready for places as doorkeepers, postmasters, marshals, and deputies, if victory perched on the banners.

Months or years before the nomination of a certain candidate, Lincoln would have cast an eye over the particular man named, and sized him up as to whether he was the one who ought to run for that office. He didn't have time, of course, for detailed canvassing and electioneering in local campaigns. But the men who did the work usually looked him up, talked things over, and got his pointers on the lay of the land.

Outside of the right and wrong of any issues of justice and humanity in politics, Lincoln enjoyed it as a game. It had some of the skill of billiards, the science of arithmetic, and the hazards of horse racing in it. The foremost national sport was politics and he was at home in the smoke, noise, and hullabaloo of it. The big angles of the game were all the more fascinating to him because he had mastered the little essential details, such, for instance, as electioneering.

"Things look reasonably well," he would write to a party worker. "If life and health continue I shall pretty likely be in Augusta on the 25th." He wrote hundreds of letters somewhat on the order of one informing Sydney Spring in Graysville: "There was no opening to nominate him (Mr. Farel) for Superintendent of Public Instruction, but through him Egypt made a most valuable contribution to the convention. I think it may be freely said that he came off the lion of the day—or rather of the

North Side of Square, Springfield, Illinois.

Newspaper print, 1858.

night. Can you not elect him to the legislature? It seems to me he would be hard to beat. What objection could be made to him? What is your Senator Martin saying and doing? What is Webb about? Please write me."

Though not a Mason, he had at hand a personal copy of the bound "Proceedings of the Grand Royal Arch Chapter of the State of Illinois," being reports of conventions of the Masonic order for the years 1851-1857.

He gave his ears to the whisperers of political gossip, seeking straws showing the wind; he wrote to an important man of "a story being whispered about here," saying, "I do not believe the story but still it gives me some uneasiness," and then instead of writing bluntly, "I would never have thought it of you," he penned the diplomatic sentence, "It was not in character with you as I have always estimated you."

Having sent ten dollars to Editor Mosely of the *Prairie Beacon*, he later mailed a political article to that editor, who refused to print it, and Lincoln laughed to Herndon that Mosely was "a real editor."

He met the Bunn brothers one day—Jacob the banker, and John W., the wholesale and retail grocer—and asked John if he didn't wish to run for city treasurer. "John will run if you want him to," said Jacob. Time went by and John almost believed his nomination was forgotten. But at the close of the convention that named the ticket, Bunn saw a young lawyer, picked by Lincoln, rise and present his name, saying: "If there is any delegate on this floor opposed to the candidacy of Mr. Bunn, I do not wish his name to be voted upon or to go on the ticket." And Bunn was nominated, his name was printed on the ticket, and the next morning, going to his grocery store, he caught up with Lincoln, who asked, "How are you running?"

Then, as Bunn himself said afterward: "I told Lincoln I didn't know how I was running. Then he said, 'Have you asked anybody to vote for you?' I said I had not. 'Well,' said he, 'if you don't think enough of your success to ask anybody to vote for you, it is probable they will not do it, and that you will not be elected." I said to him, 'Shall I ask Democrats to vote for me?' He said, 'Yes, ask everybody to vote for you.'

"Just then a well-known Democrat by the name of Ragsdale was coming up the sidewalk. Lincoln said, 'Now, you drop back there and ask Mr. Ragsdale to vote for you.' I turned and fell in with Mr. Ragsdale, told him of my candidacy, and said I hoped he would support me. To my astonishment, he promised me that he would. Mr. Lincoln walked slowly along and fell in with me again, and said: 'Well, what did Ragsdale say? Will he vote for you?' I said, 'Yes, he told me he would.' 'Well, then,' said Lincoln, 'you are sure of two votes at the election, mine and Ragsdale's.' It was my first lesson in practical politics."

If Lincoln telegraphed a friend at Alton, "Bring Joe Gillespie here

Looking along Washington Street, Springfield, Illinois.

Print owned by Joseph Husband.

immediately, don't fail," there was a scurrying in that quarter to get hold of Joe and send him on to Lincoln. He could write a letter brimming over with encouragement and hope, and full of details as to how to tackle the troubles at hand. "I do hope you are worse scared than hurt," he wrote to Gillespie, telling him, "Run down one of the poll books of the Edwardsville precinct, and take the first hundred known American names, then quietly ascertain how many of them are going to vote for Douglas. I think you will find less than fifty—but even if you find fifty, make sure of the other fifty, that is, make sure of all you can at all events."

Starting to drive Lincoln to Greenville, Gillespie said they could only go as far as Highland that evening. "He seemed delighted with the idea of stopping at Highland, as he said he had understood that place was a little Germany. We stopped there and had a good time; the house where we were stopping was crowded and jammed. I here got the first inkling of the popularity of Lincoln among the Germans. The people at Highland were enraptured." Thus wrote Gillespie.

Lincoln stayed in good standing as a member of the Illinois State Colonization Society, being included among the officers in 1857, when the *Springfield Journal* listed O. H. Browning as president, assisted by ten vice presidents, two secretaries of the treasury, and a board of managers having as its members: Rev. J. H. Brown, D.D., Rev. S. W. Harkey, D.D., Rev. J. W. Pierson, Rev. C. W. Sears, Rev. N. W. Miner, Rev. A. Hale, William Yates, Esq., J. S. Vredenberg, Hon. S. M. Cullom, Hon. A. Lincoln.

CHAPTER 105

It was in 1858, the year of the Donati comet, that Lincoln was fixing his thoughts on the fact that nothing stays fixed. Up among the fixed stars and steady constellations are explosions and offshoots of comets, sprays of comets. Even in the mathematics of the stars one had to say, "If we could first know where we are, and whither we are tending, we could better judge what to do, and how to do it."

In the spring of the year he was writing notes for a speech; at the state gathering of Republicans in June they were going to nominate him for United States senator from Illinois; and he was going to make a speech; he was to tell the world what Illinois and the Northwest would stand for. As he read the speech to Herndon in their office, it lighted Herndon into saying, "Lincoln, deliver that speech as read, and it will make you President."

Lincoln had spoken the high points of it at Bloomington during the last campaign, and a Chicago judge and a Galena congressman had warned him never to be so radical again. In the State Library in Springfield he sat in a chair and read it off to a picked dozen of political friends; they said it was too radical; it was "a fool utterance"; it was "ahead of its time"; it would drive away votes; all were against his delivering the first paragraph of the speech, except Herndon. And Lincoln was polite and decent—and couldn't see where he ought to change the speech.

The convention met in Springfield on June 17, named Lincoln for United States senator, and then sent out for him to come and make a speech. He came, bowed to the applause and cheers, murmured, "Mr. President and Gentlemen of the Convention," and then, for the first time in his life reading a speech from a manuscript, he began:

"If we could first know where we are, and whither we are tending, we could better judge what to do, and how to do it. We are now far into the fifth year since a policy was initiated with the avowed object and confident promise of putting an end to slavery agitation. Under the operation of that policy, that agitation has not only not ceased, but has constantly augmented. In my opinion, it will not cease until a crisis shall have been reached and passed. 'A house divided against itself cannot stand.' I believe this government cannot endure permanently half slave and half free. I do not expect the Union to be dissolved—I do not expect the house to fall—but I do expect it will cease to be divided. It will become all one thing, or all the other."

This was so plain that any two farmers fixing fences on a rainy morning could talk it over in all its ins and outs. And to this was added a sentence for all the more thoughtful to follow in all its exact and terrible meanings. The speaker read:

"Either the opponents of slavery will arrest the further spread of it, and place it where the public mind shall rest in the belief that it is in the course of ultimate extinction; or its advocates will push it forward till it shall become alike lawful in all the States, old as well as new, North as well as South."

In simple Bible language, in words as short as those of Bunyan's "Pilgrim's Progress," and in longer words of piercing precision, he had spoken thought as fresh, beautiful, and terrible as Donati's comet with its tail of fire in the sky. What he had said was easy to say and to understand, a common-sense telling of what millions of anxious hearts wanted told.

There was more to the speech; he put together this and that circumstance and argued that while on the face of them the people could not be sure that there was a conspiracy on foot to nationalize slavery, yet explanations were required as to why the two Presidents, Franklin Pierce and James Buchanan, a Supreme Court Chief Justice, and the United States senator, Stephen A. Douglas, had all taken parts in moves and acts that seemed to lead straight toward a time when slaves could be owned and worked in all states of the Union. And he mentioned how the Republican party, of strange, discordant, and even hostile elements, "gathered from the four winds," had fought winning battles in the last campaign and with wise counsels should go on.

He struck at the Supreme Court as a dynasty. "Put this and that together, and we have another nice little niche, which we may, ere long, see filled with another Supreme Court decision declaring that the Constitution of the United States does not permit a State to exclude slavery from its limits. Such a decision is all that slavery now lacks of being alike lawful in all the States. Welcome or unwelcome, such decision is probably coming, and will soon be upon us, unless the power of the present political dynasty shall be met and overthrown. We shall lie down pleasantly dreaming that the people of Missouri are on the verge of making their State free, and we shall awake to the reality instead that the Supreme Court has made Illinois a slave State. To meet and overthrow the power of that dynasty is the work now before all those who would prevent that consummation."

There was more to the speech—but the part that interested the country, as daily and weekly newspapers published the speech in full, was its opening paragraph. It became known as the "House Divided" speech.

CHAPTER 106

LINCOLN was charging conspiracy but not using the word conspiracy. He was saying that the President of the United States, the executive department of the Government, and the Supreme Court, the judicial department, were putting their heads together and whispering things not known at all to the country and the people, working secretly on a plan that would be beaten if worked out openly and publicly.

The Supreme Court decision or dictum in the Dred Scott case was framed by a secret arrangement between Stephen A. Douglas, the Illinois Democratic senator, Franklin Pierce, the former Democratic President, Roger B. Taney, the Democratic Chief Justice of the Supreme Court, and James Buchanan, the Democratic President succeeding Pierce.

"We find it impossible," said Lincoln, "not to believe that Stephen and Franklin and Roger and James all understood one another from the beginning, and all worked upon a common plan or draft."

Lincoln did not know that Justice Catron, on February 19, 1857, wrote to President Buchanan, saying, "My Dear Sir: The Dred Scott case has been before the Judges several times since last Saturday, and I think you may safely say in your Inaugural," following then with a draft of a paragraph which Justice Catron believed would be suitable for the inaugural, and closing the letter with a suggestion that Buchanan should "drop Grier a line, saying how necessary it is." Grier was another Supreme Court justice. "He has no doubt about the question on the main contest," wrote Catron to the incoming President, "but has been persuaded to take the smooth handle for the sake of repose."

Nor did Lincoln know that four days later Justice Grier wrote to Buchanan, the President to be inaugurated in nine days, saying, "In conversation with the Chief Justice I have agreed to concur with him," and ending the letter, "We will not let any others of our brethren know anything about our anxiety, and though contrary to our usual practice, we have thought due to you to state to you in candor and confidence the real state of the matter."

Such were a few of the secret actions operating back of the Dred Scott dictum, and pointed to as probable, and believable, by Lincoln in his homely and almost friendly declaration, "We find it impossible not to believe that Stephen and Franklin and Roger and James all understood one another from the beginning, and all worked upon a common plan or draft."

The names of agitator and blatherskite were hurled at Lincoln by Democratic newspapers, for his House Divided speech, in which he first presented this view. Political friends growled that he had been radical, gone too far. And he said: "If I had to draw a pen across my record and erase my whole life from sight, and I had one poor gift or choice left as to what I should save from the wreck, I should choose that speech and leave it to the world unerased."

CHAPTER 107

When Douglas spoke to the Senate on April 17, 1858, on the three different routes proposed for a railroad to the Pacific Ocean, he spoke as a patriot who wished to see America an ocean-bound republic, and he spoke also as a friend of the men who controlled rail transportation across the Isthmus of Panama, as well as the iron ways from the Great Lakes to the Gulf of Mexico. He said that either the northern route or the middle route to the Pacific would satisfy him as a northern man, as a man living at the centre of the continent, "the great heart and centre of the Republic, the Mississippi Valley, the point at which it is to diverge." The northern route, he had sometimes thought, furnished better grass, more timber, more water, more of the elements for construction, repair, and maintenance of a railroad; yet inasmuch as he expected never to put a dollar of money into the road nor have any agency nor connection with it, he would be willing to take the middle or Albuquerque route, if it were so decided. The cost to the Government, outside of land grants, would be limited to $25,000,000.00.

Douglas told the Senate, "I am unwilling to lose this great measure merely because of a difference of opinion as to what shall be the pass

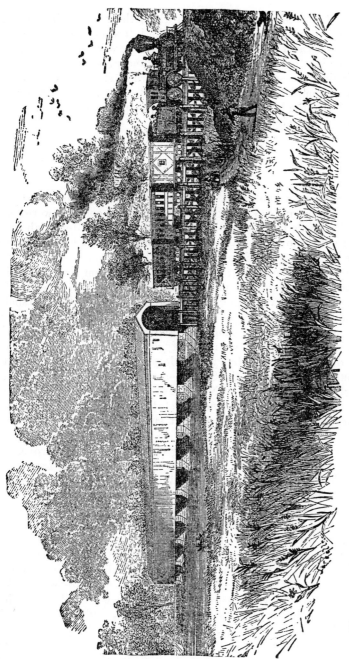

Chicago and Rock Island Railroad train, and bridge over Rock River in northwestern Illinois. Commerce wants this train to run on to the west coast instead of stopping at the Mississippi River. Politics is stopping the iron horse from crossing the Great Plains and the Rockies. Transportation to connect the two coasts is an immense underlying national issue of the late '50s.

From a print loaned by Joseph Husband.

selected in the Rocky Mountains through which the road shall run. . . . Our great substantial interests require it. The interests of commerce, the great interests of travel and communication—those still greater interests that bind the Union together, and are to make and preserve the continent as one and indivisible—all demand that this road shall be commenced, prosecuted, and completed at the earliest practicable moment. I am unwilling to postpone the bill. I have seen these postponements from session to session for the last eight or ten years."

CHAPTER 108

LINCOLN was reading a book that Herndon had brought from Boston, a book that other thousands of thoughtful men over the country were reading, a sad and terrible book, a book with the wailing of a Jeremiah in its pages, a book with a low and vague storm growling in its breath. It was entitled "The Impending Crisis of the South."

The writer was Hinton Rowan Helper, who came from a slave-holding family that had lived a hundred years in the Carolinas, and he dedicated his book "to the non-slaveholding whites of the South." He marshaled against slavery such witnesses as Mansfield, Locke, Pitt, Shakespeare, Cowper, Milton, Blackstone of England, and Socrates, Plato, and Aristotle of Greece. He called up a crowd of ghosts, such as Washington, Jefferson, Madison, Monroe, Henry, Randolph, Clay, Benton, Marshall, Bolling, Chandler, Birney—of the South—and Franklin, Hamilton, Jay, Adams, Webster, Clinton—of the North. He rested formidable chapters on the testimony of the churches and the status of the Bible as an antislavery textbook. He refused to hope that such appeals could stand by themselves.

Helper declared in italics in his opening chapter, "We can prove, and we shall now proceed to prove, that the annual hay crop of the free states is worth considerably more in dollars and cents than all the cotton, tobacco, rice, hay, hemp, and cane sugar annually produced in the fifteen slave states." Wherewith he offered statistics for 1850 to show the hay crop of the free states was worth $142,138,998 as against a total of $138,005,723, the total value of the cotton crop and the five other crops of the slave states. He began and ended the book with statistics. He quoted a governor of Virginia as saying: "Instead of having to feed cattle on a thousand hills, you have had to chase the stump-tailed steers through the sedge patches to procure a tough beefsteak. The landlord has skinned the tenant, the tenant has skinned the land, and all have grown poor together."

Helper quoted the Hon. C. C. Clay of Alabama: "I can show you, with sorrow, in the older portions of Alabama, and in my native county of

Madison, the sad memorials of the artless and exhausting culture of cotton. Our small planters, after taking the cream off their lands, unable to restore them by rest, manure, or otherwise, are going further West and South, in search of other virgin lands, which they may and will despoil and impoverish in like manner. Our wealthier planters, with greater means and no more skill, are buying out their poorer neighbors, extending their plantations, and adding to their slave force. The wealthy few, who are able to live on smaller profits, and to give their blasted fields some rest, are thus pushing off the many who are merely independent. Of the $20,-000,000 annually realized from the sales of the cotton crop in Alabama, nearly all not expended in supporting the producers is reinvested in land and negroes." Thus he massed items of information.

Before writing his book, Helper had talked with hay dealers in Baltimore, and learned that Maryland was buying seven million dollars' worth of hay from the North every year, and one million dollars' worth of cotton from the South. He listed articles the South bought from the North—Bibles, brooms, buckets and books; furniture, crockery, glassware, toys, apparel, medicines, pianos, shoes, hats, handkerchiefs. "We go to the North for them all. Instead of keeping our money in circulation at home, by patronizing our own mechanics, manufacturers, and laborers, we send it all away to the North, and there it remains; it never falls into our hands again."

And if Helper's book had stopped there and not become radical, revolutionary, it probably would have been printed and circulated in the South. But the author quoted the law of Maryland to show "why this work was not published in Baltimore." The law declared "the writing or printing any pamphlet, newspaper, handbill, or other paper of an inflammatory character, and having a tendency to excite discontent, or stir up insurrection amongst the people of color" to be a felony punishable with two to twenty years in the penitentiary. He commented on the law: "What wonder is it that there is no native literature in the South? The South can never have a literature of her own until after slavery shall have been abolished." He was insolent, scornful. "Slaveholders are too lazy and ignorant to write it, and the non-slaveholders—even the few whose minds are cultivated at all—are not permitted to make the attempt."

On the basis of the census of 1850, he showed that in a population of 6,184,477 in the slave states, only 347,525 were slaveholders. And he cried in reckless bitter accusation, and in writhing grief: "Until we examined into the matter, we thought and hoped the South was ahead of the North in *one* particular, that of agriculture; but our thoughts have been changed, and our hopes frustrated; we behold our dear native South stripped of every laurel, and sinking deeper and deeper in the depths of poverty and shame, while we see the North rising higher and higher in the scale of fame, fortune, and invulnerable power. Our soul, justly we believe, cries out for retribution against the treacherous, slave-driving legislators, who have so basely and unpatriotically neglected the interests of their poor white constituents and bargained away the rights of posterity."

Helper pointed to the white non-slaveholders of the South as in a majority of five to one. "They have never yet had any part or lot in framing the laws under which they live. There is no legislation except for the benefit of slavery, the slaveholders. As a general rule, poor white persons are regarded with less esteem and attention than negroes, and though the condition of the latter is wretched beyond description, vast numbers of the former are infinitely worse off. A cunningly devised mockery of freedom is guaranteed to them, and that is all. To all intents, they are disfranchised, and outlawed."

Unless the rich planters who controlled the South could be overthrown, the South would become to the North as Ireland to England or Poland to Russia, declared Helper's book. "How little the 'poor white trash,' the great majority of the Southern people, know of the real condition of the country is, indeed, sadly astonishing. They know what their imperious masters condescend to tell, and that is but precious little, and even that little, always garbled and one-sided, is never told except in public harangues; for the haughty cavaliers of shackles and handcuffs will not degrade themselves by holding private converse with those who have neither dimes nor hereditary rights in human flesh."

A sad, violent book it was that Abraham Lincoln read in the spring of 1858, as he was writing notes on his House Divided speech, placing the notes in his hat, taking them out, making his revisions and then putting them back in the tall silk stovepipe. As he read the book he marked passages he couldn't say yes to, such as one, "Out of our effects you have long since overpaid yourselves for your slaves; and now, sirs, you *must* emancipate them, or we will emancipate them for you."

And another he marked as too extreme: "Indeed, it is our honest conviction that all the proslavery slaveholders, who are alone responsible for the continuance of this baneful institution among us, deserve to be at once reduced to a parallel with the base criminals that lie fettered in the cells of public prisons."

Helper's book was a revolutionary appeal, as reckless and uncompromising in its passion as the speeches of Patrick Henry and Samuel Adams in the days before the American Revolution. Many Republicans, and nearly all the Abolitionists, were giving it the widest possible circulation. Some who disapproved of its violent tone believed it should be widely read because of its statistics and information.

That the book should have been produced, that the non-slaveholders of the South and the poor whites should have found a voice, that so direct and fierce a challenge should be hurled at the rich planters who controlled the South, was a symptom and a sign that Lincoln tried to analyze.

Part of his analysis went into his speech so soft, so quiet, beginning, "If we could first know where we are, and whither we are tending, we could better judge what to do, and how to do it."

The year was full of large and swift events for Lincoln—the first year in which he was so wrapped up in politics that he didn't have time to file any cases in the Illinois supreme court.

Bill Herndon had written to his Boston friend Parker, "These are curious, mysterious days," and spoken of events hard to read because there were "not facts enough out yet."

Herndon sniffed it in the air that powerful men South, North, West, were suspicious, quarreling, exasperated, desperate. "There will be many foul disclosures in this fight. They will tell each other of treachery—of each other's rascality; they will taunt each other, and the age and freedom will profit by the quarrel. Robbers have fallen out over the distribution of their bloody booty. The quarrel will be long and bitter, wild and ferocious. Let honest men look on, and laugh or weep, as suits their respective natures. I shall mourn, yet rejoice. What is your opinion of things? How do the Massachusetts men look upon this 'squabble'?"

CHAPTER 109

WHEN the newspapers brought to the eye of Stephen A. Douglas, at his Washington home, the speech of A. Lincoln saying that a house divided against itself cannot stand, the senator was more than interested. When he read that the state Republican convention had with cheers resolved, "That Hon. Abraham Lincoln is our first and only choice for United States Senator to fill the vacancy about to be created by the expiration of Mr. Douglas's term of office," he was again more than interested.

Douglas was the leading man at that hour in the great drama of American politics. Against him in his contest for reëlection he had President Buchanan and the national Democratic Administration, besides Lincoln and the young Republican party of Illinois which had two years previously elected a governor and the whole state ticket.

He was an example of success, this Judge Douglas, who as a Vermont Yankee had come to Illinois and earned his first money as an auctioneer, then as a school-teacher, a lawyer, a member of the legislature, a land commissioner, and at twenty-eight years of age a state supreme court judge, at thirty a congressman, at thirty-four a United States senator, at thirty-nine narrowly missing the Democratic nomination for President.

Among his friends Douglas could count some of the most powerful railroad financiers in the country; without his tenacity and shrewdness the rail route from the Great Lakes to the Gulf of Mexico would not have been laid so early; it was in the interest of a rail route to the Pacific that he had risked his political life in the Missouri Compromise repeal; the Illinois Central railroad company would be one of his best helpers in his Illinois campaign. He played the game on a national scale; he had sent funds from Illinois to carry Pennsylvania in the last campaign. He had earned the contempt of antislavery leaders; a Massachusetts senator who kept five different English dictionaries had compared him to "the noisome, squat, and nameless animal whose tongue switches a perpetual stench;" he had been called "a Northern man with Southern principles."

His first wife was the daughter of a North Carolina planter; at her home Douglas had seen slavery as Southern society looked at it; on her death he became the owner of 150 slaves willed to her by her father. He had grown careless of dress, bitter in speech; four years passed; clothes and manners took on fresher looks after he married Adele Cutts, a great-niece of Dolly Madison, a devout Roman Catholic; and in a gabbling underworld of politics this had been used against him; it was whispered he had on his European tour paused to kiss the foot of the Pope of Rome. He told his Illinois friends that Queen Victoria of England refused to meet him in the plain clothes of a United States senator; he therefore refused to meet the British queen.

In Russia he fared excellently; there at the palace of the Czar, he was placed on a horse with a bridle glittering with diamonds, and a saddle decorated with gold and silver. Between whiskies, he told Usher F. Linder and a circle of Illinois Democrats how a tall, fine-looking man addressed him in good English, "I have the pleasure, I presume, of receiving and welcoming to Russia, Senator Douglas of Illinois?" To which Douglas answered with a bow, "I presume I have the honor of being received and welcomed by his Majesty, Nicholas, Emperor of all the Russias."

And as Linder, after the whiskies, further recollected, the senator said: "We arrived at a cortège, and the Czar gave me the place of honor, near his own person. Linder, that was a proud day for my country. I never was vain enough to appropriate it for myself. When the little man in black was given the place of honor, it was a stroke of policy on the part of Nicholas; it amounted to saying to the hundred ambassadors from all the nations of the world: 'Gentlemen, I intend to make the great people of the great republic on the other side of the Atlantic my friends, and if any of your nations go to war with me, rest assured that that people will stand by me.' I received every attention that it was possible for mortal man to receive, all of which I knew was intended for my country."

Half the barrooms in Illinois had seen him reporting to his precinct workers what was going on in Europe and Washington, and how at Washington he let them know he was from the Mississippi Valley, which was to be the centre of a continental republic. He could put a hand on the shoulder of a young precinct worker and say, as though they had been college chums, "You—I count on your help."

Douglas could chuckle in telling of how one day he threw an arm around the shoulder of Beverly Tucker, a Virginia politician, and burbled, "Bev, old boy, I love you." Tucker asked: "Will you always love me? Will you love me when you get to be President?" "If I don't, may I be damned —and what do you want me to do for you?" was Douglas's counter-question, to which Tucker replied, "Well, when you get to be President, all I want you to do for me is to pick some public place, and put your arm around my neck, just as you are doing now, and call me Bev!" He smoked cigars in a fashionable London boarding-house, where first a manservant and later a maidservant came to his room and told him smoking was forbidden; then came the landlady herself, prim and precise in her furbelows and rustling garments; Douglas tossed back his massive, commanding head, imperiously conveyed the intelligence, "Madam, I am an American sovereign"—and went on smoking his cigar; the landlady felt the occasion an honor and let him alone as one of earth's rulers.

He had humor, and had once confessed, "I have learned enough about the tariff to know that I know scarcely anything about it at all; and a man makes considerable progress on a question of this kind when he ascertains that fact." His passion was politics and power; what he did in politics was for power first of all; as to property and cash assets he didn't have the urge. He had bought land near Chicago for a few odd dollars; and sold one tract for $90,000.00. He was ready to throw all his real-estate winnings into the coming campaign in Illinois. Ten acres of his land he had donated to the University of Chicago. When other senators had laughed at the project of a fund to help a balloonist experiment in air mastery, he argued for it. He was a strong, fearless, many-sided, colorful man, a sort of Napoleon in politics, a performer of acrobatic and equilibristic marvels, this Steve Douglas.

Hearing that Lincoln had been named to combat him in Illinois, Douglas told a group of Republicans, "You have nominated a very able and a very honest man." To John W. Forney he said: "I shall have my hands full. Lincoln is the strong man of his party, the best stump speaker in the West." And again, "Of all the damned Whig rascals about Springfield, Abe Lincoln is the ablest and the most honest."

As Douglas started West in June, his daily movements were watched by the country. The *Chicago Times* reprinted from the *Philadelphia Press:* "Senator Douglas, accompanied by his beautiful and accomplished wife, arrived at the Girard House, en route for Chicago. He was visited by a large number of our most influential citizens, holding quite an impromptu reception." The *Cincinnati Commercial* reprinted from the *Vincennes* (Indiana) *Sun,* a news letter sketching Douglas's opponent: "Lincoln is popular—the strongest man the opposition have—is nearly fifty years old—six feet two—slightly stoop-shouldered—very muscular and powerful—dark eyes—a quizzical, pleasant, rawboned face—tells a story better than anybody else—is a good lawyer—and is what the world calls a devilish good fellow. He would have been senator before, had not Trumbull's superior cunning overreached him. But in dignity, intellect, and majesty of mind it is not pretended that he is Douglas's equal."

Sixty miles out from Chicago, a special Illinois Central train with a brass band, flags, streamers, and pennants met Judge Douglas and his party on July 9th and escorted the statesman to Chicago. At the Twelfth Street depot a crowd of thousands gave him cheers of welcome, women on doorsteps waved handkerchiefs, cannon boomed a salute of 150 guns. The committee on arrangements placed the senator in an open carriage drawn by six horses and he was driven through avenues of buildings decorated with national flags. This was the city where four years before a crowd had hooted him down.

As he stepped out on the Lake Street balcony of the Tremont House that night, rockets and red fire lit the street; he gazed into what the *Chicago Times* called "an ocean of upturned faces," and his eyes met a transparent sign reading, "Welcome to Stephen A. Douglas, the Defender of Popular Sovereignty." The chairman began a speech of introduction and had to quit because the crowd in the street started a fight with hack drivers who had tried to plow through the mass of people and deliver distinguished guests at the Tremont House; as between the crowd and the hack drivers the wrangle was a stand-off; one man was knocked down with the butt end of a whip; one driver was pulled off his seat three times. As the horses, people, and hack drivers were untangled, Judge Douglas began a speech that lasted an hour and a half.

Lincoln sat near by and heard Douglas refer to him as "a kind, amiable, and intelligent gentleman, a good citizen, and an honorable opponent." He heard Douglas say to the swarming thousands amid the lights and smoke of the street: "Mr. Lincoln advocates boldly and clearly a war of sections, a war of the North against the South, of the free states against the slave states—a war of extermination—to be continued relentlessly until the one or the other shall be subdued, and all the states shall either become free or become slave."

And the night afterward Lincoln spoke from the Tremont House balcony to a crowd somewhat smaller; rockets blazed; the brass band of the German Republican Club from the Seventh Ward rendered music. And amid other issues of the day Lincoln said: "I do not claim, gentlemen, to be unselfish; I do not pretend that I would not like to go to the United States Senate; I make no such hypocritical pretense, but I do say to you that in this mighty issue, it is nothing to you—nothing to the mass of the people of the nation—whether or not Judge Douglas or myself shall ever be heard of after this night."

To Gustave Koerner, a congressman and leader of German Republicans down-state, Lincoln wrote about the importance of reaching German voters through German speakers, and noted, regarding Douglas in Chicago: "I was present at his reception in Chicago, and it was certainly very large and imposing; but judging from the opinions of others better acquainted with faces there, and by the strong call for me to speak, when he closed, I really believe we could have voted him down in that very crowd. Our meeting, twenty-four hours after, called only twelve hours before it came together, and got up without trumpery, was really as large and five times as enthusiastic. I write this for your private eye, to assure you that there is no solid shot in these bombastic parades of his."

CHAPTER 110

DURING the hot summer weeks in Illinois, as the corn was growing knee-high and then shoulder-high, Lincoln and Douglas had their coats off, making public speeches, writing private letters, listening to whisperers of gossip, watching various newspapers bawl and bark at each other.

Lincoln pointed to politicians following Douglas, expecting Douglas some day to be President of the United States. "They have seen in his round, jolly, fruitful face, post offices, land offices, marshalships."

And on the other hand: "Nobody has ever expected me to be President. In my poor lean, lank face nobody has ever seen that any cabbages were sprouting out." And effective sarcasm it was that he used in telling a crowd, "Plainly, you stand ready saddled, bridled, and harnessed, and waiting to be driven."

Not since the days of Thomas Jefferson had any American politician reached out with so direct a passion in appealing to the people as though freedom was a word that meant something to be used, as though a free country and a free people connected with causes and oaths and responsibilities. He explained the Fourth of July as a day for Americans to be thoughtful and to read the Declaration of Independence. "We are now a mighty nation; we are about thirty millions of people; and we own and inhabit about one-fifteenth of the dry land of the whole earth." He mentioned "iron men," the fathers and grandfathers of Americans then living; those iron men had fought the American Revolution. "We have among us, perhaps, half our people who are not descendants at all of these men; they are men who have come from Europe—German, Irish, French, and Scandinavian—men that have come from Europe themselves, or whose ancestors settled here, finding themselves our equal in all things."

He was speaking in Chicago where the different nationalities he named had churches, schools, saloons, gathering-places where they talked about "the old country" and "this new country," where they were asking themselves in what special and particular ways this new country was better than the old. Lincoln had looked from the Tremont House balcony into their torch-lighted faces turned up to hear his words.

And he said of the newcomers who had no grandfathers in the American Revolution: "If they look back to trace their connection with those days by blood, they find they have none; they cannot carry themselves back into that glorious epoch and make themselves feel they are part of us; but when they look through that old Declaration of Independence, they find that those old men say that 'We hold these truths to be self-evident, that all men are created equal,' and then they feel that that moral sentiment taught in that day evidences their relation to those men, that it is the father of all moral principle in them, and that they have a right to claim it as though they were blood of the blood, and flesh of the flesh, of the men who wrote that Declaration; and so they are."

And he passed on to a proud, ironic scorn: "Those arguments that are made, that the inferior race are to be treated with as much allowance as they are capable of enjoying; that as much is to be done for them as their condition will allow—what are these arguments? They are the arguments that kings have made for enslaving the people in all ages of the world. You will find that all the arguments in favor of kingcraft were of this class; they always bestrode the necks of the people—not that they wanted to do it, but because the people were better off for being ridden. That is their argument, and this argument of Judge Douglas is the same old serpent that says, You work and I eat, you toil and I will enjoy the fruits of it."

He recognized conditions, necessities; perfection is difficult. He quoted the Savior, "Be ye perfect"; it was an ideal, impossible to realize, but worth striving for. "In relation to the principle that all men are created equal, let it be as nearly reached as we can. If we cannot give freedom to every creature, let us do nothing that will impose slavery upon any other creature." Thus he would explain the meaning of the Fourth of July. It was not merely a day for the fizzling of firecrackers.

His blunt, short words in a speech in Springfield declared: "All I ask for the negro is that, if you do not like him, let him alone. If God gave him but little, that little let him enjoy." And again as to all men being born equal: "Certainly the negro is not our equal in color—perhaps not in many other respects; still, in the right to put into his mouth the bread that his own hands have earned, he is the equal of every other man, white or black. In pointing out that more has been given you, you cannot be justified in taking away the little which has been given him."

He discussed necessity, saying: "I yield to all which follows from necessity. What I would most desire would be the separation of the white and black races."

He expected trouble, a crisis, perhaps war, between the states. He didn't wish what seemed to be coming. He expected it. That was what he meant in the house-divided-against-itself speech. "I did not express my wish on anything. I simply expressed my expectation. Cannot Judge Douglas perceive a distinction between a purpose and an expectation? I have often expressed an expectation to die, but I have never expressed a wish to die."

Whenever Judge Douglas talked for an hour he pulled from inside his Prince Albert coat the opening paragraph of Lincoln's House Divided speech and read, "I believe that this government cannot endure permanently," to show that it meant Lincoln wished for a bloody war between the states. And whenever Lincoln spoke for an hour he too read the paragraph and said it meant just what it said; he expected a crisis; he didn't wish it.

CHAPTER 111

WHEN Lincoln or Herndon came back from the Springfield post office with the morning mail, they carried such newspapers as the *Chicago Tribune* and the *New York Tribune*, western and eastern Republican papers; the *Anti-Slavery Standard*, the *Emancipator* and *National Era*, Abolitionist and antislavery papers; the *Charleston* (S. C.) *Mercury* and the *Richmond* (Va.) *Enquirer*, southern proslavery papers.

Lincoln was trying to fathom what would be happening the next year and the year after. Southern newspapers at times were saying slavery would be a good thing not only for black people but for some classes of white workers. Lincoln got the *Illinois State Journal* to reprint opinions such as one from the *Richmond Enquirer*, reading: Northern free society is . . . burdened with a servile class of mechanics and laborers, unfit for self-government, and yet clothed with the attributes and powers of citizens. Master and slave is a relation in society as natural and necessary as parent and child; and the Northern States will yet have to introduce it."

In a leather-covered scrapbook, six by four inches in size, with a brass clasp, Lincoln pasted the Declaration of Independence paragraph declaring all men created equal, followed by two passionate sentences from Henry Clay of Kentucky. "I repeat it, sir, I never can, and never will, and no earthly power will make me vote, directly or indirectly, to spread slavery over territory where it does not exist. Never, while my heart sends the vital fluid through my veins—never!"

Lincoln understood well that these ideas and feelings had sympathizers in the North. He had met it in the faces of that crowd he spoke to in Petersburg when he aimed to "soak them with facts." In that same year Dumas J. Van Deren of Charleston, Illinois, became editor of the *Mattoon National Gazette*, a Buchanan organ, which advised its readers, "If

Illinois were a slave state, the best men of Kentucky, Virginia, Tennessee, and even states farther south, would be here as soon as they could remove their families." Van Deren wrote too, "The novelty of free labor is a mere humbug," and predicted the farmers of Illinois would favor slavery for Illinois if a state constitution legalizing slavery should be voted on. He wrote to a South Carolina newspaper: "Send your young men here, who can remain here and vote. If by our united efforts we shall be able to carry our point, the southern people will possess the key to the western world." The *Jackson Mississippian* joined in this view, declaring, "Establish slavery in Illinois and it would give us the key to the great West."

Lincoln felt a thing cruel and snobbish creeping farther into American philosophy. He tried to put the logic, passion, and tears of this feeling in his speeches.

With irony so sad it was musical and with sentences crowded with implications, he told three or four hundred people at Edwardsville one day: "When by all these means you have succeeded in dehumanizing the negro; when you have put him down and made it impossible for him to be but as the beasts of the field; when you have extinguished his soul, and placed him where the ray of hope is blown out in darkness that broods over the damned, are you quite sure the demon you have roused will not turn and rend you? What constitutes the bulwark of our liberty and independence? It is not our frowning battlements, our bristling seacoasts, the guns of our war steamers, or the strength of our gallant army. These are not our reliance against a resumption of tyranny in our land. All of them may be turned against our liberties without making us stronger or weaker for the struggle.

"Our reliance is in the love of liberty which God has planted in our bosoms. Our defence is in the preservation of the spirit which prizes liberty as the heritage of *all men, in all lands everywhere.* Destroy this spirit and you have planted the seeds of despotism around your own doors. Familiarize yourself with the chains of bondage, and you are preparing your own limbs to wear them.

"Accustomed to trample on the rights of those around you, you have lost the genius of your own independence, and become the fit subjects of the first cunning tyrant who rises among you. And let me tell you that these things are prepared for you with the logic of history, if the elections shall promise that the next Dred Scott decision and all future decisions shall be acquiesced in by the people."

He knew that his best hopes for listeners to such an appeal were the young people. The fifteen- and sixteen-year-old boys who had read "Uncle Tom's Cabin" when it was published six years before Lincoln's House Divided speech had grown into twenty-one and twenty-two-year-old voters. In what he was doing and saying Lincoln kept in mind the young men. He had always had an eye out in politics for those meant in his advice one time that it paid to gather in "the wild shrewd boys." His own youth was never forgotten.

He knew that the challenging, radical tone of what he was saying, about the Declaration of Independence, would interest not only the foreign-born voters but also the young people of all classes, those to whom the American Revolution still had a breath of smoke and a banner of sacred flame.

Perhaps, after all, only the young people with dreams and wishes in their eyes would understand his language. When his talk was ended and language had failed to measure off all he wanted to say, it might be the young who would best understand the desperation of his dreams, the unmeasured lengths of the adventure he was for.

For the first year in nine or ten years the prominent lawyer, Abraham Lincoln, had filed no case in the State supreme court of Illinois. For weeks and months that year his law office was shut up, for him; the cobwebs could come on the calfskin covers of Blackstone and Coke and on Chitty's Pleadings; the spiders and moths could roam with no interruption in the dust and leaves of the tall black walnut bookcase. The reader of the law books was out among the people asking them about old laws that needed making over, renewal, telling them violence and cunning had taken the place of some of the best laws, telling them too that some laws seemed to be made as excuses, as hiding-places, as barriers, as graves, as tombs where great human principles lay wrapped in shrouds and winding-sheets.

There were times when Abraham Lincoln himself seemed to be a sort of ghost standing on a platform in broad daylight before thousands of people solemnly unwrapping the sheets about their old laws and murmuring of forgotten oaths and wasted sacrifices.

CHAPTER 112

On an Illinois Central Railroad train of special coaches, with a brass cannon on a flat car at the rear, Stephen A. Douglas campaigned downstate. Republican papers said he carried his own brass cannon to make sure he would be saluted when he came to a town. The Democratic papers mentioned him as a friend of civilization in connection with his making the University of Chicago a present of ten acres of land for its buildings to stand on. At Springfield a banner with the name "Douglas" was bestowed on him as a gift from the shop workers of the Chicago and St. Louis Railroad. He spoke in a picnic grove where five thousand people stood in mud and wet grass, under trees dripping from summer rain.

Handbills notified the people that Lincoln would reply to Douglas in the evening on the courthouse square. In several towns Lincoln would stand up when calls came for him, after Douglas's speech, and notify the audience where he would speak. The *Chicago Times* told its readers: Lincoln must do something, even if that something is mean, sneaking, and disreputable. The cringing, crawling creature is hanging at the outskirts of Douglas meetings, begging the people to come and hear him."

The *New York Herald* reprinted from the *Chicago Times* an account of Lincoln's behavior at the Douglas meeting in Clinton, after Douglas finished his speech. "Mr. Lincoln gradually lengthened out his long, lank proportions until he stood upon his feet, and with a desperate attempt at looking pleasant, said that he would not take advantage of Judge Douglas's crowd, but would address 'sich' as liked to hear him in the evening at the courthouse. Having made this announcement in a tone and with an air of a perfect 'Uriah Heep,' pleading his humility, and asking forgiveness of Heaven for his enemies, he stood washing his hands with invisible soap in imperceptible water, until his friends, seeing that his mind was wandering, took him in charge and bundled him off the grounds."

At this Clinton meeting Douglas replied to Lincoln's speeches which had coupled up facts going to show that Douglas was joined in a "conspiracy" to make slavery lawful in the northern states. Douglas said, "My self-respect alone prevents me from calling it a falsehood." A few days later at Beardstown, however, he declared the conspiracy charge "an infamous lie."

Lincoln had run a grocery store and sold whisky, Douglas told a crowd one day. "But the difference between Judge Douglas and myself is just this," Lincoln replied, "that while I was behind the bar he was in front of it."

Suddenly came an event. Lincoln wrote a challenge. Douglas met it. A debate was to be staged. The two men were to stand on platforms together and argue in seven different parts of the state, with all Illinois watching, and the whole country listening.

A new way of taking down speeches as men talked—shorthand writing —had been invented; the reporters would give the country "full phonographic verbatim reports," newspapers told their readers.

Shade trees were few in the Ottawa public square and most of the twelve thousand listeners were in a broiling summer sun on August 21st when the first of the debates took place. For three hours they listened. Seventeen cars full of them had come from Chicago. By train, canal boat, wagon, buggy and afoot they had arrived, waved flags, formed processions and escorted their heroes. It took a half-hour for the speakers and committees to squeeze and wedge their way through the crowd to the platform. A lumber awning over the platform broke from men scrambling on top of it; boards fell on the Douglas committee.

During three hours the acres of people listened, and, the speaking ended, they surged around their heroes and formed escorts. Lincoln was grabbed by a dozen grinning Republicans, lifted onto their shoulders, and,

surrounded by a mass of Republicans headed by a brass band, he **was**
carried to the Glover House. "With his long arms about his carriers'
shoulders, his long legs dangling nearly to the ground, his long face **was**

[handwritten letter]

Finance and politics in a Lincoln letter of 1858 in the run for the United
States Senatorship. Body of letter reads: "When I was in Beardstown last
Spring, Dr. Sprague said if I would leave a bill, he would pay it before long—
I do not now remember that I spoke to you about it— I am now in need **of**
money— Suppose we say the amount shall be $50—? If the Dr. is satisfied
with that, please get the money and send it to me— And while you have pen **in**
hand, tell me what you may know about politics, down your way—"

Original in Chicago Historical Society Collection.

an incessant contortion to wear a winning smile that succeeded in being
only a ghastly one," said a Democratic newspaper. The reporter for **the**
Philadelphia Press noted of Lincoln as a debater: "Poor fellow! he **was**
writhing in the powerful grasp of an intellectual giant. His speech
amounted to nothing. It was made up with such expressions as 'I think **it**

is so,' 'I may be mistaken,' 'I guess it was done,' &c., &c. There were no straightforward assertions and logical conclusions, such as fall from the lips of Douglas. He spent over half an hour reading from some old speech that he had previously made on Abolitionism. As he continued reading, there were numerous voices exclaiming, 'What book is that you are reading from?' This tended to increase his confusion, and, after blundering and whining along, and endeavoring to tell anecdotes and nursery tales, he sat down. Lincoln is the worst used-up man in the United States. He has six appointments to meet Judge Douglas yet. I don't believe he will fill them all."

The *Chicago Times* had among its headlines: "Lincoln Breaks Down. . . . Lincoln's Heart Fails Him! . . . Lincoln's Legs Fail Him! . . . Lincoln's Tongue Fails Him! . . . Lincoln's Arms Fail Him! . . . Lincon Fails All Over! . . . The People Refuse to Support Him! . . . The People Laugh at Him! . . . Douglas the Champion of the People! . . . Douglas Skins the 'Living Dog'! . . . The 'Dead Lion' Frightens the Canine." The *New York Evening Post* reporter said: "In repose, I must confess that 'Long Abe's' appearance is *not* comely. But stir him up and the fire of genius plays on every feature. His eye glows and sparkles, every lineament, now so ill formed, grows brilliant and expressive, and you have before you a man of rare power and of strong magnetic influence. He takes the people every time, and there is no getting away from his sturdy good sense, his unaffected sincerity, and the unceasing play of his good humor, which accompanies his close logic, and smooths the way to conviction. Listening to him on Saturday, calmly and unprejudiced, I was convinced that he has no superior as a stump speaker. He is clear, concise, and logical; his language is eloquent and at perfect command. He is altogether a more fluent speaker than Douglas, and in all the arts of debate fully his equal."

President Buchanan's party organ at Washington wished the debaters the worst of luck and called Lincoln and Douglas "a pair of depraved, blustering, mischievous, low-down demagogues." The *New York Express* hit off a contrast. "Judge Douglas stands erect and has the bearing, the presence, and the thoughts of a statesman. Mr. Lincoln throws himself into all manner of shapes when speaking, and represents a narrow idea."

Lincoln knew there were people whose feeling about the principles and the politicians involved were like those of Mrs. William Cratty of Seneca, who said, "I felt *so* sorry for Lincoln while Douglas was speaking, and then to my surprise I felt *so* sorry for Douglas when Lincoln replied."

On the afternoon of September 8th at Clinton, Lincoln told the people, "You can fool all the people some of the time, and some of the people all the time, but you cannot fool all the people all the time." And in the office of the lawyer, Clifton H. Moore, he said on the same day, "Douglas will tell a lie to ten thousand people one day, even though he knows he may have to deny it to five thousand the next day."

Then came the debate in Freeport, far in the northwestern corner of Illinois, amid land made safe to settlers since the Black Hawk War put

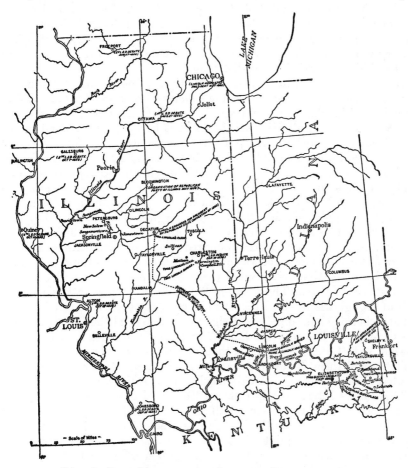

Lincoln lives fifty years in the region here mapped.

Map loaned by Ida Tarbell

the Indians west of the Mississippi. Douglas was met by a torchlight procession; the *Chicago Times* counted one thousand torches, the *Chicago Press and Tribune* seventy-four. Lincoln rode to the speaking stand in a covered wagon drawn by six white, spanking big horses. Fifteen thousand people sat and stood through three hours of cloudy, chilly weather. Mist and a fine drizzle drifted across the air occasionally. The fifteen thousand listened. Some had come on the new sleeping-cars from Chicago the night before. One train on the Galena road had sixteen cars and a thousand passengers. The platform in the grove was jammed so thick with people around it that the committees had a hand-to-hand fight in order to clear a way for the speakers. The Dred Scott decision, Kansas, the Lecompton constitution, territorial legislatures and the extension of slavery were discussed by the orators of the day. The fifteen thousand sat in the chill mist and drizzle—listening.

As Lincoln started to say, "Fellow Citizens, Ladies and Gentlemen," he heard Deacon William Bross of the *Chicago Press and Tribune* call out: "Hold on, Lincoln. You can't speak yet. Hitt ain't here." And Lincoln turned, saying: "Ain't Hitt here? Where is he?" The shorthand reporter hadn't come. The debate was put off till a reporter was found. Then the debate could go on. Not only Illinois but the whole country was listening.

From Freeport the two debaters and the shorthand reporters dropped south on the map of Illinois a length of three hundred miles—away from black-loam prairie to rocks and thick underbrush—from a point north of Chicago to a point south of Richmond, Virginia. On the way they talked to voters and asked precinct workers about the drift. The Jonesboro crowd numbered about fourteen hundred—most of them rather cool about the great debate. The place was on land wedged between the slave states of Kentucky and Missouri; several carloads of passengers had come from those states to listen. The *Chicago Times* noted: "The enthusiasm in behalf of Douglas is intense; there is but one purpose, to reëlect him to the Senate where he has so ably and vigorously defended the Constitution and the Union, and has won for himself and the State such imperishable renown." As to Lincoln's remarks, the *Louisville Journal* noted: "Let no one omit to read them. They are searching, scathing, stunning. They belong to what some one has graphically styled the *tomahawking* species."

Three days later, on September 18th, the debaters and shorthand reporters were up at Charleston, halfway between the Wabash and Sangamon rivers, and there, in the language of the *Missouri Republican*, "The regular meeting for joint discussion between the Tall Sucker and the Little Giant came off according to programme." Escorts took the two candidates along the ten miles of road from Mattoon on the Illinois Central Railroad to Charleston. A Douglas newspaper said of his procession: "This consisted of a band, thirty-two couples, male and female, on horseback, then came the Judge, the rear being supported by a large number of horsemen. On the outskirts of Charleston, they were met by the immense delegation sent out by the citizens, these being headed by a van containing thirty-two young ladies dressed in white, with wreaths of prairie flowers on their brows, and each bearing a flag inscribed with the name of the State represented by her."

A Lincoln newspaper said his procession was led by a band of music from Indiana. "Following the carriage of Mr. Lincoln was a wagon filled with young ladies, thirty-two in number, each representing a State. The wagon bearing this precious burden of destiny bore this significant motto: 'The Girls All Link to Lincoln, As Their Mothers Linked to Clay.' Immediately following this was a young lady on horseback . . . bearing the motto, 'Kansas—I Will Be Free!' In front of the procession was a banner inscribed, 'Support Abram Lincoln, the defender of Henry Clay.' At Charleston, a vast throng was awaiting the procession, and welcomed it with cheers and huzzas. From the Capitol House to the courthouse a banner was stretched, on which was sketched an emigrant wagon, drawn by two yoke of oxen, driven by a young stripling, and over the caricature the words, 'Abe's entrance into Charleston thirty years ago.' When it is remembered that thirty years ago Mr. Lincoln emigrated to this place from Kentucky, driving his father's team à la the design on the banner, this had peculiar significance. It attracted much attention during the day."

In his little reception speech, Lincoln faced the thirty-two girls whose white dresses were dusty and streaked from the ten-mile ride; above their shy eyelashes were blue velvet caps wreathed with green around one white star; Lincoln told the wagonload of them that they were "a basket of flowers." One reporter exclaimed: "Oh! how fearfully dusty candidates and cavalcades were when they arrived in front of the hotels." The *New York Evening Post* reporter noticed: "Across the main street were suspended three flags bearing Lincoln's name and a huge white banner bearing on one side the words, 'Coles County for Lincoln' and on the other an immense painting of a man driving a team of six horses. This was Abe as he appeared thirty years ago, when he drove a wagon across the country; *then* a poor teamster, unnoticed and unknown; *now* the object of almost idolatrous devotion from the people of the same county."

Twelve thousand people sat and stood at the county fair grounds—and listened. They heard Douglas accuse Lincoln of not standing by the soldiers in the field during the Mexican War when Lincoln was in Congress; and they saw Lincoln pause in his reply, step back, and take Orlando B. Ficklin by the collar and drag Ficklin to the front of the platform to testify that when he, Ficklin, was in Congress he knew that Lincoln voted the same as Douglas for the benefit of soldiers.

Even those who didn't remember anything afterward about the Nebraska Bill, Dred Scott, and a conspiracy to nationalize slavery, did remember that Lincoln stepped back, grabbed Ficklin by the collar and dragged him forward to testify. Some said they heard Ficklin's teeth rattle as Lincoln shook him. It was talked about during the next six weeks of cornhusking in the counties roundabout.

The *Chicago Times* noted that toward the south in Illinois, Lincoln "found himself among gentlemen" and was treated with courtesy, while "at

Freeport they insulted Senator Douglas, pelting him with watermelon rind and otherwise ill-using him."

As Douglas traveled from Charleston to Oquawka, one of the Buchanan Democrats, whom the Douglas Democrats had nicknamed "Stinkfingers," wrote a sarcastic letter to the *Galesburg Democrat* about Judge Douglas stopping over in Galesburg on his way to Oquawka. "It was whispered about that the Little Giant would arrive on the Peoria train at two o'clock. A self-appointed committee, numbering three persons, having hoisted their colors, straightened their hair and mustaches, and wiped the last horn off their lips with their coat-sleeves, made tracks for the depot. As soon as the cars stopped the committee rushed into the hind car. Judge Douglas was visible and G. W. Ford said, 'How d'ye do, Mr. Douglas,' as naturally as possible. Mr. Douglas replied, 'I am tolerable!' The rest of the Committee then went through the same performance, each one closing up, saying, 'This is fine weather,' then squirting a little tobacco juice and looking sidewise at Mr. Douglas. A sort of procession was now formed, consisting of one carriage and 18 or 20 persons on foot; among the pedestrians I observed 3 colored boys who seemed to be perfectly at home. Mr. Douglas had on a white hat and coat. This imposing spectacle then moved on, led by the committee, to Anthony's lumberyard, then down to Main Street. All the faithful in the city had by this time collected, and one of them went so far as to propose a cheer, but Mr. Douglas, saying at about this time that he would like some water to wash himself, put a sudden stopper on this." The letter, signed "Buccaneer," indicated only in slight degree the depths of scorn felt by the Buchanan Democrats for Douglas.

On October 7th, in the itinerary, came Galesburg, in Knox County, where Yankee settlers twenty years before had bought 10,000 acres of land for $14,000, had seen their city widen across the corn lands till it held 5,000 people, had bought stock in the Peoria, Oquawka & Burlington Railroad, established rail connections with Chicago and no longer hauled their corn by wagon nor walked their hogs 160 miles to the Chicago market. From Kentucky, Tennessee, Britain, Ireland, Sweden, Germany, had come farmers and wage workers. In the 1856 election for President there were 2,800 Republican votes as against 1,400 Democratic votes in Knox County.

Twenty thousand people and more sat and stood hearing Lincoln and Douglas speak for three hours, while a chilly northwest wind blew at a rate that tore some of the flags and banners to rags. Heavy downpours of rain the day and night before had left the air damp, and the smiling receptions to the orators during the day were carried on in raw weather.

A procession had met Lincoln in Knoxville. He had been serenaded the night before by a brass band and stepped out on the porch of the Hebard House; one man in the crowd held up a lantern to show Lincoln's face, and he opened his speech, "My friends, the less you see of me the better you will like me." In the morning he sat in a buggy to ride the five miles to Galesburg in line with a mile of buggies and wagons. Uncle Benny Hebard pointed at a house, saying, "There is where Isaac Gulliher lives." And the mile of buggies and wagons stopped ten minutes while Lincoln stepped in and drank a dipper of water with old Sangamon County friends.

West of the race track at Galesburg they met another procession of buggies, wagons, hayracks, floats, men on horses with banners; Republicans said the procession was "about long enough to reach around the town and tie in a bowknot." And they took Lincoln to the home of Mayor Henry Sanderson, a half-block from the public square.

The mayor helped with towels and warm water for Lincoln to take a bath; he saw Lincoln stripped, the lean, hard organization of muscles that sheathed the bony framework; and Henry Sanderson told men about it afterward, with a quiet lighting up of his face, "The strongest man I ever looked at."

Douglas had come in from Oquawka and taken dinner in the home of G. C. Lanphere, where he met close friends and asked them how as Douglas men they liked it that President Buchanan had thrown out the Galesburg postmaster just because he was a Douglas man. In the kitchen of the house Mrs. Lanphere was saying: "Mr. Douglas used to be very fond of my mince pies in the old days when we lived in Monmouth and he used to stop with us. I think he wanted to stay with us so that he could go out in our peach orchard and rehearse his speeches. I heard him from the kitchen window. Then he would go down to the courthouse and make the same grand speech there."

As the family took chairs and pulled up to the table with Douglas, he turned to Mrs. Lanphere and, with a shine in his blue eyes, said, "Matilda, have you got a mince pie such as you used to have in those old times?" She told him one had been baked especially for him, and, as she said to neighbors afterward: "That pie, with a cup of coffee, was all the dinner he partook of. The turkey, the oysters, and other dishes he didn't touch. He ate the pie with decided relish and remarked, 'That pie and that coffee were worth taking a long trip to enjoy!'"

To both of the candidates came committees of young men and women from Knox and Lombard colleges; they had satin banners to present. Also there came politicians, advisers, citizens, boys who wanted a peep at a famous man. And the procession that ended at the debating platform on the Knox College campus, included floats showing the methods of the Colton Foundry and the George W. Brown Cornplanter Works.

The raw northwest wind blew, ripping banners and bunting; the sky stayed gray; the damp air sent a chill to the bones of those who forgot their overcoats or who didn't have overcoats to forget. For three hours the two debaters spoke to an audience of people who buttoned their coats tighter and listened. They spilled their sentences into the air, hoping the wind would not blow away their words to be lost in the cottonwood trees and the prairie horizons.

Twenty thousand people sat and stood listening. They had come from the banks of the Cedar Fork Creek, the Spoon River, the Illinois, the Rock, and the Mississippi rivers, with hands toughened on the plow handles, legs with hard bunched muscles from tramping the clods behind a plow team, with ruddy and wind-bitten faces. They were of the earth; they could stand the raw winds of the earth as long as any two lawyers who wished to speak to them. What if one cow-milking was missed or the hogs had to root for themselves a day?

Douglas opened, speaking an hour. Then Lincoln took an hour and a half. In connection with a fraud that he accused Douglas of using, and then using over again, Lincoln said it was like "the fisherman's wife, whose drowned husband was brought home with his body full of eels." When she was asked what was to be done with him, she said, "Take the eels out and set him again."

Douglas was sitting by, in an overcoat, with a broad-brimmed white hat, smoking a cigar. When the time came for his half-hour of reply, he slipped out of his overcoat in a hurry, stepped to the front, denied Lincoln's charges, and four times walked up to Lincoln and shook his clenched fist close to Lincoln's nose. Lincoln kept his face solemn and looked Douglas in the eye, while some men in the audience got restless, started to pull off their coats, one Republican saying, "Let them come on." Then Douglas branched into another subject, and quiet came.

After the debate the *Chicago Times* reporter wrote: "The cold was intense. Mr. Lincoln, when he mounted the stand, was nervous and trembling; whether from cold or through fear of what was in store for him, we are unable to say; but before the close of the debate he was the most abject picture of wretchedness we have ever witnessed. His knees knocked together, and the chattering of his teeth could be heard all over the stand. When Senator Douglas replied, he looked pitiful beyond expression, and curled himself up in a corner to avoid facing the bitter denunciation of the Senator and the scorn and derision with which he was treated by the crowd. When Senator Douglas concluded, the applause was perfectly furious and overwhelming; he was surrounded by an immense mass of people who accompanied him to his hotel, which was thronged with people to congratulate him upon his great success, whilst Lincoln, entirely forgotten, was taken care of by a few friends, who wrapped him in flannels and tried to restore the circulation of blood in his almost inanimate body. Poor Lincoln! He was not even visible to the friends who came to weep with him."

A Galesburg newspaper dubbed Douglas "the Shortboy Senator." The Quincy *Daily Whig* reporter wrote: "Douglas actually foamed at the mouth during his speech; hydrophobia is not confined to the dog-days. When Douglas concluded, 'Old Abe' mounted the stand and was received with three such tremendous cheers as made the welkin ring. His happy, good-humored countenance—in such marked contrast with that of Douglas, which is black and repulsive enough to turn all the milk in Egypt sour—at once cheered and animated the immense crowd."

There was one disappointment in the day. Two thousand people on a train of twenty-two cars started from Peoria in the morning; it was too heavy a load; the engine broke down several times; the passengers picked hazel-nuts and rambled hillsides; just as the train arrived in Galesburg the great debate was over.

Six days later, in Quincy, on the Mississippi River, a crowd of twelve thousand people came from three states, Illinois, Iowa, and Missouri, and sat and stood listening for three hours to the debaters. And two days later, farther down the Mississippi, looking from free-soil Illinois across the river to slave-soil Missouri, the two debaters had their final match, in Alton, before 6,000 listeners.

One young man kept a sharp impression of Lincoln at Alton, beginning to speak. "He rose from his seat, stretched his long, bony limbs upward as if to get them into working order and stood like some solitary pine on a lonely summit."

CHAPTER 113

Two men had spoken from platforms in Illinois to crowds of people in broiling summer sun and raw, sour northwest winds of fall—to audiences that stretched out beyond the reach of any but a well-trained, carrying voice. And farther than that the two men had given the nation a book. The main points of the Lincoln-Douglas debates reached millions of newspaper readers. Columns and pages of the speeches of the debates were published. Some newspapers in the larger cities printed the shorthand reports in full.

A book of passion, an almanac of American visions, victories, defeats, a catechism of national thought and hope, was in the paragraphs of the debates between "the Tall Sucker and the Little Giant." A powerful fragment of America breathed in Douglas's saying at Quincy: "Let each state mind its own business and let its neighbors alone! If we will stand by that principle, then Mr. Lincoln will find that this great republic can exist forever divided into free and slave states. . . . Stand by that great principle, and we can go on as we have done, increasing in wealth, in population, in power, and in all the elements of greatness, until we shall be the admiration and terror of the world, . . . until we make this continent one ocean-bound republic. Under that principle we can receive that stream of intelligence which is constantly flowing from the Old World to the New, filling up our prairies, clearing our wildernesses, and building cities, towns, railroads, and other internal improvements, and thus make this the asylum of the oppressed of the whole earth." It was the private belief of Douglas, though he would have lost blocks of votes by saying so, that a cordon of free states could be erected on the Great Plains, with railroads crossing them to the Pacific, and that after their settlement with towns and cities there would be peace and prosperity.

Those who wished quiet about the slavery question, and those who didn't, understood the searching examination for truth in Lincoln's inquiry: "You say slavery is wrong; but don't you constantly argue that this is not the right place to oppose it? You say it must not be opposed in the free states, because slavery is not there; it must not be opposed in the slave states, because it is there; it must not be opposed in politics, because that will make a fuss; it must not be opposed in the pulpit, because it is not religion. Then where is the place to oppose it? There is no suitable place to oppose it."

So many could respond to the Lincoln view: "Judge Douglas will have it that I want a negro wife. He never can be brought to understand that there is any middle ground on this subject. I have lived until my fiftieth year, and have never had a negro woman either for a slave or a wife, and I think I can live fifty centuries, for that matter, without having had one or either." Pointing to the Supreme Court decision that slaves as property could not be voted out of new territories, Lincoln said, "His Supreme Court, coöperating with him, has squatted his squatter sovereignty out." The argument had got down as thin as "soup made by boiling the shadow of a pigeon that had starved to death."

Lincoln was trying to stir up strife and rebellion, according to Douglas, and, "He who attempts to stir up odium and rebellion in this country against the constituted authorities, is stimulating the passions of men to resort to violence and to mobs, instead of to the law. Hence I tell you that I take the decisions of the Supreme Court as the law of the land, and I intend to obey them as such." He was the sincere spokesman of powerful men. "Suppose Mr. Lincoln succeeds in destroying public confidence in the Supreme Court, so that people will not respect its decisions, but will feel at liberty to disregard them, and resist the laws of the land, what will he have gained? He will have changed the government from one of laws into that of a mob, in which the strong arm of violence will be substituted for the decisions of the courts."

Lincoln attacked a Supreme Court decision as "one of the thousand things constantly done to prepare the public mind to make property, and nothing but property, of the negro in all the states in this Union." In Kansas, the Douglas "self-government" proposed for all new western territories had been "nothing but a living, creeping lie." Why was slavery referred to in "covert language" and not mentioned plainly and openly in the United States Constitution? Why were the words "negro" and "slavery" left out? "It was hoped when it should be read by intelligent and patriotic men, after the institution of slavery had passed from among us, there should be nothing on the face of the great charter of liberty suggesting that such a thing as negro slavery had ever existed among us. They expected and intended that it should be put in the course of ultimate extinction."

Was it not always the single issue of quarrels? "Does it not enter into the churches and rend them asunder? What divided the great Methodist Church into two parts, North and South? What has raised this constant disturbance in every Presbyterian general assembly that meets?" It was not politicians; this fact and issue somehow operated on the minds of men and divided them in every avenue of society, in politics, religion, literature, morals. "That is the issue that will continue in this country when these poor tongues of Judge Douglas and myself shall be silent. It is the eternal struggle between two principles. The one is the common right of humanity, and the other the divine right of kings. It is the same spirit that says, 'You toil and work and earn bread, and I'll eat it.' No matter in what shape it comes, whether from the mouth of a king who seeks to bestride the people of his own nation and live by the fruit of their labor, or from one race of men as an apology for enslaving another race, it is the same tyrannical principle."

The high point of the debates was in Douglas framing for Lincoln a series of questions at Ottawa. At Freeport Lincoln took up these questions one by one and replied. Then in his turn he put a series of questions to Douglas, one reading, "Can the people of a United States Territory, in any lawful way, against the wish of any citizen of the United States, exclude slavery from its limits, prior to the formation of a State constitution?" The answer of Douglas amounted to saying, "Yes." It raised a storm of opposition to him in the South, and lost him blocks of northern Democratic friends who wanted to maintain connections in the South.

Lincoln showed his questions to advisers beforehand; they told him to drop the main question. He answered, "I am after larger game; the battle of 1860 is worth a hundred of this." His guess was that Douglas's answer would split the Democratic party and make a three-cornered fight for the Presidency two years later.

From a cottage on the coast of Maine, where he was resting, Jefferson Davis let it be known that he wished that the two debaters would chew each other up till there was nothing left of either, after the way of the Kilkenny cats.

Sprinkled all through the speeches of Lincoln, as published, were stubby, homely words that reached out and made plain, quiet people feel that perhaps behind them was a heart that could understand them—the

People—the listeners. His words won him hearts in unknown corners of far-off places.

CHAPTER 114

A FEW days before the first of the seven debates with Douglas, Lincoln had met on the courthouse square in Springfield a Danville Republican, Judge Beckwith. The judge was worried and told Lincoln other Republicans were worried, about how Lincoln would handle himself as against Douglas. And Lincoln sat down on the steps of a hotel, asked the judge to have a seat, and then drawled, "You have seen two men about to fight?" "Yes, many times." "Well, one of them brags about what he means to do. He jumps high in the air, cracking his heels together, smites his fists, and wastes his breath trying to scare somebody. The other man says not a word. His arms are at his side, his fists doubled up, his head is drawn to the shoulder, and his teeth are set firm together. He is saving his wind for the fight, and as sure as it comes off he will win it, or die a-trying."

He had been learning more and more to live by the two rules he had written in the book of exercises in Greek Syntax: "Deliberate slowly," and "Execute promptly." It was remembered over Fulton County that Douglas had come to Havana, and had spoken of fighting, and Lincoln began his speech the next day with saying, in his most quietly rippling and comic manner: "I am informed that my distinguished friend yesterday became a little excited—nervous, perhaps—and he said something about fighting, as though referring to a pugilistic encounter between him and myself. Did anybody in this audience hear him use such language?" And there were cries of "Yes," and "Yes, yes."

Lincoln went on, quizzical and careless: "I am informed, further, that somebody in this audience, rather more excited and nervous than himself, took off his coat, and offered to take the job off Judge Douglas's hands, and fight Lincoln himself. Did anybody here witness that warlike proceeding?" Again came cries of "Yes," with laughter and with curiosity as to what was coming next. "Well," said Lincoln, drawing himself to his full height, "I merely desire to say that I shall fight neither Judge Douglas nor his second." A fight would prove nothing. It might establish which of the two men was more muscular, but that had nothing to do with the political platforms they were running on. And if fighting Judge Douglas himself would prove nothing, still less would be proven by Lincoln fighting his bottle-holder.

Furthermore, he didn't believe Judge Douglas himself wanted a fight. "He and I are about the best friends in the world, and when we get together he would no more think of fighting me than of fighting his wife." Lincoln closed the incident by remarking: "Therefore, ladies and gentlemen, when the judge talked about fighting, he was not giving vent to any ill-feeling of his own, but merely trying to excite—well, enthusiasm against me on the part of his audience. And as I find he was tolerably successful, we will call it quits."

With only two of the debates over, Douglas knew something had hit him hard and the going would be still harder. Not only Lincoln but the Republican organization had developed a system that followed him, answered him, harassed him. The desperation of Douglas became known to the public through a telegram. What happened was told by Usher F. Linder: "A great many of Mr. Lincoln's friends followed Douglas to his large meetings, which they would address at night, attacking Douglas when he would be in bed asleep, worn out by the fatigues of the day. He telegraphed me to meet him at Freeport, and travel around the state with him and help to fight off the hellhounds, as he called them, that were howling on his path, and used this expression: 'For God's sake, Linder, come.' Some very honest operator stole the telegram as it was passing over the wire, and published it in the Republican papers. They dubbed me thenceforth with the sobriquet of 'For God's Sake Linder.' "

Shortly after the telegram to Linder, Douglas was joined by his wife, who traveled with him during most of the campaign from then on. She was a help. Lincoln referred to her when at the Capitol House in Charleston, after a debate in which Douglas had hurled wild accusations at Lincoln that he was using personalities and gossip instead of keeping the discussion on a high plane of moral ideas. Lincoln remarked to a lawyer from Greencastle, Indiana, "I flatter myself that thus far my wife has not found it necessary to follow me around from place to place to keep me from getting drunk."

From Jonesboro on it was noticed that Douglas's voice did not have the carrying power of Lincoln's. "As a stump speaker, Lincoln used Douglas up," a Galesburg lawyer observed. "In the outskirts of the crowd I could catch every word that Lincoln said, and I had difficulty hearing Douglas." One fairly accurate though slightly partisan reporter wrote from Quincy: "I was of the opinion (but I don't like to accuse Mr. Lincoln of glorying in human misery) that he even felt encouraged by the disconsolate look of his antagonist. Douglas looked very much the worse for wear. Bad whisky and the wear and tear of conscience have had their effect. So much has he changed since the commencement of the campaign that even his political enemies begin to have charitable proclivities toward him. He speaks very slowly—making a distinct pause at the end of each word, but giving as much force and accent as possible."

Lincoln had, as he promised Judge Beckwith on the hotel steps in Springfield, saved his wind, watched his reserves. His step was springy, the framework of his body elastic and rapid in doubling and undoubling as he stooped and put his hands on his knees or moved in such patterns as drove a *New York Express* reporter to say, "He throws himself into all

manner of shapes." When Douglas twisted his antislavery position into
one of race equality, Lincoln replied it was "a specious and fantastic
arrangement of words, by which a man can prove a horse-chestnut to be a
chestnut horse."

Somebody congratulated him on the sentence about the negro, "In the
right to eat the bread, without the leave of anybody else, which his own
hands earn, he is my equal and the equal of Judge Douglas, and the equal
of every living man." It had honestly pleased somebody. "Do you think
that is fine?" he asked, with a chuckle. "If you think so, I will get that
off again."

He pointed to Judge Douglas of world renown having complimented
him as a "kind, amiable, and intelligent gentleman." These were pleasant
titles. "Not being accustomed to flattery, it came the sweeter to me. I
was rather like the Hoosier with the gingerbread, when he said he reckoned he loved it better than any other man, and got less of it." At Jonesboro, farthest south: "Did the judge talk of trotting me down to Egypt
to scare me to death? Why, I know this people better than he does. I
was raised just a little east of here. I am a part of this people." And as
to the judge saying and repeating that he "had to be carried off the
platform" at Ottawa, in other words, that Lincoln was drunk at Ottawa:
"I don't want to quarrel with him—to call him a liar—but when I come
square up to him I don't know what else to call him. I want to be at peace,
and reserve all my fighting powers for necessary occasions."

Once he needed a swift illustrative cartoon, and said, "There is no
danger that the people of Kentucky will shoulder their muskets, and, with
a young nigger stuck on every bayonet, march into Illinois and force
them upon us." He told what seemed to him to be the reason for a certain
clause Judge Douglas put in the Nebraska Bill, ending, "I now say again,
if there is any different reason for putting it there, Judge Douglas, in
a good-humored way, without calling anybody a liar, can tell what the
reason was."

He gave the twelve thousand people at Charleston a free lesson in logic,
by shaking a finger at a man's face and saying, "I assert that you are here
today, and you undertake to prove me a liar by showing that you were in
Mattoon yesterday. I say that you took your hat off your head, and you
prove me a liar by putting it on your head. That is the whole force of
Douglas's argument."

He wished Douglas as a Democrat to know that the Democrat, Thomas
Jefferson, had said, "Judges are as honest as other men, and not more so."

Was one of the debaters puffed up with pride and the other humble
with a quaint Biblical humility? At Galesburg, Douglas said: "The highest compliment you can pay me during the brief half-hour that I have to
conclude, is by observing a strict silence; I desire to be heard rather than
to be applauded." At Quincy, Lincoln said: "I have had no immediate

conference with Judge Douglas, but I will venture to say that he and I will perfectly agree that your entire silence, both when I speak and when he speaks, will be most agreeable to us."

He tried to key his openings with good humor or a bit of wisdom touched with nonsense. "Since Judge Douglas has said to you in his conclusion that he had not time in an hour and a half to answer all I had said in an hour, it follows of course that I will not be able to answer in half an hour all that he has said in an hour and a half." As to Douglas's war with the Buchanan administration he would say, "Go it, husband; go it, bear."

In the southern half of Illinois, where altars still burned to Henry Clay, he referred to Henry Clay as "my beau ideal of a statesman." As to the House Divided speech and its opening paragraph, "The judge has so often made the entire quotation from that speech that I can make it from memory." A tang of the bitter touched the humor in his comment: "I agree that there are office seekers amongst us. The Bible says somewhere that we are desperately selfish. I think we would have discovered that fact without the Bible. I do not claim that I am any less so than the average man, but I do claim that I am not more selfish than Judge Douglas."

Lincoln had puzzled the shorthand reporters. Though every syllable came distinctly, he might speak several words swiftly, and then arriving at the word of phrase he wanted to stress, "he would let his voice linger and bear hard on that, and then he would rush to the end of his sentence like lightning." Thus one reporter heard him. "He would devote as much time to the word or two which he wished to emphasize as to a half a dozen less important words following."

The open air, the travel and excitement of the sixty speeches Lincoln made through the campaign threw him back to flatboating days; his voice grew clearer and stronger; in November he was heavier by nearly twenty pounds than he was at the beginning of the canvass. As he sat in his hotel room in Quincy, there came in a Toledo, Ohio, man named David R. Locke. They found each other good talkers. Would he be elected to the United States Senate? Not quite. He would carry the state in the popular vote, but because of the gerrymandered districts Douglas would be elected by the legislature. He told Locke: "You can't overturn a pyramid, but you can undermine it; that's what I've been trying to do."

They spoke of a puffed-up politician in Illinois who had just died and had a big funeral, Lincoln commenting, "If General Blank had known how big a funeral he would have had, he would have died years ago."

When Locke went away, he told of his visit. "I found Mr. Lincoln surrounded by admirers, who had made the discovery that one who had previously been considered merely a curious compound of genius and simplicity was really a great man. I obtained an interview after the crowd had departed. He sat in the room with his boots off, to relieve his very large feet from the pain occasioned by continuous standing; or, to put it in his own words: 'I like to give my feet a chance to breathe.' He had removed his coat and vest, dropped one suspender from his shoulder, taken off his necktie and collar, and he sat tilted back in one chair with his feet upon another in perfect ease. He seemed to dislike clothing, and in privacy wore as little of it as he could."

To Locke it seemed that Douglas played politics, wriggled, dodged, and worked for Douglas and nothing else. "Lincoln, on the other hand, kept strictly to the question at issue, and no one could doubt that the cause for which he was speaking was the only thing he had at heart; that his personal interests did not weigh a particle. He was the representative of an idea, and in the vastness of the idea its advocate was completely swallowed up. He admitted frankly all the weak points in the position of his party in the most open way, and that simple honesty carried conviction with it. His admissions of weakness, where weakness was visible, strengthened his position on points where he was strong. He knew that the people had intelligence enough to strike the average correctly. His great strength was in his trusting the people instead of considering them as babes in arms. He did not profess to know everything. He said wonderfully witty things, but never from a desire to be witty. He never cared how he made a point, so he made it. When he did tell a story it was for the purpose of illustrating and making clear a point. He was essentially epigrammatic and parabolic. He was a master of satire, which was at times as blunt as a meat-ax, and at others as keen as a razor."

And of Lincoln's face in the hotel room there in Quincy, David R. Locke said: "I never saw a more thoughtful face. I never saw a more dignified face. I never saw so sad a face."

CHAPTER 115

THOUSANDS of Irishmen in that year, weary of the bogs of "the Ould Sod," had come to America looking for work, and in Philadelphia, New York, St. Louis, and other cities it happened they had no jobs. And somehow the advice came to them to go to Illinois; tickets were handed them; they came in trainloads and on packed steamboats—filling the doubtful central counties of Illinois.

Lincoln wrote to Judd: "On alighting from the cars and walking the square at Naples on Monday, I met about fifteen Celtic gentlemen, with black carpet sacks in their hands. I learned that they had crossed over from the railroad in Brown County, but where they were going no one could tell. They dropped in about the doggeries, and were still hanging about when I left. At Brown County yesterday, I was told that about four hundred of the same sort were to be brought into Schuyler before the election. to work on some new railroad, but on reaching here I find that Bagby thinks that is not so. What I most dread is that they will introduce into the doubtful districts numbers of men who are legal voters in all respects except *residence* and who will swear to residence and thus put it beyond our powers to exclude them. They can, and I fear will, swear falsely on that point, because they know it is next to impossible to convict them of perjury upon it. Now the great reassuring fact of the campaign is finding a way to head this thing off. Can it be done at all? I have a bare suggestion. When there is a known body of these voters, could not a true man, of the '*detective*' class, be introduced among them in disguise, who could, at the nick of time, control their votes? Think this over. It would be a great thing, when this trick is attempted upon us, to have the saddle come up on the other horse. If we can head off the fraudulent votes we shall carry the day."

Rockford and Chicago newspapers submitted evidence that laborers drawn from Chicago, northern Illinois, Wisconsin, Indiana, and St. Louis, were being shipped by the railroads, as construction gangs, to Mattoon, Champaign, Peoria, Bloomington, and other points. Former Governor Matteson, who had interests in the St. Louis & Alton Railroad, as well as the election of his party leader, Douglas, was named as taking a hand in the shipment of voters.

The *New York Herald* was saying that agents of Douglas had appealed to the Tammany Society, and a fund of $50,000.00 had been set aside for use in Illinois. "My bones tell me that all is not safe," Bill Herndon wrote to Parker. "Quit reading and writing, if you can, and go off on a spree."

Rain fell nearly every day of the last week of October; wagon wheels sank in the roads; mud stuck to the spokes from hub to rim. Yet on Saturday, October 30, several thousand farmers out around Springfield hitched up their teams and drove in to the public square, where Abe Lincoln was to make his last speech of the campaign. Flags fluttered from wagon seats and from horse collars; red, white, and blue bunting was tied to the bridles and the whipstocks. The men and women were in their Sunday clothes, the children in their best bib and tucker.

Nine cars full of people had come from Jacksonville and way-stations. The Chicago & Alton brought thirty-two cars from McLean and Logan counties, seats and aisles full, and the tops of the cars and the two engine pilots crowded with passengers. Busts of Henry Clay and of Lincoln were pictured on one banner. Cannon and firecrackers boomed and crackled. Marchers shouting "Lincoln and Liberty" strode behind banners reading "A. Lincoln, the Pride of Illinois" and "Abe Lincoln, our next Senator." The crowd of perhaps ten thousand people swarmed around the iron railing on the east side of the Statehouse square, waves of people filling the steps of the courthouse and the Marine Bank, all facing toward the speakers' stand.

Lincoln began his speech at about two o'clock, and after a few words something happened. John H. Morgan, of Petersburg, told of it afterward: "There was a well-dressed, self-important-looking man on a fine horse who pushed his way in, up close to Lincoln, and when Lincoln said he was not in favor with interfering with slavery where it then existed, this man said in a loud voice so all could hear, 'How would you like to sleep with a nigger?' Lincoln stopped, and without replying looked the man in the eyes with a sad, pitiful look as if he felt sorry for him. The man hung his head, turning to get away, but the crowd held him, spitting all over him. Some took wet tobacco out of their mouths and threw it in his face; he was a filthy sight."

Lincoln went on with his speech. He had said: "I stand here surrounded by friends—some *political, all personal* friends, I trust. May I be indulged, in this closing scene, to say a few words of myself? I have borne a laborious, and, in some respects to myself, a painful part in the contest."

He knew that in the northern counties of Illinois he would have a far heavier vote than in most of the central counties. He was better understood politically in districts where he was personally more of a stranger. Galesburg would vote two to one for him, Jonesboro three to one against him. His final speech faced toward Jonesboro rather than Galesburg.

Facing southward, politically, he said: "The legal right of the southern people to reclaim their fugitives I have constantly admitted. The legal right of Congress to interfere with their institution in the states, I have constantly denied. In resisting the spread of slavery to new territory, and with that, what appears to me to be a tendency to subvert the first principle of free government itself, my whole effort has consisted. To the best of my judgment I have labored *for*, and not *against* the Union."

The issues were so immense, the required decisions so delicate, it was an hour for sinking personal considerations. "As I have not felt, so I have not expressed any harsh sentiment toward our southern brethren. I have constantly declared, as I really believed, the only difference between them and us, is the difference of circumstances. I have meant to assail the motives of no party, or individual; and if I have, in any instance (of which I am not conscious) departed from my purpose, I regret it."

Then came a bitterness from Abraham Lincoln's lips, spoken in words so strangely soft and lofty, that the speech was a curious bittersweet. "I have said that in some respects the contest has been painful to me. Myself, and those with whom I act have been constantly accused of a purpose to destroy the Union; and bespattered with every imaginable odious epithet; and some who were friends, as it were but yesterday, have made themselves most active in this. I have cultivated patience, and made no attempt at a retort."

And in the same tone of voice, with personal confession, he ended the speech. "Ambition has been ascribed to me. God knows how sincerely I prayed from the first that this field of ambition might not be opened. I claim no insensibility to political honors; but today, could the Missouri restriction be restored, and the whole slavery question replaced on the old ground of 'toleration' by *necessity* where it exists, with unyielding hostility to the spread of it, on principle, I would, in consideration, gladly agree, that Judge Douglas should never be *out*, and I never *in*, an office, so long as we both or either, live."

The gloaming and the dark came on that night, and the farmers had unhitched their horses and driven home; the excursion trains for Jacksonville, for McLean and Logan counties, had taken their passengers home. Trampled flags and bunting, broken whisky bottles, and the scattered rubbish of a crowd lay around the public square of Springfield.

Lincoln knew he was beaten. The Tuesday next after that Saturday might give him a popular majority, but not enough legislative districts to send him to the United States Senate. Imported voters brought into doubtful precincts would help defeat him. That was not so hard to think of as the turnabout of former political friends.

Daily newspapers had been publishing offers such as one in the *Chicago Times:* "We are authorized to announce that a gentleman of this city will bet Ten Thousand Dollars that Stephen A. Douglas will be reëlected to the Senate of the United States. Come, gentlemen Republicans, show your faith in Abe."

CHAPTER 116

NOVEMBER 2, Election Day, arrived, wet and raw in the northern part of the state. And though Lincoln had a majority of 4,085 votes over Douglas, it seemed Douglas held a majority of the legislature which would elect a United States senator in January.

To the old Kentucky Whig, Senator Crittenden, who had sent letters to Illinois Whigs urging support of Douglas, Lincoln wrote, saying: "The emotions of defeat are fresh upon me; but even in this mood I cannot for a moment suspect you of anything dishonorable."

He wrote to Judd about the senatorial contest to come two years later: "I shall fight in the ranks, but I shall be in no one's way for any of the places. I am especially for Trumbull's reëlection." And as to the expenses of the campaign just ended, he wrote to Judd: "I am willing to pay according to my ability; but I am the poorest hand living to get others to pay. I have been on expenses so long without earning anything that I am absolutely without money now for even household purposes." Lincoln's campaign contribution would amount to more than the $500.00 he had subscribed, not counting his personal expenses for travel, hotel, sundries. "But as I had the post of honor, it is not for me to be overnice." And Judd mustn't feel badly. "This too shall pass away."

He wrote to loyal friends. "Another explosion will soon come." Douglas managed to be supported as the best instrument both to *break down* and to *uphold* the slave power. "No ingenuity can keep this deception up a great while." He was glad he made the race. "Though I now sink out of view and shall be forgotten, I believe I have made some marks which will tell for the cause of civil liberty long after I am gone." Also, he joked; he was like the boy who stubbed his toe, "It hurt too bad to laugh, and he was too big to cry."

A gay lilt was in his note to Charles H. Ray, editor of the *Chicago Tribune*, asking for two sets of copies of that newspaper's reports of the debates with Douglas, and then writing: "I believe, according to a letter of yours to Hatch, you are 'feeling like hell yet.' Quit that—you will soon feel better. Another 'blow-up' is coming: and we shall have fun again."

Later he sent a draft for a year's subscription, writing: "I suppose I shall take the *Press & Tribune* so long as it and I both live, unless I become unable to pay for it. In its devotion to our cause always, and to me personally, last year, I owe it a debt of gratitude, which I fear I shall never be able to pay."

January 5 came; the legislature would ballot on a United States senator; there had been a lingering hope that Buchanan Democrats or other elements might turn to Lincoln—but Douglas had a majority in the joint ballot, and was elected over Lincoln.

Lincoln sat alone in his law office. Whitney came in, having just talked with a Republican who said he didn't like to follow a leader who was always getting defeated. "I expect everybody to desert me now—except Bill Herndon," Lincoln half groaned. Whitney went out, leaving Lincoln alone. He sat with his thoughts awhile, blew out the light, locked the door, stepped down to the street, and started home.

The path had been worn hogbacked, and was slippery. One foot slipped and knocked the other foot from under him. He was falling. He made a quick twist and caught himself, lit square, and said with a ripple, "A slip and not a fall!" The streak of superstition in him was touched. He said it again, "A slip and not a fall!"

And far off in Washington, Stephen A. Douglas was reading one telegram, from the *State Register*, "Glory to God and the Sucker Democracy, Douglas 54, Lincoln 41," and another telegram from C. H. Lanphier: "Announcement followed by shouts of immense crowd present. Town wild with excitement. Democrats firing salute. Guns, music, and whisky rampant." And to his compatriots, Douglas wired the message, "Let the voice of the people rule."

CHAPTER 117

A THUNDERSTORM had come up one night when Lincoln was campaigning at Petersburg, and he and Henry Villard, correspondent for the *New York*

Staats-Zeitung, crawled into a railroad box car to wait until their train for Springfield arrived. The two men sat on the floor of the car, chins hung over knees, and talked in the dark about the weather, crops, religion, politics.

Lincoln said he was surprised to find himself running for United States senator; when he was a country store clerk, all he asked was to get to the state legislature. And he laughed, "Since then, of course, I have grown some." As to running for senator, "My friends got me into this."

Villard felt the laughs were "peculiar" as Lincoln rambled on concerning himself for senator. "Now, to be sure, I am convinced that I am good enough for it; but in spite of it all, I am saying to myself every day: 'It is too big a thing for you; you will never get it.' Mary [Mrs. Lincoln] insists, however, that I am going to be senator and President of the United States too."

And there was light enough in the box car for Villard to see Lincoln, with arms hugging knees, roaring another long laugh, and shaking in legs and arms at his wife's ambition for him to be President. The fun of it swept him as he shook out the words, "Just think of such a sucker as me being President!"

As the raindrops ran off the sheltering box car, and the Springfield train didn't arrive, they talked on. Lincoln complimented Villard on his fluent English speech, and asked Villard, who was a German university graduate, if it were true that most of the educated people in Germany were "infidels." Villard replied they were not openly professed infidels, but most of them were not churchgoers. "I do not wonder at that," was Lincoln's rejoinder, as Villard heard it. "My own inclination is that way." This brought Villard to saying that for himself he didn't believe in the existence of God or the divinity of Christ or the immortality of the soul, as set forth in the doctrines of the Christian church.

Lincoln put more questions to Villard and drew out his anti-Christian ideas in full. And then, as Villard told about it later, "Lincoln did not commit himself, but I received the impression that he was of my own way of thinking." And when Villard later met the opinions of Herndon and Lamon, who claimed Lincoln was an "infidel," he said he wasn't surprised and he felt that he had correctly understood Lincoln in their box-car talk while waiting for the Springfield train, which lumbered in at half-past ten that night.

About this same time, however, Lincoln put into writing some interesting views of Bible characters compared with certain well-known Illinois characters. In a letter to Rev. James Lemen, Jr., son of an antislavery agitator who had stood for a free-soil constitution for Illinois, Lincoln wrote about Elijah Lovejoy: "Both your father and Lovejoy were pioneer leaders in the cause of freedom, and it has always been difficult for me to see why your father, who was a resolute, uncompromising, and aggressive leader, who boldly proclaimed his purpose to make both the territory and the state free, never aroused or encountered any of that mob violence which both in St. Louis and Alton confronted or pursued Lovejoy, and finally doomed him to a felon's death and a martyr's crown."

Lincoln saw in the two cases of Lemen and Lovejoy "a little parallel with those of John and Peter," as told in the Bible. "John was bold and fearless at the scene of the Crucifixion, standing near the cross receiving the Savior's request to care for his mother, but was not annoyed; while Peter, whose disposition was to shrink from public view, seemed to catch the attention of the mob on every hand, until finally, to throw public attention off, he denied his master with an oath; though later the grand old apostle redeemed himself grandly, and, like Lovejoy, died a martyr to his faith." Lincoln had thought a good deal over the character portraits in the Bible. He was convinced that "of course there was no similarity between Peter's treachery at the Temple and Lovejoy's splendid courage when the pitiless mob were closing round him." As between John and Peter at the Crucifixion, "John was more prominent or loyal in his presence and attention to the Great Master than Peter was, but the latter seemed to catch the attention of the mob."

The Golgotha parallel to be found in Illinois was that "Lovejoy, one of the most inoffensive of men, for merely printing a small paper, devoted to the freedom of the body and mind of man, was pursued to his death; while his older comrade in the cause of freedom, Rev. James Lemen, Sr., who boldly and aggressively proclaimed his purpose to make both the territory and state free, was never molested a moment by the minions of violence."

After twenty years the quick work of a mob, on one evening, was a lingering memory among men. It still haunted Lincoln. He wrote, "The madness and pitiless determination with which the mob steadily pursued Lovejoy to his doom marks it as one of the most unreasoning and unreasonable in all time, except that which doomed the Savior to the cross."

Lincoln and the Rev. Lemen were good friends. He closed his letter: "If ever you should come to Springfield again, do not fail to call. The memory of our many 'evening sittings' here and elsewhere suggests many a pleasant hour, both pleasant and helpful."

CHAPTER 118

GETTING railroads built and keeping them running after they were built was a peculiar process, East and West.

One day in January of 1859 the *Chicago Tribune* told its readers: "The strike on the Chicago, Alton & St. Louis Road is now becoming a serious matter. Connection of every description is almost utterly cut off between the different localities on the line and at each end of the road. The strike, be it understood, is not for higher wages but for back pay running through several months. Many of the operatives are in a famishing condition, having received no pay for a number of months. The yardmaster at Chicago took a train to Joliet yesterday where a crowd of operatives, sixty or more, took possession, ejected the yardmaster from the engine, and separated it from the train."

The strike news on the next day read, "The committee of employes at Bloomington are in quiet possession of all the offices, shops, and machinery at that point, where the general business of the company is transacted. The committee telegraphed to Governor Matteson that they would deliver up the road on condition of receiving two months' back pay and two months' wages for every month that the road was operated until all arrearages were settled. Matteson has possession of the Springfield station. We understand that all stations are in the possession of employes except Springfield."

Shortly after the strike was settled, the *Chicago Tribune* reported another curious railroad difficulty, this time in the financial field. The people of Carroll County had mortgaged their farms to the Racine & Mississippi Railroad, receiving $600,000 of bonds for mortgages of equal amount. They had hired lawyers to go into court with charges that they had been "dealt with fraudulently, emphatically swindled," and they would ask to have the mortgages set aside. Stephenson and Winnebago County sufferers had already filed suits in chancery; they held bonds to the amount of a million dollars. The *Tribune* warned farmers, "Bonds are no equivalent for mortgages on productive farms, and no farmer ought ever to touch one."

Such were a few short and simple annals of the poor, witnessed by Lincoln in the month of January, 1859.

CHAPTER 119

ONE evening in Bloomington, shortly after the November election in 1858, Jesse Fell was walking on the south side of the public square when he saw Lincoln coming out of the courthouse door. Fell was a landowner and land trader who bought and sold in thousand-acre tracts. Also he was a railroad promoter, and contracted with railroads for deliveries of large lots of railroad ties from off his timberland holdings. Also he was of Quaker blood, antislavery, Republican; he had given Lincoln a set of books by the Unitarian preacher and scholar, William Ellery Channing, on finding that Lincoln's views of religion were somewhat like his own; he was a little below medium height, smooth-faced, honest-spoken, and trusted and liked in Bloomington, which was the headquarters of his land deals.

Seeing Lincoln come out of the courthouse door, he stepped across the street and asked Lincoln to go with him to the law office of his brother, K. N. Fell, over the Home Bank. A calm twilight was deepening over the street outside and filtering through the window, as Fell said: "Lincoln, I have been east as far as Boston, and up into New Hampshire, traveling in all the New England states, save Maine; in New York, New Jersey, Pennsylvania, Ohio, Michigan, and Indiana; and everywhere I hear you talked about. Very frequently I have been asked, 'Who is this man Lincoln, of your state, now canvassing in opposition to Douglas?' Being, as you know, an ardent Republican and your friend, I usually told them we had in Illinois two giants instead of one; that Douglas was the little one, as they all knew, but that you were the big one, which they didn't all know. Seriously, Lincoln, Judge Douglas being so widely known, you are getting a national reputation *through him;* your speeches, in whole or in part, have been pretty extensively published in the East; you are there regarded by discriminating minds as quite a match for him in debate, and the truth is, I have a decided impression that if your popular history and efforts on the slavery question can be sufficiently brought out before the people, you can be made a formidable, if not a successful, candidate for the Presidency."

Lincoln heard Fell and replied: "Oh, Fell, what's the use of talking of me for the Presidency, while we have such men as Seward and Chase, who are so intimately associated with the principles of the Republican party? Everybody knows them; nobody, scarcely, outside of Illinois, knows me. Besides, is it not, as a matter of justice, due to such men, who have carried this movement forward to its present status, in spite of fearful personal opposition, personal abuse, and hard names? I really think so."

Then Fell analyzed. Yes, Seward and Chase stood out as having rendered larger service to the Republican cause than Lincoln. "The truth is," said Fell, "they have rendered *too much* service, have made long records and said radical things which, however just and true, would seriously damage them, if nominated. We were defeated on this same issue in 1856, and will be again in 1860, unless we get a great many new votes from what may be called the old conservative parties. These will be repelled by radicals such as Seward and Chase. What the Republican party wants, to insure success in 1860, is a man of popular origin, of acknowledged ability, committed against slavery aggressions, who has no record to defend and no radicalism of an offensive character. Your discussion with Judge Douglas has demonstrated your ability and your devotion to freedom; you have no embarrassing record; you have sprung from the humble walks of life, sharing in its toils and trials; and if we can only get these facts sufficiently before the people, depend on it, there is some chance for you."

And Fell went on, "Now, Mr. Lincoln, I come to the business part of this interview. My native state, Pennsylvania, will have a large number of votes to cast for somebody. Pennsylvania don't like, overmuch, New York and her own politicians. She has a candidate, Cameron, of her own; but he will not be acceptable to a larger part of her own people, much less abroad, and will be dropped. Through an eminent jurist and essayist of my native county in Pennsylvania, favorably known throughout the state, I want to get up a well-considered, well-written newspaper article, telling the people who you are and what you have done, that it may be circulated, not only in that state, but elsewhere, and thus help in manufacturing sentiment in your favor. I know your public life, and can furnish items that your modesty would forbid, but I don't know much about your private history: when you were born, and where, the names and origin of your parents, what you did in early life, what were your opportunities for education, and so on. And I want you to give me these. Won't you do it?"

Lincoln had been listening and said: "Fell, I admit the force of much that you say, and I admit that I am ambitious and would like to be President. I am not insensible to the compliment you pay me, and the interest you manifest in the matter; but there is no such good luck in store for me as the Presidency of the United States; besides, there is nothing in my early history that would interest you or anybody else; and, as Judge Davis says, 'It won't pay.' "

Rising from his chair, Lincoln wrapped a thick gray and brown wool shawl around his bony shoulders, spoke good night, and started down the stairway, with Fell calling out that this was not the last of the affair and Lincoln must listen and do as he asked.

Senator Seward of New York had told the country "an irrepressible conflict" was coming. "The United States must and will, sooner or later, become either a slaveholding nation or entirely a free-labor nation." Douglas had swept south to Memphis and New Orleans to say, "Whenever a territory has a climate, soil, and production making it the interest of the inhabitants to encourage slave property, they will pass a slave code."

Lincoln was writing letters warning Republicans of a trap. "The struggle in the whole North will be, as it was in Illinois last summer and fall, whether the Republican party can maintain its identity, or be broken up to form the tail of Douglas's new kite. Some of our great Republican doctors will then have a splendid chance to swallow the pills they so eagerly prescribed for us last spring. Still I hope they will not swallow them; and although I do not feel that I owe the said doctors much, I will help them to the best of my ability, to reject the said pills."

And Herndon was writing Parker that the Napoleonic luck-star that had shone over Douglas so often might elect him as the next President. "I shiver: there is a kind of victory fatality—a manifest destiny—hanging 'round loose' about Douglas, and this idea makes me dread the future as a child does the dark. . . . Douglas is now upon the nation, and how shall it shake him off? He is a man of no deep-hearted feelings—no wide, universal, uprising, outspreading ideas—no such thing in that little man's brains. He sits down in a mid-corner and says to the rushing world, as it sweeps by, searching for its grand ideal, 'Attend to the Here and Now—no hereafter, no higher law, no God that never slumbers, watching justice.' Well, it is too bad, but it is not my philosophy to lie down and grunt or whine. I will fight him again and again."

The man to watch was that man of many mascots, Douglas. "When you can find leisure, write me your present impressions of Douglas's movements," Lincoln wrote Senator Trumbull. Herndon had again written Parker about Greeley and others flirting with Douglas. "Are the Eastern politicians all fools? They seem to be so. I am a young, undisciplined, uneducated wild man, but I can see to the gizzard of this question. The blast of the bugle, bursting on the air, blown by Freedom, calling to her braves, rolls upon us in 1860—and where are we? Why, disorganized, hooting for Douglas, and for slavery. Pretty fix, and Greeley says, 'All right.' My dog sagacity, my mud instinct, says—fool! Let him and the world beware!"

What could the North do in 1860 with Indiana, Illinois, New Jersey Republicans, disorganized? Herndon queried, and replied, "Why, get whipped out. Greeley, horn-eyed, says 'All right, just the thing, quite practical, easy to be done.' And to which I say, 'Easy if you want to elect a proslavery Southern man for 1860.' Come, go back with me once more, and now what do you see in Illinois? Why, a well-drilled, 'Fritz'-organized, educated, liberty-loving, God-fearing Republican party, broad and wide-awake, ready for the fight, shouting for man, liberty, justice, God, and their complex duties and relations, now and forever. Greeley, shaking his Fourier head at us, may be seen, crying, 'All wrong.' Well, it may be so; but I cannot see it. We are, for Senator, whipped, but not for State officers; and so, thank God, we are this day a sober, staunch, incorrigible fact and force in Republicanism. Here we feel our nerves and muscles and bones; they are all in place, a vital, healthy, living organism, ready to function at God's order: 'Up and at them!' Excuse me. Could not help it. Must spit it out."

The *Chicago Press and Tribune*, under the editorship of Joseph Medill, gradually taking away subscribers and influence from Greeley's *New York Tribune*, spoke the independence of the Northwest Republican; "to make no alliances, offensive or defensive, with any faction, party or clique—to ask no favor—to give no quarter—to fight the great battle for the ascendancy of free principles as zealous, earnest men should—to be content with defeat as long as it must be endured—to use success wisely when we win it." A threat to Greeley and Seward and others in the East was noted. "If we are to have the coöperation of the party elsewhere, well; if not, Illinois is sovereign, and her sons can walk alone!"

Newspapers in small towns in Midwest states had begun asking, "Why not Abraham Lincoln for President of the United States?" A Chicago editor had written to Lincoln during the debates with Douglas: "You are like Byron, who woke up one morning and found himself famous. People wish to know about you. You have sprung at once from the position of a capital fellow, and a leading lawyer in Illinois, to a national reputation."

Rumors and whispers from plotters came to Lincoln's ears. As to a certain newspaper article, he wrote Trumbull he hadn't seen it and didn't wish to see it. "Any effort to put enmity between you and me is as idle as the wind. I cannot conceive it possible for me to be a rival of yours, or to take sides against you in favor of any rival." As to visiting Kansas and speaking at a convention, he would like to, but he had to keep an eye on the law practice by which he earned his living. "Last year," he wrote, "I lost pretty near all."

He struck at Douglas, speaking in Chicago on the night of the city election, March 1. Republicans who believed they could absorb Douglas would find in the end that Douglas had absorbed them. As to the judge's argument that the Almighty had drawn a line across the continent, on the one side of which the soil must be cultivated by slave labor, on the other by white labor, Lincoln urged, "Once admit that a man rightfully holds another man as property on one side of the line, and you must, when it suits his convenience to come to the other side, admit that he has the same right to hold his property there."

Lincoln softened his declaration against the further spread of slavery. "I do not wish to be misunderstood upon this subject of slavery in this country. I suppose it may long exist; and perhaps the best way for it to come to an end peaceably is for it to exist for a length of time." And to a Rock Island editor, who wrote twice that spring asking him to run for President, Lincoln replied: "I beg that you will not give it a further mention. Seriously, I do not think I am fit for the Presidency."

He sent a letter, radical in its defence of the Declaration of Independence, to a committee in Boston which had invited him to speak at a Jefferson dinner on April 6. Lincoln wrote: "Soberly, it is now no child's play to save the principles of Jefferson from total overthrow in this nation. The principles of Jefferson are the definitions and axioms of free society. And yet they are denied and evaded, with no small show of success. One dashingly calls them 'glittering generalities.' Another bluntly calls them 'self-evident lies.' And others insidiously argue that they apply only to 'superior races.' These expressions, differing in form, are identical in object and effect—the supplanting of the principles of free government and restoring those of classification, caste, and legitimacy. They would delight a convocation of crowned heads plotting against the people. They are the vanguard—the miners and sappers of returning despotism. We must repulse them, or they will subjugate us. This is a world of compensation; and he who would be no slave must consent to have no slave. Those who deny freedom to others deserve it not for themselves; and, under a just God, cannot long retain it."

Under the head of "Our Next President," J. W. Scroggs published in the *Central Illinois Gazette* at Champaign a paragraph: "We had the pleasure of introducing to the hospitalities of our sanctum a few days ago the Hon. Abraham Lincoln. Few men can make an hour pass away more agreeably. We do not pretend to know whether Mr. Lincoln will ever condescend to occupy the White House or not, but if he should, it is a comfort to know that he has established for himself a character and reputation of sufficient strength and purity to withstand the disreputable and corrupting influences of even that locality."

Then, under the subhead, "Who Will Be President?" the editor went over practically the same points that Jesse Fell had presented to Lincoln, and, under the final subhead "Abraham Lincoln," declared, "We, in Illinois, know him well, in the best sense of the word, a true democrat, a man of the people, whose strongest friends and supporters are the hard-handed and strong-limbed laboring men, who hail him as a brother and look upon him as one of their real representative men." The *Aurora Beacon* spoke likewise.

Lincoln himself was not committed as to candidates. He wrote Nathan Sargent in June: "There are as good men in the South as the North; and I guess we will elect one of them if he will allow us to do so on Republican ground. For my single self I would be willing to risk some Southern man without a platform."

Writing to the Indiana congressman, Schuyler Colfax, "for your eye only," he outlined dangers, and suggested the safe course. "The movement against foreigners in Massachusetts; in New Hampshire to make obedience to the Fugitive Slave Law punishable as a crime; in Ohio to repeal the Fugitive Slave Law; and 'squatter sovereignty' in Kansas. In these things there is explosive matter enough to blow up half a dozen national conventions, if it gets into them; and what gets very rife outside of conventions is very likely to find its way into them. What is desirable, if possible, is that in every local convocation of Republicans a point should be made to avoid everything which will disturb Republicans elsewhere." Massachusetts Republicans "should have looked beyond their noses." Likewise Ohio, New Hampshire, and Kansas Republicans.

Calls for Lincoln to speak, as the foremost Republican figure of the West, were coming from Kansas, Buffalo, Des Moines, Pittsburgh. Thurlow Weed, the New York boss, wired to Illinois, "Send Abraham Lincoln to Albany immediately."

Long John Wentworth, editor of the *Chicago Democrat,* a Republican paper, saw Lincoln looming, and told him he "needed somebody to run him"; in New York Seward had Weed to run him. Lincoln took a laugh for himself and remarked, "Only events can make a President."

He was at a governor's reception in Springfield, wore a gloomy face as he finished a dance with Mrs. E. M. Haines, and remarked that he was fifty years old. Then he braced himself, brightened, and added, "But, Mrs. Haines, I feel that I am good for another fifty years yet."

CHAPTER 120

LINCOLN was past fifty years of age, a seasoned and hardened player in the great American game of politics, the national sport of watching candidates and betting on who would win or arguing as to which was right or wrong. Without the cunning of a fox, without a wilderness sagacity, without natural instincts such as those guiding wild geese on thousand-mile flights, he would have gone down and under in stalking a presidential nomination.

Outside of himself and Theodore Canisius hardly any one in Springfield or Illinois knew that Lincoln was the owner of the German language newspaper, the *Illinois Staats-Anzeiger.* Canisius, the editor, had run into debt, and his landlord John Burkhardt took over the newspaper property and sold it to Lincoln through Canisius for $400.

Lincoln drew up a contract which he and Canisius signed. The type, press, and other equipment were declared to be the property of Lincoln, the contract read, and Canisius was free to use the property to publish a Republican newspaper in the German language with occasional articles in English.

Any time the newspaper should fail to operate as a faithful Republican mouthpiece and organ, Lincoln could take over his property and Canisius would move out; thus the contract written on legal cap paper dated May 30, 1859.

So it happened that while the leading German newspaper of Illinois, the *Chicago Staats-Zeitung,* was for Seward for President, Lincoln was the owner of a German newspaper downstate and could walk into its office, ask for favors and get consideration. Furthermore, he had kept a live political asset from falling into Democratic hands and served his party to that extent in the close fighting for control of the Northwest.

In taking possession of a printing plant and newspaper he had been "Honest Abe," with a still tongue. Not even Herndon was told, nor Swett nor Whitney nor Bunn the banker. Canisius, the editor, looked like the proprietor of the *Illinois Staats-Anzeiger* and walked the streets of Springfield as such. Lincoln had plenty else to do.

Enemies and events set traps for his feet. Friends and party workers made mistakes. Sometimes he stopped what seemed to him to be a mistake in the making. This was the case in June of 1859 when he wrote to Salmon P. Chase, the Republican governor of Ohio, to watch out or the national Republican party would look like a steamboat with the boilers blown up.

Chase and others were considering a move to have the Republican party take a stand against the Federal Fugitive Slave Law and declare for its repeal. Lincoln wrote to Chase, as one lawyer to another, a lengthy, dry paragraph on the Constitution and the Fugitive Slave Law, and then, as one politician to another, wrote for Chase the warning that the proposed move would wreck the party. "I did not write you with any view of discussing the Constitutional question. My only object was to impress you with what I believe is true, that the introduction of a proposition for repeal of the Fugitive Slave Law, into the next Republican National Convention, will explode the convention and the party." That was all he had to tell Chase. He closed, "Having turned your attention to the point, I wish to do no more." He knew that would be enough. There was a flicker of Lincoln humor in the handling of Chase, a dignified and handsome crusader who wanted to be President, and who was ranked close to Seward in the general guessing as to whom the Republicans would nominate the next year.

In northern Ohio the Fugitive Slave Law, so correctly, so absolutely, and so solemnly vouched for by the Federal Supreme Court as constitutional and American, had become a joke. State's attorneys, working earnestly, found it hard in a clear case of guilt to put an Abolitionist in jail and keep him there. Public opinion was getting tumultuous. Thousands of good men who didn't care a hoot one way or another about slavery—it was too far off to bother them—were dead set against a law that declared them criminals if they lifted a finger or spoke in a whisper to help a runaway black man. And as plans were getting under way for the realization that year of the Daily Overland Mail between the boundaries of Missouri and San Francisco, Jefferson Davis, the Mississippi senator, was declaring that Congress must protect slavery in the territories crossed by the Daily Overland Mail. Ideas and necessities snarled and showed their teeth.

Lincoln came into southern Ohio, in September, called to make speeches to help the Republicans in the state campaign. At Columbus, David R. Locke, the newspaper man, asked him why he went out of his way to go on record as favoring the Illinois law forbidding intermarriage of whites and negroes, and he remarked: "The law means nothing. I shall never marry a negress, but I have no objection to any one else doing so. If a white man wants to marry a negro woman, let him do it—if the negro woman can stand it." Public discussion was helping to doom slavery, he told Locke. "What kills the skunk is the publicity it gives itself. What a skunk wants to do is to keep snug under the barn—in the daytime, when men are around with shotguns." He opened his Columbus speech with an apology that he wasn't so great a speaker as they were used to hearing, answered a newspaper story that he had declared in favor of negro suffrage, and then took up the latest arguments of Douglas, who had been saying that as between the negro and the white man he would go for the white man.

This view, Lincoln held, was "a matter of dollars and cents, a sort of question how they shall deal with brutes." It was getting ready for legalizing the hauling of negroes from Africa to the southern states for the purposes of slavery. "If public sentiment has not been debauched already to this point, a new turn of the screw in that direction is all that is wanting. You need but one or two turns further until your minds, now ripening under these teachings, will be ready for all these things."

Addressing the Kentuckians particularly, he said: "We mean to remember that you are as good as we; that there is no difference between us other than the difference of circumstances. We mean to recognize and bear in mind always that you have as good hearts in your bosoms as other people, or as we claim to have, and treat you accordingly. We mean to marry your girls when we have a chance—the white ones, I mean—and I have the honor to inform you that I once did have a chance in that way." An interruption came when he said, "I often hear it intimated that you mean to divide the Union whenever a Republican or anything like it is elected President of the United States." A Douglas man called out, "That is so." To which flashed Lincoln's reply: "Well, then, I want to know what you are going to do with your half of it. Are you going to split the Ohio down through, and push your half off a piece? Or are you going to keep it right alongside of us outrageous fellows? Or are you going to build up a wall some way between your country and ours, by which that movable property of yours can't come over here any more, to the danger of your losing it."

He kept on with pointed questions. "Do you think you can better yourselves on that subject by leaving us here under no obligation whatever to return those specimens of your movable property that come hither? When we cease to be under obligation to do anything for you, how much better off do you think you will be?"

He was a veteran stump orator, aiming to "soak them with facts." A groan, "Oh, Lord!" came from somewhere in the crowd at one point. Lincoln caught it. "That is my Kentuckian I am talking to now." Another hearer called, "Speak to Ohio men and not to Kentuckians." To which flashed the rejoinder, "I beg permission to speak as I please." And as he took out his spectacles to read a quotation, some one called, "Put on your specs." The polite answer, "Yes, sir, I am obliged to do so. I am no longer a young man."

At Dayton, he sat for a daguerreotype, and a young man came in and began painting a portrait of him. "Keep on," he told the artist. "You may make a good one, but never a pretty one." He found personal compliments in the Dayton *Daily Empire,* a Democratic paper, commenting on his speech: "Mr. Lincoln is a very seductive speaker, and his address, although a network of fallacies and false assumptions throughout, was calculated to deceive any man, who would not pay very close attention to the subject, and keep continually on guard."

Then he went back to Springfield to the law office whose walls and bookcases he was seeing so seldom now. In a cleaning of the office one day it was found that plants had sprouted up from the dirt in one corner. They were Government seeds Congressman Lincoln had sent ten years back.

A new student, Littlefield, was digging into Blackstone and Kent. On the big table rested the feet of the new student and of the junior and senior partner—three pairs of feet. And Herndon remarked, "We ought to concentrate enough magnetism, in this way, to run a whole courtroom."

But one day in October the telegraph wires and newspapers hummed with news that none of them read with his feet on the table.

CHAPTER 121

ABOLITIONISTS had been writing, talking, singing, praying, for thirty years; Garrison had publicly burned a copy of the Constitution of the United States, calling it a covenant with hell; Henry Ward Beecher had held mock auctions of slave women in his Brooklyn church; "Uncle Tom's Cabin" was selling in editions of hundreds of thousands of copies; of writing, talking, singing, praying, there had been much. In hundreds of runaway-slave cases in the North there had been little or big riots and clashes; in Kansas had been civil war and terrorism.

Out of Kansas came a man who stole horses, ran slaves to freedom, and for the sake of retaliation and terror burned barns, stole horses, and killed men without trial or hearing. Asked why he had killed young people, he answered, "Nits grow to be lice." He had come to Kansas from Ohio and New York, a child of Mayflower Pilgrim Fathers; two of his grandfathers fought in the Revolutionary War; at his house his nineteen children had partaken in prayers and Scripture readings morning and night as they were raised up in his solemn household. As he mixed with the Abolitionists of the eastern states, he told them action was wanted, bold deeds. "One man and God can overturn the universe," he said often.

He was through with talk. Some agreed with him. The thousands of dollars he wanted for rifles, pikes, wagons, and stores were given to him by wealthy and respectable citizens who secretly agreed to call the affair a "speculation in wool," and spoke and wrote to each other asking, "How is our speculation in wool getting along?"

On Monday, October 17, 1859, telegraph dispatches to all parts of the United States carried terror, strange news. At the junction of the Shenandoah and Potomac rivers, where the states of Virginia and Maryland touch borders, in a rocky little town called Harpers Ferry, the telegraph wires had been cut, a United States Government arsenal and rifle factory captured, the gates broken and the watchmen made prisoners, Virginia slaveholders taken prisoners and locked up and their slaves told they were free and should spread the word of freedom to all slaves everywhere.

All of this happened between Sunday night and Monday daybreak. America shivered that Monday as the news spread. It was a Monday of mystery. What was happening? Was a slave revolt starting? Would the next news tell of rebellious slaves repeating the Nat Turner insurrection on a far wider scale, with a list of men, women, and children butchered in their looted or burned homes? The country breathed easier on Tuesday when Colonel Robert E. Lee, commanding eighty marines, rushed a little engine-house fort where eighteen little men inside had fought till all were dead or wounded except two.

In a corner of the engine house, they found an old man with a flowing long beard who said his name was John Brown. "Who sent you here?" they asked. "No man sent me here. It was my own prompting and that of my Maker, or that of the devil, whichever you please. I acknowledge no man in human form." "What was your object in coming?" "I came to free the slaves." "And you think you were acting righteously?" "Yes, I think, my friends, you are guilty of a great wrong against God and humanity. I think it right to interfere with you to free those you hold in bondage. I hold that the Golden Rule applies to the slaves too."

"And do you mean to say you believe in the Bible?" "Certainly I do." "Don't you know you are a seditionist, a traitor, and that you have taken up arms against the United States Government?" "I was trying to free the slaves. I have tried moral suasion for this purpose, but I don't think the people in the slave states will ever be convinced they are wrong." "You are mad and fanatical." "And I think you people of the South are mad and fanatical. Is it sane to keep five million men in slavery? Is it sane to think such a system can last? Is it sane to suppress all who would speak against this system, and to murder all who would interfere with it? Is it sane to talk of war rather than give it up?"

The state of Virginia gave him a fair trial on charges of murder, treason, and inciting slaves to rebellion; northern friends gave him able lawyers; he was found guilty; a judge pronounced the words, he must hang by the neck till he was dead, dead, dead.

And he looked the judge in the eye and spoke calmly, as though he had thought it all out long ago, and as though he might be speaking to America and to the world and to unborn generations. "Had I taken up arms in behalf of the rich, the powerful. the intelligent, the so-called great, or in behalf of any of their friends, or any of their class, every man in this court would have deemed it an act worthy of reward rather than of punishment. But the Court acknowledges the validity of the law of God. I see a book kissed here which is the Bible, and which teaches me that all things that I would have men do unto me, so must I do unto them. I endeavored to act up to that instruction. I fought for the poor; and I say it was right, for they are as good as any of you; God is no respecter of persons."

Word came from friends who planned to steal him away from the death watch. He sent back word he would be more useful to freedom when dead. He knew he could show men how to die for freedom, without a quaver or a flicker of fear. Afterward his ghost would come back and walk over the earth and tease at men's hearts with questions about freedom and justice and God. He would be a memory among young men. It is the young who count. For himself, he was fifty-nine years old, but the average age of those who had captured Harpers Ferry with him, and flamed in a scarlet deed before the world, was twenty-five years and five months.

Yes, he would go to his hanging. He would write a last message; before going to the noose he would hand another prisoner a scrap of paper with the writing: "I, John Brown, am now quite certain that the crimes of this guilty land will never be purged away but with blood. I had, as I now think, vainly flattered myself that without much bloodshed it might be done."

On the day of his doom, the Shenandoah Valley was swept and garnished by sky and weather; beyond the three thousand guardsmen with rifles and bayonets, he could see blue haze and a shining sun over the Blue Ridge Mountains. "This *is* a beautiful country; I never had the pleasure of really seeing it before." And he may have thought he had missed many other Shenandoahs of life, shining valleys that would have lighted him into pronouncing the word "beautiful" wistfully. Yet he was not a wistful man. He was a man of doom, believing in his own right to doom others, and the power of God to doom wrongdoers everlastingly.

Speaking through his bars, he had told one, "All our actions, even all the follies that led to this disaster, were decreed to happen ages before the world was made." It was all settled for him, so long before, and he was only walking as God had ages ago foreordained that he should walk. The sheriff asked, "Shall I give you the signal when the trap is to be sprung?" "No, no," came the even voice from the white beard. "Just get it over quickly."

What John Brown had believed came true; his ghost did walk. The governor of Virginia, the jailer who had kept him in the lock-up, talked about the way he died, without a quaver or a flicker, cool, serene; he died as great Virginians had died; he was an artist at dying. Emerson, Thoreau, Victor Hugo compared him to Christ, to Socrates, the great martyrs who had met death finely. Wendell Phillips said, "The lesson of the hour is insurrection." The Abolitionists shouted hallelujahs. The antislavery men had regrets; they knew the South was lashed and would retaliate.

Stephen A. Douglas called for a law to punish conspiracies, quoting Lincoln's House Divided speech and Seward's Irrepressible Conflict speech to indicate that Republican politicians and their "revolutionary doctrines" had incited John Brown.

Lincoln spoke at Troy, Kansas, on December 2, the day Brown was hanged, and made an appeal to southern sympathizers. "Old John Brown thought slavery was wrong, as we do; he attacked slavery contrary to law, and it availed him nothing before the law that he thought himself right. He has just been hanged for treason against the state of Virginia; and we cannot object, though he agreed with us in calling slavery wrong. Now if you undertake to destroy the Union contrary to law, if you commit treason against the United States, our duty will be to deal with you as John Brown has been dealt with. We shall try to do our duty."

CHAPTER 122

THE plunge of John Brown into the darker valley beyond the Shenandoah kept echoing. Sweet Louisa Alcott referred to him as "Saint John the Just," and Longfellow whispered to his diary that the hanging of Brown marked "the day of a new revolution, quite as much needed as the old one." Brown had been so calmly and religiously glad to be hanged publicly, before all men and nations, that he could not be dismissed lightly from the thoughts of men. Even those who agreed with Douglas, speaking in the Senate, that Brown was a horse thief and a murderer, were puzzled at the old man writing to his family, "A calm peace seems to fill my mind by day and by night," and to a clergyman: "Let them hang me; I forgive them, and may God forgive them, for they know not what they do."

The governor of Virginia, in a Richmond speech, said: "Brown is a bundle of the best nerves I ever saw, cut and thrust, bleeding and in bonds. He is a man of clear head, of courage, fortitude. He is a fanatic, vain and garrulous, but firm and truthful and intelligent." And to Emerson, the governor of Virginia seemed to be a "superior man." He commented: "As they confer, they understand each other swiftly; each respects the other. If opportunity allowed, they would prefer each other's society and desert their former companions."

"Crazy" was the word for Brown, said many. A Boston lawyer at a Democratic convention said Brown had aimed at "getting up a social revolution and civil war" in Virginia. Not only that, but "this traitor and murderer finds two sets of sympathizers in the northern states—one set who say that his plans and arts were so stupidly criminal, and so criminally stupid, that he must have been crazy, and should therefore go

unpunished—and another set who, moved by their own crazy false estimation of the moral quality of his acts, proceed to claim and honor him as
a hero, a saint, and a god." A plea of insanity had been made for Brown
in the trial court; in his mother's family there had been insanity, and a
dozen cases were known in his near and distant kin. For himself, he had
said: "I may be very insane, and I am so, if insane at all. But if that be
so, insanity is very like a pleasant dream." To which he added: "If I am
insane, of course I should think I know more than all the rest of the world.
But I do not think so."

The solving of John Brown as a personality was not easy. He became
a ghost, a haunting challenge. Five of his supporters crossed to the
Canadian border for safety. His chief financial backer, Gerrit Smith,
broke down in fear of indictment and social disgrace under "a troop of
hallucinations" and was taken to the Utica, New York, Asylum for the
Insane. Nine weeks previous, Smith had written: "For insurrection then
we may look any year, any month, any day. A terrible remedy for a
terrible wrong!" At that time he knew Brown's plans, except as to the
place where the interference was to begin, and he had written publicly:
"Is it entirely certain that these [slave] insurrections will be put down
promptly, and before they can spread far? Remember that telegraphs and
railroads can be rendered useless in an hour. Remember, too, that many
who would be glad to face the insurgents would be busy in transporting
their wives and daughters to places where they would be safe from that
worst fate which husbands and fathers can imagine for their wives and
daughters."

All national politics was colored by the John Brown adventure. The
New York Herald published, side by side with the news from Harpers
Ferry, the speech, in full, of Senator William H. Seward in which he
prophesied "the irrepressible conflict." Seward offered explanations in a
Senate speech; he was opposed to conspiracy, ambush, invasion, and
force as shown by Brown; he favored reason, suffrage, and the spirit of
the Christian religion. Yet his explanations could not wash off from him
the radical stripes. He knew, as Lincoln out in Illinois knew, that Seward
as a candidate for the Republican nomination had been hard hit. Jesse
Fell and Judge David Davis worked steadily on their plans to nominate
their dark horse in the coming month of May.

It interested Lincoln that testimony showed a fund of $20,000 had been
raised by Illinois Abolitionists for use in the civil war in Kansas. This
was the fund to which Lincoln had subscribed only on condition that
Judge Stephen T. Logan, of the Springfield bar, should decide that Kansas was unconstitutionally invaded by armed forces that could not be
dealt with by the legal government of Kansas. It was the fund Lincoln had
argued Herndon and others out of signing with their subscriptions.

Lincoln, on his Kansas trip, spoke in towns on the civil-war border be-

tween people who called each other "Border Ruffians" and "Nigger
Thieves"; he battered away at Douglas, rolling the words in mentioning
Douglas's "gur-reat pur-rinciple" of popular sovereignty. Politely and
decently, he recited sad political history. "Last year, as you know, we
Republicans in Illinois were advised by numerous and respectable outsiders to reëlect Douglas to the Senate by our votes." He had not questioned the motives of such advisers nor their devotion to the Republican
party. But, "Had we followed the advice, there would now be no Republican party in Illinois, and none to speak of anywhere else. The whole thing
would now be floundering along after Douglas upon the Dred Scott and
crocodile theory. It would have been the grandest 'haul' for slavery ever
yet made. Our principles would still live, and ere long would produce a
party; but we should have lost all our past labor and twenty years of time
by the folly."

As he was riding in a one-horse open buggy across prairie thirty miles
from St. Joseph, he met a two-horse wagon traveling eastward. A man
wearing corduroys, and a full face of whiskers, in the eastbound wagon,
called Lincoln's name and greeted him. Lincoln got out of his buggy,
shook hands warmly with the stranger, and searched for the face behind
the whiskers. "Don't you know me?" came the voice. "I'm Henry Villard."
They two had sat in a box car waiting, through a rain, for a train at
Petersburg, Illinois, the year before. Lincoln laughed. "Why, good gracious! you look like a real Pike's Peaker." Villard had been to Colorado
reporting for his newspaper on the gold and silver prospects there. He
noticed Lincoln shivering with the cold; a raw northwest wind was cutting
through the short overcoat that left the legs mostly without cover. Villard
offered Lincoln a buffalo robe, which Lincoln took with a promise to send
it back. They chatted on the cold, open prairie ten minutes and went
their ways—to meet again farther east.

Among the rolling gray grasses of Kansas in early winter, where lavender and silver-gray mixed on the horizons with cottonwood trees lost at
the sky-line edge, Lincoln felt how young the country was, how it had
nothing much more than a future, how its limestone houses, log cabins and
sod shanties were only a beginning. The soil, weather, and people had
promise. It was not strange that the emigrants from stony Massachusetts
and Connecticut, after arriving, had kept on in their fighting to hold it
as free soil. Nor was it strange that the squadrons on horse from Missouri
wanted to open it for slaves; it would make a sister slave state to Missouri. The nickname of "Bleeding Kansas" had been earned by two sides
visioning the future.

Amid the river bluffs of the Big Muddy, as the great clock of the midnight stars told the hours, Lincoln had his thoughts of men and history.
He knew that he had helped, possibly even he alone had accomplished,
the holding of the Northwest prairies in the political keeping of people

convinced against the spread of chattel slavery. If his life held no more, if he should lose in his dark-horse race for the Presidency of the United States, his years had held a large measure. He had been the Stubborn Man who had erected what in his phrase was "a stumbling-block to tyrants." Against what he termed "numerous and respectable outsiders" he had done this much.

If there had been any stubborn grandeur at all in the life of Lincoln, it was in his explanations of the Declaration of Independence, and his taking the words, "All men are created equal," not only seriously and solemnly but passionately. The simplest words, the shortest statements, the most blunt and direct thoughts he spoke, came from him connected with the shibboleths and passwords of the Revolutionary War. That war and the beginnings of the American nation were wrong, if those words, "All men are equal," were only phrases intended to fool men into fighting for an illusory cause.

Lincoln explained that Jefferson, Adams, Franklin, and the makers of the American Revolution understood well enough that all men are not equals. A man with so immense a feeling for the comic as Abraham Lincoln would be the first of men to understand that long men and short, fat men and lean, hard men and soft, logical men and emotional men, weak men and strong, are not equal in faculties, dimensions, capacities. The accent and stress was to be on opportunity, on equal chance, equal access to the resources of life, liberty, and the pursuit of happiness. To give men this equal chance in life was the aim, the hope, the flair of glory, spoken by the Declaration of Independence. The announcement of it was an act in line and color with Jesus of Nazareth's saying, "Be ye perfect," to people so born that they could never be perfect in mortal flesh. What then? Well then, the struggle to be perfect. Should not a young republic, a nation starting on its path of life, have a glorious and impossible ideal of perfection? So the thought of the makers of the American Revolution was that they would set up a standard, a measure of perfection for all nations as well as itself. And this standard or measure, spoken to the world boldly, hopefully, almost comically and quixotically, would be "a stumbling-block to tyrants for all time to come."

In that phrase was an approach to the bottom philosophy of politics that shaped the watchwords and actions of Lincoln. That it paid him politically in support from new American voters from Europe, and in support from antislavery and free-soil voters, who believed in the Declaration of Independence brand of equality, was a factor he reckoned with. He was a gatherer of votes with a keen eye for practical values. But it seemed that he phrased and thrust forth this very ideal of equality in such a way that it took on new meanings.

He was their thinker and spokesman. He knew what they wanted more deeply and thoroughly, more tragically and quizzically, than they knew it themselves. He made them believe that he counted the political genius and social control of the masses of people worth more in the long run than the assumptions of those who secretly will not trust the people at all. He gained and held power, votes, friends, in many and far unknown corners and byways, because he threw some strange accent into the pronunciation of the words, "The People." He made them feel he and his like were "stumbling-blocks to tyrants."

He had arrived at a sense of history. He looked into the sunburned faces of Kansans and said: "Our principle, however baffled or delayed, will finally triumph, I do not permit myself to doubt. Men will pass away —die, die politically and naturally; but the principle will live and live forever. Organizations rallied around that principle may, by their own dereliction, go to pieces, thereby losing all their time and labor; but the principle will remain, and will reproduce another, and another, till the final triumph will come."

An old legend was sometimes in his heart. "An eastern monarch once charged his wise men to invent him a sentence to be ever in view, and which should be true and appropriate in all times and situations. They presented him the words, 'And this too shall pass away.' " He had told that to his Cincinnati audience in the autumn, commenting: "How much it expresses! How chastening in the hour of pride! How consoling in the depths of affliction! 'And this too shall pass away!' " It was almost too desperate. He added: "And yet, let us hope it is not quite true. Let us hope, rather, that by the best cultivation of the physical world beneath and around us, and the intellectual and moral world within us, we shall secure an individual, social, and political prosperity, whose course shall be onward and upward, and which, while the earth endures, shall not pass away."

CHAPTER 123

LINCOLN was busy writing in the winter weeks of late 1859 and early 1860. The Young Men's Central Republican Union of New York City had asked him to be its final speaker in a course of lectures on political subjects. He was to lecture on February 27 in Cooper Institute, and he would have the chance to tell the country what was wrong and what he would do about it. So, he was writing a speech.

In the year just past he had traversed the western frontier. He had stood in Council Bluffs, Iowa, and told a man, "Not one, but many roads, will some day center here." The youth of the country, the feel of its future, was in his bones.

The winter winds blew around the public square in Springfield; he wrote his view of the Harpers Ferry blow-up. Slave insurrections couldn't be blamed on the young Republican party; twenty-three years before in the Nat Turner revolt three times as many lives were lost as at Harpers Ferry.

As to John Brown, his effort was "peculiar." It was not a slave insurrection. "It was an attempt by white men to get up a revolt among slaves, in which the slaves refused to participate. In fact, it was so absurd that the slaves, with all their ignorance, saw plainly enough it could not succeed."

Just before Christmas that winter Lincoln gave Jesse Fell a short story of his life, an autobiography. His father and mother were born in Virginia, he wrote, of "undistinguished parents," and then, feeling that "undistinguished" was too stiff and stylish and might not be understood, he added in his revision that his father and mother came from "second families, perhaps I should say." Indiana, where he grew up, "was a wild region, with many bears and other wild animals still in the woods."

And, as a dark-horse candidate for the Republican presidential nomination, he wrote: "Of course, when I came of age I did not know much. Still, somehow, I could read, write, and cipher to the rule of three; but that was all. I have not been to school since. The little advance I now have upon this store of education I have picked up from time to time under the pressure of necessity." His own drawl was in the scribbling of, "I was raised to farm work," and after various items he closed, saying he had a "dark complexion, with coarse black hair and gray eyes. No other marks or brands recollected."

In the letter sending the sketch to Fell, he noted, "There is not much of it, for the reason, I suppose, that there is not much of me." He had written the facts, for others to use. He furnished the material—for others to use. "Of course, it must not appear to have been written by myself."

To Alexander Stephens, of Georgia, he wrote with closing sentences: "This is the longest letter I ever dictated or wrote. But this is to only you alone, not to the public." It was the argument of one friendly lawyer to another. He rehearsed American history of colonial days and concluded, "All of the States' Rights which they [the colonies] wished to retain are now and forever retained in the Union, including slavery; and so I have sworn loyalty to this Constitutional Union, and for it let me live or let me die. But you say that slavery is the cornerstone of the South and if separated would be that of a new Republic; God forbid. When a boy I went to New Orleans on a flatboat and there I saw slavery and slave markets as I have never seen them in Kentucky, and I heard worse of the Red River plantations."

He had hoped and prayed that the gradual emancipation plan of Henry Clay or the Liberian colonization scheme of John Quincy Adams would work out. "Your uncle, Justice Grier of the Supreme Bench, has recently expounded the Supreme Law as I honestly accept it." And finally: "In your Oxford College orations, you say, 'I love the Union and revere its memories; I rejoice in all its achievements in arts, in letters, and in arms.' If it is a good thing, why not just keep it and say no more about it?"

Letters came asking him to explain the House Divided speech. Just what did it mean? And he would write that it meant just what it said. He would quote its opening paragraph, and write: "It puzzles me to make my meaning plainer. Look over it carefully, and conclude I meant all I said, and did not mean anything I did not say, and you will have my meaning." And to close, "If you will state to me some meaning which you suppose I had, I can and will instantly tell you whether that was my meaning."

About this time Bill Herndon cut loose with free-spoken opinions; and Lincoln in a letter to Judd remarked: "A day or so before you wrote about Mr. Herndon, Dubois told me that he [Herndon] had been talking to William Jayne in the way you indicate. At first sight afterward, I mentioned it to him; he rather denied the charge, and I did not press him about the past, but got his solemn pledge to say nothing of the sort in the future. I had done this before I received your letter. I impressed upon him as well as I could, first, that such was untrue and unjust to you; and, second, that I would be held responsible for what he said. Let this be private."

Lincoln was moving along now with some of his most important decisions and choices in politics dictated by swift-moving, inevitable circumstances.

CHAPTER 124

At the time Lincoln worked on his Cooper Union speech in the winter of 1859-60, the civilization of wood and leather was about through. Iron and coal had come. In Lincoln's own fifty-odd years of life, pig-iron production had jumped from nothing at all, so to speak, to nearly a million tons a year. Iron and coal in steam transportation had settled up the Northwest and connected that region with markets for its corn and pigs. Iron plows and iron reapers did their share in loading the thousands of eastbound box cars and stock cars with corn and pigs from the Northwest. It was the new political power of this Northwest that had broken the hold of the southern planters on the Washington Government. It was this same new power that was forcing a new political reorganization, a smashing break with the past. Pennsylvania iron, railroad tonnage, and Ohio and Illinois corn and pigs were in politics.

In the South, billions of dollars that for economic health should have been fluctuating and circulating were locked up in the ownership and maintenance of slave-labor supplies that under a wage-labor system were free operating capital. In America this locked-up capital struggled to loose itself, as in Europe it had been shaken out of feudal serfdom. The patriarchal and idyllic relations of serf or slave systems of labor instinctively set up antagonisms to wage-labor systems.

The Federal commissioner of patents issued a report, including an article by Rev. C. W. Howard, associate editor of the *Southern Cultivator*, of Kingston, Georgia, in which the writer found certain defects in southern agriculture: (1) The planter too often considers land a part of his investment to be used up, worn out, and sold as scrap; "land is with him a perishable or movable property." (2) Unsold, worn-out areas on plantations are dead capital; interest on their value must be charged to the rest of the plantation. (3) Land is allowed no value independent of the labor put on it; the negro is the investment rather than the land; market prices of negroes fluctuate with the price of cotton, but land values are comparatively unaffected. (4) The chief crops are cotton and corn, which with no rest or variation for the land soon exhaust the soil. (5) Crops require an amount of labor not known elsewhere; "the amount of labor used on an ordinary southern plantation is greater per productive acre than the amount of labor used in the most perfectly cultivated portions of Europe."

The Ohio senator, Ben Wade, replied to remarks of a Georgia senator: "We are shivering in the wind, are we, sir? You may have occasion to shiver before you are through. The question will be, shall we give niggers to the niggerless or land to the landless?" In his state it cost more to catch and return fugitive slaves than they would sell for. In Chicago, when a fugitive-slave case was on trial, the runaway negro was let out through a courtroom window; when the court asked, "Where is the prisoner at the bar?" an Abolitionist replied, "He is at rest in the bosom of the community."

A free-for-all fist-fight between northern and southern congressmen had taken place on the floor of the House of Representatives in the national capital. Three northern senators had pledged themselves each for all and all for each; if one of the three was killed the other two would "carry the quarrel into a coffin." Alexander Stephens had quoted a Greeley editorial from the *New York Tribune*, referring to the civil war in Kansas, "Better that confusion should ensue—better that Congress should break up in wild disorder—nay, better that the Capitol itself should blaze by the torch of the incendiary, or fall and bury all its inmates beneath its crumbling ruins, than this perfidy and wrong should be finally accomplished."

On the slopes of the Allegheny Mountains in slave states were thousands of white men, with contempt for negroes, yet ready to fight for the Union. In the North were men in doubt, Douglas Democrats like Ulysses S. Grant, who had moved to Galena, Illinois; Grant would not be sure whether he was against secession, two countries instead of one, until Douglas had spoken.

Lincoln the Lonely Man

Herndon the Radical   Davis the Conservative

THREE ILLINOIS REPUBLICAN PARTY MEN

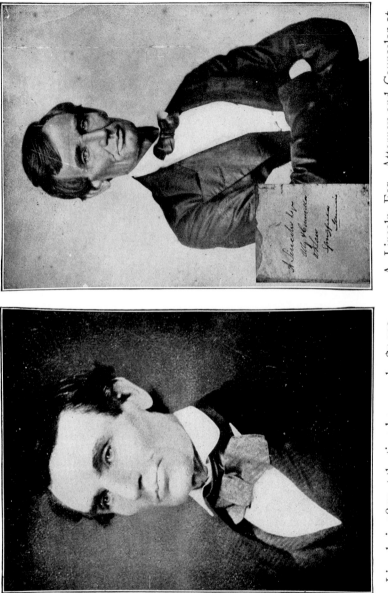

Lincoln in 1857 at the time he earned a $5,000 fee from the Illinois Central Railroad.

A. Lincoln, Esq., Attorney and Counselor at Law, Springfield, Illinois, 1860.

In the North, the South had voices, friends, spokesmen. All of New England, for instance, knew Caleb Cushing, the Boston lawyer and Democratic politician who had been minister to China, brigadier general in the Mexican War, attorney general in the Cabinet of President Pierce, close friend of Jefferson Davis. In thanking Massachusetts Democrats for naming him a delegate to the national convention of their party at Charleston, he declared the northern people were infuriated by Abolitionist propaganda, and, "I say a considerable portion of the people of the northern states are carrying on a systematic *war in disguise* against the southern states." Since the John Brown raid it appeared that Virginia must be secured against invasion from Ohio or any other state as from invasion by England or France.

"If not," said Cushing, "then are the days of the great Union numbered, and then they ought to be numbered. If not, then I say it is the right, nay it is the duty, of the southern states to separate from the northern states, and to form a confederation of their own." He threw out a warning; Republican newspapers poked fun at it; Cushing said that, unless the antislavery agitation was stopped, "it will become all persons in the eastern states to look after the condition of their property, to wind up all great local enterprises, to sell out their bank, railway, and factory stocks, and betake themselves to hoarding gold against the day of disaster, as men were accustomed to do in the troubled countries ot India—and then? Why, all history is there to tell us what then; social convulsions, hostile combats in the town streets, predatory guerrilla bands roving up and down the country, shootings and hangings, in a word, that which we have not yet had, but which all other nations have—cruel war, *war at home;* and, in the perspective distance, a man on horseback with a drawn sword in his hand, some Atlantic Cæsar, or Cromwell, or Napoleon; . . . and a line of epauletted emperors to close up the truncated series of the honored Presidents of the United States."

And while the country was sizzling with speeches, epithets, dissensions, anger, self-righteousness, Lincoln worked in the little second-story law office in Springfield, Illinois, going to the State Library nearly every day, searching the *Congressional Globe*, tracking down details of fact in history, reading clippings he and Herndon had made since 1848 from the *Charleston Mercury, Richmond Enquirer, Louisville Journal,* going through back numbers of the *Southern Literary Messenger*. He wore out the patience of Herndon with writing and rewriting some parts of the speech.

As the time came for him to go to New York and tell the country what was wrong with it, the *Chicago Tribune* came out for him for President, and he heard more reports from friends working to get the Illinois and Indiana delegations solid, and Pennsylvania on the second ballot in the coming convention. Then he left Springfield for New York as quietly as though he were going to Bloomington or Jacksonville.

In Chicago, he walked into the *Tribune* office and talked with Joseph Medill, the publisher, and Charles Ray, editor-in-chief, about how he was going to speak before the most particular and critical audience in New York and wou'd like to have them look over the manuscript of his speech; the ideas and arguments would have to stand as he had written them but he would like them to make notes as to any changes of words or phrases which they believed would improve the speech.

And the publisher and editor of the *Chicago Tribune* read the speech out loud to each other and wrote out words and phrases that would improve the text. "Ray and I buckled down to the delicate task," said Medill afterward. "One read slowly while the other listened attentively, and the reading was frequently interrupted to consider suggested improvements of diction, the insertion of synonyms, or points to render the text smoother or stronger, as it seemed to us. Thus we toiled for some hours, till the revision was completed to our satisfaction, and we returned to the office early next morning to re-examine our work before Lincoln would call for the revised and improved manuscript. When he came in we handed him our numerous notes with the reference places carefully marked on the margins of the pages where each emendation was to be inserted. We turned over the address to him with a self-satisfied feeling that we had considerably bettered the document and enabled it to pass the critical ordeal more triumphantly than otherwise it would. Lincoln thanked us cordially for our trouble, glanced at our notes, told us a funny story or two of which the circumstances reminded him, and took his leave."

CHAPTER 125

ARRIVING in New York, Lincoln was told by the lecture committee that he was announced to speak at Cooper Union. In that case, he told the committee, he would have to fix over the manuscript of his speech because he had expected to deliver it in Beecher's church in Brooklyn. He noticed that the *New York Tribune* described him as "a man of the people, a champion of free labor, of diversified and prosperous industry," and in his speeches there were "clearness and candor of statement, a chivalrous courtesy to opponents, and a broad, genuine humor." He learned for the first time that by giving to one newspaper in New York a copy of his speech it would be set in type and corrected proof "slips" would be sent to the other papers, and he would be sure of his speech being printed without mistakes.

A snowstorm interfered with traffic and Cooper Union had that night an audience that didn't fill all the seats. About 1,500 people had come, some with complimentary tickets, but most of them paying their way at twenty-five cents a head; the door receipts were $367.00. But for all that it was agreed in the *Tribune* office that "since the days of Clay and Webster" there hadn't been a larger assemblage of the "intellect and moral culture" of the city of New York. It included people who had heard Jenny Lind and Adelina Patti warble, who had seen French and Spanish dancers, who had spoken with P. T. Barnum and studied his freaks and monstrosities, who read the newspapers edited by Greeley, Bennett, and Raymond, who believed the undersea cable for instant communication from New York to London would be soon repaired. The pick and flower of New York culture was there. Some had heard of the Black Hawk War; but was Black Hawk an Indian chief or a river? Some had heard vaguely that this Lincoln person had once fought a duel and killed a man out in Illinois; at any rate, he came from a region of corn-fed farmers, steamboat explosions, camp-meeting revivals, political barbecues, boom towns, and repudiated state canal bonds. Also, they knew this Lincoln had been the first man to grapple and give stiff handling to the dramatic and powerful Stephen A. Douglas.

David Dudley Field escorted the speaker to the platform. William Cullen Bryant, editor of the *Evening Post,* author of "Thanatopsis" and "To a Waterfowl," told the audience that Lincoln had won a majority of the votes for the senatorship in Illinois and that it was the legislative apportionment that gave Douglas the victory. Closing, Bryant said, "I have only, my friends, to pronounce the name of Abraham Lincoln of Illinois [loud cheering], I have only to pronounce his name to secure your profoundest attention."

Below the platform Noah Brooks had been telling other newspaper reporters that he had heard Lincoln speak out in Illinois, and once had heard an old Democrat in an outburst: "He's a dangerous man, I tell you, a dangerous man! He makes you believe what he says in spite of yourself." But as Brooks sized up the crowd and Lincoln, he said to himself: "Old fellow, you won't do; it's all very well for the wild West, but this will never go down in New York."

Then came forward on the platform a tall, gaunt frame of bones on which hung a loose and long, new broadcloth suit of clothes, bought just before leaving Springfield, Illinois, and creased in a satchel all the way on the steam cars to New York. Applause began; the orator smiled, put his left hand in the lapel of his broadcloth coat, and stood so as the greeting slowed down. "Mr. *Cheer*man," he began with the Kentucky tang of dialect. He was slow getting started. There were Republicans who weren't sure whether they should laugh at him or feel sorry for him.

As he got into his speech there came a change. He was telling them something. It was good to hear. It was what they wanted said. He opened with a text from Stephen A. Douglas: "Our fathers, when they framed this government under which we live, understood this question [of slavery] just as well and even better than we do now." He inquired as to who these "fathers" might be. Included among them must be the thirty-nine framers of the original Constitution and the seventy-six members of the Congress who framed the amendments thereto. And he went into a crisscross of roll-calls, quotations, documents in established history connected with the sacred names of early bygone times, to prove "the fathers" were with the Republican party view of slavery and against the Democratic position.

Did any one of "the fathers" ever say that the Federal Government should not have the power to control slavery in the Federal Territories? "I defy any man to show that any one of them ever in his whole life declared that." Search all the historical records, prior to the beginning of the century, and then not only among "the fathers" but with them all other living men. "And they shall not be able to find the evidence of a single man agreeing with them." Of course, he must guard a little against being misunderstood. "I do not mean to say we are bound to follow implicitly in whatever our fathers did. To do so would be to discard all the lights of current experience—to reject all progress, all improvement." He would take all blame for John Brown and Harpers Ferry off the Republican party. And he would speak to the people of the South.

His loose-hung, dangling sleeves were by now forgotten, by himself and by his listeners. At moments he seemed to have drifted out of mind that there was an audience before him; he was sort of talking to himself. In the quiet of some moments the only competing sound was the steady sizzle of the gas-lights burning.

The audience spread before him in a wide quarter-circle. Thick pillars sprang up from floor to ceiling, white trunks, dumb, inhuman. But the wide wedges of faces between were listening. He had thought, practiced, rehearsed for this event. It was different from lecturing in Cook's Hall in Springfield, Illinois.

"His face lights with an inward fire," said Noah Brooks to himself. A *New York World* reporter was making mental notes: "His voice was soft and sympathetic as a girl's . . . not lifted above a tone of average conversation . . . a peculiar naïveté in his manner and voice produced a strange effect on his audience . . . hushed for a moment to a silence like that of the dead."

In swinging from the past to the present, Lincoln said, "And now, if they would listen—as I suppose they will not—I would address a few words to the southern people." Then he became a sad, lost, grim man, dealing in simple words with the terrible ropes of circumstance that snarled and meshed the two sections of the country.

"The question recurs, What will satisfy them? Simply this: we must not only let them alone, but we must somehow convince them that we do let them alone." What was the nub? "Wrong as we think slavery is, we can yet afford to let it alone where it is, because that much is due to necessity arising from its actual presence in the nation; but can we, while our votes will prevent it, allow it to spread into the national Territories and to overrun us here in the free states? If our sense of duty forbids this, then let us stand by our duty fearlessly and effectively."

To search for middle ground between the right and the wrong would be "vain as the search for a man who should be neither a living man nor a dead man." He finished: "Let us have faith that right makes might; and in that faith let us to the end dare to do our duty as we understand it."

There were applause, cheers; hats and handkerchief went into the air, the speaker's hand was shaken; Noah Brooks, the *Tribune* man, was blurting out, "He's the greatest man since St. Paul"; Brooks scurried away to write: "The tones, the gestures, the kindling eye, and the mirth-provoking look defy the reporter's skill. The vast assemblage frequently rang with cheers and shouts of applause. No man ever before made such an impression on his first appeal to a New York audience."

At the Athenæum Club five or six Republicans gave Lincoln a supper; over the oysters one asked which candidates would be most likely to carry Illinois. The reply was: "Illinois is a peculiar state, in three parts. In northern Illinois, Mr. Seward would have a larger majority than I could get. In middle Illinois I think I could call out a larger vote than Mr. Seward. In southern Illinois, it would make no difference who was the candidate."

The head of the lecture committee, Charles C. Nott, took Lincoln to show him the way to the Astor House. As they walked along the street, Nott saw Lincoln was limping, and asked, "Are you lame, Mr. Lincoln?" No, he wasn't lame; he had new boots on and they hurt his feet. So they waited for a street car, got on board, and rode to where Nott had to hop off for the nearest way home. He told Lincoln just to keep on riding and the car would take him to the door of the Astor House. And Nott said afterward that as he watched the car go bumping up the street he wasn't sure he had done right to get off; Lincoln looked sad and lonesome like something blown in with the drifts of the snowstorm.

In the morning in the lobby of the Astor, Lincoln saw that four morning papers printed his speech in full, and learned there would be a pamphlet reprint of it. He stayed in New York several days, sizing up "the front door" of the nation. It was a town with sights worth seeing if there was time. From his hotel room it was an easy walk to where, not so long before, the Dead Rabbits and the Bowery Boys had been in a gang fight and put up barricades and fought off the police and held their barricades till state troops arrived. Nor was it far to where Laura Keene, the actress manager, had put on her new successful play, "Our American Cousin."

He heard Beecher give a sermon and, coming away with James A. Briggs, walked past the city post office. Briggs mentioned that it was a dirty, disreputable-looking post office for a city like New York. And he put the question whether Lincoln, if he happened to be elected President, would recommend a million dollars for a new post office. Lincoln answered, "I'll make a note of that." He was taken to the studio of Brady and photographed; as the picture came out he looked satisfied with himself; it wasn't his usual face.

When New York papers carrying the Cooper Union speech arrived in the *Chicago Tribune* office, Medill and Ray were glad to see the compliments paid to Lincoln. "Ray and I plunged eagerly into the report, feeling quite satisfied with the successful effect of the polish we had applied to the address," said Medill in telling about it afterward. "We both got done reading it about the same time. With a sickly sort of smile, Dr. Ray looked at me and remarked, 'Medill, old Abe must have lost out of the car window all our precious notes, for I don't find a trace of one of them in his published talk here.' I tried to laugh and said, 'This must have been meant for one of his waggish jokes.' " And the publisher and editor promised to keep the joke a secret.

In Springfield, as the train had carried Lincoln away for his eastern trip, the *Illinois State Register*, a Democratic paper, printed a paragraph headed "Significant" with the comment, "The Hon. Abraham Lincoln departs today for Brooklyn under an engagement to deliver a lecture before the Young Men's Association in that city in Beecher's church. Subject: not known. Consideration: $200 and expenses. Object: presidential capital. Effect: disappointment." But on March 7, two weeks later, the *Illinois State Journal*, the Republican daily paper in Springfield, had received the New York papers and published the Cooper Union speech in full, commenting editorially: "The tones, the gestures, the kindling eye, and mirth-provoking look defy the reporter's skill. No man ever before made such an impression on his first appeal to a New York audience."

Senator Seward in Washington didn't exactly like to see the *New York Times* reporting, "There was a very large meeting of Republicans at Cooper Institute last night to listen to that noted political exhorter and prairie orator, Abe Lincoln. The speaker, as soon as he appeared on the platform, was vehemently cheered, and during the delivery of his address frequently applauded." It was this same week that Joseph Medill had sent to his *Chicago Tribune* an editorial showing, from his view, that Lincoln could be elected President that year and Seward couldn't. When Seward read this editorial he took his hat and hunted up Medill. And Medill told a friend: "Seward 'blew me up' tremendously for having disappointed him, and preferring that 'prairie statesman,' as he called Lincoln. He gave me to understand that he was the chief teacher of the principles of the Republican party before Lincoln was known other than as a country lawyer in Illinois."

CHAPTER 126

Two days after Lincoln's Cooper Union speech, his chief rival, Senator Seward, the man leading all others in the race for the Republican presidential nomination, delivered a speech in the Senate, soothing in tone, so different from his Irrepressible Conflict speech that it drew the criticism he was backing down and phrasing his talk "so as to suit Wall Street." Over the country there was among many of the wealthy and conservative a shifting of view: slaves were property; slave ownership was property ownership; to disturb the right to own slaves might disturb other rights and interfere with the proper conduct of business in general.

In Chicago, Cyrus H. McCormick, the harvesting-machinery manufacturer, had blamed Lincoln's House Divided speech, in part, for the John Brown raid, and in giving $100,000.00 to a Presbyterian theological seminary, McCormick insisted that the pastor of his own church should be the seminary president and an antislavery man ousted. Fitzhugh, the Virginia sociologist, was carrying on his propaganda that free society based on democracy had failed in America as in Europe. In simple words rarely heard in the United States Senate, Wigfall of Texas had said: "I am a plain, blunt-spoken man. We say that man has a right to property in man. We say that slaves are our *property*. We say that it is the duty of every government to protect its property everywhere. If you wish to settle this matter, declare that slaves *are* property, and like all other property entitled to be protected in every quarter of the globe, on land and sea. Say that to us, and then the difficulty is settled." Jefferson Davis was saying, "Slave property is the only private property in the United States specifically recognized in the Constitution and protected by it."

Robert Toombs, the Georgia senator, had spoken to a large and fashionable audience in Tremont Temple, Boston. "The great conflict between capital and labor, under free competition, has ever been how the earnings of labor shall be divided between them," said Toombs; "and in this division the southern slave has a marked advantage over the English laborer, and is often equal to the free laborer of the North." In the South the slaves were not driven to crime by hunger, while "Lord Ashley's report to the British Parliament, shows that in the capital of that empire, hunger alone daily drives thousands of men and women into the abyss of crimes."

As to marriage relations among slaves, said Toombs: "Fewer children are born out of wedlock among slaves, than in the capitals of two of the most civilized countries of Europe—Austria and France; in the former, one-half of the children are thus born, in the latter more than one-fourth." No standing armies nor police were required to keep the peace among the southern slaves "while the evidence of discontent and the appliance of force to repress it are everywhere visible among the toiling millions of the earth; even in the northern states of this Union, strikes and mobs, unions and combinations against employers, attest at once the misery and discontent of labor among them."

In the North were nearly four million wage workers; in the South nearly four million slave workers; common labor in the North was being paid from sixty cents to a dollar a day; it was a bare living wage. Toombs suggested that if so many more wage workers crowded into the northern labor market that wages reached a bare subsistence point, then slave labor in the South would automatically be abolished; it would be cheaper for Southern capital to buy wage-earning labor than to invest in slaves. Toombs did not dwell long on this point; he set it up as a little grinning skeleton of economic science and was off to other points.

At the altars of the Hebrew race it was slaveholding priests and patriarchs who received the revelations from the Most High. "The highest forms of ancient civilization and the noblest development of the individual man are to be found in the ancient slaveholding commonwealths of Greece and Rome." As to the southern people, he quoted from Edmund Burke: "These people of the southern colonies are much more strongly, and with a higher and more stubborn spirit attached to liberty than those to the northward. In such a people the haughtiness of domination combines itself with the spirit of freedom, fortifies it, and renders it invincible." The fourteen states of the South held ten millions of inhabitants, "rich, powerful, educated, moral, refined, prosperous, and happy." Thus Atlanta spoke to Boston. Old friendships were far past the breaking point.

Edwin A. Pollard of Virginia had just published "Black Diamonds," calling for the African slave trade to be made lawful again; then negroes fresh from the jungles could be sold in southern seaports at $100.00 to $150.00 a head. "The poor man might then hope to own a negro; the prices of labor would then be in his reach; he would be a small farmer revolutionizing the character of agriculture in the South; he would at once step up to a respectable station in the social system of the South; and with this he would acquire a practical and dear interest in the general institution of slavery that would constitute its best protection both at home and abroad. He would no longer be a miserable, nondescript cumberer of the soil, scratching the land here and there for a subsistence, living from hand to mouth, or trespassing along the borders of the possessions of the large proprietors. He would be a proprietor himself."

Pollard could vision steps and advances "toward the rearing of that great Southern Empire, whose seat is eventually to be in Central America, and whose boundaries are to enclose the Gulf of Mexico." Ahead were "magnificent fields of romance" for the South, as he saw its future.

The South Carolina senator, James H. Hammond, son of a Connecticut Yankee who had emigrated from New England to the South, rose one day to tell his colleagues of the North: "The difference between us is that our slaves are hired for life and well compensated; there is no starvation, no begging, no want of employment. Yours are hired by the day, not cared for, and scantily compensated. Why, you meet more beggars in one day, in any single street of the city of New York than you would meet in a lifetime in the whole South. We do not think that whites should be slaves, either by law or necessity. Our slaves are black, of another and inferior race. They are elevated from a condition in which God first created them, by being made our slaves. None of that race on the whole face of the globe can be compared with the slaves of the South. They are happy, content, unaspiring, and utterly incapable, from intellectual weakness, ever to give any trouble by their aspirations.

"Your slaves are white, of your own race; you are brothers of one blood," Hammond told the North. "They are your equals in natural endowment of intellect, and they feel galled by their degradation. Our slaves do not vote. We give them no political power. Yours do vote; and being the majority, they are the depositaries of all your political power. If they knew the tremendous secret, that the ballot box is stronger than an army of bayonets, and could combine, where would you be? Your society would be reconstructed, your government overthrown, your property divided, not as they have mistakenly attempted to initiate such proceedings by meetings in parks. with arms in their hands, but by the quiet process of the ballot box. You have been making war on us to our very hearthstones. How would you like us to send lecturers or agitators North, to teach these people this, to aid and assist in combining, and to lead them?"

The Massachusetts senator, Henry Wilson, replied: "Wages in the North are 100 per cent higher than in the South. In the iron mills in Massachusetts, they paid the laborers [1850] $30.00 a month; in South Carolina the workingmen of the same occupation received $15.00. I have lived by daily labor, but I never felt galled by the degradation."

The fresh stream of wage labor arriving in northern states from Europe would have to be met by fresh importations of slave labor from Africa, if the South was to grow and hold its own. Alexander Stephens wrote to J. Henly Smith, correcting a comment on his views: "I certainly meant to say nothing except what is clearly expressed—that was that unless we get immigration from abroad we shall have but few more slave states. This great truth seems to take the people by surprise. Some shrink from it as they would from death. Still it is as true as death."

The facts that the heart and mind had to play on and work with were troubled. It was a proper time for one of the lunatics in a New England asylum to cry out one day that he had hit it, he could solve the slavery question. "Let the niggers be whitewashed."

While the "ultras" and fire-eaters" of the South called for secession from the Union, the state of Massachusetts ran close to the act of secession in passing a Personal Liberty Bill aimed to stop operation of the Federal Fugitive Slave Law. The Massachusetts Antislavery Society resolved, "We do hereby declare ourselves the enemies of the Constitution, Union, and Government of the United States, and the friends of the new confederacy of states, where there shall be no union with slaveholders."

As the national muddle was getting more muddled, Lincoln made campaign speeches for the Republicans in New England states, and visited his boy, Robert, studying to enter Harvard in a preparatory school at Exeter, New Hampshire. Speaking at Hartford, Connecticut, he discussed property and the property angle of the slavery question. "One-sixth of the population of the United States are slaves, looked upon as property, as nothing but property. The cash value of these slaves, at a moderate estimate, is two billion dollars. This amount of property value has a vast influence on the minds of its owners, very naturally. The same amount of property would have an equal influence upon us if owned in the North. Human nature is the same—people at the South are the same as those at the North, barring the difference in circumstances. Public opinion is founded, to a great extent, on a property basis. What lessens the value of property is opposed; what enhances its value is favored. Public opinion at the South regards slaves as property, and insists upon treating them like other property. Public opinion settles every question here; any policy to be permanent must have public opinion at the bottom. The property basis will have its weight. The love of property and a consciousness of right and wrong have conflicting places in our organization which often make a man's course seem crooked, his conduct a riddle."

Lincoln knew that these statements of his, with all their delicate shadings of language, and the implication behind them, would unlock many secrets of his own conduct. At New Haven the next day he again made allusions to the property phase of slavery. He pointed to "two thousand millions of dollars invested in this species of property" being a concentrated and immense pecuniary interest that had its influence on the minds of the owners of the property. "The owners of these slaves consider them property. The effect upon the minds of the owners is that of property and nothing else." It carried them into politics "to insist upon all that will favorably affect its value as property, to demand laws and institutions and a public policy that shall increase and secure its value, and make it durable, lasting, and universal. The effect on the minds of the owners is to persuade them that there is no wrong in it." The slaveholder does not like to be called bad names; he struggles within himself and sets about arguing himself into the belief that slavery is right. The property influences his mind.

"The dissenting minister who argued some theological point with one of the Established Church was met by the reply, 'I can't see it so.' He opened the Bible and pointed him to a passage, but the orthodox minister replied, 'I can't see it so.' Then he showed him a single word. 'Can you see that?' 'Yes, I see it,' was the reply. The dissenter laid a guinea over the word, and asked, 'Do you see it now?' So here."

And with what the New York reporter had called his "kindling eye and mirth-provoking gesture," Lincoln remarked: "Whether the owners of this species of property do really see it as it is, it is not for me to say; but if they do, they see it as it is through two billions of dollars, and that is a pretty thick coating."

Shoe-factory workers were on strike in Connecticut and Massachusetts cities; they said they had the grievance that they couldn't live on wages of $250.00 a year. Douglas had said the strike was caused by "this unfortunate sectional warfare," to which Lincoln replied, "Thank God that we have a system of labor where there can be a strike."

Thus at Hartford. At New Haven, even while still a dark-horse candidate for the Republican presidential nomination, he told the striking shoe-workers: "I do not pretend to know all about the matter. . . . I am glad to see that a system of labor prevails in New England under which laborers can strike when they want to, where they are not obliged to work under all circumstances, and are not tied down and obliged to labor whether you pay them or not! I like a system which lets a man quit when he wants to, and wish it might prevail everywhere. I don't believe in a law to prevent a man from getting rich; it would do more harm than good. So while we do not propose any war upon capital, we do wish to allow the humblest man an equal chance to get rich with everybody else. When one starts poor, as most do in the race of life, free society is such that he knows he can better his condition; he knows that there is no fixed condition of labor for his whole life."

He wanted New England good will, and gave it good will in spreads. He had noticed the stony soil of New England, "and yet where will you find wealthy men so wealthy, and poverty so rarely in extremity? There is not another such place on earth!" He wished them to believe he was their friend, that he could understand how the toils of life thrust workingmen and their families hither and yon. "I desire that if you [people] get too thick here, and find it hard to better your condition on this soil, you may have a chance to strike out and go somewhere else, where you may not be degraded, nor have your family corrupted by forced rivalry with negro slaves. I want you to have a clean bed and no snakes in it!"

He battered away at Douglas. The one personal target he took shots of argument at, in every speech, was Douglas; the one man standing most in the way of the Republican party was Douglas. It was Douglas who had debauched public opinion on the Declaration of Independence more than any one else. And now "Douglas's new sedition law must be enacted and enforced, suppressing all declarations that slavery is wrong, whether made in politics, in presses, in pulpits, or in private. We must arrest and return their fugitive slaves. So long as we call slavery wrong, whenever a slave runs away they will overlook the obvious fact that he ran because he was oppressed, and declare that he was stolen off. Whenever a master cuts his slaves with the lash, and they cry out under it, he will overlook the obvious fact that the negroes cry out because they are hurt, and insist that they were put up to it by some rascally Abolitionist."

After the strain of facing intellectual and ethical New York at Cooper Union, Lincoln had a good time meeting crowds of Yankee workmen; he let loose his rippling humor in every speech. He referred to a white list got up by southern consumers; they would buy only in the North of those factories and mills considered "fair." A southern senator, Mason, had taken his seat in the Capitol one day in a queer suit of clothes, all made of southern homespun. "Senator Mason has quit buying!" said Lincoln. "To carry out his idea he ought to go barefoot. If that's the plan, they should begin at the foundation, and adopt the well-known 'Georgia costume' of a shirt-collar and a pair of spurs."

The disunionist movement thus far reminded him of a man who had a poor, old, lean, bony, spavined horse, with swollen legs. And the man was asked what he was going to do; the horse seemed to be dying. "Do?" he answered. "I'm going to fat him up; don't you see that I've got him seal-fat as high as the knees?" So with disunion. "They have got the Union dissolved up to the ankle, but no farther."

Some of the slanders on foot were a political "bushwhacking," due to the desperation of the Democrats. "At the Battle of Waterloo when Napoleon's cavalry had charged again and again upon the unbroken squares of British infantry, at last they were giving up the attempt, and going off in disorder, when some of the officers, in mere vexation and complete despair, fired their pistols at those solid squares."

CHAPTER 127

The genius of America then was swift, impetuous. "To the stars by hard ways," was written lean on many faces. "Take a chance," was a governing slogan among a million young men interested, after the day's work, in horse races, fights, dances, music, women. "The cowards never started and the weak ones died by the way." The past was, perhaps, to be forgotten, the future to be cherished. Around frontier camp fires a man might laugh of a sudden, "Let's all of us tell our real names." Many even of the unread could understand Bill Green's point: "New Salem neighborhood has no principal citizen; every man there is a principal citizen."

One summer evening Lincoln had sat on the front porch of the Judd home on Lake Shore Drive in Chicago. The plumes of steamboat smoke and the white canvas of sailboats met the eye as twilight glimmered and failed, and a red rim of a big slow moon pushed up the horizon where the sky line touched the water line of Lake Michigan. The stars came out and a silver sheen glistened on the lake waves breaking and rippling on the beach sand.

The night brought a slow surprise for Mrs. Judd. Something came into the air that evening that set Lincoln to talking to the company on the porch, and his talk was of far things, of man in old times and man in times to come. In the old times of the Bible, and earlier than that, men had looked at the stars and contemplated the mystery of the lighted clusters and forms on the sky.

Then the telescope had come, and the astronomers had found endless series of new stars, and of suns beyond our sun. The creature, man, so restless, must go on finding new worlds, would in the centuries to come be no more satisfied. It would be interesting to guess what man might do in the next thousand years.

Lincoln spoke in an easy, melodious drawl, and Mr. and Mrs. Judd felt that they had heard him in a mood when he believed that with man all things are possible. A chill came on the air; they went into the parlor, where Lincoln sat on the sofa, with his legs stretched out over the carpet, his arms folded behind his back, talking about the earliest times of various discoveries and inventions. He had got into arguments about when brass, gold, and silver instruments, besides precious metals, first came into use, had gone to the Bible for information, and made memoranda.

And when Lincoln had gone to his hotel, Mr. Judd remarked to Mrs. Judd that he was surprised at the way Lincoln was constantly perfecting himself as a scholar. As to the evening's talk by Lincoln, "A professor at Yale could not have been more interesting or more enthusiastic," Mr. Judd remarked to Mrs. Judd.

It was a year when Democratic newspapers had pictured Lincoln as oily, simpering, apologetic. Nominal friends said, "He's slick." He was the only thinker and leader in the Northwest, of wide and commanding strength, who had won a large confidence among the Abolitionist and anti-slavery forces, without coming out flat-footed for violation of the Fugitive Slave Law.

When a runaway slave was captured, and A. J. Grover at Ottawa was in danger of going to jail for helping a runaway slave, he and Lincoln sat and talked over the case. The law was wrong in taking a man's liberty away without trial by jury, Grover told Lincoln, "not only unconstitutional but inhuman." And Lincoln, with his face alive and mournful, brandishing his long right arm, brought it down on his knee, saying: "Oh, it is ungodly! It is ungodly! No doubt it is ungodly! But it is the law of the land, and we must obey it as we find it."

To which Grover said: "Mr. Lincoln, how often have you sworn to support the Constitution? We propose to elect you President. How would you look taking an oath to support what you declare is an ungodly Constitution, and asking God to help you?"

It was a stinger for Lincoln; his head sloped forward; he ran his fingers through his hair; he dropped into a sad and desperate mood, and came out of it placing his hand on Grover's knee, and saying in a mournfully quizzical manner, "Grover, it's no use to be always looking up these hard spots."

CHAPTER 128

FIVE days before Lincoln had started East to give his Cooper Union speech, he delivered a lecture in Springfield for the benefit of the Springfield Library Association, admission twenty-five cents. He stood on the platform and read the lecture, glancing through his spectacles at times to see how the audience was taking it while he rambled along with facts, but no rhetorical "fizzlegigs," on the subject of "Discoveries and Inventions." The audience was cool; a few chuckled quietly; nearly all wondered just what he was driving at. They were sure, as he was himself, that he was not in a class with lecturers like Henry Ward Beecher, who was paid $125.00 a night.

The lecture was no go; it didn't have the "git" to it. When a Galesburg committee asked if he could come there and lecture, he wrote: "I read a sort of lecture to three different audiences last month and this; but I did so under circumstances which made it no waste of time whatever." A Chicago literary institute was notified: "I am not a professional lecturer. Have never got up but one lecture, and that I think rather a poor one."

At Jacksonville the door receipts were small, and Lincoln told the committee: "Be hopeful, boys. Pay my railroad fare and fifty cents for my supper at the hotel and we'll call it square." Whitney joked about reading in a newspaper that Lincoln had gone to Clinton to deliver a lecture; nobody came to hear him and he had gone home without having lectured; and the newspaper commented, "That don't look much like his being President." Lincoln begged Whitney: "Don't mention that; it plagues me." The popular lecture audience didn't care about Lincoln; they wouldn't turn out and buy tickets to hear him.

At the Wisconsin state fair in Milwaukee in the autumn, Lincoln made free to speak as a philosopher, a scientist, even as one with kinks of invention in his mind. "I have thought a good deal, in an abstract way, about a steam plow." In the four years past the ground planted with corn in Illinois had produced about twenty bushels to the acre. "The soil has never been pushed up to one-half of its capacity." He recommended "deeper plowing, analysis of the soils, experiments with manures and varieties of seeds, observance of seasons." He told them that for the farmer with time for it, "Every blade of grass is a study," and that.

"Not grass alone, but soils, seeds, seasons—hedges, ditches, and fences—plowing, hoeing, and harrowing—reaping, mowing, and threshing—saving crops, pests of crops, diseases of crops, and what will prevent or cure them—hogs, horses, and cattle," besides many other things and ways on the farm, were "each a world of study in itself."

He had, to begin with, made a proper apology. "I presume I am not expected to employ the time assigned me in the mere flattery of the farmers as a class. My opinion of them is that, in proportion to numbers, they are neither better nor worse than other people." Also, as regards farmers: "I really believe there are more attempts at flattering them than any other class, the reason of which I cannot perceive, unless it be that they cast more votes than any other. On reflection, I am not quite sure that there is not cause for suspicion against you in selecting me, in some sort a politician and in no sort a farmer, to address you."

Farmers with big farms listened with sharp ears at his saying: "The ambition for broad acres leads to poor farming, even with men of energy. I scarcely ever knew a mammoth farm to sustain itself, much less to return a profit upon the outlay. I have more than once known a man to spend a respectable fortune upon one, fail, and leave it, and then some man of modest aims get a small fraction of the ground, and make a good living upon it. Mammoth farms are like tools or weapons which are too heavy to be handled."

Lincoln saw the country as new and young, with plenty of opportunity for the hired laborer to get a farm for himself. "There is no such thing as a free man being fatally fixed for life in the condition of a hired laborer." Some reasoners held: "Labor is prior to, and independent of, capital; in fact, capital is the fruit of labor, and could never have existed if labor had not first existed; labor can exist without capital, but capital could never have existed without labor. Hence labor is the superior—greatly the superior—of capital."

There were those who declared the working class to be the mudsills on which the structure of the upper class rested. "According to that theory," Lincoln told his farmers, "a blind horse upon a treadmill is a perfect illustration of what a laborer should be—all the better for being blind, that he could not kick understandingly." By that theory education for the workers was regarded as dangerous. "A Yankee who could invent a strong-handed man without a head would receive the everlasting gratitude of the 'mudsill' advocates."

His left hand loosened from the coat lapel, and his two long arms stretched out with quivering fingers, and he spoke strange and simple words that seemed to be part of the sun and the air and soil of Wisconsin that day. If there were laws of God or reason they must be built of the propositions he offered—almost through the shining of salt tears. "Free labor argues that as the Author of man makes every individual with one head and one pair of hands, it was probably intended that heads and hands should coöperate as friends, and that that particular head should direct and control that pair of hands. As each man has one mouth to be fed, and one pair of hands to furnish food, it was probably intended that that particular pair of hands should feed that particular mouth—that each head is the natural guardian, director, and proprietor of the hands and mouth inseparably connected with it; and that being so, every head should be cultivated and improved by whatever will add to its capacity for performing its charge. In one word, free labor insists on universal education."

After the speech he walked around and looked at the prize bulls and stallions, the blue-ribbon corn and wheat, and, chaffing with a knot of farmers, patted a boy on the head and said, "My little man, I hope you live to vote the Republican ticket." The boy's father broke in, "If he ever does, I'll break his neck." And when Lincoln came to where a strong man was lifting heavy weights, he tried his muscles at lifting, and looked down at the short strong man and said, "Why, I could lick salt off the top of your head."

During the years that Lincoln had grown, ripened, and hardened, people who had known him in earlier days talked about him. "I knew him when," and so on. Dennis Hanks had told dozens of farmers: "Abe Lincoln? Why, he's a full cousin of mine. We was raised together. I learnt him to read and write."

But when Peter Cartwright, the famous circuit rider, had published the story of his life, a notable 525-page book, in 1857, he nowhere mentioned Abraham Lincoln.

CHAPTER 129

LINCOLN wanted to be known for a genius of accuracy. He was six feet, four inches tall, "nearly"; he wouldn't count the boot heel and sock as part of his height. He liked to test his memory for accuracy. Driving toward Springfield with his boy, Bob, he recalled he had surveyed the neighborhood they were driving through. He stopped the buggy several times, and each time, with a chuckle, asked Bob to go into the woods and at a certain distance find a blazed tree, which he had more than twenty years ago marked as a survey corner. "And he never made a mistake," said Bob. He had dug into Euclid and put himself through mental discipline because he had learned that a man can be so smart that without intending to he "comes out of the same hole he went in at."

He wouldn't believe everything he saw on a government map. Zimri Enos asked him for a legal opinion on certain rules in government surveys, the opinion to be read to a convention of surveyors. After telling what he believed to be the true rule in establishing strategic lines, he wrote:

"Nearly, perhaps quite, all the original surveys are to some extent, erroneous, and in some of the Sections, greatly so. In each of the latter, it is obvious that a more equitable mode of division than the above, might be adopted; but as error is infinitely various, perhaps no better single rule can be prescribed."

Lincoln read newspapers, "skirmished through them," as he said. He had learned how to pick his way among the articles and items so as to waste little time and get at the special facts he was mousing for. It was part of his system for getting at public opinion, the temper of the people, and the spirit of the times. But this wasn't enough; for such a purpose he couldn't trust newspapers; in some particulars nearly all of them were trying to fool part of the people all the time, all of the people part of the time, or all of the people all of the time. So Lincoln talked with people, listened in while others talked, trained himself as a listener—and, in fact, developed that gift of some dramatic artists of, in a manner, standing outside himself and hearing himself talk and watching himself act. It was since this development that he had been able to wear down Douglas, and hold his own with the star political platform performer of the country, in the drama of politics. And he was well started in competing with that other star performer, Senator William H. Seward of New York.

Behind prejudiced and one-sided newspaper items, he searched his way through to the essential facts confessed. His law practice and companionship with horse thieves, slanderers, and murderers, sharpened him in getting at the truth in partisan newspapers during a time of violence, of boxes of Sharpe's rifles marked "Beecher's Bibles," of disputes as to whether old John Brown was a child of Christ or a son of the Devil. The newspapers were full of "catchwords" and in his Lost Speech he mentioned the significance of catchwords; to know the times he lives in, a man must know its catchwords; he had even lived his fifty years to see "Honest Abe" and "Old Abe" become catchwords. The art and science of plucking out the hidden motives or the probable designs of cunning men, from behind the spoken word screens and the verbal disguises, was one that challenged him.

"The language used becomes ambiguous, roundabout, and mystical," he noted of the framers of the Constitution and their alluding to slavery three times without mentioning it openly by name. He sought out in the current events the motives behind the proclaimed record. There could be such a thing as a "steady debauching of public opinion" by men with hidden motives. In Connecticut, in the shadow of Yale University, he urged, "Let us be diverted by none of those sophistical contrivances wherewith we are so industriously plied and belabored."

Two men who had watched at close hand the working of Lincoln's mind were Herndon and Whitney. Herndon said he might ask Lincoln a question and Lincoln would sit in a moody spell without replying. "Mean-

while, I would forget that I had asked him; but to my surprise a few
moments later (once it was over fifteen minutes) he would break the silence
and give me a satisfactory answer." Whitney noted a rare accuracy of
memory. "Once we all, court and lawyers, except Lincoln, insisted that a
witness had sworn so-and-so, and it turned out that Lincoln was correct,
and that he recollected better than the united bench and bar." He had not
changed since Josh Speed had said he had a quick mind and he answered:
"No, you are mistaken; I am slow to learn and slow to forget. My mind
is like a piece of steel—very hard to scratch anything on it, and almost
impossible after you get it there to rub it out."

Lincoln often read out loud to Herndon in the office, explaining: "I
catch the idea by two senses; for, when I hear what is said and also see it,
I remember it better even if I do not understand it better." In one particular he was a brother in good standing with other original thinkers of
his day and hour. He read much, but in modern books he did not read thoroughly. He skimmed, dipped for the items he could use, and never finished
a novel. The Bible, Blackstone, the Constitution of the United States, the
Declaration of Independence, and the poem, "Immortality," were among
the few writings that he seemed to have read through and through and
so lived with that they were part of him for use and service.

Lincoln was careless about mental culture for show, just as he was careless about manners and dress for show. Whitney tried to solve this careless
approach. "To all acts, accidents, incidents, he made the highwayman's
demand, 'Stand, and deliver.' Every material object or moral entity presented to his optical or mental vision conveyed to him an object-lesson.
His shrewd but apparently indifferent gaze comprehended and included
every element of the object under review. Under that mask and disguise
of nonchalance and negative dissimulation he was an eager student; and
moral objects which to the common apprehension were chaotic and
heterogeneous were orderly and homogeneous to him." He had cross-
examined himself in a stern philosophic way as to honesty, for instance,
and to be honest was a negative virtue, was merely non-stealing; whereas
justice was something positive, a power generator.

He laughed at himself for helping a pig in a gate or lifting a fledgling
bird up into a nest, and philosophized intricately to the effect that he
wasn't moral; he was selfish; his peace of heart would have been disturbed
all day if he had not helped the pig or the bird; he was paid in good feeling. It was this sort of relentless reasoning he liked in Bacon. But it surprised Whitney that Lincoln, the just man, should enjoy and approve of
Bacon, who was shown to have taken bribe money. This was true, Lincoln
admitted, but it had never made any difference in the decisions of Bacon.
In courtrooms Lincoln had a reputation for being almost uncanny in picking the moment when a crooked witness was swerving from the truth as to
essential facts.

Out of little situations in life he constructed little dramas that he carried with him in the portfolio of his memory. A line out of life was as good as anything in the books. Whitney noted: "We were together when the trial of Sickles was on, and John B. Haskin testified that he and his wife called on Mrs. Sickles when her husband was absent and found her and Key together—she mixing salad; an empty champagne bottle being on the table. As they left the house Mrs. Haskin said to her husband: 'She is a bad woman.' That expression tickled Lincoln's fancy. I heard him tell it over and over."

Whitney said Lincoln was like the race horse, Flora Temple. She was a gangling, disjointed horse that couldn't run till after she got started. She gathered speed as she got going. Highland Maid, Lancet, Rose of Washington, and George M. Patchen, fast horses, had been beaten by Flora Temple. Tacony, the first to trot a mile in 2.25½, had lost to her. So had Princess, a high-bred mare brought on from California to the East. And the small bay stallion, Ethan Allen, and the big well-bred golden chestnut horse, John Morgan. All had to take her dust. She had brought the trotting record for a mile down from 2.25½ to 2.19¾. Her pedigree, the line of bloods she came from, was in dispute, though it was published that she was sired by one-eyed Kentucky Hunter, and her dam was Madam Temple by a spotted Arabian horse. She was a rough-coated little bay with a bobtail, sold for $13.00 when a colt on account of her wild temper, and lost as a scrub horse among cattle and mules, bought and sold as a gamble at rising prices, till she began to carry away ribbons and was priceless; cigars and steamboats were given her name.

In many circles her history had the real glint of American romance.

CHAPTER 130

Bill Herndon felt sorry for Lincoln, and almost moaned at watching the "woe-struck face" of Lincoln studying the office floor, the shifting gaze out of the window, desolate with melancholy, the barriers up to all who would speak or interrupt. He tried to figure out whether it was heredity, environment, glands, slow blood circulation, or constipation, or thwarted love. Yet Herndon knew that his melancholy law partner was a steadying force in his own life, something like a big brother or a shrewd uncle. One was "Billy," the other "Mr. Lincoln," across the long years of their partnership. When Billy got blind-drunk, as had happened several times, and tarnished the firm's reputation so that others asked Lincoln if he wouldn't be wise to get rid of a tosspot partner, the answer was "No," and in a tone as though it was nobody's business but his own and Billy's.

Herndon had watched Lincoln grow. The phenomenon of Lincoln's growth was for him close to a miracle. There was no stopping; year by year Lincoln grew; it was a marvel; he was the law partner of a hero; he would some day write the life of this hero; he had his ideal of biography; it should tell everything; it should tell, even, how the man walked.

He noticed how Lincoln walked; the walk of Lincoln was a sort of poem to him. "When he walked he moved cautiously but firmly; his long arms and giant hands swung down by his side. He walked with even tread, the inner sides of his feet being parallel. He put the whole foot flat down on the ground at once, not landing on the heel; he likewise lifted his foot all at once, not rising from the toe, and hence he had no spring to his walk. His walk was undulatory—catching and pocketing tire, weariness, and pain, all up and down his person, and thus preventing them from locating." And as to general structure, "The whole man, body and mind, worked slowly, as if it needed oiling."

And the face of Lincoln? When lights sprang into the gray eyes and fires of emotion flooded out over the scarred fissures, then, "Sometimes it appeared as if Lincoln's soul was fresh from its creator."

Herndon was a transcendentalist, writing to Parker of "the All-All, forever present and eternally creative, creating world and worm, zoöphyte and man, fire and frost," reminding Lincoln by some of his talk of the Pekin witness who "came out of the same hole he went in at."

It was natural that Herndon should look on the mental Lincoln as cold, calm, precise. "Lincoln's fault, if any, was that he saw things less than they really were; less beautiful and more frigid. He crushed the unreal, the inexact, the hollow, the sham. He saw what no man could dispute, but he failed to see what might have been seen." And Herndon saw that Lincoln's life had been such that he could not trust or use what other minds offered him in certain emergencies. "Hence he tore down to their deepest foundations all arrangements of facts, and constructed new ones to govern himself."

Herndon's own kin had come from Virginia to Kentucky by the Wilderness Road through Cumberland Gap, and he mused over the fact. "The first settlers of central and southern Illinois were men of Lincoln's type. They came from the limestone regions of Virginia, Kentucky, and Tennessee, and were men of giant strength, physical force, and by nature mentally strong. They were original, were individualists. The strong alone from 1818 to 1830 could get here, and the strong alone could survive here. No one is like Lincoln, and yet many are of his type." He scrutinized Lincoln as a "critter" and found: "Lincoln's flesh is coarse, hard, harsh; color of his flesh saffron brown; no blood seemingly in it; flesh wrinkled. His flesh looks dry and leathery, tough and everlasting; his eyes are small and gray; head small and forehead receding. Beneath his rough bodily exterior Nature weaves her fine network of nerves." He may be as listless as an alligator while ideas and motives sleep. The blood has to travel far to reach from the heart to the fingers, toes—and brain.

Yet, "the convolutions of his brain are long; they do not snap off quickly like a short, thick man's brain. The enduring power of Mr. Lincoln's brain is wonderful. He can sit and think without food or rest longer than any man I ever saw."

Lincoln required not merely proof, but demonstration. He would not believe the circle was unsquarable till he had toiled the limit of his strength and found for himself it was so. "He can believe nothing unless his sense or logic can reach it," Herndon noted. "I often read to him a law point, a decision or something I fancy; he can not understand it until he takes the book out of my hand and reads the thing for himself. He is terribly, vexatiously sceptical. He can scarcely understand anything, unless he has time and place fixed in his mind." Of Lincoln and whisky he would put it down that Lincoln said: "I am entitled to little credit for not drinking, because I hate the stuff; it is unpleasant and always leaves me flabby and undone." As to eating an apple: "He disdained the use of a knife to cut or pare it. Instead he would grasp it around the equatorial part, holding it thus until his thumb and forefinger almost met, sink his teeth into it, and then, unlike the average person, begin eating at the blossom end. When he was done he had eaten his way over and through rather than around and into it. Such, at least, was his explanation. I never saw an apple thus disposed of by any one else." He would tell about the family Lincoln, the boys, Willie and Tad, in the office with their father on a Sunday morning while the mother was at church; the boys pulled books off shelves, upset ink bottles, threw pencils into the spittoon, and their father went on with his work as though the office were empty.

Lincoln would take a terribly mixed and tragic layout of human affairs, and use a fable or illustration to give his impression of it, because, as Herndon noted, "there were, in the vast store of words, so few that contained the exact coloring, power, and shape of his ideas." One morning in 1859 the two men were talking in their office about what would happen if war broke out between the states. Herndon was afraid the North would split into so many quarreling factions that there would be no unity for making war. Lincoln replied, saying the South reminded him of the fellow "who contended that the proper place for the big kettle was inside of the little one," and then branched into an illustration in war psychology: "Go to the river bank with a coarse sieve and fill it with gravel. After a vigorous shaking you will observe that the small pebbles and sand have sunk from view and fallen to the ground. The next larger in size, unable to slip between the wires, will still be found within the sieve. By thorough and repeated shakings you will find that, of the pebbles still left in the sieve, the largest ones will have risen to the top. Now, if war is inevitable and will shake the country from centre to circumference, you will find that the little men will fall out of view in the shaking. The masses will rest on some solid foundation, and the big men will have climbed to the top. Of these latter, one greater than all the rest will leap forth equipped—the people's leader in the conflict."

Time had been required to grow Lincoln. "He has had a slow build-up, a slow development; he has grown up like the forest oak, tough, solid, knotty, gnarled, standing out with power against the storm, and almost defying the lightning." Thus Herndon's hero, who knew what oaks know, and murmured out of his shadows, "I shall meet with some terrible end."

CHAPTER 131

LINCOLN had once written to a younger man his regrets over what he called "the serious, long-faced letter I wrote yesterday."

Then he told this friend in gay and rippling lines, "Let the past as nothing be—go it while you're young!"

Women registered impressions with Lincoln. Mystic women came and went sometimes in quizzical, hazy reveries. Talking with T. W. S. Kidd once, he said that when he was a boy in Indiana a wagon broke down near the Lincoln place; and the travelers on the wagon, a man, his wife and their two girls, came to the Lincoln cabin, and cooked their meals at the Lincoln fireplace till the wagon was fixed.

"The woman had books and read us stories," Lincoln told Kidd. "I took a great fancy to one of the girls. And when they were gone I thought of her a great deal, and one day sitting out in the sun by the house I wrote out a story in my mind."

He got on his father's horse and rode after the wagon with the girls in it. He caught up with them; they were surprised to see him. Thus his daydream went, sitting in the sun.

"I talked with the girl and persuaded her to elope with me, and that night I put her on my horse, and we started off across the prairie. After several hours we came to a camp; and when we rode up we found it was the one we had left a few hours before and we went in.

"The next night we tried again, and the same thing happened—the horse came back to the same place. And then we concluded not to elope. I stayed until I had persuaded her father to give her to me."

He told Kidd he had intended at one time to write out this action as a story to be published. "I began once, but I concluded it was not much of a story." And he added, "But I think that was the beginning of love with me."

One of the law students in the Lincoln & Herndon office noticed that the junior and senior partners had different ways toward women who came into the office. When a woman was through talking with Herndon about her case, she usually left Herndon at the desk and went to the door alone and stepped out. In case she was a good-looking woman and pleased the eye of Herndon, he would step to the door with her and perhaps pat her on the arm or the shoulder in bidding her good day, and close the door after her. With women callers who came to see Lincoln the action was different, as this law student observed, for no matter how homely and battered the woman might be, after the conference on her case was ended, Lincoln would step to the door with her, bid good day, and close the door. Both the good-lookers and those not so good-looking had his escort from the desk to the door, and no matter what their looks he did not risk a pat on arm or shoulder.

A law student saw Lincoln one day start to tell a story of racy color. But Lincoln paused, went to each one of three doors to the office, and looked, said the student, "to make sure there was no woman to listen." He added, "Herndon wouldn't do that."

In the matter of women, Herndon was free and easy, and Lincoln was not. When Herndon remarked to Joe Gillespie that Lincoln "ran smoothly" among the paths of the wicked, the fallen, the drunken, the disorderly, never complaining, and perfectly at home among the worst people, he added the cryptic, "Lincoln had no appetites, but *woman* must keep out of his way."

In the personal decisions as to how he should fill out those few eye-blinks between being born and dying, Lincoln was as independent and free-going as he was in shaping his own formulas of politics and law. Of two of his best friends among lawyers, one said Lincoln was "harmless as a dove and wise as a serpent," and the other, "He respectfully listened to all advice, and rarely, if ever, followed it." He was a man one Springfield old-timer tried to sketch summarily by saying: "He had the faculty of calculation," while Whitney sought to convey an elusive fugitive. "He could more effectively employ language to conceal his thoughts than Talleyrand, and, while guilty of no duplicity, could hide his thoughts and intentions more efficiently than any man with a historical record."

About women in general the lawyers of the Eighth Circuit had often joked Lincoln. But in only one case had they ever teased him about being too much in the company of any one particular woman. She was a singer, Lois Newhall, of the Newhall Family, a concert troupe who gave programs in churches and town-hall lyceum courses. Though not especially attractive in looks, she was considered a good singer; she had met Lincoln and they took a liking for each other. From the concert platform she would pick him out in the audience and send him a smile of recognition and greeting.

Whitney noticed that if the Newhall Family was to perform in a town where the Eighth Circuit lawyers had arrived, Lincoln would arrange his affairs so that he could be on hand at the church or the town hall in time to attend the entertainment. "No trial, consultation, or business engagement of any kind was allowed to interfere," said Whitney. "To most of us the thing for a time seemed more or less strange until finally the real reason developed. It was Lincoln's predilection for a woman. The attraction was a little unusual for Lincoln, who was particularly thoughtful in matters of that kind."

Judge Davis, Leonard Swett, and others close to Lincoln, saw the affair drifting along to a point where they felt it was somewhat their affair too. With sober faces they spoke of the honor of the bar of the Eighth Circuit being involved; he should be reminded of his duty as a married man; there was danger in entangling alliances; and so on. His rejoinder was easy: "Don't trouble yourselves, boys, there's no danger. She's actually the only woman in the world, outside of my wife, who ever dared to pay me a compliment, and if the poor thing is attracted to my handsome face and figure it seems to me you homely fellows are the last people on earth who ought to complain."

One evening at the Macon House in Decatur, the Eighth Circuit lawyers were having a social hour with the Newhall Family, the parents, two sisters, a brother, and a brother-in-law. The singing and fun had reached a point where one of the lawyers tried to get Lincoln to sing for the company. He urged, "Lincoln, you have been enjoying for almost a week the delightful music produced by these ladies, and it seems only fair to the rest of us that you should entertain them by singing some of the songs for which you are already famous." All the others joined in this call for Lincoln to sing. One lawyer said, "Why, over on the Sangamon Abe has a great reputation as a singer. It is quite a common thing over there to invite him to farm auctions and have him start off the sale of stock with a good song." Lincoln refused. He never was a singer in his life; what reputation he had, he wouldn't risk; they could beg; he wasn't going to offer a song.

But Lois Newhall and her sister were anxious for Lincoln to sing. "Each of us had taken a liking to him," she said afterward. "We had heard him speak several times, but that did not impress us so much as his pleasing personality and his happy manner toward women." They teased him for a song, giving a dozen reasons. Lincoln listened to them, showed a threatening face to the lawyers who were enjoying his bashfulness, turned on his heel, and told the company it was a late hour and he was going to bed.

Starting upstairs, he had to pass Lois Newhall, sitting at a melodeon; just as he passed her she looked up into his face and said: "Mr. Lincoln, if you have a song that you can sing, I know that I can play the accompaniment. If you will just tell me what it is, I can follow you even if I am not familiar with it."

"Why, Miss Newhall," he laughed, still bashful, "if it would save my soul, I couldn't imitate a note that you would touch on that instrument. I never sang in my life; and those fellows know it. They are simply trying to make fun of me." He paused; some sort of disappointment crossed her face; and he said: "But I'll tell you what I am willing to do. Inasmuch as you and your sister have been so kind and entertained us so generously, I shall try to return the favor. Of course, I can't produce music, but if you will be patient and brave enough to endure it, I will repeat for your benefit several stanzas of a poem of which I am particularly fond."

Then he stepped to the doorway leading from the hotel parlor to the stairway; he seemed too tall to stand in the doorframe, and he leaned against the casing, half closed his eyes, and brought out from the attic of his heart the quaint, faded poem, with the stains of old spinet wood in it, and the rose and gold of lost sunsets. He recited the lines beginning, "Oh, Why Should the Spirit of Mortal Be Proud?" It was the first time the Newhalls had heard the piece. The moods of joking and teasing came to an end.

Lois told her sister afterward that it was all she could do to keep back the tears as that long shadowy riddle of a man wandered through the sorrowful lines. "A flash of the lightning—a break of the wave—He passeth from life to his rest in the grave." As he was to go upstairs, she asked him who wrote the poem. "My dear Miss Newhall, I am ashamed to say that I do not know. But if you really like it, I will write it off for you tonight before I go to bed, and leave a copy on the table so that you may have it to read when you sit down to breakfast."

In the dusk of dawn the next morning, Lois Newhall came down to the hotel dining-room where candles flickered among lengthened shadows. And she had drawn a chair to the table and was eating a winter breakfast by candlelight, as she had done many times before. But as to this particular breakfast, she said at a later time: "I was eating pancakes, and was in the act of cutting one, holding it with my fork while I used the knife, when I became aware that some one was behind and bending over me. A big hand took hold of my left hand, covering it on the table, and with his right hand, over my shoulder, he laid down a sheet of paper covered with writing, in front of my plate. I realized it was Mr. Lincoln. He told me that he was due to leave town in a few minutes, and as he moved away, he looked back, waved his hand, exclaiming, 'Good-by, my dear!' and passed through the door. It was the last time I ever saw him."

One of Lincoln's sayings was, "I shall never be old enough to speak without embarrassment when I have nothing to talk about." When girls from Knox and Lombard colleges came to present him with a silk banner at the Sanderson House in Galesburg, he had said to the Galesburg mayor, "I haven't got any of that kind of spare change." The small talk, the patter of conversational nothings, the formal speeches that should be ingratiating and lubricatory, projecting ciphers while pretending to emit numbers, this he termed "spare change."

To understand Lincoln and women, one might have to begin with his feel for the comic with its quick eye for pretense and surface dignity, besides that single thing in his behavior which had ever been characterized as "exquisite." When it was mentioned of Lincoln, "He has an *exquisite* sense of justice," that was the first time anything about him had been chosen as of such peculiar inheritance and significant development that it took the character of the exquisite.

When he had written of Miss Owens as "over-size" and spoken of her "want of teeth" and "weather-beaten appearance in general" he balanced it with "No woman I have ever seen has a finer face," and in intellect "she was not inferior to any." He confessed his vanity was touched by her saying No as he proposed "over and over again" and, "I then for the first time began to suspect that I was really a little in love with her." He had closed his self-analysis with: "Others have been made fools of by the girls. . . . I made a fool of myself. . . . Now I can never be satisfied with any one who would be blockhead enough to have me."

The remark was thrown at Lincoln several times in the Sanderson house in Galesburg that he was afraid of women. He laughed it off with saying, "A woman is the only thing I am afraid of that I know can't hurt me."

He told Whitney he hated the little job of telling a hayrack full of girls in white gowns representing the states of the Union, "I also thank you for this beautiful basket of flowers." These tallied with what Mary Owens had said, that he was "deficient in the little links that make for woman's happiness." After a little tea party at the home of Mayor Boyden of Urbana one evening, the mayor and Whitney excused themselves for an hour, and left Lincoln alone with Mrs. Boyden, Mrs. Whitney, and her mother. Whitney, on returning, found Lincoln "ill at ease as a country boy," eyes shifting from floor to ceiling and back, arms behind and then in front and then tangled as though he tried to hide them but couldn't, and his long legs tying and untying themselves. Whitney pitied him. "I could not understand it unless it was because he was alone in a room with three women."

As he was arguing a case at Urbana, several ladies came in to listen, and the lawyers made room for them within the bar. Lincoln paused during the swish of the skirts and the adjustment of the new section of the audience, and then said, "I perceive, gentlemen, that you are like all the rest of the fellers in your admiration of the fair sex—in fact, I think, from appearances, that you are a little worse than the common run"; and after more remarks that raised a laugh, he took up his argument, first saying with a quizzical glance, "Now, boys, behave yourselves."

A woman wrote her admiration of his course in politics, and he thanked her in a letter which acknowledged, "I have never corresponded much with ladies; and hence I postpone writing letters to them, as a business which I do not understand." A few men knew of his saying, after he had given

> O why should the spirit of mortal be proud?
> Like a swift fleeting meteor — a fast flying cloud—
> A flash of the lightning — a break of the wave,
> He passeth from life to his rest in the grave.
>
> The leaves of the Oak, and the willow shall fade,
> Be scattered around, and together be laid
> And the young and the old, and the low and the high
> Shall moulder to dust, and together shall lie.

Reduced facsimile of "Immortality" in Lincoln's handwriting; a copy of this poem he gave to Miss Lois Newhall at winter candlelight breakfast; the above are the opening verses of a complete manuscript in the Barrett collection.

money or time or a favor in answer to a pathetic but probably bogus appeal, "I thank God I wasn't born a woman."

Lincoln's ways with women interested Herndon as much as his walk or talk. In the office, around the public square, or at Dr. Wallace's drug store or in Bunn's bank and store, or out on the Eighth Circuit, Herndon believed Lincoln cloaked his ways with women by a rare and fine code. "Mr. Lincoln had a strong, if not terrible passion for women," said Herndon. "He could hardly keep his hands off a woman, and yet, much to his credit, he lived a pure and virtuous life. His idea was that a woman had as much right to violate the marriage vow as the man—no more and no less. His sense of right—his sense of justice—his honor forbade his violating his marriage vow. Judge Davis said to me, 'Mr. Lincoln's honor saved many a woman.' This I know. I have seen Lincoln tempted and I have seen him reject the approach of woman!"

A woman charged with keeping a house of ill fame had the firm of Lincoln & Herndon for lawyers; they asked for a change of venue; and Lincoln drove across the prairies from one town to another with the madam of the house and her girls. After the trial the madam was asked about Lincoln's talk with her. Yes, he told stories, and they were nearly all funny. Yes, but were the stories proper or improper, so to speak? Well —the madam hesitated—they were funny . . . she and all the girls laughed . . . but coming to think it over she believed the stories could have been told "with safety in the presence of ladies anywhere." Then she added, without being asked, and as though it ought to be part of the story, "But that is more than I can say for Bill Herndon."

One man on the Eighth Circuit was a sort of friend and chum of Lincoln; they spent many gay hours together. Ward Hill Lamon, the Danville law partner of Lincoln, was a young Virginian of dauntless personal courage, bull-necked, melodious, tall, commanding, aristocratic, and, men said, magnificent in the amount of whisky he could carry and still pronounce the sentence, "She stood at the gate welcoming him in." Horses, women, jewelry, music, sashes of yellow and scarlet silk, the tokens of civilization after it has arrived and ripened into the overripe, had their appeal, their register of enthusiasm with him. His black hair and black mustache, the shine and the daring of him, had reminders of troubadours. The first time he and Lincoln met at Danville, Lamon wore a swallow-tailed coat, white neckcloth, and ruffled silk shirt, and Lincoln said: "Going to try your hand at the law, are you? I don't think you would succeed at splitting rails." As the years had passed a strange bond of loyalty between the two men grew stronger and was known to other men. "Sing me a little song," was Lincoln's word to Lamon, who brought out a banjo and struck up some nonsensical and rapid staccato such as "Cousin Sally Downard," or "I'll bet my money on de bobtail nag; somebody bet on de bay." Or a sailor chantey made over by mountaineers into—

> De ol' black bull kem down de medder,
> Husen Johnnie, Husen Johnnie!
> De ol' black bull kem down de medder,
> Long time ago.

Fust he paw an' den he beller,
  Husen Johnnie, Husen Johnnie!
Fust he paw an' den he beller,
  Long time ago.

Long time ago, long time ago,
  De ol' black bull kem down de medder,
  Long time ago.

The close friendship of Lincoln and Lamon was talked about among the other lawyers. Lamon was considered a second-rate lawyer, a scholar of still lower rating, and in politics and on the slavery question leaning toward the southern Illinois point of view rather than the northern. He was born two miles north of Winchester in the Shenandoah Valley from which Lincoln's grandfather had moved to Kentucky. He was pre-eminently the Good Fellow, with the grasshopper rather than the ant for his model, openly pagan; he translated the fleshpots of Egypt into the pork chops of Illinois; he was as independent in manner as young Joseph G. Cannon, slated in Danville to follow Lamon as state's attorney of Vermilion County; morals are morals but a pitcher of beer is beer; out of one somewhat like Lamon Shakespeare built Falstaff; he was Elizabethan, Hogarthian, with heavy jowls, slumbrous, dangerous eyes, and the intrepidity of famous cavalrymen. He was nineteen years younger than Lincoln, had served four years as a state's attorney, and had been sketched as "chivalrous, courageous, generous, of unquestioned integrity, inclined to be conservative"; and, "His social qualities upon intimate acquaintance are of the finest type." Yet the comment of good friends of Lincoln was that his companionship with Lamon proved that Lincoln had "a certain degree of moral obtuseness."

For driving away a spell of melancholy, probably the best friend of Lincoln was this man Lamon, whom he called Hill. Whether it was music or women or a roistering gayety he wanted for a dark mood, he treasured and kept the companionship of the reckless and romantic Hill Lamon, eater and drinker, with the swagger of a picture-book swashbuckler out of a pirate story, but a personal loyalty of tried fighting quality.

Women, music, poetry, art, science, and pure speculative philosophy, all requiring lazy days with no tumults in the near-by dusty streets and roads: to them all Lincoln's answer was spoken in the quaint gingerbread story, the Indiana boy blurting out mournfully, "Abe, I don't s'pose there's anybody on earth likes gingerbread better'n I do—and gets less'n I do."

CHAPTER 132

FRANCES AFFONSA, the black-eyed Portuguese woman who used to do the family washing for the Lincolns, had stayed on and become the regular cook. Her man, Manuel de Fraita, who said he would sometime take her for a bride, used to come to see her. They often had supper together in the kitchen, looking off in the direction of the Great Western depot.

Frances was a good woman and a good cook. The Lincolns liked her cooking and hoped she would stay many years. When Frances was asked how she got along with Mrs. Lincoln, she answered: "If I please Mis' Lincum, she like me, she treat me very well; and she very hard to please, but I please her." And that would about hit off what the husband in the house had learned about getting along with his wife. If he pleased her, she liked him, she treated him very well. And often she was very hard to please, but he pleased her.

Frances Affonsa heard the husband and wife exchange words one day. As she told it, what they said was:

MRS. LINCOLN: You're a very smart man, Mr. Lincoln.
MR. LINCOLN: Well, what have I done now?
MRS. L.: Why, you have put your coat on top of my fresh starched gowns.
MR. L.: Never mind, don't be cross. I'll take my coat away and hang your gowns over it.

As the years had passed they had learned to be more accommodating to each other, though each was so independent and their personalities were so different on important matters that often the marriage ship was in the troughs. There were stories in the talk and gossip of the town. Lincoln had been seen splitting wood at one o'clock in the morning. Hadn't he been turned out of his own house and come home when the rest of the family was in bed, to get his own supper alone in peace? Ah-h, said the tongues, that must be the explanation.

Herndon knew that his partner had come to the office sometimes at seven o'clock in the morning when the usual hour for him to arrive was nine o'clock. And in his hands at noon Lincoln had brought to the office a package of grocery crackers and cheese, and sat alone eating. The tongues in some quarters still had it that Mary Todd married him to wreak vengeance on him for not showing up on the date first set for their marriage ceremony.

Mrs. Lincoln and Herndon hated each other. He traced back to Patrick Henry stock, while she was of Covenanter offspring. And they never got along. His first compliment to her, that she danced with the grace of a serpent, was a slip from the code by which she demanded to be treated. While Herndon was careless as to where he spat, she was not merely scrupulously neat, nor merely immaculate as to linen and baths; she was among the most ambitious women in Springfield in the matter of style and fashion; she wished to be not merely agreeable and attractive, but a stunning triumph.

On such occasions as she called at the Lincoln & Herndon law office, she would walk from the door straight to the desk of Lincoln and speak with him. She might nod pleasantly to Henry B. Rankin or another law student. But she wouldn't even look toward Herndon; he was off her speaking list. The natural clash of these two temperaments and characters hadn't been helped by the fact that when the Republicans got control of the state offices in 1856, Herndon was appointed a bank examiner at a nice salary, while her husband went on dividing his fees half and half with Herndon, Lincoln being the one who earned the big fees, such as the $5,000.00 from the Illinois Central Railroad.

Mrs. Lincoln knew Herndon as an Abolitionist hothead; she knew his father had called him home from Illinois College because he had got deep into the Garrisonian doctrines; she knew definitely or had sure intuitions about Herndon's wanting to raise cash for rifles to send to Kansas besides his interest in other schemes for open combat with proslavery forces. She had told Ward Hill Lamon ten years back: "Mr. Lincoln is to be President of the United States some day; if I had not thought so I would not have married him, for you can see he is not pretty." And she felt the radical, unsteady Herndon a menace to all her dreams of her husband advancing. If Lincoln had not been the stronger and shaping personal force with Herndon, he would have been linked to political factions that would have smothered all of Mrs. Lincoln's ambitions.

She knew of such affairs as Herndon getting drunk with two other men and breaking a windowpane that her husband had to hustle the money for so that the sheriff wouldn't lock up his law partner. She didn't like it that her husband had a partner who was too easy about women and whisky, reckless with money, and occasionally touching Lincoln for loans. She didn't like it that Herndon could sometimes completely misunderstand Lincoln, as at the time Lincoln had to write from Washington asking Herndon to read his Mexican War speeches before taking the explanations of Democrats in Springfield as to how he stood on the war. At that time it looked as though Herndon had gone on a spree and was not giving his partner, so far away, ready sympathy and quick coöperation. With Herndon more on the job, and a better home guard, reporting home developments and trends of sentiment as rapidly and fully as Lincoln had done for his partner, Stuart, when Stuart was in Congress, it might have been that Lincoln's Mexican War policy as congressman wouldn't have been as muddled for the home folks as it was. Mrs. Lincoln carried suspicions and nursed misgivings of that kind.

Mrs. Lincoln would have preferred to have her husband in partnership with a kindly, mellow, easy-going scholar such as Orville H. Browning, a Kentucky gentleman of the old school, a compendium of gracious manners and fine codes. Instead there was the tavern-bred son of a tavern keeper, a swaggering upstart and interloper, radical in politics, transcendentalist in philosophy, anti-church, and calling himself an infidel as to the divinity of Christ, the Trinity of the Godhead, and the divine revelation of the Bible.

Mrs. Lincoln's instinct for politics, her views of current events, her shifting flickers of temperament, were intermingled in a letter she wrote to her sister in Kentucky at the close of the 1856 campaign when the new Republican party had taken Illinois but had lost with its national ticket headed by Frémont. She wrote: "Your husband, like the rest of ours, has a great taste for politics and has taken much interest in the late contest, which has resulted very much as I expected, not hoped. Although Mr. Lincoln is, or was, a Frémont man, you must not include him with so many of those who belong to that party, an Abolitionist. In principle he is far from it. All he desires is that slavery shall not be extended, let it remain where it is. My weak woman's heart was too Southern in feeling to sympathize with any but Fillmore. I have always been a great admirer of his—he made so good a president, and is so good a man, and feels the necessity of keeping foreigners within bounds. If some of you Kentuckians had to deal with the wild Irish as we housekeepers are sometimes called upon to do, the South would certainly elect Fillmore next time. The Democrats have been defeated in our state in their governor, so there is a crumb of comfort for each and all. What day is so dark that there is no ray of sunshine to penetrate the gloom? Now, sit down and write one of your agreeable missives, and do not wait for a return of each staid matron, and, moreover, the mother of three noisy boys."

Thus the wife wrote, a few months after the Lincoln Lost Speech, in which he set a convention on fire telling them to use bullets only after ballots had failed, and crying, "Blood will flow and brother's hand be raised against brother!" His wife was enthusiastic about Fillmore, "so good a president," "so good a man," and had told Lincoln about the goodness of Fillmore before he heard of it from the young man whom he advised to "vote for Almighty God" as being perfect in goodness and far surpassing Millard Fillmore in goodness.

Thus while the husband had campaigned for John C. Frémont, facing hostile audiences that, as at Petersburg, hooted him and tried to howl him down, the wife favored Millard Fillmore.

At parties, balls, social gatherings, she moved, vital, sparkling, often needlessly insinuating or directly and swiftly insolent. If the music was bad, what was the need of her making unkind remarks about the orchestra? Was it not to be expected that the remarks would circulate and word be sent back to her that the orchestra was not playing for her but for the colored maid?

Mary Todd Lincoln, the wife of Abraham Lincoln, in crinoline days

Lincoln in Springfield, June, 1860. Hessler, a Chicago photographer, was sent downstate by political managers who wanted more pleasant campaign pictures.

Original photograph loaned by Col. Edward J. Steichen

On her desk stood an inkstand, carved of walnut wood, in the shape of an ear of corn. Each end had an inkwell. Between was a music box. An inscription read, "Mary Lincoln."

Lighted candles in a still, dark room clothed her with invisible consolations not to be derived from the windows facing south on Eighth Street. Chills, headaches, creepers of fear came at her; misunderstandings rose in waves so often around her; she was alone, so all alone, so like a child thrust into the Wrong Room. She chose three candelabra; on each was the figure of a woman seated with her head resting in the elbow of a man's right arm. Attached to a three-candle one were ten pendent prisms of glass where flowers and stars of light ran in rainbow tints. Here was excellence—even in the Wrong Room.

At parties, balls, social gatherings, she trod the mazy waltzes in crinoline gowns, the curves of the hoop skirts shading down the plump curves of her physical figure as if fashion were coöperating to set off her lines to advantage. With middle age coming on she had spoken less often, in society, of the certainty of her husband going to the White House eventually. But there were those who recollected her replying to the remark that Mr. Lincoln seemed to be a great favorite: "Yes, he is a great favorite everywhere. He is to be President of the United States some day. Look at him! Doesn't he look as if he would make a magnificent President?" Once when talk had turned to a comparison of Lincoln and Douglas, she had said, "Mr. Lincoln may not be as handsome a figure, but people are perhaps not aware that his heart is as large as his arms are long."

Mary Todd and Abe Lincoln had good times together. How often these good times shone for them, when the ship sailed an even moonlit sea, only they two could tell. They were intense and special individuals, he having come through a siege of hypochondria which he referred to by the abbreviation of "hypo," and she moving by circling swirls toward a day when she would cry out that hammers were knocking nails into her head, that hot wires were being drawn through her eyes. They had by multiplied specific actions drawn into a tighter area, into a closer-welded definition, the meaning of the slogan that Chatterton, the jeweler, so long ago had engraved inside the plain gold band of a wedding-ring he had put on her hand. "Love is eternal." Concretely across years the man had given the woman his explanation of what his intentions were in writing to Joshua Speed as to marriage, the words of old Tom Lincoln, "If you make a bad bargain, hug it all the tighter." Between flare-ups and clashes, between collisions and regrets, the spirit of accommodation rose and offered a way out. To be strangers was to be enemies; to be free with communications was to lead toward understanding. Perhaps accommodation was a finer and surer word than Love; certainly it had been soiled less with the lies of hypocrites. He was ten years older than she, with a toiling talent for con-

ciliatory adjustment, a strict genius in the decisions of human accommodation. So he led.

Hours of pleasant reconciliations were in Whitney's mind when he said:
"Lincoln loved his wife—I had many reasons to know this." They had
good times together, days when she made herself pretty for him, wanting
him, and he willing.

She wrote to her sister in the autumn of 1857: "The summer has
strangely and rapidly passed away. Some portion of it was spent most
pleasantly in traveling East. We visited Niagara, Canada, New York and
other points of interest. When I saw the large steamers at the New York
landing, ready for their European voyage, I felt in my heart inclined to
sigh that poverty was my portion. I often laugh and tell Mr. Lincoln that
my next husband shall be rich."

She could pronounce on her husband such fine judgments as: "He
never joined a church, but still he was a religious man. But it was a kind of
poetry in his nature, and he never was a technical Christian."

The roots and the elements of their two lives ran darkly into hidden
ways and subtle crypts of life. Much of the gossip about the Lincoln
house ran on the theory that in every house there is either a master-man
or a henpecked husband, either a domineering woman or a doormat. Both
gossip and science have little to guide them in effecting a true and searching explanation of the married life of a slow-going wilderness bear and a
cultivated tempestuous wildcat.

Some of the gossip rested on solid foundations of fact. Mrs. Lincoln
had once discharged, on short notice and with sharp words, a girl in her
employ. The uncle of the girl came to ask about it. Mrs. Lincoln met him
at the door, excited, blazing, gesticulating, and sent him away with his
ears burning from a torrent of short, picked adjectives. He hunted up
Lincoln, finding the politician in a store on the public square, discussing
the news of the day and enjoying a crowd of fellow citizens. He stepped
into the store, with his ears still burning, and called for Lincoln, who came
and listened. When the man had finished telling his grievance, Lincoln
said he was sorry to hear what had been told him, he wanted to be reasonable and fair, but he would ask a question; it amounted to asking, "If I
have had to stand this every day for fifteen years, don't you think you
can stand it a few minutes one day?" The uncle would have laughed if
Lincoln had laughed. But Lincoln's face was mournful, slack, worn. It
was no laughing matter even with a man who had a knack of laughter.
The uncle apologized. The two men parted as friends.

As this scandalous morsel of gossip traveled, the identity of the
abused man who came to Lincoln took many forms. It was the iceman who
had a spat on the back doorstep of the Lincoln house, and met Lincoln
and sympathized with him at the front porch. Or it was a groceryman who
was accused of delivering decayed tomatoes, or a carpenter who had been

told by Mrs. Lincoln that he didn't know a hawk from a handsaw. The incident, however, was not merely a morsel of gossip, as it traveled. It was
also a piece of folklore, old as the human family, the Lincolns entirely insignificant figures in it. On any day when he had met unkind words from
his wife at the breakfast table, every man in Illinois who knew the story
took comfort in picturing Lincoln, saying, "If I have had to stand this
every day for fifteen years, don't you think you can stand it a few minutes
one day?" It was a farce with a moral. Men and their wives and children
told the story with a relish; in all homes something a little like it had
happened; that was why they enjoyed and understood it. In fact, sometimes the end of such incidents when repeated was separation of man and
wife by divorce. They liked the Lincolns better for it; it was common
and human.

What went on behind the doors and window blinds of the two-story
cottage at the corner of Eighth and Jackson streets was the secret of
those who lived in it, except as occasionally little accidental events revealed a momentary glint of the mirrors and a fleeting glimpse of part of
the secret. Such little accidental events were rare. One was the necessary
writing by Lincoln of an explanation to the editor of a Springfield newspaper. The letter was marked "Private," was dated at Springfield, February 20, 1857, addressed to John E. Rosette, Esq., and read in full:

DEAR SIR:—
Your note about the little paragraph in the *Republican* was received yesterday, since which time I have been too unwell to notice it. I had not supposed you
wrote or approved it. The whole originated in mistake. You know by the
conversation with me that I thought the establishment of the newspaper unfortunate, but I always expected to throw no obstacle in its way, and to
patronize it to the extent of taking it and paying for one copy. When the
paper was brought to my house, my wife said to me, "Now are you going
to take another worthless little paper?" I said to her *evasively*, "I have not
directed the paper to be left." From this, in my absence, she sent the message
to the carrier. This is the whole story.

Yours truly,
A. LINCOLN.

There was another story, quite different. A lawyer was talking business
to Lincoln once at the home. Suddenly the door opened and Mrs. Lincoln
put her head in and snapped out the question whether he had done an
errand she told him to do. He looked up quietly, said he had been busy,
but would attend to it as soon as he could. Words came wailing rapidly
from Mrs. Lincoln that she was a neglected, abused, insulted woman. The
door slammed; she was gone. The visiting lawyer looked at Lincoln open-
eyed, and muttered his surprise. Lincoln laughed it off, "Why, if you knew
how much good that little eruption did, what a relief it was to her, how she
really enjoyed it, and if you knew her as well as I do, you would be glad

she had had an opportunity to explode, to give vent to her feelings." This was not so good a story, not so quizzical an incident, and did not spread so far.

Once on a Sunday, Lincoln in his shirt-sleeves had two of his boys in a little wagon which he was pulling behind him as he walked back and forth in front of his house. His chin sunk to his bosom, he was thinking about history, discoveries, inventions, politics, when a passer-by picked him by the sleeve and told him one of the boys had spilled out of the wagon onto the sidewalk. Just then Mrs. Lincoln, coming home from church, saw what had happened, and set up a crying that could be heard at the next corner. Lincoln took a few long steps toward the house and the front door shut behind him. Thus one tale. Another had to do with an ink spot on his desk. A bottle had spilled over—and Mrs. Lincoln had pushed the desk out of the house.

Twice Mrs. Lincoln sent one of the boys to call Lincoln to dinner from a game of chess with Judge Treat; the third time the boy lined up where he could get foot action, and kicked the chessboard, kings, queens, pawns, and all, into the air. The father acted as if chessboards were made to be kicked into the air, took the boy's hand, smiled to Judge Treat, "I reckon we'll have to finish this game some other time," went to dinner and left Judge Treat puffing at the gills, with mussed-up dignity. When asked his opinion of Mrs. Lincoln, Judge Treat said he could name people who could tell about her, "if they dared to."

During six months of the year Lincoln was off practicing law on the Eighth Circuit. Other lawyers, starting home at the week-ends to spend Sunday with their wives and families, noticed that Lincoln didn't join them; they mentioned it to each other; it was sort of quietly agreed that the home life of Lincoln was not all that Lincoln would wish it; Milton Hay, a lawyer with an office on the same floor as Lincoln, used to philosophize that if Lincoln's home life hadn't sent him out over the state, with free spare hours to think for himself and to build up circles of friends that were a political asset, Lincoln wouldn't have become the powerful political manipulator that he was in the new controlling party of the Northwest.

Though the tales gathered and spread about Lincoln being a henpecked husband, his wife's conversation about him among the well-to-do and socially and politically powerful people gave the impression that she was proud of him and he had a genius that would take him farther than any man in Illinois. She joked about his failings, and defended his peculiarities. She would say: "He is of no account when he is at home. He never does anything except to warm himself and read. He never went to market in his life; I have to look after all that. He just does nothing. He is the most useless, good-for-nothing man on earth." But if somebody else had said Lincoln was the most useless, good-for-nothing man on earth,

"I would have scratched his eyes out," she flashed. "But really, he is so absorbed with his law, his anecdotes, his reading, and what not, that he is of little use at home." And could one suppose that he never gave his wife any money? "Money!" was Mrs. Lincoln's exclamation. "He never gives me any money—he leaves his pocketbook where I can take what I want."

She bought calico, cambric, muslin, oil cloth, cassimere at C. M. Smith's store; she sent Bob for ten-pound lots of sugar and Smith would enter on his books, "per Bob 10 pds Sugar $1.00"; or it might be six dozen eggs and Smith would write, "per son 6 doz. Eggs $.50." She bought candles, wood, buttons, thread, year on year managing. She bought silk, silk and luster, silk lining, plaid silk, silk lining and crêpe, silk mitts, gaiter boots, kid boots from Smith for herself. Also she picked from Smith's stock for her husband such items as "1 shirt $2.75," "1 silk cravat $1.60," and Smith wrote one entry, "Jents Stock $1.25." On April 26, 1859, Smith wrote, "per lady Silk Hat $5.00," and four days later a second entry, "per lady, for difference in exchange Hats $.50."

She was often anxious about her boys, had mistaken fears about their safety or health, exaggerated evils that might befall them. She gave parties for them and wrote with her own pen, in a smooth and even script, gracious invitations such as one received by six-year-old Isaac Diller, reading, "Willie Lincoln will be pleased to see you, Wednesday Afternoon at 3 O'clock."

Mrs. Lincoln writes to little Isaac Diller.

Between Mrs. Lincoln and Herndon fire flashed as flint upon flint. Each had peculiar personal pride. When the Republicans carried Illinois for the first time, Herndon wrote to Parker: "I commenced early in our county and spoke on every stump and in every church and schoolhouse therein, and thus carried our county by a larger majority than ever before. I turned my office into a kind of war office, took the young, active men there and got them to take an interest in favor of human liberty, human rights. You know my position here, I suppose, as a lawyer and a man; and if I had any earthly influence let me assure you that I moved this class as intensely as I could." If Parker believed what Herndon told him, then his impression was that Herndon single-handed set the prairies on fire and swept Sangamon County for the Republican ticket.

As Mrs. Lincoln and Bill Herndon came and went, holding their spites, young Henry B. Rankin, the sober, scrupulous, religious-minded law student, formed his impressions as to who was to blame. He was a reader of the Bible and of Walt Whitman's "Leaves of Grass," and as far as he could figure it out nobody was to blame. Mary Todd had married a genius who made demands; when he wanted to work, to isolate himself with every brain cell operating, he demanded to be let alone; it was no time for interruptions or errands. It was for this brooding man she was wife, housekeeper, and counselor in personal and political affairs in so far as he permitted. She watched his habits of "browsing around" in the pantry, and of skipping meals, and tried to bring him to regular eating habits. She advised with Dr. Wallace and other friends about Lincoln's tendency to consumption; they agreed to watch him closely but say nothing, as the fear of it might haunt Lincoln.

She did the shopping, picked out such things as the black satin haircloth rocking-chair in the parlor, the mahogany and haircloth sofa, the low-slung black-walnut sofa. She had kept house eighteen years before, too poor for a hired girl; they burned wood then; now they had a coal cookstove with four lids and a reservoir to warm rain water. She had chosen the beautiful, strong black-walnut cradle, into which she had put four boy babies; when one had died, the father had written to his stepbrother: "We lost our little boy. It was not our *first* but our second child. We miss him very much."

Fourteen years after her marriage she was keeping up her readings in the French language. She was not satisfied with a translation of a speech by Victor Hugo on capital punishment, published in the *Southern Literary Messenger*. She insisted on getting a copy of the speech in French, for the purpose, as she told Henry Rankin, "the better to show the strength of Hugo's oratory and the difficulty of translating into English a French oration of such intense feeling so as to preserve the true Hugo fire and force."

In bidding good night to a guest at their home, on one occasion, Mrs. Lincoln had stepped out on the front porch. The night sky was a dome of clear stars. She looked up and spoke of what a wonderful display it was; she named several planets and pointed to constellations, and explained that certain stars are suns far larger than our sun, and the centre of universes immensely larger than ours. Her interest in the stars and her talk about them was somewhat like that of Lincoln when he was at the Judd home in Chicago.

CHAPTER 133

LINCOLN was fifty-one years old. With each year of his life since he had become a grown man, his name and ways, and stories about him, had been spreading farther and farther among plain people and their children.

So tall, with so peculiar a slouch and so easy a saunter, so bony and sad, so quizzical and comic, sort of hiding a funny lantern that lighted and went out and that he lighted again—he was the Strange Friend and he was the Friendly Stranger.

Like something out of a picture book for children—he was. His form of slumping arches and his face of gaunt sockets were a shape a Great Artist had scrawled from careless clay, and was going to throw away, and then had said: "No, this one is to be kept; for a long time this one is to be kept; I made it by accident but it is better than many made on purpose."

He looked like an original plan for an extra-long horse or a lean tawny buffalo, that a Changer had suddenly whisked into a man-shape. Or he met the eye as a clumsy, mystical giant that had walked out of a Chinese or Russian fairy story, or a bogy who had stumbled out of an ancient Saxon myth with a handkerchief full of presents he wanted to divide among all the children in the world.

He didn't wear clothes. Rather, clothes hung upon him as if on a rack to dry, or on a loose ladder up a wind-swept chimney. He had clothes to keep the chill or the sun off. His clothes seemed to whisper, "He put us on when he was thinking about something else."

The stovepipe hat sort of whistled softly: "I am not a hat at all; I am the little garret roof where he tucks in little thoughts he writes on pieces of paper."

The umbrella with the name "Abraham Lincoln" stitched in, faded and drab from many rains and regular travels, looked sort of sleepy and murmuring. "Sometime we shall have all the sleep we want; we shall turn the law office over to the spiders and the cobwebs; and we shall quit politics for keeps."

People joked him on being so tall. "You're a man to look up to." In his way he belonged to the west country as Robert Burns belonged to Scotland or Hans Christian Andersen to North Europe.

Almost there were times when children and dreamers looked at Abraham Lincoln and lazily drew their eyelids half shut and let their hearts roam about him—and they half-believed him to be a tall horse-chestnut tree or a rangy horse or a big wagon or a log barn full of new-mown hay—something else or more than a man, a lawyer, a Republican candidate with principles, a prominent citizen—something spreading, elusive, and mysterious—he was the Strange Friend and he was the Friendly Stranger.

The stovepipe hat he wore had a brim one and three-quarters inches wide. The inside band in which edges of the more important letters and notes were tucked, measured two and three-quarters inches. The cylinder of the stovepipe was twenty-two inches in circumference. The hat was lined with heavy silk and measured inside, exactly six inches deep. And people tried to guess what was going on under that hat.

Written in pencil on the imitation satin paper that formed part of the lining of the hat was the signature "A. Lincoln, Springfield, Ill.," so that any forgetful person who might take the hat by mistake would know where to bring it back. Also the hatmaker, "George Hall, Springfield, Ill.," had printed his name in the hat so that Lincoln would know where to get another one just like it.

People sketched his form and look, as D. W. Wilder of Hiawatha, Kansas, did in telling how he and Lincoln sat on the river bank at St. Joseph, waiting for the ferryboat. "Lincoln had legs you could fold up; the knees stood out like that high and hind joint of the Kansas grasshopper; the buttons were off his shirt as when I saw him the summer before."

He had talked with a man on the Danville road, while sharpening his knife on the man's whetstone. They had been standing at a barnyard gate. And after Lincoln was gone, the farmer looked high and low, but couldn't find his whetstone. Lincoln had reached up and put the whetstone on top of a high gatepost, where it was found years afterward. But during those years the people at that farmhouse "allowed as maybe Abe Lincoln took that whetstone along with him."

In Pittsfield, Lizzie Gillmer was swinging on the front gate as Lincoln came out of the Gillmer house. And he took hold of Lizzie, swung her high in the air, kissed her, and put her back on the gate. And in the same town Susan Scanland had her opinion of Lincoln. "The laziest man there ever was, good for nothing except to tell stories," said she emphatically. She had fixed a turkey dinner for Lincoln and other men-folks, and six o'clock came and half-past six, and the dinner went cold, because Lincoln was spinning yarns for a crowd of men at a drug store. In Havana, Milton Logan, a juror in the Armstrong case, told his family and other families, that Lincoln addressed the jury, "Gentlemen, I appear here without any reward, for the benefit of that lady sitting there"—pointing at Hannah Armstrong—"who washed my dirty shirts when I had no money to pay her." And Lincoln, when he had freed Duff Armstrong of the murder charge, had said, "Duff, go home and be a good boy now, and don't get into any more scrapes."

The year of the big debates a boy had called out, "There goes old Mr. Lincoln," and Lincoln hearing it, remarked to a friend, "They commenced it when I was scarcely thirty years old."

Often when people called him "Old Abe" they meant he had the texture and quaint friendliness of old handmade Bibles, old calfskin law books, weather-beaten oak and walnut planks, or wagon axles always willing in storm or stars.

A neighbor boy, Fred Dubois, joined with a gang who tied a string to knock off Lincoln's hat. "Letters and papers fell out of the hat and scattered over the sidewalk," said Dubois. "He stooped to pick them up and us boys climbed all over him."

In many a prairie cabin by candlelight as the snowdrifts piled, and another crock of apples was passed to those who sat by the wood fire, the tale had been told of Abe Lincoln driving a two-horse team on a road heavy with mud. It was sunset time and Abe had his back to the sunset. And he met another driver with a two-horse wagon. Both knew that whoever turned out would be up to the hubs in mud, almost sure to get stuck in the mud. "Turn out," the other fellow called. "Turn out yourself," called Abe. The other fellow refused. Then Abe, with his back to the sunset, began to rise from his seat in the wagon, rising and rising, his tall shape getting longer and longer against the setting sun, as he was saying, "If you don't turn out I'll tell you what I'll do." And the other fellow hollered: "Don't go any higher. I'll turn out." And after he had struggled through and passed by Lincoln, he called back, "Say, what would you have done if I hadn't turned out?" Lincoln answered, "I'd 've turned out myself."

He would get on a train alone, pass a few words with men at the wood stove in the end of a car, find a seat up front by himself, arrange his legs and arms so no part of him stuck out into the aisle, fold over him the blue cloak he got in Washington after the Mexican War, and sleep.

As a young man he played marbles with boys; as an older man he spun tops with his own boys, Tad and Willie. When William Plato of Kane County came to his office with the little girl, Ella, he stood Ella on a chair and told her, "And you're not as tall as I am, even now."

A girl skipping along a sidewalk stumbled on a brick and fell backward, just as Lincoln came along and caught her, lifted her up in his arms, put her gently down and asked, "What is your name?" "Mary Tuft." "Well, Mary, when you reach home tell your mother you have rested in Abraham's bosom."

In many a courthouse, railroad depot, and drug store, the pithy anecdote had been told of the justice of the peace in Pekin who was elected circuit judge and often, when he wasn't sure about the law or the authorities, would say, "I don't know about that." And one day when Lincoln had cited the law and the authorities, he kept repeating and emphasizing to Lincoln, "I don't know about that, I don't know about that." Lincoln had looked the judge in the eye and said, "I *knew* your Honor didn't know about it and that's why I told you."

The caboose in which he was riding once during the debates with Douglas, was put on a sidetrack, while the special train and private car of Douglas whizzed by and faded. And Lincoln laughed, "I guess they smelt no royalty in our carriage." In Rushville and towns circling around, they remembered the day he was there. The whole town turned out, among them young women of Rushville society, as such. One of the belles dangled a little negro doll baby in Lincoln's face. He looked into her face and asked quietly, "Madam, are you the mother of that?" At many a corn shucking and Saturday night shindig, this incident had been told of. And likewise the one about the time he got on a train in Bloomington, after wrangling with a jury all day, and as the train got going he had turned around in his seat and told William Nichols of Bloomington, "There are two things even God Almighty doesn't know, how an Illinois jury will decide, and who a widow will marry."

As he got into an omnibus that had seen better days, he took a seat and began wheezing a tune on a mouth organ. Whitney asked the why of it. "This is my band; Douglas had a brass band with him in Peoria; but this will do me." He carried books in a handkerchief bundle. He met a weeping woman who was going to miss a train because her trunk had not been hauled to the depot; and Lincoln put the trunk on his shoulders, they met the train in time, and the woman told everybody on the train about it. He dressed any which way at times, in broadcloth, a silk hat, a silk choker, and a flaming red silk handkerchief, so that one court clerk said Lincoln was "fashionably dressed, as neatly attired as any lawyer at court, except Ward Lamon." Or again, people said Lincoln looked like a huge skeleton with skin over the bones, and clothes covering the skin.

"How tall is your wife?" he was asked in Menard County. He held his right arm straight out and said his wife could just stand under his arm. And it was told that when he was asked why the Todd name was spelled with two d's he said he guessed one "d" was enough for God, but the Todds needed two.

News was brought him one day by Tom McNeeley of Petersburg, who had been down in Mississippi and witnessed an exhibition of the taming of wild horses by Denton Offut. Offut would take a misbehaving horse, whisper in its ear and get it quiet, and then for five dollars would sell to a farmer the magic word to be whispered in the horse's ear. Offut had asked about old Petersburg and New Salem, and wished to send a special message to Lincoln. "Tell it just as Offut said it," Lincoln told McNeeley. And the message was advice. "Tell Lincoln to get out of his rascally business of law and politics, and do something honest, like taming horses." And Lincoln laughed, "That's Offut, that's just like Offut."

Two men were carrying on an old feud of their Kentucky families. One called the other a shameful name, and the other knocked him down with the blade of a hoe. Lincoln, defending the assailant, told a jury: "The important thing is that our client had a hoe instead of a revolver. It is not the day when a man can invade the property of another and apply epithets without the weight of a blow."

The "gingerbread story," which he had mentioned without telling, in one of the debates with Douglas, touched young and old. Lincoln had been asked why he seemed to have so little of the companionship of women and whether he had no pleasure from their society. "When we lived in Indiana," he said, "once in a while my mother used to get some sorghum and ginger and make some gingerbread. It wasn't often, and it was our biggest treat. One day I smelled the gingerbread and came into the house to get my share while it was still hot. My mother had baked me three gingerbread men. I took them out under a hickory tree to eat them. There was a family near us poorer than we were, and their boy came along as I sat down. 'Abe,' he said, 'gimme a man?' I gave him one. He crammed it into his mouth in two bites and looked at me while I was biting the legs off my first one. 'Abe,' he said, 'gimme that other'n.' I wanted it myself, but I gave it to him and as it followed the first, I said to him, 'You seem to like gingerbread.' 'Abe,' he said, 'I don't s'pose anybody on earth likes gingerbread better'n I do—and gets less'n I do.' "

Where he got his stories, how they would start or finish, no one could tell. "When hunting for wit he had no ability to discriminate vulgar and refined substance," said Swett, "it was the wit he was after and he would pick it up out of the mud or dirt just as readily as from a parlor table."

Old Æsop could not have invented a better fable than the one about the snakes in the bed, to show the harm of letting slavery into the new territories. "If there was a bed newly made up, to which the children were to be taken, and it was proposed to take a batch of snakes and put them there with them, I take it no man would say there was any question how I ought to decide."

That a man can tell the truth while he believes he is telling a lie, was a point Lincoln would prove in such a story as that of a negro barber in Illinois who stepped out of his shop one night to join a crowd gazing at the luminous shine of the planet Jupiter. "Sho," said the barber, "I've seen that stah befoh. I seen him way down in Georgy." Lincoln's point was, "He told the truth, but he thought he was lying."

When weathering trouble he liked to think of "Old Zach," the Mexican War hero. "General Taylor's battles were not distinguished for brilliant military maneuvers; but in all he seems to have conquered by the exercise of a sober and steady judgment, coupled with a dogged incapacity to understand that defeat was possible. He could not be flurried, and he could not be scared. He was averse to sudden and startling quarrels; and he pursued no man with revenge. It is much for the young to know that treading the hard path of duty as he trod it will be noticed, and will lead to high places."

He marked with his pencil on page 10 of "The Elements of Character" the passage reading: "A wisely trained Character never stops to ask, What will society think of me if I do this thing?" He marked also the more subtle sentence: "We are all of us perpetually liable to gross self-deception by transferring in fancy our love or our hate for the consequences of vices or virtues to the vices or virtues themselves."

His pencil drew a line on page 233 alongside this sentiment: "Let no human being think that he holds companionship with the Lord, because he loves to retire apart, to pray, or to contemplate the Divine attributes, if, at such times, he looks down upon and shuns the haunts of men." Then came the philosophy: "Every thought of self-elevation, every feeling that tends towards 'I am holier than thou,' smothers the breath of all true prayer. Neither let any one suppose himself spiritual because material life or material duties oppress him. God made the material world as a school for His children."

His thoughts dwelt on other passages he marked: "The motive power in man is Affection. What he loves he wills, and what he wills he performs. Our Character is the complex of all that we love. . . . There is no station in life where there is not a constant demand for the exercise of Charity. We cannot be in company an hour with any person without some such demand presenting itself to us."

His mind exercised itself with such distinctions as in the case of President Polk's "open attempt to prove by telling the truth what he could not prove by telling the *whole* truth." He tinted his language with a cool, strange bittersweet at the close of a campaign in which he and his associates, as he said, had been "bespattered with every imaginable odious epithet." Though he was a leader of the state bar, he could say, "Some things legally right are morally wrong." He had sought to discipline his tongue, to make it a willing instrument to bring common understandings between the alien prejudices of northern and southern Illinois. "Shades of opinion may be sincerely entertained by honest and truthful men." To hold a right opinion on all things at all times would earn bewilderment in the end; he would leave that to Horace Greeley or Henry Ward Beecher, saying for himself, "It is better only sometimes to be right than at all times wrong." In years when he had nothing to say he said it, he crept into crypts of silence and let history work and shadows pass and repass. Then when the demand came he could step forth and talk three hours a day for a hundred days, and be fresh at the finish.

He could have said that So-and-So was "reprehensible." Instead, he remarked, "He's a bad egg." His speech was at times as natural as a horse flicking its ear to shoo a fly. First-rate grammarians shivered at his commenting on a problematical issue, "Oh, that'll be got along with."

His published speeches did not always register a certain plain manner of address which he used. The *Sycamore True Republican* editor wrote of Lincoln as saying in the House Divided speech, "He *don't*"; often before final and corrected speeches were published he was recorded as saying "He don't" or "It don't." He had spoken of the "bosses" of the plan for slavery extension, according to first reports; this later appeared as "chief architects" instead of "bosses."

One who heard him reply to Douglas at Peoria reported Lincoln as saying: "He thought he could approach an argument and at times believed he could make one; but when one denied the settled and plainest facts of history, you could not argue with him: the only thing you could do would be *to stop his mouth with a corn cob.*"

He could be humble in different ways, telling the Wisconsin farmers that the privilege of addressing them was "an honor for which I make my profound and grateful acknowledgment," or saying of Douglas, "I know the judge is a great man and I am only a small man, but I feel that I have got him." As he was sitting at a table eating dinner on the fair grounds at Urbana, an old woman he knew came up and they spoke greetings. But Lincoln was surprised. "Why, Granny, have you no place to eat your dinner?" She insisted, "I just came to see you, Mr. Lincoln." "This won't do, Granny. You must have a place here. Come and take my place." And he sat down by a tree and ate a turkey leg with bread and butter. People told incidents like that, as though they had actually happened. He made plain people feel at home, so they said.

When he was in Washington as a congressman and his wife wrote letters addressing the envelopes "Hon.," the abbreviation for Honorable, before his name, he wrote to her: "Suppose you do not prefix the 'Hon.' to the address on your letters to me any more—I like the letters very much but I would rather they should not have that upon them."

At the home of Mrs. J. L. Beath in Atlanta, near Bloomington, a special cake had been baked for him. When he saw the cake, he threw his arms into the air and laughed out, "You don't expect me to eat all of that." Meeting John T. Barnett in Galesburg, he had to explain to Mayor Sanderson that years back he and Barnett were spear-fishing in the Sangamon River, and he had held a torch high up so as to keep the light out of his own eyes. And Barnett had called out: "Abe, bring down that torch. You're holding it clear out of Sangamon County." Lincoln pointed at Barnett and said to the mayor, "This is the man."

He could be so proud and simple as to say when he was asked, with Douglas present, "Do you know who Douglas is?" "Why, yes, he's a man with tens of thousands of *blind* followers. It's my business to make some of those blind followers *see.*"

He would take time, raising no fuss about it, to see that an old woman in a railway passenger car got settled with comfort in a double seat. And though nearly thirty years had gone by, he still had the same carelessness of his announcement as a candidate for the legislature, when he was twenty-one. "I am humble Abraham Lincoln. . . . If not—elected—·

it will be all the same." The remark of an Irish orator that Napoleon was "grand, gloomy, and peculiar," had sunk deep in his mind; though he would surely at times be gloomy and peculiar, he could keep off assumptions of grandeur.

When the Logan County ladies at Atlanta showed him a big cake, tinted with white frosting with stripes of red and yellow, to be cut at a dinner for him, he said, "Perhaps I'm not as hungry as I look," and had them auction the cake for a benefit of the Republican campaign fund.

"Give my love to all the connections," he would write to his stepbrother, and more than once the line, "Give my love to all, and especially to Mother." An old Quaker strain had lasted in him; he inherited some natural habit of living plainly. Often he was a slow man, sluggish as a buffalo that couldn't run till he got started running, and after he got started he was hard to slow down. Yet the personal warmth of him, his glow and shine in companionship, was swift and changeful. He often shook hands using both hands and once told a boy, "If you are my boy, you must learn to shake hands with me as my boys always do, double-handed." He had his own way of stooping to say, "How are you, Bub?" It was this often childlike man of whom John Locke Scripps of the *Chicago Tribune* said in 1860, "He has an exquisite sense of justice."

He had grown up among Kentucky and Indiana riflemen who killed the timber squirrel with a shot in the eye, but he had never pulled trigger on any animal but one wild turkey. He went coon-hunting with other boys and let them do the shooting. Then as a grown man he had spent a share of his life in saloons, among drinking men who knew him as no drinking man at all.

Respectable friends, who cared about reputations as gentlemen and scholars, took it as a little queer, a little like "a country Jake," beneath dignity, that Lincoln should carry with him the book "Joe Miller's Jests," generally called Joe Miller's joke book. English puns, Irish bulls, Greek repartee, folk tales of Jews and Egyptians, brisk anecdotes, filled the book—more than a thousand, each with a serial number. No. 997 told of "the celebrated organist Abbé Vogler, once imitating a thunderstorm so well that for miles round all the milk turned sour." The Irishman was told of, who had been living in Scotland and was asked how he liked the country, replying, "I was sick all the time I was there, and if I had lived there till this time, I'd been dead a year ago." Lord Russell on the scaffold ready to have his head cut off, handed his watch to a bishop, with the remark, "Take this—it shows time; I am going into eternity and no longer need it." Another lord, owing many debts, was asked how he could sleep at night, and answered: "I sleep very well, but I wonder how my creditors can." A wounded officer on a bloody battlefield was howling with pain when another wounded officer near by called to him: "What do you make such a noise for? Do you think nobody is killed but yourself?"

Such was some of the foolery in the book that Lincoln occasionally took out of his carpetbag and read aloud to other lawyers. Some had the pith and poignancy of the gravedigger in the play of Hamlet, one joke reading: "An Irishman going to be hanged, begged that the rope might be tied under his arms instead of round his neck; for, said Pat, I am so remarkably ticklish in the throat, that if tied there, I will certainly kill myself with laughing." Or again Joke No. 506, reading: "Lieutenant Connolly, an Irishman in the service of the United States, during the American war, chanced to take three Hessian prisoners himself, without any assistance; being asked by the commander-in-chief how he had taken them—'I surrounded them,' was the answer."

There were tales of the people. A traveler in Egypt said to a worker on the land: "I suppose you are quite happy now; the country looks like a garden and every village has its minaret." "God is great," replied the worker. "Our master gives with one hand and takes with two." Another traveler, reporting that he and his servant had made fifty wild Arabs run, said there was nothing surprising about it. "We ran and they ran after us." And again and again little tales of the people, the people. Into the street before Dean Swift's deanery came "a great rabble," waiting "to see the eclipse." And Dean Swift had the big bell rung, and a crier bawling: "O Yes, O Yes, all manner of persons here concerned take notice the eclipse be put off till tomorrow this time! so God save the King and his Reverence the dean." And the rabble went away, all but one Irishman who said he would stay because "the dean might change his mind and have the eclipse that day after all."

Thus Joe Miller's jests. They were a nourishing company to Lincoln. Once in a while he told a story that seemed to have been made over from Joe Miller and placed in Indiana. In his lighter moods his humor matched with the Rabelais definition, "a certain jollity of mind, pickled in the scorn of fortune."

He told of the long-legged boy "sparking" a farmer's daughter when the hostile father came in with a shotgun; the boy jumped through a window, and running across the cabbage patch scared up a rabbit; in about two leaps the boy caught up with the rabbit, kicked it high in the air, and grunted, "Git out of the road and let somebody run that knows how." He told of a Kentucky horse sale where a small boy was riding a fine horse to show off points, when a man whispered to the boy, "Look here, boy, hain't that horse got the splints?" and the boy answered: "Mister, I don't know what the splints is, but if it's good for him, he has got it; if it ain't good for him, he ain't got it."

Riding to Lewiston an old acquaintance, a weather-beaten farmer, spoke of going to law with his next neighbor. "Been a neighbor of yours for long?" "Nigh onto fifteen year." "Part of the time you get along all right, don't you?" "I reckon we do." "Well, see this horse of mine? I sometimes get out of patience with him. But I know his faults; he does fairly well as horses go; it might take me a long time to get used to some other horse's faults; for all horses have faults."

The instant dignity became bogus his eye caught it. He enjoyed such anecdotes as the one of a Brown County, Indiana, man who killed a neighbor's dog, and the proof of guilt was clear. The defendant's attorney cleared his throat and began a speech, "May it please the court, we are proud to live in a land where justice is administered to the king on the throne and the beggar on his dunghill." The squire then interrupted, "You may go ahead with your speech, but the case *are* decided."

Little folk tales and snatches of odd wisdom known to common people of the ancient kingdoms of the Persians and the Arabians, came to be known among the common people of the farming districts in Illinois, hitched up somehow to Abe Lincoln. When a story or saying had a certain color or smack, it would often be tagged as coming from Lincoln. He had said to a book agent, "For those who like that kind of a book, that's the kind of a book they'll like." He was the man walking along a dusty road when a stranger driving a buggy came along. And he asked the stranger, "Will you be so good as to take my overcoat to town for me?" And the man in the buggy said he would. "But how will you get your overcoat back again?" "Oh, that's easy! I'm going to stay right inside of it." And of course, said some jokers, it was Abe Lincoln who first told a hotel waiter, "Say, if this is coffee, then please bring me some tea, but if this is tea, please bring me some coffee." And on Abe Lincoln was laid the remark, after tasting ice cream, "Say, waiter, I don't want to slander this hotel, but this here pudding's froze."

He had come out of a slushy snow into a courtroom to try a case and sat down to dry his feet at the stove. The words of the lawyer arguing against him came to his ears. All of a sudden he was out in the middle of the courtroom, one shoe off, calling, "Now, judge, that isn't fair. I'm not going to have this jury all fuddled up."

Did he not say when he met a man somewhat matching his own height, "Well, you're up some"—had they not seen how the clay of the earth clung to him? Before posing for a photographer, he stepped into a barber shop, saying, "I better get my hair slicked up." Then, sitting before the camera, he ran his fingers through his hair, caught himself, and said, "Guess I've made a bird's nest of it again." It was he who agreed to make a horse trade, sight unseen, with a judge. First came the judge the next morning with a broken-down bone-rack of a horse; then came Lincoln carrying a wooden sawhorse on his shoulders, saying, "Well, judge, this is the first time I ever got the worst of it in a horse trade."

A walking, stalking library of stories he was. Some of them could have had musical accompaniments from barn-dance fiddles. The prize story-tellers of one neighborhood and another had met him and they had competed. "That reminds me." "That's like the feller down at Goose Holler." And occasionally was one with a shine of many cross-lights in it. Lincoln told of a balloonist going up in New Orleans, sailing for hours, and dropping his parachute over a cotten field. The gang of negroes picking cotton saw a man coming down from the sky in blue silk, in silver spangles, wearing golden slippers. They ran—all but one old-timer who had the rheumatism and couldn't get away. He waited till the balloonist hit the ground and walked toward him. Then he mumbled: "Howdy, Massa Jesus. How's yo' Pa?"

Lincoln had stood with two umbrellas at an imaginary rat hole, impersonating Sam'l, the Quaker boy whose father wanted to stop the boy's using swear words. The two umbrellas were blacksmith tongs. Sam'l's father had said, "Now, Sam'l, thee will sit here until thee has a rat. If I hear thee swear, thee will sit here till thee has another." And Sam'l had sat there for hours, snipping the tongs a few times, but no rat caught. At last one came out from the rat hole, the whiskers peeping up, then the black nose, and the eyes blinking. And the two umbrella tongs snapped together in a flash. And Sam'l yelled, "By God, I have thee at last!" And Lincoln with a shaking, swaying frame let out a squeal and stood holding an imaginary wriggling rat between the two umbrellas. He had told this in Illinois towns during the debates with Douglas. And Robert R. Hitt, the phonographic reporter, said he forgot himself and politics and business and nearly believed there was a live squeaking rat caught between the two umbrellas. For a roomful of men in a hotel, Lincoln would perform this drama of Sam'l, Sam'l's father, and the rat, acting subtly the rôles of the earnest father, the obstreperous boy, and the furtive rat.

He picked up comedy, as he met it, and passed it on to others. In Cumberland County, one Dr. Hamburgher, a Democrat, forced his way to the front to reply to Lincoln's speech. As Hamburgher worked into a frothy and threatening speech, a little man with a limp came over to Lincoln and said: "Don't mind *him*. I know *him*; I live here; I'll take care of *him*. Watch me." And he took the platform, and replying brought from Hamburgher the cry, "That's a lie." To which the little man with the limp called out with high defiance, "Never mind, I'll take that from *you*— yes, I'll take anything from you, except your pills." At the mention of pills, the doctor snorted, "You scoundrel, you know I've quit practicing medicine." And the little man dropped down on the knee of his best leg, raised his hands toward the sky in thankfulness, and shouted, "Then, thank God! The country is safe."

Plato, the Kane County lawyer, had told him a story about a man who had beaten a dog to death and was in such a rage that he would go out of the house and again beat the dog to death. When Plato came one day to Lincoln's office in Springfield, Lincoln's greeting was, "Well, Plato, have you got that dog killed yet?"

A family in Indiana, according to Lincoln, picked dandelion tops or other leaves and boiled "greens" for dinner in the spring and early summer. Once after a mess of greens the whole family went out of commission. After that when they had greens a big helping would first be forked out for Zerah, a half-wit boy, as the family said: "Try it on Zerah. If he stands it, it won't hurt the rest of us." And a man had a horse that would balk and settle down on all four legs like a bird dog. He traded off the horse as good for hunting birds. As the horse crossed a creek he settled down in the middle of it like a bird dog and the man who had owned him called to the new rider: "Ride him! Ride him! He's as good for fish as he is for birds."

People looked at Lincoln, searching his face, thinking about his words and ways, ready to believe he was a Great Man. Then he would spill over with a joke or tell of some new horseplay of wit or humor in the next county. The barriers tumbled. He was again a strange friend, a neighbor, a friendly stranger, no far-off Great Man at all. "His face," Moncure D. Conway noted, "had a battered and bronzed look, without being hard." He fitted the measurements, "three parts sublime to one grotesque."

A crowd was bubbling with mirth in an Ohio town as a short friend stood alongside Lincoln to introduce him. Lincoln, pointing at himself, said, "This is the long of it," and putting an arm on the friend's shoulder, "And this is the short of it."

Joe Fifer, an eighteen-year-old cornhusker, heard Lincoln at Bloomington after Sweet made the opening address. "When Lincoln was starting to speak," Fifer noticed, "some men near me said Lincoln was no great shakes as a public speaker and Swett would make a better showing against Douglas. But when Lincoln got to going they listened; they stood still without moving out of their foot tracks. Lincoln looked out on a wall of faces still as if they had been made of stone."

The Springfield doctor, William Jayne, trying to fathom why Lincoln had carried the crowds with him usually in debating with Douglas, said: "Everybody thinks he is honest and believes what he says. If he was really a great man, or if people regarded him as a great man, he could not do half so much."

He was the man who had started a little circle of people to giggling one morning in Judge Davis's courtroom, and the judge sputtered out: "I am not going to stand this any longer, Mr. Lincoln. You're always disturbing this court with your tomfoolery." The fine was $5.00, for disorderly conduct. Lincoln sat with his hand over his mouth, trying to keep his face straight. Later the judge called Lawrence Weldon to him and Weldon whispered into his ear what it was that Lincoln had told. Then the judge giggled. Getting his face straight, he announced, "The clerk may remit Mr. Lincoln's fine." The joke had to do with "taking up a subscription to buy Jim Wheeler a new pair of pants."

He could speak of So-and-So as "a quiet, orderly, faithful man." And he could hand a bottle to a baldheaded man he wished to get rid of, with the remarks: "Try this stuff for your hair. Keep it up. They say it will grow hair on a pumpkin. Come back in ten months and tell me how it works." When it was intimated to him that he was consulting too much with Judge Davis, he told of a New Hampshire judge who said: "The only time the chief judge ever consulted was at the close of a long day's session, when he turned and whispered, 'Don't your back ache?'" He liked to tell of the strict judge of whom it was said: "He would hang a man for blowing his nose in the street, but he would quash the indictment if it failed to specify which hand he blew it with."

When he presented Coles County relatives with a sad-faced photograph of himself, he said, "This is not a very good-looking picture, but it's the best that could be produced from the poor subject."

He had written angry letters filled with hard names and hot arguments. And such letters he had thrown in the stove. He gave the advice that it was healthy to write a hot letter and then burn it.

In the manuscript of a speech on the Constitution, he began, "All is not the result of accident." In a letter to a client, he closed, "Be patient— they have not got your land yet." When, twenty years previous, the Democrats had jockeyed with the supreme court and enlarged it from five to nine judgeships, and Stephen A. Douglas had taken one of the judgeships for himself, Lincoln told him, "I would not behave as well as you will have to now, for twice the money." He had a certain elusive code of behavior, varying with events. When he chose to, he could imitate a stutterer he knew who had a trick of whistling between stuttered syllables. In his earlier years as an orator, he had tried for ornamental phrases. Later he referred to such decorations as "fizzlegigs and fireworks."

The Alton Railroad conductor, Gilbert Finch, said people could get near Lincoln in a sort of neighborly way, as though they had always known him. "But there was something tremendous between you and him all the time," said Finch. "I have eaten with Lincoln many times at the railroad eating-houses, and you get very neighborly if you eat together in railroad restaurants. Everybody tried to get as near Lincoln as possible when he was eating, because he was such good company. But we couldn't exactly make him out. Sometimes I would see what looked like dreadful loneliness in his look, and I used to wonder what he was thinking about. Whatever it was he was thinking alone. It wasn't a solemn look, like Stephen A. Douglas sometimes had. Douglas sometimes made me think of an owl; he stared at you with dark eyes in a way that almost frightened you.

"Lincoln never frightened anybody," said the Alton conductor. "No one was afraid of him. But something about him made plain folks feel toward him a good deal as a child feels toward his father."

There came to be registered on Lincoln's face some of the poetry of his having said of "Popular Sovereignty" that it was "nothing but a living, creeping lie" and of one Douglas argument that it got down as thin as "soup made by boiling the shadow of a pigeon that had starved to death." Picking up a trick compliment from Douglas, he smiled it into thin air with the comment, "Not being accustomed to flattery, it came the sweeter to me."

A Boston scholar saw Lincoln as having "a plain, ploughed face; a mind, absent in part; features that expressed neither self-satisfaction nor any other Americanism but rather the same painful sense of being educated or of needing education that tormented a private secretary; above all a lack of apparent force." Many in Illinois knew him as a "learner." Lincoln told Bagby at Pekin that he was thrown in a wrestling match once, and, "I asked the fellow to show me how he did it. He showed me. And I said, 'Now, please try it again.' And I threw him as easily as he did me."

He was not merely tall, but longish. Edwin M. Stanton, referring to the reaper patent case and Lincoln as his associate counsel in Cincinnati, told Don Piatt, "I said that if that giraffe appeared in the case I would throw up my brief and leave." When Indiana people asked Dan Voorhees what Lincoln looked like he told them: "Lincoln is lean and lathy; his long, dangling, rake-handle arms are strong as steel; he stoops a little, is angular, a man of bony corners. His awkwardness is all in his looks; in his movements he is quick, sure, and graceful. Even when he crosses his spider-like legs or throws them over the arms of his chair, he does it with a natural grace."

Germans and Irishmen had greetings from him. "I know enough German to know that Kaufman means merchant, and Schneider means tailor—am I not a good German scholar?" Or, "That reminds me of what the Irishman said, 'In this country one man is as good as another; and for the matter of that, very often a great deal better.' "

Meeting Henry C. Whitney once, he told of a chat with the famous Baltimore lawyer, Reverdy Johnson, in Cincinnati. Johnson took a laugh for himself, believed it funny, that the will of Daniel Webster had made trouble for Webster's friends. The will mentioned certain silver-plate articles to be manufactured and presented to certain friends. And when the estate was settled, it was found the silver plate had been ordered but there wasn't money to pay for it. And so, Daniel Webster's friends paid their own cash to the jewelers for their remembrances from the celebrated dead man. Reverdy Johnson chuckled over the affair. And Lincoln told Whitney he couldn't see anything funny about the affair, adding that if

Johnson were to make such a will, his own friends might be in the same fix as Webster's.

His father and mother had been of the predestinarian Baptist faith, and he had a predestinarian streak, a leaning to the belief, "What is to be is to be." Among the Lincolns in Hancock County, children of Mordecai Lincoln, and among other Lincolns in Kentucky, it was said they were uneven workers, odd fellows, ringing high with laughter and then dropping to depths of gloom, "cantankerous but likable." In their blood seemed to run a melancholia they spoke of as "the Lincoln horrors," "the Lincoln hypo." They were large-boned, long-armed, long-legged men.

In Springfield and other places, something out of the ordinary seemed to connect with Abraham Lincoln's past, his birth, a mystery of where he came from. The wedding certificate of his father and mother was not known to be on record. Whispers floated of his origin as "low-flung," of circumstances so misty and strange that political friends wished they could be cleared up and made respectable. Hardin County in Kentucky, where the wedding license of Thomas Lincoln and Nancy Hanks was recorded, had been divided into two counties—and the wanted document had gone to the newly made Larue County courthouse—where no one had thought to search.

He had lived long enough to have a portrait gallery in his memory to muse over. He had seen John McNamar, once the betrothed of Ann Rutledge, turning the mother and sisters of Ann out of house and home, marrying Deborah Latimer in 1838, building a brick house that dominated the landscape, burying a first wife and marrying Eliza McNeal in 1855, a cold man of mortgages, per cents, accumulations, whose most excellent trait was always told in the words, "He's a quick man to figure." He had seen Ned Baker, the song-voiced, the reckless, the warm-hearted, move across the Great Plains and the Rockies to California and then to Oregon; the news was that Ned Baker would be the next United States Senator from Oregon.

Tom Nelson and Dick Thompson, two young lawyers and politicians over at Terre Haute, Indiana, were telling how they rode a whole day with Lincoln on the seventy-two-mile stage ride to Indianapolis. They didn't know who Lincoln was; he didn't tell them; and they were having a good time bantering him about his long legs, hayseed in his collar. In a hotel lobby that evening they saw him button-holed by important people and were told, "That's Abe Lincoln of Illinois; he's here to see the governor on business." When they apologized to Lincoln, he drawled, "That's all right; I guess I enjoyed it about as much as you did."

About three times in ten years Whitney remembered having seen Lincoln lose his temper. Once was the morning of the day when Douglas was to arrive in triumph from Washington and open the 1858 senatorial campaign. Lincoln had come to Chicago to argue a motion for a new trial before Judge Drummond. But T. Lyle Dickey, the opposing lawyer, suddenly sent word, "You go ahead and make your argument now, and I'll make mine later." The same Dickey had a short time before, in a letter the newspapers printed, drawn away from support of Lincoln for senator. As Lincoln read Dickey's message, he started walking back and forth in Whitney's office, crying in a high key, "I hain't got any argument to make! I hain't got any argument to make!" And when Whitney tried to murmur questions about the reasons for the excitement, Lincoln thrust the Dickey message into Whitney's hands and went on again, "I hain't got any argument to make!"

Usually he was easy to accommodate. "You're too late for supper but maybe we can scrape up something," a Bloomington hotel clerk told him. "All right, I don't want much," was the reply.

Taking a ten-minute walk with Owen K. Reeves before court opened one morning in Bloomington, Lincoln passed the new Gridley mansion with its large pretensions of grandeur. He remarked that for a man to live in a house like that had an effect on his character. "If he's at all sensitive he'll feel it."

When Tad was late bringing home the milk he hunted the boy and came home with Tad on his shoulders and carrying the milk pail himself. Once he chased Tad and brought the boy home, holding the little one at arm's length; the father chuckled at the son's struggle to kick him in the face. Once as he lugged the howling Willie and Tad, a neighbor asked, "Why, Mr. Lincoln, what's the matter?" The answer: "Just what's the matter with the whole world. I've got three walnuts and each wants two."

Once during a concert at the First Presbyterian Church, election returns were being discussed by the audience between the classical numbers of the program. There was a buzzing, even while music was being performed, as to which counties had been carried. And Lincoln, it was said, had turned his head and replied to some remark from the rear, in a tone heard by the entire audience, "Wait till we hear from Macoupin." At another time, while an elocutionist was reciting the satirical poem "Nothing to Wear," a clear unmistakable snort of laughter broke over the audience at a point where no one else saw anything to laugh at. All turned and looked at Lincoln, who wished that minute he could slink out of sight.

His mind had wandered in speculative humor, led by some phase of the poem, "Nothing to Wear," and his apparatus for laughter had suddenly obeyed an impulse. The act was evidence that he was a man who laughed alone sometimes, his laughing muscles coördinating in chimes with his mental reckonings in elements of the comic.

There were serious people who believed Lincoln to be a good man, a keen and a kindly man, with a smart head on him and a big heart. Yes, he was all this. But he was not a Great Man. He was hardly great enough to be a United States senator, let alone a President of the United States. They had heard of his telling stories. Or they had listened to him telling these stories. And they had laughed at the stories. They couldn't help laughing. "He makes you laugh in spite of yourself."

And these serious people didn't want a Laughing President. There never had been a Laughing President. At the head of the Government should be a solemn man who was constantly grave and dignified in his deportment. Abe Lincoln was a good fellow. But he wouldn't do for President. He was so honest that if he went to the White House he would just naturally tell visitors the same livery-stable yarns he was telling in Illinois. For President there should be a man as earnest as the Constitution and the amendments thereto. If he should be so comical that he could make a cat laugh, he wouldn't do.

And there were still other people, not so many, who wondered what it would be like to have a plain, awkward shambler like Lincoln in the White House at Washington. There never had been a Laughing President. Why not try one once? Why not see what an easy-going fellow like Lincoln would do in the presidential chair?

Everybody knew him and nobody knew him. He seemed to have more secrets about himself, that he kept to himself, than any one else in Illinois. "The most secretive, shut-mouthed man I ever knew," said his law partner. "The most reticent man I ever saw, or expect to see," said Judge David Davis, in whose court Lincoln practiced twelve years. "I doubt whether he ever asked anybody's advice about anything," said Leonard Swett.

"In eating, sleeping, reading, conversation, study, he was regularly irregular, with no stated time for eating, no fixed time for going to bed, none for getting up," said Joshua Speed. "When ignorant on any subject, no matter how simple, he was always willing to acknowledge it." A friend quoted from Calhoun, "To legislate upon precedent is but to make the error of yesterday the law of today," and said Lincoln remarked it was "a great truth grandly uttered."

"You might have made money entering land at a dollar and a quarter an acre," Gillespie told him. "Yes, that is true—but I never had any money sense."

The shifty ins and outs of politics in which he moved, and his walk when walking as if on eggshells, were intimated in his once writing to Swett: "I see no objection to the letter you have written to Shaffer. Send it to him, but do not let him know I have seen it; and by a postscript tell him to come down and see me."

He could be diplomatic, and write a note of introduction that on first reading seemed to be complimentary, but on second reading said, "For all

I know, this fellow is a deadbeat and a liar." Swett in Bloomington was handed a note by a man who had carried it from Lincoln in Springfield. It greeted "Hon. L. Swett" as "Dear Sir" and read:

This introduces Mr. William Yates, who visits Bloomington on some business matter. He is pecuniarily responsible for anything he will say; and, in fact, for anything he will say on any subject.

Yours very truly,
A. LINCOLN.

Besides the Laughing Lincoln there was the Sad Man. "He looks as if he had lost all his friends," was a common remark. Before he loosened up and hit his stride in a public speech, his eyes were the dull gray of a dead fish, as one observer saw him. He recited poetry as from the depths of grief that could not be sung nor spoken; the desperation of it might be hinted in the adumbrations of words, with low whimperings of defeated winter winds or the fugitive monotones of the mourning dove that sat summer on summer in the hopeful maples. The music of this verse pleased him:

> The mossy marbles rest
> On the lips that he has pressed
>   In their bloom;
> And the names he loved to hear
> Have been carved for many a year
>   On the tomb.

He had told Herndon he would come to some terrible end; he didn't know what; it was a fate that lurked ahead. The melancholy of Lincoln bothered Herndon, who could be desperate and wailing and vocal, but who could not understand the saturated and impregnated woe that steeped Lincoln and made Lincoln a Man Alone. Stories rose, idly as breezes. Lincoln had gone to a voodoo woman in New Orleans; she gazed with shiny eyes into his face and told him, "You will be a President of the United States." At the selling of a beautiful octoroon, he had clenched his fists and sworn, "By God, boys, if I ever get a chance to hit that thing I'll hit it and hit it hard." Of the shambling form of his law partner in one of the dark moods, Herndon said, "Melancholy dripped from him."

His very eyes and hair were baffling. Herndon said his hair was dark brown, almost black. Others saw it as black shaded to a sandy tinge. Lincoln himself described it as "coarse black." His eyes were chiefly gray; but one shrewd observer saw a tint of hazel; the color of his eyes shaded to a hint of brown just as his hair did; one who hated him said he had "a small, lascivious mouth" and "tender, bluish eyes."

Tradition had attached to him, as to storm-split oak branches grown together and leafed out. He had only wept tears instead of pronouncing a funeral oration over Bowling Green; he had shaken O. B. G. Ficklin by the nape of his neck, down in proslavery Egypt, forcing the admission that his Mexican War record was clean as to support of soldiers in the field; he had plucked from nowhere a simple almanac that saved Duff Armstrong from the gallows. He was a piece of the prairie drama of Illinois.

He defended Peachy Harrison who killed Greek Grafton, a law student in the office of Lincoln & Herndon. On the witness stand came old Peter Cartwright, the famous circuit rider, grandfather of the accused murderer. "How long have you known the prisoner?" "I have known him since a babe; he laughed and cried on my knee." And Lincoln led on with more questions, till old Peter Cartwright was telling the last words that slowly choked out from the murdered man, three days after the stabbing: "I am dying; I will soon part with all I love on earth and I want you to say to my slayer that I forgive him. I want to leave this earth with a forgiveness of all who have in any way injured me." Lincoln had then begged the jury to be as forgiving as the murdered man. The handling of the grandfather, as a witness, cleared Peachy Harrison, and set him free.

The name of the man had come to stand for what he was, plus beliefs, conjectures, and guesses. He was spoken of as a "politician" in the sense that politics is a trade of cunning, ambitious, devious men. He himself once had told the Illinois legislature that politicians are a lower breed, more often tricky than honest. He chose a few issues on which to explain his mind fully. If he had chosen more issues his time would have been spent as a talker only; he probably thought there are enough talkers. Some of his reticences were not evasions but retirements to cloisters of silence. Questions of life and destiny shook him close to prayers and tears in his own hidden corners and byways; the depths of the issues were too dark, too pitiless, inexorable, for a man to open his mouth and try to tell what he knew.

In the cave of winds in which he saw history in the making he was far more a listener than a talker. The high sportsmanship of great poets, inventors, explorers, facing adventure into the unknown and the unknowable, was in his face and breath, and had come to be known, to a few, for the danger and bronze of it.

There was a word: democracy. Tongues of politics played with it. Lincoln had his slant at it. "As I would not be a *slave*, so I would not be a *master*. This expresses my idea of democracy. Whatever differs from this, to the extent of the difference, is no democracy."

Though the years had passed, he still believed, "Improvement in condition is the order of things in a society of equals." And he still struggled under the load of that conundrum of history he had written ten years back: "As labor is the common burden of our race, so the effort of some to shift their share of the burden onto the shoulders of others is the great durable curse of the race."

There were things in politics and in everyday behavior he was stubborn about. It was whispered he could twist a friend out and twist himself in on a certain political deal. He wrote, "I would as soon put my head in the fire as attempt it."

He had faced men who had yelled, "I'll fight any man that's goin' to vote for that miserable skunk, Abe Lincoln." And he knew homes where solemn men declared, "I've seen Abe Lincoln when he played mournin' tunes on their heartstrings till they mourned with the mourners." He was taken, in some log cabins, as a helper of men. "When I went over to hear

As I would not be a slave, so I would not be a master. This expresses my idea of democracy — Whatever differs from this, to the extent of the difference, is no democracy —

A. Lincoln —

him at Alton," said one, "things looked onsartin. 'Peared like I had more'n I could stand up under. But he hadn't spoken more'n ten minutes afore I felt like I never had no load. I begin to feel ashamed o' bein' weary en complainin'."

He loved trees, was kin somehow to trees. Pine, cedar, spruce, cypress, had each their pine family ways for him. He could pick cross-breeds of trees that plainly belonged to no special family. He had found trees and men alike; on the face of them, the outside, they didn't tell their character. Life, wind, rain, lightning, events, told the fibre, what was clean or rotten.

Hearing a young woman sing, he stopped on the street sidewalk in Springfield and listened to the song that came through an open window. He sent word he would like a copy of the song; it came written on gilt-edged paper in a perfumed envelope, marked, "Mr. Lincoln—Present." He read the lines often, wrote on the envelope, "Poem—I like this." The first of four stanzas read:

Tell me, ye winged winds
That round my pathway roar,
Do ye not know some spot
Where mortals weep no more?
Some lone and pleasant vale,
Some valley in the west,
Where, free from toil and pain,
The weary soul may rest?
The loud wind dwindled to a whisper low,
And sighed for pity as it answered, No.

In going to New Salem nearly thirty years back he had been, in his own words, "a piece of driftwood floating down the Sangamon." He was, in moods, a drifter, letting the wind and weather of history have their way with him, and taking no credit to himself for the inevitable. He told Herndon he had seen great men up close who were not so great as they seemed far off.

Answering the charge that "Old Zach" Taylor was egotistical, he had said that Taylor had to have a high opinion of himself to accomplish what he did. In the same stump speech Lincoln mentioned the Democrats calling Taylor a humpback. "They say he is humpbacked, but whether his back is crooked or straight, his friends will overlook it, and his enemies will say it is so anyhow."

The left corner of Lincoln's mouth had the lines of a laughing man. Beyond a struggle in which he was loser he could see another struggle, and write in a letter, "There will be another blow-up and we shall have fun again." But the right corner of his mouth had a droop; he could say, "I laugh because if I didn't I would weep."

Sometimes a poetry of fine wisdom in short words came from his tongue as carelessly as raindrops on high corn. Milt Hay, whose law office was on the same floor as Lincoln's, told Joe Fifer and others about a goat Lincoln met on the street one morning going to the office.

"Boys had been deviling the goat to make for people and butt them off their feet," said Hay, "and this morning Lincoln with his hands folded behind him, and his chin sunk in his bosom, comes along the street. And the goat makes for him. Well, Lincoln could be pretty quick when he wanted to be. And he stooped over and his two hands got hold of the two horns of the goat."

Then Lincoln dropped down, put his face close to the goat's face and slowly drawled: "Now—there—isn't—any—good—reason—why—you—should—want—to—harm—me;—and—there—isn't—any—good—reason—why—I—should—want—to—harm—you. The—world—is—big—enough—for—both—of—us—to—live—in. If—you—behave—yourself—as—you—ought—to,—and—if—I—behave—myself—like—I—ought

to,—we'll—get—along—without—a—cross—word—or—action—and—
we'll—live—in—peace—and—harmony—like—good—neighbors."

Then Lincoln lifted at the two horns, dropped the goat over a high
fence, and walked up the street.

Drawn from Chicago Historical Society originals by Otto J. Schneider.

CHAPTER 134

In his younger days Lincoln had said on the stump that usury is wrong;
the Bible was right; to loan money at interest is unjust. But in 1859 he
loaned $3,000.00 to Norman B. Judd at ten per cent, took Judd's note
for the amount, and came into possession of a quitclaim deed, dated
November 10, 1859, from Norman B. Judd and wife to Abraham Lincoln,
of seventeen lots in Riddle's subdivision, and ten acres of land along the
right of way of the M. & M. Railway in Council Bluffs, Iowa. Besides this
property he had a lot in the town of Lincoln, Illinois, in connection with
his fee for incorporating the town; a farm of 120 acres in Crawford
County, Iowa, and forty acres in Tama County, this being land received
from the Government for his Black Hawk War service. This, with ownership of his two-story cottage and lot in Springfield, and collectible bills he
had out, made him worth between $15,000 and $25,000.

In earlier years he had been reckless about promises to pay; he exaggerated his future available cash. Since then he had grown careful in
estimates as to cash he might raise, present or future. "I could not raise
ten thousand dollars if it would save me from the fate of John Brown,"
he wrote on March 17, 1860, replying to a query as to whether he was
willing to stake that amount on his chances for political success that year.

He had come into possession of enough property to give him understanding of the feeling of property responsibility, or the fear of property

dispossession, or the slippery and fugitive character of property, and the social and political attributes and organizations that collect and cluster for mutual protection around property. That a small gold coin placed over a verse in the Bible hides that verse, was an illustration he used often. Had he chosen to develop the property instinct, and sharpen his property scent, as he had chosen to develop his political instinct, he would have rivaled Judge Davis, the millionaire landowner, who was the leading manager of the campaign to nominate Lincoln for President.

The frugal and careful ways of Lincoln in handling property, his scruples and fears about the slightest sort of cheating, his code of clean and exact justice as seen by Davis, Fell, and Judd, was an element in their support of him, and was an argument they could employ with others. They could say that Lincoln would be honest and just in the handling of property and of property owners, if he should be made President of the United States. It was true that in Connecticut Lincoln had told the striking shoe-factory workers, "Thank God we have a country where workingmen have the right to strike," but this, when discussed, was taken as political good-fellowship, or at least as not connected with the main issues of the campaign. Also the dangers that organized labor could threaten property with were not seriously thought of; labor unions were few, scattered, and weak. Their development was yet to come. Of him as man, lawyer, or politician, as custodian and caretaker of property, the managers of Lincoln as a presidential dark horse had, in their twenty years' close acquaintance with him, seen and heard nothing to indicate that he stood for anything else than stanch security for private and public property.

Lincoln had often spoken of property rights in a scornful way, as compared with human rights, but he had in mind, they believed, *slave* property, which was all in the southern states. And even of this property he did not speak in the violent way of the Abolitionists who were willing to confiscate it. In the matter of railroads, banks, gas and light companies, land corporations, they were familiar with his record as one of strict scruples; no crooked or shady deal could be named.

He took a train for Chicago, in March of 1860, on the Sand-bar case. This made four times he had taken a train to Chicago, carrying his papers on the Sand-bar case. The ownership of land at the mouth of the Chicago River, "shore land," was at issue; Lincoln was defending the title of William Jones and Sylvester Marsh as owners. Jones had hard days on the witness stand; the complainant's lawyers tore at him as if he were a swindler, cocked their eyes at him as though in the presence of a rascal; Lincoln would greet Jones as he left the stand, take his hand, and laugh: "Don't be discouraged, Mr. Jones. There are those who are better lawyers than gentlemen." The lawyers on both sides, and the judge, were dinner guests one evening, and finished with a toast, "May Illinois furnish the next President of the United States," to which all Lincoln Republicans and Douglas Democrats present drank heartily. Lincoln stopped at the Tremont House, sat for the sculptor, Leonard W. Volk, to make a life mask, visited Evanston and Waukegan, and went into a little candy store at State and Adams streets and forgot to carry away his handy pocket dictionary. The decision in the Sand-bar case was again in favor of Lincoln's clients; which started action to send the case up to the United States Supreme Court.

He looked in on Whitney's office in the Metropolitan Block. Whitney had become a Chicago lawyer. No longer would Whitney and Lincoln hitch up on hog and sheep cases in Urbana. They were getting metropolitan; they had graduated from the Eighth Circuit. Whitney had tickets to Rumsey and Newcomb's Minstrels, and queried, "Would you like to go to a nigger show tonight?" "Of all things I would rather do tonight that certainly is one," said the tickled Lincoln. "It's a high-toned troupe," Whitney guaranteed. And they went, Lincoln to rollick and clap his hands. A new song was offered. "I wish I was in de land ob cotton, Old times dar am not forgotten, Look away, look away, Dixie Land." And Lincoln rollicked, "Let's have it again! Let's have it again!"

He went into court and explained to a jury the workings of different kinds of water wheels, to show that the water wheel of his client in the case of Parker *vs.* Hoyt was not an infringement on a patent. The jury had been out two hours; Lincoln was walking the street in sight of the windows of the room where the jury was locked in; Grant Goodrich, his associate counsel, came and told him one man on the jury had held up a finger toward them. This set Lincoln wondering whether the jury were eleven to one against him. He told Goodrich it might be like the case he had in Tazewell County where the jury was eleven to one against his client, a woman seeking a divorce. Eleven jurymen had signed a verdict favoring the husband. The twelfth man said: "Gentlemen, I am going to lie down and sleep, and when you get ready to give a verdict for that little woman, then wake me; for before I give a verdict against her, I will lie here till I rot and the pismires carry me out through the keyhole." As it happened, the rights of the water wheel Lincoln argued for were upheld by the jury.

On Sunday mornings occasionally Lincoln would go to his office, take off his coat and stretch out on the sofa. "He would lie on his back and look up at the ceiling an hour or two, not saying a word," said Milt Hay. "What he was thinking about he didn't say. Sometimes after a long spell of silence he might say, 'Hay, did it ever strike you as peculiar?' and then go on with some thought he had been tracing, talking as he lay on his back looking at the ceiling. After a while he might get up and look around in some books or papers or write a letter or two. Then he'd put on his coat and hat and walk home in time for dinner."

CHAPTER 135

ONCE when Lincoln's wife came to see him in his office, he was puzzled about the business in hand, and as his face took on an absent look Mrs. Lincoln said, "Mr. Lincoln, you look like you were having your picture taken."

He had a face he could manipulate, with take-off and put-on of look and tone, shadings in a gamut of the comedy of life. He was a practiced actor and an individual artist in the use of his face, when the going was good, and the time and company proper.

Lincoln had often sat before a camera while a photographer stood with watch in hand counting the minutes till the "sitter" would be told, "All right, it's over." In front of the sitter was the black box with the negative plate taking a sun-print of his face, while behind him was an iron rack that his head fitted against while he kept his face muscles quiet, or stiff, till enough minutes had been counted off. Later, when proofs were brought to him, Lincoln left it to others to pick out the ones for final prints. Also it was others who urged him to have his pictures taken. He had greeted crowds, remarking that while they were looking into his face and he into theirs, he had "the advantage."

In his book of "Joe Miller's Jests" was an anecdote of two Frenchmen who were going to fight a duel. And one had stared long at the face of his enemy and said, "I can't fight with you," apologized, begged a thousand pardons, and explained, "If we fight I shall kill you and then I will remain the ugliest fellow in the kingdom." It was a story much like Lincoln's of his meeting with a man who handed him a pistol, saying, "I promised long ago that if I ever met a man uglier than myself I would hand him this pistol and tell him to shoot me." And Lincoln had answered, after searching the fellow's face, "Well, if I am uglier than you are, for God's sake, go ahead and shoot." Thus the story was told.

Perhaps such stories flitted through his mind as he sat one day before a mirror in a room in the Borland Block in Chicago, with plaster over all of his face except the eyes. He was breathing through quills stuck through the plaster and into his nose. It was part of what he had to go through for the sculptor Leonard Volk, who wanted to make a bust of him. Every morning after breakfast for several days he went to Volk's studio. As he came in on a Sunday morning, he remarked to Volk that a friend at the Tremont House had asked him to go to church but he preferred sitting for the bust. And as Volk told it afterward, Lincoln explained: "The fact is, I don't like to hear cut-and-dried sermons. When I hear a man preach, I like to see him act as if he were fighting bees."

Volk one day took a collection of photographs he had made in Rome and Florence, and tried to interest Lincoln in Roman art, in the way that he, Volk, was interested. And as Volk later told it: "I held the photographs up and explained them to him, but I noticed a growing weariness, and his eyelids closed occasionally as if he were sleepy, or were thinking of something besides Grecian and Roman statuary and architecture. Finally he said: 'These things must be very interesting to you, Mr. Volk; but the truth is I don't know much of history, and all I do know of it I have learned from law books.' "

As he posed, Lincoln rambled along through story after story, keeping away from politics and religion, and remarking once, "I am bored nearly every time I sit down to a public dining table by some one pitching into me on politics."

Volk finished the head, and at the final sitting had Lincoln strip off his clothes so as to show the bare shoulders and breast. Lincoln unbuttoned his undershirt, pulled it down the required distance, tied the sleeves behind him, and stood posing for an hour. The sitting came to an end. Volk offered to help him dress, Lincoln replying, "No, I can do it better alone." Volk went on working and Lincoln left in a hurry, after a warm handshake and, "Good-by, I will see you again soon."

Volk heard Lincoln's boots on the stairway, going down. Then the stairway was quiet a few moments. And again the sound of Lincoln's boots were on the stairs. He was coming at a fast pace. He came into the studio in a hurry, saying, "I got down on the sidewalk and found I had forgotten to put on my undershirt, and thought it wouldn't do to go through the streets this way."

The sleeves that he had tied behind his back had bulged out or come loose. He had forgotten to put his arms into his undershirt sleeves. Volk helped him undress and redress while they both laughed.

CHAPTER 136

THE civilization of the United States ran in elusive outlines in the months when Davis, Fell, Swett, Dubois, Herndon, Medill, and Ray were running their dark horse, Abraham Lincoln, in the race for a presidential nomination in 1860.

Lincoln murmured to Whitney one day: "Judd and Ray and those fellows think I don't see anything, but I see all around them; I see better what they want to do than they do themselves."

Lincoln had a way of slipping through a door into a roomful of men so that he was there and had seen them before they saw him. His feet, though large, had cat-sinews; he was swift and sure in movements at certain moments; when aroused there was a panther subtlety about him.

Lincoln wrote to an Ohio delegate, oi the coming national Republican convention in Chicago, that Seward "is the very best candidate we could have for the North of Illinois, and the very *worst* for the South of it." With Chase of Ohio it would be likewise in Illinois. Bates of Missouri would be the best candidate for the South of Illinois and the worst for the North. "I am not the fittest person to answer the questions you ask about candidates. When not a very great man begins to be mentioned for a very great position, his head is very likely to be a little turned." With Senator Trumbull he could be easier in speech. "As you request, I will be entirely frank. The taste *is* in my mouth a little." He did honestly have some hankerings for the Presidency. "And this, no doubt, disqualifies me, to some extent, to form correct opinions." After which he made the same points for Trumbull that he had made for the Ohio delegate.

His own philosophy of personal conduct in politics, the scrupulous caution that gave rise to the whisper of "cunning as a fox," yet which he considered sagacity, horse sense, or some quality necessary for the growth and unity of a party organization, was seen in his writing to Trumbull: "A word now for your own special benefit. You better write no letters which can possibly be distorted into opposition or quasi-opposition to me. There are men on the constant watch for such things out of which to prejudice my peculiar friends against you." The old Whig Republicans, and the former Democrats turned Republican, were sore and growling. "While I have no more suspicion of you than I have of my best friend living, I am kept in a constant struggle against suggestions of this sort. I have hesitated some to write this paragraph, lest you should suspect I do it for my own benefit, and not for yours; but on reflection I conclude you will not suspect me." He hinted at his code as to personal secrets. "Let no eye but your own see this—not that there is anything wrong, or even ungenerous, in it; but it would be misconstrued."

The Ohio delegate wrote to Lincoln again, asking "the lay of the land." Lincoln replied on May 2, the national convention that would name or reject him being just two weeks ahead: "First I think the Illinois delegation will be unanimous for me at the start; and no other delegation will. A few individuals in other delegations would like to go for me at the start, but may be restrained by their colleagues. It is represented to me by men who ought to know, that the whole of Indiana might not be difficult to get. You know how it is in Ohio. I am certainly not the first choice there; and yet I have not heard that any one makes any positive objection to me. It is just so everywhere as far as I can perceive. Everywhere, except here in Illinois and possibly in Indiana, one or another is preferred to me, but there is no positive objection." On May 12 his friends Jesse K. Dubois and Judge David Davis would probably be in Chicago "ready to confer with friends from other States." To an Indiana delegate and others, he wrote they could see Dubois and Davis.

He wrote to another Ohio delegate, expressing thanks for confidence, and pointing to his one biggest advantage as a candidate: "If I have any chance, it consists mainly in the fact that the whole opposition would vote for me, if nominated. (I don't mean to include the pro-slavery opposition of the South, of course.) My name is new in the field, and I suppose I am not the first choice of a very great many." And in two sentences there was a shading of color, an indication of the philosophy that often governed Lincoln in tight places. He wrote: "Our policy, then, is to give no offense to others—leave them in a mood to come to us if they shall be compelled to give up their first love. This, too, is dealing justly with all, and leaving us in a mood to support heartily whoever shall be nominated."

The Kansas politician, Mark Delahay, asked for money, Lincoln replying: "Allow me to say I can not enter the ring on a money basis—first, because, in the main it is wrong; and secondly, I have not, and can not get, the money. I say, in the main, the use of money is wrong; but for certain objects, in a political contest, the use of some is both right and indispensable." He had known Delahay a year or two. "With me, as with yourself, this long struggle has been one of great pecuniary loss." And the nub of the letter was reached: "I now distinctly say this: If you shall be appointed a delegate to Chicago, I will furnish one hundred dollars to bear the expenses of the trip." In a second letter to Delahay, he closed, "Come along to the convention, and I will do as I said about expenses."

Into the state Republican convention, on May 9, came John Hanks carrying two fence rails with flags and streamers tied to them, and the inscription, "Abraham Lincoln, the Rail Candidate for President in 1860: Two rails from a lot of 3,000 made in 1830 by Thos. Hanks and Abe Lincoln—whose father was the first pioneer of Macon County." Shouts followed: "Lincoln! Lincoln! Speech!"

A committee escorted him to the platform. He thanked them; a sober face; no smile. Cheers: "Three times three for Honest Abe, our next President." Again came John Hanks and a committee with fence rails, shouting, "Identify your work." "I cannot say that I split these rails," and to the committee, "Where did you get the rails?" "At the farm you improved down on the Sangamon." "Well, that was a long time ago. It is possible I may have split these rails, but I cannot identify them." Shouts from the convention: "Identify your work! Identify your work!"

The sober face of the candidate was loosening into a smile. "What kind of timber are they?" he asked, getting the swing of the fun. "Honey locust and black walnut." "Well, that is lasting timber," and scrutinizing the rails, "It may be that I split these rails," and scrutinizing further, "Well, boys, I can only say that I have split a great many better-looking ones."

Thus the Rail Candidate was baptized, and the pet name of Rail-splitter was born. It was more important that the convention instructed its delegates to the Chicago convention to vote as a unit for Lincoln; seven of the twenty-two delegates personally preferred Seward. And was there a foretoken in Dick Yates, the nominee for governor, the curly-headed and handsome Dick Yates, crying, "Let us hope that the South will not attempt to destroy this Union; but, if it should, flaming giants will spring from every cornfield in the State of Illinois"?

Yet there were peculiar undercurrents against Lincoln. Browning, for instance, who had tried cases with Lincoln and dined often at the Lincoln home, was for Bates for President. Oglesby and other delegates had walked with Lincoln out to a quiet place on a railroad track where they sat down and talked. Oglesby was in favor of cutting off Browning from the list of delegates to the Chicago national convention. Lincoln advised that this would make an enemy of Browning and he might then do more mischief than if he were sent to Chicago as a member of a delegation instructed to vote as a unit for Lincoln's nomination. "Lincoln sat on one of the railroad rails and his legs nearly reached clean across to the other rail," said Oglesby, telling later about the railroad-track conference that guided the Decatur convention.

Only two weeks earlier, the national Democratic convention had met in Charleston, South Carolina, and the Douglas delegates, holding a majority control, but lacking the necessary two-thirds to nominate their man for President, had split the party, and two separate wings of it were planning conventions in June; the powerful political body that had controlled the Government practically thirty years was staggering. The answers of Douglas to Lincoln in the Freeport debate had shown him to be a straddler; the trust of the South in him, once so loyal, was gone; he was slippery, greased with expedients; with Douglas their property was not safe.

Yancey of Alabama, tall, slender, with long black hair, spoke in a soft, musical voice for the minority, the first time in generations of men that the South was in a minority and without the votes to name the candidate for President. The southern gentlemen had cheered, the southern ladies filling the galleries had waved handkerchiefs. It was a moment of history. Yancey pronounced a swan song. "We came here with one great purpose, to save our Constitutional rights. We are in the minority, as we have been taunted here today. In the progress of civilization, the Northwest has grown up from an infant in swaddling-clothes into the free proportions of a giant people. We therefore, as the minority, take the rights, the mission, and the position of the minority."

Yancey was dealing with the fact. The Northwest had grown up; Douglas had captured it politically, and thereby made the South a political minority, in the Democratic party; and Douglas had swung its power as a big stick, and was calling for a platform pledge to abide by the Dred Scott decision or any future decision of the Supreme Court on the rights of property in the states or territories.

"The proposition you make," said Yancey, "will bankrupt us of the South. Ours is the property invaded—ours the interests at stake. The honor of our children, the honor of our females, the lives of our men, all rest upon you. You would make a great seething caldron of passion and crime if you were able to consummate your measures."

Douglas men blamed the convention chairman, Caleb Cushing, the Boston lawyer, and close friend of Jefferson Davis, for rulings; a Douglas rhymer wrote, "A poisonous reptile, many-scaled, and with most subtle fang, Crawled forward, Caleb Cush, while behind his rattles rang."

Ten days of speeches, ballots, wrangles, brought adjournment to Baltimore in June. Caleb Cushing uttered the dirge, "I fondly trust that we shall continue to march on forever, the hope of nations in the old world as in the new."

And little Alexander Stephens, weighing less than ninety pounds, with black eyes smoldering, "the little pale star from Georgia," blazed out, in a talk with a friend: "Men will be cutting one another's throats in a little while. In twelve months we shall be in a war, the bloodiest in history." But why civil war, even if a Republican President were elected? "Because," murmured the Little Pale Star, "there are not virtue and patriotism and sense enough left in the country to avoid it."

In the Senate at Washington, Davis and Douglas clashed. "I would sooner have an honest man on any sort of a rickety platform than to have a man I did not trust on the best platform which could be made," said Davis, drawing from Douglas the question, "Why did you not tell us in the beginning that the whole fight was against the man and not upon the platform?"

Senator Seward of New York gazed on what was happening and felt satisfied. He had started for his home in Auburn, New York, to write his letter accepting the Republican nomination for President. Would he not have more delegates to start with than any other candidate, and was not there a trend for him even in the Illinois and Indiana delegations? And his manager, Thurlow Weed, was rigging a plan which, according to a letter of William Cullen Bryant, was "to give charters for a set of city railways in New York, for which those who receive them are to furnish a fund of from four to six hundred thousand dollars, to be expended for the Republican cause in the next Presidential election." Bankers, railroad presidents, business men who wanted Government grants were putting their trust in Weed.

In Springfield, Judge Logan, the little frowsy-headed lawyer who used to sit on the circuit-court bench and hold court in a gray linen shirt without a necktie, was having a new silk hat made by Adams the hatter. Other delegates were outfitting with silk hats and broadcloth suits of clothes, to go to the Chicago convention on May 16. Lincoln wrote to Solomon Sturges, the Chicago banker, thanks for proffered hospitality during the convention. He had decided to stay home. "I am a little too much a candidate to stay home and not quite enough a candidate to go."

CHAPTER 137

THE Massachusetts lawyer and Buchanan Democrat, Caleb Cushing, sometimes spilled an utterance having the flow and color of poetry. Thus it was with his saying, "The sceptre of power in this Union is to be held hereafter by those vast regions of the West, state after state stretching out like star beyond star in the blue depths of the firmament, far away to the shores of the Pacific. Massachusetts and South Carolina will together be as clay in the fingers of the potter, when the great West shall stretch forth its arm of power, as ere long it will, to command the destiny of the Union."

This poetic fact had operated to give Chicago the national convention of the Republican party. The Lincoln men had made a special point of getting the convention for Chicago. But their main argument was not that Chicago was a garden city and a centre of art and traditions. They challenged the national committee, "Listen to us or run a chance of losing the West."

Chicago was the location of the heartbeats of the Northwest which Yancey of Alabama said had grown "from an infant in swaddling-clothes to the free proportions of a giant people." Its poets called it "The Queen City of the West," also "The Garden City." One guide-book styled the big stockyards four miles south on a flat prairie "The Great Bovine City of the World." It was in 1860 a city of 110,000 people, handling hogs, cattle, corn, farming machinery, and the associated finance, transportation, trade, and politics; the depot, crossroads, and point of exchange, of buying and selling, for thousand-mile prairies.

Lifted over the town as memorials and hopes were the tall, overshadowing grain elevators at the railroad yards and the river wharves; silhouettes at the sunset sky line with statements that though man doth not live by bread alone he must have bread if he is to have breath.

Bread for man's stomach, ideas and opinions for his mind radiated from Chicago. McCormick was sending out more than 50,000 reapers a year. Medill was saying, "Chicago is the pet Republican city of the Union, the point from which radiate opinions which more or less influence six states."

The *Cleveland Plain-Dealer* flung a taunt. "Lake Michigan is situated on Chicago. The principal productions of Chicago are corner lots, statistics, and wind. The population of Chicago is about sixteen million and is rapidly increasing." He was answered by Chicago newspapers. "We trust the editor of the *Plain-Dealer* will visit us again."

Grocers and butchers threw into back alleys barrels and boxes of decayed apples and oranges, scraps of meat and sheep-feet. More than a thousand saloons ran free-lunch counters; sample rooms, beer tunnels, weinstubes, summer gardens, winter gardens, road houses, liquor stores, taverns, grog-shops, bought casks of beer unloaded by brewery wagon drivers wearing leather aprons.

Ministers pointed to conditions. "Here in Chicago, we have fifty-six churches open on Sunday, during the forenoon and evening, but at the same time there are no less than eighty ballrooms, in each of which a band plays from morning till midnight, and waltzing goes on without intermission. In addition to these festivities, we have two theatres, each with its performers in tights and very short garments. Saloons have their front doors closed by proclamation, but do a thriving business through side entrances."

In and out of this place of human swarming, named Chicago, ran fifteen railways with 150 railroad trains a day; and on May 16 of 1860 they had brought 40,000 strangers and 500 delegates to the Republican national convention. At the corner of Lake and Market streets the Sauganash Hotel, kept by Alderman John Murphy, had been torn down, and a lumber shack, to hold 10,000 people, had been put up and named the Wigwam.

CHAPTER 138

On May 12 the Wigwam was opened for a mass meeting, appearing, said the *Chicago Journal*, "large with golden promise of a glorious harvest of truth." The governors of Indiana and Maine spoke, also the antislavery war horse, Joshua R. Giddings, from the cheese region of Ohio, and Delegate-at-large Johns from Iowa, who had walked 150 miles to take the steam cars to the convention; he said he was happy to look into their shining faces.

At the Richmond House, Thurlow Weed set up Seward headquarters and called in various state delegations and addressed them with pleasant arguments. Six Kansas delegates entered his parlor and sat at a round table. His face was sparkling, winning; every move and word gracious; he spoke to each delegate by name, and familiarly, a little as though he had been a college chum or boyhood schoolmate; he complimented them all on the good work border states were doing for the Republican cause, and added: "We think we have in Mr. Seward just the qualities the country will need. He is known by us all as a statesman. As governor of New York he has shown splendid executive ability. As senator he has shown himself to be a statesman, and a political philosopher. He will make a candidate to whom our people can look with a feeling of security. We expect to nominate him on the first ballot, and to go before the country full of courage and confidence."

Weed thanked them each again, and gave them each a handshake. One of the Kansas men, Addison G. Procter, said afterward: "As he stood at our table, so gracious, so assuring, so genial and friendly, with all our previous estimate of him dispelled, I was reminded of Byron's picture of his 'Corsair,' as 'the mildest-mannered man that ever scuttled a ship or cut a throat,' politically, of course." Also into the Seward headquarters came Carl Schurz, one of the Wisconsin delegation solid for Seward; he had heard of Weed, the skilled "wire-puller"; he watched Weed in the lobbies, and said afterward, "The tall man with his cold, impassive face and the mysterious whisper of his high voice, gave directions to a lot of henchmen, the looks and talk of many of whom made me fear that if Mr. Seward were elected President he might find himself burdened with obligations he would not be able to meet without dishonor." The New York boss and Seward reminded Schurz of Mephistopheles and Faust. Weed asked Schurz to mix with as many delegates as possible and tell all that no candidate could possibly receive as many German votes as Seward.

Mark W. Delahay showed Procter a telegram from Lincoln. Delahay had wired Lincoln that Seward was going to win, so it looked, and when that happened, would Lincoln be willing to run as candidate for Vice-President? Lincoln's telegram said he would take second place on the ticket if his friends thought it wise.

Delahay was not a delegate but had come along with the Kansas delegates on railroad fare sent him by Lincoln. He was mixing with delegates and telegraphing Lincoln his guesses on the race.

Delegate Knapp wrote to Lincoln two days before the convention opened: "Things are working. Keep a good nerve. We are laboring to make you the second choice of all the delegations we can, where we can't make you first choice. We are dealing tenderly with delegates, taking them in detail and making no fuss. Be not too expectant, but rely upon our discretion. Again I say, brace your nerves for any result."

Horace Greeley carried a hatchet for Seward; he listed four states sure to be lost if Seward ran. Governor Curtin of Pennsylvania was saying his state would come along with a 50,000 majority, but not if Seward ran. On the ramshackle walls of the Wigwam, Weed might have seen the shadow of a tomahawk. The Wigwam stood in a land of ambushes.

At the Lincoln headquarters in the Tremont House, Davis, Dubois, Swett, Logan, Oglesby, and others were nailing down the Pennsylvania and Indiana delegations for Lincoln. "We worked like nailers," said Oglesby. Ray of the *Tribune* came to his chief, Medill. "We are going to have Indiana for Old Abe, sure." "How did you get it?" asked Medill. "By the Lord, we promised them everything they asked."

Indiana was nailed down; Caleb B. Smith was to be Secretary of the Interior and William P. Dole, Commissioner of Indian Affairs; Indiana would vote a solid block for Lincoln on the first ballot. The next prospect was Pennsylvania, with its block of fifty-six delegates wearing white hats;

they would vote for Simon Cameron, complimenting a favorite son, on the first ballot, and then were willing to go elsewhere.

Judge Davis dickered with them; Dubois telegraphed Lincoln the Cameron delegates could be had if Cameron was promised the Treasury Department. Lincoln wired back, "I authorize no bargains and will be bound by none." Herndon brought out a message from Lincoln carried to Chicago by E. L. Baker of the Springfield *Journal;* it was a copy of a newspaper with markings of Seward speeches, with the marginal notes, "I agree with Seward's 'irrepressible conflict,' but do not agree with his 'higher law' doctrine." And the added underlined words, "Make no contracts that will bind me."

What happened among Lincoln's convention managers was told by Whitney: "The bluff Dubois said, 'Damn Lincoln!' The polished Swett said, 'I am very sure if Lincoln was aware of the necessities——' The critical Logan expectorated. 'The main difficulty with Lincoln is——' Herndon ventured, 'Now, friend, I'll answer that.' But Davis cut the Gordian knot by brushing all aside with, 'Lincoln ain't here, and don't know what we have to meet, so we will go ahead as if we hadn't heard from him, and he must ratify it.' "

In that mood they went to the room of the Pennsylvania managers. When they were through they came down to the lobby of the Tremont House, where Joe Medill of the *Tribune* was waiting. Medill had been smoking and thinking about a remark of Lincoln's that Pennsylvania would be important in the convention. "He wanted that big Pennsylvania foot brought down on the scale."

As Medill saw Judge Davis come heaving and puffing down the stairs about midnight, he stepped up to the judge and, as he told of it later, he said he asked the judge what Pennsylvania was going to do, and Judge Davis replied, "Damned if we haven't got them." "How did you get them?" "By paying their price."

Then along came Ray, who had sat in and heard. And Medill asked his editor how Pennsylvania had been nailed down. "Why," said Ray, "we promised to put Simon Cameron in the Cabinet. They wanted assurances that we represented Lincoln, and he would do what we said." "What have you agreed to give Cameron?" asked Medill. "The Treasury Department." "Good heavens! Give Cameron the Treasury Department? What will be left?" "Oh, what is the difference?" said Ray. "We are after a bigger thing than that; we want the Presidency and the Treasury is not a great stake to pay for it."

And so, with three state delegations solid, and with odd votes from Ohio and other states, the Lincoln men waited for the balloting, seeing to it, however, that the convention seating committee carefully sandwiched the Pennsylvania delegation between Illinois and Indiana. "Thurlow Weed is a sly old fellow." Also, on the night before the opening day, they had a

Pennsylvania congressman take the floor at a mass meeting in the convention hall and talk till midnight so there wasn't time for a planned program of Seward speeches.

The convention was called to order. David Wilmot, the proviso man, was elected chairman; a platform was adopted, leaving out mention of the Declaration of Independence, and old Joshua R. Giddings arose, snorted contempt and said it was time to leave the Republican party. He was about ready to put on his hat and walk out when dapper young George William Curtis stood up and shamed the convention, and the principle of the equality of men was written in so as to satisfy Giddings.

Seward victory was in the air; champagne fizzed at the Richmond House. Straw votes on all incoming railroad trains had given Seward overwhelming majorities. Six hundred friends, delegates and henchmen, marched and cheered for Seward, their band playing, "Oh, Isn't He a Darling!" The upper tier of three states of the Northwest, Michigan, Wisconsin, Minnesota, were a unit for Seward. The New York, Massachusetts, and California delegations were pledged to give their totals to Seward. Horace Greeley, a Seward enemy, wired his *New York Tribune* before nominating day that Seward seemed sure to win. Seward sat in his home in Auburn, New York, ready to send a message of acceptance, stirred with the same fond expectations that had led Henry Clay and Daniel Webster. And as with them, mice nibbled, gnawed in the cellar of fate.

Seward had a record; and Lincoln workers, in the three delegations nailed down for Lincoln, were shaking this record as a red rag; the Republican candidates for governor in these three states were saying with clenched fists and blazing eyes that they were beaten at the start if Seward ran, and they could win with 10,000 to 50,000 majority with Lincoln; the "irrepressible conflict" and the "higher law" and the New York traction campaign fund were used as arguments and flung forth with sentiment till they scared some of the politicians who wanted to win; and again there were antislavery men such as Bryant of the *New York Evening Post* who believed Seward to be the same type as Daniel Webster, much intellect, little faith, none of the "mystic simplicity" of Lincoln.

Ward Hill Lamon had been to the printers of seat-tickets to the convention hall. And a staff of young men kept busy nearly a whole night signing names of convention officers to seat-tickets so that the next day the Lincoln bucks could jam the hall and leave no room for the Seward shouters to get in.

Hour on hour the bulk of the 40,000 strangers in Chicago kept up a shouting and a tumult for Abraham Lincoln, for Old Abe, for the Rail Candidate. Judd had fixed it with the railroads so that any shouter who wished to come could set foot in Chicago at a low excursion rate. Men illuminated with moral fire, and also men red-eyed with whisky, yelled and pranced and cut up capers and vociferated for Lincoln. They swarmed around the ramshackle lumber convention hall as though they might lift it and carry it a half-block and drop it in the Chicago River.

This immense mob, the like of which had not theretofore been seen or approximated in the assemblages of American politics, was a factor; in what degree it influenced the convention in any view, decision, or emotional state, nobody could tell; it was an intangible.

The show of human force was planned by the Lincoln managers; it surpassed expectations in its noise and intensity. On the first two days of the convention the Seward men were allowed by the Chicago managers to have free run of the floor. But on the third day the Lincoln shouters were shoved through the doors till they filled all seats and standing-room, and hundreds of New York hurrah boys couldn't squeeze in.

Nomination speeches were in single sentences. Judd said, "I desire, on behalf of the delegation from Illinois, to put in nomination, as a candidate for President of the United States, Abraham Lincoln of Illinois," while Delano of Ohio said, "I rise on behalf of a portion of the delegation from Ohio, to put in nomination the man who can split rails and maul Democrats—Abraham Lincoln."

A reporter, Murat Halstead, wrote of the uproar, "Imagine all the hogs ever slaughtered in Cincinnati giving their death squeals together, and a score of big steam whistles going together. I thought the Seward yell could not be surpassed; but the Lincoln boys were clearly ahead, and, feeling their victory, they gave a concentrated shriek and stamping that made every plank and pillar in the building quiver. The New York, Michigan, and Wisconsin delegations sat together and were in this tempest very quiet. Many of their faces whitened as the Lincoln *Yawp* swelled into a wild hosanna of victory."

"The idea of us Hoosiers and Suckers being outscreamed would have been bad," said Swett. "Five thousand people leaped to their seats, women not wanting, and the wild yell made vesper breathings of all that had preceded. A thousand steam whistles, ten acres of hotel gongs, a tribe of Comanches might have mingled in the scene unnoticed."

Seward had 173½ votes, Lincoln 102, and favorite sons and others the remainder of the votes on the first ballot. On the second ballot, Lincoln jumped to 181 as against Seward's 184½. On the third ballot, of the 465 votes Lincoln swept 231½ while Seward dropped to 180.

Medill of the *Tribune* whispered to Carter of Ohio, "If you can throw the Ohio delegation for Lincoln, Chase can have anything he wants." "H-how d'-d'ye know?" stuttered Carter, Medill answering, "I know, and you know I wouldn't promise if I didn't know."

Carter called for a change of four votes from his state to the Rail Candidate. Other delegates stood up to announce changes of votes to Lincoln. As the tellers footed up the totals, and the chairman waited for the figures, the chatter of 10,000 people stopped, the fluttering of ladies fans ended, the scratching of pencils and the clicking of the telegraph dot-dash dot-dot dash-dot-dash could be heard.

The chairman spoke. Of 466 votes, 354 were cast for the candidate highest, and, "Abraham Lincoln of Illinois is selected as your candidate for President of the United States."

Chairmen of state delegations arose and made the nomination unanimous, after which O. H. Browning of Quincy spoke the thanks of Illinois. "We struggled against the nomination of the illustrious statesman of New York, solely because we believed here that we could go into battle on the prairies of Illinois with more hope and more prospect of success under the leadership of our own noble son." He thanked them again.

The nominations ended. The terrific emotional spree was over. Strong men hugged each other, wept, laughed, and shrieked in each other's faces through tears. Judge Logan stood on a table brandishing his arms and yelling; he raised his new silk hat and brought it down on somebody's head, smashing it flat.

Inside and outside the Wigwam it was a wild noon hour: hats, handkerchiefs, umbrellas, bands, cannon, explosions, the going-down of the excitement of the wild gamble over whether Abe could be nominated.

The Minnesota delegate, Aaron Goodrich, had tried to voice the feelings of the Seward men, amid cries of "Dry up." He retorted, "I am not in the habit of being hallooed down, certainly not by friends." "If you are our friend, let us adjourn," came a hint that won a ripple of laughter across the big barn. But he must go on to say: "The representatives from Minnesota feel that a seat in the presidential chair would not add one jot to the stature of William H. Seward; of all earthly fame has he seen the vanity; lasting, exalted in his fame; whenever lofty deeds——" And at that point the stenographic reporters could catch no more of his words. They wrote, "The audience here became impatient and vociferous in their calls to proceed to business and the speaker could proceed no further." Thanks were voted to the convention president, George Ashmun of Massachusetts. He made a closing speech saying he had known Lincoln in Congress: "the last two years had tried him by fire." The Republican party was headed for victory; and he struck the gavel for adjournment. One hundred guns at the Tremont House, steamboat whistles on the river and lake, steam-engine whistles in railroad yards and at factories, and the iron and brass bells of church steeples set up a clangor and a tintinnabulation that came to no quiet end for twenty-four hours; prairie towns tried to rival the Chicago jubilee.

Thurlow Weed had pressed the temples of his forehead to hold back tears. Horace Greeley wrote a letter telling a friend it was a fearful week he hoped never to see repeated. "If you had seen the Pennsylvania delegation, and known how much money Weed had in hand, you would not have believed we could do so well as we did. Give Curtin [Governor of Pennsylvania] credit for that. Ohio looked very bad, yet turned out well, and Virginia had been regularly sold out; but the seller could not deliver. We had to rain red-hot bolts on them, however, to keep the majority from going for Seward. Indiana was our right bower, and Missouri above praise."

In Albany, New York, a son of Senator Seward was working in the office of Weed's paper, the *Evening Journal*. He read a telegram up a tube to a printing-room foreman, "Abraham Lincoln is nominated for President on the third ballot." The foreman was hesitating; his voice spluttered back, "S-a-y, what damn name was that you said was nominated for President?"

CHAPTER 139

ON the Friday morning of the convention, Lincoln had walked from home, as usual, to the public square, where the horses stood at their hitching-posts with serene and sober faces, as usual, and farmers with pantaloons tucked into their boots were trudging around to buy seed corn or sell hogs, as usual.

At Chatterton's jewelry store he turned into a stairway and went up to the second-story office of James C. Conkling, the lawyer, who had just returned by night train from Chicago. With his head on a buggy cushion and his feet over the end of a settee, he listened and quizzed Conkling, and left the office saying, "Well, Conkling, I believe I will go back to my office and practice law."

Then he met E. L. Baker of the *Journal*, who had arrived by night train from Chicago, after delivering to Herndon the message from Lincoln, and watching the convention drift; Lincoln and Baker went to Carmody's ball alley for a game; the alley was full. Then, as Baker told it, they went to a saloon to play a game of billiards, but some morning billiard players had already taken the table. "We each drank a glass of beer, and then went to the *Journal* office expecting to hear the result of the convention balloting; we waited awhile; nothing came; and we parted; I went to dinner." And the horses stood at their hitching-posts around the public square with serene and sober faces, as usual, and farmers with pantaloons tucked into their boots trudged around to buy seed corn or sell hogs, as usual.

But shortly after twelve o'clock a messenger boy handed Lincoln a telegram, addressed "Abe," reading: "We did it. Glory to God!" It was from Knapp. A little flurry of telegrams followed. He told the crowd at the *Journal* office he was going out home to tell his wife the news. One heard him say, "I reckon there's a little short woman down at our house that would like to hear the news." Another heard him say: "There is a lady over yonder on Eighth Street who is deeply interested in this news; I will carry it to her."

Boxes, barrels, kindling-wood, fence rails and brushwood went up in bonfire smoke in the Sangamon River country that Friday night. As the news had come to Douglas at Washington, he smiled, "There won't be a tar barrel left in Illinois tonight." A brass band and a crowd came to Lincoln's house, surged to the front porch and asked for a speech. He told them the honor of the nomination was not for him personally but as the representative of a cause, and wished that his house were big enough so that he could ask them all to come inside. Shouts and yells of hurrah parties kept up till the gray dawn of the morning after.

When Judge David Davis was asked what it cost to nominate Lincoln, he replied, "The entire expense of Lincoln's nomination, including headquarters, telegraphing, music, fare of delegations, and other incidentals, was less than $700."

CHAPTER 140

IN its platform promise to fix the tariff, to fix land and homestead laws, to fix farm and factory laws so that workingmen and business would have "prosperity and independence," the Republican party had a sincerity, was taking care of issues that counted. Business interests that wanted to be sure of a hearing with the next Washington Administration saw to it that their political workers had front seats, committee places, and influence in the new party that had the big chance to win; bankers pleased that Simon Cameron was promised the Treasury Department, and land, mining, oil, and railway interests pleased that Caleb B. Smith was to control the Interior Department, were known to Cameron and Smith; that Lincoln had wired his managers he would be tied with no pledges was known to a small clique. Lincoln's managers were known to include a millionaire landowner, railroad lawyers, tested politicians; Lincoln himself had drawn one of the largest fees ever paid by a western railroad to a lawyer. The American political and economic diagram had its paths crossed and double-crossed; its mazy mapping sprang out of the commanding issue before which all others cracked, that of Union and the wage-labor system as against disunion and slave labor. North and South, orators spoke of freedom; both regions wanted freedom; if war came each would fight for what each called freedom.

A tone of the solemn, touched with shrill falsetto, had run through speeches and airs of the convention. Fierce challenges were sent howling, sometimes, that had in previous years been known only in Abolitionist conventions; not in any political organization with a fat chance of getting hold of the Washington Government. "We wheel into line as one man, and we will roll up our 100,000 majority, and we will give you our thirteen electoral votes," John Andrew, the Massachusetts chairman, had shouted; "and we will show you that the 'irrepressible conflict' is the 'manifest destiny' of the Democracy." Carl Schurz had yelled, to a storm of cheers, "We defy the whole slave power and the whole vassalage of hell." A cadence of exasperation, a strain of revolutionary rumble and mutter, rose, died down, and rose again.

The man in Springfield picked to carry the banner stood as a shy and furtive figure. He wanted the place—and he didn't. His was precisely the clairvoyance that knew terrible days were ahead. If he had had no reservations, if he had been in politics for power and position only, he would not have sent at least two specific messages telling his managers to make no pledges that would bind him. He had his hesitations. And he was in the end the dark horse on whom the saddle was put. He could sit and contemplate an old proverb: "The horse thinks one thing, he that saddles him another."

CHAPTER 141

THE chosen committee called on Lincoln at his house in Springfield to tell him formally he was nominated; he formally replied, and later sent the chairman a letter of acceptance. He would coöperate, "imploring the assistance of Divine Providence."

While he stayed in Springfield, an immense organization was in the field. Bills for printing, cash vouchers for speakers and their railroad fares and hotel bills, outlays for thousands of torches, oilcloth uniforms and caps for Wide-awake clubs, had to be met at campaign headquarters. And Judd's campaign slogan, as Whitney said, was, "Turn on the beer, boys." These were details manipulated by managers who aimed chiefly at carrying their states.

Swett wrote to Thurlow Weed on July 4 saying Illinois prospects were excellent, and, as to politics in general, "We have not had the experience you have, and your views, expressed to me at any time, would have controlling influence." Judge David Davis kept close track of the Midwest campaign, and on August 24 wrote from Bloomington to Thurlow Weed that he had been in Indiana and found the Republican party in danger of losing that State. "They believe that with $10,000 the State can be carried, and that without 'foreign aid' they are in trouble. Their organization is not complete for lack of money. It is difficult to raise enough money to keep campaign speakers in the field. They want a number of speakers, and they have to be paid. The state is poor and the central committee has not raised what they expected. The election may run itself, as it is doing in a great many States, but, depend upon it, without pecuniary aid, there can be neither certainty nor efficiency."

Often little hooks and crooks in the running of the campaign had to be smoothed out and straightened over. Then Lincoln would call in some one, a party worker, a friend or secretary, explain what he wanted done, and then send out on his mission one whom he called "a worker in the vineyard." A long and tangled story would lie back of such a letter as he wrote to Swett on July 16 concerning "that matter mentioned by Mr. Casey."

"Want of confidence in the Centl. Com. pains me—I am afraid there is the germ of difficulty in it—Will not the men thus suspected, and treated as proposed, rebel and make a dangerous explosion?" He advised, "When you write Mr. Casey, say to him that great caution and delicacy of action is necessary in that matter—I would like to see you and the Judge, one or both, about the matter of your going to Pa."

The two men in Illinois who probably did more than any others to keep Lincoln connected with the main cogs and campaign machinery of the Republican party through the campaign were Davis and Swett. Their relations in their errands between Illinois, New York, and Pennsylvania were indicated in a letter of Swett to Thurlow Weed, at a later time. "We should be exceedingly glad to know your wishes and your views," he wrote the New York boss, "and to serve you in any way in our power. I say this freely for myself because I feel it, and for Judge Davis, because, although now absent, I know his feelings. Of course, nobody is authorized to speak for Mr. Lincoln."

Wide-awake clubs organized and marched in torchlight processions. Seward spoke across the northern states. Batteries and flotillas of orators spoke. They argued, threatened, promised, appealed to statistics, passions, history. But the chosen spokesman of the Republican party had nothing to say. He wrote a few letters, and shook hands with orators, politicians, and reporters who came by the dozen and score out to the two-story cottage on Eighth Street. He made a short speech on August 14 when railroads, buggies, horses and ox wagons brought a crowd of more than 50,000 people to Springfield. He greeted them, half joked them. The "fight for this cause" would go on "though I be dead and gone." And he ended with the only important thing he had to say: "You will kindly let me be silent."

Five biographies of Lincoln were published in June. Medals and coins were struck, advertising soap on one side and the Republican candidate on the other. Requests for autographs came. Newspapers came. Wendell Phillips was asking, "Who is this huckster in politics?" Seward was saying, "No truer defender of the Republican faith could have been found." A *New York Evening Post* reporter sketched him: "As he gets interested in conversation his face lights up, and his gestures assume dignity. He is fluent, agreeable, and polite, a man of decided and original character. His views are all his own, worked out from a patient and varied scrutiny of life. Yet he cannot be called opinionated. He listens to others like one eager to learn. He tells a story well, with idiomatic smack, and seems to relish humor, both in himself and others."

The reporter added: "I trust I am not trespassing on the sanctities of private life, in saying a word in regard to Mrs. Lincoln. Whatever of awkwardness may be ascribed to her husband, there is none of it in her. She is quite a pattern of ladylike courtesy and polish. She converses with freedom and grace, and is thoroughly au fait. Mrs. Lincoln belongs, by the mother's side, to the Preston family of Kentucky, has received a liberal and refined education, and, should she ever reach it, will adorn the White House. She is, I am told, a strict and consistent member of the Presbyterian church."

Other newspapers came, publishing Lincoln as "a third-rate country lawyer"; he lived "in low Hoosier style"; he "could not speak good grammar"; he delivered "coarse and clumsy jokes"; he was descended from "an African gorilla." Questions came. What was his view on this or that? And his secretary, John G. Nicolay, sent them all the same letter; his positions "were well known when he was nominated; he must not now embarrass the canvass. You perceive it is impossible for him to do so. Yours, etc., John G. Nicolay."

Streets lighted with burning tar barrels and the torches of marching Wide-Awakes, heard the campaign song with its lines:

> Old Abe Lincoln came out of the wilderness,
> Out of the wilderness, out of the wilderness,
> Old Abe Lincoln came out of the wilderness,
>   Down in Illinois.

He was beginning to learn more precisely how he was food for the makers of myths. When John G. Scripps of the *Chicago Tribune* had come to him for material for a campaign biography, he told Scripps there would be nothing to it but "the short and simple annals of the poor." He toiled at shaping up a statement of the main facts of his life; it was scrupulous, careful, exact. He confessed to once shooting a wild turkey when a boy, and "never since pulled a trigger on larger game." And of young Abraham's election as captain of the New Salem Black Hawk War company, he noted, "He says he has not since had any success in life which gave him so much satisfaction."

In the Scripps sketch, as printed in the *Tribune* columns, a sentence read, "A friend says that once, when in a towering rage in consequence of the efforts of certain parties to perpetrate a fraud on the state, Mr. Lincoln was heard to say, 'They shan't do it, d—n 'em,' but beyond an expression of this kind his bitterest feelings never carried." This sentence was struck out, and not published in the Scripps biography reprinted as a pamphlet and widely circulated during the campaign.

Lincoln personally read the Scripps sketch before it was published, to correct mistakes that might have crept in. When he handed it back to Scripps he said that, before reading it, he hadn't read Plutarch, as the sketch declared, but had since gone and read Plutarch, so the statement could be published as strictly accurate.

"A scrupulous teller of the truth—too exact in his notions to suit the atmosphere of Washington as it now is," Scripps had written.

CHAPTER 142

GRIM thoughts came to Abraham Lincoln as he sat in the two-story white cottage at Eighth and Jackson streets in Springfield during the summer of 1860. He was watching the making of a legend. He saw a powerful young political party using him, shaping his personal figure into heroic stature, coloring his personality into something beyond what it actually was, picturing him as an embodiment of excellence and of genius, a creature in whom there were resident strange magnetic qualities that he knew had never been tested, never put under the fierce fire of experience.

If he should say to himself that he would make the kind of President they said he would make, he could only say it wryly with wry laughter. If he should in the days to come prove to be the man they said he was, he knew it could only be with prayers, tears, sardonic laughter, through a wild dance of death out of which he, perhaps, could not come alive. If he should in the days to come be the historic man of speech and action, of fine wisdom and chilled-steel nerves that they promised, he would be one of God's miracles, he would be one of the storm-stars lighting the history of the world.

Yet they were saying so, they were promising, the prophecies were issuing from the mouths of hundreds of stump orators, from the columns of hundreds of newspapers. "Abe," "Old Abe," "the Rail Candidate," "the Backwoodsman," "Honest Abe," "the Man of the People," the shrewd, sagacious, eloquent Man of the Hour, one who had risen from a dirt-floor cabin of poverty, who knew by first-hand acquaintance the wrongs of the poor, the exploited, the fooled—thus he was proclaimed.

What men there had been who had gone up against the test and met it and gone down before it! What a heartbreaking challenge there was in this thing of heading a government where vast sensitive property interests and management problems called for practical executive ability, while millions of people hungry for some mystic bread of life asked for land, roads, freedom, chances, open doors, release somehow from clutches that held them to monotony and toil!

On the one hand were those wanting refined mechanics of adjustment, and on the other hand those who wanted songs, slogans, words worth dying for! And between was a mass who lived, as the saying was, "by bread alone." They were the vast breathing, groaning, snarling, singing, murmuring, irreckonable instrument through which, and on which, history, destiny, politicians, worked—the people—the public that had to be reached for the making of public opinion.

He could only be solemn over the human note struck in the "Wigwam Edition of the Life, Speeches and Services of Abraham Lincoln," where it was declared: "Hitherto the backwoodsman has been powerful and important, it is true, but never until now has been conceded to him the first place . . . Whatever may be the result of the approaching Presidential election, it will always be distinguished for the elevation of one who had been a workingman to such preëminence as that accorded Abraham Lincoln . . . He has Revolutionary blood in his veins. The Lincolns of Massachusetts, known for their patriotism in the war of 1776, were his progenitors."

He could laugh low and feel hope over Dick Yates saying on the stump: "I know some folks are asking, who is old Abe? I guess they will soon find out. Old Abe is a plain sort of a man, about six feet four inches in his boots, and every inch of him *Man*. I recollect two years ago at a little party a very tall man went up to Lincoln and said, 'Mr. Lincoln, I think I am as tall as you are.' Lincoln began to straighten himself up and up, until his competitor was somewhat staggered. 'Well, I thought I was,' said he, now doubtful. 'But,' says Lincoln, straightening himself up still higher, *'there's a good deal of come-out in me,'* and he came out two inches the higher."

CHAPTER 143

THE Prince of Wales was touring America. The *New York Herald* took four columns to report a ball in Boston at which 1,080 tickets were sold at $15.00 apiece. As the prince passed through Springfield on his way to St. Louis, Lincoln told a newspaper man he would like to have welcomed or noticed the passage of the prince. "Not able to take any lead in the matter, I remained here at the Statehouse where I met so many sovereigns during the day that the prince had come and gone before I knew it." The same newspaper man to whom this was told casually asked one Springfield citizen what he thought of Lincoln, the answer being: "I like him. He talks sense, and is not too proud to sit down on his own doorstep and chat with his neighbors. I have always been a Democrat, but I am almost tempted to go for Lincoln."

An engine whistled at noon one day, bringing in a train with Senator Seward on board. Lincoln was one of the first to get on the train and shake hands with Seward. A crowd was calling, "Speech! Speech!" And Seward stepped out, to deliver the mouthful, "I am happy to express, on behalf of the party with whom I am traveling, our gratitude and acknowledgments for this kind and generous reception at the home of your distinguished fellow citizen, our excellent and honored candidate for the Chief Magistracy of the United States." Then he pledged 60,000 majority from New York, and declared that afterward New York would "ask less, exact less," from Lincoln than any other state.

Gifts arrived, a piece of white-oak wood from Josiah Crawford of Gentryville, Indiana. "It is part of a rail I cut for him in 1825 when I was sixteen years old," said Lincoln; "he sent the wood to have it made into a cane." A Terre Haute Republican sent the rib of a monster buffalo fish as a memento from a group of fishermen. "Thanks for your support and the high honor done me," he replied to letters with a certain ring of fellowship to them.

Over the country was fighting and singing. The *New York Herald* briefly reported a duel between two Missouri politicians on October 12. "Mr. Porter was addressing a political meeting at Nodaway when Col. Harlen called him a liar. Both parties were seriously though not fatally wounded."

And young men in western towns carried guitars and sang "Gentle Annie" in the streets at night:

> Shall we never more behold thee,
>   Never hear thy gentle voice again?
> When the springtime comes, gentle Annie,
>   And the wildflowers are scattered o'er the plain.

CHAPTER 144

THERE came to Springfield a correspondent for the *New York Herald*, a scribbler whose name was never signed to his articles. And while his newspaper was hurling shrapnel, javelins, and poison at Lincoln, editorially, he was sending columns of reportorial fact and impression of just the opposite character. His policy as a writer and his personal feelings about Lincoln were as different from the editorial page of the *New York Herald* as day is from night.

He liked Lincoln's looks, face, ways, and wrote: "Mr. Lincoln's face is a study—especially when lighted up. I have never seen a picture of him that does anything like justice to the original. He is a much better-looking man than any of the pictures represent. I do not understand why people call him Old Abe. He displays no appearance of age except deeply indented wrinkles on his brow, and the furrow plowed down his bony cheeks. You hardly detect the presence of frost in his black, glossy hair."

Then the correspondent did a bold deed. He compared Lincoln's looks to those of two respectable Easterners, and gave Lincoln the best of it. "I do not understand why Mr. Lincoln is represented as being so prodigiously ugly. Put him alongside Mr. Charles O'Connor and Mr. James W. Gerard—both of which eminent gentlemen have ridiculed so much his supposed ugliness—and if he would not appear 'as Adonis to a satyr,' he would at all events be set down as the finest-looking man of the trio. He affects not the elegancies of refined society, does not care to imitate New York aldermen in the matter of yellow kids, but is altogether a plain, blunt, unostentatious man. . . . In all of the photographs, his face wears a stony, rigid, corpselike expression, as if they were taken from a piece of sculpture, whereas in conversation he has great mobility and play of features. When he is thus animated, you fail to perceive anything ugly or grotesque about him."

The photographer, Hessler, came one day from Chicago. Politicians there were saying Lincoln seemed to be in "rough everyday rig" in all his pictures. Lincoln had written he would be "dressed up" if Hessler came to Springfield. And Hessler made four negatives of Lincoln in a stiff-bosomed, pleated shirt with pearl buttons. The glister of the shirt was the equal of any in a Douglas photograph, which was what the politicians were demanding.

Volk, the sculptor, arrived one day, was given a rose bouquet by Mrs. Lincoln, and presented her with a bust of her husband. As Lincoln shook him by the two hands, Volk said, "Now that you will doubtless be the next President of the United States, I want to make a statue of you, and shall do my best to do you justice." "I don't doubt it," replied Lincoln, "for I have come to the conclusion that you are an honest man."

A round stick was to be held in Lincoln's hands while Volk made casts of the hands. Lincoln stepped out to the woodshed and returned to the dining-room, whittling a broom handle. The edges didn't need such careful whittling, Volk remarked. "Oh, well, I thought I would like to have it nice."

After sittings, as the likeness emerged from the clay, Lincoln said, "There's the animal himself."

Portrait painters arrived with introductions and recommendations. One of them, Alban Jasper Conant, was secretary of the Western Academy of Art in St. Louis, which was to hold an exhibit at the coming Agricultural and Mechanical Association Fair in St. Louis, when the Prince of Wales and his suite were to be present. Conant's notion to paint Lincoln was given him by the Honorable William MacPherson, who had said in his quick way one day, "You'd better jump on a train and go paint this man Lincoln."

The new leader of the Republican party must be painted for the Fair. MacPherson said so; he was a St. Louis financial operator, builder and promoter in high favor with Morgan, Drexel & Co. of New York. Mac-

Pherson had founded Bellefontaine Cemetery and had other paying enterprises in mind, among them the Missouri Pacific Railroad. He had told Conant he was a Unionist and favored Lincoln, and a portrait would help the campaign.

"Whenever MacPherson tells people they ought to sit to me, they sit," Conant told himself, and he went to Springfield.

Lincoln read the introductions and recommendations given Conant by MacPherson, and shook his head, "No, it is impossible for me to give any more sittings." Another portrait painter edged in, "Mr. Lincoln, you can give him my sitting for tomorrow."

And Lincoln said he could sit for two as well as one, and at ten o'clock the next morning, after dictating letters to Nicolay, and leaning on his left hand while its fingers rumpled his hair, he stood up, crossed the room, threw himself into a chair, crossed his legs, and, with a sigh, was ready for the portrait painters who had easels and palettes waiting.

Conant stood dumb. Accustomed as he was to pleasant faces, he saw before him what he read to be impenetrable abstraction, sinister cross tracks of melancholy and despair. Having come to paint a meadow of contented cows and a satisfied farmer, he was unprepared for a scarred eagle flying in a black night along over a range of volcanic mountain-tops.

"Something had to be done," Conant said afterward. "And I began by asking permission to arrange his hair, which stood out like an oven broom. He nodded, and with my fingers I brushed it back, disclosing the splendid lines of the forehead. At least that was something, I thought, as I backed away. But it was not enough. All the other features seemed to me hopeless, as I stood there. His ill repute in my section flooded into my mind; his common origin—born of Kentucky 'poor white trash'; his plebeian pursuits, his coarse tastes and low associates. He seemed to me, indeed, the story-telling, whisky-drinking, whisky-selling country grocer who, they said, had been exalted to the exclusion of the astute Seward."

Thus Conant, the snob, told it. But he was not all snob. He told more. "As I sat down again before my easel, I made some flippant remark calculated to appeal to the vulgarian. It was then I got my first hint of the innate dignity of the man. He made some monosyllabic reply, and there came over his face the most marvelously complex expression I have ever seen—a mingling of instant shrewd apprehension of the whole attitude of mind back of my remark, pained disappointment of my misunderstanding of him, and patient tolerance of him. In a flash, I saw I had made a mistake." Thus Conant the artist, who learned that by asking intelligent questions he could light up a mobile face he was trying to paint.

When a barefoot boy stole on tiptoe to peep into the room and see a Famous Candidate, Lincoln joked the boy and called him to come and shake hands. Two boys came in one afternoon as he sat for the painter.

"What's your name?" Lincoln asked the first one. "Folks," was the answer. "Well, that's wrong. Don't you see that you are only one, and folks means more than one? Tell your father I say your name should be Folk. Good-by," and a handshake and a pat on the head. The second ragtag said his name was Knotts, and Lincoln laughed: "Well, if here isn't another mistake. Don't you see that you are only one and knots means more than one? Tell your father I said your name should be Knott. Good-by," and a handshake and a pat on the head.

Then his own boy, Tad, came in, with a playmate, Jim. Tad found an unfinished portrait of his father and yelled, "Come here, Jim, here's another Old Abe." Lincoln laughed to the painter: "Did you hear that, Conant? He got that on the street, I suppose."

Lincoln was thankful to Conant for one thing—the Slow Horse story. After he heard it, he told it to other people, and when introducing Conant he would say, "Did you know that I am indebted to this man for the Slow Horse story?"

A politician went to a livery stable, the story ran, for a horse to drive sixteen miles to a convention where he wanted the nomination for county judge. The horse broke down, he arrived late, lost the nomination, and came back to the livery stable feeling it was useless to be angry. He said to the liveryman: "See here, Jones. You are training this horse for the New York market. You expect to sell him for a good price to an undertaker for a hearse horse." But Jones insisted the horse was one of the best in his stable. "Now don't deny it," said the politician, "for I know by his gait that you have spent a great deal of time training him to go before a hearse. But he will never do. He—is—so—slow—he couldn't get a corpse to the cemetery in time for the resurrection."

This story stayed as a favorite with Lincoln. Conant heard him tell it, and said he embellished it. "I believe Mr. Lincoln's mind took in the whole picture in all its details—the grave, dissipated candidate, the horse moving on through the ages with the corpse, yet at a gait so slow that the end of all things comes to pass while he is still on the journey, and the corpse arrives too late for the resurrection."

Conant heard Lincoln tell stories which he said could never be printed; as with Villard they made him uneasy; he blamed them on pioneer conditions, influences far more "debasing" to the minds of the young than those in a large city. "Those born and bred in a remote country village, or reared on a farm with the hired help, will know what I mean. Those things stuck to him like a scar."

Conant believed he could see through and analyze what he called Lincoln's "humorous faculties." He noted of the stories he considered impure: "There was in them, to his mind, some striking touch of nature, emphasized by gross absurdity, of such point and power as to elevate it above the level of vulgarity. Such seeming blemishes were only the barnacles."

When the Conant portrait was finished, Mrs. Lincoln was pleased. "That is the way he looks when he has his friends about him."

And Conant was ready to go back to St. Louis with the painting for the Fair; it had been a puzzling job for him. He preferred regular features and curves, smoothly balanced lines with no gargoyle twists, and he found Lincoln's features "irregular and angular—the line of the nose straight on one side, and slightly curved on the other; the lower lip on the right side fuller than on the left, as if swollen from a blow or the sting of an insect."

The forehead was the one feature Conant found to be "very beautiful and symmetrical." The jaw, chin, nose, mouth would have to be made over before he could find "beauty and symmetry" in them.

Conant had looked at but never seen certain cathedral gargoyles that hover marvelously between tears and laughter, with mingled intimations of the tragic and comic in one breath.

Conant could hardly understand the *New York Herald* man's saying, "Mr. Lincoln's face is a study—especially when lighted up."

CHAPTER 145

Douglas was stumping the country; it seemed a losing fight; he went on, tireless; his friends were amazed at the way he wore out, went to bed, and came back to the fight again. He told a Boston crowd: "When you asked your representatives why the Pacific railroad had not been made, why the mail system had not been reformed and carried on with vigor, why you have no overland mail route to the Pacific, and no steam lines, you are told that the slavery question occupied the whole session. All great measures which affect the commercial interests, the shipping interests, the manufacturing interests, the industrial interests of the country, have been lost for want of time. There never will be time unless you banish forever the slavery question from the halls of Congress and remand it to the people of each State and Territory."

And he told a New York crowd: "If Lincoln should be elected, which God in his mercy forbid [a voice 'Amen' and laughter], he must be inaugurated according to the Constitution and the laws of the country. . . . Yet if the withdrawal of my name would tend to defeat Mr. Lincoln, I would this moment withdraw it."

Democrats of the southern wing of the party sent Jefferson Davis to dicker with Douglas; if all contenders would shake hands and join on one candidate they would sweep the election; Douglas said it couldn't be done; too many of his friends would go for Lincoln. Among business interests in the East Douglas was able to stir a fear of what would happen if Lincoln were elected and the country was split with civil war; trade would go to pieces.

"I think there will be the most extraordinary effort ever made to carry New York for Douglas," Lincoln wrote to Thurlow Weed. "You and all others who write me from your State think the effort can not succeed, and I hope you are right. Still it will require close watching." Replying to a Southerner, he wrote of receiving many assurances from the South "that in no probable event will there be any very formidable effort to break up the Union." He hoped and believed, "The people of the South have too much of good sense and good temper to attempt the ruin of the government rather than see it administered as it was administered by the men who made it."

Again and again came letters—just precisely what would he do with slavery if elected? would he interfere? would it not be wise to say plainly he wouldn't interfere? One he answered, "Those who will not read or heed what I have already publicly said would not read or heed a repetition of it." He quoted, "If they hear not Moses and the prophets, neither will they be persuaded though one rose from the dead."

Dick Yates was telling of a pretty young bride who handed a bridegroom a thousand dollars the next morning after the wedding day. And the bridegroom told her, "Lizzie, I like you very much, but this thousand dollars don't set you back any." From this Yates went on, "If Lincoln has all the other qualifications of a statesman, it don't set him back any with us who know and love him, to know that he was once a poor, hardworking boy."

"We know Old Abe does not look very handsome and some of the papers say he is positively ugly." Yates was also saying on the stump, "Well, if all the ugly men in the United States vote for him, he will surely be elected."

A child in a New York town asked whether he had a daughter, and why he didn't wear whiskers. His letter, saluting "My dear little Miss," told her: "I regret the necessity of saying I have no daughter, I have three sons—one seventeen, one nine, and one seven years of age. They, with their mother, constitute my whole family. As to the whiskers, having never worn any, do you not think people would call it a silly piece of affectation if I were to begin it now?"

He was a slow man in important decisions, slow at getting started; he hadn't shaped his decisions so that he could answer certain questions. He wrote Swett about a matter concerning Weed and others. The main point of his letter to Swett was in one sentence, "It can not have failed to strike you that these men ask for just the same thing—fairness and fairness only." But he ended the letter, "Burn this; not that there is anything wrong in it, but because it is best not to be known that I wrote at all."

Enemy newspapers raked up his past, claiming he had said Thomas Jefferson was a slaveholder who "brought his own children under the hammer, and made money of his debaucheries," particularizing that "a daughter of this vaunted champion of democracy was sold some years ago

Vanity Fair sketches Lincoln and Buchanan.

at public auction in New Orleans, and purchased by a society of gentlemen who wished to testify by her liberation their admiration of the statesman who 'dreamt of freedom in a slave's embrace.' "

This, Lincoln designated "a base forgery," which "my friends will be entirely safe in denouncing." The charge that he was a member of the

Know-Nothing organization and had attended a branch in Quincy, he dismissed with an alibi telling exactly where he was at all hours when he was in Quincy on the only evening he was ever there during which a Know-Nothing meeting was held.

And pleasant communications came, among them a letter from Nat Grigsby, a brother of the Aaron Grigsby who had married Lincoln's sister, Sarah. He replied to greetings from Dave Turnham, the constable at Gentryville who had loaned him before he was a voter "The Revised Laws of Indiana." He would like to visit again the old home and old friends. "I am indeed very glad to learn you are still living and well. I well remember when you and I last met, after a separation of fourteen years, at the crossroads voting-place in the fall of 1844. It is now sixteen years more and we are both no longer young men."

When the convention committee informing him of his nomination called at the Eighth Street cottage, he soberly brought them a pitcher of cold water; these were to be the drinks. He loosened the too stiff dignity of the occasion by calling on a tall judge to stand up and measure height with him.

A story was passing in Springfield that an Englishman in town, on hearing of the nomination, burst out: "What! Abe Lincoln nominated for President of the United States? Can it be possible! A man that buys a ten-cent beefsteak for his breakfast and carries it home himself!" And newsboys selling papers with a picture of Lincoln with his hair tousled had cried, "Here's your Old Abe, he'll look better when he gets his hair combed."

Reporters from enemy newspapers enjoyed him; one wrote: "The good-humored expression that lurks about his clear gray eye, traveling the one long, deep, curved furrow down his cheek, and making its home somewhere in the region of his capacious mouth, must always gain him friends. He dresses in the style of western lawyers, black cloth swallowtail coat and trousers fitting tightly to his long, bony frame; the inevitable black satin vest, open low down, and displaying a broad field of shirt bosom, the collar turned down over a black silk neckerchief." The silver watch chain he wore was burnished with wear; he carried the same watch key for the same timepiece he carried when the Mexican War was commencing.

"They are now using money lavishly," Thurlow Weed wrote to Lincoln three days before election, saying increased funds had fallen to the chests of the fusion leaders. "Some of our friends are nervous. I feel confident, however, that the masses are with us." Money, also "cheating," would probably cut down the New York Republican vote. Upstate, "in cities and villages their money will help them to several thousand votes, for unfortunately our state committee disbursed their funds too early, and, feeling quite safe, we have been sending money to New Jersey and Delaware that is now needed here." Oneida County would see a majority of 4,500 to 5,000, "unless the enemy buys us out." From 500 to 1,000 of the Oneida voters always went to the side with the most money on Election Day. "I fear that money against us will reduce the majority to 4,000."

CHAPTER 146

THE campaign was in its last week. Lincoln was in the Statehouse one day, alone with Newton Bateman, the State Superintendent of Public Instruction. He and Bateman were friends and talkers. He had taken a letter once to Bateman, asking corrections in syntax and structure. "I never was very strong on grammar." Bateman's head came only a little above Lincoln's elbows. He was referred to as "Little Newt." Lincoln would introduce him, saying, "This is my little friend, the big schoolmaster of Illinois."

And Lincoln had a Springfield poll book with notes on how each citizen was going to vote. "I wish particularly to see how the ministers of Springfield are going to vote." They turned the leaves, added up results, and Lincoln said: "Here are twenty-three ministers of different denominations, and all of them are against me but three; and here are a great many prominent members of churches, a very large majority of whom are against me."

Then he paused, and after a while rose and walked up and down the room. Bateman saw tears fill his eyes as he stopped in his pacing to and fro, to say: "I know there is a God, and that He hates injustice and slavery. I see the storm coming, and I know that His hand is in it. If He has a place and work for me I believe I am ready. I am nothing, but truth is everything."

And he went on in a lengthy and dark meditation on God and Christ, slavery and the teachings of the New Testament. "I may not see the end; but it will come, and I shall be vindicated; and these men will find they have not read their Bibles aright."

Suspicions were whispered, squabbles recited. In one case he advised: "I am slow to listen to criminations among friends, and never expose their quarrels on either side. My sincere wish is that both sides will allow bygones to be bygones, and look to the present and future only."

As the summer and fall drew on toward Election Day he was to those who met him the same friendly neighbor as always—but with more to think about. He shook hands with Whitney in a big crowd, and a half-hour later, seeing Whitney again, he shook hands and called him by name. "He didn't know me the first time," said Whitney.

Millions of people had by this time read his words of two years ago in the House Divided speech. They struck the soft, weird keynote of the 'hour. "If we could first know where we are, and whither we are drifting, we could better judge what to do and how to do it."

Twice, since he had first so spoken, the corn had grown from seed to the full stalk and been harvested.

In a book he had carried, it was told, "All rising to power is by a winding stair." As he went higher it was colder and lonelier.

The last leaves were blowing off the trees and the final geese honking south. Winter would come and go before seed corn went into the ground again.

CHAPTER 147

EARLY reports on the evening of Election Day, November 6, told Lincoln he hadn't won his home county of Sangamon. But he had carried his home precinct. From nine o'clock on he sat in the Springfield telegraph office. Lyman Trumbull arrived from Alton and summarized reports. "We've got 'em, we've got 'em." Then came a telegram: "Hon. A. Lincoln: Pennsylvania 70,000 for you. New York safe. Glory enough. S. Cameron."

Lincoln and his friends stepped across the street to a room where the Republican ladies' club had fixed a lunch. The ladies rushed him. "How do you do, Mr. President?" When two ladies met in a corner one said, "I've shaken hands with him," and the other replied: "Have you? Well, I was at the head of the table when he came in, and had a shake there, and then ran around and took my place at the foot of the line and shook hands with him again."

Out in the streets, and up around the Statehouse, crowds surged, shouting, "New York 50,000 majority for Lincoln"; lines of men locked arms and sang, "Ain't I glad I joined the Republicans?" till they were hoarse. The jubilee was still going as Lincoln walked to the Eighth Street cottage and told a happy woman, "Mary, we're elected."

The count showed Lincoln winning with 1,856,452 votes, a majority of nearly a half-million over Douglas, the nearest contender. A change of a few votes here and there would have given a different decision. In a total of 4,700,000 votes the other combined candidates had nearly a million more votes than Lincoln. Fifteen states gave him no electoral votes; in ten states he didn't get a count of one popular vote. And the Congress would have a Democratic majority.

In the whole Northwest, Lincoln's majority was only 6,600 over all other candidates. A change of one vote in twenty would have given Douglas the Northwest, and sent the presidential election into the national House of Representatives, where the South would probably have won.

On the day after the election, Wendell Phillips stood before an evening audience in Tremont Temple, Boston, with one hand resting on a hip, never moving out of his foot-tracks for an hour or so, while there sprang from his lips a flow of commentary, a percussion of epigrams. He shook his audience to laughter with saying: "The saddest thing in the Union meetings of last year was the constant presence, in all of them, of the clink of coin, the whir of spindles, the dust of trade. You would have imagined it was an insurrection of peddlers against honest men."

The incessant cry of "Silence!" from conservatives to agitators reminded Phillips of a sleepy crier in a New Hampshire court, who was often waking from dog-naps to shout, "Silence!" until one day the judge exclaimed, "Mr. Crier, you are the noisiest man in court, with your everlasting shout of 'Silence!'" He would say John Brown, Garrison, and the Abolitionists had so shaped politics that Lincoln, a mild antislavery man, could be elected President. But politics, the Government, wasn't so important. "To hear some men talk of the Government, you would suppose that Congress was the law of gravitation and kept the planets in their places. I think of that idle English nobleman at Florence whose brother, just arrived from London, happening to mention the House of Commons, he languidly asked, 'Ah! is that thing going still?'"

Phillips squeezed a mass of history into a little mouthful of speech. "First man walked, dug the earth with his hands, ate what he could pick up; then he subdues the horse, invents the plow and makes the water float him downstream; next come sails, windmills, and water power; then sewing machines lift woman out of torture, steam marries the continents, and the telegraph flashes news like sunlight over the globe." From this he would reason, "Every step made hands worth less, and brains worth more; and that is the death of slavery." The North and the South were like a tree trying to grow an apple one half pippin and the other half russet. "I am sure you cannot make a nation with one half steamboats, sewing machines, and Bibles, and the other half slaves."

With one hand resting on a hip, and never moving out of his foot-tracks, Phillips picked up facts, juggled and hoisted them. Forty years of industrial and mechanical revolution in transportation and machinery had brought changes worth trying to analyze. "The pulpit and the steamboat are of infinitely more moment than the Constitution. The South owes the existence of slavery today to the cunning of a Massachusetts Yankee, Eli Whitney; and Fulton did more to perpetuate the Union than a Senate chamber of Websters. The founders and presidents of our railways are a much more influential body than the Senate of the Union." It had got so that the President of the United States didn't govern; he only reigned. "Did you ever see on Broadway a black figure grinding chocolate in the windows? He seems to turn the wheel, but in truth the wheel turns him."

Phillips said, "Let us question Mr. Lincoln," and went on: "Do you believe, Mr. Abraham Lincoln, that the negro is your political and social equal, or ought to be? Not a bit of it. Do you believe he should sit on juries? Never. Do you think he should vote? Certainly not. Do you think that, when the Declaration of Independence says, 'All men are created equal,' it intends the political equality of blacks and whites? No, sir. If this be equality, surely Mr. Lincoln's mind is as yet empty. But notwithstanding the emptiness of Mr. Lincoln's mind, I think we shall yet succeed in making this a decent land to live in."

And still with one hand resting on a hip, and never stirring out of his foot-tracks, he told them: "Pictures of the mere industrial value of the Union make me profoundly sad. Is this the whole fruit of ages of toil, sacrifice, and thought? Does it result only in a workshop—fops melted in baths and perfumes, and men grim with toil?" He would have a Christian civilization with a Holy of Holies. "Crowding to the shelter of its stately arches, I see old and young, learned and ignorant, rich and poor, native and foreign, pagan, Christian, and Jew, black and white, in one glad, harmonious, triumphant procession."

Thus events marched and masked their meanings, and educated men with intellects keen as steel tried to read the future in the smoky confusions of their logic, their habits, and their geographical locations. Facts were harder to see because they were gathering motion, whisking into new shapes and disguises every day. Dream-shapes of future events danced into sight and out of sight, faded and came again, before a whirligig of triple mirrors.

CHAPTER 148

EVENTS came as by clockwork at a signal and Lincoln's election was the signal. South Carolina legislators voted to raise and equip 10,000 volunteer soldiers; Georgia and Louisiana legislatures voted $1,000,000.00 and $500,000.00 for arms and troops. South Carolina through its legislature declared itself a sovereign and independent state and seceded from the Union of States, on December 20, with a flag of its own, with oaths of allegiance; forts, post offices, customhouses of the Federal Government were taken. Before New Year's Day it was known the whole row of cotton states would follow South Carolina, with a view of forming a Southern Confederacy. And in the same weeks, for whatever it portended, there was also the accomplished fact that a great chain of railroads, making a complete rail transportation line from Bangor, Maine, to New Orleans, had been finished.

A crisscross of facts was operating. Robert Toombs was saying: "It is admitted that you seek to outlaw $4,000,000,000 of property of our people in the Territories. Is not that a cause of war?" But was secession the safest way of managing this property? Jefferson Davis had his doubts. And Alexander Stephens had written five months before, "I consider slavery much more secure in the Union than out of it if our people were but wise." Property suffers in revolutions, he pointed out. "The institution is based on conservatism." Stephens had noted the diminishing supply of slave labor and wrote his belief that, without fresh supplies from Africa, slavery would be replaced by free competitive wage labor.

Among the fire-eaters clamoring for secession were those who made a business of buying, breeding, selling slaves. A planter from Georgia had told the national Democratic convention, "I have had to pay from $1,000 to $2,000 a head when I could go to Africa and buy better negroes for $50 apiece."

On the tax list of the city of Charleston for that year were the names of 132 "colored people" who paid taxes on 390 slaves which they owned; the class included eleven Indian families who had consorted with negroes.

Secession was the creed of state sovereignty. Yet Davis, Stephens, and other high counselors of the South, in their letters and speeches at this time, did not advise secession. The leaders were Yancey, Rhett, and others. They cried, "The irrepressible conflict is about to be visited upon us through the Black Republican, Lincoln, and his fanatical, diabolical Republican party."

Once secession was accomplished by its radical manipulators, Southerners till then conservative, and advising against disunion, fell in line as patriots whose first oath of allegiance was to their sovereign state, their country. They quoted Decatur: "Our Country! In her intercourse with foreign nations may she always be in the right; but our country, right or wrong." And the *Charleston Mercury* published dispatches from northern cities under the heading, "Foreign News."

Those who demurred, reasoned, and lifted friendly warnings against disunion and secession were many, but their effort was useless against the onrush of those who took Lincoln's election as the signal for a time of change. There were those who looked on Lincoln as Alexander Stephens did in a letter to J. Henly Smith, a fellow Georgian, before the election, saying: "What is to become of the country in case of Lincoln's election, I do not know. As at present advised I should not be for disunion on the grounds of his election. It may be that his election will be attended with events that will change my present opinion, but his bare election would not be sufficient cause in my judgment to warrant a disruption—particularly as his election will be the result if it occurs at all of the folly and madness of our own people. If they do these things in the green tree what will they not do in the dry? If, without cause, they destroy the present Government, the best in the world, what hopes have I that they would not bring untold hardships upon the people in their efforts to give us one of their own modeling? Let events shape their own course. In point of merit as a man I have no doubt Lincoln is just as good, safe and sound a man as Buchanan and would administer the Government so far as he is individually concerned just as safely for the South and as honestly and faithfully in every particular. I know the man well. He is not a bad man. He will make as good a President as Fillmore did and better, in my opinion. He has a great deal of practical common sense. Still, his party may do mischief. If so it will be a great misfortune, but a misfortune that our own people brought upon us . . . We have nothing to fear from anything so much as unnecessary changes and revolutions in government . . . I shall vote for Douglas."

The "green tree" grew. One by one the six other cotton states of the lower South joined South Carolina in leaving the Union and declaring their right to self-government and self-determination. Their delegates at Montgomery, Alabama, on February 4, organized a provisional government named The Confederate States of America, electing Jefferson Davis of Mississippi as President and Alexander Stephens of Georgia as Vice President. Conventions in North Carolina and Arkansas deliberated, and joined the Confederacy. In Tennessee the voters balloted 105,000 to 47,000 in favor of secession, the Union strength coming from the mountaineers. In Virginia, three to one of 130,000 voters were in favor of "The Mother of Presidents" going into the Confederacy, the mountaineers chiefly being Unionist. In Texas, Governor Sam Houston refused to call the legislature and tried to stop secession, but was bowled over.

Arsenals, supplies, post offices, ships were taken over by the new government; fort guns fired on a ship at sea; President Buchanan proclaimed a Fast Day publicly, and moaned privately that he was the last President of the United States of America; well-meaning men of splendid intentions and large hearts sprang forward with compromises and arrangements and suggestions; special committees and conferences of duly appointed delegates met, spoke, adjourned. Southern congressmen resigned and left Washington; there were votes enough one January day to admit "Bleeding Kansas" as a state in the Union, her officially embossed motto and slogan being, as translated from the Latin, "To the Stars by Hard Ways."

At the opening session of Congress, the chaplain had prayed: "O Lord our God, we offer to Thee our humble praise for the past, the present, and for all the future. Will it please Thee, for Christ's sake, to grant us Thy special aid? Thou knowest that our good men are at fault, and that our wise men are at fault; in the North and the South, in the East and in the West, they are at fault."

While Southern radicals were calling Lincoln a fanatical, diabolical Abolitionist, Wendell Phillips sneered at him as "the slave hound of Illinois." Robert Toombs read to the Georgia legislature a defense of secession written and published by Horace Greeley; the advice of Greeley was, "Let the erring sisters depart in peace." Boston heard Phillips declare: "Let the South march off with flags and trumpets, and we will speed the parting guest. Let her not stand upon the order of her going, but go at once. Give her forts, arsenals, and subtreasuries. Give her jewels of silver and gold, and rejoice that she has departed. All hail, disunion!"

Thirty years ago, southern leaders, sixteen years ago, northern Abolitionists, announced their purpose to seek the dissolution of the Union, said Phillips. He jubilated, "Who dreamed that success would come so soon?" He paid a compliment to South Carolina, with a backhand slap at New England. "South Carolina, bankrupt, alone, with a hundred thousand more slaves than whites, four blacks to three whites within her borders, flings her gauntlet at the feet of twenty-five millions of people in defense of an idea, to maintain what she thinks her right. I would New England could count one state so fearless among her six."

This in January, while in February Phillips said disunion would be good business, declaring, "The South buys little of us and pays for only about half she gets." If the southern states put forts on the Mississippi River to bar trade, "they will graciously be allowed to pay for them, while northern railroads grow rich carrying behind steam that portion of wheat, bacon, silk, tea which would otherwise float" toward the Gulf.

Wendell Phillips welcomed disunion. "Let the border states go. Then we part friends. The Union thus ended, the South no longer hates the North. . . . The laws of trade will bind us together, as they do all other lands."

The Detroit department-store proprietor, Zachariah Chandler, senator from Michigan, a square-jawed physical bulwark, wrote his state governor "a little bloodletting" was wanted, which was matched with a Georgian's saying the people must wake up; there was a way to rouse them and get the war going: "Sprinkle blood in their faces."

CHAPTER 149

In the day's mail for Lincoln came letters cursing him for an ape and a baboon who had brought the country evil. Also letters told him he was a satyr, a negro, a mulatto, a buffoon, a monster, an abortion, an idiot; he would be flogged, burned, hanged, hampered, tortured.

Pen sketches of gallows and daggers arrived from "oath-bound brotherhoods." Some notes were scrawled with misspelled words, barking to intimidate. A one-page missive of ten lines employed the word "goddam" from one to three times in each line. Other letters were specific in statements that a rifle-shot would reach him before he reached Washington or the ceremony of inauguration as President. Some aimed at a polite and accomplished raillery. One postmarked, "Elgin, Ill., Nov. 21, 1860,' read:

Deformed Sir, The Ugly Club, in full meeting, have elected you an Honorary Member of the Hard-Favored Fraternity.—Prince Harry was lean,

Falstaff was fat. Thersites was hunchbacked, and Slawkenbergus was renowned for the eminent miscalculation which Nature had made in the length of his nose; but it remained for you to unite all species of deformity, and stand forth the Prince of Ugly Fellows. In the bonds of Ugliness—Hinchaway Beeswax, President. Eagle-Eyed Carbuncle, Secretary of the Ugly Club.

A man calling to shake hands with Lincoln one day said it was too bad that as soon as the high honor of being President had been bestowed on Lincoln he should have to deal immediately with "the vexatious slavery question." Lincoln told a story, which the *New York Herald* writer heard. "He said that many years ago an unsophisticated farmer, more honest than learned, commonly known as 'Old Zach' undertook to run for the office of Justice of the Peace in Kentucky. Being successful, the first case he was called upon to adjudicate was a criminal process for the abuse of negro slaves. Its merits being somewhat beyond his comprehension, after hearing the evidence he sought enlightenment in the Statutes of the Commonwealth and various 'handbooks for justices of the peace' with which he had provided himself on assuming the ermine. But his search for precedents proved in vain, and, growing still more puzzled, he exclaimed at last angrily, 'I will be damned if I don't feel almost sorry for being elected when the niggers is the first thing I have to attend to.' The story was, of course, intended more as a humorous reply than as an indication of Mr. Lincoln's own sentiments."

Often he took his boy Tad on his knees, and they talked. He could tell Tad many a piece of nonsense with a monkeyshine in it that would have been wasted on Horace Greeley or Salmon P. Chase. Tad came into an important conference once and in a loud whisper told his father, "Ma says come to supper." A slow smile spread over the father's face, as he said, "You have all heard, gentlemen, the announcement concerning the interesting state of things in the dining-room. It will never do for me, if elected, to make this young man a member of my Cabinet, for it is plain he cannot be trusted with secrets of state."

CHAPTER 150

As the country drifted and the muddle got worse, Lincoln had nothing to say. He delivered remarks such as, "Please excuse me from making a speech," and, "Let us at all times remember that all American citizens are brothers of a common country." He indicated he would stand for no further spread of slavery. And his close friend, Edward D. Baker, now senator from Oregon, told the United States Senate that Lincoln would respect the Fugitive Slave Law. Also, he told friends privately that the forts seized by the seceded states would have to be retaken. But as to declaration of policy on this and that, he was waiting. Those pushing him could have satisfaction later.

Newspapers twisted and misrepresented a Trumbull speech and he wrote to Henry J. Raymond of the *New York Times:* "This is just as I expected, and what would happen with any declaration I could make. These political fiends are not half sick enough yet. Party malice and not public good possesses them. 'They seek a sign, and no sign shall be given them.' "

The little financial panic and depressed business tone said to have been brought on by interests hostile to the coming administration, he dismissed with, "Nothing is to be gained by fawning around the 'respectable scoundrels' who got it up." Every once in a while he seemed to use the phrase "respectable scoundrels," and sometimes an unprintable word in place of "scoundrels."

An Indiana man, James P. Lusk, came from a talk with Lincoln, remarking, "He said he had as much curiosity to know what kind of a pronouncement the South wanted and wished, as the South had to know what kind he would make, if he made one at all." A declaration that he wasn't going to interfere with slavery would do no good, he wrote to Jesse K. Dubois. "I should have no objection to make and repeat the declaration a thousand times, if there were no danger of encouraging bold, bad men to believe they are dealing with one who can be scared into anything." He wrote to Trumbull that "Pop. Sov." was "the dangerous ground into which our friends have a hankering to run." His advice would be: "Have none of it. Stand firm. The tug has got to come; and better now than any time hereafter."

Once more Lincoln and Joshua Speed were exchanging letters. Lincoln hoped he and Speed could meet in Chicago, each with his wife. "Could you not meet me there?" he wrote. "Mary thinks of going with me; and therefore I suggest that Mrs. S. accompany you. Please let this be private, as I prefer a very great crowd should not gather at Chicago."

He went to Chicago, met Hannibal Hamlin, the Vice President elect; they held a reception in the Tremont House, went to St. James's Church together, and in the afternoon, as the *Tribune* reported it, "They visited the North Market Mission where, after the usual services, the President-elect delivered a short address which was received with much pleasure by the destitute children attending the Sabbath school."

Eight little girls stood in a row at the Tremont House; he signed his name in their autograph albums. A four-year-old boy yelled, "Hurray for Uncle Abe!" and was soon in Lincoln's hands getting tossed high toward the ceiling and hugged safe on coming down. He had a good visit with Joshua Speed, asked many questions about Kentucky. Mrs. Lincoln and Mrs. Speed went shopping.

The Lincolns went back to Springfield. Tad and Willie were singing, "Old Abe Lincoln came out of the wilderness." He resumed regular hours of ten to twelve in the morning and 3:30 to 5:30 in the afternoon, receiving visitors in the governor's room of the State House.

William Jones dropped in; he was the Jones who kept the store in Gentryville when the boy, Abe, was "the big buck of the lick." An old man from the state of Mississippi came out after his talk with Lincoln and stood at a wall, in tears; men asked the trouble; he wished more people in the South could know Lincoln. A man from the state of Alabama had a half-hour talk; what he got was jokes and illustrations, and little satisfaction.

Mark Delahay showed up, the Kansas politician whose expenses Lincoln had paid to the Chicago convention. Delahay visited the Lincoln home and scrutinized a silk banner on the parlor wall; it had been embroidered by the young ladies of Lombard College, and when they presented it Lincoln had told them, "I shall prize it." As Delahay was feeling of the banner to see if it was real silk, Lincoln remarked, "You seem to like that banner." "I do; it is a beautiful thing." "Well, I will make you a present of it." And it traveled with Delahay toward Topeka.

One political friend of twenty years' loyalty, a prospering Alton Railroad lawyer, sobbed a prayer to Lincoln to address the South and promise no war. "I live near the Missouri line; I'll be one of the first killed. Don't make a rumpus." And the man, Lincoln told Whitney, was "sobbing like a child."

The trains into Springfield unloaded hundreds of passengers on a single day, arriving to see Lincoln. Some carried shining faces; they just wanted to look at him and tell him they hoped to God he'd live and have good luck. Others, too, carried shining faces, singing, "Ain't we glad we joined the Republicans?" They said they nominated and elected him President, and inquired about post offices, revenue collectorships, clerkships, secretaryships. They wore him. Behind their smiles some had snouts like buzzards, pigs, rats. They were pap-seekers, sapsuckers, chair-warmers, hammock heroes, the office-sniffing mob who had killed Zach Taylor, who had killed Tippecanoe Harrison. They wore Lincoln—worse than the signs of war.

A joker arose, with a far sardonic snort in his jokes. He and Lincoln struck hands of fellowship. In an article in *Vanity Fair*, this joker reported with a horselaugh the tragic swarming to the trough at Springfield. "Hevin no politics, I made bold to visit Old Abe at his humsted in Springfield. I found the old feller in his parler, surrounded by a perfick sworm of orfice seekers. Sum wanted post offices, sum wanted collectorships, sum wanted furrin missions and all wanted sumthin. I thought Old Abe would go crazy. He hadn't more than had time to shake hands with 'em, before another tremenjis crowd cum porein onto his premises. The house, dooryard, barn & woodshed was all full, and when another crowd cum I told 'em not to go away for want of room, as the hog-pen was still empty.

It was the beginning of a friendship. The writer signed as "Artemus

Vanity Fair sketches Lincoln at home meeting the office-seekers.

Ward," a twenty-six-year-old wanderer born in Maine, trained on newspapers in Cleveland, Ohio, and doing one sketch a week for *Vanity Fair*. Lincoln adopted him as an unofficial spokesman who could be depended on to say things a Chief Magistrate would like to say if it wouldn't be going too far. Democracy should see and laugh. A republic should have jesters at the overstuffed shirts of dignity and pretense, such as this A. Ward.

The *Vanity Fair* sketch of the office seekers closed with, "He shook me cordyully by the hand—we exchanged picters, so we could gaze upon each other's liniments when far away from one another." This pleased Lincoln. He read such passages aloud to other people and chuckled over them.

One caller told him of a set of schemes to stop any possible war by a big wheat speculation that would make them both rich. It reminded Lincoln of the merchant who told the same sort of crank, "My advice is that you stick to your business." Then came the query, "But what is my business?" and the reply, "I don't know, but whatever it is you stick to it."

Another caller, an old woman, he greeted: "Now, Aunt Sally, this is real kind of you to come and see me. How are you, and how's Jake? Come over here." And he took her to a group of officials and political workers. "Gentlemen, this is a good old friend of mine. She can make the best flapjacks you ever tasted, and she's baked 'em for me many a time." And the old woman handed him a large pair of yarn socks, saying, "Knit 'em myself."

And Ned Baker came in, brave, warm, impetuous, extravagant, songvoiced. Lincoln had named his boy Eddie, the one who died, after Edward D. Baker, who had become United States senator from Oregon. They talked of the future and of the past. They could recall the story told twenty years before by Lincoln, to tease Baker. The story ran that Baker, who was born on the ocean, from English parents, was found sobbing alone in a timber one morning, and when asked what was the matter had answered that he had just read in a book that only citizens born in the United States could ever become President—and his chance was gone!

CHAPTER 151

THE Washington man of the *Chicago Tribune* wired on January 3 that President Buchanan had met with his Cabinet the day before, and, "The row recommenced. The President, like a pusillanimous coward, refused to take sides, and, shaken like an aspen leaf, entreated them not to quarrel, and offered them some old whisky—his unfailing remedy. The old man has become little better than a sot. He keeps saturated with Monongahela whisky. He drinks to drown remorse and stupefy his brain as he staggers along with the treasonable gang who have possession of him."

The next day was the one set apart by the President for fasting, prayer, and humiliation. Services were conducted in nearly all churches in the northern states. The Springfield man of the *Chicago Tribune* wired to his paper, "Mr. Lincoln attended church today, in obedience to the Presidential proclamation, and it is to be presumed that in his prayers Mr. Buchanan's backbone was not forgotten."

At that hour, as Lincoln was in church at fast-day services, many people believed southern forces would seize Washington, and Lincoln would have to be sworn in at some other place. Twenty-two carloads of troops were starting from Fort Leavenworth across Missouri for Baltimore. Cameron of Pennsylvania was saying, "Lincoln, if living, will take the oath of office on the Capitol steps." Newly organized artillery companies were drilling in Chicago. A thousand negro slaves were throwing up fortifications in Charleston, South Carolina. The Democrats of Illinois were ready for semi-secessionist action at their state convention that month. The governor of Illinois was writing in his message to the legislature, "Illinois counts among her citizens 400,000 who can bear arms." The Wisconsin governor was writing, "Secession is revolution; revolution is war." The governor of Massachusetts was writing that the words of Andrew Jackson of Tennessee were precious, "The Federal Union—may it be preserved!" Republican newspapers were printing the last will and testament of Jackson with his curse on "foreign foes" and "intestine traitors." Five million dollars and a hundred thousand troops would be offered by their legislature, Pennsylvania legislators were saying. "Mr. Lincoln may take his oath before any officer in the country authorized to administer an oath," the *Chicago Tribune* had said just the day before. "We have no doubt that Mr. Lincoln will be President of the United States and Commander-in-Chief of the Army and Navy, before he leaves Springfield."

"The Revolution" was the top headline under which a New York daily paper assembled the news of the country. Nine columns were required on one day to report declarations of southern conventions, and resignations from the army and navy and the training academies. A letter of Edward Everett, the classical orator, was read to a Boston mass meeting. He was saying, "To hold fifteen States in the Union by force is preposterous."

With the Union broken Stephens of Georgia could see "anarchy" at the North, "and whether we shall be better off at the South will depend on many things I am not satisfied we have any assurance of." Stephens had dug into history. "Revolutions are much easier started than controlled, and the men who begin them, even for the best purposes and object, seldom end them."

Horace Greeley dropped into Springfield, going home from a trip West. He didn't go to Lincoln's house. Lincoln walked to Greeley's hotel. Greeley was cautious, tentative, bewildered, outwardly thinking in straight lines, inwardly running circles. His original advice to "let the erring sisters depart in peace" had changed to counsel against compromise. The two men talked several hours. Lincoln knew what a wide audience of readers Greeley had through the *New York Tribune*, and was trying to join forces with him. Greeley wanted to be senator from New York. He could use

Lincoln's influence. Lincoln held off from taking a hand in New York state politics. He had written to Weed, Greeley's mortal enemy, politically, the day before, "My name must not be used in the senatorial election in favor of or against any one."

They parted—Greeley and Lincoln—with no fresh understanding of each other, no real arrangement to coöperate. Lincoln, in Greeley's eyes, was just one more common politician. In all of their hours of talk, said Greeley, "I never heard him tell a story or anecdote." The clue was sinister. But Greeley didn't know it. He believed Lincoln wanted to be charioteer of the Greeley chariot, which Lincoln didn't want at all. Lincoln wanted less zigzag driving.

Politicians swarmed in and overran Springfield. "The influx is so great that a large number nightly seek shelter in sleeping-cars," said a newspaper.

Lincoln had lost forty pounds' weight in less than a year, so Volk said Lincoln told him. "He looks more pale and careworn," said the *New York Herald* writer. "The groveling tidewaiters, fawners, sycophants, and parasites combined in the genus 'office seekers' have thus far affected him only in slight degree. . . . His ears and eyes must learn to be closed at certain times. His lips must be trained to less ready response. If not, the crowd of cormorants and place hunters will unbalance and overwhelm him."

He took a stand against Illinois sending commissioners to a peace convention called by the Governor of Virginia. Dr. William Jayne wrote to Trumbull, "Lincoln advised he would rather be hanged by the neck till he was dead on the steps of the Capitol than buy or beg a peaceful inauguration."

Day by day called for decisions. And Lincoln had no policy, as such, to guide him. He explained to a secretary, "My policy is to have no policy."

On the horizons seemed to be looming an ancient tribal Dance of Death. Men had come to the point where they wanted something done so that it would stay done, and they were acting by the theory of Emerson's neighbor with the wheelbarrow, who had said he wouldn't bother with voting at town meeting, and, "What you do with a gun will stay so."

The teachings of hate became fiercer in key. Proud and powerful men, reckless as to death and personal belongings and public peace, hunted through language and lingo to find epithets, dirty names to call the Other Side. All revolutions or wars must have their Dirty Names to begin with and to carry on. Lincoln had decided that in his First Inaugural Address he would call the southern people "My dissatisfied Countrymen." Those not his countrymen, at least, were dissatisfied. It sort of smiled through a face of tears, that salutation, "My dissatisfied Countrymen."

CHAPTER 152

THURLOW WEED, the New York boss, got off the train at Springfield. He came from Albany, where letters had kept coming from Swett, saying Lincoln wanted to see him about Cabinet matters. They talked politics and issues in general. Lincoln said he had been looking around for helpers, for great men. Perhaps he didn't know where the best available timber was. "While the population of the country has immensely increased, really great men are scarcer than they used to be."

Lincoln suggested that Weed was a Cabinetmaker, and while he, Lincoln, had never learned that trade, he had a job of Cabinetmaking on hand and was willing to have the help of friends. Weed came back saying he wasn't exactly a boss Cabinetmaker; he was a journeyman, had helped make state cabinets but not Federal. The two men had a good time.

Weed thought it marvelous that Lincoln all the time kept interspersing stories pat to the deal in hand. Weed believed two members of the Cabinet should be from slave states. "Would you rely on such men if their states secede?" "Yes, sir; the men I have in my mind can always be relied on." "Well, let us have the names of your *white crows*." For one, Weed named Henry Winter Davis of Maryland, who was elected to Congress by anti-foreigner and anti-Catholic support, calling itself the American party and nicknamed the Know-Nothings.

Lincoln knew this Davis was a cousin of Judge David Davis, and guessed that his Chicago convention manager, and the chief jurist of the Eighth Circuit, was operating through Weed. He laughed, "Davis has been posting you up on this question. He came from Maryland and has got Davis on the brain. Maryland must, I think, be like New Hampshire, a good state to move from." And he told of a witness swearing his age was sixty when the court knew he was much older; the court rebuking the witness got the reply, "Oh, you're thinking about that fifteen years I lived down on the Eastern Shore of Maryland; that was so much lost time and don't count."

Names, personalities, localities, political shadings, and shifts were talked over; they were two schoolmasters in politics enjoying each other's technic and experience. No name for Secretary of the Navy came up to suit Weed; perhaps any wooden figurehead taken off a ship and dressed up with a wig and whiskers would do. "Oh," said Lincoln, " 'wooden midshipmen' answer very well in novels, but we must have a live Secretary of the Navy."

Would Bates of Missouri do for Attorney-General? Yes, Weed was sure; he paid tribute to Bates's personal reliability, which reminded Lincoln of a story; and he sketched and wove a series of incidents leading to the office of Squire Barton in St. Louis facing a young man under suspicion of having run away with a package of bank money. The squire led the young man to an open window and said: "If you didn't steal that money, my advice is that you face the music, and I will stand by you; but if, as I strongly suspect, you were tempted and that money isn't honestly yours, I advise you [pointing through the open window] to make tracks for that tall timber, and to put the Mississippi between you and those bank fellows as soon as you can find a crossing." "And how much shall I pay you for your advice?" asked the client. "If you intend to hook it, five dollars; if you stay and prove yourself an honest lad, nothing."

Fresh December sausages were served Weed at breakfast in the Lincoln home. He asked for a second helping, with the remark that he felt safe in a section of the country where pork was cheaper than dogs. "That reminds me," said Lincoln. A Joliet grocer, doing a large sausage business, had his store full of customers one Saturday evening, and his boys were piling the scales with sausages when a neighbor, who had quarreled with him that day, came into the grocery and walked up to the counter holding two big dead cats by the tails. As he threw them on the counter, he said, so that all the customers could hear: "This makes seven today; I'll call around Monday and get my money for them."

They spent two chatty days together. Lincoln told Weed it was pleasant that he was not tied by promises of offices; it was one advantage of having been a dark-horse candidate. "I have not promised an office to any man," he told Weed. Furthermore, "Some gentlemen, who have been quite nervous about the object of your visit here, would be surprised, if not incredulous, were I to tell them that during the two days we have passed together you have made no application, suggestion, or allusion to appointments." Telegrams had come to Lincoln from prominent Republicans trying to head off appointments Weed might seek, he told the New York leader.

They talked about whether promises, assurances, laws could straighten out the wrong feeling between the peoples of the North and South. They agreed as to the people of the South, "We must not only let them alone, but we must somehow convince them that we do let them alone." Lincoln gave Weed three short resolutions to carry to Washington and give to Senator Trumbull. Then Lincoln wrote to Senator Trumbull: "Thurlow Weed was with me nearly all day yesterday, and left last night with three short resolutions which I drew up, and which, or the substance of which, I think, would do much good if introduced and unanimously supported by our friends. They do not touch the territorial question. Mr. Weed goes to Washington with them; and says he will first of all confer with you and Mr. Hamlin. I think it would be best for Mr. Seward to introduce them, and Mr. Weed will let him know that I think so. Show this to Mr. Hamlin, but beyond him do not let my name be known in the matter." Two of the three short resolutions went further than any public declarations

Lincoln had ever made in the direction of satisfying the South, while another of the resolutions was the most radical practical change he had ever suggested for the Fugitive Slave Law. The first resolution aimed so to fix the Constitution that Congress could not lawfully interfere with slavery in slave states; the second would arrange for fugitive slaves to have a jury trial; the third would ask northern states to change, to "review," their laws which interfered with the capture and trial of runaway slaves.

Weed, the New York boss, was to carry the three resolutions, all privately, but never publicly, indorsed by Lincoln, the President-elect; and Weed was to meet Trumbull and Hamlin, Illinois and Maine senators, and they would confer; if they decided after conferring that the resolutions should be introduced, then it was Lincoln's wish that Seward, New York senator, should introduce them; and Lincoln had arranged that Weed should let Seward know that he, Lincoln, thought Seward was the best man for introducing them; the letter of Lincoln to Trumbull informing him of all these arrangements and views on the part of Lincoln was to be shown to Hamlin and to nobody else; and beyond Hamlin, Lincoln's name was not to be mentioned in the matter; Lincoln was not particular as to whether his language in the three short resolutions was used; the substance of his language would do as well; and the one condition under which Lincoln believed the resolutions would "do much good" was the condition of "unanimous" support.

As it happened, the resolutions were not introduced. Trumbull, believing Lincoln to be "cunning as a fox," probably suspected that Lincoln was up to something beyond the passage of the resolutions embodying plans that Lincoln had never mentioned publicly as important. It stuck in Trumbull's mind that Swett, the lifelong friend of Lincoln, could say of Lincoln, "He's a trimmer, and such a trimmer as the world has never seen." Trumbull's impression of Lincoln was: "He is secretive, communicates no more of his own thoughts and purposes than he thinks will subserve the ends he has in view; he has the faculty of gaining the confidence of others by apparently giving them his own, and in that way attaches to himself many friends; he is one of the shrewdest men I have ever known; he is by no means the unsophisticated, artless man that many take him to be."

Lincoln had spent two days with Thurlow Weed, refreshed and loosened up Weed with stories, fables, anecdotes coming pat to each point in hand, even to the topic of fresh sausages at breakfast. Lincoln had searched his way through the upstairs and downstairs rooms of Weed's mind and heart; Lincoln had trained himself, for years, to put men at their ease while pumping them with quiet questions, learning by asking, and asking with keen, soft persistence. He knew that Weed was in communication with, and was hearing the wants of, such men of power as A. T. Stewart, the leading New York merchant, and August Belmont, New York representative of the Rothschilds, international bankers, and a leading financier among the northern capitalists to whom the South was in debt two hundred million dollars. Also Lincoln learned from Weed in elaborate detail how Weed hated and feared the extremists and radicals of the North and South; Weed was a man of compromises and adjustments, a type of the boss or leader controlling a large organization among territories, precincts, henchmen; they trade off this for that and fix arrangements that act as barriers or stopgaps; Weed was for conciliation between North and South; he believed the misunderstandings could be patched up.

Lincoln saw this and wrote three short, bold resolutions that with "unanimous support," as he wrote Trumbull, would stave off all future trouble between the South and North; he handed the resolutions in his writing, to Weed, to carry to Washington to have Seward introduce if a conference of Weed, Trumbull, and Hamlin should decide they might win "unanimous support"; and Lincoln knew that it was a foregone and absolute impossibility that such Abolitionist Republicans as Joshua Giddings or Owen Lovejoy would for a fraction of a moment consider voting for laws to take away all future power of Congress to interfere with slavery in the slave states or to ask northern states to change or "review" their laws that had been passed with the intention of defeating the Federal Fugitive Slave Law.

The proportions of some phases of the incident lifted it into the ludicrous. It helped to accomplish one thing, the cementing of loyalty between Lincoln and Weed, which was the main intention of Lincoln.

A few weeks later, however, word came to Lincoln that the New York boss claimed that Lincoln had handed over to him the say-so as to Federal jobs for New York Republicans. And Lincoln wrote to Weed: "As to the matter of dispensing patronage, it perhaps will surprise you to learn that I have information that you claim to have my authority to arrange that matter in New York. I do not believe you have so claimed; but still so some men say. On that subject you know all I have said to you is 'justice for all,' and I have said nothing more particular to any one. I say this to reassure you that I have not changed my position."

CHAPTER 153

TALK came from New York about a scheme to take that city out of the Union and set up a Free City. "I reckon," Lincoln remarked to a New Yorker, "it will be some time before the Front Door sets up housekeeping on its own account."

Important men got off the train at Springfield. Salmon P. Chase, governor of Ohio, was one. He came by invitation, Lincoln having written him: "In these troublous times I would much like a conference with you. Please visit me here at once." Not merely was Chase important; he looked so. Lincoln asked him to become Secretary of the Treasury. Chase wouldn't promise. He'd think it over. And with that he went back to Ohio. "He thinks he's a greater man than you are," said John Bunn to Lincoln, who said he would be glad if that were true; he wanted all the great men he could lay hold of for his Cabinet.

Simon Cameron, the Pennsylvania boss, came on. Judge Davis and the Lincoln managers at the Chicago convention had promised Cameron he could be Secretary of the Treasury. Cameron stayed in Springfield three days. He and Lincoln had long talks. Cameron left for his home in Pennsylvania with a letter signed by Lincoln to himself, reading:

I think fit to notify you now that, by your permission, I shall at the proper time nominate you to the United States Senate for confirmation as Secretary of the Treasury, or as Secretary of War—which of the two I have not definitely decided. Please answer at your earliest convenience.

While Cameron journeyed homeward, his enemies brought evidence to Lincoln intended to show that Cameron was, in the lingo, "crooked as a dog's hind leg" and "crooked as a corkscrew." Lincoln wrote Cameron another letter; things had developed which made it impossible to take him, Cameron, into the Cabinet. Would he, Cameron, write a letter publicly declining any Cabinet place? And Cameron's answer was a bundle of recommendations outnumbering the opposition three to one, which Lincoln looked over, and later wrote Cameron that he wouldn't make a Cabinet appointment for Pennsylvania without consulting Cameron.

Thus names slipped in and out, though Seward for Secretary of State and Judge Edward Bates of Missouri for Attorney-General were well settled from the start, besides the place of Secretary of the Interior for Caleb B. Smith of Indiana, which latter was promised by Lincoln's Chicago convention managers. He invited John A. Gilmer of North Carolina to Springfield to talk over a Cabinet appointment, but Gilmer didn't come. On January 3rd he wrote to Seward he hadn't decided who would be the heads of the War and Navy departments. "Your selection for the State Department having become public, I am happy to find scarcely any objection to it. I shall have trouble with every other Northern cabinet appointment—so much so that I shall have to defer them as long as possible to avoid being teased into insanity, to make changes."

Judge John D. Caton came. He was a Democrat. Also he was known as "the telegraph king." He was for the preservation of the Union, for a sovereign Federal Government over states with uninterrupted lines of free communication. "I advised him to avoid bringing on the war by precipitate action, but let the Southerners begin it; to forbear as long as forbearance could be tolerated," said Caton. "He listened intently, replied the struggle was inevitable, no single party could sustain him; he must rely on the great masses of the people, and he would try to pursue such a course as would secure their support."

As the lines of faces passed before Lincoln in the governor's room, he met no two alike; eyes, voices, intonations, shrugs, he gave each his own reading and met it by that; he met some arguments with argument; he met some questions with a baffling counterquestion; he told stories as he chose for those who had heard of him as a story-teller and wanted him to perform; but he picked his stories according to the faces and voices that were before him.

Henry Villard, who stayed two weeks in Springfield writing for German newspapers, was "sorry this fondness for low stories clung to him." Villard couldn't make out Lincoln at all, and wrote: "He seemed to be bent upon making his hit by fair means or foul. He never hesitated to tell a coarse or even outright nasty story, if it served his purpose. More than once I heard him 'with malice aforethought' get off purposely some repulsive fiction in order to rid himself of an uncomfortable caller. Again and again I felt disgust and humiliation that such a person should have been called upon to direct the destinies of a great nation." Yet when Thurlow Weed came and spent two days filled with hours of talk with Lincoln, he told friends, "Lincoln talked without restraint, but I never heard him use a profane or indecent word, or tell a story that might not be repeated in the presence of ladies."

When Villard arrived, Lincoln didn't recall that he had forgotten to send back to Villard the buffalo robe Villard had loaned him the year before when he was shivering in the Kansas wind. And Villard didn't remind him.

Hannah Armstrong came, the widow of Jack, the mother of Duff, strong-hearted, black-eyed Hannah Armstrong. Lincoln took her two hands. They talked, homely and heart-warming talk. He held the hands that had been good to him, so long ago, when he was young and the sap ran wild in him. They talked. And she was going. "They'll kill ye, Abe." "Hannah, if they do kill me, I shall never die another death."

Another beautiful old woman came. While on the Eighth Circuit, Lincoln had eaten at her house. "One day you came along and we had eaten up everything, and I could give you nothing but a bowl of bread and milk, and when you got up you said it was good enough for the President of the United States."

Browning dropped in from Quincy and wrote in his diary on February 7, 1861: "Changed in the night and hard frozen and very cold this morning. Met Mr. Lincoln in the basement of the State House this morning. He took me aside and gave me a very earnest invitation to go with him to Washington."

"It will do you good to get down to Washington," Joe Gillespie offered as cheer one day. "I know it will," was Lincoln's answer. "I only wish I could have got there to lock the door before the horse was stolen. But when I get to the spot, I can find the tracks."

For his regular secretary he had a trusted, reliable, accurate, scrupulous young man, sober as a work horse, earnest as the multiplication table; he had freckles and reddish hair; a young German from the *Pike County Sucker*. This was Nicolay, secretive, dependable, carrying messages not to be written but whispered, feeling equally with Lincoln the groaning loads of responsibility; the favorite word of Nicolay was "responsibility."

The other or second secretary was not strictly engaged as such, but he was going to Washington. Lincoln had said, "We can't take all Illinois with us down to Washington, but let Hay come." A keen and whimsical lad, this Hay. He had been class poet at Brown University, graduated, gone home to Warsaw, Illinois, then to Pike County, and later to Springfield to study law with his Uncle Milt, who had an office on the same floor as Lincoln & Herndon.

"I am sure to die soon," the young poet had written, and again: "I shall work out of these shadows. If not there is a cool rest under the violets." Yet he wrote notes in French to a sweetheart, and had a handsome, negligent elegance all the girls in Springfield liked. He wore a derby hat, buttoned the top button on a long loose sack coat of black, and sauntered with an ease that caught Lincoln's eye. "Let Hay come." Hay caught every accent and shading of Lincoln as an artist and as a subject for artists, an Æsop, Quixote, and Ezekiel; he was young, this Hay; he was to grow older.

Across many letters Lincoln wrote for his secretaries the notation "Need not answer this." One was from an inventor saying: "It looks like war. I have invented a machine which will fire 400 bullets simultaneously; write me if you wish me to explain it to you."

Advice arrived from a Tennessee woman who had had a dream about how to keep out of war. Another suggested he should have all his food tasted. Still another letter writer told Lincoln to resign at the inaugural and appoint Douglas as the new President.

Again Horace Greeley came, after lecturing in Chicago on "Self-made Men." He and Lincoln sat in the St. Nicholas Hotel for a three-hour talk. Greeley felt Lincoln ought to show a strong hand and be more decisive in action. In his manner toward Southerners, Greeley saw Lincoln as "apologetic, deprecatory." Again Greeley felt Lincoln reaching for him and said to himself he wouldn't be brought into the circle of Lincoln's personal influence. And again, he went away without hearing a story or anecdote from Lincoln.

CHAPTER 154

THE question whether Simon Cameron, the Republican boss of Pennsylvania, was a measurably honest man or a rascal who would do harm, used up many hours of Lincoln's time as the days went by. Several states sent delegations to stop the appointment of Cameron to the Cabinet. But Cameron kept sending more witnesses for him than the opposition sent against him.

In a letter of January 3 asking Cameron to decline a Cabinet appointment, Lincoln wrote: "Better do this at once, before things change so that you cannot honorably decline, and I be openly compelled to recall the tender. No person living knows or has an intimation that I write this letter." A postscript cried, "Telegraph me instantly on receipt of this, saying, 'All right.'"

"I learn that your feelings were wounded by the terms of my letter," Lincoln wrote to Cameron on January 13. He was referring to his letter ten days previous, asking Cameron to refuse publicly a Cabinet job. "I wrote that letter under great anxiety, and perhaps I was not so guarded in its terms as I should have been; but I beg you to be assured I intended no offense. I say to you now that I have not doubted that you would perform the duties of a department ably and faithfully." Then with this same letter Lincoln sent an inclosure, dated ten days previous, which would be the letter that Cameron could show, if necessary, to anybody who asked. It softened the sharp tone of the former letter, made the point, "You were here by my invitation, and not upon any suggestion of your own," and set forth, "With much pain I now say to you that you will relieve me from great embarrassment by allowing me to recall the offer." And he told Cameron, "Destroy the offensive letter, or return it to me."

"Another battalion of Cameron men arrived here today," a reporter wrote in Springfield on January 24. And a week later the Philadelphia *Sunday Mercury* published a report of what Lincoln told the vineyard pilgrims. It sounded so much like what Lincoln probably said that the *Chicago Tribune* reprinted it.

"Gentlemen," ran Lincoln's advice, "in the formation of my Cabinet, I shall aim as nearly as possible at perfection. Any man whom I may appoint to such position must be as far as possible, like Cæsar's wife, pure and above suspicion, of unblemished reputation and undoubted integrity." Thus he pictured the ideal Cabinet officer, and then proceeded specifically to Cameron.

"The feeling against him appears to come from Ohio and one or two of the western states. His opponents charge him with corruption in obtaining contracts, and contend that if he is appointed he will use the patronage of his office for his own private gain. I have no knowledge of the acts charged against him, but I intend to make an investigation of the whole matter, by allowing his opponents to submit their proof, and I shall give him an opportunity of explaining any part he may have had in the transactions alleged against him."

Lincoln rambled along as dryly and simply as if the case were no more involved than that of some Illinois horse thief. "For my own part I can see no impropriety in his taking contracts, or making money out of them, as that is a mere matter of business. There is nothing wrong in this, unless some unfairness or dishonesty is shown, which supposition I have no doubt General Cameron will be able to disprove."

Yet the case was one far out of ordinary politics, he would have them know. He looked them in the eye, and went on: "I shall deal fairly with him, but I say to you, gentlemen, frankly, that if the charges against him are proven, he cannot have a seat in my Cabinet, as I will not have any man associated with me whose character is impeached. I will say further that, if he vindicates himself, I have the strongest desire to place him in the position you wish him to fill, and which you think the interests of your state demand."

And he gave the men facing him something to think about in their own futures as politicians, in saying: "If, after he has been appointed, I should be deceived by subsequent transactions of a disreputable character, the responsibility will rest upon you, gentlemen of Pennsylvania, who have so strongly presented his claim to my consideration. But this is supposing a state of things which may never occur."

Early one morning in January, Lincoln knocked at the door of Gustave Koerner in a hotel room in Springfield. Koerner was still in bed; he got up and unbolted the door. In walked Lincoln, saying: "I want to see you and Judd. Where is he?" Koerner gave Lincoln the number of Judd's room. And soon came Judd and Lincoln, and, while Koerner was putting on his shirt, Lincoln said: "I am in a quandary. Pennsylvania is entitled to a Cabinet office. But whom shall I appoint?" Judd and Koerner answered in one voice, "Not Cameron." They said Cameron couldn't be trusted; he had the name of a tricky and corrupt politician. "I know, I know," said Lincoln, "but can I get along if that state should oppose my Administration?" And that was about all of the interview.

The Cameron affair was breaking in on Lincoln's sleep of nights. A telegram from A. K. McClure, the Philadelphia newspaper editor, said the appointment of Cameron would split the Republican party in Pennsylvania. But Seward, Weed, Davis, Swett, were pushing hard for Cameron.

E. Peck of Springfield wrote to Trumbull, "David Davis is quite huffy because of the objections raised to Cameron." And Trumbull wrote to Lincoln: "Cameron is totally unfit. He is very generally regarded as a trading, unscrupulous politician. He is a great manager and by his schemes has for the moment created an apparent public sentiment in

Penna. in his favor. Many of the persons strenuously urging his appointment are doubtless doing it in anticipation of a compensation. You may perhaps ask, how, if these things are true, does he have so many friends to support him, and such representative men? I am surprised at it, but the world is full of great examples of men succeeding for a time by intrigue and management."

Even the Seward appointment had left sore spots. Trumbull had written that William Cullen Bryant and other New York Republicans had fought the "gridiron" street-railway bill engineered at Albany by Weed, and believed Seward to be a Weed tool. Lincoln replied that the sentiment in New York that had sent a united delegation for Seward to Chicago "ought not and must not be snubbed." He underlined the words, "I will myself take care of the question of 'corrupt jobs.'" And he had made the Seward appointment finally, however, only after sending the documents concerned to Trumbull and Hamlin to O. K., which they did.

"Office seekers swarmed in the greatest numbers from Illinois," Horace White noticed. "Illinois could have filled every office in the national blue book without satisfying half the demands. Every considerable town had several candidates for its own post office, and the applicants were generally men who had real claims by reason of party service and personal character."

The office seekers watched Lincoln's habits, waylaid him, wedged in, and reminded him not to forget them. If personally refused, they sent appeals again to Lincoln's ear through friends who came to Lincoln on his invitation to discuss some special matter, and when that was over they would say: "There is one more thing, Mr. Lincoln: So-and-So wants to be Minister to Peru, revenue collector at Peoria, or United States marshal in Utah."

They sharpened his loneliness. As one clique of callers went out of the door and he was with an old friend, he threw his hands in the air and made motions like a man trying to scare off sheep, knowing, however, that the sheep only looked like sheep, only wore sheep's clothing.

If a man shook hands and broke into a grin, saying: "As for me, Mr. Lincoln, I just dropped in to wish you well. I don't want any office. I'm going back home with the folks and I'll do anything I can to help you," Lincoln would put both hands on the man's shoulders and nearly cry. When that happened his bones took a rest, his face lighted.

One who kept wedging in, by one device and another pressing claims on Lincoln, was Judge David Davis. Lincoln spoke to Whitney about it, and as Whitney told it: "Lincoln inveighed to me in the bitterest terms against Judge Davis's greed and importunity for office, and summarized his disgust in these words, 'I know it is an awful thing for me to say, but I already wish some one else was here in my place.'"

Strife was ahead, furious interlocked forces trying to strangle each other. The one resolve shaping far back of every act and word of Lincoln was that the Union of states must be held together. Dr. William Jayne said Lincoln told Herndon: "Billy, I hope there will be no trouble; but I will make the South a graveyard rather than see a slavery gospel triumph, or successful secession destroy the Union."

And he told Gillespie that with a Cabinet picked from the lawyers he had traveled with on the old Eighth Circuit, he believed he could head off war or settle secession without a battle. "But," said Gillespie, "those old lawyers are all Democrats." "I know it," came the reply, "but I would rather have Democrats I know than Republicans I don't know."

Sometimes, as the high howling of war threats came shriller, Lincoln would speak indirectly as though if a people want to fight there is no stopping them; wars have their own chaotic way of arriving; politicians must acknowledge tidal waves and pent volcanoes. Lincoln told of a congressman who had opposed the War of 1812, and, when asked to oppose the Mexican War, had answered it: "I opposed one war; that was enough for me. I am now perpetually in favor of war, pestilence, and famine."

CHAPTER 155

SOME of the Illinois friends of Lincoln were puzzled early in February. They couldn't figure what Lincoln was up to—if anything. It was baffling.

Next to Trumbull, Congressman William Kellogg of Canton, Illinois, was closer to Lincoln than any other Republican in the matter of favors, offices, patronage. And it was Kellogg who stood up in the House of Representatives one day and introduced a bill to amend the Constitution so that slaves could be taken into any territory south of 36° 30′ from any state where slavery then lawfully existed.

The next day the *Chicago Tribune* read Kellogg out of the Republican party, declaring another day later, "We are opposed in toto to any double-tongued proposition which shall add the crime of swindling to that of compromising with traitors." And the *Tribune* had its Springfield correspondent report on whether Lincoln was leaning toward compromise, the dispatch in reply saying there was "no belief that Mr. Lincoln was disposed to anything smacking of renunciation and humiliation."

Then the *Tribune* began printing in italics at the head of its editorial column, day after day, a decisive utterance from Lincoln, "I will suffer death before I will consent, or advise my friends to consent, to any concession or compromise which looks like buying the privilege of taking possession of the Government to which we have a Constitutional right; I should regard any concession in the face of menace as the destruction of the Government itself, and the consent on all hands that our system shall be brought to a level with the existing disorganized state of affairs in Mexico. But this thing will hereafter be, as it is now, in the hands of the people." Regarding the source of this utterance the *Tribune* said, "We have reason to know the opinions are those which Mr. Lincoln has entertained."

Kellogg's Compromise Bill had been howled down forthwith by the radical Republicans in Congress, while John A. McClernand, a Democrat from the Springfield district, arose and complimented his Illinois colleague on the ability, justice, and patriotism of the proposed plan. Also McClernand called attention to the close personal relations between Kellogg and President-elect Lincoln; high importance attached to the compromise plan if it had been handed to him by Lincoln. And Kellogg courteously interrupted McClernand to say positively it was ab-so-lute-ly his plan alone, and he and nobody else was responsible.

What was it that Lincoln had done, in letting one of his closest political friends make a public stand in favor of the extension of slavery into all western territory south of 36° 30'? Eleven weeks previous he had written to Kellogg, "Entertain no proposition for a compromise in regard to the extension of slavery. The instant you do they have us under again; all our labor is lost, and sooner or later must be done over." Then some two weeks previous, on January 21, he had held a long conference with Kellogg in Springfield. And what he had said to Kellogg, and advised was with the condition scribbled so often in postscripts to Lincoln letters, "Confidential, for your eye only." Then Kellogg had gone on to Washington, spoken for compromise, for extension of slavery into all new territories to be formed south of 36° 30', was howled down by the radicals of his party, read out by the *Chicago Tribune*—as both he and Lincoln had probably expected.

Why had Lincoln and Kellogg done this? Its first result was good will from the Democrat, McClernand. In that same week the Congress of the Confederate States of America, meeting in Montgomery, Alabama, elected a president and vice president. Strife loomed. The Democrats of southern Illinois, Indiana, and Ohio, near the slave-state borders, could say to their people that if the southern congressmen had not walked out and left the Union, there might have been a chance for the extension of slavery into the western territories. A dozen McClernands, who leaned to the Union, were strengthened. They could face their constituents with one more good excuse for Unionism. John A. Logan, "Black Jack," swinging southern Illinois politically, was wanted in Lincoln's plans, and Lincoln was reaching after him; the "half horse, half alligator men" were down in Logan's region. Then too, the slave state of Missouri had a fresh argument for staying in the Union.

The action was mazy. Lincoln wrote to Seward, four days before Kellogg introduced his Compromise Bill in Congress, "To put us on the highroad to a slave empire, is the object of all these proposed compromises." Seward got the letter just about the day that Kellogg, the close friend of the President-elect, stood up and advocated an amendment to the Constitution legalizing slavery in territory south of 36° 30′. Lincoln's letter told Seward that Kellogg, "whom you probably know, was here in a good deal of anxiety seeking to ascertain to what extent I would be consenting for our friends to go in the way of compromise on the now vexed question. While he was with me I received a despatch from Senator Trumbull, at Washington, alluding to the same question and telling me to await letters. I therefore told Mr. Kellogg that when I should receive these letters posting me as to the state of affairs at Washington, I would write to you, requesting you to let him see my letter. To my surprise, when the letters mentioned by Judge Trumbull came, they made no allusion to the 'vexed question.' This baffled me so much that I was near not writing you at all, in compliance to what I have said to Judge Kellogg."

And all the time Kellogg, who asked Congress to consider his bill to compromise with the South and make slavery lawful below the 36° 30′ line, was getting more favors, appointments of men to office whose names he put up to Lincoln, than any other politician in Illinois except Trumbull. Seward couldn't figure out the motives. He believed Lincoln was all muddled up. It was the time of the beginning of men like Samuel Bowles of the Springfield, Massachusetts, *Republican,* saying, "Lincoln is a Simple Susan," and of others saying, "Lincoln would like to have God on his side, but he must have Kentucky."

The incident was a piece of Lincoln propaganda. It came in the same first week in February in which his closest friend among newspapers, the *Illinois State Journal,* shot the fierce bolt: "Before we talk of concession we want it settled that we have a Government. Let the stolen forts, arsenals, and navy yards be returned to the rightful owners—tear down your Rattlesnake and Pelican flag and run up the ever-glorious Stars and Stripes—disperse your traitorous mobs, and let every man return to his duty. Then come to us with your list of grievances."

The North was crying, "Treason!" the South, "Freedom!" One called the Union sacred; the other spoke of State Sovereignty as holy. Propaganda was beginning to seethe. Southern newspapers were telling of riots and bloodshed in New England factory cities. Northern papers were telling of food shortages in the southern states.

Incidents in the day's chronicles were confusing. A mob in Ann Arbor, Michigan, broke into an Abolitionist meeting, smashed the doors and windows, and demolished the furniture of a church. In North Carolina, the *Raleigh Banner* was saying: "The big heart of the people is still in the Union. Less than a hundred thousand politicians are endeavoring to destroy the liberties and usurp the rights of more than thirty millions of people. If the people permit it, they deserve the horrors of the civil war which will ensue."

Five trunk-line railroads sent their head men to a conference where they reported increased receipts, and recommended the Crittenden Compromise, conciliation, and peace. In Chicago Cyrus H. McCormick, the farm-machinery manufacturer, was a leader of a mass meeting which declared for "peaceful separation" of the states. Also the McCormick interests were being denounced by the *Chicago Tribune* as "indecent" in trying to rush through Congress extensions of patents which would not expire till the following October 23. "Why should the job be put through in such headlong haste?" asked the *Tribune*. "Their indecent haste is no compliment to the present head of the Patent Bureau, for it indicates that they believe him better suited to their purpose than his successor, under Mr. Lincoln, is likely to be."

Californians in Washington were saying the only insurance against a revolution and secession in their state would be a Pacific railway. Plans for a Pacific republic were under way, they said, while Congress was doing nothing for a transportation link that would hold the West Coast in the Union.

One of the few facts all men agreed on was that the Union of States from the East to the West Coast was held together in loose and rambling cords of connection. On Christmas Day of 1860 newspapers carried a telegram from far out in Nebraska, at Fort Kearney, as far west as the wires ran. It said: "The weather is bitter cold here. The pony express, with San Francisco dates of the 12th, passed here at 4 o'clock this morning."

The iron horse had been ready for years to run and haul across the Great Plains. Politics stopped him from starting.

Henry Winter Davis of Maryland told Congress: "We are at the end of the insane revel of partisan license which, for thirty years, has worn the mask of Government. We are about to close the masquerade for the dance of death."

And the *New York Tribune* stated it as a fact that Lincoln had appointed Davis to a seat in his Cabinet. But it was not a fact.

Donn Piatt came from Springfield saying, "Lincoln told us he felt like a surveyor in the wild woods of the West, who, while looking for a corner, kept an eye over his shoulder for an Indian."

CHAPTER 156

A HATTER from Brooklyn, New York, called one January day and presented Lincoln with a black silk hat. The President-elect turned to Mrs. Lincoln and remarked, "Well, wife, if nothing else comes out of this scrape, we are going to have some new clothes."

Attentions and incidents of that sort pleased Mrs. Lincoln. She had a sprightly manner of saying, "We are pleased with our advancement."

In the hustle of deciding what to take along to the White House, asked about this, that and the other thing to be done or not done, she would sometimes burst out, "God, no!"

Pressure came on her to give her husband the names of men who should be appointed to office, with reasons why. Of one woman for whose husband she got a political appointment, Mrs. Lincoln told another woman, "She little knows what a hard battle I had for it, and how near he came to getting nothing."

She spoke of fears about her health, would mention "my racked frame" to other women, and say she hoped the chills she suffered from in earlier years would not return in Washington.

Ugly clouds shaped on the horizons, boots with nasty heel-prints on white linen and dove-gray silk. War would be messy. "If the country was only peaceful, all would be well," wrote Mary Todd Lincoln.

"I am weary of intrigue," she could remark, while in the same breath naming a former friend and saying, "She possesses such a miserable disposition and so false a tongue," rushing on with, "Such a woman no one respects," and adding, "As a child and young girl she could not be outdone in falsehood," and then, before changing the subject: "She is so seldom in my thoughts. I have so much more that is attractive, both in bodily presence, and my mind's eye, to interest me. I grieve for those who have to come in contact with her malice, yet even that is so well understood, the object of her wrath generally rises, with good people, in proportion to her vindictiveness. How far are we removed from such a person!"

Poor Mary Todd Lincoln! She was no more sure of herself as a middle-aged woman than when as a girl she had stood in the centre of a room during a thunderstorm crying, "Hide me, O my Savior!"

The city of Washington, as the time of her entry into its society approached, seemed to be a city of riddles, a city that mocked at her. The *Atlantic Monthly's* leading article in that January of 1861 was saying: "Washington is the Elysium of oddities, the Limbo of absurdities, an imbroglio of ludicrous absurdities. Planned on a scale of surpassing grandeur, its architectural execution is almost contemptible. The houses are low, the rents high; the hacks are black, the horses white; the squares are triangles, except that of the Capitol, which is oval. It has a Monument that will never be finished, a Capitol that is to have a dome, a Scientific Institute which does nothing but report the rise and fall of the thermometer. In spite of the labors of the Smithsonian Institution, it has no particular weather; it rains, hails, snows, blows, freezes, and melts in Washington, all in the space of twenty-four hours. The men are fine-looking, the women homely. The latter have plain faces, but magnificent busts and graceful figures. The former have an imposing presence and an empty pocket, a great name and a small conscience."

Small crumbs of comfort, if any, could be picked up from the *Atlantic Monthly,* regarding the city to which she was going for a home the next four years. It might be as unsatisfying as Springfield.

The *Atlantic* was saying: "If the beggars of Dublin, the cripples of Constantinople, and the lepers of Damascus should assemble in Baden-Baden during a Congress of Kings, then Baden-Baden would resemble Washington. Presidents, Senators, Honorables, Judges, Generals, Commodores, Governors, and Exes of all descriptions congregate here as thick as pickpockets at a horse race or women at a wedding in church. Add Ambassadors, Plenipotentiaries, Lords, Counts, Barons, Chevaliers, the great and small fry of the Legations, Captains, Lieutenants, Claim-Agents, Negroes, Perpetual-Motion Men, Fire-Eaters, Irishmen, Plug-Uglies, Hoosiers, Gamblers, Californians, Mexicans, Japanese, Indians, and Organ-Grinders, together with females to match all varieties of males, and you have a vague notion of the people of Washington." Mary Todd Lincoln could shiver. Perhaps the chills of earlier years would come back.

She had her method of ordering things to wear, writing such instructions as, "I am in need of two bonnets—I do not wish expensive ones, but I desire them of very fine quality and stylish." She wrote specifications to the milliner. "One bonnet, I wish fine, very fine, pretty shape. This I desire, to be trimmed with black love ribbon—with pearl edge. I cannot have it without the latter. I send you a bonnet which I think would be a pretty style—perhaps mixed with the bow on top some black sprays would not be amiss." Then further details, "The strings of the love ribbon with black pearl edge—fine, full blk inside ruche, with very finest front white face flowers, perhaps mixed with a little blk."

She would need a house headdress, "something in great taste of black gauze ribbon, with pearl edge—I am sure I need not direct you—you will send me something comme il faut. I am expecting something very choice—I am as particular about the headdress as the bonnets."

Also she included the suggestion as to one bonnet, "The bonnet will be simple and of course, not expensive, yet I wish it to be of the very finest materials."

CHAPTER 157

ONE morning in January, Lincoln, with carpetbag in hand, was starting for Coles County, and met Whitney on a street in Springfield. He asked Whitney to ride the train a few stations. "I want to talk to you." Whitney was company. "I am worrying some to know what to do with my house. I don't want to sell myself out of a home; and if I rent it, it will be pretty well used up before I get back." They came to the station. "I guess my hat hain't chalked on this road," said Lincoln, meaning he had no pass so that the conductor could chalk his hat instead of collecting fare or a ticket.

Whitney insisted he would go in and see Bowen, the railroad superintendent, and get a pass. Bowen asked that the President-elect come into his office till the train arrived. After getting settled in a chair, Lincoln queried, "Bowen, how is business on your road now?" and later, becoming personal with Bowen: "You are a heap better off than I am playing President. When I first knew Whitney, I was getting on well—I was clean out of politics and contented to stay so. I had a good business, and my children were coming up, and were interesting to me—but now—here I am——" And Lincoln paused . . . and shifted the talk into other lines.

Whitney got off the train at his station, Lincoln rode to Mattoon, missed connections with a passenger train, and took the caboose of a freight train to Charleston. The engine stopped at the station for orders, and Lincoln, with a shawl over his shoulders, and his boots in slush, mud, and ice, picked his way in the late evening dusk alongside the tracks the length of the freight train to the station, where a buggy was ready. Friends met him and took him to the house, where he was to stay overnight; the next morning he would go out to say good-by and have his last hour with his stepmother, Sally Bush Lincoln.

Among those who came to see Lincoln that evening was a lawyer, A. P. Dunbar, who had met and talked with Lincoln hundreds of times. But now that Lincoln was in five weeks to be inaugurated President, Dunbar didn't know whether he ought to be familiar and easy as in the old days. "If he is dignified and formal, I must act accordingly," said Dunbar. He knocked at the door of the house where Lincoln was staying; the family was finishing supper; Lincoln had eaten and was in the front room sitting before the fire; he heard the knock at the door and opened the door himself. In a flash he had Dunbar's right hand in his, and, resting another hand on Dunbar's shoulder, he burst out, "Lord A'mighty, Aleck, how glad I am to see you!"

Another man came in with Dunbar. They sat by the fire. Lincoln was soon drawing out one and another of his yarns, and nicely started on the fifth or sixth one, which was about a girl whose family kept a cow and who each evening would hunt up the cow and drive it home. "One day," said Lincoln, "she rode a horse bareback to the woods. On the way home the horse, frightened by a dog or something which darted from behind a bush, made a wild dash ahead, the girl still astride, when suddenly——" A knock came at the door and Lincoln halted the story, stepped across the room, opened the door, and welcomed in the Presbyterian minister, his wife, and two other ladies. Other callers arrived, the evening party began, and Dunbar and his friend went away without hearing the rest of the story.

The next day Lincoln drove eight miles out to the old farm along the road over which he had hauled wood with an ox team. He came to the old log house he had cut logs for and helped smooth the chinks; from its little square windows he had seen late winter and early birds.

Sally Bush and he put their arms around each other and listened to each other's heartbeats. They held hands and talked, they talked without holding hands. Each looked into eyes thrust back in deep sockets. She was all of a mother to him.

He was her boy more than any born to her. He gave her a photograph of her boy, a hungry picture of him standing and wanting, wanting. He stroked her face a last time, kissed good-by, and went away.

She knew his heart would go roaming back often, that even when he rode in an open carriage in New York or Washington with soldiers, flags, and cheering thousands along the streets, he might just as like be thinking of her in the old log farmhouse out in Coles County, Illinois.

The sunshine of the prairie summer and fall months would come sifting down with healing and strength; between harvest and corn-plowing there would be rains beating and blizzards howling; and there would be the silence after snowstorms with white drifts piled against the fences, barns, and trees.

CHAPTER 158

INAUGURATION DAY was less than six weeks off. Letters warned Lincoln he would be killed before he could reach Washington. As they got fiercer, and more came, Lincoln sent Thomas S. Mather, Adjutant-General of Illinois, to Washington to sound Gen. Winfield Scott, the head of the army, on his loyalty. Scott was a Virginian. "Insist on a personal interview. Look him in the face. Note carefully what he says."

Mather came back to Springfield. He had found the Mexican War commander propped up with pillows, in bed, an old worn man with flesh in rolls over a warty face and neck.

The old general's breathing was heavy, and he half choked and wheezed out the words, "You may present my compliments to Mr. Lincoln, when you reach Springfield, and tell him I shall expect him to come on to Washington as soon as he is ready." Also, the conqueror of Vera Cruz sent word: "Say to him that, when once here, I shall consider myself responsible for his safety. If necessary I'll plant cannon at both ends of Pennsylvania Avenue, and if any show their hands or even venture to raise a finger, I'll blow them to hell." Hearing these assurances that the Washington end of the inaugural was being taken care of, Lincoln went ahead with his plans to be there. When one friend warned him to have a guard, he replied, "What's the use of putting up a gap when the fence is down all around?"

He stepped into the house of Dr. John Todd one evening, holding a gripsack, and talking about the plans for his family to go to Washington.

He handed the grip to Mrs. Grimsley, a widow and the only daughter of Dr. Todd, saying it held his "literary bureau." He would leave it in her charge. Speeches, notes, writings of different sorts, filled the grip. Two tied in red tape were the manuscripts of his lecture on "Discoveries and Inventions." He might not come back from Washington, he explained, and in that case she could do what she pleased with the papers. He was a little absent-minded about it all, as though perhaps he cherished old keepsakes too dearly, and the care of them was interfering with more important errands.

He cleared out files, burned and threw away letters; a caller one day picked up an armful of letters from the floor; among them were letters Lincoln had written his wife when he was a congressman thirteen years back. He closed up odds and ends. He sold back to Canisius the *Illinois Staats-Anzeiger*.

The last week of his stay in Springfield, in Illinois, arrived. The steps up to the little two-story cottage at Eighth and Jackson streets felt the tread of several thousand people who came between seven and twelve o'clock on the night of February 6, some to say good-by, some to see what they would see.

The President-elect stood near the front door shaking hands; his son, Bob, back from school, and Mrs. Lincoln and four of her sisters assisted. Mrs. Lincoln stood in the centre of the parlor and wore, a St. Louis correspondent noted, a beautiful full trail, white moire antique silk, with a small French lace collar. Her neck was ornamented with a string of pearls. Her headdress was a simple and delicate vine. She was, the correspondent telegraphed his paper, "a lady of fine figure and accomplished address, well calculated to grace and to do honor at the White House."

Newspaper men were kindly, admiring in their sketches of Mrs. Lincoln, and references to her. She was whirling along in dizzy realizations of her fondest hopes of social importance. She had made a two-week trip East, the Cleveland, Ohio, *Herald*, saying on January 10: "Conductor Ames's train this morning brought in Mrs. Lincoln, accompanied by her brother, Mr. C. M. Smith and Hon. Amos Tuck of New Hampshire. They will proceed to New York by way of Buffalo, and, after a few days' stay to make purchases for the White House, will go to Cambridge, Mass., to visit Mr. Lincoln's son who is at Harvard College. Pres. Gardiner tendered the courtesies of the road from Toledo to Cleveland, and Supt. Nottingham set apart a special car to take the party to Buffalo."

She was a woman elevated for gaze, and could read in the *Chicago Tribune*: "At the rooms of the Wheeler & Wilson Sewing Machine Company, we yesterday saw a superb sewing machine, mounted in a solid rosewood full case, and altogether a bijou of an affair, destined as a present to the lady of the President-elect, and to find a location in one of the apartments of the White House. It is richly silver-plated and ornamented with inlaid pearl and enamel. It is worth the possession of a duchess, and indeed the very companions of this superb machine have actually been finished and sent to the English Duchess of Sutherland, and the Russian Duchess of Constantine. The Sewing Machine is well worth seeing."

In one of the farewell days, as Lincoln was meeting people in Johnson's Block opposite the Chenery House, there came to him an old farmer, in butternut jeans, who had ridden horseback many miles since daybreak. And the old man was bent and worn with age, and nearly blind. He had known the Armstrongs and what Lincoln did for Duff Armstrong. And he came and put his old eyes close to Lincoln's face, peered and studied the lines of the face, burst into tears, and murmured, "It *is* him—it's the *same*." And after mentioning the Duff Armstrong case, he shook the hand of the President-elect and said solemnly two or three times, "God preserve you, Mr. Lincoln."

Smart Alecks came, often committees of them, guffawing at their own lame jokes, with thrusts of familiarity at Lincoln as though they might next be tickling him in the ribs. Whitney saw Lincoln one afternoon, with smiling humor, usher the last member of such a committee out of the door, and Whitney remarked, "I wish I could take as rose-colored a view of the situation as you seem to." Lincoln's smiles had all crept back into the leathery fissures of his face, as he told Whitney: "I hope you don't feel worse about it than I do. I can't sleep nights."

"Lincoln is letting his whiskers grow," men were saying in January. A barber had shaved the upper lip and cheeks, leaving a stubble on the chin. Then along in February the hairs grew without interference on all the areas of the face and neck, except the upper lip.

Just why Lincoln took to whiskers at this time nobody seemed to know. A girl in New York State had begged him to raise a beard. But something more than her random wish guided him. Herndon, Whitney, Lamon, Nicolay, Hay, heard no explanation from him as to why after fifty-two years with a smooth face he should now change.

Would whiskers imply responsibility, gravity, a more sober and serene outlook on the phantasmagoria of life? Perhaps he would seem more like a serious farmer with crops to look after, or perhaps a church sexton in charge of grave affairs. Or he might have the look of a sea-captain handling a ship in a storm on a starless sea. Anyhow, with whiskers or without, he would be about the same-sized target.

CHAPTER 159

At sunset on the evening before the day set for starting to Washington, Lincoln and Herndon sat in their office for a long talk. The one older by nine years was still "Mr. Lincoln," and the other plain "Billy." Sixteen years they had been partners, and, said Lincoln, "We've never had a cross word during all that time, have we?" They reviewed old times; the office had been quite a place; they exchanged reminiscences; Lincoln was entertaining and cheerful—but suddenly blurted, "Billy, there's one thing I have, for some time, wanted you to tell me, but I reckon I ought to apolo-

Vanity Fair smiles amid chaos.

DELUSIVE DRUGGIST.—There's 'is heffigy in wax, sir, wiskers and all. Try one of them pots, and in three weeks you'll be as 'airy and 'ansom as 'im.

gize for my nerve and curiosity in asking it even now." "What is it?" "I want you to tell me how many times you have been drunk."

Herndon felt it a blunt question, made his guess as to how many times, perhaps five or six, he had brought disgrace on the law firm. Herndon expected some kind of a warning. But Lincoln changed the subject. What he had done was to give Billy a chance to say he'd keep sober and be fit for any responsible appointment Lincoln would give him.

Herndon said afterward: "I could have had any place for which I was fitted, but I thought too much of Lincoln to disgrace him. And I wanted to be free, drink whisky when I pleased." One request, however, came from Herndon, that Lincoln would speak to Governor Yates and have him reappointed state bank examiner, to which Lincoln agreed. As Lincoln gathered a bundle of papers and stood ready to leave, he told Herndon their law partnership would go on, their shingle would stay up. "If I live I'm coming back and we'll resume practice as if nothing had ever happened." He took a last look around at the old office, and Herndon and he walked downstairs together and parted.

In a third-story room over his brother-in-law's store, Lincoln had been hidden away from all callers at such times as he worked on the writing of his inaugural address to be delivered on March 4, in Washington, amid the cannon to be planted by General Scott. Two printers, sworn to secrecy, had set up and run off twenty copies of the address. That was in January. Weeks had gone by. Nobody had told or been careless. The inaugural address text was still a secret. And he had written and placed in separate envelopes copies of speeches he was to deliver on the way to Washington. "I am nothing, the Union and the Constitution everything."

Lamon was called from Danville and told: "Hill, it looks as if we might have war. I want you with me, I must have you." And Lamon was going along, banjo, bulldog courage, and all.

CHAPTER 160

A QUEER dream or illusion had haunted Lincoln at times through the winter. On the evening of his election he had thrown himself on one of the haircloth sofas at home, just after the first telegrams of November 6 had told him he was elected President, and looking into a bureau mirror across the room he saw himself full length, but with two faces.

It bothered him; he got up; the illusion vanished; but when he lay down again there in the glass again were two faces, one paler than the other. He got up again, mixed in the election excitement, forgot about it; but it came back, and haunted him. He told his wife about it; she worried too.

A few days later he tried it once more and the illusion of the two faces again registered to his eyes. But that was the last; the ghost since then wouldn't come back, he told his wife, who said it was a sign he would be elected to a second term, and the death pallor of one face meant he wouldn't live through his second term.

CHAPTER 161

Horses hitched to bobsleds stood with sober and serene faces around the public square that winter the same as other winters. When a bit of warm weather came following a spell of zero, sheets of vapor and heavy haze clung to the prairie, and the horses had hard hauling in the muddy roads. And some farmers, after tying their horses to the hitch rack, threw blankets over the beasts so they wouldn't freeze, while others let their nags stand shivering.

Lincoln took walks alone. Whitney ran across him in a section of Springfield where he had no business, unless to be walking alone. His arms were full of papers and bundles of mail. Where was he going? "Nowhere in particular," he told Whitney.

Clothes, furniture, books, the household goods, were packed in boxes and trunks. The family had taken rooms in the Chenery House; the old cottage home was gone, leased, the horse, buggy, and cow sold off.

At the hotel Lincoln had roped his trunks himself, and had written, "A. Lincoln, The White House, Washington, D. C." on cards he fastened on the trunks.

He was going to the biggest home in the country, the hardest house in the country to live in; the Atlantic seaboard was the front yard, the Rocky Mountains and the Pacific slope the colossal back yard; his body, the feet and mouth of him, would be in the White House, eating three meals a day and taking a bath every so often; but the heart and mind of him would have to be far away, roaming the immense front yard and back yard, where there were boys fighting, girls scratching each other's faces, children sticking their tongues out and calling nasty names at each other; he was to be the Father; the Red Indians would actually call him the "Great Father," negroes would call him "Massa," and punctilious white men would use the address "Your Excellency"; he would be the Supreme Counselor of the American People. "Good God, what a job!"

CHAPTER 162

A cold drizzle of rain was falling on the morning of February 11 when Lincoln and his party of fifteen were to leave Springfield on the eight o'clock at the Great Western Railway station. Chilly gray mist hung the circle of the prairie horizon. A short little locomotive with a flat-topped smokestack stood puffing with a baggage car and special passenger car hitched on; a railroad president and superintendent were on board. A thousand people crowded in and around the brick station, inside of which Lincoln was standing; and one by one came hundreds of old friends, shaking hands, wishing him luck and Godspeed, all faces solemn. Even Judge David Davis, weighing 350 pounds, wearing a new white silk hat, was a serious figure.

A path was made for Lincoln from the station to his car; hands stretched out for one last handshake. He hadn't intended to make a speech; but on the platform of the car, as he turned and saw his home people, he took off his hat, stood perfectly still, and looked almost as he had at the Bowling Green burial services when tears had to take the place of words. He raised a hand, for silence. They stood, with hats off.

Great Western Railroad Station, Springfield, Illinois.

Then he said slowly, amid the soft gray drizzle from the sky, "Friends, no one who has never been placed in a like position can understand my feelings at this hour nor the oppressive sadness I feel at this parting. For more than a quarter of a century I have lived among you, and during all that time I have received nothing but kindness at your hands. Here I have lived from my youth till now I am an old man. Here the most sacred trusts of earth were assumed; here all my children were born; and here one of them lies buried. To you, dear friends, I owe all that I have, all that I am. All the strange checkered past seems to crowd now upon my mind. Today I leave you; I go to assume a task more difficult than that which devolved upon General Washington. Unless the great God who assisted him shall be with and aid me, I must fail. But if the same omniscient mind and the same Almighty arm that directed and protected him shall guide and support me, I shall not fail; I shall succeed. Let us all pray that the God of our fathers may not forsake us now. To Him I commend you all. Permit me to ask that with equal sincerity and faith you will all invoke His wisdom and guidance for me. With these few words I must leave you— for how long, I know not. Friends, one and all, I must now bid you an affectionate farewell."

Bells rang, there was a grinding of wheels, and the train moved, and carried Lincoln away from Springfield.

The tears were not yet dry on some faces when the train had faded into the gray to the east.

Some of the crowd said afterward that Lincoln too was in tears, that tears ran down his face as he spoke that morning.

And one of the crowd said there were no tears on Lincoln's face. "But he had a face with dry tears," said this one. "He was a man who often had dry tears."

CHAPTER 163

Old Abe Lincoln came out of the wilderness,
Out of the wilderness, out of the wilderness,
Old Abe Lincoln came out of the wilderness,
Down in Illinois.

MRS. LINCOLN and the boys, Bob, Willie, and Tad, were on the train.

She noticed her husband's hair was rumpled and necktie disordered as the train was running into a town where he would face a crowd.

He put his hands under her arms and lifted her up on a seat to stand face to face with him; she "fixed him up," straightened the necktie and arranged his hair.

He bowed to ladies at one station, and his *New York Herald* friend wired, "He remarked to the ladies that he was always glad to demonstrate how well he understood the poetry of motion."

At another station he began a story to the crowd, provided they would "not let it get abroad as not compatible with dignity." The train pulled out as he was in the middle of the story. And the crowd laughed to him, "We surely won't tell the story now!"

Each mile of the railroad, and every curve, had a signalman. At one bridge a guardsman stood at "present arms" with a musket.

People on foot and in wagons had traveled since daybreak to see the train pass. A long line of saddle horses at Decatur told of old friends come for a last look.

Tolono station was the last stop in Illinois. There he said, "I am leaving you on an errand of national importance, attended, as you are aware, with considerable difficulties. Let us believe, as some poet has expressed it, 'Behind the cloud the sun is still shining.' I bid you an affectionate farewell."

And there were voices, "Good-by, Abe."

INDEX